The Conquering Tide

ALSO BY IAN W. TOLL

Pacific Crucible: War at Sea in the Pacific, 1941–1942

Six Frigates: The Epic History of the Founding of the U.S. Navy

The Conquering Tide

War in the Pacific Islands, 1942–1944

IAN W. TOLL

W. W. NORTON & COMPANY
Independent Publishers Since 1923
New York   London

For information about permission to reproduce selections from this book,
write to Permissions, W. W. Norton & Company, Inc.,
500 Fifth Avenue, New York, NY 10110

For information about special discounts for bulk purchases,
please contact W. W. Norton Special Sales at specialsales@wwnorton.com
or 800-233-4830

Manufacturing by RR Donnelley Westford
Production manager: Anna Oler

Library of Congress Cataloging-in-Publication Data

Toll, Ian W.
The conquering tide : war in the Pacific Islands, 1942/1944 /
Ian W. Toll. — First edition.
pages cm
Includes bibliographical references and index.
ISBN 978-0-393-08064-3 (hardcover)
1. World War, 1939–1945—Campaigns—Pacific Area. 2. World War, 1939–1945—Naval
operations, American. 3. World War, 1939–1945—Naval operations, Japanese. I. Title.
D767.T64 2015
940.54'26—dc23
                              2015009591

W. W. Norton & Company, Inc.
500 Fifth Avenue, New York, N.Y. 10110
www.wwnorton.com

W. W. Norton & Compant Ltd.
Castle House, 75/76 Wells Street, London W1T 3QT

1 2 3 4 5 6 7 8 9 0

To Adam

CONTENTS

LIST OF MAPS

AUTHOR'S NOTE AND ACKNOWLEDGMENTS

A decade ago, as I began the long work of assembling the research for a multivolume history of the Pacific War, I had to overcome some doubts in my own mind. A few minutes browsing in any large bookstore or library was enough to remind one of the vast historical literature of the Second World War. Even considering only the most recent publishing cycle—say, titles brought out since 1990—there appeared to be enough on the shelves to occupy even the most voracious history buff for a lifetime of reading. Was it possible, I asked myself, for any writer to add anything useful to the sea of ink that has already been spilled on World War II?

Wading chest-deep into this metaphorical sea, my misgivings soon fell away and were replaced by growing conviction in the justice of my cause. As large as the World War II literature is, it is strikingly lopsided. Certain aspects of the great conflict have been worked over to the point of exhaustion, while others have been surprisingly neglected. Studies of the Allied high command have never quite succeeded in pulling together a convincing across-the-board account of its deliberations and decisions affecting the Pacific theater. The Allies made "Europe-first" the basis of their global strategy—they agreed to regard Nazi Germany as the prime enemy, to be defeated first—but the Americans could never afford to treat the Pacific as an afterthought. The essential role of Admiral Ernest J. King, the relatively obscure wartime leader of the U.S. Navy, who insisted on an early Pacific counteroffensive over the objections of virtually everyone else whose opinion mattered, has for various reasons been overlooked or undervalued. There has been a propensity (axiomatic of all military history, one might say) to treat land campaigns as the "main plot" while demoting naval operations to the status of a subgenre to be handled by specialists. In the case of the Pacific War, that tendency has done real damage. A glance at a map of the Pacific will drive home the point: the war against Japan was chiefly a naval and air campaign, in which the destruction of the Japanese fleet was the basic strategic problem. Conquering islands was never a goal in itself, and when an enemy-held island served no purpose it was simply bypassed, its occupiers left to "wither on the vine." Specialized amphibious forces seized an island only if it was needed as a new sea or air base, with an airstrip carved out of the jungle and a harbor blasted out of the coral, to allow the fleet and bombers to consolidate their westward advance and gather strength for the next offensive thrust. The naval campaign belongs at the narrative spine of any history of the Pacific War, and I have worked in that spirit.

The Conquering Tide is the second in a projected three-volume history of the Pacific War. It resumes the narrative of *Pacific Crucible* (2011), which told the story of the first six months of the conflict, from Japan's surprise strike on Pearl Harbor to the Americans' devastating counterpunch at the Battle of Midway. The current volume covers the heart of the war, the period between mid-1942 and mid-1944, when parallel Allied counteroffensives north and south of the equator washed over Japan's far-flung island empire like a "conquering tide," concluding with Japan's irreversible strategic defeat in the Marianas. As in the previous book, my purpose has been to assimilate into one narrative many distinct and sharply contrasting points of view—the Allied and Japanese sides of the conflict, the home fronts and the battle fronts, the highest levels of political and military leadership and the perspectives from the decks, trenches, and cockpits. I have set out to tell the entire story of the Pacific War, admittedly a daunting proposition even in three books whose cumulative length will surpass 1,500 pages. I believe I can claim that this trilogy will be the first history of the entire Pacific War to be published in at least twenty-five years, and the first multivolume chronicle of the naval war since Samuel Eliot Morison's fifteen-volume series, published in the late 1940s and 1950s. In the years since, the field has been deeply enriched. New archives have opened, new oral histories have been recorded, new memoirs have been published, new and old Japanese sources have been translated, and talented writers and scholars on both sides of the Pacific have shed light on various aspects of the conflict. But a "stay in your lane" mentality prevails among drivers on these freeways. As the literature has grown richer and more varied, it has become disjointed and piecemeal. We have had a conspicuous lack of well-integrated narratives about the Pacific War in its entirety.

The obvious challenge of any big historical narrative is to do justice to the breadth, depth, and complexity of its subject. The most sensible approach (also the simplest to research and easiest to write) would be a soaring, textbook-style overview that takes each major event in chronological turn. But that sort of effort could add little to what already exists, and would fail to deliver the immediacy, intimacy, and tension that are the lifeblood of a story. The alternative is an episodic narrative, a progression of "deep dives" into selected events or themes, each chosen to illuminate another dimension of the larger subject. The episodic approach relies overwhelmingly on the direct personal account, the eyewitness description, the telling detail, and the coincident emotions and shrewd insights of observers and participants. It avails itself of storytelling techniques found in novels and (dare I say it?) even films. It requires a calculated decision to pay a lot of attention to some things and little or none to others, and can therefore be hauled up on charges of omission or neglect. The episodic narrative, as readers of my previous books will attest, also has an incorrigible tendency to stray out of the conventional lanes of military history, perhaps even to weave all over the road. I plead guilty, and I expect to be back in court again tomorrow to answer the same charges with the same plea.

The firsthand accounts in this narrative are drawn in about equal proportions from archival and published sources. I have relied heavily on oral histories recorded and transcribed in past decades by the U.S. Naval Institute and Columbia University. In analyzing strategic and tactical decisions, I have gone back to the direct testimony of commanders in action reports, letters, war diaries, or contemporary debriefings. The detailed appendices at the end of major action reports sometimes provide a more penetrating analysis (how and why a battle was won or lost) than can be found in the historical literature. As in *Pacific Crucible*, I have frequently drawn from published collections of oral histories, diaries, or letters, not because these published primary accounts are more interesting than what can be dug up in archives, but because they happened to come first to hand. I have given special emphasis to obscure and out-of-print war memoirs, many published in the 1940s and 1950s, when the writers were in the prime of their lives and their memories were fresh. Memoirists are a self-selected breed; they tend to be naturally gifted writers with sharp opinions, fearless candor, and a cunning wit. They tell us not only how the war was waged but how it was lived. Their autobiographical accounts deserve a special place in the historical record, but many have been neglected or disregarded.

Any history of this scope must be, at least in some sense, a synthesis of the best and most recent scholarship in the field. The source notes and bibliography identify what I believe to be the most important contributions. Where there is controversy, I have done my best to represent the contending points of view fairly before supplying my own conclusions.

I owe thanks to the staffs of the FDR Presidential Library, the National Archives, the Naval History and Heritage Command, and the Naval War College. Ronald Russell, former editor and webmaster of the Battle of Midway Roundtable (online at www.midway42.org), did me a generous service by reviewing this manuscript and providing detailed comments on both the history and the prose. On the same count, I offer fond thanks to my friend Floyd Beaver, a fine editor-writer and a direct eyewitness to several of the events depicted in this book. Jim Hornfischer read the manuscript and provided valuable feedback; his next book, on the Marianas, will be a must-read for all of us with an interest in the Pacific War. My friends Damian Smith, Lucy Walker, Andrew Maloney, Feyi Akindoyeni, and Kate Deverall hosted me during my research in Australia. Robyn Middleton generously turned up sources at the Australian War Memorial. Smith and Maloney went beyond the call of duty by accompanying me to Guadalcanal and Tulagi. In Japan, I especially want to express my deep appreciation for the support and assistance of Kiyohiko Arafune, Yukio Satoh, Susumu Shimoyama, Yukoh Watanabe, Naoyuki Agawa, and VADM Yoji Koda (JMSDF, ret.). For help with the photographs and bibliography, thanks to Christopher Keilman. Thanks again to my talented and dedicated mapmaker, Loren Doppenberg.

I am proud to report that Eric Simonoff, the hardest-working man in the book business, remains my agent.

I am indebted to the entire team at W. W. Norton. Ryan Harrington and Mary Babcock played significant roles in the production of this book. My editor, Starling Lawrence, has kindly accommodated my ignominious record of blown deadlines. He remains a valuable advocate, counselor, and friend.

PROLOGUE

When aiming uncertainly for a landfall, somewhere in the blue immensity of the South Pacific, navigators watched for floating leaves or coconuts. They steered to follow seabirds overhead. They noted distant columns of thunderheads, which might be hovering over islands tucked beneath the horizon. They even lifted their noses and sniffed the breeze, because every so often—especially at night or in thick weather—land could be smelled before it could be seen. Nowhere was this more true than in the Solomons, an archipelago of fetid jungle-islands a few degrees south of the equator, flung diagonally along a 500-mile axis between the Coral Sea and Bougainville Island. The larger islands of the Solomons gave off an aroma of damp soil and rotting vegetation that could travel ten to twenty miles out to sea.

To sailors on a ship approaching the source of that peculiar scent, the shoulders of the mountains loomed gradually out of the mist, even if the peaks remained hidden within impenetrable cloud caps. Plains and valleys, laid out in a patchwork of darker and lighter shades of green, spread beneath the mountains. Palm groves and mangrove swamps emerged along the shore. Finally they spied the beach, a white horizontal border between the island's verdant overgrowth and the warm cerulean sea.

The Solomons are dominated by a dozen large islands arranged in a double chain. Scattered among those mountainous landmasses are hundreds of small and mostly uninhabited islets or atolls, some rising barely 10 feet above sea level. The natural history of the region, which lies astride the southern arc of the Pacific Ring of Fire, has been fantastically violent. Subduction zones, where one part of the planet's crust is shoved under another, and sea trenches plunge to depths of 20,000 feet or more, run parallel along the archipelago's northern and southern flanks. But the islands themselves, thrust up from the seabed by the same sorts of tectonic and volcanic forces, ascend to peaks of 5,000 to 7,000 feet. Mount Popomanaseu on Guadalcanal, 7,661 feet above sea level, stands just seven miles (as the crow flies) from the island's southern shore. If that same crow flew ten more miles out to sea, it would cross the edge of the South Solomon Trench, which plunges to a depth of 17,500 feet. Only on the Ring of Fire do such extremes of ocean deeps and high peaks occur in such proximity.

On the eve of the Second World War, the Solomons were home to about 100,000 dark-skinned Melanesians, the descendants of ancient nomadic peoples who had migrated from Asia across Pleistocene land bridges or navigated across the sea in hand-carved canoes. They lived much as they had in centuries or millennia past—in small villages and isolated tribal and family units, wearing little or nothing, scratching out a Neolithic subsistence by hunting, fishing, foraging, raising pigs, and tending small plots of taro and yams. They spoke about a hundred different languages or dialects, which were, in many cases, so divergent as to be unintelligible even between neighboring tribes. Their *lingua franca* was a rough and ready derivative of English called "pidgin," whose vocabulary ran to about 600 words. They did not share any sense of nationhood; they owed devotion only to their tribal kin, their ancestors, and their sacred places.

Savage wars were recorded in their oral traditions. In the span of a few generations, history became legend; in the span of a few more, legend became myth. Young men, upon reaching a certain age, took up arms to settle their legendary and mythic blood feuds. Descending suddenly on rival tribes and villages, they killed, beheaded, and ate their enemies. Headhunting and cannibalism were rife throughout the nineteenth century, an era when the natives first came into regular contact with European seafarers. Unscrupulous whites practiced an illegal slave trade known as "blackbirding"—tricking or forcing natives aboard their ships to be transported to Australia, where they were put to work on cane plantations. The victims' tribesmen were inclined to retaliate against anyone who looked like the malefactors. A white man who went ashore thus risked being beheaded and roasted for a feast. Afterward, his severed head might be shrunken and kept by his killer as a souvenir. Before the British took control of the Solomons in 1893 (vowing to put an end to blackbirding, headhunting, and cannibalism alike), the archipelago had earned a reputation as one of the most dangerous places on earth.

Putting aside for a moment the issues of self-determination, economic exploitation, and political legitimacy, history will show that half a century of colonial rule achieved a *Pax Britannica* in the Solomons. London governed the islands as a "protectorate" rather than a crown colony, asserting a relatively narrow authority over the affairs of its indigenous people. The islanders lived much as they had in the past, under the village authority of their tribal chiefs ("headmen" or "bigmen") and according to their own inherited customs and laws. Rather than resorting to arms, the bigmen appealed to colonial officials to mediate their disputes, and were generally willing to be bound by the judgments rendered. A tribe running short of food could petition for relief, and would be fed or resettled in a place with arable land or fishing rights. It is impossible to know at this remove what proportion of the natives genuinely welcomed the British government, but by the 1930s, very few hated it enough to oppose it outright. Even in the earlier years of the protectorate, organized revolts against British authority were scattered and short-lived. By 1941, there were none, and on most islands no standing force was needed to maintain order. The Solomons natives were simply overawed by the whites—by their weapons, their ships, their technology, and perhaps most of all, their airplanes. Such unfathomable power lay beyond their ken. To think of opposing it was absurd; better to acquiesce and make the best of it. Many islanders were fervently loyal to the British, and would have occasion to prove it in the impending Pacific War.

The seat of colonial government was the somnambulant little island of Tulagi in the Nggela (or Florida) island group, twenty miles north of the much larger island of Guadalcanal. On Tulagi, three miles long and shaped like an hourglass, the British had assembled all the requisite trappings of colonial life—an officers' club, a barracks, a hotel, a stately official residence, a small golf course, a cricket pitch, a wireless station, and a waterfront with rudimentary seaport amenities. The larger outlying islands were divided into districts, and each district was administered by a district officer (DO)—generally a young, unmarried man on the first rung of a career in the British Colonial Service. The district officer had to brave primitive living conditions, suffocating heat, and recurring attacks of malaria. He lived alone, in a modest house on the coast, near the best natural harbor available. More often than not, his house doubled as the local government headquarters. His portfolio of responsibilities was very broad, but he had no staff other than the natives he recruited, trained, and employed. He was a governor, judge, police chief, coroner, tax collector, civil engineer, record-keeper, harbormaster, paymaster, and postmaster. All public funds were funneled through his hands, and he was expected to account for every penny in his official record books. He trudged from village to village on muddy jungle footpaths, or sailed a small wooden schooner along the coast, where most of the population was concentrated.

The district officer, like every other typical white islander, was absolutely sure of his innate authority over the natives, who were (after all) "only just down from the trees." (The repugnant phrase, often heard in primitive outposts of the British Empire, put the colonialist rationale in a nutshell.) But the British were well practiced in the arts of colonial oppression and shrewd enough to rule *through* rather than over the existing social order. The seasoned district officer made a show of consulting respectfully with the village bigmen, and he always deferred to local laws and customs when they did not collide with British authority.

It was a minimalist government, but it was all that was needed. In the great game of imperial empires, the Solomons had never amounted to much. They were remote and inaccessible, even by the standards of the Pacific. They offered little in the way of trade or natural wealth. Few Europeans visited, and fewer could be induced to stay. In 1941, there were between 500 and 600 whites living in the entire archipelago, variously employed as plantation managers, shipping agents, traders, mining prospectors, storekeepers, doctors, colonial officers, and missionaries. Most looked forward to the day when their careers or economic fortunes would allow them to leave. The Solomons were a hardship post. The climate was sweltering and monsoonal. Rain-sodden jungles and mangrove swamps bred exotic fevers and skin disorders—malaria, dengue fever, blackwater fever, dysentery, filariasis, clysentery, leprosy, elephantiasis, prickly heat, and trench foot. Crocodiles and leeches lurked in the rivers and swamps; aggressive sharks patrolled the fringing reefs; scorpions, spiders, centipedes, and snakes stung and bit; knife-edged *kunai* grasses sliced into the flesh of those who walked through them; cat-sized rats scurried through the jungle underbrush. The best view of the islands, said the old hands, was from the stern of a departing ship.

Those were the Solomons in 1941. A marginal outpost of the British Empire. An economic and political backwater. A strategic nonentity; an afterthought. That was to change, suddenly and violently, in 1942.

WAR ARRIVED SIX WEEKS AFTER PEARL HARBOR, on the morning of January 22, 1942, when Japanese bombs first fell on Tulagi. The air attack was a bolt out of the blue. The British had not imagined that the Japanese would strike this far south and east, into the heart of the lower Solomons, especially when Allied fleets and armies were still giving battle thousands of miles closer to Japan, in the Philippines, Malaya, and the Dutch East Indies. The following day, a Japanese amphibious force landed at Rabaul—an Australian-held seaport and advanced airbase on the island of New Britain, 650 miles northwest of Tulagi—and swiftly overran the 1,500-man garrison stationed there. The British had precious little military presence of any kind in the Solomons, so it was instantly apparent that the Japanese could swallow up the entire archipelago any time they liked.

A similar pattern of conquest was unfolding throughout the Pacific. On December 7, 1941, Japan had launched a sea-air-land *Blitzkrieg* across a vast front, and advanced everywhere against feeble and confused Allied resistance. In every case—in Hawaii, the Philippines, Wake Island, Guam, Malaya, the Dutch East Indies, Hong Kong, Burma, New Britain—they delivered the initial blows from the air. Japanese carrier- and land-based bombers struck suddenly and across unexpectedly long distances, pulverizing Allied airfields and naval bases and clearing the skies over landing beaches. Invasion forces followed in columns of troopships. Japanese infantry units went ashore and advanced quickly against poorly defended Allied airfields—often seizing them intact and without firing a shot. Japanese air groups flew in to the captured airfields and prepared to stage the next round of attacks on positions farther south or east. When pockets of Allied resistance held out behind fortified lines—notably, the joint American-Filipino forces on Bataan Peninsula and Corregidor Island in the Philippines—they were cut off and bypassed. By this rapid, tightly choreographed, leapfrogging pattern, the Japanese won an immense Pacific empire in little more than four months while sustaining only token losses.

Before December 1941, American and British aviation experts had arrogantly insisted that Japanese airplanes were poorly engineered knockoffs of Western technology, and Japanese pilots were laughably inept crash-test dummies. These delusions were upended in the opening weeks of the war, when Allied airpower throughout most of the theater was effectively wiped out. Only after the tide of conquest had washed over them did the Allies begin to understand that they had been duped. Playing cleverly on the hubris and racial chauvinism of their Western rivals, the Japanese had disguised the formidable power of their air fleets and airmen.

The Imperial Japanese Navy was equipped with two very fine twin-engine medium bombers, the G3M (Allied code name "Nell") and the G4M ("Betty"). Each could be configured to carry torpedoes or bombs with a payload capacity exceeding 1,700 pounds and a flying range of more than 2,000 nautical miles. They were often escorted by the Mitsubishi A6M "Zero," Japan's superb single-seat fighter plane, which had been designed to outclimb, out-turn, and outmaneuver any other fighter aircraft of its era. Allied pilots who survived their initial dogfighting or "tail-chasing" contests with the Zero were staggered by the machine's capacity to turn sharply and climb away at high speed. Though it had been placed in service more than a year before the bombing of Pearl Harbor, and had run up a high tally of easy victories against Chiang Kai-Shek's air force in the skies over China, the Zero had remained virtually unknown in the West. Allied aviators had received no forewarning of its capabilities and no tactical advice in countering it, and therefore were forced to discover this strange, acrobatic warplane in the unforgiving school of air combat.

The British had staked their Asia-Pacific empire on their great naval and air base at Singapore, the "Gibraltar of the East." But from the first day of the war, when a Japanese invasion force landed on the northeast coast of the Malay Peninsula and Japanese bombers battered Royal Air Force (RAF) aerodromes throughout the region, the Malayan campaign brought a relentless succession of one-sided Japanese victories in the air, on the land, and at sea. Three days after Pearl Harbor, Japanese warplanes sank the battleship *Prince of Wales* and the battlecruiser *Repulse* off the Malayan coast—the first time in naval history that capital ships at sea had been destroyed by air attack. British commanders pulled their surviving aircraft back to Singapore, yielding the skies over northern Malaya to the enemy. Japanese army forces drove south with remarkable speed, routing British Commonwealth troops from their positions and sending them into disorderly retreat. The invaders combined raging frontal charges with flanking movements and infiltration tactics, in which small groups of lightly armed Japanese soldiers penetrated the jungles and mangrove swamps and attacked the British from behind. They leapfrogged down the coast by sea lifts in small craft. In the face of such a shrewd and agile enemy, and with Japanese aircraft attacking with impunity from overhead, the British lines were quick to abandon their positions and flee.

As they joined up with other units farther south, or entered the island-city of Singapore, they spread a terrifying new image of the enemy. The Japanese were super-warriors, preternaturally endowed with superior fighting traits and an ability to live roughly off the land. They could not be defeated in the jungle, or evidently in the air or at sea; they must be invincible, and they were coming. Among many of the British and British Commonwealth troops, an attitude of despondency and resignation took hold. They were sullen and scornful of their officers, who had failed utterly to prepare for a foe they had so recently insisted on holding in contempt. Morale caved in on itself. From the wharves of Singapore, civilians began a panicked exodus, clamoring for passage on any departing ship. Officers finagled orders to be transferred to Java or anywhere else. A week after Japanese forces crossed the Johore Strait and entered Singapore, General Arthur Percival surrendered about 80,000 troops to a Japanese army less than half that size. With Singapore gone, the fate of the Dutch East Indies was preordained. An overmatched multinational Allied fleet was swiftly defeated in naval actions at the end of February, and remaining air and ground forces on Java were evacuated to Australia.

Now, in the Solomons, a stampede of panicked white refugees poured south and east, hoping to find a ship to Australia. Colonial officials faced a similarly unmanageable state of affairs—except that in the Solomons, unlike in Malaya, there were no more than a handful of British troops in place to put up any resistance whatsoever. Protectorate officials did not pretend there was any realistic hope of stopping the next stage of the Japanese advance. The enemy would take the Solomons and eject the British, and months or perhaps years would pass before the Allies could return in force. The civilians of Tulagi and the adjoining islands packed up their belongings and fled. The resident commissioner, Britain's senior official in the islands, moved to Malaita, a large island farther east. Small schooners and cutters, usually under sail, carried evacuees from the northwest on the prevailing winds. A dilapidated coal steamer, the *Morinda*, made her last trip out of the Solomons in January. At the wharf on Gavutu, an island near Tulagi, a crowd of civilian refugees demanded to come aboard. After a near riot in which a doctor was injured, the captain took the terrified evacuees on board to be spirited away to Australia.[1]

By March 1942, most of the whites were gone from the Solomons, and civil order was crumbling. But the young district officers of the Colonial Service were told to remain and carry on with their jobs. The British government even arranged to have their applications for military service denied.

Martin Clemens was one such man. He was a twenty-six-year-old Scotsman, the son of an Aberdeen choirmaster, who had won scholarships to prestigious schools and graduated from Christ's College, Cambridge. Clemens had entered the Colonial Service in 1937, had been posted to the Solomons in 1938, and had served on two of the big jungle-islands in the Solomons archipelago—San Cristobal and Malaita. He was a rugged man, mustachioed and square-jawed, but he was also a product of his era, his schooling, and the class-bound society in which he had been raised. His staunch companion was a little black dog of uncertain breed named Suinao. Fastidious in his dress and personal grooming, disciplined in his habits, and stoic in the face of danger, Clemens kept a meticulous and perceptive personal diary in which he quoted Shakespeare and punctuated his observations with modish exclamations such as "Wizard!" and "Calloo, Callay!" In the trying months of Japanese occupation, he would prove resourceful, courageous, and resilient.

As the colonial administration cleared out of Tulagi, Clemens was ordered to take over the job of district officer on Guadalcanal. The island's administrative seat was at Aola, on the north shore—about twenty miles southeast of Tulagi, across the body of water that would later take the name "Ironbottom Sound." Here Clemens moved into a modest white house built on wooden piles and thatched with palm leaves. Outside, amid frangipani and hibiscus plants and a small garden plot of yams and taro, he set up an observation platform at the top of a large banyan tree. A native scout was posted there throughout the daylight hours, watching for enemy airplanes.

Tulagi and the RAF installations on nearby Gavutu and Tanambogo were bombed every morning, as regularly and predictably as a Tokyo train schedule. Big four-engine Kawanishi flying boats flew high overhead almost daily, and often doubled back at treetop altitude for a hard, close look at Clemens's house.

One of Clemens's duties was to report these flights through a radio network known as the "coastwatching service," an arm of the Royal Australian Navy (RAN). The coastwatchers were first conceived as an informal, all-volunteer organization to provide early warning of enemy shipping and air movements. The watchers were to radio their sighting reports to a receiver station in Townsville, on the northern coast of Australia. Each man was equipped with a Type 3B "teleradio," a device that could send voice transmissions to a range of about 400 miles or tapped code (Morse) to a range of about 600 miles. A specially cut crystal enabled the machines to transmit in the seldom-used 6 MHz frequency, chosen in the vain hope that Japanese eavesdroppers might miss the transmissions. The greatest drawback to the apparatus was its size. It included more than a dozen separate elements, including a receiver, a transmitter, antennae, a loudspeaker, a set of aerials, and a large supply of spare parts. It was powered by a pair of heavy six-volt automobile batteries that had to be recharged frequently, requiring a gasoline generator and a fuel supply.

Clemens made his transmissions each day. He also listened to the broadcasts of other coastwatchers on islands up the Solomons chain, who recorded the relentless progress of Japanese forces as they swept down from the northwest. Positions fell, garrisons were routed, and coastwatchers snuck into the jungle interior. The Japanese pushed into Buka Passage, north of Bougainville, forcing the small RAF detachment there to scatter into the bush. On April 5, a surprise landing at Kangu Beach, on southern Bougainville, forced coastwatching station DMK at Buin off the air.[2] In the following week, the Japanese expanded their grip on the area around Buin and seized nearby Shortland Island.

Clemens tried to maintain civil order on Guadalcanal, but he could not be everywhere at once, and the abandoned plantations were looted and vandalized by natives and white refugees. He arrested looters, took witness testimony, and removed abandoned supplies to secure government storehouses. Much of his time was consumed in arranging food, shelter, and ship passage for groups of refugees, or repatriating native workers from other islands who had been idled by the abandonment of the plantations.

That the white inhabitants of the islands were fleeing in panic could not be concealed from the natives, who told one another, "Altogether Japan 'e come."[3] The tribal bigmen traveled to Aola from villages all over the island and put their questions to Clemens. Why were most of the whites falling all over themselves to escape the island? What would become of their villages under Japanese occupation? In his memoir, Clemens recounted his speech (in pidgin) to a delegation of chiefs in March 1942: "No matter altogether Japan 'e come, me stop long youfella. Business belong youfella boil'm, all 'e way, bymbye altogether b'long mefella come save'm youme. Me no savvy who, me no savvy when, but bymbye everyt'ing 'e alright."[4] (Even if the Japanese come in strength, I will stay here with you. Stick with me and eventually the Allies will return and save us from the enemy. I don't know who will come, or when, but we'll all be fine in the end.) Clemens recalled that he had made the promise with a "sinking heart," but the chiefs appeared to accept it.

In early April, Clemens sailed his schooner to the northwestern tip of Guadalcanal to pay a visit to a plantation manager named F. Ashton "Snowy" Rhoades. Rhoades, a hardy, stubbornly independent Australian, had watched the exodus of most of the island's other white residents with imperious disgust, and refused to join it. He had nothing but contempt for the British colonial government, which (he wrote in his diary) had simply "collapsed."[5] From his house high on a cliff at Lavoro, he commanded a broad vista of the sea and sky to the west, the direction from which Japanese ships and planes must come. Clemens convinced Rhoades to join the coastwatching network, and set him up with a teleradio.

On April 29, Allied patrol aircraft spotted a Japanese fleet moving down from the upper Solomons. Two days later, Clemens watched the heaviest bombing raid yet on Tulagi. On May 2, coastwatchers on Santa Isabel reported observing a Japanese seaplane carrier in a bay off the northwestern end of the island, just 150 miles from Tulagi. With that clear evidence of an impending invasion, the Royal Australian Air Force (RAAF) detachment on Tanambogo, where there were just four seaplanes and a small garrison, announced their withdrawal in anticipation of an enemy landing. They navigated an old steamer across the sound to Aola, towing a damaged Catalina seaplane, which they placed in Clemens's care. Clemens recruited several hundred natives to haul the aircraft up the beach and hide it under palm leaves.

At dawn on May 3, a small Japanese fleet sailed into Tulagi Harbor. Troops went ashore to find the British government gone and the island largely deserted. Clemens immediately arranged to have the damaged Catalina towed out into the sound and scuttled.

The morning of May 4 brought a stirring plot twist, as a large formation of strange planes appeared overhead at 0800. They had not come from the northwest, the direction of enemy airbases at Rabaul and at Buka Island, but from the south. The strangers were carrier bombers and fighters of the U.S. aircraft carrier *Yorktown*, and their surprise airstrike on the Japanese ships anchored off Tulagi was the opening blow in the four-day Battle of the Coral Sea (May 4–8, 1942). Snowy Rhoades wrote that he was startled to hear "a great droning overhead and saw to my amazement twenty or thirty single-engine planes flying in a course direct to Tulagi. These planes were only a few hundred feet up and I could plainly see stars on their wings."[6] Clemens was thrilled by "the magnificent spectacle of twelve dive bombers plunging down out of the clouds over Tulagi. . . . What a sight for sore eyes."[7] Having expended their bombs and torpedoes, the intruders disappeared back to the south, over the mountainous spine of Guadalcanal.

Clemens's position was precarious. The American planes had come and gone, and they had not dislodged the Japanese forces from Tulagi. His house was a stone's throw from the beach, and the Japanese might descend on him at any moment. On May 5, Clemens was on the beach at Aola when three Kawanishis suddenly roared low over his head. A few days later, another Australian coastwatcher on Bougainville reported that a large Japanese fleet was rendezvousing at Queen Carola Harbour off Buka. "For me, the issues now were clear," Clemens observed. "Here we were at Aola, and there were the Japs at Tulagi, less than twenty miles away."[8] The enemy was more likely to come to Aola than to any other part of the coast, as they would know (from the natives they had interrogated) that it was the British administrative headquarters for all of Guadalcanal. If captured, Clemens could look forward to being tortured and forced to reveal all he knew.

Snowy Rhoades, at Lavoro on the far northwestern tip of the island, was in a similarly worrying fix. Japanese patrol planes flew low over his house nearly every day. Feeling himself "as public as a goldfish," he hid in a hole covered by palm fronds whenever he heard the approaching engines. He noted in his diary, "I realized that the war had now come to us at last and that I was nothing else but a Civilian Spy and if caught would be treated accordingly."[9]

Like all the continental islands of the Solomons, Guadalcanal was large and almost entirely undeveloped. Roads were unknown except on the plantations; inland travel was done on foot, by muddy jungle trails or on streambeds. Beyond the coastal plains lay a vast, unmapped, undulating jungle landscape. The best-traveled footpaths led up knife-edge mountain ridges separated by deep ravines. A man could hide almost anywhere, concealed in the lowering jungle, and a passing column of enemy soldiers would never detect his presence.

There was much to do and little time to do it. Supplies, provisions, weapons, ammunition, and fuel cans had to be packed up and carried away to secret jungle caches. Nothing should be left behind that the enemy might find valuable; everything had to be either taken or destroyed. "There was an awful lot to do, and little time to think," said Clemens. "Things were happening very fast, and the position was very grim. I was pinned to the beach by the teleradio, yet I would have to get everything hidden away in the bush quick and lively, as a fast launch would take only two hours to come from Tulagi."[10]

Clemens ran a native constabulary, manned by trustworthy men. But he was also required to employ hundreds of others as laborers and carriers— and for every one native he employed, there were perhaps ten more who knew where he was going and what he was doing. Could he trust them? Even if he was not directly betrayed to the Japanese, could the native carriers be trusted not to plunder the secret supply caches? In late May, Clemens and Rhoades learned that a native named George Bogese, who had worked as a medical practitioner on Savo Island, was cooperating with the Japanese. The news sent a shudder up their spines because Bogese knew them personally and could give the enemy a great deal of information.

On May 19, feeling that he had already lingered too long, Clemens left Aola, leading a long cavalcade of heavily burdened carriers. Sixteen men were needed to carry the teleradio and its many component parts, which altogether weighed almost 300 pounds. Others carried vital government records, weapons, food, fuel, even his office safe with some £800 in silver coinage. Their path led up through grassy plains to a region of steeply ascending red clay hills.

At dusk they stopped, exhausted, at a little village named Palapao. Clemens moved into a small leaf hut that would double as his office and residence, and began at once to reassemble the teleradio. He strung the aerial between two trees and arranged vines to conceal it from the air. Workers began building an observation platform on one of the highest trees in the village. A native sentry would stand watch through the daylight hours, with orders to blow a note on a conch shell should the Japanese land on the beach several miles below.

Clemens's retreat was timely. The first small Japanese scouting parties arrived on Guadalcanal a week later. When questioned, the local natives pleaded ignorance of the whereabouts of any white men, replying, "Me no savvy," or "Altogether go finish."[11] On June 8, a larger force of Japanese troops came ashore and set up a tent camp on the plains near the Lunga River. Ten days later, a Japanese destroyer anchored a few hundred feet off the mouth of the Lunga and began unloading supplies on the beach. Clemens noted in his diary entry of June 20, "It looks as if the Nips are here to stay." Clemens had his trusted constables walk down to Lunga to gather information. The Japanese appeared to be building a wharf and were certainly burning fields on Lunga plantation.[12] That suggested they might be laying the groundwork for an airstrip, and Clemens promptly reported the intelligence to Townsville, where it was relayed to the navy office in Melbourne, and from there to the Allied high command in Washington and London.

In the first week of July, a twelve-ship convoy came down to Savo Sound and anchored off the new wharf. Heavy construction equipment and trucks came ashore, with several hundred more troops and laborers. That removed all doubt. The Japanese were building an airstrip on Guadalcanal, and if they were permitted to finish it, they would extend their air search capabilities deep into the Coral Sea. Clemens also learned from his scouts that the Japanese had asked after him by name. They had evidently intercepted some of his transmissions. Might they pinpoint his position using radio direction-finding gear? The natives also reported that the Japanese were planning to track him with bloodhounds. "That was cheerful news," Clemens dryly observed.

Palapao, remote as it was, was no longer safe. On July 4, Clemens moved again, farther up and back into the hills, to a tiny, impoverished village called Vungana. The trail went up a muddy ridge, with the land falling away steeply on either side. Clemens climbed the more treacherous sections with Suinao, his little dog, clutched under one arm. He watched in trepidation as the barefoot carriers struggled under the weight of his equipment, "and I died a thousand deaths as I watched the battery carriers, who had had to give up pole and sling, holding a heavy battery on their shoulder with one hand while trying to stop themselves from falling with the other."

Vungana amounted to a half-dozen thatched huts on a narrow spur of land, but it was so high in the foothills that it was probably safe from the Japanese, at least for the moment. From that altitude, more than 1,500 feet above sea level, Clemens commanded a magnificent view of the Lunga airfield and the entire sound, and could closely observe the shipping movements between Tulagi and Guadalcanal. Again he set up his teleradio, stringing the aerial between two large green bamboo trees. But the apparatus was becoming increasingly balky. It was not designed for portability, and the humidity seemed to have eaten away at its internal circuitry. Clemens found it necessary to open the case and allow the mechanism to dry in the sun all afternoon before attempting to transmit in the early evening.

July was the darkest period of the war for Clemens. The nights were cold at that altitude, and he could barely sleep. His reserves of food, money, fuel, and spare parts were running short. Even fresh water had to be carried up to the village from a stream several hundred feet below. His native scouts reported that Japanese troops were spreading out, searching along the coast and up the rivers, closely interrogating the missionaries who had remained behind. On July 8, Clemens radioed Townsville to report that 700 Japanese troops were bivouacked in tents on the plains below. The Scotsman added that he was not sure how much longer he could hold out. The radio's charging engine was increasingly difficult to start, and it seemed only a matter of time before the radio would fail for good. His native workers were hungry, and if he could not feed them, he could not expect them to stay.

On the morning of July 26, Clemens was surprised by a sudden appearance of a Kawanishi over Vungana, just a few hundred feet above his head. He dived for cover and concealed himself just as the aircraft banked sharply and came back around for a closer look. He had to assume he had been spotted. Clemens gave serious consideration to attempting the grueling and dangerous overland trek to the southern (weather) coast of Guadalcanal, in hopes of finding a hidden boat that could carry him to Australia.

Cryptic radio messages from Townsville asked precise questions. What was the exact location of the Japanese wireless station? The type and number of troops? The placement and caliber of their artillery pieces? Were any aircraft on the island? These queries fired Clemens's hopes because they seemed to presage an operation of some kind, probably an airstrike. Naturally the men on the other side of the radio link could tell him nothing, but they hinted that deliverance was imminent: "It won't be long now." So he waited, agonized, and lost weight. "The more I looked, the more impossible the situation seemed to be. With my charging engine working only intermittently, it was a struggle just to get out the traffic, let alone consult others as to what should be done."

On August 6, a scout returned from the coast to report that the airfield at Lunga had been rolled with gravel and dirt and appeared ready to receive aircraft. A hangar was under construction near the airstrip. Japanese troops on the island now numbered approximately 4,000. Clemens radioed the new intelligence and asked whether the Allies would attempt to destroy the airfield. No answer came. "All I could taste was the bitterness of defeat," he wrote.[13] He went to bed early, his stomach empty, and descended into a deep slumber.

Wrenched awake by the shock and rumble of artillery, Clemens checked his watch. It was 6:13 a.m. and still dark. Heavy naval guns were firing in Savo Sound. What ships? Whose ships? An excited scout reported that the entire Japanese navy was anchored in Lunga, and for a moment, Clemens recalled, "my heart stood still." In another few minutes, his ears pricked up at the drone of airplanes overhead. Tuning the radio, he tried different frequencies until he heard American-accented voices describing a panorama of destruction along the coast. He noted references to "Orange Base," "Black Base," and "Red Base." Three aircraft carriers! "Wizard!!!" he wrote in his diary. "Calloo, Callay, oh, what a day!!!"[14]

As dawn broke, Clemens swept the sound with his binoculars. He counted more than fifty ships, including several heavy cruisers that were raining 8-inch projectiles down on Japanese installations around Lunga Point. Buildings and fuel dumps blazed fiercely and discharged huge columns of oily black smoke. Green-clad troops descended from transports into landing boats, which then motored in toward beaches west of Lunga. It was the largest amphibious landing that Clemens—or anyone else—had ever witnessed. His teleradio was failing rapidly, the inevitable result of rough handling and humidity. But Martin Clemens did not need a radio to tell him the Yanks had come to stay.

The Pacific, 1942

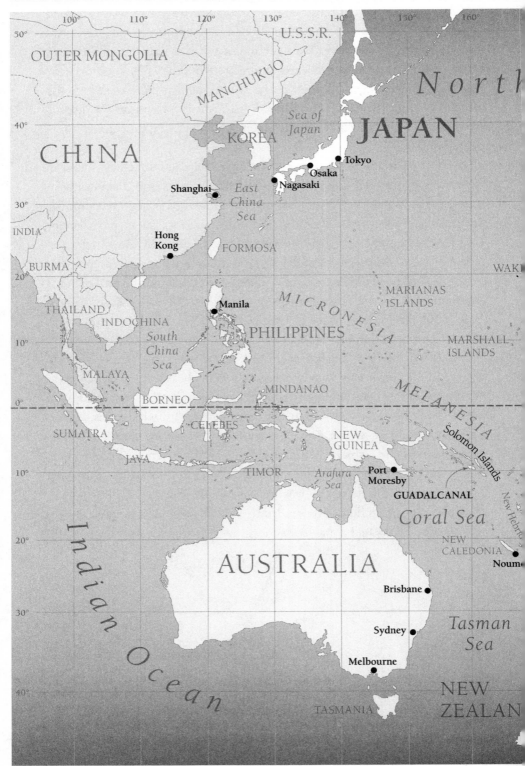

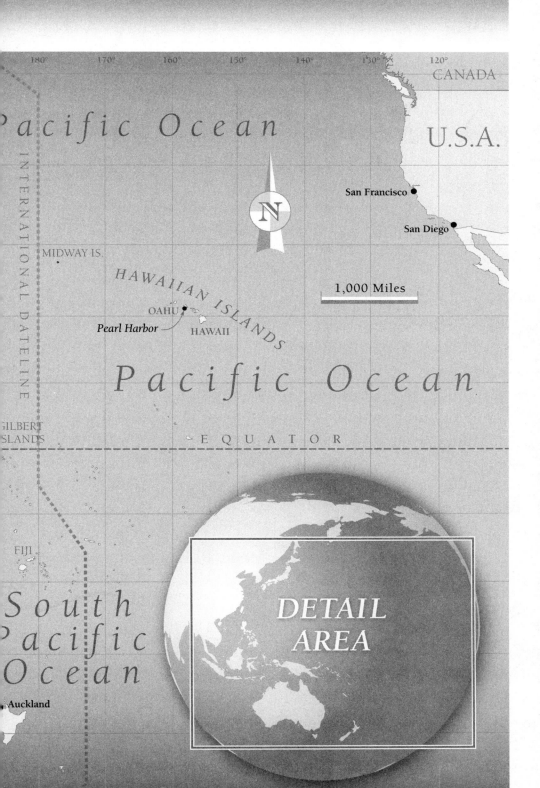

The Conquering Tide

Across the sea, water-drenched corpses;
Across the mountains, grass-covered corpses.
We shall die by the side of our Emperor,
We shall never look back.
              —"UMI YUKABA" (Across the Sea)
                  Anthem of the Imperial Japanese Navy

Yea, though I walk through the valley of the shadow of death,
I will fear no evil.
              PSALM 23

Chapter One

HENRY L. STIMSON, THE VETERAN REPUBLICAN STATESMAN WHO served as Franklin Delano Roosevelt's secretary of war, left a well-aimed barb in his postwar memoir. Recounting the bitter rivalry between the army and the navy, a struggle for influence and resources that colored every phase of the Pacific War, Stimson thought the trouble "grew mainly from the peculiar psychology of the Navy Department, which frequently seemed to retire from the realm of logic into a dim religious world in which Neptune was God, Mahan his prophet, and the United States Navy the only true Church."[1]

A navy partisan would not lack for ripostes—the messianic fantasies of General Douglas MacArthur come quickly to mind—but Stimson's characterization should not be too lightly dismissed. During past eras of peace, the navy had tended to become insular, inward looking, and parochial. Every flag officer (admiral) had passed through the same way stations: Annapolis, the Naval War College, a series of commands ashore and at sea. Whereas the army's wartime chief of staff, General George C. Marshall, had attended Virginia Military Institute (VMI) rather than West Point, there was not an admiral in the navy who had not graduated from the Naval Academy. Every senior naval commander had lived his entire adult life in the navy, beginning at the tender age of seventeen or eighteen. He had been steeped in the seapower doctrines of Alfred Thayer Mahan, the eminent naval historian and strategic theorist. He had been taught to revere the heritage and traditions of the institution, to owe it his fierce and undying allegiance: "The Navy: first, last, and always."[2]

Interservice enmity was not a specifically American predicament. Indeed, it was far more impassioned in Japan, where the generals and admirals regarded one another as virtual enemies, and a deadlock between them had been at the heart of that nation's reckless lurch into a calamitous war. But the American military leadership, thrust unexpectedly into war in 1941, was largely unprepared to function in an integrated high command. The army and navy had interacted very little in peacetime and had neglected the challenges of planning and executing joint operations. Until 1947, there was no such thing as a Department of Defense, or a secretary of defense— the navy and war departments were independent and coequal, each headed by a civilian cabinet secretary who reported directly to the president. Before December 1941, there was no such thing as a Joint Chiefs of Staff (JCS)— that body was convened as an ad hoc committee for the first wartime summit with the British. With no other mechanism on hand for interservice cooperation, the JCS continued to meet regularly for the duration of the war, but it functioned without formal statutory authority and without an official chairman. Admiral Ernest J. King, the highest-ranking officer in the navy, was not subordinate to Marshall, or vice versa. The military chiefs either muddled toward a consensus or were obliged to appeal their disputes to President Roosevelt.[3]

The acrimony was found at every rank. Vicious brawls erupted nightly between sailors, marines, and soldiers on the streets of San Francisco and Honolulu. Sailors and soldiers taunted one another as "swabbies" and "dogfaces" and settled the issue with their fists. Infantrymen begrudged sailors their hot meals and clean bunks, amenities that seemed criminally lavish when compared to the squalor and privations of war on land. The bad feeling between sailors and marines had been notorious since the founding of both services during the American Revolution. Insults crept into the "padding" inserted at the beginning and end of encrypted radio messages— for example, "U.S. Marine Corps, seagoing bellhops, ya, ya, ya."[4] On naval bases across the world, guardhouses and gates were manned by scowling marines whose customary hail to all sailors was, "Where in the hell do you think you're going?"

Senior army officers regarded the entire Marine Corps as a plot hatched by the navy to usurp their rightful function, and did their best to asphyxiate it, or at least limit its deployments to units no larger than a regiment. Naval aviators grumbled that the Army Air Forces (USAAF) handed out medals like after-dinner mints. Pilots of different services took satisfaction in "buzz-ing" a rival's airfields and aircraft, or (when on the ground) holding down their brakes while gunning their engines in order to blow clouds of dirt and dust onto their adversaries.

Every major action early in the Pacific War involved a dimension of interservice rancor. After the attack on Pearl Harbor, Navy Secretary Frank Knox often stressed that the army had been assigned primary responsibil-ity for the air defense of Oahu. After the spirited (and ultimately futile) defense of Wake Island, navy and marine public relations offices vied for public acclaim. MacArthur declared that the fall of the Philippines was "due fundamentally" to a "lack of seapower in the Pacific."[5] The Doolittle Raid, an operation in which army B-25 bombers were launched from an aircraft carrier to strike Japan in April 1942, was a rare successful example of cooperation between army and naval air units. But Colonel James H. Doolittle's airmen later faulted Admiral William F. Halsey Jr. for ordering them to launch too early, when the task force was still nearly 700 miles from Japan. At the Battle of the Coral Sea (May 4–8, 1942), MacArthur's Australian-based USAAF planes were blamed for inaccurate sighting reports and for dropping bombs on units of the Allied fleet, having mis-taken them for Japanese ships. (All fell harmlessly into the sea.)

At the Battle of Midway (June 4–6, 1942), navy dive-bombers flying from the *Enterprise* and *Yorktown* attacked and destroyed four of Japan's fin-est and largest aircraft carriers. But initial press reports mistakenly credited army B-17s flying from airfields on Midway. "BIG BOMBERS WON" was the front-page headline in the *New York Times* on June 12, 1942. Brigadier General Willis H. Hale announced that "the Battle of Midway was primar-ily won in the blasting by Flying Fortresses of a Japanese naval task force, including carriers, off the island on the morning of June 4."[6] History would eventually determine that no bomb dropped by any army plane had struck any Japanese ship. But in the immediate aftermath of the victory, the B-17 crews returned first to Honolulu and regaled news correspondents with their claims of spectacular and numerous hits on the enemy fleet. Navy pilots who knew what had really happened were incensed. When aviators of the two services came face to face at the Moana Hotel in Honolulu a week after the battle, arguments escalated into fistfights. Ensign Fred Mears, a *Hornet* torpedo pilot, noted that the navy aviators "had seen their friends risk and sometimes lose their lives going below 1,000 feet to dive-bomb, torpedo, and sink Jap warships while the army stayed at a safe 20,000 feet and not only missed but sometimes dropped on our own craft. That's why they got mad at the army."[7]

Marine General Holland M. "Howlin' Mad" Smith, in a score-settling postwar memoir, indicted the navy for "mental arteriosclerosis."[8] He cited a range of offenses. The navy had failed to provide enough gunfire and aviation support in amphibious operations. It had forced the marines to make due with second-rate, cast-off, obsolete equipment and weaponry. Admirals in offshore task forces had interfered with marine commanders' authority on the beachheads. Smith's umbrage was shared by men down the ranks. Marine infantrymen, carried to enemy beaches in navy transports, took offense at injustices large and small. Their memoirs and oral histories are rife with grievances—accounts of unequal mess privileges and berthing arrangements; of being denied the right to purchase candy or cigarettes at the ship's store; of leaving their personal effects in care of the navy and never seeing them again; of being barricaded in the lower decks and cut off from fresh air or sunshine; of being forced to abide by ridiculous rules "for the safety of the ship." Marines left a sardonic note for the crew of a navy transport that had brought them to Peleliu, site of one of the bloodiest amphibious assaults of the war:

> It gives us great pleasure at this time to extend our sincere thanks
> to all members of the crew for their kind and considerate treatment
> of Marines during this cruise. We non-combatants realize that the
> brave and stalwart members of the crew are winning the war in the
> Pacific. You Navy people even go within ten miles of a Japanese island,
> thereby risking your precious lives. Oh how courageous you are![9]

More than any other type of military operation, amphibious warfare—striking an enemy on land by way of sea—exposed and aggravated the frictions between the services. The Pacific War was the largest, bloodiest, most costly, most technically innovative, and most logistically complex amphibious war in history. To roll back the tide of Japanese conquests, the Allies would be required to seize one island after another, advancing across thousands of miles of ocean in two huge parallel offensives on either side of the equator. The army, navy, and marines were compelled to work together in sustained and intricate cooperation. They would make many mistakes, and do their best to learn from them. But even when their operations were successful, the interservice feuding left scars that even victory could not heal.

On June 13, having learned of the American victory at the Battle of Midway, British prime minister Winston Churchill cabled Roosevelt: "This is the moment for me to send you my heartiest congratulations on the grand American victories in the Pacific which have very decidedly altered the balance of the naval war. All good wishes to you and friends."[10]

Even in a routine congratulatory telegram, Churchill chose his words carefully. The battle had "altered the balance" of the Pacific War; it had not turned the tide. The Imperial Japanese Navy had lost the carriers *Hiryu*, *Soryu*, *Kaga*, and *Akagi* with all of their aircraft, and more than 3,000 veteran officers, sailors, and airmen had been killed in action. Even so, Japan retained a numerical advantage in most categories of deployed naval and air strength. The Combined Fleet could still muster five aircraft carriers to the Americans' four and had several more under construction. Except for the cruiser *Mikuma*, destroyed in mopping-up operations two days after the sinking of the four carriers, Japan's surface naval forces were intact. Midway had claimed none of Japan's redoubtable battleships, submarines, destroyers, troopships, or flying boats, or any of its potent land-based medium bombers. All but about 110 of Japan's veteran carrier aviators survived the battle, even while losing their planes, and ample numbers of replacement aircraft were still coming off the assembly lines in Nagoya, Yokosuka, Musashino, and Kure. Midway hardly diminished the violence or energy of the Japanese offensive in the South Pacific, where naval, ground, and air forces based at Rabaul on New Britain island were pushing south and east and keeping local Allied forces on a tenuous defensive.

Two weeks after Midway, Admiral King traveled from Washington to Annapolis to address the 611 midshipmen of the Naval Academy's class of 1942. Theirs was the largest class in the academy's ninety-seven-year history. The class was being graduated a year early, their course of study having been cut to three years from four, to feed the expanding fleet's demand for new officers. Standing behind a rostrum in Dahlgren Hall, the admiral warned the young men that they were to be thrown into the "greatest war in history" and that the effort would require "unremitting labor and a multitude of heartaches and sacrifices such as this country has never before known."[11]

King was the most powerful admiral in American history, the first to occupy simultaneously the two most powerful posts in the service—those of Commander in Chief of the U.S. Fleet (COMINCH) and Chief of Naval Operations (CNO). A tall, dark-haired man with a narrow face and sharply cleft chin, he was unusual among his colleagues in having risen from working-class origins. He had been born and raised in Lorain, Ohio, where his father had worked as a foreman at a railroad machine shop.

King was more respected than liked by his colleagues. Disdaining the tradition of clubby collegiality that bound Annapolis graduates to one another, he had made it his personal business to rid the service of men he regarded as indolent or inept. The admiral, according to an aide, would "tolerate almost anything in an officer except incompetence, laziness, or verbosity."[12] King was direct to the point of obnoxiousness, and he did not bother to conceal his contempt for those who opposed him. General Marshall remarked after the war, "I had trouble with King because he was always sore at everybody. He was perpetually mean."[13] In his private wartime diary, General Dwight D. Eisenhower wrote in the same vein, but less delicately: "One thing that might help win this war is to get someone to shoot King. He's the antithesis of cooperation, a deliberately rude person, which means he's a mental bully."[14]

The British military chiefs tended to suspect King of conspiring to divert forces from Europe to the Pacific. General Sir Alan Brooke, chief of the British Imperial General Staff, noted in his diary during the Casablanca conference in early 1943:

> King . . . is a shrewd and somewhat swollen headed individual. His
> vision is mainly limited to the Pacific, and any operation calculated to
> distract from the force available in the Pacific does not meet with his
> support or approval. He does not approach the problem with a world-
> wide war point of view, but instead with one biased entirely in favor
> of the Pacific. Although he pays lip service to the fundamental policy
> that we must first defeat Germany and then turn on Japan, he fails to
> apply it in any problems connected with the war.[15]

The truth was more nuanced. King never questioned the strategic wisdom of "Europe-first," the Allies' plan (agreed to in early 1941, reaffirmed after the attack on Pearl Harbor) to direct the lion's share of their collective effort against Germany. The German *Wehrmacht* was engaged on the eastern front, in the most cataclysmic ground war ever waged. Should it prevail, forcing a Russian surrender or collapse, Hitler could redeploy a hundred divisions or more to western Europe. Conversely, if Germany could be overpowered, the defeat of Japan and Italy must inevitably follow.

But the "Europe-first" (or "Germany-first") policy, stated in the abstract, left a host of subsidiary questions unresolved. If the Pacific theater was to receive a lesser share of Allied strength, what exactly should that proportion be? Ten percent? Or something closer to 30 percent? What did it mean to "hold" against an enemy that could attack anywhere across a vast ocean front? There were no foxholes at sea, no trenches or defensive fortifications. Even after its reverse at Midway, Japan posed a threat to Allied territories throughout the South Pacific, and until the theater could be stabilized, there was no prospect of the hypothetical holding action pictured in Allied planning documents. The danger was imminent, and the need to counter it imperative.

In the spring of 1942, King had pressed his colleagues to reinforce the sea route between North America and Australia. Acknowledging the scarcity of Allied troops, as well as shipping and military assets of every kind, with the unavoidable upshot that his plans might hinder the campaign against Germany, King told the other joint chiefs that the South Pacific emergency was "certainly the more urgent—it must be faced now. Quite apart from any idea of future advance in this theater, we must see to it that we are actually able to maintain our present positions."[16] He repeatedly steered discussions back to the need for "strong points," particularly in Samoa, Fiji, New Caledonia, New Hebrides, and Tonga.[17] Those islands could be held only with concentrated reinforcements of garrison troops, aircraft, and labor and equipment for airfield construction. On May 12, King asked Marshall to transfer at least three army bomber groups—with ground crews, spare parts, fuel, and ammunition—from Australia and Hawaii to New Caledonia, Efate, and Fiji.[18]

As always, however, King would not be satisfied with a purely static defense. When enough force was concentrated into this network of South Pacific strong points, the Allies should launch a more ambitious program—a northwest counteroffensive, staged from bases in the New Hebrides, into the Solomons and the Bismarck Archipelago, "after the same fashion of step-by-step advances that the Japanese used in the

South China Sea."[19] On June 24, he cabled an early warning of his contemplated offensive to Admiral Chester W. Nimitz, Commander in Chief of the Pacific Fleet (CINCPAC). Nimitz should muster naval and air forces for "the seizure and initial occupation of Tulagi and adjacent islands."[20] The following day King added that the offensive would begin "about August 1."[21]

Five weeks to launch the biggest amphibious assault since Gallipoli? In one of the most primitive and inaccessible theaters of the war? For the past several months, King had been lobbying the Joint Chiefs and the White House for a Solomons offensive, but he had never intimated that it could be launched as early as August. The timetable seemed implausibly premature.

Command responsibility would fall to Admiral Robert L. Ghormley, the newly appointed Commander of South Pacific Forces (COMSOPAC). But Ghormley had arrived in the theater only five weeks earlier, and his was an entirely new command. He was camped for the moment in Auckland, New Zealand, but he had not yet pulled together a staff or established a permanent headquarters. Immersed in the complexities of logistics, the COMSOPAC was not yet even receiving timely communications because of "inexperienced radio and coding personnel."[22]

Uppermost in Ghormley's mind was the problem of fuel. Chartered tankers had been dispatched from North America with half a million barrels of oil, and he would have three fleet oilers assigned for underway replenishment. He had small dry docks at Auckland and Wellington on New Zealand's North Island, but any major damage to larger ships would have to be handled in Pearl Harbor or North America. He had no facilities for bulk fuel storage north of New Zealand. Ammunition of every category and caliber was in dangerously short supply. The South Pacific air commander, Rear Admiral John S. "Slew" McCain (COMAIRSOPAC), was engaged in the Sisyphean tribulations of building airstrips on remote tropical islands offering nothing in the way of raw materials but coconuts and native timber. The troops that would actually land in the Solomons—the 1st Marine Division, under Major General Alexander Archer Vandegrift—had left their training base at New River, North Carolina, less than a month earlier. Two-thirds of those forces were still at sea, en route to New Zealand. They had been promised an additional six months' training before being deployed in active operations, and had not yet set in motion the colossal logistical preparations an amphibious landing would require.[23]

The South Pacific July 1942

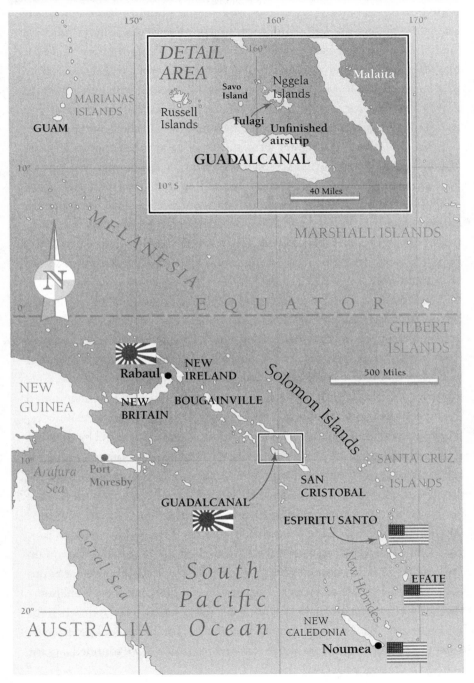

DETAIL AREA

MARIANAS ISLANDS

GUAM

Russell Islands

Savo Island

Nggela Islands

Malaita

Tulagi

Unfinished airstrip

GUADALCANAL

10° S

40 Miles

MELANESIA

MARSHALL ISLANDS

N

EQUATOR

GILBERT ISLANDS

NEW GUINEA

Rabaul

NEW IRELAND

NEW BRITAIN

BOUGAINVILLE

Solomon Islands

500 Miles

Port Moresby

Arafura Sea

GUADALCANAL

SAN CRISTOBAL

SANTA CRUZ ISLANDS

ESPIRITU SANTO

Coral Sea

South Pacific Ocean

New Hebrides

EFATE

AUSTRALIA

NEW CALEDONIA

Noumea

Operation PESTILENCE, the code name assigned to this first attempt to wrest territory from the Japanese, would quickly fall to pieces unless supported by well-appointed sea and air bases in the island groups immediately east of the Solomons. With King's deadline just five weeks away, those bases did not yet exist. Noumea, capital of the Free French colony of New Caledonia, offered a serviceable airfield and a capacious harbor with rudimentary port facilities. But it was 986 miles southeast of Guadalcanal, far too distant to provide direct air support. Farther north, in the southern New Hebrides, the island of Efate had been occupied by a marine battalion, and construction was underway on a fighter airstrip. But Efate was 800 miles southeast of Guadalcanal, still too far to serve the purpose. A sea base and airstrip were needed in the remote northern reaches of the New Hebrides, within a 650-mile flight radius of Guadalcanal. Scouting the area from the air, Admiral McCain peered down at the island of Espiritu Santo, the largest in the group, and spotted a heavily forested plain nestled amid hilly jungle terrain. It was just inland of Segond Channel, a fine natural harbor. It would have to do.

Captain M. B. Gardner, McCain's chief of staff, later told a panel of officers in Washington, "Robinson Crusoe should be required reading for anyone who is setting up an advanced base in the South Pacific islands. There is nothing to start with, except the jungle."[24] The frenetic month-long race to hack a 6,000-foot bomber strip out of the jungle at BUTTON (the code name for Espiritu Santo) exposed the scale of the challenges encountered by the construction battalions ("Seabees") in the South Pacific. All necessary equipment and supplies were brought into Segond Channel by ship, but there were no wharves, warehouses, or cranes in the harbor, and all heavy equipment had to be hauled onto the beach from pontoon lighters. Fuel drums were pushed off the decks and "swum" into the beaches, then lifted manually onto trucks to be dispersed to more than two dozen concealed fuel dumps. Marston mats, the pierced steel planking used to surface runways, came in monstrous two-and-a-half-ton bundles that had to be run up the beaches in tank lighters. When the destroyer USS *Dale* arrived at Santo on July 28, her crew had expected a proper naval base, but for several hours they could not even find the anchorage: "We couldn't figure out where to go, so we just cruised slowly around the island. Finally the lookout spotted some mastheads sticking up above some palm trees and we rounded a point to find an entrance to a little bay."[25]

The primeval conditions required manpower, and plenty of it—but man-power, in turn, created its own logistical problems. All provisions, clothing, and medical supplies had to be brought in directly from the United States, and the prevalence of malaria called for Quonset huts or at least screened tent cabins.

For a month, thirty-five Seabee equipment operators and a company of African American labor troops did battle with the jungle. They worked around the clock, under floodlights at night. The Seabees ran the trac-tors, bulldozers, and rollers, and the infantrymen wielded axes and shovels. Trucks and earthmoving equipment were often idled for lack of a single minor part, and a seaplane had to be dispatched to Efate or Noumea to obtain it. With a desperate spasm of effort the work was completed on July 28, the deadline McCain had ordered. The first squadron of B-17s flew in the next day, but they had to be fueled manually, and each of the big four-engine bombers drank 50 drums of fuel. (Almost a year would pass before the base could be equipped with bulk aviation gasoline storage tanks and a pipeline to the harbor.) Seaplanes could operate out of Segond Chan-nel, but there was no seaplane tender available until the end of July. The harbor was unprotected by either mines or torpedo nets. The construction teams had worked themselves to exhaustion; they were "full of malaria and need rest."[26]

THE *WAKEFIELD*, A ONCE-SUMPTUOUS LUXURY LINER now doing service as a squalid and overcrowded troop transport, passed through the heads of Wellington Harbour, New Zealand, on June 14. She carried General Vande-grift, most of his staff, and the first echelon of the 1st Marine Division. The voyage had been grueling. The *Wakefield* was under-provisioned, requir-ing the men to manage on short rations. Many had lost fifteen to twenty pounds at sea.

Vandegrift had counted on a period of rest and recuperation, followed by an additional six months' training in New Zealand. But on June 26, at a conference with Admiral Ghormley in Auckland, the admiral wordlessly handed him King's June 24 dispatch to Nimitz warning of pending orders for an amphibious attack in the Solomons, with D-Day set for August 1. Vandegrift was dumbfounded. "I could not believe it," he recalled. "I read the typewritten words again. There was no mistaking their content."[27]

Most of the marines of the 1st Division had enlisted immediately after Pearl Harbor. They had received little or nothing in the way of amphibious training. Two-thirds of the division was in Samoa or still at sea. Operation WATCHTOWER (code name for the first stage of PESTILENCE—the capture of Tulagi and Guadalcanal) would throw those new marines into an assault on enemy-held islands in just five weeks' time. Insofar as Vandegrift knew, the beaches would be fortified and defended by the same battle-tested veterans who had routed the British in Malaya and the Dutch in the East Indies. His equipment, weaponry, and supplies were crated in the holds of seven transports. All had to be unloaded, reclassified, and combat-loaded onto smaller assault transports, a colossal logistics problem that alone might require a month or more to solve.[28] Vandegrift did not believe the operation was feasible, certainly not by August 1. Ghormley was even more pessimistic: "I don't see how we can land at all, and I am going to take it up with MacArthur."[29]

King's dispatch had not come in the form of an affirmative order. Rather, the COMINCH had written that "the following arrangements are contemplated" and Nimitz should "prepare" accordingly.[30] King was maneuvering to force the operation through the Joint Chiefs over the objections of MacArthur, who wanted to command it himself. After several rounds of heated argument, followed by some hard bargaining, Marshall agreed to a three-phase offensive through the Solomons and New Guinea, concluding with the capture of Rabaul. The orders were distributed on July 2. Task One, the "seizure and occupation of Santa Cruz Islands, Tulagi and adjacent positions," would remain under the command authority of Nimitz and his sub-theater commander, Admiral Ghormley.[31] (King subsequently altered "adjacent positions" to specify the island of Guadalcanal.) Tasks Two and Three, involving the capture of Japanese airfields on the northeast coast of New Guinea, followed by the seizure and occupation of Rabaul, would be General MacArthur's show. In order to keep Task One entirely within Ghormley's domain, the line of demarcation dividing the SOPAC (South Pacific) and SOUWESTPAC (Southwest Pacific) areas was moved one degree westward, to latitude 159° east, skirting the western end of Guadalcanal.

Ghormley's instinct was to scuttle PESTILENCE, or at least to have it postponed. In this view he found a provisional ally in MacArthur. One month earlier, the imperious general had proposed to mount a direct assault on Rabaul itself, asking that two carrier task forces be transferred from the

Pacific Fleet into his command. (King had shot that proposal down.) Now, a month later, Ghormley found the general willing to join in opposition to the more indirect line of attack envisioned in PESTILENCE.

Following a hasty conference in Melbourne, MacArthur and Ghormley sent a long joint dispatch to Washington, proposing that the operation be "deferred." They cited a lack of trained amphibious troops, a shortage of adequate shipping, and a dearth of sufficient land-based bomber or fighter strength. Japanese air reconnaissance flights would likely discover the incoming invasion forces, and therefore "surprise is now improbable." The fleet and supporting carrier groups would be obligated to linger in the area for one to four days, during which time they would be "exposed to continued hostile air, surface, and submarine attack," posing a "danger of destruction by overwhelming force." It was their joint recommendation that PESTILENCE be postponed pending a buildup of sea, air, and ground forces in the region.[32]

King was disappointed with Ghormley and incensed with MacArthur. "I take note," he complained to Marshall, "that about three weeks ago MacArthur stated that . . . he could push right through to Rabaul. Confronted with the concrete aspects of the task, he now feels that he not only cannot undertake this extended operation but not even the Tulagi operation."[33]

King refused to entertain any deferral of PESTILENCE, but he offered a fig leaf in the form of additional naval and logistical forces to support the operation, including carrier task forces built around the carriers *Enterprise*, *Wasp*, and *Saratoga*, and logistical vessels including tankers and troop transports. "With these and other considerations in mind, [the Joint Chiefs] do not desire to countermand operations already underway for the execution of Task One."[34]

GENERAL VANDEGRIFT AND HIS STAFF moved into the Hotel Cecil in downtown Wellington—a once-elegant, now-shabby institution that had been reserved for their exclusive use—and faced the daunting task of writing a plan. More than any other military organization in the world, the Marine Corps had studied and planned for amphibious warfare, and they were keenly aware of its risks. To land on a hostile shore was the most perilous of all major military operations. To be confident of victory, the attacker must possess overwhelming advantages—control of the surrounding sea and of the air above; and heavy bombardment of enemy positions to precede the landing, followed by rapid delivery of ground forces and heavy weaponry to the beaches. If he could achieve surprise, that would greatly mitigate the initial risks. But even if the first attack was successful, he would have to receive constant resupply by sea and reliable air protection overhead. Ghormley and MacArthur doubted those conditions could be guaranteed, and had placed their doubts on the record. King, half a world removed from the scene of action, had locked the operation into a seemingly impossible schedule.

The grave problems confronting the marines could easily give way to dark pessimism. Vandegrift, aware that morale was brittle, would tolerate no negative chatter. He was a native Virginian of medium height, with thinning hair and gathering jowls—a genial and gentle man, known for his steady and unflappable demeanor, even when under great stress. That trait had earned him a nickname among his Marine Corps colleagues: "Sunny Jim." Once it was clear that WATCHTOWER was inevitable, a staff officer recalled, Vandegrift "refused to engage in any chitchat concerning its merits. Those who questioned it were immediately rebuffed. . . . Vandegrift rejected all doubts and cavils about what we were ordered to do and regarded those who offered them with condign and unforgiving contempt."[35]

Next to nothing was known about the Solomons. Aerial photos of the area, forwarded from MacArthur's headquarters in Melbourne, were misdirected and lost in a file at Ghormley's headquarters. What few maps and charts they obtained were spread out on a table, but these were too old or drafted on too large a scale to be useful. One identified Guadalcanal incorrectly as "Guadalcanar."[36] Rivers were misidentified or inaccurately located. The sea charts forwarded by the navy were decades old and provided little detail about coral heads.

The marines put out word that they would like to interview anyone who had personal knowledge of the islands, and the New Zealanders managed to collect some of the refugees who had lived and worked in the Solomons before the Japanese invasion. Charles Widdy, a former Lever Brothers plantation director, made a crude hand-drawn sketch identifying from memory the position of ditches, swamps, hills, barbwire fences, grass plains, coconut palms, and rivers. But Widdy, like most Europeans, had stuck mainly to the coasts and knew little of the island's interior. Even when his memory was reliable, the distances and scales were not much more than guesswork.

An aerial reconnaissance mission was plainly needed, and Colonel Merrill B. Twining arranged to fly over Savo Sound in an army B-17. Looking down from 3,000 feet, Twining noted and photographed an extensive network of coral reefs in the azure waters south of Tulagi. When the aircraft banked south to reconnoiter the north coast of Guadalcanal, Twining was relieved to see that the situation there was much better—deep blue water reached almost to the shoreline, and no Japanese defensive fortifications were visible along the beach. Dogged by three floatplane Zeros, the sturdy bomber escaped by dodging into a cloud bank, and returned safely to Port Moresby on New Guinea.

King's stringent deadline required around-the-clock logistical preparations. The 1st Division's supplies, ammunition, and heavy equipment had been embarked haphazardly in ships that had sailed from Norfolk, New Orleans, San Francisco, and San Diego. All had to be unloaded onto the Wellington quays, then sorted, repackaged, and reloaded for combat into smaller attack transports. The scale of the work was unprecedented.

Wellington, a graceful English city enclosed by green hills, offered the best port facilities in the SOPAC command area. Aotea Quay, the largest in the harbor, could accommodate five large vessels, and the waterfront was spacious enough to allow crates to be stacked and concealed under tarps. An early New Zealand winter brought cold rains and high winds. Cardboard boxes disintegrated under the driving rainstorms, reducing dry foodstuffs to an unsalvageable mush. Much of the division's fresh eggs, meat, and dairy products had spoiled for lack of refrigeration.

Wellington stevedores were organized into a semi-militant union and ruled by a port director who barely disguised his hostility to the Americans. The wharf workers ("wharfies") were always on the verge of striking and often refused to work for reasons that seemed obscure. Turning a deaf ear to suggestions that they work at a wartime pace, they spurned any references to the danger posed by Japan. They broke for morning tea, afternoon tea, and cigarettes, and laughed at the idea of working past the customary quitting time. They walked off whenever it began to rain, sometimes explaining that they had not brought their "Macintoshes." The stoppages were usually of short duration, often less than an hour, but they were maddeningly frequent. In one twenty-four-hour period the wharfies walked off the job fourteen times. Most of the stevedoring was done by the marines themselves, who worked around the clock, under floodlights at night, and kept at it through driving rainstorms. One marine approvingly noted graffiti left on a Wellington wall: "All wharfies is bastards."[37]

FROM THE START, PLANNING FOR the forthcoming expedition was encumbered by an awkward and unwieldy chain of command. Admiral Ghormley, to whom King had assigned principal responsibility for WATCHTOWER, would remain shorebound at his embryonic headquarters in Noumea. Ghormley gave seagoing command of the entire expeditionary force to Vice Admiral Frank Jack Fletcher, the carrier task force commander who had come south with the carriers *Enterprise* and *Saratoga*. (The third carrier, the *Wasp*, was en route from the United States, but required several days' repairs in Tongatabu.)[38] Fletcher's carrier groups (Task Force 61) would soften up the beaches with a heavy schedule of aerial bombing and strafing attacks, and provide fighter cover to intercept any incoming Japanese aircraft. The cruisers and destroyers of Task Group 62.6, commanded by Rear Admiral Victor A. C. Crutchley of the Royal Australian Navy, would bombard the beaches prior to the landings. MacArthur's air forces, operating from Port Moresby, would attack the Japanese airfield at Rabaul and the other satellite airfields in the region to suppress the inevitable enemy airstrikes on the invasion forces. Before the fleet set sail for the Solomons, it would rendezvous in the Fiji group and conduct a rehearsal landing on the island of Koro, in the southern Fijis. "Dog-Day" was set for August 7, approximately one week later than the original deadline established by King.

To command Operation WATCHTOWER's amphibious forces (Task Force 62), King tapped a member of his own staff—Admiral Richmond Kelly Turner, who had headed the navy's War Plans Division since 1940. Turner was, like King, a brilliant but touchy character. A short, balding man with steel-rimmed glasses and heavy black eyebrows, Turner was habitually irritable and quick to raise his voice. "Balls!" was a favorite exclamation. Relentlessly driven, he expected colleagues and subordinates to match his pace. He had a keen analytical mind—even his critics acknowledged that much—but he did not take kindly to criticism even when it was offered in good faith. Rarely did Turner give fulsome praise for a job well done, and he was not slow to lay blame on others, especially when the culpability was arguably his own. He often lapsed into a hectoring, didactic style more suitable to a courtroom lawyer than an admiral. These qualities had earned him the nickname "Terrible Turner."

In preparing operational plans for WATCHTOWER, Turner would have liked to begin with a blank page, but he did not reach New Zealand until mid-July, only a week before the fleet must ship out to meet King's deadline. He was therefore obliged to work backward from the draft plan prepared by Vandegrift's staff.

The task force sortied from Wellington on July 22, a long column of transports and cargo vessels under the protection of cruisers and destroyers. A passage of four days through calm seas brought them to the appointed rendezvous, 367 miles south of Fiji. Each ship lay wallowing on the swell, engines throttled back. As the afternoon wore on, new masts and super-structures peaked over the horizon in every direction. Veteran sailors pointed and identified ships by type or name: cruisers, destroyers, trans-ports, cargo ships, minesweepers, fleet oilers, and (most encouraging to the marines) the big boxlike profiles of aircraft carriers. Grumman fighter planes patrolled the skies above. Near the carrier *Enterprise* was an even rarer sight—a battleship, the *North Carolina*. "There will never be a feeling like the feeling we had when we first made out a task force coming up over the horizon with an aircraft carrier and supporting cruisers and destroyers," recalled Major Justice Chambers of the 1st Raider Battalion. For the first time since leaving the United States, the marines "realized that whatever we were going to do we were going to have a lot of friends with us."[39]

For the good of secrecy and stealth, no one who was not directly involved in planning WATCHTOWER had been permitted to know what was afoot. Scuttlebutt had held that the 1st Division would relieve a garrison of New Zealanders at Fiji.[40] But here was a vast and majestic display of seapower—a fleet of eighty-two ships, the largest yet assembled in the Pacific War. It could only mean that a major combat operation was at hand. "All over the sea and as far out as eye could reach the armada mottled the water," an *Enterprise* pilot recalled. "Everybody aboard became excited at the prospect of being part of what looked like the first big American offensive of the war."[41]

The fleet converged on the little island of Koro, where Turner had arranged for a dress rehearsal. The southern beaches of Koro were pounded by cruiser shells; Grumman F4F fighters roared overhead in a pantomime of engaging and shooting down Japanese Zeros; carrier dive-bombers hurtled down from high altitude and planted hundred-pound bombs on locations designated as enemy positions. Koro, they soon discovered, was unlike Guadalcanal in one critical respect. At low tide, shallow coral heads blocked the approach of the Higgins landing boats. The first wave of boats, filled with fully equipped marines, ran aground and the propellers jammed. Because he did not have boats to spare, Turner cancelled the landings.

On the afternoon of July 27, Admiral Fletcher summoned the task force commanders to a conference on his flagship, the carrier *Saratoga*. Rough seas made for difficult and even dangerous ship-to-ship transitions by boat or breeches buoy. Turner, on the destroyer *Dewey*, came alongside the looming shape of the big carrier. Vandegrift, accompanied by several 1st Division officers, came on the destroyer *Hull*. Admiral McCain, while hauling himself up a heaving ladder, was drenched by a flood of spoiled milk and garbage spewing from a waste chute. The brass convened in Fletcher's wardroom. Notably, Ghormley did not attend the conference—the COMSOPAC was represented by his chief of staff, Rear Admiral Daniel J. Callaghan.

According to several participants, Admiral Fletcher was in a foul temper and opened the meeting with a distinctly unconstructive tone. He cleared the room of all officers below the rank of admiral or general. Vandegrift judged Fletcher to be "nervous and tired," and ill informed about the details of WATCHTOWER. The admiral seemed to think the entire operation was a misadventure, and "quickly let us know he did not think it would succeed."[42] All could agree that the operation had been rushed, and lamented the lack of time for careful and thorough preparation. There were not even sufficient copies of Fletcher's and Turner's operational orders and annexes, and many fleet staff officers and ship captains would have to work from notes.

Discussion ranged over details of logistics, refueling, schedules of airstrikes on Tulagi and Guadalcanal, the occupation of the Santa Cruz island group, and the planned relief of the marines by army garrison troops. The discussions took an ugly turn when the subject changed to the controversial issue of air protection for the landing operations. Turner estimated that four or five days were needed to unload equipment, ammunition, and supplies onto the beachheads. Fletcher tersely replied that he intended to keep his aircraft carriers in the vicinity for only two. A tense debate brought from Fletcher a begrudging concession: the carriers would stay for three days. Beyond "Dog-Day plus two," Turner's amphibious force would have to manage without air cover. With that, Fletcher dismissed the conference, and the commanders parted on edgy terms. As the marines descended into the boat that would carry them back to their ship, a staff officer found Vandegrift "deeply disturbed and in no mood to talk."[43]

THE PASSAGE TO THE SOLOMONS was pleasingly uneventful.[44] The combined task forces, zigzagging to thwart enemy submarines, shaped a westerly course north of New Caledonia and into the Coral Sea, leaving Guadalcanal well to starboard. The seas were calm, the breezes mild, and a low cloud ceiling sheltered the fleet from Japanese reconnaissance planes. "It didn't seem like war at all to me at first," said Roland Smoot, captain of the destroyer *Monssen*. "We cruised those beautiful southern waters just as casually and unconcerned as though we were going to a Sunday school picnic."[45]

On the transports, marines cleaned and oiled their rifles, machine guns, and cartridges; they belted ammunition, sighted along their rifles, sharpened their bayonets and knives. They scattered their gear over the decks, took inventory, and repacked. They secured their packs, with bed rolls folded carefully on top, and stood them in rows along the bulkheads. Their personal belongings went into sea bags to be entrusted to the crews of the ships. Each man was to carry six cans of C rations, enough to feed him for two days. One hundred rounds of ammunition in a cartridge belt, one hundred more in a bandoleer. Two grenades. A pickaxe or shovel (one or the other, as he chose). Two canteens, a gas mask, a first aid kit, a bed roll, a poncho, a mosquito net, a mess kit.[46] To pass the time, they sang, smoked, played cards, or wrote home. At night, they slept in hot, dirty holds, in bunks four or five tiers high. To escape the heat, some of the men curled up on deck or bedded down in a lifeboat.

On August 5, with the three carrier groups leading the column, the fleet turned northward for the final leg of its approach. That afternoon, the weather cleared and the sun beat down for several hours. But their luck held: no Japanese snoopers appeared overhead, and in the mid-afternoon they entered another frontal area, and were blanketed by dense overcast and intermittent rainsqualls. On the following afternoon, Dog-Day minus one, Fletcher's three carrier groups turned away to take up their position south of the weather coast of Guadalcanal. Turner's amphibious force continued north toward Cheetah Shoals, off the mountainous island's westernmost point.

At 11:05 p.m., the northbound fleet divided into two double columns, separated by 1,000 yards. The first (Transport Group XRAY) turned east to hug the north coast of Guadalcanal; the second (Transport Group YOKE) proceeded north of the stratovolcanic cone of Savo Island and then turned east toward Tulagi and the Nggela group. The night was dark, the sea calm. Not even a lit cigarette was permitted on deck. A crescent moon rose above the horizon in the east.[47] Lieutenant Herbert L. Merillat recalled "tension in the air and complete silence save for the steady throbbing of engines, the gentle splash of ships' prows cutting through the water, and the hushed movements of men on the open decks."[48] The cruisers and destroyers surged ahead at 27 knots, fast enough to throw salt spray over the rails. At that speed the warships would show "bone in teeth," a long white bow wave that could be seen even on dark nights. Would Japanese lookouts detect them and raise the alarm? No shore guns opened fire; nothing stirred along the shore. "It was a most prosaic type of thing," said Captain Smoot. "We had achieved complete surprise."[49]

From the rails of the transports, the marines studied the looming shape of Guadalcanal. It was a high black jagged mass, with contours barely distinguishable against the backdrop of a slightly lighter sky. They could see little in the predawn darkness, but their nostrils took in the rich, fetid odor of damp vegetation. With the first flush of dawn, they gradually discerned the rugged bluish-green mountains, the heavily forested ridgelines, the light patches of open plain, and the serpentine columns of trees and foliage that followed the rivers down to the coast. Binoculars swept over the native villages just beyond the beaches—little clusters of fiber roofs and garden plots. Every few miles along the shore, a river delta protruded to form a point. One of these marked the mouth of the Lunga River, just west of "Beach Red," where the marines would put ashore. A few miles inland was their main objective, the nearly completed airfield.

The marines had been warned to expect a bloody fight on Beach Red. Those who survived the initial assault would have to fight their way inland, storming across drainage ditches that might double as trenches, fording rivers under fire, and advancing through fields of razor-sharp *kunai* grass. At every stage they would encounter thousands of well-armed and fanatical Japanese. A marine lieutenant told the journalist Richard Tregaskis that he expected one in four men to die in the first wave.[50] Even so, spirits were high. Private William Rogal felt "a knot in my stomach, but it was no greater or more intense than the knot associated with stage fright." More than death or injury, Rogal feared disgrace, or "showing the white feather."[51] William Manchester, the marine private who would earn literary fame as a memoirist and biographer, wrote that "vitality surged through you like a powerful drug, even though the idea of death held no attraction to you."[52] More than anything, he just wanted off the filthy, crowded transport that had been his universe for more than a month. A reserve captain who had been a grocery wholesaler in Boston said he felt "no more nervous than if I were being sent out to do a tough job in civilian life—you know, like trying to sell a big order, when there's a lot of sales resistance."[53]

At 6:13 a.m., as veins of gray light spread from east to west through the overcast, the heavy cruiser *Quincy* trained her main battery on Lunga Point and opened fire. The blast force of her 8-inch guns punched craters into the sea alongside the ship. Heavy concussions reverberated across Savo Sound and echoed back from the hills on the surrounding islands. To Colonel Twining it was "an unforgettable moment of history"—the first Allied counterinvasion of the war, the first step on the long bloody road to Tokyo.[54] Four cruisers and six destroyers joined the *Quincy*, their greenish-yellow muzzle flashes lighting up the sea and the ships and the hills and ridgelines of the surrounding islands. Red tracer lines arced toward the shore, and powerful explosions backlit the palms along the beach. One shell found a fuel dump in the village of Kukum, just west of Lunga Point. The result was a tremendous detonation, a sheet of flame a hundred feet high, and a tower of oily black smoke. Lookouts on the light cruiser *San Juan*, in the northern fire support group, opened fire on Tulagi, Gavutu, and Tanambogo at a range of 2,000 yards. Within two minutes the waterfronts were reduced to smoking wreckage.

Five minutes after the first salvo, the ships' guns fell abruptly silent. That was the cue for the Grumman F4F Wildcat fighters, launched from the carriers before dawn, to begin their initial strafing runs over the unfinished airstrip. Red tracer lines reached down from the .50-caliber guns and ricocheted back into the sky, forming a shallow luminescent "V" pattern.[55] Sixteen Grummans of the *Wasp*'s Fighting Squadron 71 (VF-71) flew low over the bay south of Nggela and riddled the seaplanes moored off Tulagi and Tanambogo with .50-caliber incendiary fire.[56] Several of the enemy's Kawanishi flying boats and floatplane fighters were transformed into floating infernos.[57] Turning back for a second strafing run, VF-71 laid waste to landing craft, fuel barges, and machine-gun emplacements. SBD Dauntless dive-bombers planted 1,000-pound bombs on assigned targets along the Guadalcanal shoreline. As the bombers pulled out of their dives and turned west to return to the carriers, the cruisers and destroyers opened up again.

From the *McCawley*, General Vandegrift and Admiral Turner inspected the scene through binoculars. The landing beaches were marked by colored smoke pots that had been dropped by cruiser floatplanes. On Guadalcanal, plumes of smoke were uncoiling along a three-mile length of shoreline between the Lunga and Tenaru Rivers. The naval guns and carrier planes had done their work—Japanese buildings, barracks, radio stations, wharves, camps, warehouses, and antiaircraft batteries were burning brightly. There were no muzzle flashes ashore, or any enemy troops to be seen. Cruiser planes scouting the island from overhead reported no enemy activity. Even the natives seemed to have fled into the bush. Vandegrift and his staff officers noted the imposing mass of Mount Austen a few miles behind Lunga Point. Their maps had identified it as a "grassy knoll" of uncertain elevation. But it evidently stood more than 1,000 feet above the surrounding plains. They would have to pull in their lines and exclude it from their perimeter.

"H-Hour," the landing on Tulagi, had been set for 0800; "Zero-Hour," the landing on Guadalcanal, was to be half an hour later. At 0630 Turner passed the word to begin lowering boats. Each craft was lowered away to the harsh clank of chains running through davits. The coxswains circled cautiously, engines muffled at low rpm, exhaust clouds wafting across the sea, and awaited the signal flag that would summon them to return and embark troops. A few minutes before seven, the marines began going down the cargo nets. They took care to grasp the vertical lines (not the horizontal ones, where fingers might be crushed under another man's boot). Heavy gear was rigged with quick-release straps, a precaution against drowning should they fall into the sea. Each marine stepped into the flat bottom of a Higgins boat and took a seat. When a boat was full, the coxswain pulled away and began to circle. Conditions were near perfect—the sea was as calm as glass. Cargo nets were lowered on both sides of the transports, allowing for simultaneous port and starboard disembarkation. There were no overturned boats, no casualties, and no delays. After the comedy of errors of Koro, the smooth execution of the landing operations came as a welcome surprise—Major Donald Dickson called it "one of the slickest things I have ever seen."[58]

At 7:41 a.m., the first wave of boats passed the line of departure (formed

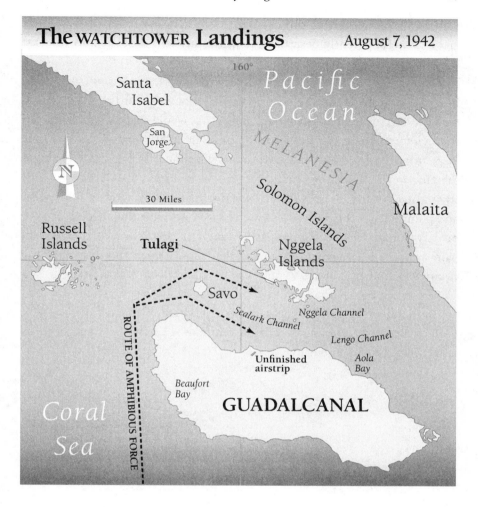

The WATCHTOWER Landings   August 7, 1942

between two destroyers) and opened their throttles. The marines crouched
down, heads below the gunwales. Spray flew over the sides and into their
faces. The small American flag at the stern of each craft snapped briskly in
the wind. A sailor watching from the *Vincennes* thought that "it looked like
a Newport boat race with our flags flying from the sterns headed into the
beach. It was thrilling to watch such an undertaking, and still there wasn't
any artillery fire or anything of that sort, and we were beginning to get a
little apprehensive because we knew it was bound to come sooner or later."[59]
The destroyers continued raking the shore with their 5-inch guns, then fell
silent as the first boats scraped onto the sand. The marines clambered over
the sides and trudged through the surf. They met no resistance at all. From

Kukum to the mouth of the Tenaru, the beaches and adjacent coconut groves were apparently deserted. A white star shell shot up into the sky, signaling an unopposed landing.

When the third and fourth waves arrived later that morning, the beach-head was weirdly serene. An occasional rifle shot was heard in the distance, but no concentrated and sustained bursts that would suggest a firefight. On the incoming boats, marines lined up in leisurely fashion; one by one they leapt from the bow, over the surf, to avoid soaking their boots. Men were relaxing in the shade, smoking cigarettes, or trying to open coconuts with their knives or bayonets. A few had even stripped down to their underwear and plunged into the surf for a swim. Native huts with thatched roofs were being commandeered as shore-party command posts, and signs nailed to palm trees indicated where cargo handlers should stack and sort incoming equipment and provisions. A medical tent had been set up under a Red Cross banner, but at 10:30 a.m. the only casualty was a young man who had cut his hand while trying to open a coconut with a machete.[60]

It all seemed too easy, even a bit ominous. Did the Japanese hope to draw them into an ambush?

Chapter Two

AWAKENED BY THE NAVAL BARRAGE, THE JAPANESE ON TULAGI HAD been caught completely by surprise. Captain Shigetoshi Miyazaki, commander of the seaplane base, fired an initial radio warning to Rabaul. As the first landing boats scraped ashore on what the marines had designated Beach Blue, he and his small force of Special Naval Landing Force troops withdrew into the island's hilly interior, but not before sending a final spirited broadcast: "We will defend to the last man. Pray for our success."[1]

Rabaul, 650 miles to the northwest, was headquarters of the Eighth Fleet, commanded by the newly arrived Vice Admiral Gunichi Mikawa—and of the Twenty-Fifth Air Flotilla, a land-based aviation command with about ninety operational aircraft, including bombers, reconnaissance planes, and Zero fighters. With two working airfields and two more in reserve, Rabaul was the axis of Japanese airpower in the region, the backstop to smaller satellite airfields at Kavieng, Lae, Salamaua, Buin, and Buka. It offered a superb natural harbor, a flooded caldera more than a mile in diameter. But the Japanese conquerors had little affection for the place. It was a hot, dusty, primitive township, disturbed by frequent earthquakes and choked with pumice and gray-black ash from the volcano Tavurvur, whose imposing black cone dominated the view to the south. Admiral Mikawa's headquarters was in a cramped, dilapidated colonial building. Enlisted men were quartered in crude barracks and fed mostly barley rice and *miso* soup, with open-pit cesspools for toilets. The best thing about Rabaul, according to an officer stationed there, was a bath house erected by the Japanese over the hot springs at the base of Tavurvur. Nothing boosted Japanese spirits like a hot bath.

Upon receiving word of the American invasion in the Solomons, Rear Admiral Sadayoshi Yamada prepared to strike the American fleet. Twenty-seven twin-engine G4M bombers and nine Zero fighters had been fueled and armed for a scheduled attack on Rabi, an Allied airfield in New Guinea. Yamada now ordered that the flights be diverted to the Tulagi-Guadalcanal area, and launched immediately. He would not even allow the bombers to be rearmed with aerial torpedoes, which were far more effective against ships than land bombs, for fear that his planes might be caught on the ground and destroyed.

When the Zero pilots examined their charts, they whistled in disbelief. Six hundred and fifty miles down, and then all the way back: their single-seat fighter had never flown a combat mission of that range. The flight leader told his men that conserving fuel must be their overriding concern. They would fly with belly tanks, which would diminish the Zeros' performance in air combat, and they could afford only a brief visit to the enemy fleet. Under these conditions they would fight at a severe disadvantage.

Shortly before 10:00 a.m. (Guadalcanal time), the big G4Ms began roaring down the runways, followed a few minutes later by the Zeros. The forty-five planes coalesced into an "arrowhead" configuration, with the bombers locked in three stepped-down "Vee of vee" formations and the Zeros trailing closely on either flank. The long flight took them directly over the large island of Bougainville, which was home to two intrepid coastwatchers who had pulled well back into the bush. W. J. "Jack" Read was concealed at an advanced observation post in the northern jungle hills. Paul Mason was ensconced in a remote hideaway called Malabita Hill, near the south end of the island. In preparation for WATCHTOWER, and to avoid coding delays, both men had been instructed to report hostile aircraft sightings immediately, by voice transmissions in plain language.

Shortly before 11:00 a.m., Mason heard the drone of aircraft overhead. Looking up through the canopy of foliage, he saw an armada of Japanese bombers. He counted twenty-four. Immediately he transmitted, "FROM STO, 24 BOMBERS HEADED YOURS."[2] The report was copied in Port Moresby, relayed to Townsville, sent immediately to Pearl Harbor, and then broadcast to the WATCHTOWER task forces.

In spite of its circuitous route, Mason's message arrived on the *Saratoga* and the *McCawley* when it was just thirty minutes old. Flight time from south Bougainville to Guadalcanal was more than two hours, so Fletcher and Turner had plenty of time to react. Turner got his ships dispersed and underway for emergency evasive action, and the carriers launched fighters to intercept the incoming planes.

Even with ample warning, Fletcher faced daunting logistical problems. His Grummans had to protect two task forces separated by sixty to seventy-five miles, requiring about thirty minutes of flight time. Dogfights would burn fuel and oblige their early return to the flattops—and once the fighters returned, there was the problem of clearing the flight deck so that they could land and be refueled. The day's crowded flight-operations schedule placed heavy demands on all three flight decks. (It was essentially the same problem that had lost the Battle of Midway for the Japanese.) At 1:15 p.m., as the Japanese strike closed on Savo Sound, just eight Wildcats were in position to defend the amphibious fleet. They were at 12,000 feet, below an opaque layer of overcast. The Japanese G4Ms approached at 16,000 feet—above the cloud ceiling, thus invisible to the Wildcats. The fighter control circuits rang with radar warnings.

All at once, the bombers broke through the clouds in a shallow dive. Lieutenant James J. Southerland, leader of a division of *Saratoga* F4Fs, radioed a "tally-ho": "Horizontal bombers, three divisions, nine planes each, over Savo, headed for transports. . . . Let's go get them, boys."[3] Southerland dropped to his left and opened a few bursts on the nearest Japanese aircraft, at a range of just 500 yards. He pressed this promising attack and sent one G4M down in flames, but seconds later the Zeros descended through the clouds and found three of his wingmen in their sights. Two Wildcats went spinning into the sea, and the others were forced to dive for their lives.

Taking in the view from below the overcast, the Japanese airmen were astonished by the size of the American fleet. The bombers continued east, descending to 10,000 feet, and opened their payloads over the XRAY transports maneuvering at high speed off Lunga Point. The sky was mottled with the dark smudges of antiaircraft bursts, but the Japanese planes stayed in formation. As the sticks of bombs fell behind them in a glinting diagonal tail, the American helmsmen coolly steered to avoid them. Every bomb fell harmlessly into the sea near Lunga Point. The G4Ms banked west for the long run back to Rabaul.[4]

A furious fighter melee continued over Savo Island and western Guadalcanal. Among the Zero pilots were two of the most lethal fighter aces in the Imperial Japanese Navy: Hiroyoshi Nishizawa, who would eventually be

credited with eighty-seven kills, making him Japan's top-ranked ace; and
Saburo Sakai, who would survive the war with about sixty claimed kills.
(Sakai authored a fascinating and credible postwar memoir, *Samurai*, which
was translated into English in the 1950s.) Southerland, after flaming one of
the G4Ms, went into a spiraling dive to avoid two pursuing Zeros. Lieutenant Joseph R. Daly's aircraft, riddled with 7.7mm machine-gun fire, began to
turn over and descend toward the sea. His fuel tank ignited and the flames
spread into his cockpit: "My clothes were on fire; my pants and shirt burning: I could see nothing but red fire all around me."[5] Daly wrenched open
the canopy and leapt out. He dropped through the cloud cover at 7,000 feet
and pulled his chute.

Saburo Sakai had never seen an F4F until this moment. Looking down,
about 1,500 feet below, he saw a lone Wildcat in a skirmish with three Zeros.
Lieutenant Southerland was flying a series of tight left spirals that denied
his pursuers a clean shot at him. He repeatedly forced the Zeros to overtake
him and peppered their wingtips with .50-caliber fire. Sakai dived into the
fight, and was immediately taken aback by Southerland's skill: "Never had I
seen an enemy plane move so quickly or so gracefully before."[6] In a dance of
snap rolls and sudden throttle-chops, Sakai and Southerland maneuvered
for advantage, until both aircraft slipped into a vertical spiral, with one
wing pointed down at the sea and the other up at the sky. Intense g-forces
shoved both men into their seats and forced them to strain their necks to
keep their heads erect. After the fifth spiral Southerland broke out into a
loop, and Sakai locked on to his tail. "I had him," Sakai wrote. "The Zero
could outfly any fighter in the world in this kind of maneuver."[7]

Sakai fired a long burst of 7.7mm caliber rounds into Southerland's
cockpit, but the sturdy Grumman flew on, apparently unperturbed. The
Japanese pilot then fed fuel to his engine and flew alongside the Wildcat.
The two men made eye contact. Sakai saw that Southerland was badly
wounded, with blood on his shoulder and chest. Southerland lifted his hand
and waved; Sakai shook his fist and shouted for the American to fight on
"instead of flying along like a clay pigeon."[8] But Southerland's guns had
jammed. His aircraft had been hit hundreds of time, and the aluminum
skin of the fuselage and wings was shredded so badly that the frame was
bared to Sakai's view. His instrument panel was completely destroyed; his
canopy was shattered; his radio was dead; his flaps were not responding; and
oil was coursing into the cockpit. He had eleven separate wounds. He had

no choice but to bail out. As Sakai fired several 20mm cannon rounds into the Wildcat's wing root, setting the plane afire, Southerland unbuckled and got free of the cockpit. He had just enough altitude to pull his chute before hitting the treetops. Though suffering severe wounds, including a 7.7mm round that passed through his foot, Southerland managed to make his way overland to the American lines.

Sakai then chased a formation of eight American dive-bombers, elements of VB-6 and VS-5 of the *Enterprise*. The SBDs held formation, and the rear-gunners concentrated their fire into the engine and cockpit of the oncoming Zero. A .30-caliber round grazed Sakai's skull and blinded his right eye. Somehow he managed not only to survive this grievous wound, but to fly 650 miles back to Rabaul and land safely. Sakai would lose the eye but return to flight service in 1944.

A flight of nine type Aichi D3A2 (Allied code name "Val") dive-bombers, armed with sixty-kilogram bombs, dived on the XRAY transports off Lunga Point. One bomb hit the superstructure of the destroyer *Mugford*, killing twenty-one men but doing little damage to the ship. Wildcats chased the retreating dive-bombers and peppered them with .50-caliber fire. All the Vals were destroyed, either in air combat or by ditching at sea; twelve of eighteen crewmen were also lost.

Off the weather coast of Guadalcanal, the mood in Task Force (TF) 61 was decidedly upbeat. A destroyer officer watched the first wave of planes as they returned to the *Wasp*: "Jubilant pilots circled us, rocking their wings and waving as they passed overhead."[9] As the planes recovered, the word spread quickly—the initial bombing and strafing attacks had put every Japanese plane in the area out of action before they could get into the air. But the carriers' air operations were only beginning. Between first light and dusk, the three flattops completed an extraordinary 704 plane launches and 686 recoveries. Beginning long before dawn, with a bleary-eyed breakfast, followed by the call to General Quarters at 0500, the crews had worked to the brink of exhaustion. Flights had been planned in painstaking detail and down to the minute—Admiral Thomas C. Kinkaid, commander of Task Force 16, compared the day's operations to a "railroad schedule."[10] Planes were landed, refueled, rearmed, replenished with oxygen, respotted, and sent back up at a record-breaking pace. In one case, the *Wasp* turned around an eight-plane squadron in sixteen minutes.[11] Inevitably, there were mishaps. Planes spun into the sea or catapulted over the crash barrier and had to be jettisoned over the side. Some failed to find their carriers on the return and were forced to ditch at sea.

The air groups had successfully protected Turner's fleet, but the day's fighter losses were worryingly high. Fifteen Grummans had been destroyed or forced to ditch, and five more had been badly damaged. In the initial melee with the Zeros, which were piloted by some of the top aces in the Japanese navy, the Wildcats had suffered 50 percent losses. The superior speed and maneuverability of the Zero remained a grave concern. Grummans were needed over the carriers to provide air protection; they were needed to protect Turner's fleet in Savo Sound; they would be needed to escort any outbound airstrike, should Japanese carriers appear on the scene. Eighteen fighter planes per carrier were "nowhere near enough," Admiral Kinkaid concluded, and the fighter complement would be doubled by the end of 1942. For now, however, Fletcher had to do the best with what he had, and he had good reason to wonder whether he had enough fighters to cover the fleet on D-Day plus one.

SHORTLY BEFORE THREE THAT AFTERNOON, General Vandegrift went ashore. A Higgins boat filled with senior officers of the 1st Division churned in toward Beach Red, picking its way through dozens of boats plying the waters between the anchored transports and cargo ships. As he set foot on Guadalcanal, the general noted that cargo was beginning to pile up on the beach. There were too few men available to handle it properly. The problem would have to wait, however; his first concern was the state of his defensive perimeter. Units were advancing inland and along the shore, but the enemy was nowhere to be seen. "I'm beginning to doubt whether there's a Jap on the whole damned island," he remarked.[12]

To the west, forward elements of the 1st Battalion, 5th Marines had halted on the bank of the Ilu River. Vandegrift, coming up from the rear in a jeep, found them "moving as if it were about to encounter the entire Imperial Army."[13] He ordered them across. Engineers were summoned to improvise a makeshift bridge. They laid spare lumber over the riverbed with the help of an amphibious tractor. It was not much to look at, but it bore the weight of jeeps and artillery.

Beyond the Ilu, the natural terrain barriers of Guadalcanal began to work against them. Troops wielded machetes to hack a four-foot-wide path, wide enough for ammunition carts to follow, but soon became bogged down in a huge mangrove swamp. To the east, advance parties pushed along the coconut-strewn beach, through abandoned native villages, to the Tenaru River. They hesitated to cross. The absence of enemy resistance seemed bizarre and even ominous. Major Dickson thought the men "expected to bump into the Japs any minute and were wondering why they didn't. . . . [T]hey said, 'These damn Japs are setting a trap for us and we are going to walk into this trap one of these minutes.' That wasn't a very pleasant feeling."[14]

A wealth of first-rate assets had been left behind by the enemy—two power houses supplied with new electrical generators and ample fuel; a radio receiver station stocked with equipment and spares; 50,000 to 60,000 gallons of gasoline and diesel fuel; a fleet of trucks; two working water pumps; nine road rollers; and several tons of cement.[15] Weapons of various categories and calibers fell into the Americans' hands, including two working antiaircraft batteries. A hospital tent, stocked with excellent medical supply kits and water purification tablets, was commandeered by navy corpsmen.

In a laborer's camp across the Ilu River, Sergeant James Hurlbut found a hot iron left on a pair of officer's trousers. It had burned all the way through to the ironing board. Half-eaten meals had been left on dining tables with "chopsticks left propped on the edges of the dishes, or dropped in haste on the floor mat."[16] All around the camps was evidence of the terrific cannonading delivered earlier that morning—coconut palms torn to pieces and tents shredded by high explosive fragments.

Major Dickson's unit was the first to reach the Japanese headquarters building near the airfield.[17] Among the officers' possessions, they found a souvenir-hunter's bonanza—swords, medals, capes, and starched white uniforms. In an adjoining quartermaster's supply building was a large supply of rice, dried fish, canned crab, beer, sake, candy, and cigarettes. A guard was posted to prevent looting.

The main Japanese wharf at Kukum was placed under the direction of a coast guard detachment, and rear echelon units—engineers, motor transport operators, radiomen—began claiming the huts and tents left by the Japanese. By nightfall on August 7, the little village was beginning to look like a conventional ship-to-shore depot.

On Tulagi, across Savo Sound, the marines had likewise gone ashore unopposed. The naval barrage had been superb—the cruiser *San Juan* had put some 800 rounds of 5-inch shells into the high ground above Beach Blue prior to the landing, and then lifted the onslaught precisely three minutes before the first boats touched the beach. Beach Blue had been left completely undefended by the Japanese, who apparently had concluded that the shallow coral heads offshore would discourage any landing attempt there. The raiders crossed the narrow waist of the island without much difficulty, taking the little settlement known as Sasapi village—but when they turned east, resistance stiffened. Japanese snipers had concealed themselves in trees and the underbrush. The rattle of machine-gun fire was heard offshore and even on Guadalcanal, twenty miles away, where Colonel Twining recalled, "We felt left out."[18]

The remaining enemy troops, bottled up in the southeast corner of the island, went to ground in dugouts and caves. Demolition teams were brought up to destroy those positions, but many were connected by subterranean tunnels. The fight for Tulagi was savage and bloody. As Major Justice Chambers recalled, "When you would blast them out of one dugout, you would find that there was nobody in there and you would find a hole through which they had crawled to another place." That night, Japanese soldiers "were sniping, shouting at us, throwing grenades at us, whistling, and carrying out all the tricks of the trade we had read about in the pamphlets, but I suspect none of us ever believed."[19]

East of Tulagi lay the minuscule islands of Gavutu and Tanambogo, connected to one another by a wooden causeway. Some 500 Japanese naval infantrymen (sometimes called "Japanese marines") were on these islands, dug into trench lines and artillery emplacements, and they put up an even more desperate fight than their comrades on Tulagi. A pre-landing naval bombardment leveled most of the trees and buildings, but the defenders emerged as soon as the marines went ashore on Gavutu's northeast coast, and pinned the invaders down in a mangrove swamp.

The marines put two tanks ashore on Tanambogo, but one was destroyed almost immediately. George Kittredge, a gunnery officer on the *Chicago*, watched through his turret's periscope as a platoon of Japanese troops swarmed over the tank, poured gasoline over it, and set it afire. The hatch opened and a marine emerged. He was knocked down immediately and beaten to death with rifle butts. A Japanese soldier dropped a grenade into the tank, killing the remaining occupant. Kittredge's 8-inch gun fired, and in the next moment the entire scene had vanished—no tank, no enemy soldiers, "just a pall of white smoke and a very large hole in the ground."[20] Seventy marines would give their lives in the conquest of these islands, which were not secured until midday on August 8.

Guadalcanal remained largely peaceful that first night. Scattered gunfire along the perimeter kept the marines on edge, but no counterattack developed. At dawn on the eighth, increasingly confident that the Japanese did not intend to make a stand at all, they advanced in force onto the Lunga Plain and took possession of the unfinished airstrip. They encountered no one but a few unarmed Korean workers, who broke and ran at the first sight of the marines. Those who surrendered told the same story: the Japanese troops had fled to the west. The airfield was nearly finished; only a few hundred feet in the middle section remained to be filled in and graded. Another week of work would bring it to completion.

At sunrise, Task Force 61 cruised south of Guadalcanal at 8 knots. It looked to be another day of light easterly winds, requiring the task force to run at high speed to create sufficient wind over the decks for flight operations. The *Wasp* air group would fly search patterns to the north and west, while the *Saratoga's* planes remained deckbound in case an enemy carrier group should appear in striking range. After the previous day's losses, Fletcher would be operating with an acute shortage of fighters. Fuel limitations would require their frequent return to the carriers. The air protection scheme was beginning to fray, and there was every reason to expect another round of air attacks from Rabaul.

FROM HIS HIDEOUT IN THE JUNGLE HILLS of northern Bougainville Island, coastwatcher Jack Read watched over the Buka Passage, a narrow and strategically vital seaway between Bougainville and Buka Island. A dark, sinewy, thickly bearded lieutenant of the Australian Royal Navy, Read had served for more than a decade in South Pacific postings as a patrol officer. His observation post lay directly in the flight path between Rabaul and Guadalcanal, and that alone made him a critical node in the coastwatching network. Constant movement was a precaution against being caught by the Japanese, who were hunting him diligently. On August 8, Read was preparing to move to a new post at a remote native village named Porapora. After a regularly scheduled radio check-in with station VIG (Port Moresby), he dialed in to a 7-megacycles frequency in hopes of picking up stray aviation communications. Immediately his ears were filled with radio chatter of the American carrier pilots. It did not take Read long to put the pieces together: the Americans had descended in force on the southeastern Solomons.

As he was pondering the significance of this development, one of his native scouts heard the drone of aircraft engines overhead. Through a break in the jungle canopy, a large formation of torpedo-armed G4Ms came into direct view, only a few hundred feet above their heads. Read counted twenty-four. He immediately got back on the teleradio, raised VIG, and blurted out in plain English: "Bombers now going southeast."[21]

For the second consecutive day, a coastwatcher had provided vital forewarning of an incoming airstrike. It was a pattern that would continue throughout the Solomons campaign. Every day, or nearly so, the Japanese sent airstrikes down from Rabaul—and every day, Jack Read or Paul Mason spotted the southbound formations overhead and relayed the warning. Read was especially well situated for this purpose, because his vantage point at Porapora commanded a panoramic view of all of Buka Island to the north, the eastern sea channels leading down the "Slot" (the body of water between the double file of islands that formed the Solomons archipelago), and the skies through which Japanese aircraft must pass. "The whole lay before you as a huge mosaic of detail and tropical splendor," he wrote in a 1943 report to the Australian navy.[22] Moreover, Read's lookout camp at Porapora was difficult to approach overland, and he had won the stalwart loyalty of the native tribesmen, who gave him advance warning of any Japanese search parties. He was never caught.

READ'S TRANSMISSION WAS PICKED UP at Pearl Harbor and relayed to the American commanders, who received it twenty-five minutes after it was broadcast. That provided ample time for Turner's transports and screening ships to get underway for evasive action, and for the carrier planes to gain altitude so as to be in proper attacking position when the enemy arrived.

The twin-engine bombers, painted green with the rising-sun disk on their fuselages, made a shrewd approach. The low-flying formation approached from the north, over Indispensable Strait, concealing themselves in the radar shadow of the Nggela island group, then turned back over Sealark Channel to attack from the east. The American fighters were at 27,000 feet above Savo Island, far out of position to repel the attack. At precisely noon, the intruders were spotted by gunners on the cruiser *Australia*. They were roaring in over the reefs, just 20 to 30 feet above the sea. Richard Tregaskis, watching from Guadalcanal, saw "flat sinister shapes, prowling low over the water, darting among the transports."[23] The fleet was wheeling and circling in anticipation of the attack. As the enemy planes came into close range, the heavy repeating concussions of the big antiaircraft guns were joined by the higher rattle of the shorter-range weapons.

All but five of the Japanese planes blew up, broke into pieces, cartwheeled, or dived into the sea. Only three managed to launch a torpedo, and only one of those struck home—the destroyer *Jarvis* was hit near the bow. (She limped away and was later sunk by a second air attack, resulting in the loss of her entire crew.) American Grummans, diving from high altitude, chased the survivors as they withdrew to the west. A stricken G4M crashed into the upper deck of one of the transports, the *George F. Elliott*. The ship's marines had disembarked, so casualties were limited, but she burned fiercely from stem to stern, and trailed a plume of thick black smoke into the sky.

Two hours later, as the remnants of the flight passed over northern Bougainville, Jack Read counted only eight survivors.

VAST QUANTITIES OF MUNITIONS, EQUIPMENT, and supplies remained to be brought ashore. A thousand drums of aviation gasoline for Gavutu, 1,500 drums for Guadalcanal; small arms and machine-gun ammunition; aviation lubricating oil, engine spares, radio equipment, water distillation equipment, and water cans. Semaphore flags, Aldis lamps, smoke signaling devices, binoculars, typewriters, pencils, message blanks. Sixty days' rations for all troops.[24] Crates and drums had been landed haphazardly on Beach Red, and the shoreline was so congested with unsorted supplies that General Vandegrift had to ask Turner to suspend landing operations. With no advanced port facilities available, everything had to be transferred into small craft, manhandled up the beach, and sorted into supply dumps. Two days of air attacks had left barely a scratch on the fleet, but the recurring threats had required Turner's ships to maneuver evasively for hours on end, during which time nothing could be unloaded.

The danger of beach congestion had been anticipated, but in the rush to plan and execute WATCHTOWER, the commanders had never faced it squarely. The landing craft were poor substitutes for proper cargo lighters.

Navy beachmasters had neither the training nor the experience to do the job properly—but even if they had, there were not enough laborers. Turner's operation plan specified that "Shore Party Commanders will call upon troop commanders in their immediate vicinity for assistance in handling supplies from landing beaches to dumps. Prisoners and stragglers will be used to assist in this task."[25] But no marine unit had been detailed to the task in advance, and the navy boat crews were not numerous enough to do the work. More hands were needed on the beaches.

The chaos prompted mutual recriminations. Citing doctrine and precedent, the marines insisted that the commander of troops ashore should be authorized to put a stop to unloading if the beachhead was not yet prepared to receive supplies. Turner blamed the marines for bringing a "vast amount of unnecessary impediments" and for failing to provide labor for the unloading. "The Marines have got to do this," he wrote a colonel commanding the 7th Marines. "Ships' crews can't run boats and winches, operate the ship, man guns, furnish personnel to handle boat traffic, repairs and evacuation at the beach and at the same time furnish unloading details."[26] Navy landing boat crews offered some barbed comments to a number of marines on Beach Red who were neither fighting nor working.

Vandegrift was unwilling to pull combat troops back off the perimeter, but Turner (who planned to land forces on Ndeni in the Santa Cruz Islands) refused his request for a replacement battalion to provide beach labor. Not until the morning of August 9 was the problem addressed with the simple expedient of dropping supplies farther down the beach. Ammunition, crates, shells, and other materials were simply stacked among the palm trees, left for the marines to sort out in good time.

ADMIRAL MIKAWA, NEWLY APPOINTED COMMANDER of the Eighth Fleet, had arrived in Rabaul little more than a week before the invasion of Guadalcanal. Japanese command arrangements in the theater were fragmented and illogical. The navy's Eighth Base Force had responsibility for garrison defense of New Britain and adjoining territories, while the Twenty-Fifth Air Flotilla controlled all air operations, but a cold rivalry divided them and rendered any effective cooperation unlikely. The Seventeenth Army staff, also headquartered at Rabaul, was heavily engaged in operations against Port Moresby on New Guinea.

No one seemed to welcome the arrival of Mikawa's Eighth Fleet, as all of the suitable administrative buildings and barracks in Rabaul had already been occupied. Mikawa decided to station most of his cruisers at the rear base of Kavieng, on New Ireland, where they would be less vulnerable to Allied air attack. Mikawa, a cerebral and soft-spoken officer, had served as Chuichi Nagumo's second in command through the first six months of the war. He had commanded the battleships and cruisers of *Kido Butai* (the carrier striking force) and had witnessed firsthand the disaster at Midway, which would weigh heavily on his mind in the action to come. On July 30, he broke out his flag above a tumbledown house in Rabaul township. Lacking even a toilet, it was far beneath his station, but he had bigger problems.

On August 7, immediately after receiving word of the American invasion in the lower Solomons, Mikawa mustered his surface naval forces for a counterstrike. The Seventeenth Army was unwilling to provide reinforcements for Guadalcanal—the army staff took the view that the Americans could be ejected with ease, and in good time—so Mikawa pulled together a pitifully small force of 315 riflemen and "Japanese marines" to be embarked on a transport. (It was subsequently torpedoed by U.S. submarine S-38 off Cape St. George, New Ireland.) The *Chokai* put into Rabaul to embark the admiral and his staff, and then put to sea at 2:30 p.m., in company with the light cruisers *Tenryu* and *Yubari* and the destroyer *Yunagi*. They rendezvoused with Cruiser Division 6—*Aoba*, *Kinugasa*, *Kako*, and *Furutaka*—off Cape St. George shortly before nightfall.[27]

Mikawa intended a surprise nighttime raid into Savo Sound to destroy Turner's vulnerable transports and cargo ships. Though the eight vessels in his column had not previously operated together, each ship and its crew were superbly outfitted, armed, and trained for night surface combat. Since the early 1920s, Japanese naval planners had envisioned a scenario for war with the United States that would require *Zen-Gen Sakusen*, "attrition operations."[28] Assuming that a naval war would be decided by a Mahanian clash of battleships in waters south of Japan, the planned "attrition operations"—submarine, air, and night torpedo attacks—were intended to sink American battleships as they advanced westward across the central Pacific. Night torpedo strikes by high-speed cruiser-destroyer forces (the *Senken Butai*, or "Advanced Force") were held to be the most essential component of *Zen-Gen Sakusen*. The Japanese had devoted intense efforts to developing the weaponry, doctrine, and training of *Senken Butai* for these all-important night torpedo attacks.[29] The fruits of their labors included first-rate night optical rangefinders and spotting sights, the skillful use of night illumination tactics (including star shells, searchlights, and flares dropped by cruiser floatplanes), and the exceptional aptitude of Japanese lookouts, chosen for their superior eyesight. In addition, the Type 93 "Long Lance" oxygen torpedo, which was 24 feet long and weighed more than a ton, carried a 1,100-pound high-explosive warhead and could travel at 50 knots to a range of 24,000 yards, or at lesser speed to a range of 48,000 yards. The Long Lances would inflict appalling punishment on the Allied fleet in the night to come, and in many more night actions in the ensuing campaign for Guadalcanal.

Reasoning that a simple formation would reduce the risk of collisions or confusion, Mikawa arrayed his seven cruisers and one destroyer into two columns. He placed his heavy cruisers (including his flagship, the *Chokai*) in the van and his destroyer in the rear.

Having witnessed the annihilation of four carriers by air attack at Midway two months earlier, Mikawa knew his planned dash into the Savo-Guadalcanal area might prove disastrous. Two or more American carriers were known to be in the vicinity, and if their air groups found him in daylight, they might destroy his ships at their leisure. Mikawa would manage the odds by traversing the last 200 miles of the run under cover of darkness, and then get away to the west before dawn. But he could not avoid being sighted farther up the Slot. Allied reconnaissance flights, including a B-17 and two Royal Australian Air Force (RAAF) Hudson bombers, passed overhead on the morning of August 8. Though Mikawa did not know it, his force had also been reconnoitered by an American submarine, S-38.

Passing the island of Choiseul at 4:00 p.m., Mikawa signaled his squadron to increase speed to 24 knots for the final leg of the approach. He planned to pass south of Savo Island, shell and torpedo the transports lying off Lunga Point, turn north and attack the ships lying off Tulagi, and retreat to the north of Savo Island.[30] He hoped to be at least 120 miles up the Slot by first light.

AT DUSK, ADMIRAL CRUTCHLEY'S CRUISERS and destroyers maneuvered into their night deployment positions north and south of Savo Island. In conformity to Turner's plan of operations, they divided into two groups, each built around three heavy cruisers, to guard one of two possible western entrances to the sound. Two destroyers, the *Blue* and the *Ralph Talbot*, were positioned as radar pickets farther west. The main eastern entrance to Savo Sound, Sealark Channel, was deemed a less likely route of attack. It was left in care of the light cruisers *Hobart* and *San Juan*.

At eight that evening, Turner summoned all senior commanders afloat and ashore to his flagship, the transport *McCawley*, for a late-night conference. Though Admiral Crutchley could have traveled to the *McCawley* by whaleboat, he elected to take his flagship *Australia* out of the southern line. In departing, he left Captain Howard D. Bode of the *Chicago* in command of the southern group. The northern group commanders were not informed of the admiral's absence.

On the *McCawley*, Turner shared unwelcome news. He had copied a radio signal from Fletcher to Ghormley asking permission to withdraw the aircraft carriers to the east. Ghormley had assented. Having previously committed to stay for two days (less than half the time Turner thought necessary to unload), Fletcher was now pulling out eight hours early. Turner was dismayed, and so was the normally mild-mannered Vandegrift. Without air protection, Turner's transports and cargo ships would be vulnerable to the inevitable Japanese airstrikes on August 9. He believed that he had no alternative but to move the rest of the fleet out at sunrise the next day. When Vandegrift insisted that he needed more supplies, Turner agreed to leave the cargo ships behind for another day of unloading. But the transports and warships must leave at dawn.

At no point in the conference did Turner refer to an approaching Japanese fleet. He had received spotty and contradictory sighting reports, and apparently did not fit the pieces together. The two RAAF Hudson bombers flying from Milne Bay, southeastern New Guinea, had seen Mikawa's force that morning, but their reports had given different headings. One had identified two seaplane tenders in a column of ships on a course of 100 degrees. That misidentification—two seaplane tenders—led Turner astray. The admiral assumed they would anchor in Rekata Bay off Santa Isabel Island, about 200 miles northwest, and launch seaplane torpedo attacks the following day. Turner had also assumed (mistakenly) that Consolidated PBY Catalinas (flying boats) based in Espiritu Santo had searched up the Slot that afternoon. Poor weather had scrubbed those flights, but Admiral McCain had failed to inform Turner that the searches had not been completed. For that reason, perhaps, Turner had not ordered Crutchley's cruiser planes to be dispatched to reconnoiter the same area.

The various communication failures and conflicting and erroneous reports seemed to have left Turner with a wholly unwarranted sense of invulnerability, at least until daylight brought the renewed threat of air attack.

It was a dark and moonless night, warm and humid, with mists hanging low across the sea. Passing rain showers repeatedly shrouded the area north of Savo Island, so the northern and southern screening groups could rarely see one another. Among the marines on Guadalcanal, rumors circulated that a major naval counterattack was impending. That impression multiplied at about 1:40 a.m., when the drone of a small aircraft engine was heard above the patchy cloud ceiling over Lunga Point. An air officer at the 1st Division command post correctly deduced that it was a cruiser floatplane, "and not ours."[31] Lieutenant Charles P. Clarke, officer of the deck on the *Quincy*, warned the executive officer that the strange planes must be enemy, as all Allied cruiser planes had been recovered earlier in the evening. But the executive disagreed and declined to awaken Captain Samuel N. Moore. Clarke later wrote that the brusque dismissal "was such that I was made to feel as if I were a jittery school boy."[32] (According to later reports by navy lookouts, one cruiser plane was sighted with running lights on, and therefore assumed friendly.) Only one ship broadcast a warning, but it apparently did not get through to Turner.

The scout dropped several parachute flares over Lunga Roads. They descended slowly through the overcast, emitting an intense greenish-yellow light that illuminated the entire transport fleet. A surge of false contact reports circulated through the marine lines. Some believed that the enemy was actually landing on the beach, and intermittent small-arms fire was directed at American patrol craft offshore. Then the engines faded as the planes headed west, and the flares came to rest on the sea.

The screening group crews had been at Readiness Condition One for forty-eight hours, and collective exhaustion was taking its toll. Rumors and bogus contact reports had continued to circulate without respite, and the contradictory and phantom sightings gradually eroded readiness. The cruisers ran in a monotonous oval pattern, crisscrossing the passages north and south of Savo Island. At nightfall on August 8, the alert level was downgraded to Condition Two, allowing half the watch to turn in and get some badly needed sleep in their bunks. The captain of one of the Allied cruisers wrote, "The enemy can reach this position at any time in the mid-watch," then went to sleep.[33] Physical and mental fatigue had exposed the fleet to precisely the sort of surprise attack that Mikawa was preparing to spring on them.

Between 12:44 and 12:54, Japanese lookouts first reported a visual fix on the destroyer *Blue* at a distance of about five miles. Mikawa ordered a slight northerly course change and cut his column's speed in order to reduce its bow waves. A few minutes later, lookouts spotted the *Ralph Talbot*. Both ships (which were supposed to function as the eyes of the Allied fleet) had reached the far northern and southern ends of their patrol circuits, placing them at near-maximum distance from the approaching enemy column. Their lookouts did not see Mikawa's ships, and their radar sets were apparently foiled by the radar shadow of Savo Island's volcanic cone. At least a dozen Japanese guns were trained on the *Blue*, and the little destroyer would have been blown out of the water had she shown any indication of having spotted the enemy. But the cool-headed Mikawa, in order to preserve the element of surprise, allowed her to continue on her way.

As the Japanese column passed into the channel between Savo and Guadalcanal, Mikawa ordered the speed resumed to 30 knots. The still-burning transport *George F. Elliott* lit up the southern horizon—faintly, but enough to reveal the silhouettes of the two southern group cruisers, *Canberra* and *Chicago*. The *Chokai*'s lookouts were soon able to discern the northern and southern forces simultaneously. The Japanese ships remained undetected. Mikawa's bold tactics had been dramatically vindicated. At 1:31, he signaled, "Every ship attack."[34]

The destroyer *Patterson* was the first to raise the alarm. By TBS ("talk-between-ships," a short-range voice radio used for tactical communications) she signaled, "Warning, warning, strange ships entering harbor."[35] But the Long Lances were already away, and the Japanese cruiser planes, circling overhead, dropped flares directly over the two cruisers, lighting them up for the gunners. At 1:44, Mikawa's ships opened a devastating salvo of 8-inch and 6-inch armor-piercing shells. The *Canberra* and *Chicago*, on a course of 310 degrees at a speed of 13 knots, were caught by surprise. Struck by at least twenty shells and two torpedoes, the *Canberra* blazed all along her length. Most of her senior officers, including Captain Frank Getting, were killed by direct hits on the bridge and superstructure. She lost all propulsion and electrical power, took on a ten-degree starboard list, and shuddered to a stop.[36]

The *Chicago*, just astern, steered to avoid her. Captain Bode ordered star shells fired in the direction of the enemy salvos, but they either failed to fire or were duds. Two torpedoes narrowly missed the *Chicago*, but a third hit and tore open her starboard bow. A gunnery officer recalled, "The deck beneath me came up under my feet, and the turret door to the officer's booth flew open. . . . Through the open turret door I could see two broad pencil streaks of phosphorescence in the water, parallel to the hull of the ship. They were the wakes of two torpedoes that had missed."[37] *Chicago* could fight no more. She had no power, her cruiser planes were spilling burning aviation fuel all along her upper works, and her forward compartments were flooding rapidly. Captain Bode apparently made no attempt to radio a warning to the other ships of the task force, a failure for which he would later be censured.

The action south of Savo Island had consumed less than ten minutes. Mikawa's column, racing east at 30 knots, veered north. While executing the turn, the cruisers *Tenryu*, *Yubari*, and *Furutaka* diverged from the rest of the column and took a more westerly course. Though Mikawa had not intended it, this maneuver had the effect of dividing the Japanese force into two roughly parallel columns that enveloped the three American cruisers and two destroyers of the northern group, which were steaming at 10 knots on a heading of 315 degrees in a column led by the *Vincennes*. The gunfire to the south had been heard, but officers in the northern cruiser group apparently assumed it must be friendly. The radio rooms on *Quincy*, *Astoria*, and *Vincennes* had each copied the *Patterson's* warning, but on the *Vincennes* it did not reach the captain, who remained fast asleep in his emergency cabin near the pilothouse. Men went to battle stations, but the speeding attackers overtook their quarry quickly.

Flares dropped by Japanese cruiser planes descended through the overcast and bathed the three American cruisers in brilliant greenish-yellow light. A few seconds later, the *Chokai's* searchlight flashed over their sterns. Once again, the Japanese launched torpedoes and then—before the fish reached their targets—opened a salvo of devastating and accurate shellfire. One of Mikawa's officers, Toshikazu Ohmae, observed that the *Chokai's* searchlight served the double function of leading the column and spotting targets. As if by an unspoken seaman's language, wrote Ohmae, the flagship was "fairly screaming to her colleagues: 'Here is the *Chokai*! Fire on *that* target! . . . Now *that* target! . . . This is the *Chokai*! Hit *that* target!'"[38]

Battle of Savo Island August 8, 1942

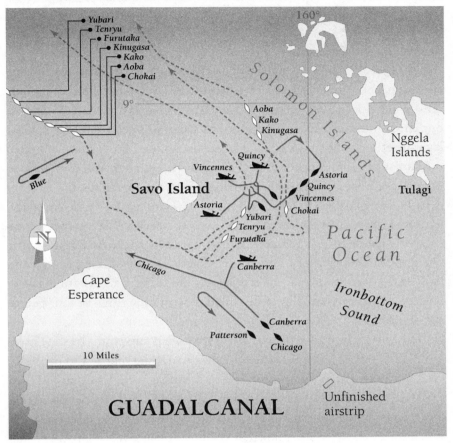

On the *Astoria*, Captain William G. Greenman was shaken awake, but his first order upon reaching the bridge was to cease fire. The bleary-eyed skipper was sure the southern group had somehow blundered into the northern group and was firing on it in confusion. In these critical moments, *Astoria* was battered by 5- and 8-inch shells on both quarters and peppered along her length by 25mm machine-gun fire. One heavy projectile struck the barbette of turret No. 1, knocking the weapon out of action and killing all personnel in the area. Another slammed home in the No. 1 fireroom, and a third struck a kerosene tank on the starboard side amidships, spilling blazing fuel across the well deck. According to the damage report, the ship quickly "become a raging inferno from the foremast to the after-bulkhead of the hangar. These fires eventually necessitated the abandoning of the fire-rooms and engine rooms due to intense heat and dense smoke."³⁹ Steering control was lost on the bridge, but that was moot as the ship soon lost all headway. All the forward fire main risers having ruptured, no water could be pumped to the hoses.

The *Quincy* was badly mauled on both quarters as her crew was rushing to stations. She was struck several times in the 1.1-inch antiaircraft mounts on the main deck aft. Firing back gamely, her main batteries delivered an 8-inch shell into the *Chokai*'s operations room, just abaft her bridge. *Cho-kai*'s turret No. 1 was knocked out of action, and her floatplanes, mounted on catapults, burst into flame. The *Quincy*'s skipper, Captain Moore, ordered a starboard turn to avoid colliding with the *Vincennes*. But another devastating salvo severed the steering leads, jammed the rudder in place, and held the ship in her turn until she was struck by two torpedoes on the port side near her firerooms, killing her propulsion. At 2:10 a.m., the *Quincy*'s bridge was wiped out by two direct shell hits, killing Moore and most of the senior officers. Upon reaching the scene, an assistant gunnery officer "found it a shambles of dead bodies with only three or four people still standing."⁴⁰

The *Quincy* listed heavily to port. As the sea poured into the shell holes in her hull, her upper decks were soon awash and she rolled onto her beam ends. Survivors threw rafts and other floatable objects into the sea, and then followed. Lieutenant Commander Bion B. Bierer, a supply officer, dived into the sea and swam about a hundred feet away. Treading water, he turned to watch the finale: "She went down by the bow and at a very sharp angle, her stern with propellers and rudder clearly outlined against the fire-lit sky."⁴¹

Captain Frederick Lois Riefkohl of the *Vincennes*, shaken awake by a crewman, likewise hesitated to engage the searchlights for fear that they might be friendly. Before the ship's signalmen could send recognition sig-nals, the ship was battered by too many projectiles to count—perhaps as many as seventy-four, fired by four or five different Japanese cruisers. The initial salvos struck the bridge, the carpenter shop, the hangar, and the antenna trunk. All the *Vincennes*'s gun turrets were disabled by direct or near shell hits. Fires sprang up throughout those areas, the floatplanes in the hangar lit up like tinderboxes, and the enemy fire did not let up for a moment. Direct shell hits were sustained on sky aft and sky forward. To add to her tally of grief, the *Vincennes* caught two torpedoes on her port side, near the forward magazine. Fires raged out of control all along her length, and great rippling explosions threw sheets of flame into the sky. An analysis published by the navy's Bureau of Ships later concluded, "It is not possible for any lightly protected vessel [i.e., a non-battleship] to absorb such punishment and survive."[42] Riefkohl ordered the crew off the ship at 2:14, and the *Vincennes* went down thirty minutes later.

At 2:16 the Japanese ships, still steaming at 30 knots, cleared Savo Sound and headed up the Slot. The *Ralph Talbot*, belatedly attempting to join the action, found herself directly in Mikawa's path. Lit up by searchlights and mauled by five shell hits, her radar, radio communications, and fire control equipment were all destroyed.[43] The hull plating on her starboard quarter was torn open at about the waterline, and she took on a 20 percent starboard list. Had a timely rain shower not descended over her, shrouding her from the enemy's view, she would likely have been blown out of the water.

To the marines on Guadalcanal and Tulagi, and the crews of the XRAY and YOKE transports in Savo Sound, the terrific roar and reverberations of the big guns had been accompanied by distant flashes in the mist. A searchlight occasionally stabbed through the night, and red tracer lines spat out here and there, but it was impossible to draw any firm conclusions from what they could see and hear. "We could clearly hear the thunder of guns, and see the sky light up from explosions," said a witness on Tulagi, "but knew only what the crews of the landing boats told us, that there was a naval battle going on."[44] On the *McCawley*, Turner and Vandegrift came up on deck to watch the pyrotechnics. Sailors on the flagship cheered wildly, assuming that the American ships were letting the enemy have it. Very soon silence returned, and all that could be seen were a few distant fires, apparently blazing ships. It was not yet known whether they were Allied or enemy.

Richard Tregaskis watched the show from Lunga Point. He had known that a counterattack by sea was likely, but the tremendous cannonading brought home a terrible truth. The marines on Guadalcanal were not in charge of their fate. "In that moment I realized how much we must depend on ships even in our land operation. . . . The terror and power and magnificence of man-made thunder and lightning made that point real. One had the feeling of being at the mercy of great accumulated forces far more powerful than anything human. We were only pawns in a battle of the gods, then, and we knew it."[45]

The sea was littered with debris and dead bodies. Hundreds of men who had abandoned the sinking ships clung to rafts or wreckage and struggled to remain afloat. Lieutenant Harry Vincent of the *Vincennes*, having leapt into the sea about fifteen minutes after Riefkohl's order to abandon ship, found himself among a group of sixteen sailors, all treading water. The stronger swimmers removed their life belts and gave them to the men who appeared most in need. Vincent recalls, "We discovered we could tread water without a belt for thirty minutes and then hang on to a sailor with a belt for thirty minutes and then do it again and again."[46] The battle and the sinking ships had stirred up the phosphorus in the sea, and men could look down to a depth of 15 or 20 feet. Sharks occasionally patrolled beneath their feet, but none attacked. Fred Moody, also of the *Vincennes*, was similarly proud of his shipmates. "Even these boys that were wounded out there, I didn't hear anyone calling for help for himself. Everyone seemed to want to help the other guy. That was my impression. I know certainly it was that way for the rest of the night."[47] They stayed afloat in this manner until daybreak, when the destroyer *Chambers* came alongside and lowered a cargo net.

MIKAWA ELECTED TO RETIRE AT HIGH SPEED TO THE NORTHWEST, rather than return to Savo Sound to engage the XRAY and YOKE transport groups. That was a fateful decision, and for the Americans a very lucky one. If the admiral had taken the more aggressive course, as some of his officers had urged, Turner's fleet might have been wiped out. In that case, the logistical underpinning of WATCHTOWER might have collapsed, with bleak consequences for Vandegrift's marines.

Mikawa's caution has been criticized, particularly by Western historians. But the admiral later offered a trenchant defense of the decision. He had been informed, incorrectly, that the Japanese air raids on August 7 and 8 had destroyed a large portion of the American transport fleet, so he did not expect to find a great wealth of targets. His column was traveling at high speed, and its formation had become disordered. Herding them back into a coherent formation and charging back into Savo Sound might have taken as long as two or three hours. Most importantly, he could not know that Fletcher's carriers had retired to the east and posed no danger.

Mikawa had thus far wagered his ships, and won. To renew the attack, he believed, would expose his force to a carrier air attack while he lacked any defense except antiaircraft guns; he would be inviting the same sort of catastrophe that he had recently witnessed at Midway. After the war, the admiral acknowledged that he might have scored a fantastic victory had he chosen differently, but he insisted that he could act only on the basis of what he knew at the time:

> Knowing now that the transports were vital to the American foothold on Guadalcanal, knowing now that our army would be unable to drive American forces out of the Solomons, and knowing now that the carrier task force was not in position to attack my ships, it is easy to say that some other decision would have been wiser. But I believe today, as then, that my decision, based on the information known to me, was not a wrong one.[48]

THE CANBERRA, AFLAME AND LISTING HEAVILY, drifted on the tide. The surviving crew worked valiantly to save the ship, but there was little they could do. The *Patterson* came alongside, and its crew ran hoses across to assist in quelling the fires, but boxes of ready service ammunition exploded sporadically along the *Canberra*'s deck, and the destroyer had to sheer off. The *Canberra*'s fuel was dumped overboard, her remaining torpedoes jettisoned, and her magazines flooded. Her starboard list gradually increased, and the fires worsened. At 5:30 a.m., Turner sent word that the fleet was preparing to depart by Sealark Channel, and if the *Canberra* could not be navigated safely, she must be destroyed. The ship was abandoned in orderly fashion, with the crew leaping directly onto the decks of the destroyers or into the sea, where they were lifted by cargo nets. The burning, listing *Canberra* did not succumb willingly to the destroyers' attempt to sink her. The *Patterson* and *Elliott* had to fire 263 rounds of 5-inch shells and four torpedoes before she finally slipped beneath the waves.

There remained some hope of salvaging the *Astoria*. Shortly after 2:00

a.m., with her fires raging out of control throughout the upper decks amidships, Captain Greenman ordered survivors out of the bridge and foretop
and sent them forward into the forecastle. Though the skipper did not
yet know it, his executive officer had organized another party of survivors aft, on the fantail. Both groups formed bucket brigades and managed
to keep the flames at bay, but between them—on the well deck, hangar,
and superstructure—a ferocious inferno consumed whatever fuel it found,
including the floatplanes, the boats, the paint locker, the mattresses and
furniture in wardroom country, the clipping room ammunition, and shells
on the 5- and 1.1-inch hoists. A welcome rainsquall washed over the burning ship at 3:30 a.m., but it provided only momentary relief, and as it passed,
the flames flared up more intensely than before. Shortly before dawn, the
destroyer *Bagley* came alongside and began taking men off the bow. The
fires advanced relentlessly until 11:30 a.m., when an explosion tore open
the ship's port side at the waterline. The sea poured into the *Astoria*, and
she rolled radically to port. Officers and sailors leapt clear and swam for
their lives. The *Astoria* rolled all the way onto her beam ends, and her stern
went under. By a quarter past noon she was gone.[49]

The transport fleet, ignorant of its salvation, was left in an uproar.
Enemy cruiser planes continued to circle overhead for about an hour after
the Japanese fleet's departure, dropping flares off Tulagi and the adjoining islands. It stood to reason, or so it seemed, that the flares portended
another round of attacks. Rain showers and shrouding mists made for poor
visibility, and recognition signals were difficult to pick out. Landing boats
and patrol craft raced this way and that, apparently in distress. Collisions
were narrowly averted. Rumors and spurious sighting reports proliferated.
Lookouts, believing they had seen periscopes and torpedo wakes, raised the
alarm, and destroyers laid down patterns of depth charges across the heart
of Savo Sound (which now took the name "Ironbottom Sound"). Although
no friendly exchanges of major-caliber naval gunfire were reported, sporadic "intramural" small-arms firefights persisted until dawn. Men who had
been at Pearl Harbor the previous December 7 felt an unpleasant sense of
déjà vu.

Among the marines, news spread that the navy had suffered a terrible
defeat. As dawn broke, and it finally became apparent that the enemy
had left the scene, the American fleet was scrambling to get underway

via Sealark Channel. To the west were the drifting, burning hulks of the *Canberra* and *Astoria*. General Vandegrift, watching the disorderly scene from the beach on Guadalcanal, wondered aloud, "What's happened to the navy?" A staff officer replied, "I don't believe the first team has taken the field, General."[50]

The marines urgently needed more vital provisions and supplies delivered to the beaches, but Turner was determined to clear his ships out of the area. The admiral agreed to leave several cargo ships behind until that afternoon, but without air protection the rest of the fleet must go. Beach Red remained congested with unsorted crates. The frenzied state of the fleet—false contact reports, air-raid warnings requiring high-speed maneuvering, boats racing around in search of their ships—repeatedly interrupted unloading operations. An hour after dawn there were no landing barges at work in Lunga Roads. Wounded sailors had to be collected from the stricken cruisers. Fierce Japanese resistance continued on the little island of Tanambogo, and reinforcements had to be put ashore there. The diary of the cargo ship *Betelgeuse* contained the following observation: "The major part of this time was used up in awaiting orders to land after a beachhead had been secured, ceasing unloading due to orders from the beach, getting underway and coming to anchor, underway at sea to avoid the enemy, manning general quarters stations, scattering and recalling boats, diversion of ship's boats to assist in unloading of other ships."[51]

Meanwhile, Vandegrift had to fortify his shoreline against an expected enemy counterinvasion. An intelligence alert had warned that a Japanese invasion force was gathering at Rabaul and was expected to arrive within four days. Preparation of defenses required manpower, diverting men from the unloading work. Turner refused Vandegrift's request to be reinforced with the 1,400 officers and men of the 2nd Marines, which the admiral continued to insist on holding in reserve for possible deployment to Ndeni.

Throughout the morning, ships filed out of Sealark Channel. Hundreds of marines watched glumly as the battle-mauled *Chicago*, still smoking and with most of her bow blasted away, vanished beyond Taivu Point. By sundown, none remained. A supply officer estimated that fewer than half of the crates packed into the transports in New Zealand had been landed. The marines, now alone, were precariously short of such vital necessities as food, ammunition, heavy artillery, antiaircraft guns, communications equipment, barbed wire, fuel, and spare parts. And still they wondered: where was the Japanese army, and when and where would it reveal itself?

Chapter Three

ADMIRAL KING, SOUND ASLEEP ON HIS DOCKED FLAGSHIP *DAUNTLESS* at the Washington Navy Yard, was shaken awake in the early morning hours of August 12. "Admiral, you've got to see this," said his duty officer, who had never before interrupted the boss's sleep. "It isn't good."[1]

With disbelieving eyes, King read Turner's dispatch reporting the loss of four Allied cruisers with heavy loss of life, and the hurried withdrawal of the transports and cargo ships from Ironbottom Sound. He asked that the dispatch be decoded again, in the vain hope that it was somehow mistaken. It was not.

The news kicked King in the teeth. WATCHTOWER was his invention, his hobbyhorse, and his responsibility. He had insisted on the risky expedition with full knowledge that Allied shipping resources and airpower were strained to the snapping point. He had trodden over the well-reasoned joint objections of the region's two theater commanders. "That, as far as I am concerned, was the blackest day of the war," he later said. "The whole future became unpredictable."[2]

The next morning, in his office on the second "deck" of Main Navy (the headquarters building on Constitution Avenue), he studied the track charts forwarded by Turner and tried to envision how the Japanese fleet could have stolen into Ironbottom Sound undetected. "I just can't understand it," he admitted to Admiral Harry W. Hill, who had dropped in to see him.[3] The analogy to Pearl Harbor was impossible to ignore. The earlier surprise attack had inflicted greater casualties and material damage, but the beating at Savo had been meted out in wartime, against ships operating in enemy-dominated seas, when their commanders and crews ought to have been hypervigilant to every likely threat. The navy's honor, reputation, and self-respect were on the block.

FDR received the news from his naval aide, Commander John L. McCrea, who drove the dispatch from Washington to "Shangri-La," the president's rural presidential retreat in Maryland (later renamed Camp David). The president, McCrea recalled, "was heartsick about it. There wasn't anything he could do about it."[4]

King ordered that news of the defeat be concealed from the press. He dispatched two trusted officers, Admiral Arthur J. Hepburn and Captain DeWitt C. Ramsey, to fly to Noumea to investigate its causes. Not for a moment did he consider scaling back the commitment to WATCHTOWER, however—indeed, he moved at once to reinforce Ghormley. In a memorandum to the president on August 13, King outlined his plan to send the battleships *South Dakota* and *Washington*, accompanied by a cruiser and six destroyers, through the Panama Canal and on to Noumea. Two more cruisers would be transferred from Britain to the east coast and kept in readiness for possible transfer to the Pacific.[5] On the same day, King asked General Marshall to provide more army air units to the region, "regardless of commitments elsewhere. . . . In my opinion, the Army Air Forces in Hawaii and the South Pacific Area must be reinforced immediately to a much greater extent than appears now to be in prospect."[6] Marshall acquiesced without dissent, even though the USAAF chief Henry "Hap" Arnold was adamantly opposed to diverting any of his strength from Europe or the pending invasion of North Africa. Marshall was perfectly aware that King had FDR's ear, and that the commander in chief wanted it done.

As Turner's ships limped back toward Noumea, survivors of the sunken cruisers began the grim work of reconstructing the fatal events. The senior surviving officer of each ship was required to submit an action report—but the loss of records and the death or disablement of many key witnesses and participants required them to work largely from memory. All knew the action would receive intense scrutiny. Admiral Crutchley, to his credit, did not mince words. On the morning of August 10, he wrote Turner: "The fact must be faced that we had an adequate force placed with the very purpose of repelling surface attack and when that surface attack was made, it destroyed our force."[7] How had it happened?

Hepburn and Ramsey's investigation shone a harsh light on the failure of air and submarine reconnaissance to discover Mikawa's force and alert the task force to its approach. The division of the region into two theaters, one controlled by Ghormley and the other by MacArthur, had posed a communications hitch right at the vital boundary that Mikawa crossed on the night of August 8–9. Several Allied planes had spotted the Japanese ships farther up the Slot, but some of the sighting reports failed to get through to Turner in time, and others were inaccurate or incomplete. A report of "seaplane tenders" among the Japanese ships threw Turner off the scent—he assumed they must be headed for Rekata Bay on Santa Isabel and would launch a seaplane torpedo attack on August 9. Admiral McCain's PBYs had been foiled by bad weather, but McCain had failed to inform Turner that the patrol flights had not occurred. Turner might have used the cruiser planes in his task force to conduct his own air searches, but he did not.

A fateful convergence of errors and bad luck was behind the debacle, and no senior naval commander in the WATCHTOWER expedition could count himself entirely blameless. Hepburn's report concluded that the defeat could not be attributed to a single root cause. Captain Bode, of the *Chicago*, was the only officer formally censured (for failing to send an alert when his ship was attacked). In his comments on the report, submitted to Secretary of the Navy Frank Knox five weeks after the battle, King stressed that "this was the first battle experience for most of the ships participating in the operation and for most of the flag officers involved, and that consequently it was the first time that most of them had been in the position of 'kill or be killed.' . . . They simply had not learned how and when to stay on the alert."[8] The officers and men had been on Condition One Alert, with virtually the entire crew on watch, for more than forty-eight hours. The men were human; they could not function indefinitely without rest. Collective physical and mental exhaustion had overcome the task forces, rendering them vulnerable to surprise attack.

A more contentious question was Fletcher's abrupt decision to withdraw the aircraft carriers on the afternoon of August 8, which the Hepburn report called "a contributory cause" of the disaster. Had he stayed until the morning of the ninth, as previously planned, Fletcher could have done nothing to prevent the catastrophe off Savo Island—but it is possible that his air groups could have delivered retribution from the air on Mikawa's fleeing column. Fletcher's early withdrawal has remained one of the livelier controversies of the Pacific War. It drew pungent criticism from Turner and

Vandegrift, both of whom seemed to have regarded it as a personal betrayal. In his memoir, the normally even-tempered Vandegrift used the incendiary term "running away," with its blunt intimation of cowardice, to describe Fletcher's departure.[9] Fletcher's decision was pilloried by the influential Samuel Eliot Morison in his quasi-official history of U.S. naval operations in the Second World War.

The subject has been parsed, scrutinized, and debated by generations of historians. Little more can be usefully said, except to bring out some of the most salient points. Fletcher, in almost perfect contrast to Turner, seemed content to accept history's judgment of his conduct. He did not, like Turner, review and provide detailed notes on Morison's draft manuscript covering the events of WATCHTOWER. He published no memoir. Retiring in 1947 to a farm in rural Maryland, he largely removed himself from the cut and thrust of historical debate. He either forgot or falsely denied that he and Turner had clashed, during the July 26 planning conference on the *Saratoga*, over the question of how long the carriers would stay. "Turner and his staff were very pleased" with the arrangements made at the conference, Fletcher told a *New York Times* reporter in 1947, and added: "At no time was there any friction between Turner and myself."[10] That was plainly inaccurate, as several other witnesses have attested.

In his dispatch to Ghormley on the evening of August 8, Fletcher had offered two reasons for his proposed withdrawal: the low-fuel state of his task force, and heavy losses of F4F fighters on August 7 and 8. In preparing his volume on the Guadalcanal landing (volume 5, *The Struggle for Guadalcanal*) Morison obtained the navy's records of the actual fuel state of each of the ships in Fletcher's task force, and showed that Fletcher's fuel situation was far from critical. All the cruisers were at least half full. The destroyers' fuel condition varied, but none had less than 40,000 gallons of fuel, and their daily fuel expenditure ranged from 12,000 to 24,000 gallons. Morison's biting conclusion: "Thus it is idle to pretend that there was any urgent fuel shortage in this force. . . . Fletcher's reasons for withdrawal were flimsy. . . . [H]is force could have remained in the area with no more severe consequences than sunburn."[11] John B. Lundstrom provides evidence that Fletcher may have received incomplete or inaccurate information about the fuel state of his screening vessels.[12] The admiral could act only on the basis of what he knew. On the other hand, it is a task force commander's responsibility to obtain proper reports from ships under his command.

The second issue, heavy fighter losses in air combat on August 7 and 8, cannot be idly dismissed. On Dog-Day, half of the American fighters that engaged the enemy in air combat were sent down in flames. Overall fighter losses in the two days had come to twenty-one, leaving reserves of seventy-eight Wildcats on the three carriers. Fighters, by a wide margin, were the most valuable weapon in Fletcher's arsenal. They were the only aircraft that could properly defend Turner's ships against air raids, but they were equally needed to fly cover over the carrier task forces throughout the daylight hours. Fletcher's air operations during the first two days of WATCH-TOWER had been the busiest in the history of carrier warfare. Wear and tear to equipment, and the simple exhaustion of the aircrews, were considerations that no responsible task force commander could afford to ignore.

The heart of the controversy was the value of the carriers themselves. Their best protection was constant movement and finding concealment in thick weather whenever possible. Operating for several days "chained to a post," in a fixed location south of Guadalcanal, invited devastating counterattack by air or submarine. Japanese twin-engine medium bombers, armed with torpedoes, had the range to reach Fletcher's task force from Rabaul. The submarine menace grew inexorably the longer his ships remained corralled in a finite geographic zone. Three months earlier, in these very same waters, Fletcher had lost the *Lexington* to air attack at the Battle of the Coral Sea. The *Yorktown*, his former flagship, had been shot out from under him at Midway. The *Saratoga*, his current flagship, had been torpedoed by a Japanese submarine in January and knocked out of action for four months. Though Fletcher did not yet know it, the *Saratoga* would catch another torpedo on August 31, and the *Wasp*, the newest carrier to arrive in the theater, would be destroyed by submarine attack in mid-September. The *Hornet* would succumb to air attack in October (at the Battle of the Santa Cruz Islands), leaving just one American flattop (the *Enterprise*) in the Pacific.

This much is incontrovertible: the risk that one or more American carriers would be lost during the WATCHTOWER expedition was not negligible. But how should that risk be balanced against Turner's need for continued air protection? The carriers had provided most of the navy's offensive striking power since escaping destruction on December 7, 1941. For the time being (until the new *Essex*-class carriers could be commissioned and brought into the fleet) they were scarce and valuable assets. Fletcher correctly assumed that the Japanese aircraft carriers would sooner or later come down into the lower Solomons. In that case it would be his overriding duty to fight another carrier slugging match like those of Coral Sea or Midway. It was in that context that Fletcher's withdrawal must be judged.

The proper use of the carriers during WATCHTOWER was a first-order strategic question, and it should have been resolved in advance. That it was not is unsurprising, given how hastily WATCHTOWER had been planned and executed. Turner had hoped for a full five days to unload the division's cargo, but plans for the operation had specified that the transport fleet would withdraw in three days, and neither Turner nor the marines had ever been promised longer than "two or three" days of carrier air cover. Neither King, Nimitz, nor Ghormley had provided clear instructions to resolve the discrepancy. The decision therefore fell to Fletcher, whom Ghormley designated the overall commander of the expedition. Many officers who took part in the July 26 command conference on the *Saratoga* were taken aback by the evident rancor between Fletcher and Turner and came away with the impression that Fletcher lacked confidence in the operation. Ghormley's presence had been urgently needed at that conference—had he been at the table, he could have adjudicated the question and resolved any doubt. A reasonable share of culpability must be attributed to WATCHTOWER's cumbersome and ambiguous command arrangements, and thus to King himself.

SUNRISE ON AUGUST 10 found Task Force 62 zigzagging generally east, at about the midpoint between Guadalcanal and Noumea, with the damaged *Chicago* and *Ralph Talbot* struggling to remain in company. Turner's ships were loaded with hundreds of wounded marines and sailors, 831 hospitalization cases in all. Four submarine contacts were reported between dawn and dusk, and a torpedo wake was once observed to pass by the bow of the *McCawley*. The destroyers hunted the surrounding waters with depth-charge barrages, and the task force executed a series of radical turns. The stricken *Chicago*, falling behind, was ordered into Efate with a destroyer screen. No ship suffered a torpedo hit, and on August 15, the bulk of Task Force 62 arrived safely at Noumea Harbor. The wounded were removed to hospital ships by stretcher. All would be sent to Australia or the States.[13]

The 1st Division's hopes now depended on constant and generous supply by sea. On August 15, four old flush-deck "four-piper" transports dropped anchor at Lunga Roads and began unloading supplies—aviation gasoline

(400 drums), aerial bombs (300), .50-caliber ammunition, lubricating oil—and ground personnel for Marine Aircraft Group 21, which would fly in as soon as the airstrip was in a condition to receive planes. On the following afternoon, the Fomalhaut, loaded with heavy construction equipment for Guadalcanal and Tulagi, stood out of Noumea accompanied by three destroyers. On that same date, Turner asked McCain to "load all APDs [high-speed transports] to capacity with food and send one division to Guadalcanal and the other to Tulagi."[14]

With 16,000 mouths to feed, Vandegrift grew concerned about his food reserves. According to Turner's records, entered into his war diary on August 9, "Sufficient food was landed at the Tulagi area for about eleven days and at the Guadalcanal area for about thirty-six days."[15] The marines did not agree with those figures, however—Vandegrift radioed this on August 15: "From rations on hand and consumed to date estimate about twelve days' rations landed Guadalcanal. Further loss due to weather and handling reduced this to ten days. No opportunity should be lost to forward rations to this command."[16] In the 1st Division's final report, submitted in 1943, the figures recorded for August 15 were seventeen days of regular field rations, three days of Type C Rations, and another ten days' supply of captured Japanese food. The discrepancies are likely explained by the spoilage of rations packed in cardboard boxes, which tended to disintegrate in the rain, and by the uncertain amount of captured enemy food. At any rate, there is no doubt that the marines went hungry during those early weeks in the Solomons. Vandegrift ordered reduced rations on August 12, and most men subsisted on two meager meals per day. Private William Rogal, manning a foxhole on Tulagi, was issued one C ration per day "and sometimes not even that." He and his fellow marines scavenged for Japanese provisions in warehouses along the Tulagi waterfront and found a few sacks of barley. They made a kind of barley soup, an awful mush, but ate it avidly. On the transports, Rogal recalled, sex had been the habitual topic of conversation among bored marines. Now it was food, because "the single overriding emotion during the weeks we existed in that jungle retreat was hunger!"[17]

Turner continued to pressure Fletcher to shield his cargo ships, but Fletcher was keen to keep his task force together and on the move. He anticipated a major Japanese counterstrike, and with good reason. The intelligence picture remained clouded, but air reconnaissance, coastwatcher reports, and bits and pieces of "Ultra" (decrypted enemy radio intercepts) seemed to portend a major Japanese fleet movement into the lower Solomons. Overflights of northern Bougainville confirmed that the Japanese were building new landing strips south of Buka Airfield.[18] MacArthur's B-17s flew over Rabaul and Kavieng almost every day and snapped aerial photographs. Between August 12 and August 16, these photos revealed a significant buildup of naval force, and the airfields at Rabaul appeared to have been reinforced with fighters and bombers. The Japanese were apparently constructing another airfield at Buin on southern Bougainville, about 400 miles northwest of Guadalcanal, which would give them a much closer springboard for air attacks. Considerable enemy air activity was reported at Lae, on the northern coast of New Guinea. On August 15, Japanese aircraft dropped six loads of ammunition and food to Japanese troops scattered on the western end of Guadalcanal (four fell within or near the marine lines and were captured). The Americans still had not pinpointed the location of Japanese carrier forces, but they could be at sea and on their way to the Solomons. On August 21, Fletcher told Ghormley that he considered it "inadvisable to send cruisers and destroyers into CACTUS [Guadalcanal] nightly," because of their exposure to submarine attack.[19] Better to keep them at sea, on the move, and prepared to repel the expected enemy naval offensive.

The struggle for Guadalcanal now settled into a repetitive daily pattern. Each day, shortly after noon, Japanese bombers appeared overhead and pounded the island, concentrating their bombs on marine installations, defenses, and the airstrip. A single battery of four 90mm antiaircraft guns, set up on the edge of the airfield, usually discouraged the pilots from descending lower than 20,000 feet. Still, the bombing arrested construction work and forced the units positioned around the airfield to spend hours each day in hastily dug slit trenches and foxholes. Occasionally Zero fighters made low-altitude strafing runs. The twin-engine bombers flew lazy circles above the island even after having released their payloads. Vandegrift's officers correctly deduced that they were snapping aerial photographs of the airfield and the various installations and weaponry in the marine perimeter.

Air attacks did not claim heavy casualties, but the absence of any friendly planes overhead ate away at morale. If the Japanese could send their Zeros all the way from Rabaul, why couldn't the American fighters come up from Espiritu Santo, which was slightly closer? The answer, as an aviator could explain, was that the heavier Wildcats did not have the range to make such a flight. Guadalcanal needed its own air force—it was urgently necessary to complete "Henderson Field," the name now given to Guadalcanal's not-quite-finished airstrip in honor of Major Lofton R. Henderson, who had perished while leading a squadron of marine bombers against the enemy fleet at Midway.

At 11:00 a.m. on August 18, eight G4M "Betty" bombers appeared suddenly over Henderson at well under 5,000 feet. Radar had failed to pick them up. Men standing along the side of the field scattered and ducked into foxholes and trenches. A tightly concentrated pattern of 500-pound bombs fell around the antiaircraft batteries and down the length of the strip, leaving seventeen craters that would have to be filled in by the engineers. In flying so low, the G4Ms exposed themselves to antiaircraft fire, and several were observed to trail smoke as they turned northwest for home.

The near-daily midday raids were followed by harrowing nighttime bombardments—at first by submarines and then (on August 16) by destroyers that snuck into Ironbottom Sound after dark. Often these ships disgorged Japanese troop reinforcements and supplies onto Guadalcanal's northwestern beaches. Lacking heavy shore guns or air cover, the marines could do nothing to interfere with Japanese ships even in broad daylight. On the afternoon of the sixteenth, several dozen marines on a hill near Kukum watched as a Japanese destroyer disembarked about 200 troops on the beach to the west.

Almost every night, a floatplane circled over the marine perimeter, dropping occasional bombs here or there. Collectively known to the Americans as "Washing Machine Charley" or "Louie the Louse," these nocturnal visitors usually did little damage. But they kept the marines awake, and that may have been their purpose. The marines spoke of "shoes on" and "shoes off" nights.[20] Most of the division was sleeping on the ground, curled up on ponchos against the wet earth. Some attempted to rig crude hammocks, but every sleeper had to be positioned near his foxhole so that he could execute the half-awake rolling maneuver called the "Guadalcanal twitch." The marines, almost none of whom had experienced combat before setting foot on this miserable island, were on edge. Any noise in the jungle beyond their lines might signal the beginning of an enemy attack. Men on the perimeter threw away a lot of ammunition in that first week. On the fourth night, marine units dug in on opposite sides of the airfield held an "intramural" (friendly) firefight, exchanging a large volume of fire before their officers put a stop to it. Mercifully, none was injured.

The stultifying heat and humidity, oppressive swarms of insects, gnawing hunger, and sleepless nights wore the men down. The first two weeks felt like two months. Sickness soon began to take its inevitable toll. Most of the 1st Division marines would suffer dysentery and malaria at some point during the campaign, often at the same time. When overtaken by a malarial fever, a marine was taken off the lines to the hospital tent near Lunga Point, where he and a hundred or so fellow sufferers lay bathed in sweat from head to toe, oscillating between blazing fevers and teeth-rattling chills. When the fever broke, usually after twenty-four to forty-eight hours, the man put his boots back on and went back to his foxhole. Chronic dysentery was so common as to be universal, but it did not normally require hospitalization. Rogal recalled, "It was so bad and so prevalent that a solid bowel movement was a cause for rejoicing."[21]

The marine perimeter was semicircular in shape, bounded by Ironbottom Sound on the north and the jungle foothills to the south. It was about five miles wide (east to west) and about two miles deep (north to south). It covered most of what had been, before the war, the three largest and most prosperous Lever Brothers coconut plantations on Guadalcanal (named Kukum, Lunga, and Tenaru). For that reason, it was the most developed part of Guadalcanal—which is not to say it was well developed, but it did have a network of reasonably passable dirt roads running between the beach, Lunga Point, and Henderson Field. Much of the land was covered with coconut palms planted in neat and orderly rows, offering some cover against daytime bombing and strafing attacks.

General Vandegrift had to consider many unpleasant possibilities. The greatest danger, he concluded, was a counter-landing in force on the same beach that the marines had taken on August 7. He drew up his beach-facing defenses behind Lunga Point, running from the Tenaru River to a hill about 1,000 yards southwest of Kukum. The marines dug foxholes and trenches, swinging picks and turning dirt out with shovels in the sweltering heat. At first they had no sandbags or barbed wire, as these items had not been unloaded from the cargo ships before their withdrawal on August 9.[22] Automatic machine guns were emplaced along these lines and positioned to sweep the beach. Units detailed men to start moving the piled-up supplies off the beach and back into secure supply dumps. Vandegrift also had to consider the possibility of a concerted attack anywhere along his perimeter; the enemy might attack from the east and west simultaneously. That danger prompted Vandegrift to pull in the eastern flank from the Ilu River to the Tenaru. This shortened his perimeter and made it more defensible, a decision that would very soon be vindicated.

Company commanders gathered each morning at Vandergrift's command post. All were fatigued: worn down by the heat, the stress, and the difficulty in getting a decent night's sleep. In his memoir, the general left a portrait of his officers sitting on the wet ground, sipping cold coffee from tin cups and listening to the sound of "rain hissing on a pathetic fire."[23] They were haggard, filthy, and unshaven. All wore brave faces, but Vandegrift sensed that morale was fragile. They wondered if they had been abandoned by the navy. When a radio broadcast mentioned decorations awarded to navy crews, a low growl of anger circulated through their ranks.

Vandegrift moved to fortify the division's spirits by issuing a series of upbeat announcements. Japanese resistance on Tulagi had been snuffed out. Patrols had not encountered any strong enemy force outside the lines. Work on the airfield was progressing rapidly, and marine fighter squadrons would soon arrive. The general made a point of touring the lines at midday, timing his visits to precede the daily Japanese airstrikes. He often posed for photographs with the troops, "a morale device that worked because they thought if I went to the trouble of having the picture taken then I obviously planned to enjoy it in future years."[24]

Not least among the marines' difficulties was a nearly complete lack of intelligence about enemy troops on the island. Except for a few minor skirmishes in patrols outside the perimeter, the enemy had not yet shown his hand. Vandegrift did not know how many Japanese troops were "out there," or where they were bivouacked, or how well armed or provisioned they were, or what they intended in the way of counterattack. The stillness of the jungle exerted subtle psychological pressure on men who had been trained for a quick, hard-fought amphibious assault. The few prisoners taken by patrols outside the lines seemed to be laborers rather than soldiers ("termites" as the marines called them), and they could offer little information about the Japanese army's presence on the island.

On August 12, a Japanese naval warrant officer was taken prisoner near the Matanikau River. Interrogated by Lieutenant Colonel Frank Goettge, the 1st Division intelligence officer, he revealed that there were several hundred Japanese stragglers encamped on the west bank of the river who might be willing to surrender. Another report referred to a "white flag" displayed near an enemy position. Goettge proposed to take a combat patrol down the coast in a Higgins boat, land near Point Cruz, and go up the river in search of these prospective prisoners. Vandegrift gave his reluctant assent. The party landed after nightfall on the twelfth and was ambushed immediately. Goettge was the first man killed in an action that quickly developed into a massacre. Only three survivors managed to escape and make their way back into the marine perimeter. A reinforced company was sent back out to look for the lost patrol, but no one and no bodies could be found. Lurid stories later appeared in the press, suggesting that the Goettge patrol had been enticed by a sham surrender. But there is no evidence to suggest any such trickery on this occasion, and it is likely that the "white flag" spotted the previous day was a "Rising Sun" in which the red disk was concealed from view.

As if in answer to the marines' urgent need for better local intelligence, the coastwatcher and former colonial district officer Martin Clemens appeared on August 14. Clemens had been invited down from his high mountain aerie by Charles Widdy, the former Lever Brothers plantation manager who had landed with the marines, by a handwritten note delivered by a native runner: "American marines have landed successfully in force. Come in via Volanavua and along the beach to Ilu during daylight—repeat—daylight. Ask outpost to direct you to me at 1st Reg. C.P. at Lunga. Congratulations and regards."[25] Beginning at dawn, Clemens had packed up his radio gear and came down the hill, a cavalcade of native carriers in train. He took a circuitous route, taking care to avoid the enemy lurking in the jungle, and hailed the marines from a position just east of Volanavua. The marines raised their rifles but held fire, and then welcomed Clemens warmly with cigarettes and chocolate bars. It had been months since the Scotsman had spoken English, except over the radio. He was speechless with emotion.

Late that afternoon, after having cleaned himself up, Clemens was taken to division headquarters and introduced to Vandegrift. He perched on a ration box in the general's command post and told the entire story of his activity since the Japanese had landed on Tulagi more than three months earlier. The general described his visitor as a "remarkable chap of medium height, well-built and apparently suffering no ill effects from his self-imposed jungle exile."[26] He wore shorts and black dress oxfords that had been polished to a high sheen. It was obvious that he knew a great deal of the island and its people, and he already had intact a native constabulary that would serve well as a patrolling force. Vandegrift placed him in charge of "all matters of native administration and of intelligence outside the perimeter." The Scotsman would contribute invaluable intelligence through his native scouts—brave and steadfast fighters who could, when necessary, shed their uniforms and blend into the native population. Guadalcanal had been a campaign of extermination from the beginning, and the islanders understood that sort of fighting well. Traveling quickly and silently over secret paths through the jungle, they were to prove fearsome guerrilla fighters.

THE JAPANESE NAVY APPARENTLY BELIEVED it had crippled the invasion fleet in Ironbottom Sound. According to Mikawa's Eighth Fleet war diary, Allied losses in naval and air action between August 7 and August 9 amounted to twelve cruisers (eight heavy, four light) and "several destroyers."[27] The Fifth Air Attack Force jacked these estimates up to "twenty some cruisers, destroyers, transports, and other types" of ships.[28] When the buoyant reports reached Tokyo, however, the Imperial General Headquarters (IGHQ) apparently deemed them too conservative: a press communiqué declared that at least twenty-eight Allied warships and thirty transports or freighters had been sent to the bottom. An unnamed source boasted that "American and British naval strength has been reduced to that of a third-rate power."[29]

Gross inflation of claimed air and naval combat results was a pervasive syndrome in the Pacific War. Throughout the conflict, for example, American aviators and submariners consistently overestimated the number and tonnage of enemy ships sunk. (Those discrepancies would cause embarrassment after the war, when the U.S. Strategic Bombing Survey published revised estimates based on Japanese records.) But Japanese military leaders were often led astray by even the most improbable claims. If Japanese naval and air forces had slaughtered the invasion fleet, then the enemy troops on Guadalcanal must be underequipped and under-provisioned. They could be mopped up without much trouble. Admiral Osami Nagano, chief of the Naval General Staff (NGS), hastened to the summer palace in Nikko to soothe the emperor's concerns. The capture of Guadalcanal and Tulagi, he said, was "nothing worthy of Your Majesty's attention."[30]

The local army headquarters in Rabaul was largely unconcerned about the American move into the Solomons. Far more important, or so it seemed, was the campaign in eastern New Guinea, where the Twenty-Fifth Air Flotilla was preoccupied with a buildup of Allied air strength in Rabi, and the Japanese army was determined to take the dusty colonial outpost of Port Moresby by marching troops over the soaring hump of the Owen Stanley mountains.[31] A Japanese prewar assessment had emphasized the importance of Moresby as a "stepping stone." Its airfields and naval base would guarantee Japan "control of the air and sea in the Southwest Pacific."[32] The interior offensive against Moresby would eventually be defeated by the valor of Australian troops, assisted by an awful climate and grueling terrain. But for the time being, it remained the chief priority of Japanese ground forces in the region.

From the beginning, the Japanese badly underestimated the number of marines in the lower Solomons. They were apparently misled by an intelligence report filed by a Japanese attaché in Moscow, who had picked up rumors in conversation with unidentified Russians. The Guadalcanal landing was a raid rather than a sustained invasion, the attaché reported, and American troop strength on the island was only about 2,000.[33] (Vandegrift had five times that number on Guadalcanal and another 6,000 on the islands across Ironbottom Sound.) Aerial photo reconnaissance in mid-August failed to correct the misimpression. Perhaps the Americans would attempt to dynamite the airfield and supporting equipment and then withdraw. If so, it was no matter; Guadalcanal could be reoccupied and the airfield completed in good time.

Nevertheless, Admiral Isoroku Yamamoto, the commander in chief of the Combined Fleet and the highest-ranking seagoing admiral of the Japanese navy, committed the bulk of his available naval forces to a counteroffensive known as "KA-Go." His paramount objective—unaltered since the debacle at Midway two months earlier—was to flush out and destroy the American aircraft carriers, which he knew to be operating in the waters south and east of Guadalcanal.[34] KA-Go involved four main elements. A landing force of army and special naval landing troops would be embarked in four troopships. They would sail for Guadalcanal in a convoy under the command of Rear Admiral Raizo Tanaka, who flew his flag on the light cruiser *Jintsu*. These forces were first dispatched from the Inland Sea in Japan to Truk Atoll, from which they departed on August 16. A carrier task force built around the *Zuikaku* and *Shokaku* (with the baby flattop *Ryujo*), and commanded by the veteran Vice Admiral Chuichi Nagumo, would descend on the Solomons from the north. The two big carriers would hang back until the American carriers revealed themselves; then they would strike. Nagumo's carriers would be heavily reinforced with surface ships, including the powerful battleships *Hiei* and *Kirishima* and heavy cruisers *Tone* and *Chikuma*. Two other forces, comprised chiefly of surface ships, would backstop the carriers and invasion convoy—Rear Admiral Hiroaki Abe's Vanguard Force, with two battleships, three heavy cruisers, and one light cruiser, and Vice Admiral Nobutake Kondo's Advance Force, including six cruisers, the seaplane tender *Chitose*, and sundry destroyers. If Nagumo could find, engage, and destroy Fletcher's carriers, the entire Japanese fleet would advance into Ironbottom Sound and wipe out whatever American naval resistance remained, and then land ground forces on the island to recapture the airstrip.

VANDEGRIFT'S 1ST ENGINEER BATTALION RACED TO COMPLETE Henderson Field using captured Japanese construction equipment and materials, including six road rollers, two tractors, and fifty handcarts. A gap of about 180 feet in the middle of the strip remained to be filled and graded. "Worked on the field just as Japs had, with their equipment," read an early draft of the 1st Division report. "No bulldozer, power shovel, or dump truck. Seemed endless work."[35]

On August 12, the airfield was continuous to a length of 2,600 feet, and a navy PBY amphibious patrol plane landed to the cheers of hundreds of marines. Among the passengers was Lieutenant William Sampson, who had been sent personally by Admiral McCain, the SOPAC air chief, to assess the field's condition. Sampson thought it ready to handle fighters, but too short and soft for bombers. A number of tall trees obstructed the approach on the eastern end of the field, and would have to be cut down. The muddy surface was not yet overlaid with steel Marston matting, nor did it include taxiways or revetments (earthen walls to shield parked planes against explosions). Henderson was badly exposed to the south—its western end was only about 300 yards from the perimeter, and thus vulnerable to light artillery fire, sniper fire, and an attack in force. But McCain had made it his personal business to get as many planes into Guadalcanal as quickly as possible, even if it meant stripping the airbases at Espiritu Santo and Efate. "The best and proper solution of course is to get fighters and SBDs onto your field," he told Vandegrift in a handwritten letter delivered by Sampson.[36] He promised marine fighter and dive-bombing units by August 18 or 19. Three days later, the first Seabee unit arrived with a "carryall," a machine that could scoop about twelve cubic yards of earth out of the ground at one stroke. The work accelerated rapidly, and Henderson was declared ready to receive any type of airplane on August 18.

The promised airplanes were those of Marine Aircraft Group 23 (MAG-23), which included two squadrons of F4F Wildcat fighters and two of Dauntless (SBD) dive-bombers.[37] They had been training since May at Ewa Field in Oahu. The skipper of Marine Fighter Squadron 223 was Captain John L. Smith, who had just recently transferred from a dive-bombing squadron. Most of his pilots were second lieutenants, recently out of flight training; a few were lucky survivors of the air defense of Midway the previous June. Their combat experience to date had given them little cause for confidence. Marine Bombing 232 was manned by aviators just out of flight school, many of whom had never dropped a live bomb from an SBD. The marine squadrons were dangerously green, but circumstances did not allow for more training. They were needed on Guadalcanal immediately. As Nimitz's CINCPAC headquarters war diary observed on August 13, "Opinion here is that no squadron is ever sufficiently trained. . . . At any event they are well enough trained to go to work down south."[38]

The marine F4Fs and SBDs launched by catapult off the escort carrier *Long Island* (which had ferried them down from Pearl Harbor) on the afternoon of August 20. The carrier lay about 190 miles southeast of Guadalcanal, about an hour's flight to Henderson Field. About fifteen minutes after takeoff, the island's green mountains loomed over the horizon.

Loren D. "Doc" Everton, one of the most experienced fighter pilots in the group, gazed down at the unfolding northern plains and was struck by how peaceful and beautiful the island appeared from the air. But as they arrived over Lunga, neither he nor his wingmen liked the look of Henderson Field. The approach had been cleared of tall coconut palms, leaving a meadow strewn with stumps and heaps of rotting foliage. At 3,600 feet, the field was long enough but very rough and uneven, with patches of mud amid the gravel. David Galvan, a marine radioman-gunner on an SBD, recalled

seeing "a very small pasture with a whole lot of holes in it. . . . I mean a
narrow one too. When you come into Guadalcanal there was a grove of
coconut trees, maybe three-quarters of a mile, then you go into an opening:
a little kind of meadow that extended from Tenaru River running east by
southeast. On the opposite side was jungle—thick jungle: a solid mass of
trees and brush."[39]

About 4:00 that afternoon, men on Guadalcanal first caught the distant
drone of aircraft engines. Many moved instinctively toward their trenches
and foxholes, but these planes were approaching from the east rather than
from the west (as the enemy planes usually did). The antiaircraft gunners
tensed but held fire. Then the drone ascended to a roar, and thirty-one blue
carrier planes flew low over the field and then circled back to line up their
landing approaches. Shouts of joy rose up all throughout the perimeter, and
men waved their helmets above their heads. "I just looked up and grinned
till I felt the mud crack on my whiskers," a marine remarked. "It looked so
damn good to see something American circling in the sky over the airfield.
It was like being all alone, and the lights come on, and you've got friends
from home in the same room with you."[40]

Nineteen Wildcats and twelve Dauntlesses lined up in an orderly pattern and touched down one by one. Most bounced once or twice before settling on the field. The thirty-one propellers threw gravel pebbles and kicked
up clouds of dust that hovered in the air even after they cut their engines.
As the planes taxied to a stop, men clambered onto the wings to greet the
pilots with handshakes and backslaps. Vandegrift, overcome with emotion,
took the hand of Major Dick Mangrum, commander of Marine Bombing
232, and said, "Thank God you have come."[41]

No event of the Guadalcanal campaign lifted morale so much as the
arrival of those first planes. The "Cactus Air Force," as it was immediately
dubbed, offered protection against attack by air, sea, and land. It gave Vandegrift eyes over the shipping approaches to the northwest. Martin Clemens
wrote that the planes' arrival was "a gladsome sight, and gave me a tingle
right down the spine."[42] Colonel Merrill Twining thought it "one of the
great turning points" of the campaign.[43]

Climbing from their planes, the marine aviators were greeted by their
new ground crews—sailors of CUB-1, a navy mobile advanced base construction team. The unit had no special training to work on airplanes, but
they were mechanically gifted and quickly learned what they needed to

know. Their work was complicated by the primitive conditions at Henderson. All fueling was done by hand pumps fastened to gasoline drums. Bombs were transported on trucks to the airfield from ammunition caches hidden in the palm groves; they had to be muscled up to the underbellies of the SBDs by hand. It was backbreaking, exhausting work. Henderson had no taxiways, no revetments, and no drainage. Steel matting had not yet been laid, and the middle section of the field was soft and uneven. Carrier aircraft, built to withstand hard impact on a flight deck, would stand up to the abusive landings at Henderson. More delicate types were likely to suffer considerable wear and tear.

There were signs that afternoon of an impending attack on the eastern flank of the American lines. A night earlier, ships had been heard passing through the sound from west to east. Some minutes later, several large waves washed up on the beach. Three hours later, another set of waves washed up on the beach, and ships were heard to return to the west. It did not require clever deduction to conclude that Japanese troops had probably landed somewhere to the east of the marine lines. (A detachment of 916 troops under Colonel Kiyonao Ichiki had landed at 11:00 p.m. that night.) Throughout the twentieth, Japanese cruisers and destroyers operated in Ironbottom Sound with complete impunity, unchecked and unmolested. Clemens had received native reports of a Japanese force "of unknown size" down the coast to the east. On the afternoon of August 19, he sent a patrol under the native constable Jacob C. Vouza to creep across the American lines into the heavily forested ridge south of Henderson Field, and then to turn east and back north to the coast, in hopes of gaining information about Japanese movements in that area.

Vandegrift strengthened his lines on the right bank of the Tenaru River by summoning reinforcements from Tulagi, where the fighting was finished. As darkness fell, the marines were on edge. Any sound in the jungle beyond their lines was liable to signal the beginning of an enemy attack. At midnight, the floatplane "Washing Machine Charlie" arrived on his normal schedule, dropped a single bomb, and then continued circling noisily overhead. At 2:00 a.m., the plane dropped a brilliant green parachute flare over the sandbar at the mouth of the Tenaru. Observers discerned shadows moving through the underbrush. Marine outposts on the far side of the river were withdrawn to the defensive lines on the right bank.

At 2:30 a.m. came the first "*banzai* charge"—several hundred screaming Japanese hurtled across the sand spit and breeched the marine lines.
A cacophony of machine-gun, rifle, and mortar fire rose from the engaged
front. That charge was bloodily repulsed, with about 200 enemy soldiers
hung up in barbed wire and cut down by enfilading machine-gun fire. The
Japanese tried again, this time north of the river's sand spit; this too was
stopped dead, with heavy losses to the attackers. Japanese positions east of
the river concentrated light mortar and rifle fire on the point at which they
had first attempted to break through, but the line held fast as reserves were
brought up.

The screams of "*Banzai!*" intermingled with the rattle of machine-gun
fire and the repeating crescendos of mortar and artillery fire. The .50-caliber
guns, held down in long bursts, made a sustained roar. The .30-caliber guns
made a sharper staccato sound. The American mortars thumped deeply.
The Japanese 25mm bursts were shorter and higher pitched. To men who
could recognize the different weapons by their sounds, one thing was agreeably obvious—the Americans were generating a much greater volume of
fire. Clemens watched from the intelligence division headquarters adjacent
to the airfield, half a mile away: "Tracers ricocheted up into the sky, together
with red and white flares as Japanese columns came into the attack. We
could see the coconut palms silhouetted in pink flashes and, in that strange
light, debris being thrown heavenward. Everything appeared to be going
all right, but it all seemed dangerously near, and as the din increased I had
the eerie feeling that the battle was creeping closer."[44] For the newly arrived
aviators, still settling into their new accommodations, the battle was an
eye-opener. Doc Everton had moved into a Japanese tent and fashioned
a bed with woven rice straw bags, two deep. Though he knew he needed
sleep, he sat up all night with his .45 sidearm in one hand and his helmet in
the other. He kept his shoes on.

Shortly before dawn, the 1st Battalion, 1st Marines, under Lieutenant
Colonel L. B. Creswell, was ordered across the river to attack the enemy's
left flank and rear. The battalion crossed the river about a mile above
its mouth and enveloped the Japanese forces entirely, cutting off their
retreat. The remaining enemy soldiers, about 500 men, were trapped in
a coconut grove and slaughtered methodically throughout the morning
of August 21. At first light, F4F fighters took to the air and flew strafing
runs over the enemy position. By late afternoon, it seemed that the few

remaining Japanese troops could be overrun in a concerted counterattack across the river.

While this last act of the Battle of the Tenaru River was playing out, Jacob C. Vouza crawled back into the American lines. He was nearly dead for loss of blood. His patrol had run into an advance scouting force of the Japanese invasion group. Vouza had been brutally interrogated, enduring prolonged torture while tied to a tree. He had been smashed repeatedly in the face by rifle butts, and his face was a swollen bloody mass; he had been stabbed by bayonets and was bleeding freely from the throat and chest. Against the odds, his torturers had struck no vital artery, and he had managed to chew through the ropes and crawl back to the American lines. Taken to the field hospital, he was stitched up and fed blood intravenously. In twelve days he recovered and returned to duty. His heroism was recognized by two nations: the United States awarded Vouza the Silver Star and Legion of Merit, and the British knighted him and named him a Member of the Order of the British Empire.

In the aftermath of the battle, the marines quickly learned that the enemy owed no allegiance to the norms of "civilized war." Wounded Japanese soldiers would call for medical attention and then shoot the corpsmen who came in response. Others would pretend to lie dead, clutching a grenade, hoping to take a marine with them to the afterlife. "I have never heard or read of this kind of fighting," Vandegrift wrote the commandant of the Marine Corps. "These people refuse to surrender. The wounded will wait until the men come up to examine them and blow themselves and the other fellow to pieces with a hand grenade. You can readily see the answer to that."[45]

A platoon of light tanks was deployed to finish off the remaining survivors. They fired canister shot into the fields of dead and wounded, and ran over the bodies with their treads. Vandegrift, visiting the scene late that afternoon, remarked that "the rear of the tanks looked like meat grinders."[46] Another marine officer had this recollection: "Japanese bodies lay piled together in stinking heaps—burned, crushed, and torn. A tide flowed and ebbed before all could be buried, and here an arm, there a head, stuck up through the new-washed sand on the beach."[47] In losing forty-three killed and fifty-seven wounded, the marines had annihilated Ichiki's entire attacking force of 800 men. (The rest of the detachment, numbering about 120 men, had been left behind to the east as a rear guard.)

The psychological repercussions of the Tenaru action were far-reaching. That victory, and the actions on Tulagi and Gavutu two weeks earlier, had put an end to the myth of the Japanese soldier as an untouchable jungle warrior. The fanaticism of the Japanese was unnerving, but it prompted them, again and again, to fight in tactically idiotic ways.

Vandegrift lost no time in circulating word of the victory. Attacked by a large force, the marines on the Tenaru "defended their position with such zeal and determination that the enemy was unable to effect a penetration of the position in spite of repeated efforts throughout the night. The 1st Marines, counterattacking at daybreak with an envelopment which caught the enemy in the rear and on the flank, thus cutting off his withdrawal and pushing him from inland in the direction of the sea, virtually annihilated his force and achieved a victory fully commensurate with the military traditions of our Corps."[48]

IN TWO PREVIOUS CARRIER DUELS, Frank Jack Fletcher had enjoyed timely intelligence about the enemy's plans. Now the picture was murkier. The Japanese had updated their naval code again on August 13, setting the cryptanalysts back by several weeks. Radio traffic analysis had detected the southward movement of naval forces from Japan's home waters to Truk, which might presage a move into the lower Solomons, but the Americans lacked hard evidence of the whereabouts of the Japanese carriers. Commander Joseph Rochefort, chief of Pearl Harbor's codebreaking unit, who had set up the American victory at Midway, believed they were in Japan's Inland Sea.[49] No data had emerged to challenge that theory, and if Nagumo's task force was practicing good radio discipline, it might have moved south to Truk or even into the Solomons. Ghormley radioed Fletcher on August 22: "Indications point strongly to enemy attack in force CACTUS area 23–26 August." COMSOPAC believed the enemy fleet might include one or two battleships, fifteen cruisers, and many destroyers: "Presence of carriers possible but not confirmed."[50]

Since his withdrawal on August 9, Fletcher's mandate had been to fly cover over the sea-lanes linking bases in New Caledonia and the New Hebrides to the Solomons, and to assist in transferring aircraft to Henderson Field. He had taken care to keep his ships well fueled, in case of any sudden contingency. Receiving news of the Japanese ground attack on the Tenaru

River, he turned north on the night of August 19–20 and advanced to an aggressively far northwest position, just east of the island of Malaita. But radio intelligence continued to posit that the Japanese carriers remained at Truk, more than 1,000 miles northwest—and if that was so, the earliest they could be expected to give battle was August 25. Fletcher, supposing he had a two-day refueling window, sent the *Wasp* and her escorts south to rendezvous with a fleet oiler. As it happened, she would not return in time to join the impending battle.

On August 22 and 23, as each combatant probed for the other, the skies above the region were congested with reconnaissance planes. Admiral McCain's PBYs and B-17s flew long missions from Espiritu Santo; marine dive-bombers spread out from Henderson Field; six more PBYs operated from a lagoon on Ndeni in the Santa Cruz Islands. From Rabaul, big four-engine Kawanishi flying boats radiated out in 700-mile search vectors to the south and east.[51] On August 22, shortly before 11:00 a.m., the *Enterprise* radar scope picked up a blip to the southwest. Four fighters were sent to investigate. They tracked a Kawanishi and quickly sent it down in flames.

The next morning brought a confusing flood of contact reports. PBYs from Ndeni reported a column of four transports escorted by four destroyers east of Bougainville Island, about 300 miles north of Guadalcanal. This was Tanaka's occupation force. Aware that he had been snooped, and fearing a punishing air attack on his vulnerable transports, Tanaka turned north. Radioing from his flagship *Yamato*, Admiral Yamamoto ordered Nagumo to send the "Diversionary Force"—light carrier *Ryujo*, heavy cruiser *Tone*, destroyers *Amatsukaze* and *Tokitsukaze*—to race south and attack Henderson Field the following morning. The scheduled date for Tanaka's troop landings was pushed back to August 25.

With the PBYs' sighting report in hand, Fletcher launched a powerful strike from the *Saratoga*, thirty-one dive-bombers and six TBF Avenger torpedo planes, to attack Tanaka's column. Commander Harry D. Felt, the *Saratoga* air group commander, led the flight. They were joined en route by another nine SBDs, one TBF, and thirteen fighters from Henderson Field. The formation ran into a wall of impenetrable wet white haze. Felt arrayed his planes by sections in a line abreast, flying just 50 feet above the sea. No one could see anything but the sea below and the planes on either side. "We must have flown in this stuff for an hour," Felt remembered, "and all of a sudden, broke through into an open area, and there was the whole damned group right there. Just magnificent discipline!"[52]

Tanaka having dodged north to avoid just this attack, Felt and his squadrons found no sign of the enemy fleet. The *Saratoga* planes followed the marine planes back to Guadalcanal, where they managed to land on the muddy field in the failing light. The exhausted *Saratoga* pilots spent the night in their cockpits, ready to take off at dawn.

The two carrier forces were mutually blind. They were only 300 miles apart, just beyond extreme air-striking range, but neither had pinpointed the other's location. Between 5:55 and 6:30 a.m. on August 24, the *Enterprise* launched twenty-three SBDs. From the carrier's position, 200 miles east of Malaita, they fanned out in a 120-degree arc to the north and west. The PBYs at Ndeni were also in the air before first light. The Japanese fleet, converging on Guadalcanal from the west, was still just beyond the edges of the American morning search, and none of the *Enterprise* planes reported a contact. But one of McCain's PBYs spotted the *Ryujo* force roaring south at 9:05 a.m., and another found the heavy surface warships of Kondo and Abe's force half an hour later.

Now Fletcher faced a dilemma. Should he pounce on the *Ryujo*, or should he keep his powder dry, hoping for word of the big carriers? The PBY's report had put the *Ryujo* 275 miles north of Tulagi, a long flight of about 250 miles from the *Saratoga*—but if the target kept her southerly course, she would come closer. When Felt's planes returned from Guadalcanal, landing at 11:00 a.m., Felt told the admiral that his pilots were dog-tired and could use a rest. "You keep getting intelligence and when those things are within our range, we'll go," he suggested.[53] Fletcher assented. At 11:38 a.m., another PBY reported the *Ryujo* force, this time farther south.

Confronted with a mass of conflicting and uncertain data, and with so much at stake, Fletcher hesitated to make a precipitous decision. Shortly after noon, he assigned the *Enterprise* air group to conduct a search to the northwest to a distance of 250 miles. Sixteen SBDs and seven TBFs departed the carrier at 1:15. In short order, Charlie Jett of VT-3 found the *Ryujo* and radioed back a contact report. Jett and a wingman attempted a horizontal bombing attack at 12,000 feet. Dropping bombs from altitude on ships maneuvering at speed was usually futile, and this was no exception. They missed and turned back toward the American task force.

Still having heard nothing about the enemy's big carriers, Fletcher elected to commit his reserve strike to finish the little *Ryujo*. Twenty-eight SBDs and eight TBFs led by Commander Felt flew a heading of 320 degrees. By that time, *Ryujo* had already launched six Nakajima B5N "Kates" and fifteen Zeros against Henderson Field. Marine fighters defended the airfield in a pitched dogfight over the island, downing three Nakajimas and three Zeros, losing only three American aircraft in the melee. (Bombers from Rabaul were supposed to have arrived over the target at about the same time, but thick weather had forced them back to base.) Importantly, the *Ryujo* planes did not do any significant damage to the marine installations around Henderson or to the airfield itself.[54]

At 3:36 p.m., the *Saratoga* strike closed in on the *Ryujo*. She went into a tight starboard turn and continued to circle throughout the attack. One after another, the dive-bombers rolled into their dives and released their bombs. Several missed close aboard, but Felt personally planted the first of three 500-pound bombs on the flight deck, and one of the TBFs sent a torpedo into her starboard side. The attack, said Felt, "was carried out just like a training exercise."[55] The *Ryujo* was soon blazing out of control while still circling clockwise. From the air, Felt observed her "pouring forth black smoke which would die down and then belch forth in great volume again."[56] She was abandoned by her crew, most of whom simply leapt over the side. The skipper of the destroyer *Amatsukaze* watched the blazing wreck through his binoculars. "A heavy starboard list exposed her red belly," he recalled. "Waves washed her flight deck. It was a pathetic sight. *Ryujo*, no longer resembling a ship, was a huge stove, full of holes which belched eerie red flames."[57] A total loss, she would be scuttled four hours later. Her returning planes were forced to ditch at sea.

Meanwhile, a cruiser scout from the *Chikuma* sighted the two American carriers at 2:30 p.m. The sluggish floatplane was shot down by *Enterprise* fighters, but not before the pilot managed to get a transmission off to Nagumo. Radio direction-finding gear on the *Shokaku* gave the Japanese an accurate bearing to the doomed plane, and thus to the American task force. Nagumo now held the advantage. He had not yet been discovered, but he had pinpointed Fletcher's position, and it was well within striking range. At 2:55 p.m., the first of two big strikes took off from the *Shokaku* and *Zuikaku*: twenty-seven Aichi D3A2 "Vals" escorted by fifteen Zeros.

As the planes left the decks, two *Enterprise* SBDs caught sight of the Japanese carriers and radioed a report to Fletcher. The American communications were very poor, however: the airwaves were clogged by heavy static and gratuitous pilot chatter, and the admiral received no word of the contact until more than an hour later. The two SBDs dived and bravely attacked the *Shokaku*, but missed. About an hour after the first wave, Nagumo launched a second wave of twenty-seven Aichis and nine Zeros.

Now Fletcher had two large waves of enemy dive-bombers incoming, and had not yet replied. When the contact report belatedly got through to him, he realized he may have repeated the error he had committed three and a half months earlier in the Battle of the Coral Sea—aiming his strike at a small carrier when the enemy's big carriers were still in the vicinity. He tried to redirect the outbound flight, but was again defeated by feeble radio communications. As one *Enterprise* dive-bomber pilot ruefully observed, "We had been outsmarted strategically with the tactical battle still to be fought—it was Coral Sea all over again."[58]

The *Enterprise* radar plot detected the first wave of incoming planes at 4:32 p.m., when they were eighty-eight miles to the northwest.[59] F4F Wildcats roared off both flight decks and "dangled on their propellers" (climbed at maximum speed), their 1,200-horsepower Pratt & Whitney radial engines straining mightily. The Japanese now enjoyed the tactical upper hand. A broken cloud ceiling gave them good visual cover.[60] Knowing that the F4Fs were slow climbers, the attackers approached at abnormally high altitudes, between 18,000 and 24,000 feet. After the initial radar return, the American scopes went dark for seventeen minutes, and when they lit up again at 4:49, the leading edge of the enemy wave was only forty-four miles away. American fighters were diverted by the escorting Zeros, allowing most of the dive-bombers to slip through the screen unmolested. The *Enterprise*'s fighter director officer (FDO) struggled to get through to his pilots while the radio circuit was congested with their chatter: "Look at that one go down!" and "Bill, where are you?"[61] (Captain Arthur C. Davis of the *Enterprise* later observed, "The air was so jammed with these unnecessary transmissions that in spite of numerous attempts to quiet the pilots, few directions reached our fighters and little information was received by the Fighter Director Officer.")[62]

Both carriers rang up maximum speed for evasive maneuvering and turned southeast in order to bring wind across their decks for flight operations. All strike planes spotted on deck were ordered to launch. The pilots were simply told to get away, to clear the area—it was not that important where they went, so long as they were not on deck when the enemy

Battle of the Eastern Solomons — August 24, 1942

dive-bombers hurtled down from overhead. If both flattops went down, or were damaged and incapable of landing planes, they could fly to Henderson Field on Guadalcanal. Once aloft, the *Enterprise* and *Saratoga* strike planes were instructed by radio to head northwest in search of the big twins *Zuikaku* and *Shokaku*. With only two hours of daylight remaining, their odds of attacking the enemy and returning safely were very long.

At 5:09, the *Enterprise* radar plot informed the captain that "the enemy planes are directly overhead now!"[63] The antiaircraft gunners, with helmets pushed back on their heads and kapok life vests drawn up tight around their necks, studied the sky. For a moment, nothing seemed amiss. The afternoon was absurdly peaceful. A few black specks moved above and between the high, thin wisps of cloud. Then a few of those specks stopped and seemed to fix in place. Gradually, the rising drone of aircraft engines could be heard. The larger specks began to take shape—a blurred disk, bisected by wings, with fixed landing gear under the wings, sun glinting off the cockpit canopies, and a second, smaller speck (the bomb) tucked under the fuselage. Witnesses who had never seen a dive-bombing attack were surprised at how long the enemy planes took to come down. They dived at angles of 70 degrees or even steeper, most on the port beam and quarter of the *Enterprise*. The attack, according to Captain Davis, was "well executed and absolutely determined."[64]

With the *Enterprise* tearing through the sea at 27 knots, Davis ordered maximum rudder right, then maximum rudder left, and the ship heeled radically to port and then to starboard. Behind her stretched a long, foaming, serpentine wake. The gunners threw up a wall of 5-inch, 1.1-inch, and 20mm antiaircraft fire. Black, brown, and white bursts blemished the sky. The *South Dakota*, said a witness, was "lit up like a Christmas tree," emitting so much fire and smoke that the battleship appeared to be herself ablaze. The sea all around was mottled by falling antiaircraft shell fragments, as if under a heavy rainstorm. Several dive-bombers were blown to pieces. Ensign Fred Mears watched the burning remains of one Aichi "flutter down like a butterfly and kiss the water."[65] Several more flew through the 5-inch bursts and emerged with fire or smoke training behind. But it was a huge attack—Davis estimated one plane every seven seconds for four consecutive minutes—and many got through unscathed.

The Aichis released their bombs about 1,000 feet above the ship. Each black cylindrical shape separated from the fuselage and took a steeper trajectory as the pilot pulled out of his dive. Some bombs flew straight and true like a missile; others tumbled end over end. Nine fell close aboard to port and starboard and detonated upon striking the sea, throwing up columns of whitewater that crashed down over the flight deck. Men in the catwalks were thoroughly drenched.

At 5:14 p.m., the *Enterprise* took her first hit. A 1,000-pound, armor-piercing, delayed-action bomb smashed through the flight deck just forward of the aft elevator and continued through four steel decks and two bulkheads before detonating deep in the ship. The blast claimed the lives of thirty-five men in an elevator pump room and the adjacent chief petty officers' quarters. Seventy more were injured. A chain of explosions blew down all the bulkheads in the area and tore a hole through the starboard side at the waterline.[66] The force of the explosion caused the after part of the hangar deck to bulge upward, leaving a two-foot "hump." The aft No. 3 elevator was jammed and out of action. But the *Enterprise* surged ahead, her speed undiminished.

Three minutes later, after several more near misses, a second 1,000-pound bomb struck the aft starboard 5-inch gun gallery. Thirty-eight men were killed outright. The blast ignited the ready service ammunition casings, and fires raged throughout the area. The *Enterprise* plowed ahead, still making 27 knots, but she trailed a nasty column of oily black smoke. Hoses were put on the fires, wounded men were brought up on deck, and the ship was ventilated to release any flammable gases. Less than two minutes later, a third bomb struck just forward of the No. 2 elevator. The explosion gouged a ten-foot hole in the flight deck and put the No. 2 elevator out of commission. Photographer's Mate Marion Riley, stationed on the island veranda, pressed his shutter button at exactly the moment it detonated. The photograph—expanding spikes of flame and smoke, rushing out from the midline of the *Enterprise*'s flight deck—was to become one of the most famous of the war.

At the Battle of Midway, four Japanese carriers had taken similar punishment and been destroyed by secondary explosions and uncontrollable fires. Aboard the *Enterprise*, damage-control measures quickly brought the fires under control, and the ship continued to maneuver deftly and keep pace with the task force. Counterflooding corrected the starboard list. Wood planking was used to patch the holes torn in the flight deck. The rupture in the starboard side was plugged by whatever came first to hand, including mattresses, lumber, wire mesh, and wooden plugs. Most of the *Enterprise* dive-bombers, launched just before the Japanese attack, flew into Henderson Field. Orphaned by the damage to their ship, they would operate as part of the Cactus Air Force for the next several weeks.

Based on the reports of his returned dive-bomber crews, who believed they had destroyed an American fleet carrier, Nagumo celebrated a tactical victory. Losing the little *Ryujo* was not a calamity. She was the smallest flattop in the Combined Fleet, and her sacrifice (as intended) had drawn most of the American carrier planes away from the *Shokaku* and *Zuikaku*. As more was learned about the fate of Tanaka's transport group, however, the picture darkened. His ships had suffered heavily under air attack. Marine dive-bombers and fighters flying from Guadalcanal had planted a bomb on his flagship, the cruiser *Jintsu*, and sank a transport, the *Kinryu Maru*. Later that afternoon, B-17s operating from Espiritu Santo sank a destroyer, the *Mutsuki*. The Japanese were learning that they could not safely operate ships in the Slot without first suppressing the airpower of Henderson Field. As in the earlier carrier battles at Coral Sea and Midway, the encounter ended with the Japanese forced to abort a planned invasion. On the following day, August 25, Yamamoto cancelled Operation KA and recalled his forces.

So concluded the Battle of the Eastern Solomons, the third carrier duel of the Pacific War. It had been a confused and scattershot encounter, in some respects analogous to the Battle of the Coral Sea three months earlier. Fletcher had been plagued by dreadful radio communications and spotty intelligence. Still, he had won a modest tactical victory by destroying the *Ryujo* while saving the *Enterprise*, and by losing only twenty-five aircraft while claiming seventy-five of the enemy's. In forcing back the Japanese troop convoy, the Americans had also earned a strategic victory. The temporary loss of the *Enterprise* (to major repairs at Pearl Harbor) was counterbalanced by the arrival in SOPAC of the *Hornet*. Most importantly, perhaps, the battle had bought time for Ghormley—time to expand the supporting bases, to bring in air reinforcements, to transfer more cargo ships from North America, and to improve Vandegrift's supply situation.

The *Enterprise* had suffered heavy casualties: two officers and seventy-two men killed, six officers and eighty-nine men wounded. The first bomb had detonated deep in the ship, and the carnage was appalling. Most of the dead had perished quickly, but their bodies had subsequently roasted in the fire, making individual identification impossible. On August 26, as the *Enterprise* and her screening ships headed south toward Noumea, the bodies were collected and prepared for burial at sea. Fred Mears left a visceral impression:

> The majority of the bodies were in one piece. They were blackened but not burned or withered, and they looked like iron statues of men, their limbs smooth and whole, their heads rounded with no hair. The faces were undistinguishable, but in almost every case the lips were drawn back in a wizened grin giving the men the expression of rodents.

The postures seemed either strangely normal or frankly grotesque. One gun pointer was still in his seat leaning on his sight with one arm. He looked as though a sculptor had created him. His body was nicely proportioned, the buttocks were rounded, there was no hair anywhere. Other iron men were lying outstretched, face up or down. Two or three lying face up were shielding themselves with their arms bent at the elbows and their hands before their faces. One, who was not burned so badly, had his chest thrown out, his head way back, and his hands clenched.[67]

Lack of time and manpower on the stricken ship ruled out committing each body individually to the deep. Under the supervision of the ship's chaplain, a single unidentified sailor was buried with the traditional honors. The remains were laid on a pantry board under an American flag. A bugler played "Taps." The marine guard presented arms. Four sailors lifted the board, and the remains slid into the ship's wake. Some seventy other dead, collected in canvas sacks and weighted with spare metal, were dropped from the fantail without ceremony.

Chapter Four

———————

F OR A DECADE, FDR'S CRITICS HAD HAMMERED AWAY AT HIS MUDDLED and sporadically anarchic style of presidential leadership. He reversed major decisions without admitting or even seeming to know what he had done. He hated to fire a man no matter how egregious his performance had been, and blithely piled one new government agency on top of another without spelling out their relative spheres of authority. He seemed to agree with whatever advice-giver had most recently held his ear. Not even his most ardent loyalists would call him a talented administrator. "He was just not a routine executive," said Robert H. Jackson, who served as Roosevelt's attorney general and was appointed to the Supreme Court in 1941. "He certainly was not accomplished as an administrator and in normal times . . . it is doubtful if he could have been a distinguished president."[1] When FDR had not made up his mind about a given policy, Jackson observed, it was impossible to elicit a presidential decision. The president would stall, procrastinate, filibuster, and refuse to act for months on end. At other times, he would render far-reaching decisions "with an apparent nonchalance that sometimes took away the breath of his advisers."[2] Harold Smith, the White House budget director, admitted that many of Roosevelt's domestic programs were poorly conceived, but defended the president as an instinctual and intuitive visionary, "a real artist in government."[3]

From the school of Jackson Pollock, the critics might have riposted. Or the Marx Brothers. "Bold experimentation" had been a New Deal lodestar, but could a nation at war afford to tinker with unproven methods? If not, would the price of failure be paid in American blood?

To defeat the Great Depression, the president and his men had brewed up an "alphabet soup" of new federal agencies. To beat back the Axis, they concocted another—OPA, OPM, DPC, WPB, OWI, WRB, SPAB, and too many more to cite here without cluttering the page.* The veteran newspaper columnist Walter Lippmann, by no means a partisan critic of the Roosevelt administration, threw up his hands at the inveterate backbiting and turf-skirmishing among the heads of these various outfits. "A great deal of the trouble arises from Mr. Roosevelt's inability to remove even the lamest of his lame ducks," he wrote in the *Washington Post*:

> Since no one has to give up his titles and emoluments, no matter how inadequate he is or how badly he has failed, Mr. Roosevelt at the top of the Government sets an example which destroys the discipline down the line. It is taken for granted that if an official is out of place, his functions may be removed but that he will remain. This makes intrigue, indirection, and slickness a habit in getting things done, good things and bad things alike. If everything has to be done by beating around the bush, men lose the habit of going forward on a straight line.
>
> The amount of nervous energy that is burned up by the able men as they move in and out and around and across the immovable lame ducks, the fossil remains of Mr. Roosevelt's earlier political commitments and previous political mistakes, would, if it were released, electrify the whole conduct of the war.[4]

Though his party commanded towering majorities in both the House and the Senate, its prospects in the 1942 midterm elections were dismal. The Democrats' once-unassailable New Deal coalition—the urban-union-liberal-ethnic-Catholic vote in the North and upper Midwest combined with the dependably solid South—had been fractured and diluted by the war's disruptions. Millions of servicemen and war workers had been uprooted from their homes and hereditary polling precincts. Voter turnout was expected to hit record lows, and the remaining electorate skewed toward older, rural, and affluent voters who leaned toward the Republicans.

---

* Office of Price Administration; Office of Production Management; Defense Plant Corporation; War Production Board; Office of War Information; War Resources Board; Supply, Priorities, and Allocations Board.

By the early summer of that year, the post–Pearl Harbor mood of bipartisan unity had taken an ugly turn, and the customary thrust and parry of political combat had returned with undiminished vehemence. All recited the shopworn mottoes of patriotic unity, but criticism of the administration grew freer and more vigorous, both in the anti-Roosevelt press and on the floors of Congress, and Republicans angrily spurned any suggestion that politics be suspended for the war's duration. What were the Allies fighting for, if not the right of democratic opposition? In April 1942, the Republican National Committee had pledged to work for a "complete victory" over the Axis powers, but added "solemn protestations" that the GOP would "preserve the constitutional form of government . . . and the two-party system." When the president proposed that the party organizations be reconstituted as civil defense associations, Senator Robert A. Taft of Ohio barked to reporters, "I'll be goddamned if I'll bow to Roosevelt and stand on the street corner as an air raid warden with a tin hat, flashlight and a bucket of sand."[5]

The newspaper tycoons whose broadsheets had fought the New Deal and carried the torch of prewar isolationism—most prominently Robert McCormick, Cissy Patterson, and William Randolph Hearst—now purported to support the war, but they assailed the president for waging it ineptly. Roosevelt's enemies in Congress, among them the leading isolationists of 1940 and 1941, now agitated for a concentration of resources against Japan rather than Germany, and complained bitterly about American combat losses. More out of habit than real conviction, perhaps, they seemed determined to undermine the administration by any means at hand. Many observant pundits doubted that their hearts were really in the war. Marquis Childs, a Washington correspondent for the *St. Louis Post-Dispatch*, was unsparing: "No matter what they said for the record on December 8, the blindest and the stubbornest would continue to believe that Pearl Harbor was no more than [what] America deserved for not having remained pure and isolated as such wise men had counseled."[6]

The critics were of two minds. Even when lashing out at the administration, they declared that all Americans must eschew bickering and unite to win the war. Democrats indignantly accused the president's wartime critics of doing the bidding of Axis propaganda. Oratory in Congress grew venomous. On June 25, Senator Harry Schwartz of Wyoming took the floor to deliver a long philippic aimed at the "whisperers who inculcate class,

racial, and religious hatreds. They unwittingly are using Hitler's most effective weapons of propaganda. . . . Following in the wake of this Nazi machine
are camp followers, blinded by private ambitions and secret hatreds, intent
on gathering unto themselves personal advantage. They do not consciously
seek the loss of this war or the defeat of democracy, but by their course they
imperil both."[7]

Conservatives of both parties wrung their hands over the war's inevitable
expansion of federal and presidential powers. Washington's business was government, and business was booming as it had never boomed even at the zenith
of the New Deal. There seemed every reason to fear that the war would yoke
the country to an elephantine bureaucracy. The president's congressional foes
acquiesced in providing the colossal sums needed to mobilize and equip the
armed forces, but Republicans and conservative southern Democrats moved
to eliminate or defund several landmark New Deal programs, including the
Civilian Conservation Corps, the Works Progress Administration, and the
National Youth Administration. Roosevelt did not even bother trying to save
them. The war itself would provide more than enough employment to offset
the loss, and his core legislative achievements (notably Social Security, collective bargaining, and bank regulatory laws) would survive.

Congress was determined not to act as a mere "rubber stamp," but members of both parties were aware that a fine line lay between constructive
oversight and deadly obstruction. The Republican Party was sharply divided
between its historically isolationist leadership and its rising internationalist
bloc, headed by the party's defeated 1940 presidential nominee, Wendell
Willkie. Total war could be waged only by a concerted and centralized executive power, and Congress was inevitably relegated to the policy-making
sidelines. It was expected to fund military budgets fully, promptly, and without offering more than token dissent. Members could point to ample evidence of bungling, waste, overspending, corruption, internecine feuding,
and monopolistic practices—but no function of oversight could be permitted to slow the progress of mobilization.

BY THE SWELTERING SUMMER OF 1942, the federal government employed
about a quarter of a million civilians in the District of Columbia, but it still
lacked the scale and manpower needed to wage a global war. The population of Washington would nearly double between the day Pearl Harbor

was attacked and V-J Day. About 10,000 new workers were arriving in the city each month, drawn by high wages and a seemingly bottomless demand for clerks, secretaries, stenographers, statisticians, and mid-level managers. The state-of-the-art information technologies at the time were the electric typewriter, the carbon copy, and the steel file cabinet. Washington's administrative command-and-control apparatus was the typewriter battalion, deployed in phalanxes of wooden desks under fluorescent lights in long sweeping halls, with memoranda, requisitions, and requests typed in octuplicate and copies dispersed to cross-indexed files across the city. The OPA alone churned out more paper between 1940 and 1945 than the entire federal government had generated since 1789.[8]

More than half the new arrivals were young women responding to recruiting drives that promised a generous paycheck to any high school graduate who could type. They staffed the "tempos" ("temporary" prefabricated cement-asbestos office buildings, so named because they were to be torn down at war's end) that crowded across almost every part of the Washington Mall. The dreary, gray edifices lined both sides of the Reflecting Pool, and were connected by pedestrian bridges spanning the pool; they walled in the Washington Monument; they abutted the entire length of Constitution Avenue to the foot of Capitol Hill. Dirt excavated from their foundations was simply bulldozed into tremendous mounds and left there. Before the first anniversary of Pearl Harbor, twenty-seven of the temporary monstrosities were thrown up. In one case, construction from groundbreaking to ribbon-cutting took just five weeks. Together these twenty-seven buildings provided 3.3 million square feet of office space.[9] They were pitilessly hot in the summer and glacial in the winter. Floors, walls, and ceilings clattered unnervingly. Plumbing and electrical systems were prone to chronic malfunction. Outside these buildings, on any weekday morning, long lines stretched down the sidewalk and around the block, as employees waited to show their credentials to an armed guard, or visitors on official business pleaded for permission to enter. Each building was made to accommodate an average of 40,000 workers, the very limit allowed by health and safety. In many agencies, work was conducted around the clock in eight-hour shifts, with each shift taking over the desks as the previous departed. Janitors strained to service the human avalanche, and the buildings grew filthy and even unsanitary.

The War Department sought a more permanent solution across the Potomac River, in the leviathan War Department Building. The huge pentagonal structure, not yet called the "Pentagon," was the largest in the world; it covered forty-two acres and included more than five million square feet of floor space. In September 1942, it was not yet completed and seemed likely to overrun its original budget by about 100 percent, raising an outcry in Congress, but 17,000 workers were already at work in its completed sections.[10]

In 1942, Washington remained a somnolent midsized city—culturally southern, devoid of private industry, and entirely unprepared to accommodate a population boom. As in other cities, landlords gouged tenants and made money hand over fist. Government recruiters warned married applicants that they could not relocate their families to the capital, as no housing was available. The young women of the typewriter battalions crammed together into small apartments, with as many as four beds per room. Makeshift trailer parks were set up in vacant lots. Tract housing developments overran the farmland of suburban Virginia and Maryland. Dilapidated houseboats, with laundry hanging from the rigging, moored beam to beam along the Potomac riverfront. Owners of private homes were enjoined by authorities to rent out their vacant rooms. "If the war lasts much longer," observed *Life* magazine in January 1943, "Washington is going to bust right out of its pants."[11]

Public services buckled under the strain. Trolleys and buses could accommodate perhaps a third of the daily commute. At peak transit hours, the cavernous terminal at Union Station was immobilized by crowds. Garbage piled up on the sidewalks. The telephone system was so overloaded that the telephone company ran newspaper advertisements begging the public not to make calls except in case of emergency. Long lines stretched down the sidewalk from retail businesses of every category—restaurants, grocery stores, dry cleaners, movie theaters, newspaper stands. Hospitals were so overcrowded that pregnant women scheduled induced deliveries when the occasional vacancies occurred. Public schools were oversubscribed; churches offered standing-room-only on Sundays; servicemen bribed doormen to be let into packed nightclubs. Crime, prostitution, and sexually transmitted diseases were rife, but the police were overwhelmed and the prisons overflowed.

THOUGH HE HAD NEVER WORN A UNIFORM, Roosevelt was entirely comfortable in the role of commander in chief, and not in the least bit overawed by stars or gold braid. When a larger consideration of politics or diplomacy intruded, the president never hesitated to overrule the Joint Chiefs. "I am a pigheaded Dutchman," he might say, "and I have made up my mind about this. We are going ahead with it and you can't change my mind."[12] Marshall and King quickly learned to limit opportunities for presidential mischief by presenting the White House with joint consensus recommendations. When they did so, the president almost always gave his categorical assent.

That the president was a navy man at heart was obvious to all, including Marshall and Stimson, who regarded it as a manageable problem. But for the admirals, his affection was a mixed blessing. Roosevelt's habit of "running" the navy dated back to 1913, when the newly elected president Woodrow Wilson had appointed the thirty-one-year-old former New York state senator to be assistant secretary of the navy. Serving under the unobtrusive Secretary Josephus Daniels, the young FDR had overseen the daily operations of the service and had personally directed its mobilization in the First World War. He had been briefly acquainted with most of the up-and-coming midlevel naval officers of that period—King, Nimitz, Halsey, Stark, Leahy, Towers, Spruance, Fletcher, Turner—when they had been lieutenants and lieutenant commanders.

By long-ingrained habit, President Roosevelt demanded information about individual ships and officers—information that would ordinarily fall far beneath the attention of a commander in chief. When he threw out impromptu ideas for new ship designs or weapons systems, the Navy Department was obliged to study these proposals and explain (tactfully) why they were impractical. The president nonchalantly short-circuited the chain of command—ordering a particular ship to a particular theater, for example, or dispatching officers on fact-finding missions with instructions to report back to him directly.[13] On the other side of the ledger, Roosevelt had a flair for placing the right admirals in the right jobs at the right moments. His record in this respect was not perfect, but in the immediate aftermath of Pearl Harbor he made two vital personnel decisions that were superbly vindicated. He recalled King to Washington to run the navy, and sent Nimitz to Hawaii to command the Pacific Fleet.

When voices in the press and Congress suggested that the president confer supreme command on a properly qualified military authority such as Douglas MacArthur, Roosevelt gave the idea the back of his hand. "My crime is that I have read the Constitution and stand by it," he remarked to Ross T. McIntire, his personal physician. "What is clearer than that the framers meant the President to be the *chief executive* in peace, and in war the *commander in chief?*"[14]

Blurring the lines between labor and leisure, the wheelchair-bound Roosevelt did much of the substantive work of his presidency in the Oval Study (in the White House residence) or even his bedroom. Military leaders naturally and very properly preferred to maintain a professional distance when dealing with the president. (To sit at the foot of the commander in chief's bed while he ate breakfast from a tray, for example, was asking too much of Ernest King or George Marshall.) But when an issue required immediate presidential attention, decorum was a secondary consideration. Marshall and King were frequent visitors to the Oval Study, and each man grew accustomed to briefing the president while he peered absent-mindedly through a magnifying glass at his stamp collection. On summer weekends, the military chiefs often drove the sixty-odd miles to "Shangri-La" and sat with Roosevelt on a screened porch overlooking a pastoral vista of the Catoctin Valley. In receiving the president's written communications, the chiefs had no choice but to acquiesce in his warm and familiar tone ("Dear Ernie") and steadfastly reciprocated with the correct forms of address ("Memorandum for the President").

Much could be accomplished by working through Harry Hopkins, the president's principal adviser and alter ego. More than any other member of Roosevelt's official family, "Harry the Hop" (who lived in the White House, in a bedroom down the hall from the president's) elicited rational presidential decisions when they were urgently needed. This was no small achievement, and all the chiefs came to respect Hopkins immensely. But Hopkins was spread thin, and he lacked military training or experience. In June 1942, Marshall proposed that a new man be inserted into the White House to act as a senior liaison to the Joint Chiefs. This "military chief of staff" ought to be a gray eminence of one of the services, a man who had worked with Roosevelt in the past and was acquainted with his eccentric ways.

King's first instinct was to resist the idea, probably because he did not want another officer interposed between himself and the president, and because he assumed Marshall would nominate a general. Marshall defused the second objection by proposing Admiral William D. Leahy, a retired chief of naval operations. Leahy had known Roosevelt since 1915, when he commanded the *Dolphin*, the secretary of the navy's dispatch boat. He and his wife were close friends of the Roosevelts, and had often been guests at Hyde Park. After Leahy's retirement from the navy in 1939, the president had appointed him governor of Puerto Rico. In 1941, Leahy had been sent to France to serve as Roosevelt's ambassador to the Vichy regime of Marshal Pétain. On July 7, 1942, Roosevelt lunched with Leahy in the Oval Study and offered him the job. Leahy took it.

Returning to active duty with four stars, Leahy was now the senior-most American officer of all the armed services (by date of first commission). In deference to that seniority, he was recognized as the ad hoc chairman of the Joint Chiefs of Staff. As a former chief of naval operations, he was sympathetic to the navy's concerns in the Pacific, but his appointment in Vichy had fortified his commitment to the Europe-first principle. It was hoped that Leahy, the mild-mannered diplomat, would provide a moderating effect on King's volcanic temper.

Most mornings Leahy went straight up to the president's living chambers, where he found Roosevelt reclining in his four-poster bed, a monogrammed navy cape worn over his pajamas, the blankets pulled up over his wasted legs, reading the newspapers and eating his breakfast from a tray—or perhaps he was in the bathroom, shaving with a straight razor. The admiral took a seat in the corner and began summarizing the latest incoming dispatches from field commanders and outgoing orders from the Joint Chiefs, or he summarized important studies published by the military planning staffs.

Having heard descriptions of Churchill's fine "map room," located in the prime minister's underground bunker in London, Roosevelt decided that the White House ought to have a similar command center. A large room on the ground floor was vacated for the purpose, and a navy lieutenant commander, John L. McCrea, was placed in charge.[15] Large maps of Europe and the Pacific were mounted on opposite walls. Smaller maps of Southeast Asia, the Mediterranean, and North Africa were mounted between them. All were positioned low enough that the president could scrutinize them without rising from his wheelchair. Flags and multicolored pins marked the known locations of Allied and Axis naval, ground, and air forces. The current locations of the "big three" (Churchill, Stalin, and FDR himself) were indicated by special pins—a cigar for Churchill, a briar pipe for Stalin, and a cigarette holder for FDR. Updates were relayed hourly from the navy and war departments by secure dedicated telephone lines.

The Map Room was staffed twenty-four hours a day, eventually by six navy and six army officers. An armed guard stood watch at all times, and only half-a-dozen members of the White House staff were cleared for access. (After learning that her son's location was updated daily, Eleanor Roosevelt dropped in whenever she pleased; the guards did not have the courage to stop her.) Roosevelt appeared each afternoon after his daily sinus treatment with Dr. McIntire, whose office was next door. Leahy and Hopkins often accompanied the president. When he was in town, Churchill haunted the place at all hours. It became, for all purposes, the brain center of the Allied war effort. "McCrea," Leahy said, "I think there is more information about the war concentrated in your Map Room than there is in any other one place in Washington."[16]

ROOSEVELT HAD PLEDGED TO RENDER no military decision for the sake of domestic politics. But he was beset on all sides by amateur "typewriter strategists" who aired their unsolicited advice in public, and he repeatedly warned that the war could not be waged by referendum. Even after the Battle of Midway, a vociferous segment of public opinion wanted to intensify the campaign against Japan. William Randolph Hearst's newspapers demanded a rebalancing of American military power from Europe to the Pacific, for "the war in the Pacific is the World War, the War of Oriental races against Occidental races for the domination of the world."[17] The congressional delegations of Washington and Oregon were distressed by the presence of some 10,000 Japanese troops on two outer islands of the Aleutian archipelago. The Japanese must be driven off the islands at once, they warned, lest they storm into Alaska and imperil the entire West Coast. (Professional strategists knew the scenario was impossible, given Japan's military and shipping limitations, but they could not say so in public without tipping off the enemy to their indifference.) Others looked toward Europe, especially to southern Russia, where the Red Army was fighting a desperate stand against the *Wehrmacht* on the outskirts of Stalingrad. The Allies had agreed to a "Europe-first" policy, but the United States had not yet directly engaged the forces of the Third Reich. Wendell Willkie clamored for a second front against Hitler to relieve the pressure on Russia. In a single week Willkie called for an urgent increase in military aid to Russia *and* China. Eyes rolled in the White House—did Willkie suppose ships and armaments grew on trees?

Nevertheless, the Russian apprehensions were well founded. A collapse of the Red Army would be an unmitigated disaster. Stalin had demanded a second front in France, and the Allies had thus far failed to supply one. Twenty-five years earlier, the Bolsheviks had sued for peace with Germany. A similar armistice in 1942 would permit Hitler to redeploy more than a hundred divisions to Western Europe. "The biggest question mark in the latter half of 1942," Leahy wrote, "was can the Russians stop the Germans, and when?"[18] In the White House Map Room, small black pins edged left to right across the huge wall-mounted map of the Atlantic. The pins, whose locations were updated hour by hour, marked the locations of the all-important Allied convoys to Murmansk as they ran the gauntlet of Germany's submarine wolf packs. Harry Hopkins often ducked into the room to observe their progress, and McCrea later recalled that the president's gaunt *consigliere* always seemed to know exactly what armaments each ship carried in its hold. The hopes of the Red Army, and by association the entire Allied cause, seemed to depend on the convoys' getting through to Murmansk.

With circumstances in Europe pressing so heavily on their minds, it is remarkable that Roosevelt and his advisers had not only agreed to WATCH-TOWER in the first place, but also continued to send reinforcements to the South Pacific in the critical months of August and September 1942. Since Pearl Harbor, the Allied high command had found itself sharply divided over the question of how and when to come to grips with Germany. The Americans had committed to a massive buildup of ground and air forces in Britain (Operation BOLERO). In negotiations that spring, the American chiefs had pressured Churchill to agree to a direct assault across the English Channel by mid-1943 (ROUNDUP). Marshall had further proposed an emergency contingency if the Soviet Union seemed on the verge of collapse—a landing of six divisions (mostly British) on the French coast in September 1942, code-named SLEDGEHAMMER.

The British had first agreed to ROUNDUP and paid lip service to SLEDGE-HAMMER, but with no intention of supporting it. At successive Allied conferences (Washington in June, London in July) the British had stiffened in their opposition to SLEDGEHAMMER and voiced increasing skepticism about ROUNDUP. General Sir Alan Brooke, the acerbic chief of the British Imperial General Staff, left some choice observations in his diary on the subject. Even if an Allied expeditionary force could get ashore safely, he had asked

Marshall on April 15, what would they do? "Whether we are to play bac-
carat or chemin de fer at La Touquet, or possibly bathe at Paris Plage is not
stipulated! I asked him this afternoon—do we go east, south or west after
landing? He had not begun to think of it!"[19] The expedition was almost
certainly doomed to fail, and a failed invasion could do nothing to help the
Russians. Why rush into a campaign that entailed such grave risks, when
the *Wehrmacht* was being bled white on the eastern front and the American
war mobilization had not yet reached its high tide? "Marshall had a long
time to go at that time before realizing what we were faced with," Brooke
later commented.[20]

On July 8, Churchill cabled Roosevelt with definitive notice that the
British would not consent to a landing in France that year: "No responsible
British general, admiral, or air marshal is prepared to recommend SLEDGE-
HAMMER as a practicable operation in 1942."[21]

SLEDGEHAMMER was always a chimera, and British arguments effectively
demolished the American position on the merits. But Marshall, backed zeal-
ously by King and Secretary of War Henry Stimson, held out for the implau-
sible operation even to the point of threatening to abrogate the American
commitment to "Europe-first." In what must be reckoned as one of the most
peculiar episodes of the war, Marshall and King sent a joint memorandum
to Roosevelt on July 10, 1942:

> If the United States is to engage in any other operation than forceful,
> unswerving adherence to full BOLERO plans, we are definitely of the
> opinion that we should turn to the Pacific and strike decisively against
> Japan. In other words, assume a defensive attitude against Germany,
> except for air operations; and use all available means in the Pacific.
> Such action would not only be definite and decisive against one of our
> principal enemies, but would bring concrete aid to the Russians in case
> Japan attacked them. It is most important that the final decision in
> this matter be made at the earliest possible moment.[22]

Roosevelt was not interested in reorienting the global war toward the
Pacific, however, and slapped the suggestion down: "It is of utmost importance that we appreciate that defeat of Japan does not defeat Germany and
that American concentration against Japan this year or in 1943 increases
the chance of complete German domination of Europe and Africa."[23]

In fumbling toward some sort of plan to attack German forces, the Americans had been pitted against the British, the Army Air Forces against the army ground forces, and MacArthur against everyone who did not share his view that he should immediately receive more ships, troops, and planes regardless of what was happening elsewhere. Admiral King, while pressing his plans for WATCHTOWER, had loyally backed Marshall's determination to invade Europe.

Out of these astringent deliberations came Operation TORCH, the invasion of North Africa. The proposal originated with Churchill, who was well aware that his American allies were determined to come to grips with Germany in 1942 and must have an option to do so. British fortunes in North Africa had been battered by General Erwin Rommel's Afrika Korps throughout the spring and early summer, culminating with the surrender of 33,000 troops at Tobruk on June 21. Churchill now argued that the Allies had much to lose in the theater unless the rampaging German armies could be stopped. Roosevelt listened. The president had decreed that his forces must clash with Germany, somewhere, in 1942. The British had ruled out a landing in France. North Africa was the only operation under discussion that fulfilled both conditions. After registering Marshall's opposition, Roosevelt agreed to it. The first landings would occur on November 8.

Plans proceeded in the strictest secrecy. While the president's domestic critics clamored for action, none could be told (even in a whisper) of the planned invasion. November 8 happened to fall five days after the midterm elections. The American people would not learn of this first major counterthrust against the Third Reich until they had already visited the polls (and delivered a sweeping Republican victory).

For the moment, in that political season of 1942, Guadalcanal was the only place in the world where major American ground forces were engaged against the Axis. The island and the 1st Marine Division inevitably loomed large in the American imagination. The campaign received fulsome press coverage, thanks to the presence on the island of more than half-a-dozen gifted military and civilian correspondents. Dick Tregaskis, whose lucidly detailed stories were published by the International News Service, would win fame with the publication of his bestselling *Guadalcanal Diary* in 1943. Hanson Baldwin, a navy correspondent, filed stories for the *New York Times*. Tom Yarbrough wrote for the Associated Press, Bob Miller for the United Press, John Hersey for *Time* and *Life*, Ira Wolfert

for the North American Newspaper Alliance, Sergeant James Hurlbut for
the Marine Corps, and Mack Morriss for *Yank* magazine. Vandegrift published no communiqués, but he encouraged the reporters to go wherever
they liked and write whatever they wished. Lieutenant Herbert L. Merillat,
the 1st Division public relations officer, provided able service to that pack
of willful newshounds while also submitting stories of his own—many of
which appeared, unbeknownst to him, under banner headlines in newspapers across the United States.

"Solomons Action Develops into Battle for South Pacific" was the
front-page, above-the-fold headline in the *New York Times* on September
27, 1942. In a 5,000-word story, Baldwin reported that the "toughened, sunburned marines—veterans of innumerable jungle skirmishes, several large
actions, and continuous bombing and shelling—still clung tenaciously to
the beachhead on Guadalcanal that they seized six weeks ago."[24] When
hopes of holding the island seemed dubious, Baldwin asked General Vandegrift point blank, "Are you going to hold this beachhead?" Vandegrift
replied, "Hell yes, why not?"[25] The exchange, as reported by Baldwin, fired
American spirits. The "toughened, sunburned" marines would not know
it until months later, but Guadalcanal was a household name across the
United States, and the people at home were fervently wishing and praying
for the survival and triumph of the beleaguered 1st Marine Division.

To be at Henderson Field in the fall of 1942 was to live life constantly under fire. Japanese infantry units were concealed in the hills and
forests, some as close as 300 yards to the western end of the strip. Snipers
crept in close to the perimeter and shot at men who stuck their heads up.
Japanese artillery pieces lobbed 75mm shells into the bivouac and aircraft
parking areas. "Every now and then you hear a dull 'ka-boom' off in the
distance," a torpedo plane pilot recalled, "and then would come a little
screaming and ripping noise, and a shell would explode in the field. It didn't
make anybody very happy."[26] Flights of G4M bombers arrived from Rabaul
nearly every day at about noon and dropped their sticks of bombs across the
heart of the marine perimeter. Very often, at night, Japanese destroyers or
submarines lobbed shells into the field from Ironbottom Sound. No one got
enough sleep; the enemy made sure of that. The Japanese cruiser floatplane
they called "Washing Machine Charlie" circled overhead most nights after

midnight. The plane's single rattling engine awakened the marines and kept them awake. "Charlie" usually dropped only one or two small bombs, which rarely took any lives or did any noteworthy damage, but he kept the Americans on edge and deprived them of rest. As soon as the engine was heard each night, each man awoke, took his rifle, and descended into his shelter or foxhole. "You never knew where Charlie would drop a bomb," said the soldier Robert Ballantine. "Sometimes you could hear the bomb-bay door kind of click open. You sure could hear the bombs coming down. If it makes a kind of swooshing, whirling noise the bomb is by you and will miss. If it's hissing it's going to be close, and you might have to change your underwear."[27]

The tedious daily cycle spun without respite: long sleepless nights yielding to drowsy dawns, heavy airstrikes each midday, firefights and artillery duels all day long—an endless lethal routine of sniping, strafing, bombing, and shelling. When it rained, it rained hard and long, and the foxholes and trenches flooded and made everyone miserable. When the rain let up, the ground dried and clouds of dirty gray dust rose from the airfield and got into eyes and lungs and made everyone miserable. The men ate two meals a day and were always hungry. The food was awful—cold C rations, stale biscuits, powdered eggs, dehydrated potatoes, soggy boiled fish, and canned Australian sheep's tongue. They drank green, bitter coffee brewed in a rinsed-out fuel drum. Everyone lost weight, often at an alarming pace. Told to remain close to their planes, pilots tried slinging hammocks underneath the wings. In the middle hours of the day, the machines baked in the sun and a man could burn himself by touching the aluminum surface. For lack of enough ground personnel, the pilots had to learn how to do some of their own maintenance, but as one squadron leader recalled, most of them "didn't even know how to gas their airplanes."[28]

Long-range airstrikes from Rabaul were a daily ordeal, but the Americans usually received two hours' warning from coastwatchers on Bougainville. Jack Read, from his fine vista at Porapora, scrutinized the Japanese formations as they were still climbing to altitude overhead. He would radio directly to Hugh Mackenzie's station KEN, located in a bunker on the edge of Henderson Field. On August 29 at 8:25 a.m., for example, this message came through: "18 TWIN-ENGINE BOMBERS, 22 FIGHTERS NOW HEADING SOUTHEAST."[29] Mackenzie relayed the contact by field telephone to Air Control, located in the pagoda-style administrative building a few hundred feet north of the airfield, and to "D-2," Vandegrift's intelligence staff. A white flag went up, signaling "condition yellow." The Wildcats usually took off about fifty minutes before the enemy's expected arrival—enough time to climb to 30,000 feet, an altitude from which the heavy fighters could make diving attacks on the intruders. Two hours after the Japanese had come and gone, Read was back on the radio to report how many survivors had passed overhead en route back to Rabaul. In the second week of September, the marines finally installed an air search radar on Guadalcanal. But it was effective only to a distance of about eighty miles, and it did not provide ample warning to allow the F4Fs to claw to altitude. It would be difficult to exaggerate the importance of Jack Read's coastwatching reports to the success of the air war over Guadalcanal.

Most of the interception work was done by Marine Fighter Squadron 223 (VMF-223), commanded by Captain John L. Smith. Smith's F4Fs took position at very high altitude, a few miles northwest of Henderson. The big formations of G4M "Betty" bombers generally arrived at about 25,000 feet. The Wildcats attacked in two-plane sections—diving runs from overhead, at an angle that kept them out of the G4M's machine-gun turrets' line of fire. The G4M was not nearly as tough as the B-17 Flying Fortresses or other American heavy bombers. The pilots soon learned to aim their .50-caliber fire into the engines or the wing root, where a short burst normally sufficed to set the aircraft afire or even blow it apart.

Zeros flew high cover over the G4Ms, but they were often positioned too far behind the bombers to interfere with the Wildcats' initial diving attacks. Day after day, the Zeros entered the fray only after the Americans had sent several bombers down in flames. Joe Foss, a marine fighter ace, scratched his head at the tactics employed by his Japanese counterparts. Most were obviously highly skilled, but they failed to adapt to changing tactics and became predictable: "They tried the same thing all the time."[30] The Americans had long since learned to avoid "chasing tails" with the quick and maneuverable Zeros, and did not hesitate to dive out of a dogfight if the enemy gained an advantage. Foss praised the sturdy construction of the F4F and noted that many Americans claimed aerial victories after their planes had been shot up. "We were hit with Japanese cannons as well as their machine guns," he said. "This was unable to knock us down unless it happened to hit the oil cooler or some oil line or gas line in the motor. On a head-on run at each other, we would usually blast the opponent out of the sky and when he was on our tail our armor plating kept the pilot from getting injured, and at no time did any Grumman blow up." The Zero, by contrast, was agreeably easy to destroy: "At any time that you got a direct hit at the base of the wings, the plane exploded like a toy balloon."[31]

For most of the six-month air campaign over Guadalcanal, the Japanese airstrikes flew all the way from Rabaul and back, covering more than 600 miles each way in a single combat flight. It was too much time in the cockpit, too wearing on the Japanese pilots. "My God!" exclaimed Alex Vraciu, a navy fighter ace with Fighting Squadron Six (VF-6). "That's one thousand miles total both ways, plus any air action over the target area. That's a lot of time. Fighter pilots don't like to sit on their seats for too long a stretch. Three hours in a combat air patrol is enough."[32] Some of the Zero pilots behaved strangely and even seemed to avoid combat. They flew inexplicably acrobatic maneuvers, almost as if they were trying to impress their foes. "Oh, they put on lots of acrobatics, slowovers, loops," Foss said. "The only reason that we could figure out for their doing all those stunts, they wanted to show us just how 'hot' they were. So, we showed them how hot we were, and shot them down."[33] One afternoon over Ironbottom Sound, Jack Conger of VMF-223 had a Zero riding his tail and thought he might be finished. But then:

> he did the damnedest thing you ever saw. He came down from above
> and behind, and instead of riding it out on my tail and filling me
> full of bullets, he let himself go too fast so that he went by me. He
> should've dodged off to one side and got out of there, but instead of
> that the fool rose right up under my nose and did a roll. What was he
> trying to do? Impress me with his gymnastics? I don't know. Apparently those fellows have been told that they were the best flyers in
> the world, and so they were like little children with toys; they had to
> show their tricks when they had an audience. Or maybe he thought I
> couldn't hit him if he kept his plane tumbling like that. As a matter of
> fact, he was just making himself a bigger target. I used a three second
> burst, and he was dead before I stopped firing. . . . He made a splash no
> bigger than a porpoise. Then he was just part of the soup.[34]

Zeros sometimes flew surprise strafing runs at treetop altitude directly over Henderson Field. Men scattered and dived into the nearest foxhole;

some were inevitably cut down in their tracks. Strafing runs also damaged or destroyed parked aircraft. On August 23, eight Zeros suddenly strafed Henderson, sending men running for cover. Eventually, these runs were effectively countered by P-400s of the Army Air Force's 67th Fighter Squadron. The P-400s—a slightly modified version of the P-39 Airacobra—were practically useless at altitude, but they were fast and maneuverable close to the ground. Marine Clifford Fox was driven into his trench by a strafing Zero when a P-400 appeared suddenly over the trees and "caught the Jap plane with his cannon and the Zero disintegrated in the air. It floated right down into this ravine in the jungle in front of us. You could see the pilot and the engine of this Zero coming down together. They were the heaviest objects and going forward the fastest. The rest of the plane was sort of floating earthward, shot to smithereens. We were all cheering."[35]

Vandegrift and his marines had a friend in Admiral John S. "Slew" McCain, Commander of Aircraft South Pacific (COMAIRSOPAC), who was determined to saturate Henderson Field with air reinforcements. A week after the 1st Division landed on Guadalcanal, he became the first high-ranking visitor to the island, dropping in for an overnight stay with a bottle of bourbon under his arm. That night, an enemy destroyer lobbed 5-inch shells into the perimeter from Ironbottom Sound, driving the general and the admiral (both dressed in skivvies) into Vandegrift's bomb shelter. "By God, Vandegrift, this is your war and you sure are welcome to it," McCain said. "But when I go back tomorrow I am going to try to get you what you need for your air force here."[36]

Before he left the next morning, McCain told Colonel Twining that the 1st Division's fight was not really about Guadalcanal. It was not, as Twining paraphrased, "a grudge fight between some raggedy-assed Marines and the Japanese. . . . In the admiral's view, Guadalcanal was a rampart, not an outpost. Its successful defense could lead to the destruction of Japanese naval power in the Pacific."[37] McCain wrote in the same vein to Nimitz and King shortly after returning to Espiritu Santo. If adequately reinforced, Guadalcanal could become "a sinkhole for enemy air power."[38] So long as the Japanese arrogantly insisted on sending airstrikes across 600 miles of sea, the long flights alone would whittle down their numbers. Guadalcanal could finish the process begun at Coral Sea and Midway—the gradual extinction of Japan's remaining cadre of irreplaceable veteran aviators.

In the following weeks, McCain lobbied persistently for air reinforcements. He asked for additional army planes, particularly P-38s (which performed much better than the P-39/P-400 at higher altitudes). He summoned air reinforcements from throughout his COMAIRSOPAC domain and asked Nimitz and MacArthur for more. Aviation gasoline, bombs, ammunition, spare parts, tools, and ground personnel were urgently needed. VMF-223 ran out of oxygen canisters three days after the squadron's arrival on the island. The transport *William Ward Burrows* would carry a large load of supplies and the marine air group's ground personnel to Guadalcanal. In the interim, the marine Wildcats were serviced by sailors attached to the CUB-1 base construction facility. Turner sent another battalion of Seabees to the island to upgrade and lengthen Henderson Field so that it could handle B-17s. Land immediately northeast of Henderson was cleared and graded for a shorter auxiliary grass airstrip to be called "Fighter One." When aviation gasoline stocks dipped dangerously low, fuel drums were loaded onto B-17s and flown into the island. The *Hornet* had come south with a squadron of unassembled fighters stored overhead in her hangar deck. They were assembled and flown into Henderson. From August through November, the Cactus Air Force would field a total of eight fighter, twelve dive-bomber, and two torpedo squadrons from three branches of the armed services.

Enterprise and *Saratoga* squadrons, orphaned by the maiming of their ships, were sent into Guadalcanal and told to operate from Henderson until further notice. Lieutenant Commander Harold H. "Swede" Larsen led his squadron of TBF Avengers, Torpedo Squadron Eight (VT-8), into Henderson in mid-September. McCain urged that the bombers be sent on late-afternoon and evening missions up the Slot to destroy Japanese ships before they could land troops and supplies on the island. "Your whole existence up there," he wrote Vandegrift and General Roy Geiger (commander of air forces on Guadalcanal) on September 14, "depends on hitting those Jap ships consistently *before* they get there, while they are there, or during departure."[39] Four days later he added, "The planes must find those ships that come in and hit you at night, and must strike them before dark. Should I die now, those words will be found engraved on my heart."[40]

Each morning, marine and navy SBDs flew "the milk run," a long scouting patrol up the Slot. Every plane at Henderson typically scrambled aloft at midday, if only to avoid being caught on the ground during an airstrike. In the late afternoon, a flight of six to eight SBDs again left Guadalcanal to scout up the Slot for incoming Japanese shipping. These late-day flights were productive, as they forced enemy ships to hang back in the northwest until dark, and thus limited the amount of time they could spend in Ironbottom Sound. The Cactus Air Force also began flying night missions by the light of the moon. Dive-bombing at night was still a fairly low-percentage game, however, and operational losses were high. Swede Larsen's torpedo planes flew scouting and attack missions, but they were rarely able to press home a coordinated attack with dive-bombers, and the hit rate was frustratingly low throughout September. In a debriefing recorded at the Navy Department in January 1943, Larsen recommended "fighting a war that is a very aggressive war. . . . If you can possibly attack and continue attacking—which means a continuous series of replacement supplies and aircraft and provisions, you certainly ought to do it. It was a black eye that we had to let a lot of those Jap ships get away from there, but there really wasn't anything to do about it."[41]

AFTER THE ANNIHILATION OF ICHIKI'S FORCE at the mouth of the Tenaru, General Vandegrift asked his brain trust—Colonel Twining and Colonel Gerald C. Thomas—to consider where the Japanese might attempt their next attack. The colonels had previously expressed concern about an amphibious landing on the beaches around Lunga Point. But the Japanese did not possess the amphibious equipment to make a hostile landing under fire, and any fleet large enough to mount such an attack would inevitably be discovered from the air. With good roads around Lunga Point, moreover, reinforcements could be moved into that area quickly.

A more worrisome problem was the exposed ridge directly south of Henderson Field. In that direction, the jungle provided cover for an enemy approach by stealth. With a concerted attack, the Japanese might break through to the airfield, which lay only a few hundred yards north of the perimeter.

The ridge—remembered later as "Edson's Ridge" or, alternately, "Bloody Ridge"—ran from northwest to southeast for a distance of some 1,000 yards. It rose to a series of bumps or spurs just a few hundred yards from the jungle tree line. Vandegrift deployed Colonel Merritt Edson's battalion of raiders and parachutists to dig into defensive positions on one of the forward spurs. A battery of howitzers was brought up from Lunga Point to provide fire support. Two battalions were kept in reserve.

Admiral Tanaka's "Rat Express" continued to run supplies and troop reinforcements into the island almost every night. Costly experience had taught Tanaka that he must not attempt daylight operations in air-striking range of Guadalcanal. To make matters worse, the Japanese navy's command setup in the region was in evident disarray, and Tanaka was receiving contradictory orders from the Combined Fleet and the two rival subordinate naval commands at Rabaul: the Eleventh Air Fleet and the Eighth Fleet. On August 29, a new invasion force under Major General Kiyotake Kawaguchi arrived at Shortland Island in the transport *Sado Maru*. Two nights later, General Kawaguchi and most of his force, about 3,000 men, were landed successfully from eight destroyers on a beachhead east of the marines, near Taivu Point. The rest of his force attempted to reach the island in landing barges from Gizo Harbor, a tactic Tanaka had warned against, to no avail. More than a dozen of these heavily loaded barges were caught in the open sea and sunk by sixteen SBDs of Scouting Squadron Five (VS-5 of the *Enterprise*). But Tanaka's persistent destroyer operations gradually added to General Kawaguchi's force. By September 12, it numbered more than 6,000 troops. They bivouacked around the villages of Kokumbona and Tasimboko, about twelve miles east of the American beachhead.

September 11 and 12 were as intense as any two-day period the marines had yet experienced. A large strike of G4Ms crossed overhead at noon and walked a pattern of bombs across the populated area just south of the field. Not enough fighters were aloft to break up the attack. That afternoon, twenty-four Wildcats of VF-5, made homeless by the torpedoing of the *Saratoga*, set down on Henderson Field. Their arrival was welcome, but it also put pressure on the gasoline reserve, which was running dangerously low. That night, the marines enjoyed especially heavy shelling by cruisers and destroyers in the sound. September 12 was one long unremitting series of Japanese air raids, and many marines spent the entire day in bomb shelters. At nine that night, the ships returned to give the Americans a three-hour working over with the big naval guns. Harold Buell recalled "a monstrous shelling on a scale unlike any before. . . . The shells were cutting trees off right over our heads, and the shrapnel was falling around us like hailstones. All of us in the trench survived, but the marines of VMSB-232 nearby were not so fortunate. A shell hit on top of their shelter, killing Lieutenants Rose and Baldinus and wounding two others. The whole thing was a nightmare."[42]

Kawaguchi's attack on the ridge began at 7:30 p.m. on the thirteenth. A red flare was fired from the tree line, and a wave of Japanese soldiers charged Edson's line. The fighting quickly degenerated into a series of vicious hand-to-hand encounters. One wave of attackers followed another, and the weight of these repeated attacks threw the marines back to within a quarter mile of the airfield. A counterattack on Kawaguchi's east flank by the reorganized Parachute Battalion forced the Japanese to pull back into the tree line. Constant artillery fire by a battery of 105mm howitzers apparently claimed heavy casualties among the Japanese. "That night was hell: savagery on both sides," recalled David Galvan, a radioman-gunner in one of the SBD squadrons. "That night everything was firing; nothing was held back. Shells went flying over our head: We were very close to the battle and could hear the artillery, the gunfire, the screaming."[43]

At the height of the battle, small groups of Japanese soldiers broke through Edson's lines, and a few reached the edge of the airfield before they were cut down. Several SBDs were positioned so that their rear-facing, .30-caliber machine guns could be trained toward the ridge. A marine assigned to guard one of the SBDs killed an enemy soldier as he climbed onto the wing. "I knew that any Jap that got this far would try to destroy the plane by putting a hand grenade into the cockpit. So I just sat there waiting, and sure enough here came this gook right up onto the wing. I put my automatic piece against his chest and gave him a short burst—bastard never knew what hit him."[44] Vandegrift's command post, about 300 yards south of the ridge, came under direct attack at dawn, but the attackers—two soldiers and an officer wielding a samurai sword—were killed within direct sight of the general.

Morning found the Japanese in retreat and Edson's battalion in possession of the ridge. General Geiger sent up several P-400s to strafe the remaining enemy units. Patrols went into the jungle and killed a few stragglers, but Kawaguchi was in headlong retreat. More than 800 Japanese dead were counted on the ridge and adjacent positions. The total number of Japanese casualties was about 1,200, most of whom were killed in action or later died of wounds. The marines lost 143, killed and wounded combined.

The Japanese infantryman was fast losing whatever mystique he had earned in the early phase of the war. For more than twenty years, the Japanese army had emphasized "fighting spirit" over tactics or technology, and adopted the *banzai* charge as its main offensive doctrine. Against disciplined troops dug into fortified lines and supported by artillery, those tactics were ruinous. Twice in three weeks, a fanatical bayonet charge had been repelled, with casualty loss ratios of about ten to one. Among the marines, spirits rose. They listened to Radio Tokyo's broadcasts with mordant good humor. At the village of Kukum, a big billboard was erected at a crossroads known as "Times Square." On it was reported all of the news of the day, including the numbers of enemy aircraft claimed in air combat overhead and the latest baseball scores from home.

Morale was further boosted on September 18, when an unexpectedly large transport fleet anchored off Lunga Point and began disembarking supplies and 4,000 marine reinforcements (the 7th Marines). These fresh troops were warmly welcomed, as were the lavish quantities of food, medical supplies, ammunition, and construction equipment unloaded onto Beach Red. Martin Clemens later recalled, "We were terribly excited, and licked our chops at the prospect of a square meal."[45]

THE *ENTERPRISE*, MAIMED AT THE BATTLE of the Eastern Solomons, had been obliged to part ways with the *Saratoga* and withdraw to Pearl Harbor for extensive repairs. Fletcher's Task Force 61 was soon reinforced by the arrival in the Solomons of two more carrier groups—Task Forces 17 and 18, built around the *Hornet* and the *Wasp*, respectively.

Ghormley deployed this powerful task force between San Cristobal and the Santa Cruz Islands, in a rectangular zone measuring approximately 160 miles (east-west) by 60 miles (north-south). In this "centrally-located" position, Fletcher could move quickly to counter any Japanese advance into the Solomons while also providing air cover to Turner's transport fleet as it ran supplies and reinforcements into Ironbottom Sound. But Ghormley's orders had the perilous effect of tying Fletcher down in a specific area. The carriers, ringed by their accompanying cruisers and destroyers, continually traversed the same waters—heading southeast at night, then reversing course and steaming northwest in the early morning hours. Enemy air and submarine reconnaissance was bound to discover these patterns and react accordingly. Captain Davis of the *Enterprise* reported to Nimitz on the quandary after his arrival in Pearl Harbor:

During the past month the strategic situation has required long continued presence of carrier task forces in limited areas within at least approximate range of the enemy. Such risks, of course, must be accepted. They should, however, be minimized in every possible way. The percentage should always be played. The widest possible variation should be made in general location from day to day while still meeting strategic requirements. Higher speeds, even at some increase in fuel expenditures, should be used. There should be no hovering during a given day in the same general vicinity. . . . Occasional departure, whenever the strategic picture permits, entirely away from the area should be undertaken so as to leave the enemy guessing where we have gone and when and where we will appear next.[46]

Unhappily, these astute remarks were also prophetic. Knowing full well that the Americans must run convoys between Noumea, Espiritu Santo, and Guadalcanal, Admiral Yamamoto had deployed a scouting line of submarines 150 miles southeast of San Cristobal. The Allied sailors whose duty it was to navigate that submarine-infested corridor gave it a nickname: "Torpedo Junction." On the last day of August, at 7:48 in the morning, the *Saratoga* took a single torpedo in her starboard side, just aft of the island. The explosion tore away her blister plating and destroyed the electrical controls for her propulsion system, bringing her to a dead stop. The blast injured a dozen men (including Fletcher) but killed none. Her destroyers scattered depth charges all around the task force, but the attacker (Japanese submarine *I-26*) dove deep and escaped. *Saratoga*'s crew got the damage under control, and the carrier was able to limp away under her own power, but she would have to follow the *Enterprise* to Pearl Harbor for dry-dock repairs and would not get back into the war until November.[47]

The following two weeks brought almost daily submarine contacts, either by sound gear or by aerial sightings. On September 6, the pilot of a *Hornet* TBF Avenger, flying antisubmarine patrol over Task Force 61, caught sight of a torpedo track pointed at the *Hornet* and dropped a depth charge on it. The torpedo broached, veered off course, and detonated harmlessly. Another torpedo exploded prematurely a few seconds later. A third narrowly missed the *Hornet*, continued on its course, and also narrowly missed the battleship *North Carolina*. Later that afternoon, one of the *Hornet*'s long-range scouts saw an enemy submarine on the surface and dropped depth charges on it, with uncertain results. The next day, as Nimitz reported to King, "Four different contacts, which may or may not have been false, kept the Task Force dodging most of the day."[48]

In mid-September, Ghormley deployed his two remaining carrier groups to provide distant cover for the transport convoy carrying the 7th Marines to Guadalcanal. The reinforcements were landed successfully, but Task Force 61 again tested its luck in the treacherous waters of Torpedo Junction, and this time its luck ran short. On the afternoon of September 14, the *Wasp*—in company with the *Hornet*, the battleship *North Carolina*, and more than a dozen screening ships—was proceeding at 16 knots on the familiar northwesterly course. At 2:15 p.m., she turned into the wind to launch planes, then at 2:42 turned back toward her base course of 280 degrees. Before she had completed the turn, her lookouts sang out and pointed to three incoming torpedo tracks close off the starboard bow. The fish were on target and nearly home; the *Wasp* had no chance of evading any of the three.

The first struck home just forward of the island. The powerful blast lifted the entire ship and hurled her forward, flinging two F4F fighters into the sea and throwing hundreds of her crew from their feet. Ensign John Jenks Mitchell, a twenty-two-year-old Naval Academy graduate, was thrown 30 feet into the air and landed 60 feet away. He recalled the impact of the first torpedo as "a loud, unruly noise—something like a railroad train going up a flight of stairs—and the next thing I knew it was ten days later and I wanted a cigarette." (From his hospital bed in Noumea, two weeks after his injury, Mitchell joked to a reporter: "I am thinking of putting in my chit to qualify for landings on the flight deck.")[49] The second and third torpedoes struck in quick succession, each causing the entire length of the ship to leap again. On the hangar deck, planes were lifted and dropped with such force that their landing gear was crushed, and two fighters that were triced up overhead broke loose and fell on the planes below.

The U.S. Navy could take justifiable pride in its damage-control equipment and training, and with a little luck the *Wasp* might have survived. Captain Forrest P. Sherman conned his stricken ship with sangfroid even while a maelstrom of secondary explosions blew debris around the bridge. He maneuvered the *Wasp* to put the wind on her starboard quarter so that the flames were blown forward and to port.[50] That allowed many hundreds of her crew to take refuge astern. Commander William C. Chambliss noted that the men reacted coolly and efficiently, "cracking their usual gags with their usual vivacity."[51]

But the *Wasp* had been struck at the worst possible moment in the most vulnerable part of her hull—near the aviation gasoline storage tanks, which exploded into incandescent flames. Having just launched planes, the *Wasp*'s fuel lines were full and the fires traveled through the hoses to the forward part of the hangar deck. (The deadly predicament was similar to that of the Japanese aircraft carriers on the morning of June 4 at the Battle of Midway.) Secondary explosions occurred quickly and with devastating effect. In the hangar, the inferno enveloped fueled-up planes. Their wing tanks exploded, their bombs and torpedoes detonated, and their .30- and .50-caliber guns began firing haphazardly. Lieutenant Chester M. Stearns, an engineering officer, made his way up to the hangar deck and noted that a torpedo was roasting under a burning TBF Avenger. He dived flat on deck in time to protect himself against the powerful explosion. When he looked up, "neither plane nor torpedo nor deck were there." Several bombs left on racks near the bomb-arming station had apparently detonated, leaving a "vast hole through [the] elevator pit," with a "seething mass of flames."[52]

The *Wasp* listed 15 degrees to starboard. Electrical lines and fire mains cut out throughout the forward part of the ship. Rivets popped out of the platings and shot through the air like bullets. Most of the communication circuits were knocked out, so the bridge could not communicate with stations belowdecks. Ready service ammunition by the starboard forward antiaircraft guns detonated and rained debris down along the *Wasp*'s entire length.[53]

The devastating attack had been launched by Japanese submarine *I-19*. She had fired six torpedoes; five of these struck an American ship. Three hit the *Wasp*, one the destroyer *O'Brien*, and another passed under the keel of the destroyer *Dale*, narrowly missed the stern of the destroyer *Mustin*, and struck home into the *North Carolina*, sending a column of water and fuel oil to the height of the battleship's masts. The *O'Brien*'s bow was torn cleanly off forward of frame 10, but she limped away. (She was lost en route to the American mainland.) The *North Carolina*'s starboard side was gouged open, but she likewise managed to steam away under her own power. Shortly thereafter, *I-19* fired another spread of torpedoes at the *Hornet* from her stern tubes, and they missed narrowly. The screening ships began zigzagging prodigiously and dropped depth charges throughout the area, driving the enemy submarines away but destroying none.

At 3:05 p.m., a tremendous gasoline vapor explosion ripped through the *Wasp*. Flames ascended to a height of 150 feet. A quadruple 1.1-inch anti-aircraft mount forward of the island was plucked from its foundation and ejected high into the air. The weapon's entire crew was killed. Admiral Leigh Noyes, who had taken command of Task Force 61 two weeks earlier, was thrown down on the deck of his signal bridge. He suffered third-degree burns on his face, scalp, and ears. The interior of the island was completely engulfed in smoke, requiring everyone to retreat aft. A steady rain of burning debris fell on the heads of men gathered on the flight deck. A pilot circling above said that the *Wasp*'s "whole island structure was white, as if the skin had been burned away from the flesh."[54]

Less than an hour after the attack, Sherman realized the game was up, and ordered the crew off the ship. Men went down lines into the sea or simply leapt feet first. Spectacular explosions continued, and debris rained down around the ship to a distance of about 200 yards. Whaleboats from the cruisers and destroyers moved among the swimmers and picked them up.[55]

The *Wasp* burned fiercely through the afternoon, settling gradually by the bow. After sunset, when darkness began to descend over the scene, Chambliss recalled that the ship was "completely enveloped in flames, and presented a weirdly fascinating picture. Against the night tropical sky, she looked like some ship of neon fantasy."[56] The steel plating around her upper works glowed bright orange. Her ruptured tanks spilled bunker oil and aviation gasoline into the sea, and the fires spread around her to a radius of several hundred feet. Shortly after eight, destroyers fired several torpedoes into the burning hulk to be sure she went down. At nine, she rolled a bit to starboard, and the bow went under. She slid into the sea, very slowly, until only her stern remained; then she was gone.

The *Hornet*, now the last battle-worthy carrier remaining in the South Pacific, recovered all of the *Wasp*'s twenty-six planes that were aloft during the attack. Forty-five more went down with the ship. Remarkably, given the carnage, only 173 of the *Wasp*'s officers and men were lost, a consolation owed to Sherman's fine seamanship and the quick work of the escorting destroyers.

The sudden and devastating loss of the *Wasp* at a time when the task forces were under omnipresent threat of submarine attack finally prompted

Nimitz to lay down the law. "For three weeks Task Force 61 and its elements remained in the same waters adjacent to our supply route to the Solomons in an area known to be infested with submarines. The mission did not require that the Task Force be restricted to that area." Henceforth, wrote CINCPAC, "The area of operations of our Task Forces should be changed radically at frequent intervals."[57]

Chapter Five

Tokyo in autumn: the parks were painted with every shade of yellow, orange, and red, and the air was pleasantly cool and not too humid. On a clear morning, from a hilltop, one might catch a distant view of Fuji. Nothing filled a Japanese heart like a glimpse of that regal snowcapped cone.

More than anywhere else in the country, Tokyo was a study in the contrasts of old and new Japan. Throughout the sprawling city, the ancient and the modern coexisted side by side. Men in tailored three-piece suits and fedora hats strolled alongside women in brightly colored kimonos. Automobiles, streetcars, and bicycles vied for the right of way with rickshaws and ox-drawn carts. Billboards and neon signs drew the eye away from hanging lanterns and banners fluttering on wooden poles. Power lines, construction cranes, and elevated railways rose above a sea of dark tile rooftops. The metropolis had only recently begun to grow vertically; large office and apartment buildings were a rarity outside the core finance, business, and government districts. Most urban Japanese lived in miniature wooden houses, crammed into teeming neighborhoods linked by cobblestone streets barely larger than alleys. Steel-framed concrete buildings were going up all over town, but the workers who built them wore split-toed shoes and loincloths and nothing else, just as they had in decades or centuries past.

Hirohito, the emperor of Japan, had been seldom seen by his people in peacetime. Now, as the spiritual leader and sovereign of a nation at war, he was allowed a higher profile. In October 1942, as the struggle for Guadalcanal approached its savage climax, the emperor's red Rolls-Royce twice carried him beyond the gray stone walls of his Imperial compound.

On the fifteenth, he presided over the ceremonial induction of the spirits of 15,021 war dead at Yasukuni Shrine. A crowd of 30,000 came to pay respects. A news photographer captured a sea of solemn, reverent faces under the shrine's huge *tori*. On the twenty-ninth he appeared at the 13th Meiji Shrine National Athletic Games, where one popular competition was a "bayonet charging race." That month also witnessed a wave of public veneration for the fallen crewmen of the "midget" submarine that had shelled Sydney, Australia, the previous June. The cremated ashes of four seamen were transported aboard a truce ship from Sydney, arriving in Japan on October 9, 1942.[1] Newspapers and magazines eulogized the men who had given their lives in a virtual suicide mission against the hated Australians, but none dared acclaim the enemy's chivalry in repatriating their remains.

Insofar as the public was permitted to know, Japanese forces were continuing to trounce the Allies on land, at sea, and in the air. The print and radio media, under exacting state control, rang with exultant declarations of victories and expressions of contempt for the enemy. The editors of *Kokusai Shashin Joho* (International Graphic Magazine) scoffed at the American slogan "Remember Pearl Harbor." ("Yes, Nippon will remember too," they remarked, "the same day and the same harbor.")[2] Prime Minister Hideki Tojo, an army general who dominated the regime with Hirohito's support, declared in a publicized speech at the War Ministry, "The British-Americans want obstinately to continue their counterattack. But making use of our great material resources, we are ready to annihilate them at any moment at any point on the globe."[3] Japan had brought a vast Pacific empire under the flag of the "Rising Sun." From north to south, they ruled from the western Aleutians to the East Indies; from east to west, the Solomons to the Burma-India frontier. Admiral Kichisaburo Nomura, a former ambassador to Washington, explained that the Allied position in the Pacific was hopeless, for Japan "need only hold out in conquered positions."[4] Perhaps peace would come if the two arch-villains and warmongers Roosevelt and Churchill were driven from office by their own people. Only then would the Allies take a more constructive attitude and acknowledge Japan's Asian ascendancy. So it was said.

The Japanese came out to the rallies, mouthed the slogans, waved their hats, marched in the lantern parades, and bowed to the departed spirits at Yasukuni. To all appearances they continued to support the war no less fervently than they had in the heady early months, when spectacular victories came in rapid and uninterrupted succession. Beneath the surface, however, were symptoms of discontent. The Japanese people had obediently submitted to harsh privations for the sake of the war—stringent rations, labor drafts, censorship, repression of political parties, and civil defense regulations promulgated by the *tonarigumi*, or "Neighborhood Associations." But living conditions were deteriorating, and the austere regimentation of daily life was losing whatever charm it had once held. Restaurants closed for lack of food. Intercity train tickets were treasured commodities to be sold or scalped for more than their face value. In December, to arrest falling share prices, the stock market was placed under direct government control.[5] Japanese of that generation were accustomed to war as a quasi-permanent condition; the country had been waging war, to a greater or lesser degree, since the invasion of Manchuria in 1931. War with all enemies, waged indefinitely, had seemed natural enough in the past. But by the fall of 1942, the people began to grasp that this was a total war, which must end either in total victory or in total defeat.

On street corners, women called out to other women to sew a crimson stitch into a 1,000-stitch belt, a traditional talisman believed to protect the wearer against enemy bullets. Millions of soldiers and sailors went off to war with these cotton bands concealed under their uniforms. Japanese public opinion could barely envisage the enormous casualties their forces would suffer in 1944 and 1945, but the death toll was rising alarmingly in late 1942, and the military drafts had started to creep up and down the age scale for Japanese men. According to Hiroyo Arakawa, a Tokyo baker, "Everyone lived in dread of their impending call-up."[6] Nothing inflamed the resentment of ordinary Japanese against the rich and well connected as much as exemptions from military service. Parents with sons overseas were incensed by rumors that strings had been pulled to keep an upper-class lad out of uniform. Arakawa recalled that her husband's cousin—a man from an influential family, employed at Mitsubishi Heavy Industries in Tsurumi—had received several call-up notices but each time arranged to be excused from service: "The big shots always get the best deal."[7] She was likewise exasperated by military men and police officers who felt entitled to help themselves to food or other store items without paying.

As servicemen circulated back into the country, either wounded or on leave, they brought whispers of a war that was progressing much differently than the public reports let on. Saburo Sakai, the fighter ace wounded in combat over Guadalcanal on August 7, returned to Tokyo on leave that autumn. He was appalled by the shrill, vainglorious propaganda—the ubiquitous handbills, the martial orchestral music blaring through loudspeakers, the sham assurances that Japan was still running up a score of one-sided victories. "The nation was drunk on false victories," he wrote. "It was hard to believe that a destructive war was going on." But he soon realized that not everyone on the home front believed what they read in the papers or heard on the radio. His own mother asked him, in a low conspiratorial voice, whether it was true that Japan was winning the war. "We must win," he told her. The alternative was too awful to contemplate.[8]

ISOROKU YAMAMOTO LIVED IN A PLUSH SUITE of air-conditioned cabins on the superbattleship *Yamato*, which rested at her moorings, wrapped in anti-torpedo nets, in the huge cobalt lagoon of Truk Atoll in the Caroline Islands, about 1,600 miles south of Japan. As commander in chief of the Combined Fleet, he did not work particularly hard, and when he did work, his attention was not always on the problems of the war. He read and wrote letters to friends and strangers. He played *shogi* (Japanese chess) against staff officers, often for money. He wrote poetry quickly and (according to his Japanese biographer) not very well, but he had a good hand for calligraphy and provided samples to admirers who asked for them. He read, often late into the night. That Yamamoto did not work obsessively was no mark against him, at least in the view of his loyal chief of staff, Admiral Matome Ugaki. Ugaki reproved staff officers who burdened the commander in chief with minutiae; he preferred that the boss reserve his mental energy for decisions of the highest strategic order.

Tradition demanded that Yamamoto live in sumptuous luxury, and he did. He dined in his wardroom, at a polished teak table covered with a white tablecloth, and his meals easily rivaled those that one might find in an expensive Tokyo restaurant. The navy had recruited professional chefs to man the galley. Luncheons were Western-style, served with silver and finger bowls; dinner was usually Japanese cuisine, with such delicacies as broiled sea bream, egg custard, and sushi. Yamamoto's particular favorites, such as *urume-iwashi* (sardine), were brought from Japan by sea or air. The ship's bakery turned out fresh bread and other baked goods. Crewmen were sent to fish in the lagoon to provide the freshest sushi for his table.

The admiral liked his food and ate with gusto. Finding little opportunity for exercise, he grew portly, as any man must who carries extra weight and stands just five feet three inches tall. But he had the sturdy build and bull-necked confidence of an athlete. His salute was famous in Japan, often captured in wartime newsreels. It was a casual gesture, almost laconic—his meaty right hand raised, straight up at the elbow, to the right edge of the visor on his uniform cap. His orderlies kept his uniforms in scrupulous condition: in the tropics he always appeared in whites, starched and pressed, with gold buttons and chrysanthemum-crested epaulettes reflecting the sun. He was not a dandy, but he had a part to play. Yamamoto was a warm man, always kind and considerate to his officers, yet he maintained an Olympian distance from the crew of his flagship, who snapped to attention at his appearance and did not twitch until he was out of sight. Only occasionally did Yamamoto show himself on deck, usually to raise his cap for a departing ship or a flight of aircraft overhead.

In the West, Yamamoto is best remembered as the prime mover behind Japan's surprise attack on Pearl Harbor and the disastrous attempt to seize Midway six months later. In Japan, his legacy is more multifaceted. It owes more to his prewar career as a subcabinet minister and diplomatic representative. In the militarist regime of Japan's "dark valley" period (1930–45), there was no such thing as civilian control of the military; rather, the military directly controlled all domestic, economic, and international functions of government. Military leaders suppressed the political parties, stripped the Diet (parliament) of its power, placed the media under state supervision, and controlled the appointment of cabinet ministers. In both fact and effect, generals and admirals became politicians, civilian ministers, and foreign diplomats. Western historians are predisposed to evaluate Yamamoto's career using the same standards, benchmarks, and gauges one would apply to any professional naval officer in such nations as the United States or Britain. To do so misses the point. Quite apart from his naval career, Isoroku Yamamoto was a major player in Japanese politics from the mid-1930s through the outset of the Pacific War, and probably the nation's most revered public figure after the emperor himself.

Disdainful of the army and the ultranationalist right, Yamamoto had consistently opposed the Japanese radicals who used revolutionary violence and assassinations to achieve their ends. He was a leading figure in the navy's moderate "treaty faction," known for its support of unpopular disarmament treaties. His rivals charged him with courting fame and celebrity, cultivating newsmen to ensure favorable press coverage, and maneuvering for his own advantage in politics. There is undoubtedly some truth in these charges. If Yamamoto had not been so politically adept, he could not have survived the repeated purges of like-minded officers in the turbulent 1930s. But it is also true that he put his life on the line to prevent the slide toward war with the United States and Britain.

Yamamoto had represented Japan at the 1935 London Naval Conference, and advocated ratifying an extension of politically unpopular arms-control limitations. These and other positions had placed his life in jeopardy, as right-wing zealots explicitly threatened to assassinate him and attempted to do so on at least one occasion. In August 1939, he was transferred from the Navy Ministry in Tokyo to command of the Combined Fleet; the move was intended, at least in part, to place him beyond the reach of his would-be murderers. From his flagship, often moored in Hiroshima Bay, Yamamoto continued to insert himself into national policy debates. He opposed signing the Tripartite Pact (allying Japan to Nazi Germany and Italy), and had called for a withdrawal of Japanese troops from China.

Yamamoto was one of the few Japanese of that era who found the courage to oppose war with the United States. As a younger man, he had twice been posted to America (once as an English student at Harvard, once as naval attaché in Washington), and he had made a close study of the country's vast economic resources and industrial base. "Anyone who has seen the auto factories in Detroit and the oil fields in Texas," he would later remark, "knows that Japan lacks the national power for a naval race with America."[9] He foresaw that the Pacific War was likely to become a long, drawn-out conflict in which titanic American production would overwhelm Japan's much smaller and less advanced war industries. Under no circumstances could Japan hope to inflict a total defeat on the United States. A war against the United States could be "won" only by a negotiated settlement favorable to Japanese interests. Against such odds, Yamamoto could "see little hope of success in any ordinary strategy."[10] When it became clear that war was coming whether he liked it or not, he groped for a way to force it to a quick conclusion. His proposed raid on Pearl Harbor, he admitted, was "conceived in desperation."[11] The raid was an all-or-nothing gambit, a throw of the dice, designed to prompt a political calculation in Washington that war with Japan was not worth the cost: "We should do our best to decide the fate of the war on the very first day."[12]

The raid was a spectacular tactical success. All eight battleships of the Pacific Fleet were knocked out of action, and more than 180 American planes were destroyed, mostly on the ground. The Japanese carriers escaped with the loss of just twenty-nine planes. That success, and the rapid conquest of Pacific and Southeast Asian territories in the early months of the war, lifted Yamamoto to new heights of popularity and prestige. With the power to dictate his wishes to the Naval General Staff (NGS), he forced through a plan to hurl the entire force of the Japanese navy against Midway Atoll in June 1942. The Midway operation, like the raid on Pearl Harbor, was an attempt to force the war to a premature conclusion by inflicting a knockout blow on the U.S. Navy. Instead, the gambit ended with the loss of four Japanese aircraft carriers and all of their aircraft, one of the most cataclysmic defeats in the history of war at sea. Though the debacle was carefully hidden from the Japanese people, Yamamoto lost his leverage over the NGS. The Tokyo admirals recovered their primacy in strategic policy-making.

The debacle at Midway left a mark on Yamamoto. His outlook grew gloomy, detached, and fatalistic. Japan was now engaged in precisely the war of attrition he had often warned against, without any means of escaping it short of abject surrender. Although he could never say so, Yamamoto must have known, by mid-1942, that his country was careening toward an apocalyptic defeat. In a sense, he would be vindicated by that defeat, but that could come as no comfort. He could no longer make his influence felt in Tokyo; he could do nothing but revert to his proper place as the navy's top seagoing commander. It was his duty to wage war against the enemies of Japan. He would do so until the bitter end, whatever that might be and whenever it might come. He did not expect to survive it: "Within a hundred days," he predicted in September 1942, "I will wear out my life entirely."[13]

In the ranks of the fighting navy, there was a good deal of irritated chatter about the *Yamato*'s long sojourns in port. She and her sister, the equally enormous *Musashi*, were the two largest warships in the world. Each weighed more than 70,000 tons when fully loaded, each carried a complement of 2,700 men, and each was armed with nine mammoth 18.1-inch guns. They had been constructed at grand expense by battleship admirals who believed that they would be the key to destroying the

American battleships in a traditional naval gun duel, and thus winning the naval war. But neither of the leviathans had engaged in combat, and neither would until 1944. They had spent most of the war at anchor, first in Hashirajima anchorage in the Inland Sea, and now at the great southern fleet base of Truk. *Yamato* was derided as the "Hotel Yamato." An officer of a freighter later observed, "We were always being sent to the very front lines, and those battleships never even went into battle. People like us . . . were shipped off to the most forward positions, while those bastards from the Imperial Naval Academy sat around on their asses in the *Yamato* and *Musashi* hotels."[14] The truth was that neither of the big battleships was of much use as a combatant vessel. In any theater of the war, they would likely come under air attack long before they could bring their guns to bear on an enemy ship. More significantly, the two superbattleships drank so much fuel (each had 6,300-ton tanks) that operating them at sea would strain the navy's resources, especially as the American submarines were beginning to take a bite out of the seaborne oil-supply line.

Admiral Ugaki left a running daily assessment of the war in his personal diary, which fortuitously survived the war. The invaluable document is a candid firsthand account of the Guadalcanal campaign as viewed from the flagship. In earlier pages, covering the beginning of the war through the Midway operation, Ugaki often recorded Yamamoto's decisions and directives. By the summer of 1942, however, the commander in chief appears to have taken a step back from the management of daily operations, leaving his chief of staff to pick up the slack. Ugaki began to write in the first person ("I decided . . . ," "I ordered . . . ") and often issued directives in his own name rather than Yamamoto's.

On August 7, Ugaki fretted over the news that marines had landed on Guadalcanal, and opined in his diary that they must be driven off at once. But a month passed before he grasped that the struggle for Guadalcanal was the decisive campaign of the Pacific War, and that it must take precedence over every other operation, even if it required suspending the offensive against Port Moresby in New Guinea. He complained of poor radio communications, which caused delays in orders sent and reports received aboard the *Yamato*. All along, he was plagued by a recurring toothache, which seemed to multiply his despair at the repeated failures to recapture Henderson Field.

Was the key to Guadalcanal the air war, the ground war, or the naval war? In Ugaki's rolling analysis, he vacillated. On August 13, six days after the invasion, he wrote, "The most urgent thing at present is to send a troop [sic] there to mop up the enemy remnant, rescue the garrison, and repair the airfield."[15] A week later, on August 20, he was convinced that the "most urgent thing" was to "render the airstrip unavailable by launching air raids and night bombardments."[16] Four days later, he concluded that air reinforcements for Rabaul were "as urgent" as troop reinforcements for Guadalcanal, because the Japanese must "destroy the enemy air arm on the island as soon as possible."[17] He grasped that the great distance from Rabaul to Guadalcanal was encumbering the air campaign, but he was willing to accept heavy air losses. On September 1, however, he concluded that the American forces must be defeated on the ground: "In the end, Guadalcanal must be secured by land warfare, even with sacrifices. There is no other way."[18]

After the indecisive carrier skirmish of August 25, Ugaki wanted the Japanese fleet to remain in the forward area so that it could engage any new American attempt to resupply Guadalcanal by sea. He noted that Tokyo had finally "become aware of the gravity of the situation" and was rushing ships, aircraft, and troop reinforcements into the theater. But the supply problem was growing more critical, especially with respect to oil—tankers were in short supply, and the major fleet movements into the lower Solomons had consumed a tremendous quantity of fuel. Truk did not yet have any fuel storage capability ashore. Ships sometimes drew alongside the *Yamato* and drank from her cavernous tanks.

Betraying a naval officer's archetypal disdain for the army, Ugaki blamed a lack of aggressiveness on the ground for the repeated failures to break through Vandegrift's lines. When Ichiki's forces were wiped out on August 20–21, he assumed that the men had fallen under attack on the beachhead and should have "advanced recklessly."[19] The admiral had it exactly wrong. Ichiki had indeed advanced recklessly, against a heavily fortified riverbank, and his 800 men had been annihilated by the marines' withering defensive fire. After what the marines called the Battle of the Bloody Ridge in mid-September, when General Kawaguchi's forces were repulsed, with heavy losses, and forced to retreat to the west, Ugaki's army liaison seemed "at a loss about what to do." Ugaki surmised that the army had "made light of the enemy too much," which was true enough.[20] But neither he nor his army counterparts suspected that their estimates of American troop strength on Guadalcanal were too low. The Japanese believed that about

7,500 marines were on the island; actually there were more than 11,000, and another 4,000 arrived on September 18.

With growing naval and army forces at their disposal, the Japanese commanders prepared an all-out campaign to break the six-week deadlock and seize the airfield. The pressure for a decisive victory emanated from the throne itself. After the war, Hirohito would portray himself as a powerless figurehead, but in September and October of 1942 he continually goaded his army and navy ministers to take the offensive and drive the Americans off Guadalcanal. Appeals from the *Showa Tenno* ("Emperor of the Era of Illustrious Peace, Light, and Harmony") were tantamount to commands handed down from heaven. But neither the army nor the navy needed much encouragement. The struggle for the island had become an issue of national will. The Japanese army, in particular, had suffered an intolerable loss of face. Two elite Japanese army detachments had been defeated by enemy troops that they had insisted on holding in contempt. In early October, Imperial General Headquarters committed a full division of the Seventeenth Army, some 20,000 troops, to the campaign. The navy's Eleventh Air Fleet was heavily reinforced; a new fighter strip at Buin, on southern Bougainville, was made operational; and a new commander in chief, Vice Admiral Jinichi Kusaka, was dispatched to assume command in Rabaul. The navy would redouble and intensify its night bombardments, dispatching the battleships *Kongo* and *Haruna* with a large escort of cruisers and destroyers, to pulverize Henderson Field with 14-inch anti-personnel shells.

On October 11, as Yamamoto and Ugaki watched from the *Yamato's* weather deck, an enormous fleet steamed out of Truk's north channel—four carriers, four battleships, ten cruisers, and thirty destroyers. The carriers would sweep north of the Solomons, hanging back until the airfield was overrun, and then race south or east to hunt down and destroy enemy fleet units. Ugaki confided in his diary that the coming offensive would commit "most of the Combined Fleet." Failure was therefore unthinkable: "Whatever happens, we must succeed in the coming operation of recapturing Guadalcanal at any cost."[21]

CHESTER NIMITZ, THE FIFTY-SEVEN-YEAR-OLD Commander in Chief of the Pacific Fleet (CINCPAC), was a gentleman of the old school. Unlike Ernest King, who stood above him in the chain of command, Nimitz never yelled at a subordinate, drank to excess, chased women, or let a word of profanity fall from his lips. He had inherited a shattered, demoralized command after December 7, 1941, and very swiftly restored confidence and morale. He was the most respected naval officer of his generation; today he is fittingly revered as the greatest leader in American naval history. He was of medium height and had a ruddy complexion and pale blue eyes, set in striking contrast to a pair of white eyebrows and an equally white head of hair. Born and raised in a landlocked corner of Texas, Nimitz came from a humble family of German American innkeepers. As a boy he had spoken as much German as English. Long hikes, swims, and bouts of tennis kept him fit. For relaxation, he shot at targets with his pistol, tossed horseshoes, played cribbage, and listened to classical music on a phonograph.

Within the constraints of his lofty rank, Nimitz was a genuinely warm and outgoing man. He was compulsively social and always used a personal touch. He let it be known that the commanding officers of all ships that put in to Pearl Harbor were expected to pay him a visit, and his office established an "open house" each day at 11:00 a.m. for the purpose. His command was vast—two and a half million men and more than a thousand ships—so these daily meetings were a tax on his time, but they kept him in direct touch with every level of the fleet. Nimitz was a natural-born warrior, one who always insisted on carrying the war to the enemy. He had the inborn military bearing of his Teutonic ancestors; his family had once held a title of nobility and coat of arms in rural Saxony. His chief of staff, Rear Admiral Raymond Ames Spruance, later attested that Nimitz was the only man he ever knew who seemed to be completely fearless, and added, "The one big thing about him was that he was always ready to fight. . . . And he wanted officers who would push the fight with the Japanese. If they would not do so, they were sent elsewhere."[22]

When Admiral King had first devised his ambitious and risky WATCH-TOWER operation, Nimitz had kept his cards close to his vest. There is little in the historical record to indicate whether he agreed with King's reasoning. When Ghormley and MacArthur recommended a deferral of the offensive, Nimitz again remained conspicuously silent, neither supporting nor disputing their arguments. But when King overruled their objections and reaffirmed WATCHTOWER, the CINCPAC threw everything he could into the operation. He knew that the position on Guadalcanal was precarious, but he thought Ghormley's dispatches too pessimistic. Having lived through

the menacing weeks after Pearl Harbor, and the knife's-edge vicissitudes of
Coral Sea and Midway, Nimitz was not easily shaken by the recurring setbacks in the South Pacific. The sinking of four Allied cruisers at the Battle
of Savo Island was a heavy blow, as was the destruction of the *Wasp*. But
even if Guadalcanal could not be held, the Japanese were frittering away
their strength, little by little. In the long run they would stagger under the
weight of America's growing military power. "Remember this," he had told
his staff after learning of *Lexington*'s loss in the Coral Sea; "we don't know
anything about the enemy—how badly he's hurt. You can bet your boots
he's hurt too. His situation is no bed of roses either."[23] He could have made
the same point about the struggle for Guadalcanal.

On September 24, Nimitz left Pearl Harbor for an extended inspection
tour with half-a-dozen members of his staff. A big four-engine PB2Y Coronado flying boat roared down the East Loch and staggered into the sky,
then banked south and set a heading for tiny Palmyra, 960 miles distant.
Palmyra was one of several remote mid-Pacific atolls on the daisy chain
of refueling stops and emergency airstrips that formed the air route to the
South Pacific. The pilots flew a compass heading over eternally monotonous
blue seascapes, aiming for a tiny horseshoe-shaped tendril of sand and scrub
that was easily missed when cloud cover was thick. They flew through thunderheads that tossed the aircraft sickeningly. The navigator might hope to
pick up a radio beacon, but when there was none, it was a matter of dead
reckoning—watching the compass, keeping track of course and speed, and
applying estimated corrections for cross winds, which might be guessed by
watching the play of the wind on the waves. Nothing provided a more visceral sense of the immensity of the Pacific than flying across it in a World
War II–era aircraft.

The Coronado was a very large snub-nosed airplane with a single high
wing and a cockpit positioned high and forward of the fuselage. Its range
was only about 1,000 miles, but it was strongly armed and therefore better
prepared than the Catalina PBY to ward off unfriendly advances by enemy
fighters. Less than 200 miles from Palmyra, one of the engines on Nimitz's
aircraft conked out. The plane landed safely, but a replacement had to be
summoned from Pearl, requiring a long delay. The next leg down to Canton
Island, 800 miles southwest of Palmyra, passed without incident, and there
Nimitz rendezvoused with Admiral McCain, who had been relieved as
COMAIRSOPAC and was on his way north. McCain gave the CINCPAC

his views about the air fight for Guadalcanal. He was more upbeat than Ghormley but urged that reserve planes be sent into Espiritu Santo and readied to reinforce the contested island. McCain also stressed the critical problems of aviation fuel supply and pilot fatigue.

The next day brought another long hop to Fiji for refueling. The party arrived at Noumea on the afternoon of September 28 and went straight into a conference on Ghormley's flagship, the transport *Argonne*, at 4:30 p.m.

Ghormley did not look well. Nimitz had seen symptoms of fatigue in leaders before.* It was typically manifested in weight loss and a slightly manic gleam in the eyes. Ghormley appeared gaunt and hunted. His surroundings could not have helped. Unable to obtain suitable quarters and a staff headquarters from the French colonialists on the island, Ghormley had chosen to run his command from his overcrowded and sweltering flagship, berthed at a pier in Dumbea Bay. Nimitz learned that Ghormley had not left the ship in a month. When a staff officer handed Ghormley an urgent dispatch, he appeared shaken by whatever he read and was heard to murmur, "My God, what are we going to do about this?"[24] The COMSOPAC's nerves were brittle; he was not looking after his physical or mental health.

The September 28 conference in the *Argonne*'s wardroom was one of the largest concentrations of senior Pacific commanders ever to sit around one table. General MacArthur had declined to travel outside his command area (as was his normal practice throughout the war, until he was ordered to meet the president in Hawaii in July 1944), but he sent his chief of staff, Major General Richard K. Sutherland, and his air commander, Lieutenant General George C. Kenney. SOPAC was represented by Ghormley, Turner, and Major General Millard F. Harmon, commanding general of U.S. Army Forces in the theater. General Henry "Hap" Arnold, the ranking officer of the USAAF and one of the four members of the Joint Chiefs, was passing through on an inspection tour.

Admiral Nimitz opened the meeting with cursory pleasantries and then turned to Ghormley and asked for a briefing on the state of play. The chief problem with Guadalcanal, said Ghormley, was the difficulty in providing logistical support to the marines. Only two fast transports were left; aviation gasoline reserves were down to 5,000 gallons; and the ships bringing

---

* In May, Admiral Halsey had been laid low by a skin breakout after several months of continuous command of a carrier task force.

additional supplies and material from the United States had been loaded carelessly, so that the ships' manifests did not provide an accurate record of what cargoes they carried or where they were stowed. A lack of advanced port facilities in Noumea and everywhere else north of New Zealand made it nearly impossible to reload the attack transports for runs into Guadalcanal. Nimitz sympathized, observing that "cargo handling, living arrangements, and gas storage are terrible everywhere we go."[25] Turner predicted the Japanese could take Guadalcanal at "any time with a good landing force, three or four carriers, and proper ships." If the Japanese forces on the island had been quiet since the battle on the ridge, it was only "a lull in their efforts."[26]

The three-hour conference exposed all of the cross-service and cross-theater tensions in the South Pacific, and indeed in the entire global conflict. General Sutherland, speaking for MacArthur, said that the fight for Guadalcanal was not nearly as critical as the defense of Port Moresby and Milne Bay on New Guinea, where the Allies had 55,000 vulnerable troops. Ghormley's naval forces should operate farther west, he said, to counter Japanese moves toward those positions. Excerpts from CINCPAC staff notes summarized the exchange that followed:

Nimitz: Doubts that Jap will "come around the corner for Moresby." Easier to stop us at Guadalcanal.

Sutherland: Gen. MacArthur wants Ghormley to cover the whole area. . . . Fleet shouldn't be restricted to a line. Should base more ships on Australia, including TF-1 [the battleships] which would be better located strategically than at Pearl.

Nimitz: TF-1 must remain in Hawaii.

Kenney: The Japs have lots of bauxite; can increase plane production.

Nimitz: The Jap is not happy. Shipping losses 1,000,000 tons. . . . Avgas shipped from Japan.

Kenney: With bauxite Japan has, they can increase production to 2,000 planes per month.

Nimitz: I don't believe the Japs can build 2,000 planes per month.

Kenney: We should take Rabaul.

Turner: We can't take Rabaul now. We must continue to eat away at the edges. Can do nothing but attrition until we have local air and naval superiority . . . covering air and naval forces.

Sutherland: We want to establish a school of amphibious warfare.

Turner: We have no amphibious training going on. Our school is CACTUS.

Nimitz: On question of Ghormley covering MacArthur, we must counter Jap air with our carriers, which cannot operate in restricted areas. We now have only one, *Hornet*; *Enterprise* will be ready 6 Oct.

Sutherland: Once on north coast Papua we will put our fighters there, bombers at Moresby.

Kenney: If Japs take Milne they can get at Moresby easily.

Nimitz: I still say he isn't comin' round the corner.

Kenney: If they do they'll stop our supply line, and starve out our 55,000 at Moresby.

Nimitz: Tell MacArthur we have sent him everything we have. [27]

The problems in both theaters were plain to see, but Hap Arnold had come from Washington with an entirely different agenda, and a message that must have galled all of the men around that green baize–covered table. The future five-star general believed that the South Pacific was "oversaturated" with army air units. He reminded the Pacific commanders that the Allies' global strategy called for defeating Germany first. They could not afford to let American airpower be sucked into the vortex of the Pacific War when the more dangerous enemy was still rampaging across Europe. Between MacArthur's and Nimitz's commands, he counted some 1,314 airplanes, and another 302 on the way, for a total of 1,616. That was against his best estimates of Japan's airpower in the theater: 554 airplanes. The only way the navy's request for more air could be met was by drawing them away from Europe. Arnold was against it. Air reinforcement of the Pacific should be halted and even reversed—the Allies should be moving planes from the Pacific to Europe. These arguments, he knew full well, did not "make a hit with either the high ranking officers of the navy, or, probably, with General MacArthur." [28]

More than any other member of the Joint Chiefs, Arnold backed rigid adherence to the "Germany-first" principle. By prior agreement with the British, the Army Air Forces were to concentrate a tremendous force of bombers and fighters at airfields in southern England, where they would operate with the Royal Air Force in the bombing campaign against Germany. The planned buildup had been substantially delayed by deployments to support WATCHTOWER and TORCH. In July 1942, nine heavy air groups were on their way to the Pacific and another eleven to Africa. In a strongly worded private memorandum to Harry Hopkins on September 3, 1942, Arnold expressed "growing apprehension" over the dispersal of American airpower to peripheral theaters and reminded Hopkins that the war was to be fought according to the "Germany-first" strategy. He could rely on neither Marshall nor King to back the strategy reliably: "At this writing, the major effort of the Navy is from the Southwestern Pacific to the Northwest against Japan. . . . The Army, for one reason or another, has changed its primary objective from time to time as circumstances, policies, and politics dictated." The cost of these "piecemeal dispersals and petty diversions all over the world," he wrote, was to cripple the air campaign against the industrial heartland of Germany:[29]

> [The navy's] main objective is in the South Pacific. Little by little, bit by bit, the Navy is increasing its strength down there, calling for large air and ground support. Every increase in strength that the Navy gets for its operations in the Pacific necessitates taking something away from some other theater. These reinforcements may save our Navy or prevent the recapture of South Pacific islands occupied by us, but there is a strong possibility that the Navy could withdraw entirely from that theater and we would not lose the war. Furthermore, if we capture all the islands up to and including New Britain, we still would not necessarily win the war. On the other hand, if we beat the Germans we know that we will win the war.[*][30]

Nor was this attitude of Pacific localism limited to the navy. When Arnold met with MacArthur in Brisbane the following day, the imperious commander in chief of the Southwest Pacific area demanded 500 more planes of any kind. When Arnold referred to commitments in Europe, MacArthur offered his professional opinion that "a sufficient number of air bases could never be established in England to provide air cover for a second front."[31] Arnold was incredulous. "Germany-first" was the sanctioned basis of the Allies' entire global strategy, and here was a major Allied theater

---

* Churchill was receiving similar jeremiads from his RAF commanders. See "Air Marshal A. T. Harris to Prime Minister, Personal and Secret," June 17, 1942, Harry L. Hopkins Papers, Book 5: The Air Offensive, Box 313.

commander who did not accept it even in theory. All subordinate commands, Arnold concluded, ought to be "indoctrinated with the idea that there is a United States plan—An Allied plan—for winning the war, and all must conform to it."[32]

ON THE AFTERNOON OF SEPTEMBER 29, Nimitz boarded his Coronado for the three-hour flight to Espiritu Santo, the advanced air and supply base that provided direct support to the garrison on Guadalcanal. There he was greeted by Admiral Aubrey "Jake" Fitch, who had succeeded McCain as the commander of SOPAC air forces.

Nimitz could not have been surprised by the retrograde conditions at Santo. He had been well informed of circumstances on the airfield since it had been hewn out of the jungle two months earlier. Still, to see it with his own eyes must have made an impression. There were no circulating runways, no traffic control, not even a control tower. The aircrews lived in primitive huts and tents, getting very little recreation or rest. They were plainly exhausted, and many were sick. At Segond Channel, he watched as the fuel drums were dropped from the transports and "swum" into shore, then lifted onto the backs of trucks and dispersed to uncovered fuel dumps. Every day, 20,000 gallons of aviation fuel was landed on the island by these grueling means.

Nimitz awarded decorations to several marine and navy pilots, and a Distinguished Service Medal to Fitch. Then he and his retinue boarded an army B-17, provided by Fitch, for the 620-mile hop to Guadalcanal.

The B-17 had plenty of range to make the flight, and in case of a sudden ambush the Fortress was a rugged and well-defended airplane. But the young pilot flew into a weather front and soon admitted that he was not sure of his position. That was a gentle way of saying he was lost in the lowering white murk. All hands scanned the seascape below. Lieutenant Arthur Lamar fished a *National Geographic* map of the South Pacific out of his bag and tried to match it up to the contours of passing islands. They found Guadalcanal and flew up the north coast. Finally they glimpsed the small, muddy airfield littered with junked airplanes and surrounded by bomb craters and tent camps. A torrential rain was beating down as the aircraft sloshed and skidded to the edge of the runway. Nimitz stepped down into the downpour and was greeted by Vandegrift.

As the skies cleared that afternoon, the general took the admiral on a tour of the defense perimeter. Nimitz met several of the regimental commanders, who spoke in low tones about the action they had seen and their preparations for the future. He observed the still-unburied hundreds of Japanese dead strewn across the hill south of Edson's Ridge. In the Pagoda, General Geiger briefed him on the air campaign, and Nimitz took in the exhausted and hunted appearance of the airmen who had been on the island for a month or more. At the field hospital, he spoke to men wounded in battle and men laid low by malaria or other tropical ailments. "The grim appearance of the command noticeably impressed him," Vandegrift wrote of his visitor; "I was not exactly sorry since I wanted Nimitz to see what we were up against."[33]

The next morning, Nimitz was to award decorations, and Vandegrift's staff was up late that night writing citations. Lieutenant Herbert L. Merillat found the entire process shockingly arbitrary. The number of decorations to be handed out, he noted, was not determined by any impartial standard of heroism, but by "the number and types of medals the admiral totes along." Officers lobbied on behalf of their units and horse-traded so that each received its share. Marginal cases were dressed up, and many deserving men were undoubtedly neglected. Merillat confided to his diary that he was relieved he did not have the responsibility to decide the awards, because "there are so many real heroes here."[34]

The ceremony took place at 6:30 a.m. in a bamboo grove in front of Vandegrift's shack. Lieutenant Lamar read the citations as the admiral went down a line of marines and pinned medals to chests. The solemnity of the occasion was broken by some singing and shouting of marines up the hill, who were ignorant that a ceremony was taking place, and had to be told to quiet down. A sergeant keeled over in a dead faint as Nimitz approached to pin a medal on his chest. When he came to, he apologized and explained that he had "never seen a four-star admiral before and he was scared to death."[35] Vandegrift was genuinely surprised and moved when he received the Navy Cross.

The flight back to Espiritu Santo was delayed by the condition of Henderson Field, which remained a quagmire after the previous day's downpour. One thousand feet of the runway still lacked steel matting. The first of the two planes to attempt takeoff (it carried Nimitz) could not get airborne. It skidded down the last unmatted section of the strip, did a ground loop, and came to a stop at the edge of a ravine. Nimitz descended from the plane and went to lunch with Vandegrift. They would wait for the sun to dry the strip. At midday they tried again, and this time the Fortress wobbled into the sky and droned away to the east.

THE MARINES ENDURED. They suffered the enervating heat and humidity, the endless torture of insects, the hours of pelting rains that swamped their foxholes and tent camps. They sweated and shivered through the malarial fevers. When they had an hour or so of relief, they took a bar of soap and went down to the Lunga River. With their mates manning machine guns and watching for enemy soldiers or estuarine crocodiles, they scrubbed their bodies and their dungarees, washing themselves as thoroughly as they could in the brown water. But no amount of scrubbing did away with the "jungle rot," the blisters and open sores that accumulated on their wrists, in their armpits, under their testicles. Scratching made it worse, and they warned themselves and each other not to scratch, but sooner or later the temptation overcame the will to resist. The "prickly heat," as it was called, was just another inescapable annoyance of life on the stinking, godforsaken island. The marines carried away their dead and buried them respectfully, marking their graves with wooden crosses or a stick with a helmet slung on top. They stripped the Japanese dead of whatever valuables or interesting souvenirs were found on their persons, and even smashed out their gold teeth and pocketed them as spoils of war. The stench of their rotting flesh wafted on the breeze. The unburied bodies were overrun with ants. In time, nothing would be left but polished bone.

Since August 9 they had been asking one another, "Where's the fucking navy?" It was a rhetorical question, of course. They were marines; they could rely on no one but themselves. The 1st Marine Division had become the "1st Maroon Division." "U.S.M.C." stood for "Uncle Sam's Miserable Children." They had been played for suckers. By training and doctrine, they were elite shock troops—amphibious specialists brought in to storm an enemy beach and secure a beachhead. They had done their job. They were not supposed to be left to defend that beachhead for months on end. The plan, as the officers and men had always understood it, called for the army to come in behind them and take over the position. The marines would be pulled back to a rear area for a period of rest, recuperation, and additional training, and later deployed to another amphibious attack on another island closer to Tokyo. Two months after the invasion of Guadalcanal, a new question was on the lips of every marine: "Where's the fucking army?" It was another rhetorical question, of course. It was their lot to be left behind, as they had been at Wake Island. They were "George," and the sister services had agreed to "Let George do it." Singing voices rose in bitter unison from the foxholes. Their profane anthem had been adapted from the old British expeditionary soldiers' song "Bless 'em All":

> They sent for the Navy to come to Tulagi,
> The gallant Navy agreed;
> With one thousand sections
> In different directions,
> My God! What a fucked-up stampede!
>
> (Chorus)
> Fuck 'em all! Fuck 'em all!
> The long and the short and the tall;
> Fuck all the swabbies and dogfaces too,
> Fuck all the generals and above all fuck you!
> So we're saying goodbye to them all,
> As back to our foxholes we crawl;
> There'll be no promotion on MacArthur's ocean,
> So cheer up marines, fuck 'em all![36]

Turner's handful of suitable attack transports continued irregular runs between Noumea, Port Vila (Efate), Espiritu Santo, and Guadalcanal, but the supply shortfalls were endemic. Food was often in dangerously low reserve, and although the marines were never reduced to a starving condition, they were required to subsist on reduced rations, which sapped their energy and strength. Everyone lost weight, as much as twenty to thirty pounds. Ammunition was landed on Lunga Point and then distributed to caches as directed by the quartermaster. The reserves were usually low enough that the marines had to be warned not to waste a shot unless they were sure of hitting an enemy soldier. Even when the transports arrived in Ironbottom Sound, always a welcome sight, unloading them into the rudimentary port facilities at Lunga Point required meticulous attention and backbreaking labor. Constant harassment by Japanese air attacks required the ships to raise anchor and maneuver at high speed in the sound, losing precious hours. The single most critical shortage, in early October, was aviation gasoline. So critical was the avgas situation that fifty-five-gallon fuel drums were flown into Henderson on DC-3 transports.

The Tokyo Express, variously known to the marines as the "Cactus Express" or the "Tojo Express," landed small numbers of Japanese troop reinforcements and supplies on the beaches west of the American perimeter night after night. Tanaka's fast destroyers continued to do double duty as transports. Their speed allowed them to hang back until nightfall, far up the Slot, beyond the flying range of the Henderson-based bombers, and then race in under cover of darkness. If they unloaded quickly enough, the destroyers managed to lob a few shells into the marine perimeter and then race westward to be out of range again by daybreak.

But Tanaka's destroyers could not land an entire division, at least not on the timetable demanded by the ambitious Japanese plans. Lieutenant General Harukichi Hyakutake, commander of the Seventeenth Army, needed proper troop transports to do the job. The Japanese had learned through bitter experience that they could not bring transports into Ironbottom Sound as long as planes based at Henderson Field could attack them as they approached. It followed that the Japanese must find some means of putting Henderson out of business long enough to land a division of troops. They had been trying to do exactly that for two months, and thus far failed. This time they would not fail—or to put it more precisely, they *could* not fail, because the emperor himself had insisted that they succeed.

VANDEGRIFT REPEATEDLY APPEALED for more troop reinforcements. But Admiral Turner, who stood above him in the chain of command, held very different ideas about the deployment of ground forces. Again and again the two commanders found themselves at cross-purposes. Turner was inclined to disperse ground forces across many islands or beachheads, whereas Vandegrift and his staff preferred the virtues of concentration. The admiral obstinately insisted on holding back the 2nd Marines (assigned to replace the 7th Marines, which had been deployed in Samoa) for a subsequent landing on Ndeni in the Santa Cruz Islands, 300 miles east of Guadalcanal. Vandegrift's officers thought Ndeni irrelevant and urged Turner to hold troops in reserve to reinforce Lunga if the fight grew hotter than expected. Only after the admiral had personally witnessed the ferocious combined ground assault and naval bombardment of Henderson on September 11 (taking a bottle of scotch with him to his foxhole, as one marine staff officer noted) did he agree to deliver the regiment to Lunga.

As for the marines already on the island, Turner believed that they should take the offensive. On September 28, he urged Vandegrift to storm across the Matanikau River and hunt down the "nests of enemy troops" lurking along the coast to the west: "I believe you are in a position to take some chances and go after them hard."[37] The embattled marines were understandably irked by the suggestion that they had been too passive. Moreover, a ground offensive at that stage of the campaign was neither feasible nor sensible. The 1st Division lacked the equipment, weaponry, and ammunition to pursue the Japanese down the coast. The marines controlled the island's only airfield, and their overriding priority should be to defend that asset and keep it supplied with adequate airpower. The Japanese, true to form, would continue to hurl themselves against the well-fortified American lines—and if those lines held, the attackers would suffer disastrous losses, as they had in the past.

But Turner would not be dissuaded. In early October, the argument flared up again over the deployment of the 164th Infantry Regiment of the U.S. Army's Americal Division. Vandegrift wanted the regiment on Guadalcanal, as reinforcement; Turner wanted to land it on Ndeni. Ghormley at first gave tentative approval to Turner's plan. But General Harmon, on October 6, weighed in strongly in favor of sending it to Guadalcanal. Ndeni, he told Ghormley, would be "a diversion from the main effort and dispersion of force." He warned that "the Jap is capable of retaking CACTUS-RINGBOLT [Guadalcanal-Tulagi] and . . . will do so in the near future unless it is materially strengthened."[38] Ghormley overruled Turner, and the 164th was landed at Lunga Point on October 13.

The landing of the Americal troops led to another night naval action off Savo Island—eerily similar to the Battle of Savo Island two months earlier, but with a result more pleasing to the Americans. The transports carrying the Americal troops had been accompanied by a small task force of four cruisers and five destroyers, under the command of Rear Admiral Norman Scott. On the night of October 11–12, Scott's warships ambushed a Japanese column of three cruisers and two destroyers as they headed into Ironbottom Sound to bombard Henderson Field. The surprise attack destroyed a Japanese cruiser and a destroyer and heavily damaged another cruiser. The Japanese commander, Rear Admiral Aritomo Goto, was critically wounded and later died. Scott lost a destroyer, the *Duncan*, and suffered damage to the cruisers *Boise* and *Salt Lake City*. The short, vicious fight, which would pass into history as the "Battle of Cape Esperance,"* was a tactical victory for the Americans, though not by the margin they apparently believed. (Scott reported that he had sunk three Japanese cruisers and four destroyers. That inflated result was reported as fact in the American press.) But the victory, such as it was, did little good for the marines. Later the same night, another of Tanaka's convoys successfully landed troop reinforcements and supplies (including artillery field pieces) near the cape that gave the battle its name. Two nights later, a larger Japanese surface force would pour the heaviest barrage of the campaign down on Henderson Field.

Between bombing raids by day and naval shelling at night, nothing could be done to stop the Japanese from punching holes in Henderson Field. But the airfield was kept in reasonably good repair by the diligent exertions of the Seabees, who filled in the craters as soon as they appeared. Each Seabee unit manned a repair station directly alongside the airfield. When a bomb landed on the runway, the nearest unit raced to the smoking hole, tore up the ruined Marston matting, and hauled it away. They dumped dirt and gravel into the hole from a dump truck, then hauled in the replacement steel and laid it over the fill. "We found that a 500-pound bomb would tear up 1,500 square feet of a Marston mat," said one, "so we placed packages of this quantity of mat along the strip, like extra rails along a railroad."[39] When the work was interrupted by low-flying, strafing Zeros, they dived for cover into trenches alongside the field—or into the bomb crater itself, if that was possible.

Marine, navy, and army air reinforcements flew in every few days to replace aircraft lost or damaged beyond the possibility of repair. The Cactus Air Force now included more than a dozen USAAF pursuit planes, but the workhorses of the air campaign remained the carrier-type aircraft—F4F Wildcats, SBD Dauntlesses, and TBF Avengers, flown by marine and navy aircrews. Aircraft designed to operate from carriers were equipped with landing gear that could sustain plenty of punishment, and that suited them

---

* Known in Japan as the "Second Battle of Savo Island."

to a beaten-up airfield like Henderson. In a month on Guadalcanal, the navy pilots flew more combat hours than they would fly during six months of typical carrier operations.

The bombers and torpedo planes flew long daily scouting missions to the northwest. In the late afternoon, they might discover Japanese shipping inbound for Guadalcanal—the "Tokyo Express coming down Broadway"—and if they did, General Geiger launched an airstrike with whatever planes he could muster. Those long daily flights "up the alley" were grueling and dangerous, and not only because the Japanese shot back. In the Solomons, visibility could deteriorate quickly and at any time. Swede Larsen badgered his VT-8 pilots to write down their navigational checkpoints. Memory was unreliable, especially under the strain of combat flying: "You would see points of land in low visibility when the Russell Islands or the lower tip of the New Georgia islands would look like Cape Esperance. The first thing you knew, if you were not actually checking yourself in speed, time and distance, you would be lost; it's very easy to do."[40]

When the cumulus clouds descended almost to sea level, the aviators flew on instruments, in formation, shrouded in mist and rain showers. They struggled to maintain contact with their wingmen, keeping their eyes locked on the blue exhaust flames of the planes ahead. When one young TBF pilot lost visual contact with the plane ahead, he would "rudder back and forth until I felt the slip stream, and then I crept slowly straight ahead until I picked the exhaust up again."[41] Planes in formation drifted apart, lost contact, and turned back alone. Now and again, flashes of light cut through the gloom. Were they gunfire flashes? Lightning? Flares? Was a friendly plane flashing his running lights to guide his wingmen back in? It was often hard to tell. Under the stress of such flying, pilots sometimes misread their altimeters and flew into the sea.

Four or five weeks of daily combat flying was about the limit of the aviators' endurance. The routine was physically, mentally, and emotionally punishing. After six weeks, even the toughest among them seemed to buckle under the strain. Aviation and medical authorities were coming to accept that "pilot fatigue" was a real and unavoidable syndrome that must be countered by rotating squadrons out of the theater every four to six weeks. Aviators pushed past the limit became listless, haggard, and hollow-eyed; they lost weight rapidly even if well fed; they crashed more often, or made navigation errors and got lost; their reflexes slowed and their aggressiveness diminished. In extreme cases, pilots were known to crawl under the wings of their airplanes, curl up in a fetal position, and cry like children. When coaxing and threats failed, they had to be literally kicked until they staggered to their feet and climbed back into their cockpits.

Admiral Kelly Turner had once dismissed talk of pilot fatigue, supposing it sounded too much like coddling, but now he declared himself a believer: "When the medicos used to tell us about pilot fatigue, I used to think they were old fuds. But now I know what they meant. There's a point where you just get to be no good; you're shot to the devil—and there's nothing you can do about it."[42]

Joe Foss, one of the mentally toughest aviators in the South Pacific, told a navy panel that pilots could endure no more than six weeks in combat. "The fourth week you start to slip," he said. "And the fifth week you'll lose a lot of men that are really good men that just get a little bit tired and dope off so that will result in their being shot down." Moreover, Foss added, when pilots were rotated back into the theater after an extended rest, "you'll find that you tire a lot easier. . . . On our second trip in I noticed that the second week the boys seemed to be failing again."[43]

The stoic Larsen took a less forgiving view. He believed the fault was to be found in poor training and leadership. Fear was natural and inevitable, but it had to be managed. If the pilots understood their own fear and anticipated it, they would be better prepared to master it. Speaking for himself, Larsen observed, "I know that I felt a reaction to my first engagement for a couple of days afterwards; you get filled up with a lot of nervous tension which gradually wears off. After we had made a few attacks on Guadalcanal, however, the nervous reaction would last only from 10 to 15 minutes after you landed. That is, you were excited and keyed up; then it would die away and you wouldn't feel especially tired."[44] Larsen suggested a whiskey ration at the end of each flight: "I know that might sound strange, but if you give a man a drink of whiskey after an attack, he thinks it's fine. . . . Those little extra privileges make the men feel a hell of a lot better."[45]

AFTERWARD, THE MARINES WOULD REMEMBER IT simply as "The Night."[46] It was the night, October 13–14, when the battleships *Kongo* and *Haruna* stood into Ironbottom Sound and rained 14-inch shells down on Henderson Field for an hour and a half. The marines had long since grown accustomed to night bombardments, but never before had they been on the receiving end of such monstrous projectiles, which made every previous encounter seem picayune by comparison. Each of the two battleships had been armed with 500 rounds of a new type of shell designed to inflict the greatest possible damage on parked aircraft and fortified positions. Firing tests in Truk Lagoon had demonstrated that these shells (a thin casing loaded with incendiary and shrapnel, instantaneously fused) were most effective when striking the target at an angle of 25 degrees.[47] That gave the Kongo and Haruna their ideal firing range: 16,000 meters, or about ten miles. At that distance, the American shore batteries had no prospect of returning effective fire.

The Night had been preceded by an afternoon of relentless and unusually heavy airstrikes. For some reason, coastwatcher alerts had not been timely, and several F4F Wildcats were caught on the ground and destroyed. Aerial bombing punched craters in Henderson Field and the auxiliary grass field at Fighter One. An avgas fuel dump took a direct hit and went up in a mushroom cloud of blue-orange flame. At sunset, when the western sky lit up in a typically majestic palate of tropical colors, a new sound was heard to the west. "Pistol Pete," the marines' nickname for a Japanese 150mm artillery battery, was shelling the airfield from an unseen position at the base of Mount Austen. General Geiger ordered his grounded planes to taxi to Fighter One, out of range.

As darkness fell, Japanese floatplanes circled overhead and dropped stray bombs here or there, nothing more obnoxious than usual. Shortly after eleven, the sirens signaled "Condition Green" (all clear), and men dragged themselves out of the foxholes and dugouts and back to wherever they were sleeping. "Pistol Pete" was intermittently active throughout the night. Men snatched sleep in twenty- to thirty-minute increments. At about one, the sirens sounded "Condition Red," and men went wearily back to their shelters. At 1:30 a.m., a cruiser plane dropped a flare, and then a star shell fired from a ship offshore burst directly over the airfield.

Then came an ascending scream often compared to a freight train's whistle, and a series of gigantic detonations that seemed to turn the night into day. They were, Lieutenant Merillat recorded in his diary, "the heaviest blasts I have ever heard."[48] Each explosion gouged a truckload of soil out of the ground and flung it into the air. Entire trenches were buried in showers of earth and rock. The air was choked with dust and smoke that worked its way into the men's noses, ears, eyes, and throats. Ensign Mears was in a foxhole with several other pilots:

> We could see the flash from a salvo light the sky, hear the report, then the whistle of the shells, and finally the terrible crack-crack of the shell exploding. Coconut trees split off and crashed to the ground, shrapnel whirred through the air, a few duds came crashing and bounding through the jungle without exploding. We smelled the powder of detonating shells. The sky was now ghostly, now brilliant with fires which had been started and with pin-wheel star shells. Some of the shells hit not more than twenty or thirty feet from our dugout. When a big one struck, the walls of the dugout trembled the way chocolate pudding does when someone spats it with a spoon.[49]

Even in the deepest and best-constructed bomb shelters, the immense concussions lifted men into the air and hurled them against the walls. A crowded dugout was preferable to an empty one. Where there were enough men, they could hang on to one another for mutual support—but if a man found himself alone, a Seabee noted, "you'd rattle around in your foxhole like a ping-pong ball."[50] General Vandegrift and several of his staff were in the command post's bomb shelter when an explosion outside "bowled us down like a row of ten pins." The general picked himself up, "unhurt except in dignity."[51] Each salvo shook dirt loose from the coconut log roofs. Colonel Twining recalled that "the earth seemed to turn to the consistency of Jell-O, making it difficult to move or even remain upright."[52]

At the height of the barrage, some of the men in Mears's shelter laughed uncontrollably. One pilot was overcome with violent trembling. Another struggled physically to burrow under the other men. The top of a nearby tree was severed from its trunk and crashed down across the foxhole.

When the big guns fell silent, at about 3:00 a.m., men on the ground could make out the familiar rattle of "Washing-Machine Charlie" overhead. Bombs continued to fall at erratic intervals for the rest of the night. Those blasts were puny compared to the battleship shells, but they were steady and dangerous. No one slept. Vandegrift vowed that he would never judge a man suffering from combat fatigue or shell shock. No one who has not suffered under that kind of bombardment, he wrote, can "easily grasp a sensation compounded of frustration, helplessness, fear and, in case of close hits, shock."[53]

Dawn exposed the carnage. Bleary-eyed men stumbled out of their trenches and dugouts, some dressed and some half-naked, some barefoot and some bleeding. They gratefully sipped coffee brewed in fuel drums, the bitter brown fluid comforting their jangled nerves. Sifting through the wreckage, men found heavy steel base plates larger than dinner plates, and sections of 14-inch casing, some weighing nearly twenty pounds.[54] Dugouts adjoining the airfield were entirely buried by earth and trees torn out of the ground, and men still trapped inside had to be excavated.[55] Martin Clemens discovered, within a hundred-yard radius of his position, "six tremendous craters, any one of which could have hidden a jeep."[56]

Blackened, smoking, deformed lumps of aluminum wreckage occupied the aircraft parking areas around Henderson Field. An inventory of the Cactus Air Force revealed that five SBDs and perhaps seven or eight Wildcats remained in flyable condition. No Avenger could fly without major repairs. VT-8's chief mechanic judged all but three TBFs a total loss, and of the three that might be salvaged, only one could be repaired inside of a week. The surviving planes had to be dispersed to less vulnerable positions and, if possible, hidden from the enemy. Wrecked planes were lined up in neat rows, wingtip to wingtip, in hopes of diverting the enemy's attention. A new aircraft parking area was established near the eastern extremity of the perimeter, and a strong force of marines posted to guard it.

Several of the Avenger airmen, made redundant by the loss of their machines, walked back to their camp and found it a near-complete loss. Every tent had either vanished or been left in a heap of shreds, and all their contents of "mosquito netting, cots, tables, and papers and luggage, had been riddled and tangled and scattered by shrapnel holes and explosions." The survivors were tense, but also a bit giddy. Ensign Robert E. Ries Jr. drew a laugh from his squadron mates by "pulling the corners of his eyes toward his ears and saying, 'So sorry. Which way to Henderson Field, please?'"[57]

Hundreds of drums of precious avgas had gone up in flames. An urgent appeal went out to quartermasters and supply officers to hunt down any reserves. Many small fuel dumps had been dispersed and hidden in small caches around the field and in the woods. Several hundred drums were discovered, and another 200 were transferred from Tulagi. At one point, Geiger reported that his entire reserve had been pumped into the tanks of the flyable planes on the island. Another night of similar bombardment, he warned, might put the entire air force out of action.

Forty-one men lay dead. That figure was lower than it might have been, a testament to the depth and strength of the bomb shelters and the determination of all to keep their heads down for the duration of the barrage. One dugout took a direct hit, killing nine men at one blow. A newly arrived marine dive-bombing squadron had lost both its commanding officer and its executive officer.

Heavy air attacks, artillery fire, and nighttime naval barrages (though not by battleships) continued throughout the next several days and nights. On the morning of October 15, Americans standing on the bluff above Kukum watched six Japanese troop transports "brazenly unloading" off Tassafaronga, about ten miles west. Japanese destroyers patrolled protectively in the sound, little more than a mile offshore. Clemens observed the incoming troops through his field glasses as they mustered in smart lines. He could not tell how many there were, but their numbers certainly ran into the thousands. Geiger managed to throw his few operable SBDs against the Japanese transports and set two afire, but only after they had unloaded their cargos and troop reinforcements.

That mid-October was the bleakest moment of the campaign. The long shadows of Bataan and Wake Island were cast across the Lunga perimeter. Many men seemed dazed and listless, and gazed vaguely off into the distance. The marines called it the "thousand-yard stare." Aviators who had lost their planes collected whatever weapons they could find and joined the infantrymen in the trenches. Since August 7, the besieged marines had bucked themselves up with mordant humor and a brawny *esprit de corps*. Now, increasingly, they flared up at one another and exchanged heated words over small annoyances. "Everyone made mistakes," wrote Colonel Twining. "Orders miscarried. Communications failed. Execution was sluggish."[58]

The Japanese army, now heavily reinforced on the western flank, began probing attacks along the Matanikau River. Vandegrift fortified his lines, but he was not entirely confident they would withstand a concerted assault. Retreat and even surrender became a thinkable prospect. D-2, the 1st Division intelligence staff, began burning their classified records. Units made plans to melt into the jungle hills, live off the land, and wage a guerrilla war as long as they could. "We all feared defeat and capture, I think," recalled Tony Betchik, an F4F crew chief. "We were afraid they were going to leave us there."[59] A navy air officer, Lieutenant Commander John E. Lawrence, recalled the insidious effects of "the hopelessness, the feeling that nobody gave a curse whether we lived or died. It soaked into you until you couldn't trust your own mind."[60]

According to Twining's postwar memoir, Ghormley authorized Vandegrift to surrender his forces if the position became hopeless. (No such dispatch has survived, but it is precisely the sort of document one might expect to slip into oblivion.) Among the 1st Division staff, there was hushed talk of a last stand. Vandegrift ordered contingency plans for a fighting retreat up the Lunga River. Twining studied the issue and recommended another option—moving the marines down the coast to the east, where they could establish interim defensive lines at each river and preserve the possibility of evacuation by sea.

The despair reached all the way back to the United States. The *New York Times* wrote about the Guadalcanal campaign in a valedictory tone. Speaking to reporters in Washington, Secretary Knox refused to guarantee that the island could be held. He had been embarrassed by his boastful confidence immediately before the Japanese attack at Pearl Harbor, and was determined not to commit another such gaffe.

IF THE GRIM DISPATCHES FROM GUADALCANAL were not enough, Admiral Ghormley was badly shaken by an October 16 aerial sighting report placing a Japanese aircraft carrier just to the west of Ndeni—an island that lay 330 miles *east* of Henderson Field, dangerously near the supply route between Espiritu Santo and Guadalcanal. The report was in error, and was soon corrected, but not before it elicited from Ghormley a pitiable *cri de coeur*. To Nimitz and King, he cabled, "This appears to be all out enemy effort against CACTUS possibly other positions also. My forces totally inadequate [to] meet situation. Urgently request all aviation reinforcement possible."[61]

The embattled South Pacific commander had never really bought into the WATCHTOWER offensive. King had thrown it into his lap when he was still setting up the rudiments of his new command, before he had assembled an adequate staff or even established a permanent headquarters. His logistical problems were undoubtedly more severe than those faced by any other Allied theater commander, but Ghormley had made a bad habit of asking for reinforcements that he knew did not exist. From the start of the campaign, he and his staff had seemed stressed and uncertain. When the French colonialists at Noumea had resisted providing an administrative building, he had accepted the rebuff with a born diplomat's equanimity, and operated from the cramped and fetid precincts of his flagship. He had failed to appear in person at vital command summits, particularly the planning conference on board the *Saratoga* (July 26) that preceded the landing at Guadalcanal. Unlike McCain, Turner, Harmon, and Nimitz, he had never set foot on Guadalcanal.

During his recent inspection tour, Nimitz had observed his old friend closely. His observations confirmed the reports that he must have been gathering from many sources. Ghormley was not up to the job; he would have to be relieved and replaced.

No less a figure than FDR bore a share of the responsibility. Ghormley had been special naval observer in London until he was replaced in that job by Admiral Harold "Betty" Stark, who in turn yielded the job of chief of naval operations (CNO) to King. Stark's transfer to London in April 1942 was really a face-saving demotion that allowed King to wield simultaneously the two most powerful commands in the navy (CNO and COMINCH). But it put Ghormley out of a job, and that didn't sit right with the president, who had known the admiral for more than a quarter of a century. FDR asked his naval aide, Commander John L. McCrea, "What's going to happen to Ghormley?" McCrea had no idea and said so, adding that Ghormley was likely to lose his temporary three-star rank and revert to his permanent rank of rear admiral. FDR replied, "Well, tell Ernie King for me that I think it rather unfair because we have to find a place for Stark that Ghormley is to lose his rank as vice admiral."[62] Coming from the commander in chief, that amounted to an order to find Ghormley another three-star billet.

In retrospect, Nimitz should probably have relieved Ghormley in September, during or immediately after his inspection tour to the South Pacific. There is evidence that King and Nimitz had discussed a change at SOPAC as early as their meeting in San Francisco on September 7.[63] But Ghormley was an honorable officer who had given forty years of his life to the service. He had been one of the stars of his class, a man (like Nimitz and King) whose talent, dedication, and hard work had marked him at an early age for rapid promotion. There was no way around the fact that relieving him would leave the stain of failure on his career and legacy. It was a painful duty to strike such a blow against a brother officer, and Nimitz hesitated to do it.

In a meeting at Pearl Harbor on October 15, senior members of the CINCPAC staff put the issue to their boss with a forcefulness and candor that crept up to the edge of insubordination. According to fleet intelligence officer Edwin Layton, they urged that "personalities should be set aside and that the commander South Pacific should be replaced by someone who could do a more effective job."[64] Whatever the merits of their case, that was not the way things were supposed to be done in the navy, and Nimitz hotly reprimanded them for "mutiny." Undeterred, a delegation of officers reiterated their case later that night during a visit to Nimitz's Makalapa quarters, where the CINCPAC greeted them in his pajamas. Bill Halsey had orders to take over command of the carrier task forces, and was at that moment en route to the South Pacific. It would be a simple matter of directing Halsey to Noumea, and then ordering him to relieve Ghormley as COMSOPAC. Nimitz was subdued, but noncommittal.

The following morning came Ghormley's dispatch (160440) bewailing his "totally inadequate" forces. Nimitz fired off an ultra-secret dispatch for King's eyes only: "In view Ghormley's 160440 and other indications, including some noted during my visit, I have under consideration his relief by Halsey at earliest practicable time. Request your comment."[65] King briefly replied: "Approved."[66]

Halsey, overnighting at Canton Island, was directed to fly directly to Noumea. His Coronado let down in the harbor at 2:00 p.m. on October 18. A whaleboat carrying Ghormley's flag lieutenant came alongside, and the lieutenant handed Halsey a sealed envelope, inside of which was another sealed envelope marked "SECRET." It was a dispatch from Nimitz directing Halsey to relieve Ghormley as COMSOPAC immediately.

One of Halsey's staff recorded the admiral's exact words: "Jesus Christ and General Jackson! This is the hottest potato they ever handed me!"[67]

Chapter Six

THE MEMOIRS, DIARIES, AND ORAL HISTORIES ARE UNANIMOUSLY agreed. The news that Halsey had taken charge brought a sudden upwelling in morale through the theater. "I'll never forget it," recalled a navy air officer on Guadalcanal. "One minute we were too limp with malaria to crawl out of our foxholes; the next, we were running around whooping like kids. . . . If morale had been enough, we'd have won the war right there."[1] Halsey was known as an aggressive, emotional, risk-taking warrior who loved nothing more than to attack. The marines called him a "rough brush"[2]— that is, an artist who painted in big strokes rather than a draftsman who drew fine lines. He would not be deterred by subtle arguments of strategy and tactics—he would simply throw everything he had at the enemy and slug it out until the issue was decided.

The "rough brush" was an old and venerated tradition of American naval leadership, dating back to John Paul Jones's "I have not yet begun to fight!," James Lawrence's "Don't give up the ship!," and David Farragut's "Damn the torpedoes, full speed ahead!" In October 1942, it was precisely the attitude needed in the South Pacific. It lifted men's spirits and gave them hope. But it is also worth considering how close the Allies came to the brink of ruinous defeat in the Solomons. If the fortunes of war had turned a bit differently in the climactic naval battles of late October and November, American seapower might have been garroted and the marines cut off and overrun. In that case, Halsey's characteristic daring and aggression would have been condemned as unreasoning and rash (as indeed it would be two years later, at the Battle of Leyte Gulf).

At the very outset of his command, the new COMSOPAC faced a stark choice. He could push all his chips into the middle of the table, or he could fold and wait to be dealt a better hand. It was his duty to give due consideration to the second option, demoralizing as it was. His long-term chief of staff, Admiral Robert B. Carney, maintained that Halsey was never quite as madcap or impulsive as the newspapers liked to portray him. His garish boasts and his exhortations to "Kill more Japs!" and "Keep 'em dying!" were always aimed down the ranks, as a spur to morale. When Vandegrift flew into Noumea for a command summit on October 23, Halsey listened more than he spoke. He listened to Vandegrift, then to Turner; he let silence fall over the wardroom while he smoked a cigarette, drummed his fingers on the table, and turned the issues over in his mind. Finally he asked the general, without fanfare, "Can you hold?"[3]

"Yes, I can hold," Vandegrift replied. "But I have to have more active support than I have been getting."[4] Halsey promised to send everything he had.

It was evident that a big Japanese naval offensive was shaping up. Communications intelligence was far from perfect, at the moment, but the new COMSOPAC knew the Japanese fleet would include more than two flattops (perhaps as many as four) and a large force of surface ships, including at least four battleships. Halsey had two carrier task forces, built around the *Hornet* and *Enterprise*. The latter, having been damaged in August and patched up at Pearl Harbor, rendezvoused with the *Hornet* northwest of Espiritu Santo at 3:45 p.m. on October 24. The two groups were combined into Task Force 61, under the command of Admiral Thomas C. Kinkaid—the two carriers, the battleship *South Dakota*, six cruisers, and fourteen destroyers. That force was little more than half the size of the Japanese fleet descending on the region. In an aggressive and potentially dangerous move, Halsey threw virtually everything he had into the fight. Kinkaid was ordered to sweep north of the Santa Cruz Islands and seek battle with the enemy.

RADIO MONITORS ON THE YAMATO had picked up a United Press report, broadcast from Hawaii, referring to plans in the making for "a major sea and air battle soon near the Solomons."[5] It did not escape Admiral Ugaki's attention that Americans were about to go to the polls for midterm congressional elections. Would FDR order a major operation to coincide with America's Navy Day (October 27), in hopes of stirring up voter support for his party? That chain of reasoning was badly flawed, but the Combined Fleet staff had nonetheless surmised correctly that Halsey would throw all available naval forces into the defense of Guadalcanal. The Japanese army and navy gathered strength for an all-out sea-air-ground offensive, with the dual ambitions of seizing Henderson Field and wiping out the American fleet.

The Japanese fleet was the largest assembled since the Midway offensive: two fleet carriers, two light carriers, and four battleships, with many supporting cruisers, destroyers, and auxiliaries, sixty-one ships altogether. As at Midway, the Japanese plan called for a partition of naval forces into several, widely separated groups. The advance or van of the Japanese fleet would be led by Vice Admiral Nobutake Kondo, who flew his flag in the cruiser *Atago*, and would include two battleships, five cruisers, ten destroyers, and a light flattop, the *Junyo*. A scouting line (and decoy force) of surface warships and one light carrier would steam about a hundred miles ahead of the two big fleet carriers, *Shokaku* and *Zuikaku*. As in the August battle, the Japanese commanders hoped that the Americans' initial carrier airstrike would fall on the scouting line. The various elements would converge on Guadalcanal after the Japanese army had broken through Vandegrift's perimeter and overrun the airfield.

The Japanese army was in force on Guadalcanal, but it continued to operate under the heavy disadvantages of poor communications and the rigors of an unforgiving jungle terrain. The scheduled assault on Vandegrift's lines was twice delayed (from October 22 to October 24, local date), and when it began, it quickly deteriorated into a series of small, confused unit encounters. The marines held their well-fortified lines and exacted a bloody toll on the attackers, who suffered casualties at the ratio of about seven to one. At dawn on the morning of October 25, however, a Japanese soldier thought he saw green-white flares over Henderson, the agreed signal that the airfield had been captured, and the Japanese army radioed the defective information to Rabaul. It was relayed to Ugaki and Yamamoto, and the *Yamato's* towering radio antennae told Kondo and Nagumo to charge south toward the island and seek battle with the American fleet. The advance force passed through Indispensable Strait, north of Malaita. There it was intercepted by five SBDs from Guadalcanal, which planted bombs on a destroyer and a light cruiser, the *Yura*. The ships turned tail and ran, leaving the stricken *Yura* to be abandoned and scuttled.

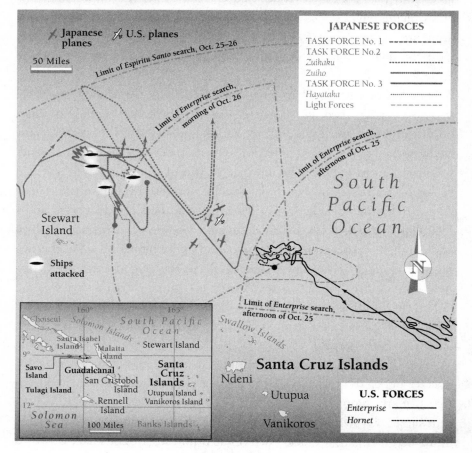

Battle of the Santa Cruz Islands October 25–26, 1942

Task Force 61 had meanwhile advanced along the northern shoals of the Santa Cruz group, and then turned southwest toward a point just east of San Cristobal. Throughout the long daylight hours of October 25, the two fleets steamed toward one another as air patrols reached out and probed ahead. A PBY spotted two big Japanese carriers at 11:03 a.m., but in a position 355 nautical miles from Task Force 61, far out of range. At 12:50 p.m., the seaplane tender *Curtiss* relayed a sighting report from one of her seaplanes, reporting two Japanese carriers to the northwest, 360 miles away. Closing on the enemy at near-maximum speed, Kinkaid made the chancy decision to launch a twenty-nine-plane composite strike. The planes went out to the end of their search vectors, continued eighty miles to the northwest, and finally turned back in the failing light. The F4F pilots of Fighting Squadron Ten flew for three and a half hours at 17,000 feet, exhausting themselves, their oxygen supply, and their fuel.[6] As they spiraled down through broken cloud cover, the *Enterprise* was nowhere to be seen. Running on fumes, they descended to just 15 to 20 feet above the sea, until Swede Vejtasa caught sight of an oil slick reflected in his own running lights. The Wildcats followed that greasy trail for forty-five miles and found the ship.[7] Several were forced to ditch at sea due to fuel exhaustion, or crashed while trying to land on the *Enterprise* in darkness.[8]

A full moon rose in the east and threw enough light across the sea to accommodate nighttime air searches. PBYs from Ndeni continued to blanket the area. At 3:10 a.m., one spotted the long, darkened flight deck of the *Zuikaku*. Kinkaid cocked his air group for a night bombing attack, and the aircrews remained in their ready rooms all night. But without further confirmation of the enemy fleet's position, the admiral prudently chose to keep the strike on deck until dawn.

At first light on October 26, the two groups were only about 200 miles apart. The weather was fair, with clear visibility above and below a 2,000-foot layer of scattered cumulus and stratocumulus clouds. The sea was smooth and the northwest breeze less than 10 knots.[9] Passing rainsqualls would continue throughout the day. Two Dauntlesses of Kinkaid's morning search flight discovered the *Zuiho* at 7:40 a.m. and attacked her directly. Both dive-bombers scored, pitching their 500-pound bombs into the middle of her flight deck. The little flattop survived but could neither launch nor recover aircraft for the remainder of the battle.[10]

About ten minutes later, some miles north, two more *Enterprise* SBDs discovered the *Shokaku* and *Zuikaku*. They radioed the contact report and prepared to dive, but defending Zeros broke up the attack. Both planes escaped by dodging into a cloud bank.

Nagumo and Kinkaid now hurled their principal airstrikes at one another. Strung out over fifty or sixty miles in three separated groups, the American planes were vulnerable to the concentrated attentions of the Zeros passing on a reciprocal heading. Nine Japanese fighters dived unseen out of the sun on the *Enterprise* torpedo planes of VT-10, and sent three TBFs down in flames before the American aircrews had even registered the enemy's presence.[11] Misleading oddments of radio chatter confused and mis-led aviators in the trailing squadrons. The surviving *Enterprise* Avengers had lost altitude in their tussle with the Zeros, thus shrinking their visible horizon. Finding no carriers, they attacked the *Chikuma*, inflicting heavy damage on the Japanese cruiser but failing to sink her.[12] At 10:50, the first wave of *Hornet* planes converged on the *Shokaku*. Lieutenant Commander William J. "Gus" Widhelm, commander of the *Hornet's* VS-8, kept his trac-ers centered on a Zero coming directly toward him in a head-on run and blew the plane apart, then dived sharply to evade the oncoming debris. A second Zero darted in from a high side and fired two or more 20mm rounds into his engine with a full deflection shot. Widhelm's engine emitted black oil smoke, then seized, and he dropped out of the battle. (He ditched safely and was recovered later with his radio-gunner, George D. Stokely.) Though he had been roughly handled by the Zeros, Widhelm's determination to manage his aircraft like a fighter rather than a dive-bomber had diverted the enemy's attention from the remaining *Hornet* SBDs, which reached their attacking positions and pushed into their dives.[13]

The *Shokaku*, according to a VB-8 radio-gunner, was lit up all along her length by antiaircraft fire, "like a Christmas tree,"[14] but the Dauntlesses plunged through the flak and released their 1,000-pound armor-piercing bombs. Three smashed through the flight deck and exploded in the inte-rior of the ship, with spectacularly destructive effect.[15] From the bridge of a screening destroyer, Captain Tameichi Hara saw "two or three silver streaks, which appeared like thunderbolts, reaching toward the bulky carrier. . . . The whole deck bulged quietly and burst. Flames shot from the cleavages. I groaned as the flames rose and black and white smoke came belching out of the deck."[16]

By 10:30 a.m., the Americans had knocked two Japanese carriers out of action, an impressive score even if neither ship was destroyed. In the meantime, however, more than a hundred Japanese planes were converg-ing on the *Hornet* and *Enterprise*. The American radar sets first detected the incoming Japanese strike at 9:05 a.m., and the task force raised speed for evasive maneuvering. The combat air patrol first made contact with the enemy planes at 9:59, when they were at 17,000 feet altitude, about forty miles northwest of the task force. The *Enterprise* managed to take cover in a passing rainsquall, but her disappearance diverted the full brunt of the enemy air attack to the *Hornet*.

"Stand by for dive bombing attack," warned the *Hornet*'s loudspeakers at 9:09, and down came a long convoy of steeply diving Aichi "Val" dive-bombers. Tearing through the sea at 28 knots, the carrier S-turned radically and her antiaircraft guns threw up a dense barrage, but several planes made accurate releases at the near-suicidal altitude of 800 feet. Three 250-kilogram bombs crashed through the *Hornet*'s flight deck in quick succession and exploded in the lower decks. A damaged Aichi dived vertically into the island, its pilot apparently determined to trade his life for a chance to destroy the ship's brain center. The burning plane glanced off the stack, sheered through the signal bridge, and crashed into the flight deck amidships.[17] Saturated with burning aviation gasoline, the *Hornet*'s entire superstructure burst into flames. According to Alvin Kernan, stationed in a repair shack just below the island, "a bright red flame came like an express train down the passageway, throwing everything and everybody flat."[18]

At about the same time, low-flying Japanese torpedo planes approached on the starboard and port sides simultaneously. They attempted to fly over or around the screening ships to get to the *Hornet*. One of the *South Dakota*'s 40mm quad mounts destroyed an oncoming Nakajima when it was just thirty yards away—"sawed the wing right off it," a witness recalled.[19] Another enemy plane hopped over the *South Dakota* and crashed, apparently deliberately, into the port side of the *Hornet*. Burning wreckage skittered across the flight deck and fell into the No. 1 elevator pit.[20] Two aerial torpedoes slammed into the wounded carrier's starboard side, lifting the entire hull and shaking it violently. Propulsion, fire main pressure, power, and internal communications were lost, and the *Hornet* listed 10 degrees to starboard.[21]

At 9:50, the *Enterprise* CXAM radar detected a second wave of incoming enemy dive-bombers. The *Enterprise* and her nearby escorts put up a prodigious barrage and destroyed half the Aichis in that first dive, but the survivors pressed the attack with skill and determination and planted three bombs on the flight deck. The first struck near the bow, destroying one airplane and ejecting another off the *Enterprise*, then punched through four layers of steel plating before detonating just outside the bow.[22] A second hit just aft of the forward elevator on the centerline of the flight deck and exploded below the hangar deck. A third bomb was a near miss to starboard, causing the entire ship to shudder and tossing another plane overboard.

Those heavy blows did not slow the *Enterprise* at all, and even while maneuvering radically, the ship somehow managed to recover several of her returning planes. But the second explosion jammed her forward elevator in the up position, reducing her plane-handling capabilities by at least 50 percent. Damage-control parties put hoses on the fire and fitted steel plates over the holes on the flight deck. The hangar was a mess, however—the entire deck was bulged upward and strewn with bodies and parts of bodies and blazing aircraft wreckage.

Fifteen dark-green "Kate" torpedo planes approached the *Enterprise* at 11:35. They divided into two groups and maneuvered to set up an "anvil attack" on both bows. Captain Osborne B. Hardison ordered the helm hard right, turning the *Enterprise* toward one group and leaving the other far astern. Floyd Beaver watched from the signal bridge as the second group attempted to overtake the ship, flying parallel on the beam at about 1,500 yards' range, "strung out like tin ducks in a shooting gallery."[23] The 40mm Bofors quadruple-barrel mounts cut them down methodically, one by one. The second group released their torpedoes, and Hardison deftly turned the ship toward the oncoming tracks and threaded them neatly. Men in the port gun galleries looked down and watched one of the long black cylindrical shapes speed away in the opposite direction, just beneath the surface. At 12:20, the injured *Enterprise* took cover in another passing rainsquall.[24]

With the *Enterprise* severely damaged and the *Hornet* crippled, and with new Japanese airstrikes arriving every thirty to sixty minutes, Admiral Kinkaid sensibly chose to put some distance between Task Force 61 and the enemy. All ships but the *Hornet* and a cohort of her screening destroyers and cruisers steamed away to the southeast and disappeared over the horizon.

The *Hornet* was a blazing, listing, foundering wreck. Her engineering spaces were heavily flooded, and her propulsion gone. At half past noon, the cruiser *Northampton* was summoned to tow the ship. A steel cable, run from the cruiser to the carrier's anchor chain, promptly broke. Two hours later, another attempt was made with a two-inch cable stowed on the *Hornet*, muscled up to the bow by the sweaty, backbreaking effort of more than 500 men. "With a 15-degree list then on the ship, this was pretty difficult," one officer remarked. "There was foam all over the hangar deck, so it was slippery as hell."[25] The *Northampton* gradually got the listing giant underway at 3 to 4 knots, but in the ensuing seven hours a relentless series of air attacks fell on the ship.[26]

When the last torpedo hit the *Hornet*, at 6:15 p.m., Commander E. P. Creehan was in one of the repair shacks below: "The deck on the port side seemed to crack open and a geyser of fuel oil which quickly reached a depth of two feet swept all personnel at Repair V off their feet and flung them head long down the sloping deck of Repair V compartment to the starboard side. Floundering around in the fuel oil, all personnel somehow regained their feet and a hand chain was formed to the two-way ladder and escape scuttle leading from the third deck to the second deck."[27]

The escorting destroyers drew in close and began removing wounded men from the fantail. Pitching and rolling on the waves, the little ships clanged violently against the carrier, and their rigging fouled into the *Hornet*'s catwalk, tearing away their radar and fire control equipment.

With the list increased to 25 degrees, posing an imminent danger of capsize, the captain ordered the crew to abandon ship. Most went over the side, either down knotted lines or by simply swimming from the hangar deck, which was awash along the length of the starboard side. In the water, the swimmers stayed together and kept excellent discipline. One officer was impressed to see thirty men on a small life raft, paddling toward a destroyer, singing "Sidewalks of New York" at the top of their lungs and badly out of tune.[28]

The destroyers *Mustin* and *Anderson* were given the grim order to scuttle the ship. But it was no easy task to sink an aircraft carrier, even one as badly damaged as the *Hornet*. The two tin cans put at least sixteen torpedoes into the ship, nine of which detonated. They followed with hundreds of rounds of 5-inch ammunition, antiaircraft fire, and even star shells aimed at the avgas storage tanks. These efforts set the ship ablaze, but they also apparently flooded the port side of the ship, because she returned to an even keel, albeit much lower in the water. At last, the two destroyers were called away to the south so that they would not be sitting ducks for a morning air attack. The Japanese destroyers *Makigumu* and *Akigumo* finally delivered the *coup de grace*, putting four torpedoes into the burning ghost ship at 1:25 a.m. on October 27. As the enemy sailors watched, she slipped beneath the waves and set out on her journey into the abyss.

THE BATTLE OF THE SANTA CRUZ ISLANDS, as it would be called, was the fourth carrier battle of the war and the last until the Battle of the Philippine Sea in June 1944. As at Coral Sea, the contest would go into the books as a tactical victory for the Japanese but a strategic victory for the Americans. The destruction of the *Hornet* left the Allies with just one carrier in the theater. In exchange, the Americans had damaged two Japanese carriers but destroyed neither. Plane losses were roughly comparable—eighty-one for the Americans, ninety-nine for the Japanese. But the Americans, as usual, did a much better job of recovering their downed aviators. They lost only twenty-six airmen while the Japanese lost 148, and among the latter's dead were twenty-three squadron or section leaders, all prized veteran flyers who could not be easily replaced.

The Japanese claimed and apparently believed they had inflicted catastrophic losses on the American fleet. Admiral Nagumo, in his post-action report to Yamamoto, stated that four American carriers had been "attacked and sunk."[29] The commander of Cruiser Division 8 (CruDiv8) reported three carriers sunk, including the *Enterprise*, the *Hornet*, and "a third vessel [that] may be the *Saratoga*."[30] The CruDiv8 report also claimed sinking the *South Dakota*, three cruisers, and a destroyer. (In fact, the Americans had lost the *Hornet* and the destroyer *Porter*, and suffered damage to the *Enterprise*, the *South Dakota*, the cruiser *San Juan*, and several destroyers.)

The Japanese press reported another triumph, and the rank and file cheered another fantastic victory. But the senior commanders of the navy privately acknowledged that the result had been, at best, a pyrrhic victory. Cumulatively, in the four carrier fights that took place in the five months between the Battles of the Coral Sea and the Santa Cruz Islands, the Japanese had lost more than 400 carrier airmen, more than half the number that had been on active duty at the start of the war. Admiral Nagumo was well aware that the recurring carrier slugging matches were draining away the Imperial Navy's strength. "Considering the great superiority of our enemy's industrial capacity," he told Tameichi Hara, "we must win every battle overwhelmingly. This last one, unfortunately, was not an overwhelming victory."[31] Nagumo was relieved of his command and transferred back to the home islands, where he would assume command of the Sasebo Naval Station on the southern island of Kyushu.

The encounter ended as all previous carrier duels had ended, with a mutual retreat of all naval forces from the area. The *Enterprise*, severely damaged though she was, was patched up in Noumea and put back into action in time for the climactic naval battles in Ironbottom Sound less than three weeks later. The two injured Japanese flattops, *Shokaku* and *Junyo*, had to limp back to Japan for repairs. *Shokaku*, the more valuable of the two, would not return to action until June 1943, half a year after the campaign to recapture Guadalcanal had been abandoned. With postwar hindsight, Halsey summed the battle up thus: "Tactically, we picked up the dirty end of the stick, but strategically we handed it back."[32] The judgment seems incontrovertible.

TANAKA'S INDEFATIGABLE "TOKYO EXPRESS" managed to put more than 20,000 troops ashore in mid-October and the first week of November. Those reinforcements brought Japanese and American troop strength to approximate parity, although the Japanese chronically underestimated the size of Vandegrift's force and by November believed they had superior numbers. But the rapid buildup of Japanese troop strength also left them more vulnerable to air and sea attack, because it was no easy task to hide 20,000 men and their supplies under jungle canopies and in dark ravines. Day after day, the Cactus Air Force worked over their encampments, fortifications, and supply dumps with bombs and lethal strafing runs.

Since September, the Japanese had often brought their big naval guns into Ironbottom Sound to shell Henderson Field and the American positions on Lunga Plain. On the night of October 29–30, the Americans gave their adversaries some of the same consideration. The light cruiser *Atlanta* and four destroyers shelled Japanese camps inland of Point Cruz for eight hours. Five nights later, the cruisers *San Francisco* and *Helena* trained their guns on Japanese positions east of Koli Point and laid waste to newly landed supply dumps. Troops bivouacked in the area were forced back into the jungle, where the harsh toll of starvation and disease would gradually cull their numbers. The Japanese army now had many more mouths to feed on Guadalcanal, but it lacked the logistical capability to provide for them. Men living on fewer than 500 calories a day could not be expected to work or march, let alone fight.

On November 1, Vandegrift ordered an offensive to the west, aimed at overrunning the headquarters of the Seventeenth Army (located near the coast just west of Point Cruz) and capturing enemy supplies recently landed at Tassafaronga. Six battalions of the 5th Marines, led by Colonel Merritt Edson, crossed the Matanikau River on pontoon bridges and attacked the Japanese army's Fourth Infantry Regiment. In two days of hard fighting around Point Cruz, some 400 Japanese were killed, and the rest retreated across the Poha River. The rout secured Henderson Field from the enemy's artillery fire. But Tanaka's destroyers continued to land troop reinforcements on the island's western beaches—and these fresh troops, not yet weakened by hunger and tropical diseases, were deployed to positions around the mouth of the Poha. For the moment, that stymied any further near-term progress in that direction.

The marines remembered October 25 as "Dugout Sunday." The sirens churned two or three times an hour, signaling "Condition Red" (enemy planes approaching). Japanese bombers were overhead for much of the day, and the Zeros flew a relentless series of strafing runs, riddling the parked planes and dugouts and field installations with incendiary ammunition. Torrential rains in the preceding days and nights had made a mud bath of the landing fields and prevented the fighters from getting aloft until midday, after the sun finally dried the field. When the Wildcats managed to take station at high altitude, however, they gave a good account of themselves, and the army P-400s pounced on Zeros winging in at 10,000 feet or less. Clemens fondly remembered the sight of a Zero blown to pieces above Henderson Field: "The tail plane floated down, turning over and over like a falling leaf. And so it went on all day."[33]

The balance of power in the air war had shifted gradually but decisively in the Americans' favor. The long daily "milk run" from Rabaul wore the Japanese airmen down and reduced their chances of returning to base. They were no less susceptible to fatigue than were the Americans, but the Japanese navy did not systematically rotate their veteran pilots out of the combat zone. "They won't let you go home unless you die" was an unofficial motto of the Japanese naval air corps.[34] The *Yamato* spirit, a nationalist creed rooted in the emperor's divinity, would sustain the energy and determination of every warrior. So it was said and believed. As combat attrition reduced the numbers of veteran aviators, they were replaced with green men recently graduated from truncated flight-training programs. The newcomers did not press home their attacks in the face of antiaircraft fire and were more easily shot down. Their formations tended to come unglued during the long southbound flights, and they were more likely to get lost when visibility was poor. The long return to Rabaul was a deadly disadvantage.

Belatedly, the Japanese began to build or expand airfields between Rabaul and Guadalcanal—Kahili on southern Bougainville, Ballale Island (in the Shortland group), Buka Island (north of Bougainville), Lae on New Guinea—but none of these achieved the status of a major forward airbase, and they were most often employed as emergency strips for aircraft staggering back toward Rabaul. Japanese construction battalions were underequipped and manned by largely unskilled draftees from Korea, Okinawa, or Taiwan. Lieutenant Commander Iyozo Fujita, a Zero pilot based at Rabaul, recalled that in the last extremity pilots were told to ditch their planes near islands occupied by the Japanese army. "Unfortunately, there was no guarantee that you could get back to your home base from there."[35]

The Bougainville-based coastwatchers continued to send their priceless forewarnings of southbound enemy air formations. Jack Read, whose beard had descended almost to the neck of his shirt, enjoyed the afternoon ritual of watching the surviving remnants of Japanese flights as they flew overhead in groups of two or three.[36] The Japanese knew perfectly well that two Allied coastwatchers were hiding in the bush at the northern and southern ends of Bougainville, and were determined to get rid of them. Paul Mason learned from native spies that a hundred Japanese troops and a number of tracker dogs had gathered at Buin and would soon come after him. He called in an airstrike that killed the dogs in their cages. Both men had remarkable success in holding a tenuous grasp on the loyalty of native villages. Though their presence was known by hundreds of people in dozens of villages, none betrayed them to the Japanese.

IN WASHINGTON, HAP ARNOLD TOLD HIS COLLEAGUES on the Joint Chiefs of Staff that the South Pacific was oversupplied with airpower. He had returned from his inspection trip through the region armed with statistics purporting to show that Halsey's and MacArthur's theaters held a commanding margin (by number of aircraft) over the enemy. His accounting was close to the mark, but the rapid attrition on both sides required constant reinforcement. Guadalcanal was becoming the "sinkhole" for Japanese airpower that Admiral John S. McCain had advertised, but the scale and ferocity of the South Pacific air war could be sustained only by drawing down commitments to Europe, especially to Britain. As Washington's most tenacious custodian of the "Germany-first" principle, Arnold was impatient to expand the bombing campaign against the Reich. He had opposed the North African invasion (TORCH) on the same grounds.

Admiral McCain, having been succeeded as COMAIRSOPAC by Aubrey Fitch, returned to Washington to assume command of the navy's Bureau of Aeronautics. There he instigated a quiet campaign to relieve Arnold of his job. McCain told anyone who would listen that the USAAF "did not know how to operate over the sea, that they have not been trained for this work, and that, instead of admitting their failure, they were try-ing to discredit the performance of the navy's air arm."[37] In budget talks for 1944, the two services were at loggerheads over the expansion of naval shore-based aviation. McCain believed the army would put up with aircraft carriers but was determined to control all land-based aircraft, even those engaged in attacking the enemy's naval forces. The admirals were irritated by the USAAF's tendency to publicize exaggerated claims of bombing suc-cess. Ten months of warfare had established that bombs dropped from alti-tude almost never hit ships operating at sea. In defiance of the evidence, the army's public communiqués declared large numbers of Japanese fleet units sunk or "probably sunk" by B-17s or other army bombers. When those same ships later appeared off Guadalcanal, the navy was not amused.

But the political winds were blowing against Arnold. Admirals King and Leahy, two of the four joint chiefs, had the ear of the president. While preparations for TORCH progressed in secrecy, the South Pacific was the only theater in which American forces were heavily engaged. As the site of the first offensive taken by the Allies in any theater, the Solomons had attained outsized symbolic and political importance. The raid on Pearl Har-bor was being avenged on Guadalcanal, and the American people heartily approved. On October 23, FDR backed Leahy's request for twenty more 7,000-ton cargo ships to resupply the South Pacific. That same day, when news reached the White House of the sinking of the *Hornet*, the commander in chief penned a strongly worded memorandum to his military chiefs:

My anxiety about the S.W. Pac. is to make sure that every possible weapon gets into that area to hold Guadalcanal, and that, having held in this crisis, that munitions, planes and crews are on the way to take advantage of our success. We will soon find ourselves engaged in two active fronts and we must have adequate air support in both places even tho it means delaying our other commitments, particularly to England. Our long-range plans could be set back for months if we fail to throw our full strength in our immediate and impending conflicts.[38]

After the war, Arnold acidly observed that the president, with a stroke of his pen, had upended the "Europe-first" strategy. But what could he do but swallow his pride and obey?

"I HAD TO BEGIN THROWING PUNCHES almost immediately," Halsey wrote Nimitz shortly after assuming command at Noumea.[39] There was no transitional period, no time to attend to the details of setting up his headquarters or staff. Urgent decisions confronted him right away.

Ghormley had never visited Guadalcanal, and Halsey was not about to make the same mistake. On November 8, he flew into Henderson Field. Vandegrift met him at the airfield and conducted him on a jeep tour of the front lines. The admiral's uniform was nondescript khaki, so many of the marines in the trenches had no idea who or what he was until he disembarked from the jeep and stood among them.

Security required that the arrival of such an exalted figure as COM-SOPAC never be announced in advance. There was no "Potemkin village" effect—no sprucing up, no turning the men out in their best uniforms, no parade-ground reviews. Urged by his staff to stand up in the jeep or to wave as he passed, Halsey refused: "It smells of exhibitionism. The hell with it!"[40] The marines were dumbstruck by the three stars on his collar, but the admiral quickly put the men at ease. He asked questions and listened. He noted their malarial emaciation and witnessed the deplorable conditions in which they lived and fought, and agreed with Vandegrift that they must be relieved by the army as soon as possible. In impromptu remarks to the island's press representatives, Halsey first coined the bloody-minded motto that would make him famous: "Kill Japs, kill Japs, and keep on killing Japs!"[41] Asked if victory would require an invasion of the Japanese home islands, he replied that he hoped so and looked forward to the carnage such an operation would inevitably entail.[42]

For all his bravado, Halsey did not mind owning up to his own fear. When a Japanese destroyer in Ironbottom Sound exchanged fire with marine artillery, Halsey could not sleep. "It wasn't the noise that kept me awake," he wrote, "it was fright. I called myself yellow—and worse—and told myself to 'go to sleep, you damned coward!' but it didn't do any good; I couldn't obey orders."[43]

ADMIRAL TURNER RUSHED A CONVOY OF FAST TRANSPORTS, accompanied by cruisers and destroyers, out of Noumea and Espiritu Santo between November 8 and 10. Sighting reports and intelligence estimates suggested that another major enemy naval force would descend on Ironbottom Sound the night of November 12–13, and Turner wanted his ships clear of the area before they arrived. Turner's plan depended on the rapid unloading of the transports and cargo ships—at all costs the troops and supplies must be put onto the beach by Thursday night, November 12. The cargo ships and transports were supported by two cruiser-destroyer squadrons commanded by Rear Admirals Daniel J. Callaghan and Norman Scott. In hopes of avoiding air detection, they would approach Guadalcanal by the long route south of San Cristobal. The first elements entered Ironbottom Sound in the small hours of November 11.

Later that morning, the *Enterprise* threaded the intricate channel out of Noumea Harbor and put to sea. The carrier was still licking her wounds sustained in the Battle of the Santa Cruz Islands. Her forward elevator remained jammed in the up position, her hull was taking on water, and the warren of corridors and staterooms known as "officers' country" remained a blackened and misshapen wreck.[44] In company was Task Force 64, under the command of Rear Admiral Willis A. "Ching" Lee: the two fast battleships *Washington* and *South Dakota* with supporting destroyers. By Halsey's orders, the combined task forces (still under the overall command of Admiral Kinkaid) were designated Task Force KING. They were to take station well south of Guadalcanal, avoiding the better-traveled sea-lanes to the north in hopes of eluding submarine predators and enemy reconnaissance flights.

On November 11 and 12, the transport fleet anchored off Lunga Point and carried out their race-against-the-clock unloading procedures. On the afternoon of the second day, a flight of torpedo-armed Mitsubishi Type 1 planes approached low over the green hills of the Nggela Islands. They fanned out into two groups, skimming over the water at an altitude of 30 to 40 feet, evidently intending to attack simultaneously from the north and south.[45] The fleet threw up an antiaircraft barrage so thick that it appeared almost as a wall of black smoke. The *San Francisco's* 5-inch guns, fired at near-maximum depression, took down two planes in the first salvo. The Mitsubishis veered right and left, maneuvering radically to avoid being hit. Lieutenant (jg) Flavius J. George of the *Pawnee* left a contemporary description of the raid in his diary: "One plane, then another and another exploded in a burst of flame or nosed over into the sea with a tremendous splash. In a matter of seconds only four were left and these launched their torpedoes wildly, and frantically banked away from the deadly fire."[46]

Of the four torpedoes dropped, none registered a hit on an American ship. One "porpoised" and then seemed to dive; another made a circular run and did not detonate; one actually rebounded off the sea and nearly struck the plane that had dropped it. Antiaircraft fire from the ships and the Guadalcanal-based fighters destroyed all the planes save one, which managed to dodge into a low bank of dark cloud. But one of the damaged aircraft suicide-crashed into the *San Francisco's* superstructure and exploded in a ball of fire. The attack killed fifteen men and wounded twenty-nine, most of whom suffered grievous burns.[47]

Air searches up the Slot revealed several inbound columns of enemy warships, including *Kongo*-class battleships. Turner pulled the fleet out through Sealark Channel at sundown. He placed his cruisers and most of his destroyers under the tactical command of Admiral Callaghan, who would be left behind to grapple with the incoming Japanese force. Lacking battleships, Callaghan's thirteen warships would be badly overmatched. But if they could inflict enough punishment on the enemy, they might at least spare the marines another holocaust of 14-inch bombardment. Kinkaid's group could follow the next day to despoil the enemy's planned troop landings.

American officers who knew of the reported presence of Japanese battleships were none too happy. The captain of the destroyer *Fletcher* remarked caustically: "Seems funny to be fighting battleships with destroyers and a few cruisers."[48] Cassin Young, captain of Callaghan's flagship *San Francisco*, was overheard telling the admiral that the mission amounted to suicide.[49]

At exactly midnight, Callaghan's ships crept back into Ironbottom Sound. It was a dark night, with dense overcast and no moon. There was no breeze, and the sea was as smooth as a mill pond. Men could barely make out the other ships in the column, though they were only about 500 yards apart. The glowing greenish phosphorescence stirred up by their wakes trailed away to the south. The date was Friday the thirteenth.

The enemy revealed itself only gradually. Radar scopes showed blips in the northwest at ranges between 27,000 and 32,000 yards. The Japanese seemed to be arranged in two parallel columns of four and six ships, and Callaghan steered toward the gap between them. When the radar range had dropped to about 1,100 yards, American lookouts first perceived vague silhouettes moving across the landmasses of the islands to the north.[50]

The action began when a powerful searchlight suddenly illuminated the upper works of the San Francisco. Both sides opened fire simultaneously, and the battle quickly degenerated into a general melee, with ships drifting out of position and firing indiscriminately on whatever enemy units they could bring to bear. Callaghan ordered, "Odd ships fire to starboard, even to port," but it was often difficult to distinguish friend from foe. The scene was intermittently lit by searchlights, flares, muzzle flashes, star shells, streams of tracers, and the yellow thunderclaps of exploding ships. Lieutenant C. Raymond Calhoun of the Sterett was reminded of "a no-holds-barred barroom brawl, in which someone turned out the lights and everyone started swinging in every direction—only this was ten thousand times worse. Shells continued to drop all around us, star shells and flares flung overhead, tracers whizzed past from various directions, and everywhere we looked ships burned and exploded against the backdrop of the night sky."[51]

The American TBS circuits became overloaded and confused, and not all the ships heard the instructions coming from the officer in tactical command (OTC). Destroyers altered course to bring their broadsides to bear on enemy ships, deranging the American formation. The destroyer O'Bannon had to steer aggressively to avoid her sister the Sterett, but her movements placed her in the course of the cruiser Atlanta, which also had to execute an emergency turn. The San Francisco fired on and badly mauled her sister the Atlanta. At 1:51 a.m., Callaghan ordered a cease-fire and attempted to identify his own ships. The order went out by TBS: "Turn on lights for about three seconds."[52] But the circuits were badly overloaded, and in the deadly chaos the order did not get through to most American ships.

On the whole, it was now a case of every ship for herself. "Occasionally a blinding flare and rumbling blast would indicate that some ship had blown up," wrote Lieutenant George in his diary, "and we would catch momentary glimpses of black and smoke shrouded shapes belching flame."[53] An observer on the beach at Guadalcanal thought the scene "resembled a door to hell opening and closing, opening and closing, over and over."[54]

The *San Francisco* headed off to starboard and became separated from her sisters, and then found herself staring down the giant 14-inch barrels of the battleship *Hiei*. She opened fire and struck first, and the *Hiei* was slow to respond, possibly because she could not depress her guns quickly enough. Several American destroyers also crossed paths with the leviathan. The *Cushing* fired six torpedoes at the *Hiei* from a range of 1,200 yards, scoring perhaps three hits. The *O'Bannon* added three more torpedoes. The *Laffey* crossed the *Hiei*'s towering bow with barely a few yards to spare, and was almost overrun by the monstrous ship. She fired two torpedoes, which failed to arm before they were stopped by the *Hiei*'s hull, then followed with several 5-inch rounds fired into the battleship's bridge structure.

From a range of 1,000 yards, the *Sterett* poured nine salvos of 5-inch into the *Hiei*'s bridge—thirty-six shells—and every one hit. The *Sterett* crossed her bow at a range of only about 500 yards, close enough that the crew could see Japanese sailors running along the deck with their clothes on fire. The *Hiei* burned brightly from stem to stern; explosions rippled along her length; men leapt from her decks into the sea; and burning debris rained down on ships all around her.

The abandoned *Cushing* drifted and burned out of control. The *O'Bannon* steered wildly to get out of the way of her sister, the badly stricken *Laffey*. A torpedo struck the destroyer *Barton* and tore her in half. Her bow section bobbed one way, her stern the other, and both sections sank within seconds. About forty of her crew survived and swam through her debris and the oil slick she had left on the surface. Some were overrun and drowned by other ships, or killed or injured by depth-charge explosions in the water nearby.

Both the *Portland* and the *Juneau* were struck by torpedoes and made their way out of the action as best they could. The *Portland* circled aimlessly, her steering and propellers damaged, but she still managed to fire a few salvos at a damaged *Shiguri*-class destroyer south of Savo Island. The *Helena*, in better shape than most of her sisters, fired at strange ships off her starboard beam.

The *San Francisco* drifted through the center of the action, bruised but

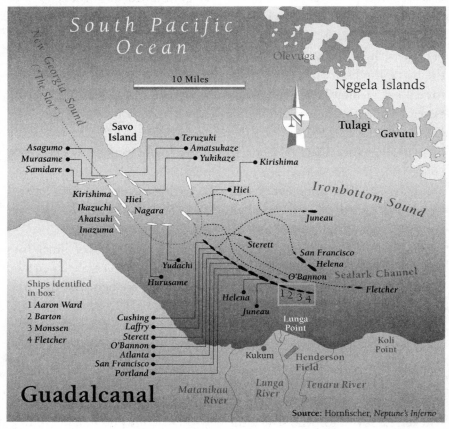

Naval Battle of Guadalcanal, Phase One
November 13, 1942

South Pacific Ocean

New Georgia Sound ("The Slot")

10 Miles

Olevuga

Nggela Islands

Savo Island

N

Tulagi
Gavutu

Asagumo
Murasame
Samidare

Teruzuki
Amatsukaze
Yukikaze

Kirishima

Kirishima
Ikazuchi
Akatsuki
Inazuma

Hiei
Nagara

Hiei

Ironbottom Sound

Juneau

Sterett

San Francisco
Helena

Yudachi

Hurusame

Helena

Juneau

O'Bannon

Sealark Channel

Fletcher

1 2 3 4

Ships identified in box:
1 Aaron Ward
2 Barton
3 Monssen
4 Fletcher

Cushing
Laffry
Sterett
O'Bannon
Atlanta
San Francisco
Portland

Lunga Point

Kukum

Henderson Field

Koli Point

Guadalcanal

Matanikau River

Lunga River

Tenaru River

Source: Hornfischer, *Neptune's Inferno*

not knocked out, firing everything she had at the *Hiei*. In turn, however, the *Hiei* planted several large-caliber shells on the *San Francisco*, including one that struck the bridge on the starboard side and killed Admiral Callaghan and most of his staff. Both Captain Young and his executive officer were grievously wounded and died within a few hours. One of the senior surviving officers went up to the navigation bridge and found not a living soul, then went looking for Admiral Callaghan or his staff and "found them all in one heap on the starboard side of the signal bridge, all apparently dead."[55] Lieutenant Commander Bruce McCandless, officer of the deck, took the conn and made for Cape Esperance, taking the badly mauled cruiser out of the line of fire. But the *San Francisco*'s main battery continued pumping out one salvo after another until the *Hiei* silenced her entirely.

Dawn revealed an awful scene. Ironbottom Sound was littered with burning wreckage, oil, and floating bodies. Hulks of ships drifted and burned, their smashed superstructures leaning drunkenly over the sea, their gun turrets collapsed and hanging over the hulls. Hundreds of oil-saturated survivors clung to debris and called for assistance. Small boats plied to and fro, picking them up. With rare exceptions, the Japanese sailors in the water refused to be picked up, and some attempted to drown themselves rather than be taken prisoner. The *Hiei* was seen brightly afire, moving slowly north of Savo Island, apparently without control of her rudder, accompanied by several smaller ships. Lieutenant George of the *Pawnee*, detailed to take survivors off the *Atlanta*, described the mortally wounded ship: "Her entire superstructure had been shot away and her three forward turrets were like shattered egg crates out of which stuck distorted and twisted guns. Her main deck was almost awash and on it huddled the grimy and dazed remnant of her crew."[56] The survivors were taken off by landing boats, and a demolition party went aboard to set charges in the engine room. She sank shortly after 8:00 a.m.

The *Helena*, least damaged of the American cruisers, led a column of six smashed ships toward Sealark Channel. The *San Francisco* appeared so badly maimed that it seemed incredible she could make way at all—one witness on another ship counted twenty-six shell holes in her side.[57] Dead men were buried at sea in hasty ceremonies. Crewmen, utterly exhausted, snatched short periods of sleep wherever they could find a place to stretch out.

The *Juneau* was running low in the water, her decks almost awash. She could make only 13 knots and was slow to answer her helm.[58] At 11:01, some miles east of Guadalcanal, a torpedo fired by Japanese submarine *I-26* struck the ship in the port side and touched off the torpedo warheads in her magazine. The blast was so powerful that it blew men standing on the *San Francisco* flat on the deck.[59] Men glancing up from the other ships saw entire 5-inch gun barrels and large sections of the *Juneau*'s superstructure hurled high into the air. An enormous cloud of mostly yellow smoke hung there for several minutes, obscuring her position. Gradually, as the cloud rose off the surface, observers on the other ships scanned the sea and saw nothing. "There was not a stick, or a spar, or a boat, or a life buoy; nor was a single man visible," recalled an officer of the *Sterett*. "I strained to see a head, or a body; but as the smoke cleared, I could see absolutely nothing."[60] Lieutenant Graham C. Bonnell of the *San Francisco* agreed: "I looked over to the spot where the *Juneau* had been and saw only a large cloud of smoke. . . . And in a short space of time this smoke had completely cleared and you could see nothing but a wake going along and immediately stopping."[61]

The destroyers could establish no sonar contact on the submarine, nor was there any sign of it. Captain Gilbert Hoover of the *Helena*, eyeing the danger posed to the other ships, made the hardheaded decision to keep the remnants of the task force on course and underway. Officers would later say that they did not believe a single man on the *Juneau* could have survived the attack, and that impression was echoed by dozens of witnesses. In fact, 120 of her crew did survive the sinking. They drifted at sea for five days, clinging to three rafts connected by life nets, and dying one by one. Ten survivors washed up on Santa Catalina Island on November 18.

ADMIRAL KINKAID, on the *Enterprise* about 270 miles south of Guadalcanal, launched his dawn search on a wide arc from north to west, with the planes ordered to fly to a range of 200 miles. The still-wounded flight deck of the *Enterprise* was kept "cocked" to launch a large airstrike should enemy carriers be discovered. But the search found nothing. Later that morning, Kinkaid decided to send his torpedo planes on an offensive sweep up the Slot, with orders to land at Henderson Field and place themselves at the disposal of General Vandegrift's air department.

The Cactus Air Force, thus reinforced, turned its attention to the burning, listing *Hiei*, which was drifting north of Savo Island. The once-mighty battleship had absorbed about eighty-five shell hits and six or seven torpedoes. Her after turrets were smashed and hanging limply over her side. Smoke poured out of ruptures in her upper works and her forward turret. The *Enterprise* Avengers dropped torpedoes on her, scoring two hits on the port side and one on the starboard side. Several more flights from Henderson of both marine and navy planes assailed the smoking hulk, but she was a remarkably tough customer. At sunset she was not only still afloat but still making way. At dawn on the fourteenth, however, there was nothing to be seen but an enormous oil slick almost two miles in diameter.[62]

Henderson Field had come under bombardment that night by cruisers and destroyers, but the shelling was not particularly unnerving to men who had endured much worse. PT boats operating from Tulagi fired torpedoes on the hostile fleet and apparently drove them away. The Japanese ships were chased and taken under attack the next morning by *Enterprise* and Henderson-based planes, which probably scored some hits on one of the cruisers. Most important, however, was a sighting report at 9:49 that morning. An *Enterprise* scout spotted a large Japanese force north of New Georgia island, headed toward Guadalcanal at 14 knots. The pilot saw destroyers and "many enemy transports."[63]

This was Tanaka's latest attempt to land a major reinforcement—eleven troop-loaded transports screened by eleven destroyers, on a course of 140 degrees. By decree of Vandegrift, the transports were the overriding target for all Allied aircraft that could reach them. Throughout the afternoon, every plane that could fly from Henderson was fueled, armed, and sent up the Slot to attack. The pilots ignored the destroyers and concentrated all their efforts on the troopships. One *Enterprise* aviator judged that afternoon to be "the most hectic, frantic period of many that took place at Henderson Field. A coordinated effort between the Navy carrier pilots and their Marine brothers-in-arms, combined with a superhuman effort from the aviation ground support personnel, kept a steady stream of SBDs and TBFs carrying bombs and torpedoes shuttling back and forth from the field to the convoy targets."[64]

The slaughter was cold and meticulous. Jimmy Flatley's VF-10 fighters dived at 60-degree angles and raked the crowded troopships with their .50-caliber machine guns. Japanese soldiers leapt over the sides to escape the onslaught.[65] Army B-17s flying from Espiritu Santo got into the act later that afternoon. A torpedo dropped by a TBF ripped out the bowels of a 10,000-ton transport, which rolled over and sank in minutes. Planes circled overhead, then flew low over the debris and strafed the troops struggling to stay afloat. "There were rafts and boats all over the sea floating on an oil scum amidst chunks of wood and other stuff," recalled one of the Avenger pilots. "There were three transports still afloat when we opened up with our guns. We strafed the transports, the boats in the water, and everything else we saw, and so did the fighters."[66] It was hideous work, even "sickening," as one pilot said.[67] But not all the aviators were so squeamish; some proudly hailed themselves as the "Buzzard Brigade." The *Enterprise* action report observed that the work was done "with methodical and devastating effect."[68] By the end of the day, four troopships were sunk, and three more were on fire and limping back up the Slot toward Rabaul. Two more sank that night. Admiral Tanaka later reported that only 400 troops were killed, but that number seems unrealistically low.

IN SHARP CONTRAST TO THE METHODS OF HIS PREDECESSOR, Admiral Halsey chose to move the chess pieces around the board on his own initiative. By his prior instruction, the partially disabled *Enterprise* and her screening vessels remained well away to the south of Guadalcanal to avoid crossing paths with enemy aircraft or submarines.[69] At 3:42 p.m. on November 14, Halsey detached the *Washington* and *South Dakota* and directed them to proceed north, skirting the western edge of Guadalcanal, to take station south of Savo Island. The two big battlewagons, accompanied by four destroyers, were designated Task Force LOVE, commanded by Admiral Lee. They were to intercept enemy surface forces expected to enter Ironbottom that night.

Zigzagging north at 23 knots, Lee's force rounded the western shoals off Guadalcanal and arrived off Savo at midnight. He did not have to wait long for the enemy fleet to reveal itself. Strange lights were seen in the sky above the horizon to the west. Officers speculated that they might be the fires of burning ships around the Russell Islands. Radio monitors tuned in to the enemy's low-power ship-to-ship frequencies and caught some excitable Japanese chatter. Tulagi-based PT boats zoomed around Ironbottom Sound, and Lee's staff radioed urgent identification messages to avoid taking a friendly torpedo in the hull of one of his ships. It was another calm night. A light breeze blew from the south. A quarter moon was setting in the west, and visibility at sea level was good.

At midnight, the newly installed SG search radars began to pick up blips in the northwest. As the enemy ships came down the Slot, they entered the radar shadows of the landmasses of surrounding islands. Soon the American spotters, peering through optical sights, made out distant shapes moving on the horizon. Admiral Lee altered his course to 300 degrees and ordered the *South Dakota* to open fire once she obtained a good firing solution.

At 12:16 a.m., when the first ship in the enemy column was at a range of 18,500 yards, the *Washington*'s 16-inch batteries spoke up. Her first salvo of 16-inch armor-piercing shells straddled the target. The splashes could be seen on radar, and the gun elevations and trains adjusted accordingly. The second (or at least the third) salvo connected. The *South Dakota* opened up about a minute after her sister. With the benefit of radar fire control, she landed her first or second salvo on one of the closer ships in the Japanese column at a range of about 15,700 yards. The target blazed fiercely, providing a gratifying spectacle to the spotters. *South Dakota* turned her guns to the second ship in the column and scored several more hits. The Japanese task force was slow to respond and scored no hits in this first phase of the action.

The four American destroyers had held fire because the range was near the extreme limit of effectiveness of their 5-inch guns. At 12:20 a.m., a column of Japanese destroyers and light cruisers emerged from the southwestern edge of Savo Island. The *Walke*, the first destroyer in the American van, opened fire first, followed quickly by the *Benham*, *Gwin*, and *Preston*. One or more targets appeared to burst into flames. But the quartet of American destroyers soon took heavy punishment in turn. Several 6-inch projectiles landed on the *Preston*, laying waste to her fire rooms and killing dozens of her crew. The *Preston*'s stack collapsed, crushing the ship's searchlight. A Japanese heavy cruiser managed to sneak up on the port side of the four destroyers and added several 8-inch rounds to the *Preston*'s tally of woe. The little ship burst into flames, listed deeply to starboard, and began going down by the stern. Her captain ordered the crew to abandon ship. As the men were going over the side, fires reached her magazine and she went up in a yellow thunderclap. Debris rained down around the ship.

At about the same time, the *Benham* was struck by a torpedo on her starboard side. The foundering destroyer executed a sluggish starboard turn and limped away from the action. The *Walke* soldiered on, pumping 5-inch rounds at enemy ships off the south coast of Savo, until she was silenced by a series of heavy shells fired by an unidentified cruiser. Violent explosions blew slabs of her superstructure into the sea and set fires raging along her length. Her ready 20mm ammunition began "cooking off," and her deck began to buckle. Captain Thomas E. Fraser ordered the men to abandon ship as she began to go down by the head. She sank at 12:42 a.m. Her depth charges had been set to safe, but a few apparently detonated as the ship went down, injuring or killing several of her surviving crew.

The *Gwin* took a heavy salvo in her engine room. As her damage-control parties struggled to save the ship, her captain ordered an emergency starboard turn to avoid the sinking remains of the *Preston*. She took more shell hits as she limped out of the battle.

The *Washington*'s spotters, blinded by their ship's 16-inch muzzle flashes, lost visual contact with the enemy. Like their counterparts in the destroyers, they found the enemy by scanning the horizon for *his* muzzle flashes, and targeted them in return. The Japanese ships seemed to retreat beyond the black conical silhouette of Savo Island, perhaps fleeing the catastrophic punishment inflicted by the *Washington*'s 16-inch shells.

A brief lull in the action followed as repair crews scrambled to correct electrical failures apparently caused by the concussion of the *Washington*'s own guns, and her spotters scanned in vain for suitable targets. Where were the Japanese battleships?

The *Washington* increased speed to 26 knots and turned onto a course of 282 degrees. Her radar identified four large enemy ships coming into range south of Savo. While the *Washington* passed through and around the wreckage of the several crippled destroyers of the American van, her crew dropped life rafts over the side. The destroyers were in no condition to continue the fight, and the officer in tactical command ordered them to withdraw toward Guadalcanal as best they could.

South Dakota surged ahead at 26 knots on a course of 290 degrees, firing on targets off Savo at a range of about 14,000 yards. The blast force of her tremendous weapons set her own floatplanes on fire and then blew them off their catapults and over the side. Circuit breakers tripped and power was cut to much of the ship. At about 12:45, steering clear of the sinking remains of the van destroyers, the *South Dakota* drew up on the *Washington*'s starboard quarter.

The two battleships, without screening vessels, continued to the northwest. But the *South Dakota* diverged onto a more northerly course, which took her into illumination range of Japanese searchlights. That was a tactical blunder, as it would render moot the American advantage in fire control radar. The *Washington*'s main battery fired on the battleship *Kirishima*, the first ship in the enemy line. The *Kirishima* returned fire, and the two behemoths dueled for the next several minutes at what amounted to close range for guns of that caliber.

The superstructure of the *South Dakota*, illuminated by searchlights, was

Naval Battle of Guadalcanal, Phase Two
November 14–15, 1942

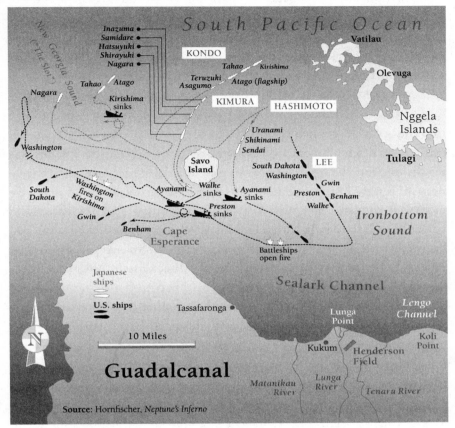

Source: Hornfischer, *Neptune's Inferno*

pounded by shells of many different calibers. The salvos destroyed much of her radar and communications equipment. She was unable to hail the flagship or even to see her. She was taking on water. Her turret 3 was inoperable, her fire control systems were seriously impaired, and she was leaking fuel.[70] A sailor recalled that "her decks were stacked high with dead, and sharp jagged edges from ripped steel were everywhere."[71]

All the Japanese guns fell silent at about 1:10 a.m., and the ships that could still make way began withdrawing to the northwest in apparent disorder. The *Washington* continued to pound away at the *Kirishima* and her screening vessels as they retired. Admiral Lee gave chase for the next twenty minutes, and his ship continued to land shells on the enemy. But he was wary of a torpedo attack, and at 1:33 a.m., he decided to turn south. Dodging the odd torpedo track (launched by the retiring Japanese ships or perhaps even American PT boats), the *Washington* made radar contact with the *South Dakota* and the surviving American destroyers. Lee coaxed them in via TBS. At 6:49 a.m., after dawn, Lee received a radio dispatch from Halsey ordering him to pull his wounded ships together and bring them back to Espiritu Santo.

Lee had routed the enemy. The Japanese had brought a stronger force into the action, but it had been taken by surprise and been beaten by superior gunnery. The American advantage in radar fire control systems was readily evident; the Japanese systems were at least a year behind. Six Japanese ships were lost, including the *Kirishima*, which sank at 3:25 a.m. Five more were damaged. The survivors were in full retreat. The *Washington* had come through the action without significant damage. The *South Dakota* had been roughly handled but would be repaired and returned to service. The American destroyers had been decimated—three of four sunk, with heavy loss of life—but they had played an essential part in the action by absorbing much of the enemy's punishment, both gunfire and torpedoes, allowing the battleships to concentrate their guns on the larger Japanese ships. Henderson Field was spared another shelling, and Tanaka's four surviving transports would be obliged to attempt a landing without naval protection.

TANAKA JUDGED THAT HIS ONLY HOPE of unloading the four ships was to run them aground near Tassafaronga Point. He asked for permission to do so and received an affirmative reply from Rabaul. As November 15 dawned, the Americans could plainly see the four hulls propped up on the beaches to the west. About 2,000 troops got ashore before daylight, and stacks of crates and rice bales were left in and among the palm groves just inland of the beach.[72] Henderson-based planes worked over the ships and supplies throughout the morning. Except for brief and largely ineffective resistance by a few floatplane Zeros, the Japanese had no air protection. A marine 155mm artillery piece even managed to reach the nearest of the four ships, beached near the mouth of the Poha River. By midmorning all four ships were burning fiercely, and by early afternoon they were little more than charred husks emitting columns of greasy black smoke.

TBFs flying from Henderson targeted the supplies on the beach with the incendiary weapons nicknamed "Molotov bread baskets."[73] A Dauntless pilot detected a trail leading from the beach inland to a circular clearing. Guessing it was an ammunition dump, he aimed his 1,000-pound bomb in the middle of that clearing. He had guessed right. A titanic explosion turned the heads of marines at Lunga, several miles away, and a column of smoke reached up to a height of 2,000 feet. The fire burned all night and was still burning sixteen hours later.[74]

Chapter Seven

IN THE THREE-DAY STRUGGLE KNOWN TO HISTORY AS THE "NAVAL Battle of Guadalcanal," the Japanese navy had been soundly defeated and driven back up the Slot. But Admiral Tanaka's beleaguered "Tokyo Express," relying on fast destroyers darting into Ironbottom Sound under cover of darkness, had achieved the signal feat of putting more than a division of fresh troops ashore on the island. Added to the remnants of the Kawaguchi Corps, Japanese troop strength on Guadalcanal reached approximately 30,000 in mid-November. The Imperial General Headquarters had not anticipated that so many "sons of heaven" could fail to overrun the American position, but every successive assault on Vandegrift's lines had been bloodily repulsed. Now the immediate problem was logistics. It was becoming terribly clear that the Imperial Japanese Navy, having strained its capabilities to put so many troops ashore, had no practical means of feeding so many mouths. Even as early as September, Japanese units on the island had begun to waste away for lack of provisions, medicine, and other supplies. By the first week of December, they were succumbing en masse to plague and famine. Guadalcanal, for its Japanese inhabitants, had become "Starvation Island."*

Newcomers who came ashore at Tassafaronga Point were taken aback. Wraithlike soldiers approached and begged for food. Their uniforms, little more than rags, hung from emaciated limbs; their hair had grown long and crawled with lice; their skin was dirty and pocked with open sores that were

---

* The name is a play on the term *Gato*, the abbreviated Japanese name for Guadalcanal, and *Ga*, which translates as "hunger" in certain inflections.

fed on by flies.[1] Many had thrown away their rifles because they either felt too weak to carry them or had no ammunition.

But the Japanese stationed along the coast were among the most prosperous on the island. There they could fish or forage for coconuts or plunder the meager supplies of rice brought ashore from the destroyers. Units posted deeper in the jungle had been reduced to eating lizards, snakes, worms, roots, grass, and insects. Trails into the hills were littered with the bodies of dead or dying men. Those immobilized by malaria, dengue fever, or beriberi were often abandoned to die where they lay. As one officer observed, food was the overriding obsession of starving men: "All senses, except hunger, went out. No laugh, no anger, no tear."[2]

Japanese soldiers' diaries, captured during and after the Guadalcanal campaign, told a pathetic story of deteriorating morale and wasted hopes. The malnourished soldiers were repeatedly exhorted to stir themselves to greater efforts: "We must by the most furious, daring, swift and positive action deal the enemy annihilating blows, [and] foil his plans completely. . . . It is necessary to arouse the officers and men to a fighting rage."[3] But the officers made too many promises they could not keep. A fleet of Japanese transports, laden with food and other supplies, was always just over the western horizon; Japanese warplanes would soon darken the sky; one more *banzai* charge would cause the cowardly marines to throw away their weapons and run for their lives. But for days or even weeks at a time, no Japanese aircraft appeared overhead and no Japanese ships were seen offshore. "Every day enemy planes alone dance in the sky, fly low, strafe, bomb, and numerous officers and men fall," noted a diarist on December 23. Three days later, he added, "O friendly planes! I beg that you come over soon, and cheer us up!"[4]

Discipline collapsed. Soldiers bickered over their paltry rations. Food was stolen and hoarded. Enlisted men accused their officers of diverting extra portions to themselves. They refused to work, fight, or march unless fed. From the summit of Mount Austen, where a detachment of about 450 Japanese troops kept watch over Henderson Field, the lookouts watched miserably as American cargo ships anchored off Lunga Point and delivered a seemingly limitless quantity of supplies, weapons, and fresh troops into the American lines. A sub-lieutenant posted at the top of Austen devised a mortality table to predict each starving soldier's remaining life span:

Those who can stand upright: 30 days.

Those who can sit: 3 weeks.

Those always lying down: 1 week.

Those who pass urine lying: 3 days.

Those who cannot speak: 2 days.

Those who cannot wink: On the morrow.[5]

On December 8, the Seventeenth Army headquarters on Guadalcanal reported that only 4,200 troops (about 15 percent of the total on the island) were strong and healthy enough to fight. Combat deaths were running at forty to fifty per day, mainly as a result of air attacks, but some three times that number were succumbing to disease or starvation.[6]

Tanaka's mid-November resupply effort had been a debacle. He had lost eleven valuable transports in three days. From the four ships he had sacrificed by running them aground on the beaches, he had disembarked just 2,000 troops, 360 cases of ammunition for field guns, and 1,500 bales of rice.[7] By consuming so many scarce cargo ships, the fight for Guadalcanal threatened to cripple the entire Japanese war economy, which could not function without raw materials imported into the home islands.

A new supply tactic was urgently needed. Tanaka's hard-run destroyers would again be deployed as transports, this time using the "drum method." Empty fuel drums were sterilized and filled with ammunition and provisions. The drums, linked together by ropes, were secured to the outboard railings of the destroyers. A column of destroyers would approach the island at high speed and cast away the drums, which would be retrieved by small craft (or even swimmers) and towed or hauled ashore. All supply drops would be attempted at night, as Tanaka dared not expose his ships to air attack.

The first run was attempted on November 30, 1942. Shortly after ten that evening, a single column of eight destroyers roared into Ironbottom Sound at nearly 30 knots. Admiral Tanaka knew that his ships had been spotted from the air, but hoped to launch the drums and withdraw up the Slot before daybreak. The weather was fair, with a gentle breeze and good visibility at the surface. Six of the eight ships were loaded with between 200 and 240 supply drums each. To offset the added weight topside, those six ships had sailed with only eight torpedoes (one per tube) and half their usual supply of main battery ammunition.[8]

American search flights had tracked Tanaka's movements carefully. He had staged through Rabaul and the Buin and Shortland harbors, where a large increase in shipping during the last week of the month had clearly signaled another supply run. To counter it, Halsey dispatched Rear Admiral Carleton H. Wright with a cruiser-destroyer force (Task Force 67) from Espiritu Santo. Wright passed through Lengo Channel at 9:45 p.m. and arrived in the waters north of Tassafaronga Point just as Tanaka closed from the north.

At 11:06 p.m., SG radar on the flagship cruiser *Minneapolis* discovered two ships at a distance of 23,000 yards. The blips gradually resolved into seven or eight ships on a southeasterly course. At about the same time, Japanese lookouts noted flares dropped from cruiser planes overhead, and obtained a visual fix on "what appear to be enemy ships, bearing 100°."[9] Without waiting for Tanaka's order, the lead destroyer *Takanami* launched torpedoes and opened fire.

The Americans had brought superior firepower into the action—five cruisers and six destroyers matched against Tanaka's eight destroyers, six of which were short of munitions and heavily loaded with supplies. But Wright was slow to give the order to open fire, and the delay mattered. The American torpedoes were fired at an awkward angle, and none struck home. Their 8- and 5-inch projectiles were better aimed, but they were concentrated on the lead ship *Takanami*, which was quickly set ablaze all along her length and began going down by the head. *Takanami*'s sacrifice effectively decided the action in favor of the Japanese, because she absorbed all the American gunners had to offer while her explosions and fires screened her seven sisters. No other Japanese ship suffered a direct hit in the battle, or even a destructive near miss.[10]

Tanaka ordered a hard port turn to take his column on a course parallel to that of Wright's. As they rotated their broadsides toward the enemy, the undamaged Japanese destroyers launched their deadly spreads. The Long Lance torpedoes ran true. Beginning at about 11:27, as the warheads connected with their targets, the big cruisers at the heart of Wright's column lurched upward and erupted in flames. The *Minneapolis* took two crippling blows on her port side. The first tore off the ship's bow and ignited gasoline storage tanks; the second struck amidships and flooded her engineering spaces. Less than a minute later, the *New Orleans* was hit on her port bow. The explosion detonated her magazines, tore off a large section of her bow, and killed the entire crew of turret 2.[11] The *Pensacola*'s fuel tanks were ignited by a torpedo hit; she would burn through the night. The venerable *Northampton*, the last cruiser in Wright's column, gave chase to the retreating Japanese ships and sent several 8-inch salvos after them. For that she was rewarded with two devastating torpedo hits that put an end to her. She was abandoned and sank early the next morning.

Not for the first time, the U.S. Navy had suffered a dreadful beating in a night torpedo action. In fifteen minutes, and at a cost of one destroyer, Tanaka had sent one heavy cruiser into the abyss and critically damaged three more. The naval historian Samuel Eliot Morison, a free-handed critic but a miser with praise, rated Tanaka's performance "superb."[12] Admiral Nimitz ruefully observed that "we are made painfully aware of the Japanese skill, both in night and day action, in the use of guns and torpedoes. To date there has been no reason to doubt his energy, persistence, and courage."[13]

Wright estimated that his force had sunk four Japanese destroyers and damaged two more. That rosy claim was viewed with suspicion even by the crews of his own ships, especially when dawn revealed no sign of enemy wreckage. If there was anything to console the Americans, it was the exceptional valor and skill of the damage-control parties that saved the *Minneapolis*, *New Orleans*, and *Pensacola*. The action had left the three cruisers ablaze and in near-sinking condition, but all somehow managed to quell the fires and hobble into Tulagi Harbor, and all would be returned to service later in the war.

Tanaka chose to withdraw to Shortland without attempting the supply drop. His reasons were sensible enough—his destroyers had expended all torpedoes, and he could expect attack from the air if he did not get well away to the west before morning. But the decision exacerbated the privations of the army on Guadalcanal, and apparently angered his superiors at Rabaul and Truk. He must try again, without delay. On the night of December 3, ten destroyers managed to drop 1,500 supply drums off Cape Esperance. But only a fraction, perhaps one-fifth of the drums, reached the Japanese army. The units assigned to recover them had been undermanned and physically exhausted. The following morning, American fighters flying from Henderson Field strafed and destroyed several hundred drums found drifting in Ironbottom Sound. Tanaka tried another run on December 7, but his ships were harried by bombers and fighters, then attacked and driven away by six PT boats west of Savo Island.[14]

Even in their anchorage at Shortland, the Japanese could not rest. B-17s and fighters raided the area every day. On December 10, two fuel tankers were struck and set afire, with heavy damage. Tanaka sortied with nine destroyers the following afternoon and managed to drop 1,200 supply drums. American PT boats swarmed out of Tulagi Harbor and launched torpedoes, one of which struck Tanaka's flagship, the recently commissioned *Teruzuki*. "The ship caught fire and became unnavigable almost at once," he wrote. "Leaking fuel was set ablaze, turning the sea into a mass of flames. When fire reached the after powder magazine there was a huge explosion, and the ship began to sink."[15] She was scuttled at 4:00 the next morning; more than half her crew went down with her. The eight surviving destroyers withdrew to Shortland. Tanaka, injured in the action and confined to a hospital at Buin, was disgusted to learn that only 220 of the 1,200 drums launched that night had been recovered by the army.

With the moon waxing, the PT boat attacks were growing more deadly every night, and Admiral Mikawa ordered a temporary halt to the supply runs. Tanaka privately advised him that the game was up—Guadalcanal must be abandoned. For his trouble, Tanaka received orders transferring him to an administrative post in Singapore. This talented officer, who had done his best to supply Guadalcanal with the limited tools at hand, and who had scored a mighty naval victory less than a month earlier, would never command at sea again.

Talk of pulling out of Guadalcanal was strictly taboo. The Japanese army, even more than the navy, had staked its honor and reputation on the recapture of Henderson Field. Lieutenant General Hitoshi Imamura, recently arrived at Rabaul to assume command of Eighth Area Army, intended to summon the Sixth and Fifty-First Divisions from China and put them ashore on Guadalcanal by the end of the year.[16] Senior naval commanders thought the plan absurd but were reluctant to say so. Even if 50,000 more troops could somehow be transported to the island, an unlikely prospect in light of November's events, how could they be supported? If 30,000 men currently on the island were starving, how could 80,000 be fed?

In the privacy of his diary, Admiral Ugaki contemplated the inevitable. The interservice politics were extremely delicate, and considerations of "face" would certainly come into play. But it would not do to persist in a futile campaign for the sake of maintaining cordial relations between the army and the navy. On December 7, he wrote, "Deeming wrong as wrong and impossible as impossible, and without being obstinate because of face-savings or without coaxing others, we should deal with this important matter with the utmost frankness." The army would have to arrive at the conclusion independently—"it is essential to let them realize its inevitability by themselves."[17] At any event, the question was out of his hands. Such a momentous change in policy could be decided only by the high command in Tokyo.

IN JAPAN AND OTHER POINTS WEST of the International Date Line, the eighth day of December marked the first anniversary of the attack on Pearl Harbor. The date was feted with the usual self-congratulatory bunkum. The Imperial Navy headquarters released a grossly inflated tally of enemy ships sunk in the first year of the "Greater East Asia War": eleven aircraft carriers, eleven battleships, forty-six cruisers, forty-eight destroyers, and ninety-three submarines. (More accurately, it also reported a cumulative total of Japanese officers and sailors killed in action: 14,802.)[18]

Newspapers and magazines published annual retrospectives highlighting the notable victories achieved by Japanese forces. *Kokusai Shashin Joho*, the International Graphic Magazine, published gun camera photos depicting burning enemy ships and aircraft.[19] In a speech carried over the airwaves, Foreign Minister Masayuki Tani declared that American leaders "are truly running their nation in a laughable manner. They may be high in producing capacity, but without the more essential qualities, such as lofty war ideals, America cannot win over us."[20]

Japanese servicemen returning from the South Pacific were confounded by the elation they found at home. No one in Tokyo seemed to grasp how precarious Japan's position had become. There might be some compelling purpose in firing up the spirits of the public, but the boundaries dividing fact and fantasy were blurred even in the inner councils of power. Prime Minister Hideki Tojo, in a December 8 speech to military leaders at the War Ministry, declared that the Allies "want obstinately to continue their counterattack, but making use of our great material resources, we are ready to annihilate them at any moment at any point on the globe."[21] That very week, as Tojo undoubtedly knew, the Imperial General Staff had begun a joint army-navy strategic review with an eye toward cutting losses and pulling out of Guadalcanal. In Truk, Admiral Ugaki judged that a visiting delegation of army staff officers "didn't seem to have enough knowledge of the fervent fighting spirit of the American forces. Neither did they show much interest in comparative strength, theirs and ours."[22] Captain Tameichi Hara, who had returned to Japan for repairs to his ship, dined with a group of naval staff officers in mid-December. "I don't know how you who are stationed here view things from the homeland, but it is hell at the front," he told them. "As professionals you all know better than to base your judgments on the official bravado announced by headquarters in Tokyo. We have had some tactical victories, but we are suffering a strategic defeat."[23] The mood grew tense, and one of the others told Hara that it was a social occasion and he ought to lighten up.

In mid-December, Colonel Joichiro Sanada of the Imperial Headquarters staff was dispatched on a fact-finding mission to the South Pacific. At Truk and Rabaul, he solicited and recorded the views of senior officers of both the army and the navy. Even accounting for what is lost in translation, one is struck by the temporizing, evasive, and subtext-laden character of the answers given. More than one officer remarked that recapturing the island "is difficult." Several kicked responsibility up to the "ultimate authorities." All were preoccupied with army-navy sensitivities. The army called for more ships; the navy called for more army airpower. Neither was willing to be the first to advocate giving up Guadalcanal, but neither was keen to commit its strength to a renewed offensive. "If the army can undertake it with confidence," said a senior member of Yamamoto's staff, in a typical reply, "the navy will pitch in, too." General Imamura, who had recently spoken of landing two fresh divisions on Guadalcanal, offered Sanada this master stroke of equivocation: "At present, we are searching for a plan to lead us out of the difficulty, but we alone cannot say that the operational policy be changed. I hope that the central authorities will make a decision from the overall viewpoint after deliberating on the relationship with the navy."[24]

In conferences at the Imperial General Headquarters, it was customary for officers of the two services to sit on opposite sides of the table, an arrangement that could only dramatize the rift between them. Recriminations proceeded until all arguments were exhausted. The army blamed the navy for failing to maintain adequate supply lines. The navy criticized the ground tactics employed on Guadalcanal, and demanded more army air support. General Kenryo Sato recalled "heated discussions exchanging clenched fists over the table between the army and navy."[25] Neither side could afford an impasse, however, and not only because both services were suffering ruinous losses in the Solomons. The emperor had lost patience with the sniping between his two military branches and had issued stern warnings against disharmony. The generals and admirals had no choice but to grapple toward some sort of face-saving consensus. Gradually it became clear that everyone was looking for a way out of Guadalcanal. As one conference followed another, and the regime stumbled toward a new accord, about 200 Japanese soldiers on the island perished each day.

Colonel Sanada reported to Tojo upon his return to the capital on December 29. His formal recommendation, couched in terms only slightly less paralytic than those he had heard in Rabaul and Truk, was that "it is not advisable to hurry the recapture of Guadalcanal Island."[26] He had expected a furious rebuke, but was relieved to learn that Tojo had apparently reached the same conclusion. Sanada's report and recommendation were "adopted much more readily than I had feared."[27]

According to Ugaki, an "understanding" had been reached between the services on December 16, 1942, but another two weeks passed before the issue was put to the emperor. At a conference at the Imperial Palace on the last day of the year, the high command offered a unanimous recommendation that Guadalcanal be abandoned. The navy would attempt to evacuate as many of the surviving army troops as possible. The emperor was displeased, and he questioned Admiral Nagano closely concerning the laggardly pace of new airfield construction in the South Pacific.[28] Hirohito gave his approval to the recommendation, as he always did when his advisers were unanimous, but added that it was "unacceptable" to pull out of Guadalcanal without simultaneously mounting a new offensive in New Guinea.[29] Japan's forces must not be seen to shift to a merely defensive posture. Some days later, the man-god conveyed an imperial message to the high command, transmitted through his chief aide-de-camp: "The evacuation from Guadalcanal Island was regrettable. Further cooperation between the Army and Navy is requested hereafter for the attainment of operational objectives."[30]

Disguised though it was, the new policy called for a retreat to a new defensive line running north and south through the central Solomons. The army would fortify and garrison islands north of New Georgia and Santa Isabel. The navy would accelerate work on the new airstrip at Munda on New Georgia, making it the region's principal forward fighter base. As for the remnants of the army on Guadalcanal, the navy would continue supply runs, but these would be little more than missions of mercy—there would be no further offensives against the American lines. Admiral Tomiji Koyanagi, with ten cruisers under his command, made supply drops on January 2 and January 10, 1943. As in the prior month, provisions were crammed into fuel drums that were dropped into the sea off Tassafaronga Point.[31] More than half of these drums were apparently recovered, providing life-saving relief to the Japanese forces on the island, whose number had diminished to fewer than 15,000.

"Operation KE" was the name given to the evacuation and the covering operations that disguised it. On January 14, a fresh infantry and artillery battalion (the "Yano Battalion") was landed on the island to act as a rear guard. Naval and air forces moved down the Solomons in strength. These were discovered (as the Japanese knew they would be) by Allied air reconnaissance. Daylight and nighttime air attacks against Henderson Field rose sharply. Radio traffic analysis misled American intelligence to believe that the Japanese were mounting another naval offensive and troop landing, and the American commanders reacted accordingly. Major General Alexander Patch of the army (who had relieved General Vandegrift as commander of American ground forces on the island on December 7) had some 50,000 army and marine troops under his command. Patch began to press into the hills south of the village of Kokumbona, the Seventeenth Army headquarters on the island's north coast. The Americans found Japanese resistance surprisingly light, and elements of the 25th Infantry Division walked into the village unopposed on January 23. The Japanese were evidently withdrawing in a hurry to the west, but Patch did not commit to a pursuit in force, as he still believed another large-scale amphibious landing was at hand. Halsey deployed his remaining cruisers and carrier task forces to the waters in and west of Ironbottom Sound. On January 30, Japanese air attacks destroyed the cruiser *Chicago*.

On February 1, as the Japanese evacuation runs began, the Americans received a cascade of sighting reports from coastwatchers and scouting aircraft. Some twenty Japanese destroyers were headed down the Slot. A small Japanese infantry force had been put ashore in the Russell Islands, a small group just thirty miles west of Guadalcanal (and visible from the high bluffs on the western shore, where the colorful Australian coastwatcher Snowy Rhoades had once lived in his airy lodge). Allied flights over the Japanese anchorage off Buin noted a sharp increase in the number of ships. Japanese air activity intensified to levels unseen since December. Halsey asked MacArthur for "all air support possible against an expected major offensive following the same general pattern as that of mid-November."[32] The COMSOPAC sent most of his remaining American naval forces south of Guadalcanal to await the expected incursion.

Given the wasted condition of their forces, the withdrawal of Japanese units to the northwest corner of the island was surprisingly deft. The evacuation order was disseminated at first only to a small circle of officers, who kept their men in the dark. Most Japanese soldiers expected to be reinforced right up until the moment they were told to abandon their positions. (The misdirection was thought necessary to keep the men at their posts until the last minute.) The Thirty-Eighth Division fell back toward Cape Esperance, covered by the Second Infantry Division and the Yano Battalion. The rear guard, once safely disengaged, followed to the west. Men immobilized by disease or malnutrition were persuaded to take their own lives.

The first evacuation run was completed on the night of February 1. Twenty-one Japanese destroyers, under the command of Rear Admiral Shintaro Hashimoto, lifted 4,935 soldiers off the island, nearly half those remaining. On the night of February 4–5, Hashimoto returned with twenty destroyers. Fighting off air and PT boat attacks, he nonetheless embarked 3,921 troops of the Second Division and returned them safely to Bougainville the next day. The third run, on the night of February 7–8, lifted 1,796 men off Guadalcanal and the Russell Islands.

The bodies of some 16,800 Japanese were left behind on Guadalcanal, many unburied. Those who were rescued were little more than scarecrows. Their knees and elbows bulged out from their shrunken limbs. Their hair and fingernails had stopped growing. Their buttocks had wasted away to the extent that their anuses were exposed, and they suffered uncontrollable diarrhea. Some carried urns with the ashes of their dead comrades.[33] Yahachi Ishida, a young soldier posted on Bougainville, helped some of the starving men from the landing barges:

Waiting at the shore, we gently lifted out the soldiers retreating from Guadalcanal one by one and laid them on the sand. What a sad and pitiable sight they presented. Hardly human beings, they were just skin and bones dressed in military uniform, thin as bamboo sticks.

They were so light, it was like carrying infants. Only their eyes were bright; they must have been living on their strong will alone. When I put a spoon with some lukewarm rice gruel to their mouths, large teardrops rolled down their faces, and they said thank you in tiny mosquitolike voices. I too felt something hot unexpectedly welling up in my eyes. My blood roiled with anger at those who had given the orders to these men.[34]

Patch held back, expecting to meet resistance in force at any moment. The general and his staff continued to believe that the enemy had been landing fresh reinforcements throughout the past week. As American forces advanced along the north and west coasts of the island, however, they encountered no one but a few Japanese stragglers, mostly sick and dying, and some bewildered natives. At Tassafaronga, the Americans captured the deserted remains of a major Japanese base, including ten artillery pieces, a machine shop, medical stores, and a radio station. In the late afternoon of February 9, the two columns met at the village of Tenaro on the west coast. Patch finally realized that he had been swindled. He radioed Halsey: "Total and complete defeat of Japanese forces on Guadalcanal effected 16:25 today . . . the Tokyo Express no longer has a terminus on Guadalcanal."[35]

The Guadalcanal campaign was over, and it had ended in a humiliating defeat for the Japanese. Yet at least they had saved 10,652 men of the approximately 36,000 who had landed on the island. The evacuation was a small Dunkirk, an unlikely tactical getaway right under the noses of superior ground, air, and naval forces. The Japanese had accomplished the bold rescue operation with the loss of just one destroyer sunk and three damaged. American radio intelligence, which had so often divined the enemy's intentions, had failed to foresee the evacuation. Admiral Yamamoto congratulated Koyanagi, adding, "You did it very well, indeed. . . . The Army will be pleased to know we can send back its soldiers in great mass."[36]

Yamamoto's opposite number, Chester Nimitz, was equally generous in his praise. "Until almost the last moment it appeared that the Japanese were attempting a major reinforcement effort," he wrote in his report to Admiral King. "Only skill in keeping their plans disguised and bold celerity in carrying them out enabled the Japanese to withdraw the remnants of the Guadalcanal garrison. Not until after all organized forces had been evacuated on 8 February did we realize the purpose of their air and naval dispositions;

otherwise, with the strong forces available to us ashore on Guadalcanal and our powerful fleet in the South Pacific, we might have converted the withdrawal into a disastrous rout."[37]

King could not have faulted Nimitz or Halsey or any of the other American commanders on the spot. He had expected another major offensive against Guadalcanal, and had predicted it in an off-the-record interview with a group of journalists on December 2, 1942. The COMINCH had told the newsmen that the Japanese "had lost a lot of face, and were set on regaining [Guadalcanal] by hook or by crook."[38]

IN THE SIX-MONTH FIGHT OVER GUADALCANAL, the two sides had suffered roughly equivalent naval and air losses. Sixty-seven ships had been sunk in the contest over the island—twenty-nine Allied, thirty-eight Japanese. The Japanese had destroyed two valuable American aircraft carriers and damaged another (leaving the *Enterprise* the sole remaining Allied carrier in the theater), but the Americans had claimed two light aircraft carriers and two battleships. Both sides had lost many cruisers, destroyers, and noncombatant transports and cargo ships that could not be easily replaced. On several occasions, the Japanese navy had given proof of its excellence in night surface combat, but its advantages had gradually given way to the Americans' adroit use of radar for range finding and fire control. By the fall of 1942, an American ship could land its first salvo on an unseen enemy without the benefit of searchlights or flares. That was a valuable technical advantage over the Japanese, and it largely offset the superior skill, training, and torpedo weaponry of the Japanese surface fleet.

Each side lost between 600 and 700 aircraft in the campaign, but the fraction of downed aviators who were recovered told a different story. The Allies lost about 420 pilots and aircrew in the Solomons; the Japanese, more than three times that number. Since the Battle of the Coral Sea in May 1942, Japanese aircrew losses had consistently exceeded those of the Allies, often by a wide margin. The stark disparity could be partly explained by circumstances—throughout the period, but especially during the fight for Guadalcanal, air combat had been concentrated in skies closer to Allied than to Japanese air and naval bases. It is also true that the Japanese had not devoted much effort to search-and-rescue operations, a failure that must be attributed (at least in part) to the influence of *bushido*, the traditional samurai warrior code that exalted an honorable death in combat.

Replacement pilots emerging from Japan's wartime training pipeline lacked the skill or confidence to carry on the air war effectively. As early as November 21, 1942, Admiral Yamamoto confessed to a visiting army officer that Japan was losing the air war in the Solomons. "In the Navy they used to say that one 'Zero' fighter could take on five to ten American aircraft, but that was at the beginning of the war. Since losing so many good pilots at Midway we've had difficulty in replacing them. Even now, they still say that one 'Zero' can take on two enemy planes, but the enemy's replacement rate is three times ours; the gap between our strengths is increasing every day, and to be honest things are looking black for us now."[39] Blacker even than he knew or cared to admit, for the American fighter pilots had already learned how to neutralize the Zero's advantages in maneuverability and climbing speed.

Most striking was the disproportion in troop losses. The U.S. Army and Marine Corps had suffered casualties of 5,875, of whom 1,592 were killed in action. The Japanese army had lost two full divisions on the island, and the great majority were killed (or died of other causes) rather than wounded and evacuated—14,700 killed or missing in action, an estimated 9,000 dead of starvation or disease, and more than 4,300 lost at sea while in transit to or from the island. That asymmetric result debunked the myth of the Japanese army's fanatical and invincible "fighting spirit." Guadalcanal was not the name of an island, concluded General Kawaguchi. "It is the name of the graveyard of the Japanese army."[40]

Insofar as the Japanese people were permitted to know, the withdrawal from Guadalcanal was a tactical redeployment. *Tenshin*, roughly translated as "advance in a new direction," was the euphemism offered by the Imperial General Headquarters. Japan's attacking naval, air, and ground forces had merely "turned" toward another sector of the front, where they would undoubtedly achieve new triumphs in short order. Japan's state-controlled news media had long since acquiesced to the regime's Orwellian abuse of truth, and had adopted the necessary tone of elation and righteous zeal. But there were many servicemen who had returned to the home islands from the theater of combat, and their hushed accounts did not sustain the official version of events.

Several Japanese officers who survived the war later recorded their

unvarnished postmortems. Even with the benefit of hindsight, and allowing for the likelihood that English-translated accounts were self-serving
and shaped to fit the preconceptions of the victors, Japanese officers who
had participated in the campaign offered keen and hard-hitting critiques of
their nation's strategic failures. Captain Hara judged that the Japanese navy
really lost the war as a result of a "series of strategic and tactical blunders by
Yamamoto after Midway." The commander in chief had failed to commit
the bulk of his naval power immediately after the marines' invasion, and had
instead "flung into the area one small fleet unit after another. His strategy
seems ridiculous when judged by hindsight."[41] Admiral Nobutake Kondo,
commander of the Imperial Navy's Second Fleet, agreed that Yamamoto
should have thrown everything he had at Guadalcanal in August, even if
it required abandoning the offensive against southeastern New Guinea. He
quoted a Japanese proverb: "He who pursues two hares catches neither."[42]
The seventeenth-century samurai and philosopher Miyamoto Musashi,
whose *Book of Five Spheres* was an essential text for Japanese officers of both
services, had written of "arresting shadows." To hold a psychological edge
over a weaker opponent, a combatant must "arrest the enemy's action at the
point of the very impulse to act." That is, the enemy must know immediately that his attack will be opposed and foiled; he must not be permitted
to think that he will gain the advantage by his initiative: "If you show the
adversaries strongly how you control the advantage, they will change their
minds, inhibited by this strength."[43]

The Guadalcanal campaign had exposed all of the internal rifts and
rivalries that divided the Japanese military regime and paralyzed its ability to craft coherent strategies. Major decisions, especially those involving
joint action by the army and navy, were reached gradually. Consensus had
to be given time to congeal. Considerations of "face" were always near
the surface. The Japanese army had first discounted the significance of
the enemy's move into Guadalcanal, assuring themselves and their navy
counterparts that the Americans could be dislodged at any time. Piecemeal and ineffective troop landings followed. First, a lightly equipped
regiment was sent in and annihilated; then a lightly equipped brigade;
eventually a full division, but without adequate munitions, equipment, or
provisions. Again and again, frontal attacks on strongly fortified marine
lines were beaten back, with devastating losses to the attackers. Even
within the ranks of the navy, command rivalries were debilitating. More

than once, Admiral Raizo Tanaka received contradictory orders from the Eleventh Air Fleet and the Eighth Fleet. One headquarters had dominion over the entire region, and the other stood directly above Tanaka in the chain of command. Each seemed to regard the other as an interloper, and they tussled over issues large and small. Tanaka thought it "inconceivable" that the two commands did not confer effectively with one another, since both were (usually) seated at Rabaul. "When their orders were conflicting and incompatible, it was embarrassing at least, and utterly confounding at worst."[44]

Once a course of action was chosen, a prevailing inertia inhibited modification. The rigidity inherent in Japanese operations led to repeating patterns that could be analyzed and predicted by the Allies. Even when communications intelligence failed to discover the Japanese intentions, American commanders could often foretell when, where, and how the enemy would mount his next assault. "In fighting it is bad to repeat a formula," Musashi had written, "and to repeat it a third time is worse. When an effort fails it may be followed with a second attempt. If that fails, a drastically changed formula must be adopted. If that fails, one must resort to another completely different formula. When the opponent thinks high, hit low. When he thinks low, hit high. That is the secret of swordsmanship."[45]

GUADALCANAL WORE THE SCARS of the long, vicious conflict that had raged on, over, and around it. The Lunga Plain was pockmarked with craters and strewn with broken and splintered palm trees. Everywhere there was wreckage, shoved to the edges of roads or airstrips or lying half-awash on the beaches. Foliage was beginning to creep over the rusting remains of smashed tanks and crashed aircraft. Copper telephone wire was draped haphazardly over standing palms. West of Point Cruz, the bows of Tanaka's four bombed-out transports jutted up onto the beach. Even months after the last naval action, Ironbottom Sound was still littered with floating debris, and brown coils of fuel oil marked the sites of sunken wrecks.

On the ridges south of Henderson Field, trees and foliage had been mowed down by artillery and machine-gun fire. Beyond the coils of barbed wire marking the American lines, the bloated and stinking remains of Japanese soldiers lay half-buried in the muck. The stench was awful, but the Americans were in no hurry to bury the enemy dead. The Japanese had been known to booby-trap the corpses of their fallen friends. Ants and other scavengers would eventually strip them to the bone.

Among these relics of past carnage were ambitious new building projects. It has been cleverly observed that the bulldozer was one of the most significant weapons of the Pacific War, and the point was never better showcased than on Guadalcanal in 1943. Ten new 1,100-man Seabee battalions arrived to join the pioneering 6th and 14th (which had landed under fire in November 1942), and all were reorganized into the 18th Naval Construction Regiment. Airfields were expanded, regraded, and resurfaced with concrete made of coral or red volcanic rock. Networks of taxiways connected them to revetments, machine shops, barracks, warehouses, and camouflaged munitions dumps. The hills inland of Koli Point were leveled and developed into "Carney Field," a new airbase for USAAF bombers. Tank farms mushroomed around Lunga Point and Henderson Field, and were linked by miles of piping to the airfields and wharves. Bulldozers uprooted the trees and flora around Koli, Lunga, and Cruz Points, where modern seaport complexes—concrete piers, cranes, pipelines, narrow-gauge railways running into warehouses—would serve the constantly arriving transports and tankers. Fresh troops, airmen, maintenance crews, and civilians poured into the island day by day, arriving on ships or on the big Douglas C-47s of the South Pacific Combat Air Transport Command (SCAT). Paved roads were built through recently impenetrable jungle; steel-framed bridges were flung across rivers; electrical power lines were strung between utility poles; tent cities appeared suddenly in palm groves and *kunai* fields. The social nexus of the growing community was the "Hotel De Gink," a row of Quonset huts providing lodging for transient airmen and other visitors. A spacious dining hall served coffee and hot meals around the clock.

As the counteroffensive rolled up the Solomons, the island groups to the south and east—New Caledonia, New Hebrides, the Santa Cruz group, Samoa, the Fijis—were demoted to the status of holding zones, rest areas, and way stations. The war had passed them by, but they remained populated by large and growing numbers of Allied personnel. Pacific War memoirs tend to dwell at length on these tropical paradises, safely removed from the fighting, where young servicemen (and women, particularly nurses) sojourned for weeks, months, or years of their lives. They were the setting for James Michener's postwar novel *Tales of the South Pacific*, a thinly fictionalized series of vignettes drawn from the author's experiences as a reserve naval lieutenant stationed on Espiritu Santo and other islands east of the Solomons.* Life in those quiescent islands figures very little in histories or even films about the war, but it retains a potent hold on the memories of the men and women who were there.

Visitors who set foot on those remote shores were easily enchanted by the exotic beauty of the region—by the azure lagoons and white beaches; by the brilliantly colored fish, flowers, and birds; by the soft rustle of palm fronds and the metrical thump of the surf. Limes and lemons grew wild along the beaches. Flying fish leapt from the wakes of passing boats. Sunsets were unlike anything they had seen before: a sublime palette of colors ranging from blue to orange to green to red to purple. The stars were wrong, at least in the southern half of the sky. One might find a familiar constellation near the northern horizon, but it would appear upside down. Wartime letters, diaries, and memoirs are full of such observations.

The islands also had a sinister aspect. Observers described dark volcanoes shrouded in steaming mists. Land crabs the size of dinner plates scurried around their tents at night. Fruit bats with four-foot wingspans took flight at sunset. Insects were relentless, and the mosquitoes carried malaria. Americans and other Westerners were alternately fascinated and repelled by the natives—their loincloths and bare breasts, their betel-reddened incisors filed to sharp points, the vaguely intelligible version of English they spoke. Rumors circulated that the tribesmen still practiced headhunting and cannibalism, a prospect both enthralling and hideous. *Long pig* was the pidgin word for human flesh. Harold Buell recalled that islanders on Espiritu Santo liked to joke about cannibalism. "A favorite native joke was to pinch your arm or stomach and state solemnly: 'You makeum fine long pig.' They would then grin broadly showing their front teeth."[46] Americans would barter handsomely for a shrunken head, and at least a few of those gruesome souvenirs were smuggled aboard ships and taken back to the United States.

Units left on rear-area islands for weeks or months suffered paralyzing boredom. Poker games went on for days, as they did in every other part of the Pacific. Men played checkers, backgammon, and cribbage, and read

---

* Michener's book, which won a Pulitzer Prize in 1948, bears little resemblance to the better-known musical stage and screen adaptations. *Tales* was his first book, perhaps his best. He turned forty the year it was published, but somehow managed to turn out fifty more books before his death in 1997.

months-old magazines, comic books, and newspapers. Bloody "grudge matches" were fought between feuding soldiers or sailors of rival ships, with wagers placed on the outcome. Everyone lived for mail, which arrived more regularly as the war progressed; reading letters, however, only took up a fraction of their time, and wartime censorship limited what they could write. Movies were screened each night in makeshift outdoor amphitheaters, with the men sitting on the ground or on coconut logs, but because new reels were scarce, the men were often condemned to watch the same film twenty or more times. They often recited the dialogue mechanically, in unison with the actors. Eventually, on the better-developed islands, the Seabees built tennis courts, horseshoe pits, and baseball diamonds. USO tours stopped at the larger islands, and the shows got bigger and more lavish in the final two years of the war. The smaller islands were lucky to receive any entertainment at all. Marine Private John Vollinger, who spent eight months on a lesser island in the Samoa group, saw "only one U.S.O. show consisting of two old vaudeville guys that told dirty jokes while juggling. Back in the States they would have been booted off the stage, but we wanted entertainment in any form." [47]

Heavy drinking was a time-honored outlet. Every island had an officers' club, though on smaller islands it might amount to a wooden table covered by a thatched roof. Admiral Aaron Stanton Merrill liked to say that "if we could find a palm tree and a bottle we'd set up an officer's club." [48] Enlisted men had to work harder to procure a supply. Throughout the Pacific, one could find an illicit trade in "torpedo juice," the high-proof fuel used in torpedoes. Beer was usually rationed at two cans a week. When a larger quantity of beer was obtained by backhanded means, it could be chilled by taking it to high altitude for thirty minutes. Pilots would provide that service in exchange for a share of the spoils. Whiskey was more scarce and expensive, but there was a price for everything on the black market.

"War everywhere is monotonous in its dreadfulness," wrote the newsman Ernie Pyle, when he toured the theater later in the war. "But in the Pacific, even the niceness of life gets monotonous. . . . [T]he days go by in their endless sameness and they drive men nuts. It's sometimes called going 'pineapple crazy.'" [49] Morale in the South Pacific boondocks was a growing concern in 1943. The Joint Chiefs discussed the problem at length. General Marshall worried about the state of mind among army garrisons on rear island bases, and thought it essential to move them forward into combat areas as soon as it became feasible. His views on this subject likely factored in the support he often gave to King's demands for offensive action in the Pacific.

ADMIRAL HALSEY, WHO PRESIDED OVER the far-flung islands from his COMSOPAC headquarters in Noumea, was one of those rare military leaders who did not attach much importance to his own dignity. He laughed out loud at jokes made at his expense. He wore khaki shorts that flaunted his pale, spindly legs. He was not too proud to admit that he had graduated in the bottom third of his Naval Academy class of 1904, or that he had run up enough demerits to put his career there in peril. He had been a star fullback, he often said, on the worst football team in the navy's history. (The team lost to Army every year he played, always by lopsided scores.) Halsey agreed with Ernest King's maxim that a sailor who didn't drink, smoke, or chase women was not to be entirely trusted. His bony hands were usually clutching a cigarette. He once stepped off a plane in Espiritu Santo and kissed his girlfriend, an army nurse, while a row of officers stood at attention. Now and again he drank until the break of dawn, slept for four hours, then grumbled about his hangover at the 9:00 a.m. staff meeting: "It seemed like a good idea last night."[50] Liberty with Halsey, said the admiral's long-term chief of staff, was "more damned fun than a circus."[51]

Halsey had a fine sense of the absurd. He threw out wisecracks that would not have been out of place in a Bob Hope monologue. Overhearing one sailor tell another, "I'd go through hell for that old son of a bitch," Halsey accosted the pair and said, "Right here I want to tell you that I object to being called 'old.'"[52] In 1945, upon receiving word of Japan's surrender, he sent the following instructions to all carrier air groups: "Investigate and shoot down all snoopers—not vindictively, but in a friendly sort of way."[53] He was willing to be kidded about his lack of fortitude under fire. When the *Enterprise* was attacked by Japanese warplanes off the Marshall Islands in February 1942, Halsey threw himself flat on deck, forsaking the grandeur of his three-star rank. As he picked himself up, he noticed that one of his young signalmen was stifling a laugh. "Who the hell are you laughing at?" he asked. "You don't have rank enough to laugh at an admiral." As the man began to apologize, perhaps fearing he was in serious trouble, Halsey cut him off, saying, "I'm going to make you a Chief Petty Officer—that will make it look better."[54]

Halsey knew perfectly well that stories of these antics would circulate widely, with variations and embellishments, all up and down the ranks. Together they crafted an image of a happy warrior, a fighting man who loved war and wanted everyone else to have as much fun as he was having. There was plenty of truth in that representation, but it was not complete. More than any other major military commander of the Pacific War, Halsey wore his emotions on his sleeve. He wept openly, frequently, and without pretense. When inspecting ships returned from battle, or visiting wounded men in hospital wards, or pinning medals to men's chests, or stepping up to a microphone to address the crew of a ship, he was never far from tears. Upon receiving the Distinguished Service Medal for leading a carrier raid into the Marshall Islands, he choked up and told the officers and men of the *Enterprise* that they had won it for him. His peculiar style of leadership was full of contradictions: simultaneously cold-blooded and tender-hearted, bombastic and coolly logical, overbearing and self-deprecating, sentimental and ridiculous. Whatever it was, it resonated powerfully. Sailor James J. Fahey of the *Montpelier* undoubtedly spoke for the fleet when he told his diary, in November 1943, "The men would do anything for him."[55]

He was taller than average, with broad shoulders and an exceptionally large head. His eyes were pale blue and crowned with graying, disheveled eyebrows. He had an old sailor's complexion, weather-beaten and spotted. His posture was not his greatest virtue; the cameras often caught him with his hands on his broad hips and his head set very far forward on his shoulders. Unlike King, Nimitz, Turner, or Spruance—in fact, unlike any other senior figure in the U.S. Navy—Halsey always made a point of smiling for photographers. He was a warm and cheerful man who liked people, even journalists. He was far more obliging with newsmen than either Nimitz or King, and always quick with a quotable line. They reciprocated his affection and gave him plenty of good copy. The press (and perhaps the American people) appeared eager to cast someone in the role of a Hollywood admiral. Halsey never auditioned for the role, but he did not recoil when it was thrust on him.

Today he is best remembered for his exuberant loathing of the enemy, summed up in his signature slogan: "Kill Japs, kill Japs, and then kill more Japs."[56] His messages to the fleet typically concluded with the refrain "Keep 'em dying." In a private letter to Nimitz, written shortly after he took command in the South Pacific, Halsey vowed that he was "obsessed with one idea only, to kill the yellow bastards and we shall do it." In the same letter he proposed new submarine operations as a means of "securing more monkey meat."[57] Killing enemy soldiers and sailors was the duty of every man in uniform, and Halsey was not the only senior Allied leader to indulge in exterminationist wartime rhetoric. But Halsey, more than any other officer of his generation, made himself famous (or infamous) for fudging the distinction between Japanese fighting forces and civilians, and for seeming to advocate a vengeful occupation of postwar Japan. "When we're done with them, the Japanese language will only be spoken in hell" was his (probably apocryphal) remark upon returning to Pearl Harbor the day after the December 7 attack. He told reporters, in early 1944, "When we get to Tokyo, where we're bound to get eventually, we'll have a little celebration where Tokyo was."[58] In private, Halsey suggested (presumably in jest) that the Allies should castrate all Japanese males and spay all Japanese women. He told Kelly Turner that he looked forward to parading Isoroku Yamamoto in chains through the streets of Washington, "with the rest of you kicking him where it would do the most good."[59] In several publicly reported remarks, he seemed to imply that Hirohito, the *Showa* emperor who was adored by ordinary Japanese as a benevolent father-god, would be executed following the Japanese defeat. On January 2, 1943, Halsey shared his vision for the postwar occupation of Japan: "We will bypass all smaller towns and let [occupation forces] loose in Tokyo. That will be a liberty town they'll really enjoy."[60]

Words are not deeds, and there is no reason to believe that Halsey, given the opportunity, would actually order a city sacked, a population neutered, or a prisoner degraded and abused in defiance of the Geneva Convention. Halsey's hatred of the enemy was genuine, and his sentiments were widely shared by servicemen and civilians of the Allied nations. In the peculiar context of a savage war, his more outlandish rants are best understood as figurative rallying cries rather than literal threats. Behind the bellowing thespian was a complicated man with a nuanced conscience. The crowning irony of his career came after the Japanese surrender in 1945, when Halsey (of all people) publicly criticized the decision to drop atomic bombs on Hiroshima and Nagasaki.

The more interesting questions are practical ones. How, if at all, did Halsey's virulent wartime rhetoric serve the Allied cause? Did it do any harm? After the war he explained that his purpose had been to embolden his fighting forces by deflating the myth of the Japanese "super-warrior," an artifact of Japan's extraordinary triumphs in the opening phase of the war. But it seems more likely (based on a reading of his wartime correspondence, and the opinions of those who worked closely with him) that Halsey's swashbuckling oration had no calculated purpose at all. He simply gave vent to his feelings without pausing to think through the consequences. He apparently never considered that he might be playing directly into the hands of Japanese propagandists, who could more or less truthfully report that an American theater commander had threatened to wipe out the entire Japanese race.

Dehumanization of the enemy was one of war's necessary evils, but it was every officer's responsibility to arrest the descent into bestiality. On Guadalcanal, a small minority of American infantrymen had engaged in the practice of mutilating enemy dead. Most common was the practice of extracting teeth for the value of their gold fillings—but there were also instances of men wearing severed ears on their belts, of necklaces made of teeth, of heads erected on poles, of skulls mounted on tanks. As early as September 1942, Nimitz had ordered that "no part of the enemy's body may be used as a souvenir," and warned that violators would face "stern disciplinary action."[61] That order was subsequently reinforced by several directives issued by the Joint Chiefs. But the practices of mutilation and trophy-taking continued throughout the war, and they were even reported in the American press. In May 1944, a *Life* magazine picture of the week depicted a woman admiring a Japanese skull sent to her as a gift by her boyfriend, a navy lieutenant. A month later, FDR was presented with a letter-opener carved from the bone of a Japanese soldier's arm. (The president accepted it at first, but later returned it with the request that it be buried.)

The Japanese news media was quick to seize on such reports. Cross-edited with excerpts of Halsey's bloody-minded tirades, they provided plenty of grist for the mill of Japanese wartime propaganda. Truth was cleverly combined with fiction. The Americans were represented as beasts, savages, and demons. Surrender to such a foe was unthinkable. The fight to protect the homeland must therefore be waged to the last man, woman, and child. In 1944 and 1945, when the inevitability of Japan's defeat was no longer in doubt, the cost would be paid in American as well as Japanese lives.

ON NEW YEAR'S EVE, 1942, Halsey met with a group of reporters aboard his flagship *Argonne* in Noumea Harbor. Asked for a preview of the war to come in 1943, he obliged. "Victory," he declared. "Complete, absolute defeat for the Axis powers."[62] Pressed to elaborate, he was unequivocal: the Allies would be in Tokyo by the end of the year. The reporters, presumably stunned by their good fortune, filed their copy, and the rash prophecy was splashed across the front pages of newspapers across America. In New Zealand two days later, Halsey stuck to his guns. "We have 363 days left to fulfill my prediction," he told *The New Zealand Herald*, "and we are going to do it."[63]

In his postwar memoir, Halsey confessed that he had known that the promised timetable was impossible. The war could not be won in 1943, or even in 1944. He had offered the spurious prediction as a means to bolster the morale of his forces and to fortify the political standing of New Zealand's prime minister, Peter Fraser. Within a matter of weeks, he began to understand that he had hoisted himself with his own petard. Draft boards complained. American production leaders feared that workers would leave the factories. Secretary Knox and Admiral King were obliged to deny rumors that Halsey had been drunk when he spoke to the press. The admiral's batty prediction would be flung back in his face, again and again. Eventually he would be forced to disavow it, to his own embarrassment and the glee of the Japanese copywriters.

According to DeWitt Peck, a marine officer who served in the COM-SOPAC headquarters, Halsey's loose tongue and high-spirited bluster-ing were strictly for public consumption. "The impression that people got from newspaper stories and so on [was] that he was impulsive and a damn-the-torpedoes-full-speed-ahead type. He wasn't. . . . I never saw him making a lightning damn-the-torpedoes decision at all. He was a thought-ful, intelligent, forceful leader."[64] Halsey insisted on a full airing of views before any decision. He wanted to hear every possible objection, every counterargument, and he encouraged even junior officers and enlisted men to speak up if they had something to say. As a strategist he was bold but not reckless. He had a fine command of details; he saw the entire picture; he weighed risks properly. A British officer who visited Halsey in Noumea was amused by the admiral's appearance and manner—his informality, his folksy humor, his shorts, his plain khaki shirt without insignia. "I remember thinking that he might well have been a parson, a jolly one, an old-time farmer, or Long John Silver. But when I left him and thought of what he had said, I realized that I had been listening to one of the great admirals of the war."[65]

Halsey had brought several key members of his carrier task force staff with him to the South Pacific. Miles Browning, who had served for more than a year as his chief of staff, retained that role and title in the South Pacific. Others included Julian Brown (intelligence), Doug Moulton (air operations), and Bill Ashford (flag lieutenant). Marine General DeWitt Peck, who had served ably as a war plans officer since before the Guadalcanal landings the previous August, stayed on in that capacity. Harold Stassen, a former governor of Minnesota, came on board as assistant chief of staff in March 1943. Rear Admiral William L. Calhoun, Nimitz's service force commander, came south to take over logistics in the South Pacific. Captain John R. Redman took over as COMSOPAC communications officer. Even with this talented line-up, however, the SOPAC headquarters organization remained shorthanded and overstressed until late 1943. More than once, Nimitz had to prod Halsey to provide timely action reports.[66] In Ray Spruance's tactful opinion, "Bill Halsey was a great fighter and leader of men, but he did not shine as an administrator."[67]

Halsey was determined not to repeat Ghormley's mistake of allowing himself to be bogged down in details. He would delegate as much authority as possible to others, preserving his time and energy for essential decisions. He received his fourth star shortly after taking over in Noumea, making him the sixth admiral to hold that eminent rank. It gave him leverage in Washington, which he employed to prevent the recall of some of his key officers to the capital, while demanding that more be sent to him. He also lobbied for promotions, and then threatened to promote officers on his own authority if his requests were not granted in timely fashion. The SOPAC organization grew steadily, eventually numbering over 300 officers and enlisted men of the navy, marines, and army. Halsey had an extraordinary ability to remember names and faces; he called enlisted men by their first names and summoned from memory minor details of their past service. He had an "open door" attitude. One of his officers recalled, "Halsey would see the janitor if he wanted to come in."[68]

The SOPAC staff developed a vital *esprit de corps*, symbolized by their practice (decreed by Halsey) of not wearing neckties. "He wants his men to be comfortable," a sailor observed in his diary. "He doesn't go in for this regulation stuff."[69] The "no-ties" policy was not entirely for the sake of physical comfort in a sweltering climate, however—army officers did not normally wear them, and Halsey did not want them to become a symbol of service divisions. "I don't want anybody even to be thinking in terms of Army, Navy, or Marines," he told his officers. "Every man must understand this, and every man *will* understand it, if I have to take off his uniform and issue coveralls with 'South Pacific Fighting Force' printed on the seat of his pants."[70]

Noumea was a languid little colonial capital, a bit tumbledown but still charming in contrast to almost any other seaport in the South Pacific. Vandegrift recalled it as "ramshackle in a pleasantly unpainted way with galleries encircling the second stories of residences and louvered doorways flanked by brilliantly blooming flowers."[71] Being French, the town offered good food and wine to those who could afford it. Plantation grandees lived in airy mansions on hills, flanked by elegant rows of coconut palms. Their daughters, usually dressed in immaculate white silk dresses, were local icons. Thousands of Americans who had never met them nonetheless knew their faces and names, but they were accessible only to officers and available only for marriage. The French colonialists were not overjoyed by the inundation of Americans, but granted that if they had to be overrun by Allied servicemen, better the Americans than the British.

As Halsey's staff expanded and the hot southern summer approached, it became increasingly evident that the flagship *Argonne* could not accommodate a major command. Local French officialdom had been uncooperative in responding to Ghormley's requests for quarters ashore, but Halsey was determined to succeed where his predecessor had not. He sent Colonel Julian Brown as an emissary to the French governor, His Excellency Marie Henri Ferdinand Auguste Montchamp. Having previously served in French forces, Brown had been awarded a fourragère and the Croix de Guerre, which he wore when he went to meet the governor. Brown asked for suitable housing in town or elsewhere on the island. "What do we get in return?" asked Montchamp. Brown replied, "We will continue to protect you as we have always done." At a subsequent meeting Brown added, "We've got a war on our hands and we can't continue to devote valuable time to these petty concerns. I venture to remind Your Excellency that if we Americans had not arrived here, the Japanese would have."[72]

To his credit, Halsey did not behave with the hubris of a conqueror. He took a personal liking to Governor Montchamp, whom he thought "a nice old boy, a good and tried soldier—albeit a bit futile."[73] But Charles de Gaulle's man in the South Pacific was Admiral Georges Thierry d'Argenlieu, the High Commissioner for Free France in the Pacific, who was often away and generally unresponsive to American wishes. Among the local colonists there were layers of intrigue that Halsey and his officers only gradually fathomed. The politics were complicated by political tensions between those sympathetic to the Vichy regime and those loyal to de Gaulle's Free French. The French had about 2,000 troops in New Caledonia, and Halsey thought they could easily be moved into one or two barracks. Halsey offered to feed all French troops in the island in return for an allocation of space—but when the question was appealed directly to de Gaulle, the answer was negative. "This whole situation is really a pain in the neck," Halsey wrote Nimitz on January 8, 1943. "We have very few dealings with them fortunately, but every time we do they are inclined to get in our hair. . . . It is the usual story: we do all the giving and they reciprocate by doing all the taking."[74]

Promises and small concessions followed. Eventually, the French allowed the COMSOPAC staff to relocate into an old barracks building near town. For living quarters, Halsey and his senior staff moved into the former Japanese consulate, a modest but comfortable brick house on a hill overlooking the harbor. The consul, who had been interned in Australia, had left behind his furniture, art, and housewares. Halsey relished living among paintings and embroideries depicting geishas, carp, and Mount Fuji, especially when a marine color guard raised the American flag over the house each morning. "We are enjoying his silverware, china and many other comforts," he told Nimitz. "Unfortunately the furniture (chairs, sofa, etc.) was designed for those short bandy-legged bastards. We must perforce sit on the back of our necks."[75] When a Filipino mess attendant broke a piece of the consul's china, Halsey told him, "The hell with it! It's Japanese."[76]

Captain Miles Browning, the chief of staff, had served with Halsey since 1938. He was one of the navy's early aviators, having earned his wings in 1924, and had done as much to develop aircraft carrier doctrine and tactics as any man in the service. Browning had always been an irritable character with an explosive temper, but in early 1943 he seemed to be cracking under the strain of prolonged service. He was drinking heavily, feuding with various officers, and attempting to restrict others' access to Halsey. He was rumored to have had an affair with another naval officer's wife, a grave offense. When Secretary Knox visited Noumea in January 1943, he was taken aback at Browning's brusque and disrespectful behavior. Complaints reached all the way to navy headquarters in Washington, and Admiral King, over Halsey's passionate objections, recalled Browning to the States, where he would take command of the new USS *Hornet* (CV-12). The new COMSOPAC chief of staff was Robert B. Carney, who would serve with Halsey for the rest of the war.

THE NEW SUPERBATTLESHIP *MUSASHI*, whose colossal proportions matched those of the *Yamato*, put in to Truk Lagoon on January 23.[*] She entered by the North Channel at low tide and anchored among the other big ships of the Combined Fleet, not far from her twin sister. Like the *Yamato*, she was manned by an elite, handpicked crew, was armed with a main battery of mammoth 18.1-inch guns (the largest naval weapons in the world), and was said to be "unsinkable." Like her sister, the *Musashi* would spend most of the war at anchor, draped in anti-torpedo nets. At the high cruising speed required for naval combat operations, the two behemoths drank prodigious quantities of fuel—and by 1943, Japan's oil supply was a matter of life or death to the empire.

One day after the final evacuation of Japanese forces from Guadalcanal, Admiral Yamamoto shifted his flag from the *Yamato* to the *Musashi*, the latter having been specially outfitted to function as the Combined Fleet's flagship. His launch brought him aboard while a military band played the national anthem. He passed in review, dressed as always in a pristine white uniform with gold braid and white gloves, and moved into his new suite of air-conditioned cabins, as upscale and spacious as those on the *Yamato*. Ugaki followed later that afternoon.

Yamamoto had aged considerably in the fourteen months since the raid on Pearl Harbor. His close-cropped hair had turned almost completely gray, and his eyes appeared discolored. Rarely did he emerge from his quarters, and when he did, it was only briefly, usually to acknowledge (with cap waved in the air) a departing ship or a squadron of aircraft. Occasionally he joined

---

[*] The ship was named not for the samurai-author, but for Musashi Province (an ancient name for a region encompassing part of Tokyo and points south).

his staff officers for a game of ring-toss on deck. In a letter written at the end of January 1943, he claimed to have set foot ashore only four times since the previous August, and only to visit sick or wounded men at the hospital or to attend funeral services. Other sources suggest Yamamoto was a regular patron of a "naval restaurant" on an island in the lagoon. The establishment was actually a franchised satellite of a well-known brothel near Yokosuka Naval Base in Tokyo Bay.

The commander in chief seemed resigned to his fate. When he was asked, in October 1942, what he would do after the war, he replied, "I imagine I'll be packed off either to the guillotine or to St. Helena."[77] On other occasions he declared that he did not expect to live through the war. He mourned the loss of so many of the fleet's officers and sailors, and was especially saddened by the loss of commanders who refused to leave their doomed ships. Yamamoto had campaigned to reform the principle that a captain could not honorably survive the destruction of his ship—but to little avail, as the belief was deeply inculcated in the Japanese naval officer corps. He was prone to existential ruminations. To a friend he wrote, "I wonder what heaven must think of the people down here on this small black speck in the universe that is earth, for all their talk about the last few years—which are no more than a flash compared with eternity—being a 'time of emergency.' It's really ridiculous."[78]

Though he could not say it overtly, Yamamoto must have known Japan was staggering toward a catastrophic defeat. He had thrown the entire weight of his considerable political influence against the decision to wage war on the United States. He had warned that the great industrial power of America must eventually overwhelm Japan. His attack on Midway in June 1942 had been a gambit aimed at forcing the war to an early conclusion. The failure at Midway had ensured that the conflict would become a prolonged war of attrition that Japan could not hope to win. He often criticized the "facile optimism" that Japanese commanders in the navy and especially the army carried into battle against the Americans.

On the morning of April 3, 1943, Admirals Yamamoto and Ugaki, accompanied by more than a dozen officers of the Combined Fleet staff, boarded two Kawanishi flying boats and flew to Rabaul. From there they would supervise "I-Go," an aerial counteroffensive against Allied shipping and bases in the southern Solomons and New Guinea. Yamamoto was quartered in a cottage high on a hill behind Rabaul town. He spent the following week inspecting airfields and other military installations, and meeting with local army and navy commanders in the various headquarters concentrated on New Britain. As always, he bid good luck to the departing air squadrons by standing in some prominent vantage point and waving his uniform cap over his head.

For ten consecutive days, heavily reinforced bomber and fighter groups attacked Allied shipping and airfields on Guadalcanal, Port Moresby, Milne Bay, and the Russell Islands. More than 200 aircraft attacked Guadalcanal on April 7, a raid larger than any attempted during the five months the Japanese had contested the island's ownership. As usual, the Japanese aviators and aircrews returned with fantastically exaggerated claims of success: they had destroyed dozens of ships and hundreds of planes. (In fact, I-Go claimed twenty-five Allied planes, one destroyer, one corvette, one oil tanker, and two transports. The Japanese lost forty aircraft in the operation.) Yamamoto, his spirits buoyed by the ostensible triumph, ordered the operation wound down. He announced that he would conduct a one-day tour of forward bases at Buin, Ballale, and Shortland Island on the eighteenth. The commander in chief's itinerary was radioed from Rabaul to those commands on April 13.

The signal was picked up by Allied listening posts. Cryptanalysts in Pearl Harbor went to work on it immediately, and it soon gave up its secrets. Major Alva B. Lasswell, duty officer at Joseph Rochefort's Combat Intelligence Unit ("Station Hypo"), translated the first version of the decrypt and pronounced it a "jackpot."[79] That the message referred to Yamamoto was easily deduced, and the geographic designators for Rabaul, Ballale, and Buin were quickly extracted. Better than that, the message contained the specific information that Yamamoto would travel on a medium bomber escorted by six fighters, and would "Arrive at RYZ at 0800." That would put the admiral's plane over the southern end of Bougainville on the morning of the eighteenth. The location was just within fighter range of Henderson Field. Lasswell and intelligence analyst Jasper Holmes took the decrypt to CINCPAC headquarters and handed it to the fleet intelligence officer Ed Layton, who laid it on Nimitz's desk a few minutes after eight on the morning of April 14.

Nimitz scrutinized the chart on his wall and confirmed that Yamamoto's plane would enter airspace that could be reached by American fighters operating from Guadalcanal. "Do we try to get him?" he asked Layton.[80]

The question could be broken into two parts.

First, was it wrong to target the Combined Fleet chief based on a conventional understanding of military chivalry? Like most naval officers of his
vintage, Nimitz had interacted socially with Japanese officers in the prewar
period. He was not a particularly vengeful or bloody-minded man. In eras
past, an American flag or general officer would certainly have refused to
single out his opposite number for assassination. Under no conceivable cir-
cumstance would George Washington have ordered a hit on William Howe,
or Robert E. Lee on Ulysses S. Grant. But war in the twentieth century was
not war in the eighteenth or nineteenth century. Even by the standards of
the Second World War, the Pacific campaign had been unremitting in its
brutality. Japan had not waged a limited war in the Pacific, nor had it asked
for one. As recently as the Russo-Japanese War (1904–5), Japanese ground
and naval forces had strictly adhered to the rules of war. Russian prisoners
had been housed comfortably, fed well, and provided with excellent medical
care. Their requests for cigarettes, spirits, and reading materials had been
readily granted. Those few who died in captivity had been buried with military honors. Had Japan carried those chivalrous inclinations into the present war, Nimitz might have hesitated to give the order. But the behavior
of Japanese forces in China, the Philippines, Malaya, Hong Kong, the East
Indies, and the Solomons had simplified the issue.

The second question was strategic. Was it wise to kill Yamamoto? This
was the man who had planned and executed the disastrous foray against
Midway, losing four aircraft carriers with all their aircraft. Yamamoto had
badly mismanaged the Guadalcanal campaign by deploying air and troop
reinforcements in piecemeal fashion. He was evidently doing a fine job of
losing the war. Shouldn't he be permitted to continue? But Layton, who
had known Yamamoto personally, argued that he was the best-respected
military leader in Japan, and that his death would strike a "tremendous
blow" at the enemy's morale. "You know, Admiral Nimitz, it would be just
as if they shot you down," he said. "There isn't anybody to replace you."
Nimitz, persuaded, sent Halsey an "eyes only" message alerting him to the
break and ordering a fighter interception. He concluded, "Best of luck and
good hunting."[81]

As it happened, Halsey had already learned of the operation in a chance
encounter in Melbourne, Australia. Halsey, who was inspecting naval
facilities in that city, had dropped in to the communications intelligence

office. A yeoman, Kenneth A. Boulier, was working on one of the draft decrypts when the COMSOPAC stopped at his desk and asked, "What are you working on, son?" When Boulier explained, Halsey raised his voice and addressed the entire unit: "Goddamit, you people knock off this Yamamoto business! I'm going to get that sonofabitch myself!"[82]

Southern Bougainville lay more than 400 miles from Henderson Field, but the planes would have to take a roundabout route to evade detection. The mission would require about 1,000 miles of flying, a range that would test the capabilities of even the longest-legged American fighters. The marine air commander on Guadalcanal assigned the job to the army's 339th Fighter Squadron, whose Lockheed P-38 Lightnings had a range comparable to that of the much lighter Zero. With a lean fuel mixture and drop tanks, the P-38s could (just) make the long flight. But the timing would have to be precise, as the planes would not have fuel to burn while awaiting the appearance of the enemy planes. Major John Mitchell of the 339th was assigned to lead eighteen P-38s piloted by handpicked airmen. Four of those aircraft were designated as "killers," the ones that would attack the medium bombers carrying Yamamoto and other high-ranking officers; the others would fly cover against the escorting Zeros. Mitchell's flight plan would put the squadron directly over the final approach to Ballale airfield at 9:35 a.m.

Yamamoto and his party arrived at Rabaul's Lakunai Field a few minutes before six. They climbed into the two waiting G4M "Betty" medium bombers—Yamamoto into one, Ugaki into the other. The men wore green khaki uniforms with airmen's boots. (Yamamoto's customary white dress uniform was thought too formal for the front lines.) The planes roared down the runway and climbed past the gray caldera guarding the entrance to the harbor. The weather was clear, with excellent visibility above and below a high ceiling of intermittent cumulus. Leveling out at about 6,500 feet, the two bombers flew in such close formation that Ugaki could clearly see Yamamoto through the windshield of the other plane, and even feared that the wingtips might collide. Zero escorts converged alongside, and drifted in and out of view. They droned on to the southeast for an hour and a half, hugging the southern coast of Bougainville.[83]

Ugaki nodded off as the group began its descent toward Ballale. At 9:43 a.m., he awoke to find his plane in a steep diving turn. The pilot was unsure of what was happening, but the sudden evasive maneuvers of the escorting Zeros had alerted him that something was awry. The dark green canopy of the jungle hills reached up toward them. The gunners opened up the gun ports to prepare for firing, and between the wind blowing in and the sound of the machine guns, things got very noisy. Ugaki told the pilot to try to remain with Yamamoto's plane, but it was too late; as his plane banked south, he caught a glimpse of his chief's plane "staggering southward, just brushing the jungle top with reduced speed, emitting black smoke and flames." His view was again obscured, and the next time he looked, there was only a column of smoke rising from the jungle.[84]

Ugaki's pilot flew over Cape Moira and out to sea, descending steadily to gain speed. Two Lightnings were in close pursuit, however, and .50-caliber rounds began slamming into the wings and fuselage. The pilot tried to pull up, but his propellers dug into the sea and the plane rolled hard to the left. Ugaki was thrown from his seat and slammed against an interior bulkhead. As the water entered the sinking aircraft, he thought, "This is the end of Ugaki."[85] Somehow, however, he and three other passengers managed to get free and swim toward the beach. They were helped ashore by Japanese soldiers and transported to Buin.

Yamamoto's plane had gone down about four miles inland, in remote jungle. Search parties took more than a day to find the site. There were no survivors. Yamamoto, according to eyewitnesses, was sitting upright, still strapped into his seat, with one white-gloved hand resting on his sword. A bullet had entered his lower jaw and emerged from his temple; another had pierced his shoulder blade. His corpse was wrapped in banyan leaves and carried down a trail to the mouth of the Wamai River, where it was taken to Buin by sea. There it was cremated in a pit filled with brushwood and gasoline. The ashes were flown back to Truk and deposited on a Buddhist altar in the *Musashi*'s war operations room.

News of Yamamoto's death was at first restricted to a small circle of ranking officers, and passageways around the operations room and the commander in chief's cabin were placed off limits. But the truth soon leaked out to the *Musashi*'s crew. Admiral Ugaki was seen in bandages; the white box containing Yamamoto's ashes was glimpsed as it was carried on board; and the smell of incense wafted from his cabin. Admiral Mineichi Koga was quickly named the new commander in chief, and flew in from Japan on April 25. At last an announcement was made to the crew. In Japan the news was kept under wraps for more than a month.

On May 22, Yamamoto's death led the news on NHK, Japan's national

Yamamoto Slain April 18, 1943

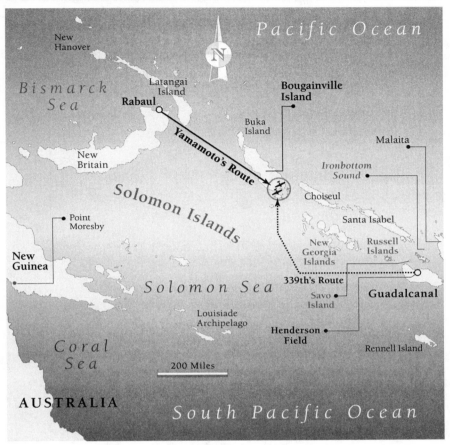

radio network. The announcer broke into tears as he read the copy. A special train carried the slain admiral's ashes from Yokosuka to Tokyo. An imperial party, including members of the royal household and family, greeted its arrival at Ueno Station. Diarist Kiyoshi Kiyosawa noted, "There is widespread sentiment of dark foreboding about the future course of the war."[86]

On June 5, 1943, the first anniversary of the Battle of Midway, a grand state funeral was held in Hibiya Park. Hundreds of thousands came to pay their respects. Pallbearers selected from among the petty officers of the *Musashi* carried his casket, draped in a white cloth, past the Diet and the Imperial Palace. A navy band played Chopin's funeral march. The casket was loaded into a hearse and driven to the Tama Cemetery, on the city's outskirts, where it was lowered into a freshly dug grave alongside that of Admiral Togo.

Yamamoto's old friends and colleagues waved away talk of establishing a "Yamamoto Shrine." Admiral Mitsumasa Yonai recalled that the admiral had always deplored the deification of military officers. "Yamamoto hated that kind of thing," said Yonai. "If you deified him, he'd be more embarrassed than anybody else."[87]

Chapter Eight

EXHAUSTED, BEDRAGGLED, AND BEARDED, WITH BOOTS COMING APART at the seams and fraying dungarees hanging from gaunt limbs, the veterans of the 1st Marine Division left Guadalcanal the first week of December 1942. Many were so emaciated and disease-ridden that they lacked the strength to climb from the boats into the transports anchored off Lunga Point. Agile and well-fed sailors had to descend the cargo nets, seize them under the armpits, and haul them up and over the rails to the deck, where they lay splayed in bone-weary bliss, finally sure that they had seen the last of the odious island. At least eight in ten were suffering recurrent fits of malarial fever, barely kept in check by regular doses of Atabrine. After they were initially sent to Camp Cable, a primitive tent camp about forty miles outside Brisbane, Australia, they were transferred by sea to Melbourne, the graceful Victorian city in that nation's temperate south, where they would spend the next several months recuperating and training for their next combat assignment.

That year the War Department had published a handbook entitled *Instructions for American Servicemen in Australia*. It offered a digest of information that would be found in any civilian travel guide: statistics concerning population ("fewer people than there are in New York City"), geography ("about the same size as the United States"), natural history ("the oldest continent"), and history (largely skirting the touchy subject of the nation's origin as a penal colony). The authors took pains to emphasize the similarities between Americans and Australians. Both were pioneer peoples who spoke English, elected their own leaders, coveted personal freedom, loved sports, and had spilled blood to defeat the Axis in every theater of the war.

There were differences too, in traditions, manners, and ways of thinking—
the handbook warned that *bahstud* was no smear, and could even be taken
as a term of affection—"but the main point is they like us, and we like
them. . . . No people on earth could have given us a better, warmer welcome, and we'll have to live up to it."[1]

That last point was evident from the moment the marines strode down
the gangways onto the Melbourne docks, where they were greeted by a
brass band playing the "Star-Spangled Banner." Herded onto a train that
would take them to the city center, they could hardly believe their eyes
or their good fortune. The railway was lined with cheering and shouting women. They blew kisses, waved little American flags, and reached
up to touch the marines' outstretched hands. Regiments were to be billeted in various suburbs—Balcombe, Mount Martha, Ballarat—but the 1st
Marines were the most fortunate because they were sent to the Melbourne
Cricket Grounds, near the heart of the city, where tiers of bunks had been
installed in the colossal grandstand. In that semi-protected barracks, the
veterans would live out of their packs, partly exposed to wind and rain.
None complained. According to Robert Leckie, they were mainly interested in a female mob that had gathered just outside the pitch. The women
were "squealing, giggling, waving handkerchiefs, thrusting hands through
the fence to touch us."[2] They asked for autographs and gave their telephone numbers in return.

Discipline collapsed. Men went AWOL for days. Women reported to the
officer of the day and requested "a marine to go walking with."[3] At night,
guards left their rifles leaning against the fence and disappeared into the tall
grass of Victoria Park. In the entire history of the Marine Corps, a sergeant
cynically observed, there had never been so many volunteers for guard duty.

A large proportion of young Australian men had shipped overseas,
leaving a gender imbalance at home. War and the threat of invasion had
upended conventional moral strictures and dramatized the ephemeral—life
might end tomorrow, so better live for today. Many Australian women did
not mind admitting that they found the newcomers charming and alluring.
Before the war, they had heard American-accented English only on the
wireless or at the cinema, when it was on the lips of screen idols like Clark
Gable and Gary Cooper. In person they found it exotic and magnetic. In
early and mid-1942 they had feared invasion with all its horrors, and the
flood of Allied servicemen gave them a longed-for sense of security.

In contrast with the Aussie "digger," the Yank wore a finely tailored uniform and was instinctively chivalrous. He had money in his pocket and was willing to spend it. He danced outlandish jazz steps like the Jitterbug, the Charleston, or the Shim Sham. He stood when she entered a room, he held the door, he pulled out her chair, he filled her glass, he lit her cigarette, he brought flowers, and he gave gifts. She had not been brought up to expect any of that, and was not accustomed to it. The novelty was intoxicating.

Alex Haley, future author of the novel *Roots*, was a young messboy on the cargo-ammunition ship *Muzzim*. Haley had been submitting love stories to New York magazines; all had thus far been rejected. When the ship departed Brisbane in 1942, the crew enlisted his talents to compose letters to the women they had met while on liberty. Haley lifted and transposed passages from his unpublished stories. He made carbon copies so that the letters could be recycled, and even established a filing system—eventually 300 letters filled twelve binders—to ensure that the same woman did not receive the same letter twice. When the ship returned to Brisbane, Haley recalled, one after another of his shipmates "wobbled back" from a night at liberty on the town, "describing fabulous romantic triumphs."[4]

By no means did the Australian male lack a decent sense of etiquette. He was affable, plainspoken, and honest. There was no artifice in him, and he was ready to welcome any man as his friend. "Good on you, Yank!" was his customary hail. If an American approached him on Flinders Street and asked for an address, he did not point and give directions; he walked half a mile or more to be sure the visitor found his destination. But it was not the digger's practice to mollycoddle his woman, as if she were a princess or a porcelain doll. He drank with his mates, and not in mixed company. The Yank knew of no such constraint and saw no reason to abide by it. The moment a woman appeared, he was up out of his chair and playing at his pusillanimous and unmanly courtship routines. In the Land Down Under, a man who said "ma'am" or "please" or "after you" too bloody many times was marked as a pantywaist. Late at night, when all the girls had gone off with all the Yanks, the diggers had a good laugh among themselves at the visitors' effete and sissified ways.

James Fahey, sailor on the *Montpelier*, polled his shipmates in early 1944. Given the option to take liberty in any port in the Pacific, which would they choose? Sydney won by a commanding margin, beating Honolulu, San Francisco, and San Diego. The sentiment was universal. "It was everyone's dream to go to Australia," wrote a PT boat skipper in the Solomons.[5] And it would be too cynical by half to say it was just the girls. Australia was paradise—a fairer, friendlier, more honest and open-hearted version of America. Before movies and other performances, all stood and uncovered for the "Star-Spangled Banner" as well as "God Save the King." The climate, landscape, and wildlife were magnificent. Families opened their homes to the Americans as if they were long-lost sons. Homesick farm boys from Kansas or Arkansas took a train into the country and volunteered to work a few days in the paddocks. "When you go to Australia it is like coming home," Fahey mused in his diary. "It is too bad our country is so far away. Our best friends are Australians and we should never let them down, we should help them every chance we get."[6] Even in a fight, the Australian was trustworthy—he did not pull a knife or throw a low punch. Like the Yank, he guarded his rights and was not cowed by authority. Mobs of Yanks and diggers often fought baton-swinging constables and MPs, with international alliances on either side. With the arrival of the wireless a generation earlier, Australia had felt the pull of America's cultural gravity, but now it was the Yanks who were calling one another "mate," "bloke," or "cobber." First Division marines sang "Waltzing Matilda" at the top of their lungs, and added old British campaigning songs to their drunken repertoire—especially "Bless 'Em All," with the refrain profanely amended when no respectable citizen was in earshot. Intermarriage, discouraged by both civil and American military authority, was nonetheless relatively common. Many hundreds of Americans would settle in Melbourne and Sydney after the war.

Even the differences were familiar. The Yanks recognized and approved of the Australian obsession with sports, even if they privately found the antipodal versions of baseball and football incomprehensible and plainly inferior. The racetracks looked much the same as those in America, except the horses ran clockwise and the punters muttered darkly about the murder of someone called "Phar Lap." Beer was cheap and plentiful even if the pubs shuttered at the unreasonable hour of six. The locals relished their steaming caffeinated doses even if the cup was filled with tea instead of coffee. Mutton was not a great hit with the Yanks, but they couldn't get enough of the Australian meat pies and "styke and aigs." The currency was almost farcically esoteric. The pound note was simple enough, but the coinage was a ludicrous mob of copper and silver pieces, engraved with the images of kangaroos and emus, divisible by two, three, four, twelve, or twenty—the shilling, the florin, the sixpence, the penny, the halfpenny, and the three-penny, but one also heard mention of the bob, the copper, the thrippence, the zac, the deener, the traybit, the quid, and the guinea. (Regarding the last of these, *Instructions for Servicemen* recommended, "Don't bother about it.") With rare exceptions, however, the Australians did not exploit the Americans' ignorance to cheat or shortchange them.

Inevitably, as the novelty faded and the "friendly invasion" swelled to near a million American servicemen, the limits of Australian hospitality were put to the test. With the cities overrun by sweet-talking, free-spending Yanks, the local economy boomed but the locals were pinched. Pubs sold bottles out the back door at inflated prices, and then announced to the reg-ular clientele that the shelves were empty. Some thoughtless Yanks offered insult when none was intended, remarking that they had arrived to "save Australia," or referring to the country as a "colony," or comparing cricket unfavorably to baseball, or disparaging the taste of mutton. A spate of deadly road accidents was blamed on boozed-up Yanks driving on the right (wrong) side of the road. A serial killer terrorized Melbourne in the spring of 1942: three women were strangled and left with their genitals exposed. The per-petrator was a U.S. Army private named Edward Joseph Leonski, who was arrested, convicted, and hanged. To some Australian commentators, the ghastly crimes seemed emblematic of the Yanks' predatory sexual depravity.

Girls no older than fifteen or sixteen commandeered boats and rowed out to American naval vessels anchored in Sydney Harbour. Some learned semaphore so that they could get ahead of the competition by signaling incoming ships. Wives whose husbands were fighting overseas were seen in the company of Yanks; couples grappled openly in the parks and on the beaches; epidemics of syphilis and gonorrhea swept through the urban populations. Untold hundreds of women died after botched back-alley abor-tions. Fathers were appalled to hear their daughters bicker among them-selves: "I saw him first, and anyway Vera is engaged."[7] Bishops, editors, and politicians rushed to man the barricades of morality. Sir Frank Beaurepaire, the Lord Mayor of Melbourne, urged parents to exert "stricter control over their young daughters" and to "control the older girls who claim the right to do as they like."[8] Newspapers joined the campaign to police female sexual-ity, publishing censorious editorials under headlines such as "Behaviour of Girls Causes Concern," "Street Scenes Problem," and "Girl's Yearning for

Yanks."[9] W. J. Tomlinson, a Methodist minister in Queensland, wrote to the *Courier-Mail* to lament that Brisbane had sunk deeper into wickedness than Sodom and Gomorrah.[10] A Japanese leaflet dropped on New Guinea depicted an American soldier embracing a woman. "Take your sweet time at the front, Aussie," says the smarmy Yank, whose slick-backed hair is parted down the middle. "I've got my hands full right now with your sweet tootsie at home."[11] Every propagandist knows that the most potent appeal is founded on a modicum of truth.

In Brisbane, Queensland's state capital, heavy concentrations of both American and Australian troops overwhelmed the city's public services, housing, and retail and trade establishments. The population doubled in less than a year, to about 600,000. There was not enough of anything to go around, but the highly paid Yanks usually contrived to obtain superior service in the shops, pubs, and restaurants. The diggers were barred from shopping in the American PXs, which offered subsidized prices for hard-to-get goods such as cigarettes, razor blades, food, candy, liquor, and nylon stockings (highly prized as gifts). The Australians understandably resented being relegated to second-class citizens in their own country, and their grievances inevitably boiled over, especially when fueled by alcohol.

Street brawls erupted nightly throughout October and November 1942, climaxing in a major disturbance in the heart of the city on November 26, which would go into the history books as the "Battle of Brisbane." Beginning in the early afternoon, sporadic battles broke out throughout the downtown area, becoming more sustained and violent as the crowds grew larger and drunker. As night fell, a melee raged outside an American PX on the corner of Creek and Adelaide Streets. Touched off when a group of baton-wielding American MPs harassed an American soldier, on whose behalf a group of diggers generously intervened, the fracas swelled as hundreds of enraged soldiers and civilians poured into the intersection and the Americans retreated into the building. A siege ensued. Bottles and rocks crashed through the windows and the mob tried to batter down the door with a signpost uprooted from the sidewalk. The Americans unwisely broke into the PX's inventory of weapons and brandished shotguns at the angry rabble. One of the weapons discharged as several pairs of hands grappled for it. An Australian soldier was shot dead and several others were injured. Fighting continued and spread through the city. For the rest of the night and into the next day, hundreds of Americans were beaten badly, especially around the Allied headquarters on the corner of Queen and Edward Streets.

Except for a brief and heavily censored report in the Brisbane *Courier-Mail*, no reference to the incident appeared in the press. This attempt to suppress the news boomeranged, however—too many witnesses had seen the riots. In the absence of official statements or corrections, their stories grew lurid in successive retellings. It was said that American forces had massacred unarmed crowds and that heaps of bodies were piled in the streets of Brisbane. (In truth, there had been many scores of injuries but only one death.) Smaller riots followed in the weeks ahead, both in Brisbane and in other communities, including Townsville, Rockhampton, Melbourne, and Bondi Beach in Sydney.

THE AUSTRALIAN CULTURE OF "MATESHIP" was a conscious rejection of English class hierarchies. Instinctive distrust of authority was paired with a fondness for the underdog. The country was royalist only in the sense that it was faithful to its British heritage. In Australia, a rich man might be better off than his neighbors, but that did not make him better and he had better not forget it. Power, privilege, and individual achievement were tolerable only if conjoined to an attitude of genuine humility. According to a local maxim, the "tall poppy" was the first to be cut down. Probably there was not another society in the world less inclined to elevate an individual to the status of idol or messiah.

Douglas MacArthur was the first and probably the last man in Australian history to put that proposition to the test. In the national emergency of 1942, Australians opened their arms and embraced him as a savior. Enormous crowds gathered each day outside the Menzies Hotel in Melbourne, where he and his family lived for four months after their arrival in the country. The day of his arrival was declared "MacArthur Day." Newspapers serialized one of the many instant hagiographies that had been published in the United States. "Douglas" was one of the most popular names for Australian boys born between 1942 and 1945. Photographs of him appeared in shop windows. They were often autographed, as his headquarters always accommodated requests for signed portraits. The *Truth*, a Brisbane paper, told its readers that "MacArthur is the man to whom the civilized world looks to sweep the Japs back into their slime."[12] When he visited Canberra in May 1942, the House of Representatives gave him the privileges of its floor. Without delay and apparently without dissent, Prime Minister John Curtin acted to abolish the military board and invest its powers in MacArthur as supreme commander of Australian forces. MacArthur placed his thumb on the scale of Australian politics when he said that Curtin, whose Labour government held a knife's-edge majority in Parliament, was the "heart and soul of Australia."[13]

MacArthur did not add a single Australian officer to his personal headquarters staff, and he refused requests from Washington to do so. His staff would be dominated by his chief of staff, the high-handed and mercurial General Richard K. Sutherland, and other members of the "Bataan Gang" who had joined his audacious cover-of-darkness escape from Corregidor by PT boat. The blow was softened a bit by his nomination of an Australian officer, General Sir Thomas Blamey, as commander of Allied land forces in the theater. He and Curtin together lobbied Churchill to send British naval forces to the theater, and were refused.

In time, many Australians would come to resent MacArthur's aversion to crediting Australian troops in his portentous press communiqués, and they could not have overlooked the fact that the general was broadly unpopular among the hundreds of thousands of American servicemen pouring into the country. According to the anti-MacArthur chatter heard among American servicemen of all branches, he was "Dugout Doug," an arrogant potentate who had remained cosseted with his wife and young son in an opulent Corregidor bunker while his army starved on Bataan; who had fled the scene with suitcases of clothing, furniture, and valuables, leaving sick nurses behind to be defiled by the Japanese; who had run all the way down to Melbourne, as far from the enemy as he could go without continuing south to Tasmania or Antarctica; and who insisted on monopolizing all glory and honor while denying it to the men actually doing the fighting and the dying. When American servicemen in Australia tired of eating so much mutton, a rumor circulated that MacArthur owned a sheep ranch and was being enriched at their expense.

Most of these charges were false, and some were perverse. Whatever MacArthur was, he was no coward. His service in the Great War had left no doubt of his exceptional personal courage, but he proved it again on Corregidor, where he stood erect and unflinching at an observation post while Japanese planes flew low overhead, bombs burst nearby, and his staff dived for cover. He left Corregidor with his family and a core of his staff only after FDR ordered him to do so. He and his party took one suitcase each. MacArthur was a deeply flawed man whose Olympian ego and garish vanity warped his perceptions and even stained his personal integrity. As a commander of armies, he would have been more at home in the eighteenth century. But he was also an officer of rare and brilliant ability, who combined an expansive perspective with an exceptional memory and a quick grasp of detail.

More than any other Allied military leader, MacArthur instinctively perceived the larger context of the Pacific War. The Japanese had vowed to drive the Western interloper from Asia, and Asian peoples must inevitably be enticed by that proposition. It was not enough to reverse Japanese conquests. Japan's imperial pan-Asian ideology had to be smashed and replaced with something better. MacArthur's greatness—and his greatness is indisputable—would not be fully revealed until after the war, when he would rule as a latter-day *shogun* over the reconstruction of a democratic Japan.

In July 1942, MacArthur moved his family and his headquarters north to Brisbane, to be closer to the combat theater. His headquarters staff moved into the abandoned offices of the AMP Society, an insurance company that had evacuated to the south. For his personal office, MacArthur claimed a grand boardroom on the ninth floor. Here he had a secure telephone that connected directly with the War Department in Washington. The MacArthur family lodged in three adjoining suites on the top floor of the graceful Lennons Hotel on George Street. Crowds gathered outside each morning, hoping for a glimpse of the supreme commander as he walked from the lobby to his black Wolseley limousine with the license plate "USA-1." At eleven each morning, a phalanx of policemen cleared the street, and the four-year-old Arthur, accompanied by his Filipina Chinese governess, crossed to the state's Parliament House. The tall wrought-iron gate was solemnly unlocked, the boy and his nurse entered, the gate was locked behind them, and the police stood by while the boy played in the grounds.

MacArthur liked to work while on his feet. He paced his office tirelessly, and would not talk to an officer on the telephone if he could walk to the man's office and lean on his desk. His standard opener was, "Take a note." General George C. Kenney, who relieved George Brett as commander of Allied Air Forces in the theater in August 1942, resolved to confront MacArthur's despotic chief of staff, General Sutherland, directly early in

his tenure. When Sutherland began issuing orders to the air groups, infringing on what Kenney believed to be his rightful purview, he drew a dot on
a blank sheet of paper and told Sutherland, "The dot represents what you
know about air operations, the entire rest of the paper what I know."[14] Kenney demanded that they ask MacArthur to clarify their respective spheres
of authority. Sutherland, according to Kenney, capitulated and gave him no
more trouble.

Admiral Thomas C. Kinkaid, who replaced Arthur S. Carpender as
commander of Allied Naval Forces, Southwest Pacific Area (SWPA) in
November 1943, likewise contrived to circumvent Sutherland. MacArthur
was not as isolated and remote as his reputation suggested. Senior officers
whom he respected felt free to walk into his office whenever they wanted a
word with him. In Kinkaid's telling, he would often walk in and say, "General, I just came up to smoke a cigarette."

> He'd say, "Fine," and hand me the cigarette box and I'd take a ciga-
> rette. "Won't you have a seat?" And then, "You don't mind if I walk?"
> So he'd walk up and down the room, which was his habit, while we
> talked.
>
> Sometimes I would have things that I knew the General didn't
> approve of and might object to, and then I would say, "Well, General,
> I've got something this morning that I don't think you approve of."
>
> "All right, what is it?"
>
> So I'd tell him, while he walked up and down. He never inter-
> rupted. And when I finished, then he'd start to talk. I knew that the
> General would eventually get off base. If I had a good case, I'd just let
> him talk until he did and then I'd say, "General, you know damned
> well what you said isn't so."
>
> He'd look around at me over his shoulder and say, "Well, maybe
> not," and go on walking and puffing his pipe.[15]

As commander of the U.S. Seventh Fleet—"MacArthur's Navy"—
Kinkaid had to straddle the awkward command setup that made him simultaneously answerable to MacArthur and Admiral King. That he succeeded
in the job was a credit to his tact and diplomatic talents. Much like Kenney,
Kinkaid was an outsider who stood apart from MacArthur's intensely loyal
staff, a coterie of army officers who shared and amplified the boss's paranoia

and prejudices and were loath to challenge his views when he was wrong on the merits. Both Kenney and Kinkaid discovered to their surprise that MacArthur was more amenable to dissent than his overawed staff seemed to realize. "Nobody could take MacArthur as an average man," Kinkaid observed. "They either put him up on a pedestal, or else they damned him, and neither is correct."[16]

No military leader ever took a greater interest in the press. For both Australians and Americans, MacArthur's resounding communiqués provided the essential narrative of the war in the South Pacific. Colonel LeGrande "Pick" Diller, recruited by Sutherland to run MacArthur's publicity department, was armed with the powers of wartime press censorship. He scrubbed all press copy of any implied or actual criticism directed against the SWPA command, whether or not legitimate issues of military secrecy were at stake. Reporters who laid the praise on thick were rewarded with favored treatment and access. Kenney acerbically noted that news did not see the light of day unless it "painted the General with a halo and seated him on the highest pedestal in the universe."[17]

MacArthur managed to transfix and overawe a room filled with veteran reporters—pacing the room, entertaining no questions, and speaking off the cuff for an hour or more without repeating himself. He had the facility to "write on his feet"—to communicate in polished, well-constructed, multi-clause sentences. Reporters came away with a sense of having been enlightened, even if they were not free to write what they wished. When MacArthur was emotional, his rhetoric was prone to career from the gallant to the purple, as when he eulogized the American soldiers fallen on Bataan: "To the weeping mothers of its dead, I only say that the sacrifice and halo of Jesus of Nazareth has descended upon their sons and that God will take them unto himself."[18]

Seeing the name of a subordinate officer in print put MacArthur in a foul temper. He favored the antique rhetorical device of substituting the singular pronoun "I" for the forces under his command. Arriving in Australia from Bataan, he insisted on the formulation "I came through and I shall return." Asked by the Office of War Information to amend that to "We shall return," MacArthur refused. "I shall return" had a Caesarian ring, and was the most memorable phrase of the entire Pacific War. To the Filipino people, suffering under an atrocious occupation, the first-person declaration was a thunderbolt of hope and inspiration. But the singular pronoun was unpopular among the troops, who found it bombastic and ungenerous. As the war moved north, men in the line of fire were chagrined to learn that "MacArthur," from his headquarters in Brisbane, had bombarded an enemy airfield or secured a new beachhead. In May 1942, the general deftly seized credit for the Battle of the Coral Sea, a naval victory won in Nimitz's theater by forces under Nimitz's command. General Robert L. Eichelberger, who led a grueling and bloody campaign against Japanese forces at Buna on southeastern New Guinea, believed MacArthur conspired to convince the press and public that he was personally at the head of the Allied fighting forces. Eichelberger vented his resentment in private letters to his wife. Following MacArthur's brief trip to Port Moresby, wrote Eichelberger, "the great hero went home without seeing Buna before, during, or after the fight while permitting press articles from his GHQ to say he was leading his troops in battle. MacArthur . . . just stayed over at Moresby 40 minutes away and walked the floor. I know this to be a fact." [19]

The close of the Guadalcanal campaign would take the fight west of the 159th parallel—into Douglas MacArthur's domain. Based on the division of command responsibilities negotiated by the Joint Chiefs a year earlier, Halsey remained in Nimitz's chain of command, and his forces would continue to "belong" to Nimitz. But as SOPAC ships, aircraft, and troops were deployed into the central and upper Solomons, they would fall under MacArthur's strategic authority. The navy had often avoided sending its ships to Australia for fear of losing them to MacArthur. In March 1942, for example, King had stipulated that Admiral Fletcher's task force should avoid Sydney because the appearance of American aircraft carriers in that harbor might "inspire political demands to keep him in Australian waters." [20] Worse, the awkward arrangement ruled out direct discussions of strategy between Halsey and MacArthur. If protocol was to be strictly observed, any major operation Halsey wished to undertake west of the 159th must be proposed to Nimitz, who would pass it to King, who would consult with Marshall, who would forward it down the chain to MacArthur. The reply would take the absurdly roundabout path back through Washington and Pearl Harbor to Noumea.

The command setup, as Halsey shrewdly put it, had been intended "to maintain equilibrium between the services." But it was plainly ineffective and fraught with risks. On February 21, 1943, Halsey had landed 10,000 soldiers and marines in the Russell Islands. As soon as they were secure,

Halsey poured Seabees into the islands and supplied their two new fighter strips with lavish amounts of ammunition and aviation fuel, in anticipation of an expanded air offensive against the central Solomons. But the Russells were at the absolute limit of his demarcated border (slightly over it, in fact), and no more westward progress could occur without MacArthur's blessing. Halsey had his eye on Munda Point, a new Japanese fighter strip in the New Georgia group 120 miles farther west, as a site that offered terrain suitable for a large bomber field. The COMSOPAC wisely decided to see if the issue could be resolved in a face-to-face summit. In early April 1943, he crossed the Coral Sea and presented himself at the AMP building in Brisbane.

There was no reason to expect the two to establish a warm personal rapport. Halsey had not appreciated MacArthur's credit-snatching communiqués, and an aide remembered him referring to the general as a "self-advertising son of a bitch." MacArthur had imperiously declined Nimitz's invitation to attend the command conference in Noumea in September 1942, sending Sutherland and Kenney in his place. (The minutes of the conference, prepared by one of Nimitz's staff officers, began with a sarcastic comment: "MacArthur found himself unable to be present."[21]) To his surprise, however, Halsey took an instant liking to the general. Within five minutes, Halsey later wrote, "I felt as if we were lifelong friends. I have seldom seen a man who makes a quicker, stronger, more favorable impression. He was then sixty-three years old, but he could have passed as fifty. His hair was jet black; his eyes were clear; his carriage was erect. If he had been wearing civilian clothes, I still would have known at once that he was a soldier."[22] MacArthur, for his part, was equally impressed with Halsey: "He was of the same aggressive type as John Paul Jones, David Farragut, and George Dewey. His one thought was to close with the enemy and fight him to the death. . . . I liked him from the moment we met, and my respect and admiration increased with time."[23]

Even making allowances for interservice and inter-theater diplomacy, there is no reason to suppose that these opinions were less than sincere. In the year that followed, the admiral and the general would effectively coordinate their operations in the South Pacific. As Kenney and Kinkaid had learned, and as Halsey found in turn, MacArthur was accustomed to deference but did not bristle at well-reasoned opposition. He would yield to sound arguments. Army-navy frictions were more often attributed to his subordinates, and could be resolved in direct communications between the two theater commanders, whose mutual respect and affection did not fade away even when they were at odds. Halsey's long-term chief of staff, Robert Carney, was witness to a heated argument between the two theater commanders later in 1943. The admiral, with his "chin sticking out a foot," told MacArthur that he was placing his "personal honor . . . before the security of the United States and the outcome of the war!" In Carney's recollection, the accusation brought MacArthur up short. "Bull," he said. "That's a terrible indictment. That's a terrible thing to say. But, I think in my preoccupation, I've forgotten some things. . . . You can go on back now. The commitment will be met."[24]

As it turned out, Halsey's proposed attack on the New Georgia group was exactly in line with MacArthur's thinking, and he approved the operation on the spot. It would intersect admirably with MacArthur's existing plans for an offensive up the north coast of New Guinea and the occupation of Woodlark Island and the Trobriand Islands. ELKTON, the Maryland town famous as a destination for quick marriages, was the code name given to the two-front offensive. D-Day on New Georgia was originally set for May 15, subsequently postponed to June 30.

THE 1943 CAMPAIGN BEGAN with a perceptible lull. For the first time since December 1941, the Allies were entirely on the offensive, but they were not yet strong enough to mount an all-out assault on the Japanese stronghold at Rabaul, on New Britain. The campaign would require "climbing the ladder" formed by the Solomons chain. Japan shortened and fortified its new defensive line, running from Munda on New Georgia to Salamaua in New Guinea. Above all, it was an air war. New beachheads and rapid airbase construction extended the ranges of bombers and fighters northwest toward the great enemy bastion at Rabaul.

The Cactus Air Force was reorganized and expanded into Air Command Solomons (abbreviated as AIRSOLS), an amalgamation of army, navy, and marine air groups, combined with bombers and fighters of the Royal New Zealand Air Force. The first commander of AIRSOLS (COMAIRSOLS) was Rear Admiral Charles P. Mason, whose multiservice and international staff was based at Henderson Field. The effective radius of most strikes was about 200 to 300 miles, and Rabaul lay more than 600 miles away. New airfields were needed farther up the Solomons, and they would be

Joint Chiefs of Staff (JCS) at a luncheon meeting, mid-1943. From left to right: General Henry H. "Hap" Arnold (USAAF), Admiral William D. Leahy, Admiral Ernest J. King, General George C. Marshall. *Official U.S. Navy Photograph.*

Rear Admiral Richmond Kelly Turner, USN (left), and Major General Alexander A. Vandegrift, USMC, on the flag bridge of the transport *McCawley* during the WATCHTOWER Operation.
Official U.S. Navy Photograph.

Japanese G4Ms armed with aerial torpedoes fly through antiaircraft bursts to attack the American fleet off Guadalcanal on August 8, 1942. Note the skilled wave-top approach.
Official U.S. Navy Photograph.

Henderson Field, Guadalcanal, in late August 1942. This aerial view looks northwest, with the Lunga River and Ironbottom Sound in the background. Bomb and shell craters pockmark the entire area. *Official U.S. Navy Photograph.*

Wreckage of a SBD scout bomber on Guadalcanal, still afire after being destroyed on the ground by a Japanese air attack.
Official U.S. Navy Photograph.

Battle of the Eastern Solomons, August 24, 1942. This photograph, taken from the island veranda of the *Enterprise* (CV-6), recorded the third of three bombs to strike the carrier in a huge Japanese dive-bombing attack.
Official U.S. Navy Photograph.

South Pacific command conference on USS *Argonne* at Noumea, New Caledonia, on September 28, 1942. From left to right: Major General Richard K. Sutherland, chief of staff to General MacArthur; Admiral Chester W. Nimitz, CINCPAC; Vice Admiral Robert L. Ghormley, COMSOPAC; and Major General Millard F. Harmon, USAAF.

Official U.S. Navy Photograph.

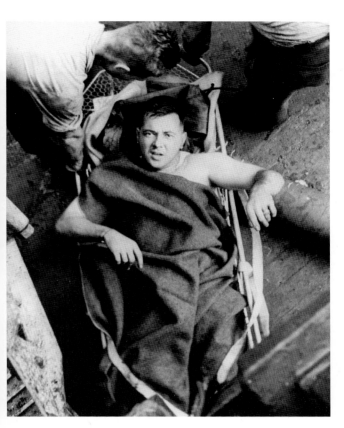

Battle of Tassafaronga, November 30, 1942. A wounded man is evacuated from the torpedo-stricken cruiser *Minneapolis*, flagship of Rear Admiral Carleton H. Wright.
Official U.S. Navy Photograph.

U.S. amphibious troops transfer into landing craft for the landing at Empress Augusta Bay, Bougainville, November 1943.
U.S. National Archives.

An LST transports troops of the 1st Marine Division to a landing on Cape Gloucester, the western extremity of New Britain, in December 1943. Note the wealth of supplies and munitions loaded into trucks and jeeps on deck.

U.S. National Archives.

Marines encounter rough surf as they wade ashore unopposed at Cape Gloucester on December 26, 1943. *U.S. National Archives.*

The Gato-class submarine *Wahoo* (SS-238) is launched at Mare Island, California, February 1942. *Courtesy of Mare Island Historic Park Foundation.*

The newly commissioned *Wahoo* gets underway in the Napa River, July 1942.
Courtesy of Mare Island Historic Park Foundation.

Richard O'Kane, executive officer, and Dudley "Mush" Morton, captain of the *Wahoo*.
Courtesy of Mare Island Historic Park Foundation.

The Japanese destroyer *Harusame* struck by an audacious "down the throat" torpedo shot in Wewak Harbor, northern New Guinea. Photograph taken through the periscope of the *Wahoo*, January 24, 1943. *Courtesy of Mare Island Historic Park Foundation.*

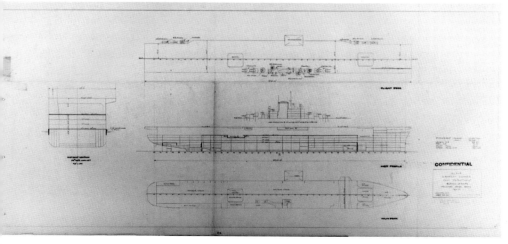

Preliminary design plan for the *Essex*-class aircraft carriers.
U.S. Naval Historical Center Photograph.

USS *Essex* (CV-9), underway in May 1943. She was the first in a new class of powerful fleet carriers that would spearhead the advance into the western Pacific. A squadron of SBD scout bombers (lacking folding wings) are parked aft on the flight deck. Amidships, with wings folded, are F6F Hellcat fighters and TBF torpedo planes.

Official U.S. Navy Photograph.

Marines advance across a devastated landscape on Betio Island, Tarawa Atoll, November 1943.
U.S. National Archives.

Hangar deck of the *Yorktown* (CV-10), circa October–December 1943. Ordnancemen are working on bombs among several parked F6F Hellcats. In the background, a movie is being screened for their shipmates.

U.S. National Archives.

won by the same sort of naval and amphibious operations that had won Guadalcanal. AIRSOLS could put about 300 planes into action in March 1943; by midyear, the total would exceed 450. The venerable F4F Wildcat, SBD Dauntless, TBF Avenger, B-17, and P-38 Lightning—more of those long-legged army fighters were gradually pried from Hap Arnold's reluctant grasp—would continue to do the arduous and deadly work of reducing Japanese airpower in the South Pacific. They were reinforced by new, fast, powerful arrivals, including the F6F Hellcat, Grumman's next-generation carrier fighter, and the Vought F4U Corsair, a gull-winged fighter-bomber issued to marine fighter squadrons on Guadalcanal. AIRSOLS operations were supported by the heavy bombers of General Kenney's Fifth Air Force, staging from airfields on southeastern New Guinea. Kenney received ample USAAF reinforcements, including the 475th Fighter Group (all P-38s, with elite and highly trained pilots), and a new medium-bomber group, the 345th. Old, dilapidated, and combat-weary B-17s were replaced with newly commissioned B-24 Liberators.

Halsey and MacArthur were still operating under the Joint Chiefs' directive of July 1942, which had set a deadline of September of that year for the conquest of Rabaul. The headquarters in both SOPAC and SWPA had simply ignored that deadline, which was obviously so unrealistic as to be absurd. Task One had been completed with the expulsion of Japanese forces from Guadalcanal in February 1943; Tasks Two and Three called for a coordinated advance up the Solomons and New Guinea followed by the reduction of Rabaul. New orders and deadlines were needed, but Admiral King now proposed another characteristically audacious stroke. Why not penetrate deep into Japanese territory by bypassing all of the Solomons and all of New Britain, instead landing an invasion force in the Admiralty Islands west of Rabaul? The latter could be suppressed in an air offensive but never actually taken.

Nimitz, Halsey, and MacArthur joined in opposition to the idea, arguing that the bypassed Japanese positions would represent thorns in the side of the elongated supply lines. MacArthur told the chiefs that he needed Rabaul as a forward naval base, and leaping over it "would involve hazards rendering success doubtful."[25] American carrier forces, much reduced in the sea battles of 1942, could not compensate for a lack of land-based air support. The Pacific commanders favored a stepwise advance, with a chain of newly constructed airfields supporting each new landing. King yielded to this united front of opposition, but his conception of the bypass would eventually be adopted by Halsey and MacArthur as a tactical linchpin in the South Pacific offensive.

On March 28, 1943, the Joint Chiefs issued a new directive for the advance toward Rabaul. MacArthur and Halsey would push north and west in two parallel advances through the Solomons and up the coast of New Guinea, culminating in landings on western New Britain (MacArthur) and Bougainville (Halsey). The two-pronged operation was given the name CARTWHEEL.

INTERSERVICE COORDINATION BETWEEN THE Japanese generals and admirals remained intermittent and largely ad hoc. General Imamura's Eighth Area Army headquarters at Rabaul stood above Hyakutake's Seventeenth Army, comprising three divisions spread over the Solomons and New Britain, and General Hatazo Adachi's Eighteenth Army, which had another three divisions on New Guinea. Troop reinforcements were arriving in Rabaul, and the garrison there would soon exceed 90,000. Vice Admiral Jinichi Kusaka remained in command of navy forces at Rabaul and held responsibility for the defense of the central Solomons. Admiral Mineichi Koga had succeeded the slain Yamamoto as commander in chief of the Combined Fleet, based at Truk. Nowhere in the theater was there a blended command; the army and navy had to coordinate their operations through a meticulous process of nemawashi, or "digging around the roots," for a consensus. The Japanese moved new air units into the theater, including more of the elite carrier aircrews that had trained and honed their skills before the war—but the loss ratios in air combat continued to move sharply against the Japanese in 1943.

Facing the growing effectiveness and confidence of Allied bombing runs, Japanese shipping became more vulnerable than ever before. Because of the distances involved, the Japanese army on New Guinea could be reinforced only by daylight convoys. In March 1943, USAAF and RAAF aircraft based at Moresby and Milne Bay slaughtered an entire convoy of transports attempting to land troops in the Lae-Salamaua area. The army bombers employed a new technique called "skip-bombing," which involved attacking at masthead altitude and "skipping" bombs off the sea and into the sides of the target ships. Kenney's Fifth Air Force bombardiers employed slow-fused bombs that gave the pilots time to pull up and get out of range of the explosions. Reiji Masuda, a crewman on the destroyer *Arashio*, left a vivid account of the harrowing attack:

> They would come in on you at low altitude, and they'd skip bombs across the water like you'd throw a stone. That's how they bombed us. All seven of the remaining transports were enveloped in flames. Their masts tumbled down, their bridges flew to pieces, the ammunition they were carrying was hit, and whole ships blew up. . . . They hit us amidships. B-17s, fighters, skip-bombers, and torpedo bombers. On our side, we were madly firing, but we had no chance to beat them off. Our bridge was hit by two five-hundred-pound bombs. Nobody could have survived. The captain, the chief navigator, the gunnery and torpedo chiefs, and the chief medical officer were all killed in action. The chief navigator's blackened body was hanging there, all alone.
>
> Then a second air attack came in. We were hit by thirty shells from port to starboard. The ship shook violently. Bullet fragments and shrapnel made it look like a beehive. All the steam pipes burst. The ship became boiling hot. We tried to abandon ship, but planes flying almost as low as the masts sprayed us with machine-guns. Hands were shot off, stomachs blown open. Most of the crew were murdered or wounded there. Hundreds were swimming in the ocean. Nobody was there to rescue them. They were wiped out, carried away by a strong current running at roughly four or five knots.[26]

At least 3,600 Japanese troops were killed in this "Battle of the Bismarck Sea." MacArthur, in a statement released for radio broadcast in the United States, called it "one of the most complete and annihilating combats of all time."[27] He marked it as a signal moment in military history, when airpower had finally and forever asserted its preeminence over seapower.

FAR TO THE NORTH, in the western reaches of the Aleutian archipelago, Japanese forces remained in possession of Kiska and Attu. The two bleak, fog-mantled islands had been seized in June 1942, during the Midway operation, by a task force under the command of Vice Admiral Boshiro Hosogaya.

Thanks to a phenomenal effort by his radio intelligence analysts, Nimitz had known of the move against the Aleutians before it happened (just as he had known of the attack on Midway). Concluding that the islands would be of little value to the Japanese, and could be retaken in good time, the CINCPAC had chosen not to oppose the invasion.

Both sides had once regarded the Aleutians as a potential route of invasion of northern Japan, by way of the Kurile Islands and Hokkaido. But the Americans eventually abandoned the northern line of attack, mainly because the dreadful weather conditions prevailing in those latitudes would pose severe challenges for sea and air operations. Since the islands lay near the "Great Circle" shipping route, the Japanese had imagined that they might serve as useful watch posts against naval incursions—but this theoretical advantage was defeated by persistently bad visibility over the surrounding seas. Possession of the two islands—the only incorporated territory of the United States to fall under enemy occupation during the war—provided the Japanese with a propaganda triumph of sorts. After the crushing defeat of the Imperial Japanese Navy at Midway, Tokyo noisily acclaimed the capture of American territory and implied that the offensive would continue into mainland Alaska and beyond. In military terms, however, Attu and Kiska were never more than a liability. Provisioning and resupplying their garrisons consumed shipping and other resources that the Japanese urgently needed in other regions.

The Aleutians were a terrible theater in which to live, to fight, or to get anything done at all. Soldiers, airmen, and sailors generally hated to be sent north. Flying conditions were among the worst of the war, and operational losses exacted a heavy toll on both sides. In the summer, the sea and islands were habitually carpeted by heavy fog. Planes lost their way and ditched at sea, or descended through a low cloud ceiling and flew directly into terrain. Between September and May, a frigid climate and long nights made for even more atrocious flying conditions—before an aircraft could even leave the ground, its engines had to be warmed with blowtorches, and ice had to be chipped off its wings. The great distances lying between the Japanese and American bases exacerbated the challenges on both sides. Rear Admiral Robert A. Theobald, Commander of the North Pacific Area (COMNORPAC), was based in Kodiak, Alaska, 1,000 miles east of Kiska. USAAF bombers could reach Kiska from the U.S. airbase at Dutch Harbor, on Unalaska island—but the flying distance (about 500 miles) was too far to permit a fighter escort. Attu, some 190 miles west of Kiska, lay entirely out of air-striking range.

Hosogaya lacked forces to mount any sort of eastward offensive, and remained chiefly concerned with repelling air attacks and securing his seaborne supply line against a gauntlet of American submarines. Efforts to build an airfield on Kiska were thwarted by a combination of weather, soft soil, and a dearth of equipment, materials, and labor. Air defense was chiefly provided by floatplane Zeros, which were cumbersome and easily destroyed in air combat; air reconnaissance was provided by flying boats, but many of these big aircraft were lost to accidents or navigation errors.

In September 1942, as days shortened and temperatures plummeted, it became clear that the Japanese could not be driven off the islands until the spring of 1943 at the earliest. As the Guadalcanal campaign heated up, it pulled the sea and air forces of both combatants south. American submarines continued to claim a few victims, American cruisers and destroyers periodically shelled the Japanese garrisons from offshore, and Theobald's air forces continued to pester Kiska with regular air raids.

In Kodiak, service frictions between the navy and the Army Air Forces deteriorated steadily through the fall of 1942. Admiral Theobald pressured his USAAF subordinates to bomb at lower altitude—descending below the cloud ceiling for the sake of accuracy—but that drove up operational losses. The Americans needed air strips farther west, nearer to the enemy objectives, but the two services could not agree on a location for a major new airbase—the navy wanted Adak, the Army Air Forces insisted on nearby Tanaga. The issue was appealed to the Joint Chiefs, who chose Adak. But that island was so often shrouded in fog that another one was needed for an emergency strip. In January 1943, an advance force landed on Amchitka, which lay only ninety miles east of Kiska.

When the Imperial General Headquarters in Tokyo learned of the new airfields on Adak and Amchitka, it made the belated decision to pour resources into Kiska and Attu in hopes of fortifying them against an expected counterassault. But the rigors of winter and a tenuous supply line continued to hobble the Japanese airfield construction program. Coastal defenses were improved on Kiska and to a lesser extent on Attu, but the Japanese had been late off the mark and were racing against the calendar. Late spring would bring better weather for air and sea operations.

Washington was determined to recapture the islands in 1943, if only to silence the outcry in Congress—members of the Washington and Oregon delegations were warning that the Japanese might land in Alaska and sweep down on Seattle. That scenario was incredible, but no one could say so in public without tipping off the enemy to American indifference. Moreover, should the Soviet Union enter the war against Japan, the Aleutians would provide a useful staging area for aircraft deliveries to Siberia. Nimitz's planners estimated that sufficient forces could be assembled by May for a landing on Attu, but there would not be enough to attempt a landing on Kiska until midsummer. In March, Nimitz requested and received clearance from the Joint Chiefs of Staff to aim the first landing at Attu instead of Kiska, even though the former was 190 miles west of the latter.

That month a radio intercept revealed that a Japanese supply convoy was inbound for the Aleutians. Rear Admiral Charles "Soc" McMorris, a future chief of staff to Nimitz, took a cruiser-destroyer squadron north from Pearl Harbor in hopes of intercepting and destroying the enemy freighters. Contact was made at dawn on March 26. The winds were light and the seas unusually mild. Under a 2,500-foot cloud ceiling, visibility was extraordinarily clear. McMorris's flagship, the cruiser *Salt Lake City*, obtained radar returns on five ships several miles due north. As light came up, lookouts gradually perceived the profiles of several destroyers and at least one cruiser. The Japanese column turned southeast to engage, and McMorris continued gamely into range. The enemy force included four cruisers and four destroyers, altogether commanding about twice McMorris's aggregate firepower. He had not expected to encounter enemy warships, certainly not a powerful surface force.

At 8:40 a.m., the Japanese cruiser *Maya* opened fire from long range, about 20,000 yards. The second salvo straddled the *Salt Lake City*. That was unnervingly accurate shooting. The *Salt Lake City* returned fire and landed two hits on the cruiser *Nachi*. McMorris turned to port, and the American ships began "chasing salvos" to avoid taking hits—that is, continuously altering course toward the last splash in order to foil the enemy gunners' targeting corrections. The two columns fought a long running battle. *Salt Lake City* was battered by the *Nachi*'s and *Maya*'s 6-inch shellfire, taking several hits between 9:00 and 11:00 a.m. Seawater entered her boilers and shut them down, leaving her dead in the water with a 5-degree list. Several American destroyers closed around her and began making smoke.

At this stage, McMorris's prospects appeared grim. Two Japanese cruisers and several destroyers were closing the range on his port quarter. They would undoubtedly fire torpedoes on the immobilized flagship when they came within optimal range. The admiral ordered his three destroyers to charge the approaching enemy and launch a spread of torpedoes. Before the destroyers could get into range, however, the Japanese ships broke off contact and turned away to the west. The Americans watched in surprise as the enemy withdrew over the horizon. By noon, the *Salt Lake City*'s boilers were back in operation and the ship was able to make 30 knots. McMorris's squadron retired toward Dutch Harbor.

The six-hour "Battle of the Komandorski Islands"—named for a Russian island group that lay some miles north—had nearly ended in an American debacle. If Admiral Hosogaya (who had personally led the Japanese force from his flagship *Nachi*) had pressed his advantage, he would likely have destroyed the *Salt Lake City* and might have claimed several of her consorts as well. Hosogaya later explained that he had withdrawn because he expected an American airstrike at any moment. Some of his crew had mistaken the *Salt Lake City*'s high-explosive shells for bombs dropped from above the cloud ceiling. The Japanese ships were also low on fuel and ammunition. Nevertheless, Hosogaya's conservative decision was condemned by superiors, and the admiral was forced into retirement.

McMorris's force had suffered damage to three ships and had lost seven men, all killed. Two Japanese cruisers were damaged, later repaired; casualties were fourteen men killed and twenty-six wounded. The Battle of the Komandorski Islands marked the last attempt of the Japanese to resupply the Attu and Kiska garrisons with surface ships; all future supply runs would be made by submarines.

Attu, among the most remote and inhospitable places on earth, was a lump of treeless muskeg plains rising to bare, bleak peaks about 2,500 feet high. Though it was American territory, the Americans knew almost nothing of the island's interior terrain. The best and most recent maps covered only part of the island, and only to a distance of about 1,000 yards inland. The offshore approaches were not well charted.

Troops assigned to seize Attu were drawn from the army's 7th Infantry Division, which had completed an amphibious training course overseen by Marine General Holland "Howlin' Mad" Smith. Task Force 51, consisting of more than fifty ships, with 34,000 troops embarked in transports, closed in on the island before dawn on May 11. A small scouting force landed on the northern coast, near Holtz Bay, from submarines and a destroyer transport. The main landings were to follow in the south, at Massacre Bay—but the southern group was forced to wait most of the day for the fog to lift, and the first units did not reach the shore until about 3:30 p.m. They encountered little opposition, however—and by nightfall, 1,500 troops were ashore in the north and another 3,500 in the south.

The Japanese defenders did not contest the landing, remaining in defensive positions on high ground. Colonel Yasuyo Yamazaki, the Japanese commander, concentrated his 2,650 troops in the hills between the two landing sites. Knowing that he could not defeat the Americans, and that he could count on no naval or air support from Japan, he burned all sensitive documents. The American naval task force pounded the island from off the shore, but Yamazaki's force was strongly entrenched and the persistent fog helped to conceal the Japanese positions. Throughout the afternoon of May 11 and into the following night, Japanese artillery rained projectiles down on the American troops of the southern force. The Americans advanced steadily inland, but their progress was impeded by the difficult terrain. The island's spongy soil would not support the weight of trucks and armored vehicles. On May 17, Holtz Bay was cleaned out and the first contingents of the northern and southern forces made contact.

The last Japanese troops retreated to a ridge above Chichagof Harbor. At dawn on the twenty-ninth they broke out of their position in an all-out *banzai* charge. The mass of men moved through the American lines and penetrated deep into the rear areas. In a fierce battle, including much hand-to-hand fighting, nearly the entire Japanese garrison was killed.

The Americans had not yet mastered their skills in amphibious warfare, and the Attu operation exposed many shortcomings. The force did not have enough landing craft. It had not prepared sufficient contingencies for bad weather and poor visibility. The assault troops were not adequately equipped with cold-weather uniforms and gear. Key supplies were late to the beach or were not landed at all. The American casualties were 580 killed and 1,148 wounded in combat; another 1,200 suffered frostbite and other cold-related injuries.

The landing on Kiska, ten weeks later, was one of the greatest anticlimaxes in the history of amphibious warfare. For a week in August the island was battered by bombing raids and heavy naval gunfire. On August 15, a big transport fleet arrived and put 34,000 Canadian and American troops ashore. (The invasion force was twice the size of the one that had participated in the WATCHTOWER landings in the Solomons a year earlier.) The invaders advanced inland cautiously, but they found no one and encountered no hostile fire at all. The Japanese garrison had been evacuated under cover of fog two weeks earlier.

Considering the expenditure of naval ordnance and aerial bombs on an island that had been vacated by the enemy, and the tremendous investment of shipping and troops in a bloodless invasion, the Kiska operation had been slightly farcical. In Pearl Harbor, the news was received in good humor. Nimitz liked to tell visitors how advance elements of the huge invasion force, creeping inland with weapons at the ready, were warmly greeted by a single affable dog that trotted out to beg for food.

IN THE SOUTH PACIFIC, the Munda operation began on June 30, 1943, when Admiral Turner's Third Amphibious Force put troops ashore on Rendova Island, five miles south of the assault beaches on New Georgia. This island would have offered an ideal platform for artillery fire directed onto the landing site, but the Japanese had not secured it and the small garrison was swiftly overrun.

With the cover provided by newly installed batteries, landing boats ferried army and marine units across the sound to New Georgia. AIRSOLS put hundreds of planes into the air to support the landing. Japanese air attacks were brushed off with little trouble, but the American ground troops ran into forceful resistance as they closed the ring around the Munda airfield. The 4,500-man Japanese garrison had dug in deeply and well, and the terrain was abysmal. The Munda campaign was a photonegative of the fight on Guadalcanal, with the Japanese and Allied positions reversed. Now it was the American soldiers and marines who struggled through swamp and underbrush, losing contact with adjacent units and suffering heavily under harassing attacks by the enemy. Japanese units launched nighttime *banzai* attacks, accompanied by shouted profanities and taunts in broken English. Two green American army regiments broke and ran, throwing down their weapons; several were shot by other American soldiers who mistook them for enemy, and several dozen had to be evacuated because of "psychoneurosis." One officer recalled that fear was like a disease that spread through the ranks, eventually transmuting into mass panic. Discipline and morale crumpled. "By morning, in an unmanageable mass, men were huddling in groups along the trails to the rear and pursued savagely by the enemy that caught up with many of them and—to use an archaic phrase—put them to the sword."[28]

Eventually, all available reserves were committed to the capture of Munda. Three army divisions required a full five weeks to secure the airfield; 1,195 Allied servicemen were killed in the effort. Most of the defenders died or took their own lives, but a few managed to evacuate by sea to Vila airfield on nearby Kolombangara.

As if more evidence was needed, the Allies now had another exhibit in the case against the wisdom of frontal attacks on strongly entrenched island positions. The road to Rabaul was not open. The Japanese had another dozen airfields, large and small, on islands to the north, east, and west. The complex on southern Bougainville, in particular, would require a long and bloody effort to capture. Commanders in Washington, Pearl Harbor, Noumea, and Brisbane began to study and debate the concept of bypassing or "leapfrogging" strongly defended positions, as a means to speed the campaign and contain the cost in Allied lives. Ernest King's proposal (in March 1943) to pole-vault over Rabaul to the Admiralties had been an idea ahead of its time, but it would soon be adopted as the centerpiece of the Allies' grand strategy in the Pacific.

In his widely read memoirs, *Reminiscences*, MacArthur named himself the mastermind of the leapfrogging strategy. "I intended to envelop them, incapacitate them, apply the 'hit 'em where they ain't—let 'em die on the vine' philosophy," he wrote. "There would be no need for storming the mass of islands held by the enemy."[29] The truth is that MacArthur was a late convert to the cause. Robert Carney, chief of staff to Halsey's "Dirty Tricks Department"—the insiders' affectionate nickname for SOPAC headquarters—recalls obstinate opposition from his counterparts in Brisbane. "MacArthur felt that you simply couldn't go away and leave strong forces . . . upon your flank or behind you. This thinking in his outfit was quite different from the thinking in ours."[30] MacArthur apparently adopted the leapfrogging philosophy some time after the bypass of Rabaul was ordered by the Combined Chiefs of Staff (the American-British supreme command) in August 1943. Even then, he initially opposed several bypassing maneuvers, notably Halsey's leap past Kavieng in March 1944.

Immediately northwest of New Georgia was the island of Kolombangara, a perfectly round stratovolcanic cone soaring out of the sea to an altitude of 5,800 feet. A Japanese garrison was dug in at Vila Airfield, on the island's southern shore. Admiral Kusaka expected the next amphibious landing to fall on Vila, and had been reinforcing the position for weeks. Japanese troop strength in the perimeter had reached about 10,000 troops, more than double the number the Allies had faced at Munda. On August 15, the Third Amphibious Force instead circumvented Kolombangara and seized a beachhead on the island of Vella Lavella, about fifty miles north, where the enemy garrison numbered only 250 men. The invasion force suffered minimal casualties, and the Seabees had a new airfield operating within three weeks. Realizing that Kolombangara was to be ignored by the enemy, Admiral Kusaka ordered the garrison evacuated to Bougainville, under cover of darkness, by submarines and destroyers.

In attempting to reinforce their beleaguered positions in the New Georgia group, Japanese cruiser and destroyer squadrons clashed with Allied task forces in several minor naval battles. The Japanese retained their customary excellence in night torpedo actions, and their Type 93 "Long Lance" torpedoes remained the best weapons of their kind in the theater, but the Americans were learning to use their superior radar systems to advantage. Each ship now correlated information from radar and other sources in the Radar Plot, which later evolved into the Combat Information Center (CIC). During this period the U.S. Navy also benefited from the exceptional leadership of seagoing commanders such as Rear Admirals Walden Lee "Pug" Ainsworth and Aaron Stanton Merrill, and Commander Frederick Moosbrugger and Captain Arleigh "31-Knot" Burke. During the battle for Munda, Admiral Ainsworth twice intercepted inbound Japanese forces at the Battles of Kula Gulf (July 6) and Kolombangara (July 13). In each engagement, the Americans approached in a single column with cruisers in the center, fired on the lead ships in the Japanese column, and then turned away to avoid the inevitable torpedoes. In both battles, the Allies and Japanese suffered in about equal measure; in each, the Japanese force was beaten back and failed to reinforce Munda.

On the night of August 6–7, Commander Moosbrugger led a division of six destroyers in two parallel columns (the tactic had been developed by Burke, recently recalled to higher command) against another incoming Japanese squadron. One column fired a spread of torpedoes and turned away. As the Japanese fired on the withdrawing ships, the second column crossed the enemy's "T" and opened a devastating salvo of gunfire. Three Japanese destroyers, crammed with troops intended for Kolombangara, blew up and went down. One spectacular explosion, as described by one of the American action reports, "took the form of a large semicircle with the water as the base, extended six to seven hundred feet into the sky."[31]

A thousand Japanese soldiers and sailors were killed in the explosions or drowned afterward. Tameichi Hara, commanding the one Japanese destroyer to escape the action, concluded that "the enemy had ambushed us perfectly."[32] The tactics employed by the Americans in this "Battle of Vella Gulf," faithfully executed by Moosbrugger, served as a template for several surface actions to come in the fall of 1943.

The tide of battle in the South Pacific had decisively turned. Japanese naval operations became increasingly concerned with evacuating troops as their positions grew hopeless. During the retreat from Kolombangara, the Japanese had established a staging base for barges and landing craft at Horaniu, on the northeast shore of the island of Vella Lavella. An Allied landing at Horaniu on September 14 dislodged the 600-man Japanese garrison and sent them in a disorderly overland retreat to Marquana Bay on the northwest shore. Admiral Kusaka ordered a rescue operation. Rear Admiral Matsuji Ijuin sailed from Rabaul with a force of six destroyers and two transport groups, the latter including three transport destroyers. About twenty small craft joined up from Buin on southern Bougainville.

On October 6, this small armada—seemingly disproportionate to the task at hand—was discovered by American air search. Six American destroyers were in the area, and they moved to intercept, but they were divided into two divisions separated by about twenty miles. The northern group—the *Selfridge, Chevalier,* and *O'Bannon,* under Captain Frank R. Walker—charged into action without waiting for Captain Harold O. Larson's southern group (the *Ralph Talbot, Taylor,* and *La Vallette*). Since the days of John Paul Jones, American naval lore had honored and applauded the bold attack on superior enemy forces. In this case, however, Walker's daring proved rash. His three-destroyer squadron advanced on Ijuin's nearest division of four destroyers and fired projectiles and torpedoes. Ijuin turned away and blew a smoke screen to cover his withdrawal, but one of his destroyers, the *Yugumo,* continued toward the Americans and exchanged fire as she closed. She was lit up by at least five 5-inch shell hits and quickly exploded into flame. A few minutes later, Walker's ships ran into a deadly spread of Long Lances. The *Chevalier* and the *Selfridge* each had their bows torn off, and the *O'Bannon* was unable to avoid colliding with the injured *Chevalier*. The *Selfridge* continued firing gamely on the second division of enemy ships, passing in column at a range of about 11,000 yards, but took a torpedo in her port side at 11:06 p.m. The *Chevalier* was finished, while the heavily damaged *O'Bannon* and *Selfridge* managed to hobble back into Purvis Bay. As the Americans cleared the area, the Japanese small craft completed the evacuation of the troops at Marquana Bay. The Japanese had won a tactical and strategic victory in this "Battle of Vella Lavella." It was to be their last sea victory of the war.

At the first Allied conference in Quebec (code-named QUADRANT and held in August 1943), the British chiefs—tilting toward any arrangement that would release more forces to the campaign against Nazi Germany—had backed King's case to consolidate offensive resources into a single drive across the central Pacific. That would have sidelined the South Pacific operations and marooned MacArthur in a strategic backwater. FDR was swayed by Marshall's insistent demands to continue the southern push toward the Philippines. The president was likely influenced by MacArthur's political weight and his implicit threat to accept the Republican nomination for the presidency in 1944.

Pursuant to the conference directives, the Combined Chiefs of Staff (CCOS) promulgated a revised plan entitled RENO III, which directed MacArthur to "seize or neutralize Eastern New Guinea as far west as Wewak and including the Admiralties and the Bismarck Archipelago. Neutralize rather than capture Rabaul."[33] The document reasoned that "direct attack to capture Rabaul will be costly and time-consuming. Anchorages and potential air and naval bases exist at Kavieng and in the Admiralties. With the capture and development of such bases, Rabaul can be isolated from the northeast."[34]

The next and last major landmass on Halsey's road to Rabaul was Bougainville. Here the bypass principle would again save time and lives. The Japanese had poured troop reinforcements into its bases on and around the island—at Buin and Shortland in the south, and at Buka and Bonis in the north. By mid-October, total Japanese strength in these areas exceeded 40,000 men. Halsey and his Dirty Tricks Department elected to land forces on the west coast, at Cape Torokina in Empress Augusta Bay, where the enemy presence was negligible. By now the pattern was familiar. Assault troops stormed ashore, heavy equipment and munitions followed behind them, the forces established a strong perimeter, and Seabees raced to build a working airfield. The Japanese army would naturally counterattack—but to do so they were obliged to struggle over primitive jungle terrain, their strength draining away by starvation and disease, before running up against well-entrenched American defenders.

For this operation (CHERRY BLOSSOM), Halsey could muster about 34,000 troops under the command of General Vandegrift—the 3rd Marine Division and the army's 37th Infantry Division, combined into the First Marine Amphibious Corps. As an immediate prelude to the landings, the New Zealand 8th Infantry Brigade Group seized the small Treasury Islands. On November 1 before dawn, 3rd Division marines stormed ashore at Cape Torokina from a dozen transports and swiftly overpowered the meager Japanese forces in that area. Furious air battles raged overhead throughout the day, but the AIRSOLS fighters managed to prevent any sustained attack on the beachhead. Kenney's Fifth Air Force poured an unprecedented amount of punishment down on Rabaul's airfields to suppress the Japanese air response. By nightfall, 14,000 troops were safely ashore with 6,000 tons of equipment, munitions, and supplies.

The Imperial Japanese Navy was determined to interrupt the operation. Kusaka organized a cruiser-destroyer task force at Rabaul and sent it south under the command of Rear Admiral Sentaro Omori. This force was discovered by air search as it steamed down the Slot, and Halsey ordered his only naval force in the area, Admiral Merrill's Task Force 39, to protect the beachhead. The crews of Merrill's four light cruisers and eight destroyers had been hard at it for more than twenty-four hours and were nearing the point of exhaustion, but no other forces were on hand. Merrill employed the tactic of deploying his destroyer divisions in a separate group to launch unseen attacks on the enemy's flank. His cruisers guarded the approach to the beaches, kept up a continuous fire with their 6-inch guns, and looped around in coordinated "figure-8" patterns to confuse the enemy and avoid his torpedoes. Arleigh Burke, recently promoted captain, commanded Destroyer Division 45. The tactics had been well rehearsed, and the commanders were perfectly attuned to one another.

James Fahey, a sailor on Merrill's flagship *Montpelier*, described a long night illuminated by lightning, flares, star shells, and muzzle flashes. "The big eight inch salvos, throwing up great geysers of water, were hitting very close to us," he recorded in his diary. "Our force fired star shells in front of the Jap warships so that our destroyers could attack with torpedoes. It was like putting a bright light in front of your eyes in the dark. It was impossible to see. The noise from our guns was deafening."[35] Merrill's ships destroyed a Japanese cruiser and destroyer and drove the intruders away, securing the beachhead. Two American ships were disabled, but none were lost.

Admiral Koga sent another cruiser-destroyer task force down from Truk, under the command of Vice Admiral Takeo Kurita. When Kurita's ships were sighted by AIRSOLS scouts north of Rabaul on November 4, Halsey decided to deploy his two available carriers, the *Saratoga* and the light carrier *Princeton*. As heavy attacks on the airfields in and around Rabaul kept Japanese airpower on the defensive, the carriers charged into the Solomon Sea. On the morning of November 5, a massive ninety-seven-plane strike rained bombs down and launched aerial torpedoes on the Japanese fleet, inflicting ruinous damage on seven cruisers.

A week later, three American carriers on loan from the Fifth Fleet (then moving toward the Gilbert Islands to strike the opening blow in the central Pacific offensive) detoured south and launched another attack on the Japanese fleet at anchor in Rabaul's Simpson Harbour. One was the recently commissioned *Essex*, namesake of a new class of fleet carriers that would dominate the air war as the fight moved into the western Pacific in 1944 and 1945. More than a hundred Japanese aircraft attacked the carrier group, and the executive officer of the *Essex*, Fitzhugh Lee, recalled an edgy night in the ship's Combat Information Center: "We were trying to use our new radar, which worked well at long range in the early stages of the battle, but it soon became too much of a melee in which we didn't know whether we were shooting at our own planes or the Japanese planes."[36] Lee was surprised and relieved that the *Essex* avoided taking a single bomb or torpedo hit in the action, and that it came through unscathed except for a few bullet wounds in strafing runs. The Japanese lost forty-one of the planes committed to the attack. In Nimitz's view, the November 1943 carrier strikes on Rabaul "settled once and for all the long-debated question as to whether carriers could be risked against powerful enemy bases."[37] Admiral Koga summoned the surviving elements of his fleet back to Truk.

Beginning in December, the skies over Rabaul were darkened by Allied bombers from dawn to dusk. For the defenders on the ground, their only respite from unremitting aerial punishment came when the weather closed

in and cut visibility to zero. Kenney's Fifth Air Force pummeled the airfields
and supporting installations. Marine Major General Ralph J. Mitchell took
over as commander of AIRSOLS, but most of the previous staff was kept
in place. (AIRSOLS had become, perhaps, the single-best-integrated multiservice command in the world.) Mitchell began moving units northwest from
months-old airfields on New Georgia and Vella Lavella to his new airfields
on the Treasury Islands and at Torokina on Bougainville. Shorter-legged
navy and marine fighters and bombers could now comfortably reach Rabaul,
and began pouring down destruction on the Bismarcks in hundreds of daily
sorties. Admiral Koga continued feeding air reinforcements into the theater
from Truk, including his last reserve of trained carrier airmen. The South
Pacific had become a meat grinder for Japanese airpower.

Air officer Matasake Okumiya, who arrived at Rabaul from Buin on
January 20, noted that exhaustion and despair permeated every rank. The
ground crews were worked to the edge of collapse, and their aircraft gradually succumbed to mechanical failures. Night bombardments interrupted
their sleep. At Kusaka's Twenty-Sixth Air Flotilla headquarters, officers and
pilots were "quick-tempered and harsh, their faces grimly set. . . . The men
lacked confidence; they appeared dull and apathetic. . . . Their expressions
and actions indicated clearly that they wished to abandon Rabaul at the
earliest possible moment."[38] The influx of inferior pilots degraded the quality of the squadrons that had flown together in the past. Japanese air resistance gradually deteriorated, whether measured by numbers of aircraft or by
the prowess of the aircrews. The loss of so many elite flyers in air combat,
day after day, plunged the entire staff into a paralyzing malaise. Okumiya
remembered the heady days of early 1942, when the Japanese naval airmen
were accustomed to sweeping their adversaries from the skies. Now he found
"an astonishing conviction that the war could not possibly be won, that all
that we were doing at Rabaul was postponing the inevitable."[39] Since the
Japanese navy did not concede the inevitability of combat fatigue, neither
pilots nor staff officers were ever rotated out of the theater:

American air pressure increased steadily; even a momentary lapse
in our air defense efforts might lose us Rabaul and our nearby fields.
The endless days and nights became a nightmare. The young faces
became only briefly familiar, then vanished forever in the bottomless
abyss created by American guns. Eventually some of our higher staff

officers came to resemble living corpses, bereft of spiritual and physical strength. The Navy would replace as quickly as it could the necessary flight personnel, but failed at any time during the war to consider the needs of its commanding officers. This was an error of tragic consequence, for no leader can properly commit his forces to battle when he does not have full command of his own mental and physical powers. Neither did the Navy ever consider the problems of our base maintenance personnel, who for months worked like slaves. From twelve to twenty hours a day, seven days a week, these men toiled uncomplainingly. They lived under terrible conditions, rarely with proper food or medical treatment. Their sacrifices received not even the slightest recognition from the government.[40]

Since mid-1943, MacArthur's forces had been advancing up the northern coast of New Guinea. Admiral Daniel E. Barbey's Seventh Amphibious Force, part of what was colloquially known as "MacArthur's navy," had landed assault troops on Kiriwina and Woodlark Islands and at Nassau Bay, a few miles south of the Japanese stronghold at Salamaua. Allied troops were transferred up from Milne Bay in a series of small-craft sea lifts, which moved safely under cover of darkness and avoided the risk of using larger fleet units in waters infested with Japanese submarines. The Japanese at Salamaua were reinforced by troops rushed down from Lae, but MacArthur planned only a diversionary attack on Salamaua. His main objective was on the other side of Huon Gulf. Barbey's amphibians struck next on the night of September 3–4, landing 8,000 Australians east of Lae; the next day, 1,700 U.S. Army paratroopers jumped out of transports and captured an airstrip west of Lae. Lae was bracketed, and pulverized relentlessly by air in daylight and by sea at night. The surviving Japanese garrison abandoned the town and melted into the jungle, where hundreds would succumb to disease and starvation.

Another surprise sea lift put an Australian force ashore north of Finsch–hafen in late September, and the town was taken on October 2. With a reliable supply line by sea, the diggers pushed up the coast toward Sio and Madang. In a three-month campaign, MacArthur had deftly seized control of the Huon Peninsula, leaving the bulk of Japanese forces far to his rear, or as fugitives dispersed into the unforgiving jungle.

From Finschhafen, it was a leap of less than fifty miles across the Vitiaz

Strait to Cape Gloucester, the western extremity of New Britain. Though the chiefs had decreed that Rabaul (on New Britain's opposite end) was to be bypassed, MacArthur wanted to capture the smaller enemy aerodromes on the western side of that island. Lieutenant General Walter Krueger's Alamo Force landed a regiment at Arawe, a village on the southern coast, on December 15. The landing was a diversionary feint, intended to draw the enemy away from Cape Gloucester. The 1st Marine Division, proud veterans of Guadalcanal who had replenished their strength and spirits in Melbourne, stormed the beaches of Cape Gloucester on December 26, 1943. The weakly defended enemy airfields of western New Britain were quickly secured. Surviving Japanese forces retreated toward Rabaul and prepared for what they assumed would be the largest land battle of the South Pacific campaign.

As an airbase, Rabaul had been very nearly neutered by unrelenting air attacks. But with units streaming into the lines from points west, Japanese troop strength approached 100,000. Surrender was beneath consideration, of course, so the garrison began to prepare for a climactic fight to the last man. Defeat might be inevitable, but it would be honorable. Heaven beckoned—they would sell their lives dearly, and take plenty of American soldiers and marines with them. For almost two years the Japanese had been building and improving their defensive fortifications, their intricate networks of subterranean bunkers and tunnels, and they were well stocked with provisions and ammunition for a long siege.

So they waited. And waited. And waited. And the Americans did not come. The defenders were denied even the consolation of dying for the emperor. A Japanese intelligence officer interviewed after the war admitted that the Japanese "hated" the leapfrogging strategy, perhaps because it offended their sense of honor; but he added that they respected it and understood its wisdom. "The Japanese Army preferred direct assault, after the German fashion, but the Americans flowed into our weaker points and submerged us, just as water seeks the weakest entry to sink a ship."[41]

The weak points, in this case, were the lightly garrisoned island groups north and west of New Britain. MacArthur and Halsey seized and secured a ring of bases around Rabaul that rendered the once-formidable bastion entirely impotent. Nor would Kavieng, Rabaul's principal satellite naval base on New Ireland, fall to direct assault. In February 1944, Halsey's Third Amphibious Force put New Zealand troops ashore on the Green

South Pacific Counteroffensive
Advance of MacArthur, Halsey, 1943 to 1944

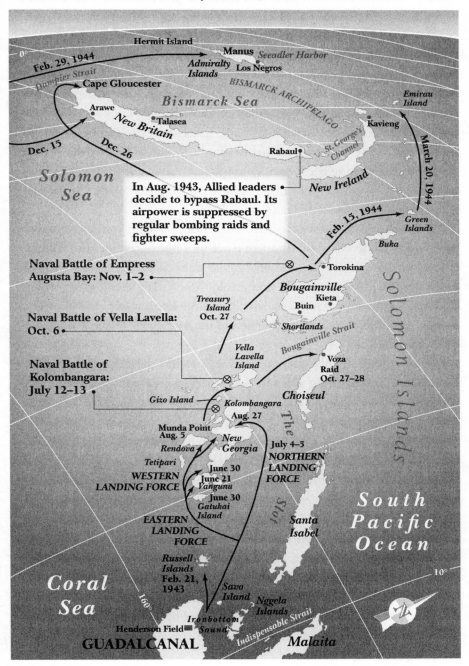

Hermit Island

Feb. 29, 1944

Manus Seeadler Harbor

Admiralty Los Negros
Islands

BISMARCK ARCHIPELAGO

Dampier Strait

Cape Gloucester

Bismarck Sea

Emirau
Island

Arawe

Talasea

New Britain

Kavieng

Dec. 15

Dec. 26

Rabaul

St. George's
Channel

March 20, 1944

Solomon
Sea

In Aug. 1943, Allied leaders
decide to bypass Rabaul. Its
airpower is suppressed by
regular bombing raids and
fighter sweeps.

New Ireland

Feb. 15, 1944

Green
Islands

Buka

Naval Battle of Empress
Augusta Bay: Nov. 1–2

Torokina

Bougainville

Kieta

Solomon   Islands

Treasury
Island
Oct. 27

Buin

Naval Battle of Vella Lavella:
Oct. 6

Shortlands

Bougainville Strait

Vella
Lavella
Island

Voza
Raid
Oct. 27–28

Naval Battle of
Kolombangara:
July 12–13

Gizo Island

Kolombangara
Aug. 27

Choiseul

The   Slot

Munda Point
Aug. 5

New
Georgia

July 4–5

Rendova

NORTHERN
LANDING
FORCE

Tetipari

WESTERN
LANDING FORCE

June 30

June 21
Vangunu

June 30
Gatukai
Island

Santa
Isabel

South
Pacific
Ocean

EASTERN
LANDING
FORCE

Russell
Islands
Feb. 21,
1943

Savo
Island

Nggela
Islands

10°

Coral
Sea

160°

Ironbottom
Sound

Indispensable Strait

Henderson Field

GUADALCANAL

Malaita

Islands, about midway between Bougainville and New Ireland. Then, in mid-March, the Third Amphibious Force leapt all the way north to Emirau Island, seventy miles northwest of Kavieng, in the Bismarck Archipelago. "The only casualty we had was some marine sprained his ankle jumping out of the boat," said Carney. "But it placed us athwart their line of communication from Truk or from the westward. And from that time on, Kavieng was a dead bird. They stayed there and rotted."[42] Carney added that leapfrogging destabilized the psychology and morale of the Japanese fighting forces. "Once the Japanese had launched a plan," he remarked, "he apparently had no alternative plan, because in his mentality, in his psychology, there could be no such thing as failure. There could be no such thing as turning back, once committed." When the Americans went around a Japanese position, rather than attacking it directly, "his whole military campaigning morale collapsed."[43]

MacArthur took Los Negros, 220 miles from Kavieng, in the Admiralty Islands. From there it was a short step across a narrow channel to Manus, which offered a superb natural anchorage in Seeadler Harbor. There the Seventh Fleet would gather its strength for MacArthur's next giant step to the west—Operation RECKLESS, which would take him to Hollandia. The Bismarcks barrier had been shattered and the route back to the Philippines was wide open.

Admiral Koga finally understood that Rabaul was now a liability, and he ordered his remaining air units flown back to Truk. His reasoning was certainly helped along by the Fifth Fleet's devastating surprise carrier air raid on Truk on February 16–17, 1944.

At the end of 1943, Allied victory in the South Pacific appeared certain. What remained in doubt was the cost to be paid in lives, and (relatedly) the time it would take. The Allies had bypassed and rendered impotent about 125,000 Japanese troops. The cream of the Japanese navy's air arm had perished, and the rookie successors were undertrained and underprepared for war. The Japanese had lost more than 2,000 aircraft in the South Pacific campaign, and their economy had no realistic prospect of replacing those losses. The remaining Japanese carriers had been pulled back to the home islands, presumably because the enemy knew they would be destroyed if committed to battle. New and better U.S. ships, aircraft, and weapons were arriving in the Pacific as the American war economy approached peak production.

Among the American rank and file, morale rode at a new high. An officer writing from the Pacific in the last month of the year observed, "We've got so much equipment in the Pacific now, it's like shooting ducks out of your front living room."[44] Lieutenant Bonnell, veteran of several horrific sea fights in Ironbottom Sound, noted that the "cynicism" prevalent in those desperate months of 1942 had given way to a pervasive confidence and optimism. The fleet was expanding rapidly while simultaneously becoming qualitatively better in training, experience, doctrine, and technology. Officers and sailors knew what they had to do, and they knew how to do it. "In other words," he said, "they're sending out men to do boy's jobs now where it used to be boys to do men's jobs."[45]

Chapter Nine

T HE HILLS OF SAN FRANCISCO MADE A MOCKERY OF WARTIME SECRECY. Except when the fog was in (as it very often was, at any time of year), any citizen, sightseer, or spy could ascend to some commanding urban vista and survey the ships as they stood out to sea. Warships, troopships, freighters, oilers, submarines—more ships went under the Golden Gate Bridge than ever before in history. San Francisco and its eponymous womblike bay, once the continent's "back door," had become the vital supply and transshipment hub for the Pacific War.

Ships were berthed at every finger pier and wharf from Fort Mason to Hunters Point. The longshoremen worked in shifts, around the clock, under floodlights at night. Retailers and landlords sustained the city's Gold Rush traditions of price-gouging and rent-gouging. Movie theaters ran films around the clock, but still managed to sell out every showing. Long lines of hungry citizens and servicemen stretched outside of restaurants, down sidewalks, and around corners. Inside, the waiters badgered the customers to eat up and get out. Hotel stays were limited by house policy to one or two nights. (Generals and admirals could usually wangle an exception.)

At the foot of the hills in the city's northeast quadrant, on the dirty streets of the Tenderloin, Chinatown, and North Beach, a sea of men clad in green, white, or khaki went looking for whatever was on offer in one of the world's most renowned liberty ports. They had money in their pockets and good reason to wonder if they would ever have another chance to spend it. On streets lit by garish neon, crowds elbowed into seedy nightclubs, burlesque joints, and all-night tattoo parlors. The military police and shore patrol worked to keep the peace, patrolling in pairs and armed only with nightsticks. It was perilous work because no one liked to see a mate arrested. Two men with nightsticks could not hold back a mob determined to liberate a malefactor. Once or twice a night, the riot squad and paddy wagon were summoned and a mass of men were hauled into the Hall of Justice on Kearney and Washington Streets, which had been converted into a military jail for the duration.

Eleven o'clock was closing time, when well-served crowds flooded out onto narrow sidewalks. It was the most dangerous moment of the night. Brawls pitting sailors against marines (or soldiers against sailors, or marines against soldiers) were always a prospect, but all-navy crews of rival ships were likewise liable to mix it up. In early 1942, the piers along the Embarcadero north of the Ferry Building were converted into the new Battleship Row, as the big ships torpedoed at Pearl Harbor underwent lengthy repairs. "Market Street commandos" was the derisive sobriquet attached to the sailors of those long-berthed warships, but a man flinging the term at a battleship sailor had better be willing to back it up with his fists. "You could start a fight pretty easy that way," recalled Floyd Beaver of the cruiser *Indianapolis*.[1]

As the war matured, San Francisco (and every other American liberty town overrun with servicemen, including Honolulu and San Diego) became jaded and unfriendly in a way that Sydney, Brisbane, and Melbourne never did. Theodore C. Mason, a battleship sailor and memoirist, left a poignant impression of wartime Market Street:

> From the Ferry Building tower to the Civic Center more than a dozen long blocks away, San Francisco's broad, dirty and noisy main stem was always awash with the flotsam of a large city—the lame, the misshapen, the poor, the blind, the self-appointed soul-savers. Now they had to compete for sidewalk space with a flood tide of uniforms in Navy blue, Army khaki, and Marine green. Most of the uniforms were worn by seamen or privates fresh from boot camp or recruit training who had little money and even less sophistication about the ways of sinful San Francisco. Generally, they were too young even to buy a drink.
>
> Restlessly they roamed the great, world-weary street, past the bars, pawn shops, and movie-theater marquees, the hotels, office buildings, and restaurants, each hoping he would beat the odds and meet a girl like (or perhaps very unlike) the one he had left behind. Unless he was

a "jive hound" who lucked out at the El Patio Ballroom, the only girl
he was likely to meet was a streetwalker, or a "conductorette" who collected 10-cent fares on one of the four streetcar lines that kept Market
Street perpetually aroar.

The harshly lighted coffee shops offered a last chance at romance.
The waitresses, however, were as blasé as the street itself. They had
heard the pitches and propositions of these young men from the hills
and farms and towns many times before. Rejected again, the boots
and recruits were reduced to congregating at the Fun Center, a penny
arcade where they could vent their frustration by shooting Japanese
Zeros and warships, drawing a bead on Adolph Hitler, or posing with
buddies in front of a cardboard battleship. San Francisco, I learned,
could be a cold city indeed.[2]

In the panicked weeks after Pearl Harbor, the Twelfth Naval District
had moved with preemptive swiftness to seize whatever land it wanted or
felt it needed to meet the emergency. The navy had taken over Treasure
Island in April 1942, before having worked out the details of a lease with
the City and County of San Francisco. The issue was acrimonious. Certain grandees of the city's political elite wanted the 300-acre island as an
airport, and they were unsatisfied with the navy's offer of $44,801 to remu-
nerate the city for prior improvements. Threats of litigation were quashed
by the filing of a "declaration of taking and deposit," signed the same day
by a federal judge. That hard-hitting legal maneuver transferred title to the
navy. Civilian officials were unaccustomed to being manhandled in such
fashion. The Twelfth Naval District likewise decided that it must have the
shipyard at Hunters Point, and not just the docks and yard facilities but the
entire adjoining neighborhood. One hundred civilian families were told to
be prepared to move at forty-eight hours' notice. In the East Bay, the navy
absorbed an old Bethlehem Steel Company shipyard and expanded the
Alameda Naval Air Station by plunking landfill into shoal water.

The North Bay was home to teeming shipbuilding complexes in Sau-
salito (Marinship Corporation) and Richmond (Kaiser Shipyards). A
quarter-mile-long Ford Motor Company plant was speedily retooled to
assemble jeeps and tanks, which were loaded onto transports at a 500-foot
concrete pier. Winehaven, a compound of great stone wine cellars and port
facilities erected at the turn of the century, was converted into a naval fuel

depot, and pipelines ran up to brown fuel tanks that sprouted like mush-rooms on the hills above Richmond. The huge factories and shipyards were surrounded by chain-link fences topped with coils of barbed wire and guarded by armed men. Their daily rhythms were punctuated every eight hours by the shift change, when a multitude entered by one gate and another emerged on the opposite side. Exhaust-belching buses discharged a full load at the first gate, then drove around and took on another. And so it went on, twenty-four hours a day, seven days a week, until the Axis was crushed.

As in every other wartime boomtown, it was a seller's market for labor. A job applicant who could not read and had dug ditches all his life could be working on an assembly line the following morning. Wage prospectors, chasing paychecks double or triple what they had ever dared to expect, crowded into the region on trains or buses, in their cars, or by their thumbs. People crammed into makeshift shantytowns reminiscent of a decade earlier, or "hot-bedded" in overcrowded apartments (where roommates arranged their schedules to work different shifts and alternate in the same beds), or lived in their cars, parked alongside roads or in vacant lots. Henry Kaiser apportioned part of his manic energy into throwing up new wartime housing projects, such as the 450 duplexes and quadplexes of Atchison Village in Richmond.

Native Californians had not yet forgotten their inborn contempt for "Okies" and "Arkies," the Dust Bowl migrants who had arrived in over-whelming numbers the previous decade. Now they turned that same brand of scorn on the hayseeds who came seeking "big money jobs" in the war industries, and aimed those same shopworn epithets at all rural migrants, whether from Idaho, Indiana, Kentucky, or North Carolina. Families newly arrived from the hinterlands, with children barefoot and braided, looked around in open-mouthed astonishment. They had never seen such conges-tion, so many cars and people, or such a paucity of manners. Laura Briggs, a young girl fresh from Idaho, was amazed to learn that urban neighbors did not automatically offer greetings. "In the morning they'd walk right by you—'Walk right by you!' my dad said—and not even say hello, not even acknowledge you were there."[3]

Men, women, and racial minorities were thrown together and compelled to work in conditions of enforced intimacy. The West Coast's reputation for racial tolerance and moderation was a beacon to African Americans, who migrated to California in great numbers during the war. By executive order, the shipyards and factories were integrated, and photographs of cafeterias in munitions plants depict men and women of different races sitting shoulder to shoulder, with no evidence of segregation or hostility. But blacks were subjected to humiliations and injustices, large and small, in step with the racial attitudes prevailing in the 1940s. Generally they found themselves stranded at the bottom of the "shipyard pecking order." Bay Area shipyards and factories also hired many tens of thousands of women. "Wendy the Welder" was the title favored at Kaiser, more than the now-familiar "Rosie the Riveter." At first, shipyard union bosses insisted that women receive lesser wages, but soon realized that the disparity would only incentivize management to hire more women. Misogynistic paroxysms were chronic and contagious. Salacious rumors made the rounds: lurid tales of philan-dering and trick-turning in the dark recesses and interior compartments of factory floors and ships under construction. Female shipyard workers were pressured to wear head scarves and to remove jewelry, lipstick, and nail polish. The dress codes were policed indirectly by men and directly by self-appointed guardians among the women workers. Katherine Archibald, who worked at the Moore Dry Dock Company in Oakland, wrote a tren-chant memoir after the war. "Like soldiers infiltrating enemy lines," she wrote, "women in the shipyards had to be camouflaged lest the difference in sex be unduly noted and emphasized."[4]

The shipping crisis of 1942 and 1943 was to be alleviated by veloc-ity. Many more ships were needed as quickly as they could be built and launched. Quality control and product lifespan were not important. Nor was economy. For the shipbuilding industry, the new routines required a profound and far-reaching change in culture and attitudes. The shipyard had always been the province of highly skilled craftsmen who guarded their privileges and prerogatives against outsiders. Welders, electricians, pipefitters, and lathe operators had patiently ascended the rungs of their profession, always taking pride in their work. By dint of organizing and col-lective bargaining, they had won wage hikes and protections against the owners and managers, their mortal enemies and paymasters. Henry Kaiser, without any industry experience at all, had shouldered his way into this tradition-bound brotherhood, bringing with him the radical idea that ships could be built on an assembly line by unschooled and unskilled laborers from far-flung regions and walks of life. Prefabricated sections of hulls were brought into the yard, each marked with numbers indicating where they were to be riveted together. Kaiser was no union buster, and his yards paid good wages, but veteran workers were dismayed by the sudden expansion of the unions, which had once been exclusive havens of privilege and prestige. The wartime shipyard had become (except for the actual existence of the union) akin to an open shop. The old guilds were overrun by unwanted outsiders—women, racial minorities, and illiterate farmers. More scandalously, some of those interlopers were promoted into positions that would have taken a decade or more to achieve in the prewar period.

Uncle Sam attempted to persuade this distended and restless workforce that they were "production soldiers" in a noble and patriotic cause. The results were mixed. In Katherine Archibald's emphatic opinion, none of her fellow workers at Moore felt patriotically motivated to do the job. Many younger men frankly preferred shipyard work as both safer and more lucrative than serving overseas in uniform, and arranged to have their status as "essential war workers" extended so that they could avoid the draft. A man who talked of enlisting in one of the services was "scoffed at as a fool or disliked for setting a bad precedent."[5] Union leftists, veterans of the labor struggles of the 1930s, insisted that the war was a conspiracy to enrich politicians and fill the coffers of their capitalist benefactors. Archibald writes of "an atmosphere of lassitude" that "flooded like a heavy vapor over the yards, and everywhere was evidence of an incredible waste of time."[6] Loafing was widespread, and it was organized. Newspapers were smuggled into the yard and passed around. In out-of-the-way corners of the ships and machine shops, men and women played cards, threw dice, or exchanged gossip. Lookouts were posted at doors, and coded signals warned of an approaching superintendent. The malingerers maintained that the front office did not really care how hard they worked, because the yard would go on making money hand over fist no matter how many ships it turned out.

MARE ISLAND, DESPITE ITS NAME, was actually an estuarine peninsula cut off from the mainland by a marshy, cattail-choked slough. It squatted near the mouth of the Napa River, opposite the sun-baked town of Vallejo, about twenty-five miles northeast of San Francisco. Since 1854 it had been home to the Mare Island Navy Yard, the oldest naval installation on the West Coast, and among its many new concrete and steel facilities were a few redbrick buildings dating back to the Civil War. Even before the attack on Pearl Harbor, it was the largest integrated industrial plant west of the Mississippi, with shipbuilding and repair facilities amounting to a capital investment of about $100 million. By late 1942, the yard employed more than 45,000 workers, and Vallejo staggered under the influx of migrants seeking any sort of accommodation. Because there was not adequate housing to shelter the brimming workforce, a fleet of 300 chartered Greyhound buses was called into service to shuttle workers in and out, seven days a week, on routes extending to a radius of seventy-five miles.

Mare Island's riverfront was a congested warren of machine shops, pipe shops, warehouses, rigger's lofts, ammunition depots, administrative buildings, launch ways, finger piers, and dry docks. In the crowded and floodlit workshops, men in overalls pored over the engine lathes, planer mills, and shaft bearings. Specialized teams calibrated periscopes for the dozens of submarines built or overhauled at the yard. A paint factory mixed 200,000 gallons of paint each month. A dozen large cafeterias turned out food at all hours, and a long train of "pie wagons" circulated through the yard and allowed workers to bolt down their victuals while on their feet. Mare Island built more than a hundred new ships during the war, repaired or overhauled more than a thousand, and turned out about half of all landing craft deployed in the Pacific War. It was one of the two principal submarine construction and repair centers in the nation, the West Coast counterpart to New London, Connecticut.

In the late months of 1941, a sleek new *Gato*-class submarine took shape on one of the shipbuilding ways, her long steel hull wedged between towering steel gantries. She was coal black, with only a plain white number stenciled on her bridge structure: "238." Her name would be known only to the enigmatic and tight-lipped officers and men of the submarine force. Like every other boat of her class, SS-238 was to be named for a fish—in her case, the *Wahoo*. She was launched stern first, in a ceremony small and modest by the standards of Mare Island, on February 14, 1942.

Every submariner was a volunteer. The submarine force did not want men who did not directly aspire to wear the twin-dolphin insignia. In most circumstances, any officer or sailor who wanted out was granted a prompt transfer back into the surface fleet. Many of the *Wahoo*'s enlisted men had come directly from submarine school, or from other schools in which they learned their particular trades. Several of her petty officers had trained at the manufacturers' plants, learning the systems from the ball bearings out. The skipper, Marvin G. "Pinky" Kennedy, was a tall, slender redhead with a ruddy Irish complexion (thus the nickname). He was a hard-driving task-master and a bit of a pedant, but an efficient administrator. The executive officer (XO), Richard H. O'Kane, struck some of his shipmates as slightly high-strung and socially awkward, but he was automatically admired because he was one of those rare men (rare in early 1942) who had a wartime cruise under his belt. O'Kane had served as a junior officer on the *Argonaut* during a mine-laying mission off Midway Atoll, and had tracked two Japanese destroyers the night of December 7.

Operating independently of the fleet, and ranging far from welcoming ports, the submarine must be a self-contained and self-sustaining vessel. It followed that the officers and crew must know every inch of her, intimately. At any time, they might be obliged to make repairs as best they could, even when proper tools and parts were not at hand. Every submariner ran a gauntlet of grueling tests—first in writing, then in an oral examination conducted during a bow-to-stern walk-through—to prove he knew the function of every valve and electrical panel. Those who flunked were sent back to the fleet or assigned to work in one of the shore-bound relief crews. A qualifying officer on another boat told the men under his charge, "Learn the old girl inside and outside, learn about everything that makes her tick so that you can treat her well. She'll keep us alive only if she's able to do so; it's up to all of us to keep her that way."[7]

Reasoning that there was no better way to learn a boat's systems than to take a direct hand in installing them, the navy assigned officers and crew to supervise the latter stages of construction and commissioning. The *Wahoo*'s crew supervised the work from a tumbledown wooden building just opposite the submarine's berth. One officer remembers the building's aroma "of diesel oil and tired sailors."[8] A surprising degree of customization was allowed, based on the penchants of the captain, his subordinate officers, and the all-important veteran petty officer known as the "chief of the boat." As a result, each submarine, though largely indistinguishable in appearance from others of her class, developed her own personality and quirks.

The yard laborers and the crew worked themselves to the fine edge of mental and physical exhaustion to commission the *Wahoo*. Her eighteen torpedoes, each as heavy as a four-door sedan, were wrestled through the hatches using a block-and-tackle rig that would not have been far out of place on an eighteenth-century man-of-war. Sailors who had not graduated from submarine school practiced a deepwater escape drill. They entered a high-pressure chamber at the base of a water tower, and then ascended to the top with the help of a dreaded escape apparatus, an airbag with a carbon dioxide absorbent called the Momsen lung. Men sometimes emerged from the drill with a trickle of blood running from an ear.

On June 15, Lieutenant Commander Kennedy read his orders, a commission pennant was broken out on the main, and the *Wahoo* was formally entered onto the list of Pacific Fleet units. At dawn on July 16, the boat sounded her whistle and backed into the Napa River. She motored on two engines at 14 knots, following the channel markers into the Sacramento River and the narrow, dredged channel that cut through San Pablo Bay. Gliding along on the surface, a *Gato*-class submarine was a dark and stealthy shape, menacing and quiet. The East Brother Island Station, an old wood-frame lighthouse west of Point San Pablo, marked the entry to San Francisco Bay. With the city's skyscrapers dead ahead, the *Wahoo* turned into the main ship channel and pointed her bow at the long red bridge, where there would be a last bit of delicate navigation to avoid the antisubmarine nets. Then the *Wahoo* stood out to sea and her war had begun.

THE WAR THEY WOULD FIGHT was not the war they had trained for. Interwar doctrine, influenced by study of the Anglo-German naval clash at the Battle of Jutland (1916), had conceived the submarine as an appendage to the navy's main fleet of battleships. Its primary role was that of a scout. It would forge ahead of the fleet by a hundred miles or so, making periscope observations of the enemy and sending contact reports by radio. Its offensive power was secondary and opportunistic. Torpedo attacks might peck away at the margins of the enemy fleet, but the killing blow was to be delivered by the big guns. Thus the misnomer "fleet boat" was attached to the *Gato*-class vessels and to their immediate predecessors and successors. Longer than a football field, the World War II submarine was in point of fact a ship, not a boat, and it rarely operated with the fleet. Naval tradition being impregnable, however, the submarine was and is the only ship that can properly be called a boat.

From the submariner's point of view, operating anywhere in the vicinity of a friendly fleet was potentially lethal. Throughout the war, but especially in its early stages, American submarines were relentlessly bombarded, strafed, dive-bombed, and depth-charged by American ships and aircraft. On December 7 and 8, 1941, the *Tambor*-class *Thresher* (SS-200) was twice attacked and nearly destroyed by American depth charges as she attempted to enter Pearl Harbor. Falling in with a major task force was a nail-biting event. No submarine failed to provide prompt and correct recognition signals, knowing that any error or delay might be fatal, but American pilots and destroyers were apt to ignore or misinterpret them. Many submarine skippers were forced to reckon with the high-stakes alternatives of repeating a misunderstood signal or ordering a crash dive. In October 1944, off the Philippines, the *Flying Fish* was attacked by the destroyer *Cogswell* after having provided the correct recognition signals. Her captain ordered a crash dive and took her deep; the *Cogswell* dropped several depth charges. When the *Flying Fish* managed to transmit the signal by sonar, the *Cogswell* signaled, "Sorry, are you damaged?" *Flying Fish*: "I don't think so." *Cogswell*: "Come on up." *Flying Fish* : "Go to hell. We'll wait until you're gone."[9]

Not so distantly in the past, Americans had deplored the use of submarines against merchant shipping. Unrestricted German U-boat attacks in the Atlantic had brought the United States into the First World War. The London Naval Treaty (1930), to which the United States was a signatory, had proscribed unrestricted submarine warfare against merchant ships. (Article 22 bound submarines to antediluvian "prize rules," requiring that unarmed merchantmen be stopped and searched, and their crews removed to safety before the vessels are sunk.) Among Americans, and even among naval officers, the idea lingered that unrestricted submarine warfare was a war crime. But no twentieth-century naval war was going to be waged by the rules James Madison had urged on the Royal Navy of King George III. The London agreement was both impractical and toothless. Less than an hour after the raid on Pearl Harbor, the American government simply shrugged it off, and the order went out to the entire fleet: "Execute unrestricted air and submarine warfare against Japan."

From the start of the war, submarines did the most good in long, solitary cruises into the interior sea-lanes of the Japanese empire. "It is my belief that enemy shipping is one of the most vulnerable functions involved in continuance of his operations," Admiral King wrote Nimitz on February 22, 1942, "and that every submarine that can be spared . . . should be sent to attack enemy lines of communications in Western Pacific."[10] Japan's war economy could not carry on without constant imports of raw materials, especially oil; nor could Japan feed and supply her overseas forces without dependable access to sea routes. The American fleet boats, designed to scout and attack enemy naval forces, proved superbly well matched to the very different role thrust on them in the Pacific War. They were self-supporting, self-reliant, and fast on the surface, and they could remain at sea for six to ten weeks. Freighters, troopships, and tankers were slower than warships, and thus more susceptible to torpedo attack. When the results were tallied at war's end, it was found that American submarines had taken a considerable bite out of the Japanese navy—almost as much as American carrier airpower had, for example—but their invaluable part in the Allied victory was in wiping out Japan's merchant shipping, or *marus*.* By August 1945, the submarine force would sink more tonnage than Japan had possessed at the outset of hostilities.

Prewar doctrine and training had favored caution. Submarine officers were taught that high-periscope observations in daylight invited attack and were extremely perilous. Better to raise the scope only to wave-top height for a quick peek and then retract it quickly. Early in the war, Pacific Fleet submarines were ordered to remain submerged in daytime if they were within 500 miles of a Japanese airbase. The injunction drastically curtailed their effective cruising radius. Admiral Thomas Withers Jr., Commander of the Pacific Submarine Force (COMSUBPAC) at the war's beginning, had been a proponent of the submerged sonar-ranging approach, in which the boat lined up its torpedo attacks by sound bearings alone. Skippers were encouraged to think first of preserving the boat; scoring hits on targets was a lesser concern. It was thought that a Japanese destroyer hunting on the surface would stand a very good chance of pinpointing a submerged boat by sonar, and officers were instructed to seek temperature gradients as a buffer. Wartime experience would soon prove that the enemy's countermeasures were not nearly as lethal as had been believed, and that a more aggressive spirit was needed.

The year 1942 was one of abject disappointment for the submarine force. The Asiatic submarine fleet, based at Cavite Naval Base in Manila Bay, had failed to repel or even seriously disturb the Japanese invasion of the

---

* *Maru* was the suffix applied to the names of Japanese freighters, troopships, and oil tankers. American submariners employed the term to refer to any such vessel.

Philippines. Post-defeat analysis exposed many problems. Admiral Thomas C. Hart's aged and leaky S-boats had been unprepared for the rigors of wartime cruising; their crews' training had been unrealistic; there had been a rigid emphasis on sonar approaches and attacks, and undue worry about vulnerability to enemy air attack. The Asiatic Fleet skippers had little experience in long-distance patrolling. Cavite was vulnerable to air attack. On the third day of the war, a stockpile of 233 torpedoes was lost in a Japanese bombing raid. No boats were deployed in the perilously shallow waters of Lingayen Gulf, where the major Japanese amphibious landings occurred. The remnants of the fleet retreated to Freemantle and became the nucleus of the Western Australia command. Here the overworked and short-ranged S-boats would struggle under adverse conditions. They were chronically undersupplied and too far from their patrol areas in the East Indies and South China Sea to be effective.

Indoctrinated and promoted in peacetime, the first cohort of skippers was generally unequal to the task. Caution and acquiescence to organizational politics had been the qualities that marked a man for promotion. Peacetime exercises, mattering greatly for the career prospects of a submarine officer, had penalized adventurous tactics. War gradually exposed a "skipper problem." Cautious captains had to be identified and relieved so that younger and bolder men could assume command. The process took about eighteen months.

The war likewise required juggling the men in the top jobs. In March 1942, Nimitz relieved Tommy Withers as COMSUBPAC and gave the job to Rear Admiral Robert Henry English, a former submariner who had most recently commanded the light cruiser *Helena*. (He had also served as a chief of staff to a previous Pacific submarine commander and had served on the "submarine desk" at Main Navy in Washington.) English demanded aggressive tactics and was hard on skippers he judged to be too timid, even when they had been victims of bad luck or faulty equipment.

For the first half of the Pacific War, the submarine force was grievously handicapped by bad torpedoes. The weapons ran too deep, passing harmlessly under a target's keel. Magnetic detonators either failed to explode or exploded prematurely. Torpedoes often bounced pathetically off the hull of a Japanese ship. The flaws were not discovered until the war was long underway, partly because the peacetime economy had precluded live firing tests and partly because apathetic time-servers in the Bureau of Ordnance stonewalled all reasonable requests for study and improvement. Eventually it was discovered (and the bureau acknowledged) that torpedoes ran an average of 10 feet deeper than their settings. The problems with the secret Mark 6 magnetic exploder—which detected the presence of a hull overhead and was timed to explode directly underneath the target's keel, with the blast force directed upward—took longer to rectify. As more submarine officers became convinced that the magnetic exploder was unreliable, they lobbied their commanders to allow them to deactivate the device and set the torpedoes to run shallower. Admiral Withers refused these proposals, partly because it would require firing three-fish spreads, and the supply of torpedoes at Pearl was dangerously low throughout 1942. In many cases, skippers deactivated the devices on their own and then fudged patrol reports to cover their tracks. But that tended to obscure the problem and further delay an adequate response. At any rate, a torpedo relying on the older contact trigger was also faulty because the poorly engineered firing pin was often crushed on impact and failed to detonate the warhead.

Diffident captains and abysmal torpedoes tended to eclipse the saving fact that the submarine force was stocked with talent further down the ranks. The executive officers and third officers, most of whom had graduated from the Naval Academy in the early and mid-1930s, would supply the skippers of 1943–45. The "chief of the boat" (senior-most petty officer) was often the oldest man aboard; he might have served twenty or more years in submarines. The submarine service was small and proud, a self-conscious elite that prized their inimitable *esprit de corps*. Submariners relied on one another for mutual survival and success; they were bound together not only by common interest but by good humor, camaraderie, and respect. The oppressive distinctions of rank faded in importance among the seventy to eighty men living cheek to jowl in a warren of cramped and gloomy compartments. No one saluted or threw his rank around. Officers and men called one another by first names. "It's a whole different world when it comes to discipline," said Alan Polhemus, who served on diesel boats for more than a decade. "It was all handled just in interpersonal relationships, persuasion—saying 'You need to do this, and if you don't I'm going to kick you where it really hurts.' One of the reasons why a submarine crew is so cohesive is because there's constant daily contact. There's never a day where you don't rub elbows with everybody at least once."[11] There were no laggards, no malingerers—there was nowhere to hide in a submarine, and anyone who failed to pull his weight endangered the life of every man aboard. Personal rivalries, petty privileges, interdepartmental grievances, antagonism between officers and enlisted men or between reservists and Annapolites—all the inveterate pathologies of naval life were scarcely to be found among the men who served under the sea in a long steel tube.

IN JULY 1942, IN SUPPORT OF the impending WATCHTOWER landing on Guadalcanal, Nimitz sent a strong force of submarines to the great Japanese fleet base at Truk. The boats were to patrol the sea routes into the atoll with the twofold purpose of providing early notice of enemy naval movements south into the Solomons, and of sinking ships when opportunity offered. Admiral English sent eleven boats to Truk between July and September. One was the *Wahoo*. It was to be her first war patrol.

She left Pearl Harbor on August 23. Day after day she ran submerged, with occasional quick periscope observations; night after night she motored on the surface, recharging her batteries, with position checks by celestial sightings. Two weeks passed before the *Wahoo* sighted an enemy ship, a small tanker of the *Hyogo Maru* class. Kennedy stalked the target and fired a three-torpedo spread at a range of 1,430 yards. All missed, and the skipper ordered the boat deep to run under the target. Feeling that air patrols posed a risk to the *Wahoo*, Kennedy declined to attempt a second attack. That decision did not sit well with the other officers. Lieutenant George W. Grider, the third officer, recalled that "it was demoralizing to creep away submerged from that first target."[12]

More than two weeks passed before the *Wahoo* attempted another attack, this time on a 6,500-ton freighter. After a cautious submerged approach, the *Wahoo* fired four torpedoes and apparently scored a single hit on the target. Kennedy observed the ship listing to port and settling by the stern. (Postwar records turned up no information on a sinking at that time and place.) The *Wahoo* played cat and mouse with a destroyer escort and escaped by ducking into a welcome squall of rain.

The greatest disappointment of this first cruise was a missed opportunity to sink the seaplane tender *Chiyoda*, which crossed paths with the *Wahoo* on September 30. The valuable target, first observed by periscope at a range of 12,000 yards, was apparently unescorted. Kennedy made a cautious approach, declining to use full power for fear of running down the batteries.

The *Chiyoda* zigged instead of zagged and quickly went out of position. The missed opportunity was more a case of bad luck than negligence, but it ate away at the crew's morale. The incident left them "brooding and discouraged," wrote Grider. "It played havoc with our self-confidence, our faith in our boat, and our aggressiveness in general."[13]

On October 5, Kennedy sighted an even more precious target, a light carrier. She had two destroyers as escorts, and Kennedy chose another conservative approach, holding the *Wahoo* to one-third speed. The target slipped through their grasp.

To his credit, Kennedy faulted himself for failing to make a good attack in this instance. His approach, he wrote in his report, "lacked aggressiveness and skill. . . . Watched the best target we could ever hope to find go over the hill untouched at 0800."[14] Admiral English strongly agreed with Kennedy's self-criticism and amplified it in his endorsement.

The patrol was marred by several mechanical mishaps, some more critical than others. The SJ radar shaft was misaligned and would not turn properly. Two men had to muscle the hand wheel while a third lubricated each bearing on the shaft with a grease gun. Their efforts were of little avail. The bow buoyancy-tank vent jammed shut, making the boat balky in a dive. A botched routine test left a torpedo partly jammed through one of the bow tube's doors, with its brass-capped warhead protruding from the hull. The weapon could not be removed from the tube or pulled back in. Would it arm itself? Not likely, but if it did, it might detonate and blow the ship to kingdom come.

Since there was nothing to be done but hope for the best, the crew resorted to gallows' humor. Of a subsequent minor mishap, someone remarked, "Well, it doesn't matter. That torpedo's going to go off pretty soon anyhow."[15]

Returning to Pearl Harbor, the *Wahoo* sighted three PBY patrol planes on October 15 and 16 and encountered their escort ship dead ahead on Saturday, October 17. With the boat rigged for surface running, and a section of sailors on deck, they crept down the channel into Pearl Harbor. The skipper conned the ship into the East Loch, around the end of Ten Ten Dock, and approached the submarine base. A navy band and a delegation of officers and sailors were gathered on a pier to welcome her. Kennedy had radioed ahead to request a port-side berth. Either the transmission had not been copied or the request had been ignored, and a starboard berth had been cleared. The submarine waited in the channel, her diesels rumbling idly, while a signalman sent another message via blinker light. "Have possibly armed torpedo protruding to Starboard. Still recommend port side mooring."[16] The delegation and band retreated to a safe distance as the request was fulfilled.

IN THE 1930s, JAPANESE ANALYSTS had postulated that Americans were culturally unsuited to the rigors and deprivations of submarine warfare. Luxury-loving layabouts, fond of good food and soft beds, were ill prepared for the mental and physical strain of prolonged operations. So it was said and apparently believed. The crude caricature goes a long way to explain the Japanese navy's inattention to antisubmarine warfare (ASW). But it is true that the Americans emphasized comfort and habitability in their new diesel fleet submarines, and long-serving veterans thought the *Gato*-class boats almost absurdly opulent when compared to their predecessors. They were air-conditioned, well lit, and equipped with washing machines and freshwater showers. Well-appointed galleys turned out the best and freshest food in the navy, including ice cream and baked bread. A separate bunk awaited almost every member of the crew. Leather-upholstered benches lined the bulkheads in the wardrooms. Record players and movie projectors provided entertainment. Time would prove the wisdom of such crew comforts, large and small—the crews functioned well in grueling voyages lasting as long as two and a half months.

Upon putting into port, a submarine crew was given liberty right away, and a relief crew took over the boat. The plush Royal Hawaiian Hotel, queen of Waikiki Beach, had been reserved by the navy for submariners on R&R. For two weeks, the men were encouraged to forget about their recent patrol, about the submarine, even about the war itself. They had nothing to do but immerse themselves in complete relaxation. Each ship was assigned a "refreshment room," freely accessible to every officer and enlisted man, in which a bathtub was filled with ice and stocked with beer, champagne, and soft drinks. "Whoever established the tradition knew what he was doing," Grider commented. "It took just about two weeks to get over the strain."[17] Returning to the boat for the next patrol, they found it scrubbed clean, freshly painted, and reprovisioned. Even the mattress covers had been replaced. One sailor remarked that it was like entering a hotel room after maid service. All the "housework" had been done, "except that they didn't lay any bath towels out."[18]

To Dick O'Kane's surprise, Lieutenant Commander Kennedy had retained command of the *Wahoo* even after her disappointing first patrol. Kennedy's patrol report had been abjectly self-critical, and Admiral English had bluntly seconded those criticisms. But English had softened the blow by remarking that Kennedy seemed to have learned from his mistakes, and credited the *Wahoo* with one 6,441-ton freighter (postwar analysis disallowed the claimed sinking). Despite the patent frustrations of the *Wahoo*'s first cruise, the results had been no worse than average for all the submarines sent to Truk.

O'Kane worked quietly through back channels to have a PCO, or "prospective commanding officer," assigned to the ship on her second cruise. The PCO was a senior officer, usually with the same rank as the skipper, who was slated to take command of another boat. He would come aboard as an observer, with no duties other than acquiring information and experience prior to being inserted into his own command. The navy's wry pet name for this slightly clumsy arrangement was "makey-learn."

The newcomer was Lieutenant Commander Dudley W. Morton, who had acquired the nickname "Mushmouth" in his plebe year at the academy, later shortened to "Mush." He was a big, broad-shouldered man with large hands and a powerful handshake. He was gregarious and high-spirited, with a contagious grin and a tendency to roar with laughter. "He was built like a bear," said Grider, "and as playful as a cub."[19]

Born in Owensboro, Kentucky, Morton had arrived at the Naval Academy with a thick Kentucky drawl. Four years at Annapolis had flattened out that accent, but he was still recognizably a southerner. Some said Morton had been tagged as "Mushmouth" because of that hill-country brogue, although a rival explanation traced the origin to a popular comic-strip character of that name, thought to resemble Morton. In either case, Morton liked his nickname and encouraged his shipmates, officers and enlisted men alike, to use it. He had played football and wrestled at the academy. He loved high jinks and rough physical horseplay, even while on patrol. The crew of the *Wahoo* soon found that the new PCO might seize a shipmate in a headlock and throw him to the deck. He did not affect the aloof style of a ranking officer; his puckish roughhousing might be sprung without warning on a crew member of any rank. Forest Sterling, the ship's yeoman, was tending to his paperwork in the yeoman's shack when "a bolt of lightning landed on my back and drove me into the typewriter." Wheeling around, with fist clenched to throw a punch, he came face to face for the first time with Morton, towering over him in the doorway. The grinning lieutenant commander pointed to his insignia and said, "Go ahead and strike me."[20]

Wahoo departed for her second patrol on November 8, 1942. Her diesels rumbling and belching blue exhaust, her dock lines were uncleated and thrown back on the deck, and she backed gingerly from her berth. Her piercing whistle sounded. The colors were broken out at the main. She went down the channel and steamed out to sea with an escort vessel in company. She made a trim dive, received an "indoctrination depth charge," fired her deck guns, and then put them to bed.[21] At dark the escort parted ways, and the *Wahoo* set a course of 230 degrees. She had 3,000 miles to travel to her patrol area in the central Solomons, north of Bougainville. She was to seek out and destroy Japanese ships headed south toward Ironbottom Sound, where the navy and marines were waging their desperate struggle to hold Guadalcanal. Passing over the latitude 7°50' north, the boat entered into the SOPAC domain of Admiral Halsey.

Spirits were distinctly elevated on this second patrol. Kennedy had agreed to do away with the Dantesque red interior lights that had depressed the crew's mood on the previous voyage. No major mechanical problems tormented the engineers. A handful of enlisted men began publishing a ship's "newspaper," the *Wahoo Daily Gazette*. It offered a mockingly earnest summary of news gathered from Radio Tokyo broadcasts, along with satirical bits of doggerel and even a comic strip. The wardroom phonograph was sometimes cranked up to high volume, and big-band melodies boomed through the boat.

Mush Morton's good-natured and rambunctious presence lifted the crew's mood. He was none too exacting about his uniform, often walking around the ship in a red bathrobe. Without particular duties, he spent much of his waking hours playing cribbage with other officers in the wardroom. He was also happy to chew the fat with the petty officers and enlisted men. "He was best described as a big, overgrown Kentucky boy who had never been told that adults weren't supposed to smile," wrote O'Kane.[22] Morton was often found in the engine room, chatting with shipmates while scrubbing his clothes in a bucket of water. He instructed Forest Sterling not to address him as "sir," a protocol that flew in the face of naval regulations and traditions.[23] Morton's relaxed informality and chumminess with enlisted men was unusual even on a submarine, the most democratic of all naval vessels. It may have had an underlying purpose: Morton was quietly gathering information on the boat and its internal crew dynamics. Later, in Brisbane, he was to argue that Kennedy should be relieved of command.

In their long discussions of tactics, O'Kane and Morton found that they were very much of the same mind: The *Gato*-class submarine would achieve its full potential only with more aggressive and determined tactics. A skipper could and should take more risks to sink enemy ships. Kennedy had been too slow to let go of prewar doctrine and ideas limiting the role of the submarine to a "submerged vessel of opportunity." Custom and etiquette required that the officers steer clear of disparaging their skipper, but the implied criticism was understood. The ship could afford to remain on the surface longer, to make higher and more frequent periscope observations, and to run fast on the surface at night or use maximum submerged speed in daylight to gain an attacking position in the path of oncoming enemy ships.[24] The officers appreciated the belligerent attitude, though Grider wondered whether Morton was too much of a daredevil. "It is one thing to be aggressive, and another to be foolhardy . . . ," he observed. "Most of us, in calculating the risk, threw in a mental note that we were worth more to the Navy alive than dead . . . but when Mush expressed himself on tactics, the only risk he recognized was the risk of not sinking enemy tonnage."[25]

Operating off Bougainville in late November and December 1942, when the campaign for Guadalcanal was in its climactic last phase, the *Wahoo* was hindered by dirty weather, with hard rain and gale-force winds. At night, on the bridge, lookouts peered through a tumultuous seascape of towering seas, occasionally lit up by lightning flashes. The *Wahoo* sighted several targets but repeatedly failed to attain a viable attack position.

On December 10, the *Wahoo* fired three torpedoes at a convoy of three cargo ships accompanied by a destroyer. One freighter was hit and sank quickly. The crew's cheers were silenced by O'Kane's urgent order: "Rig for depth charge! Rig for depth charge!"[26] The destroyer laid down a pattern of depth charges on the diving *Wahoo*. Lights went out as bulbs exploded, men were thrown against bulkheads, and showers of cork dust rained down from the overhead. But the damage was minor, and there were no leaks.

The freighter was *Wahoo*'s first kill, but the encounter seemed to exhaust Kennedy, whose nervous strain grew after each periscope observation.

A few days later, *Wahoo* received a message carrying the "Ultra" designation, which meant that it contained intelligence regarding enemy shipping and must receive the highest priority. A tanker was proceeding from Truk to the Shortland Islands and was expected to arrive on December 8. Oil tankers were among the highest-priority targets throughout the war, but that was especially true in those critical closing weeks of the Guadalcanal campaign, when one lost tanker might have fatally limited Japanese shipping movements.[27]

Kennedy maneuvered the *Wahoo* into the target's expected track and searched with all three dimensions available—sonar, radar, and lookouts on the bridge peering into the darkness through powerful binoculars. A passive sonar search obtained a "weak echo ranging on a broad front to the north." The SJ radar returned a range of 18,000 yards bearing 62 degrees. The tanker was headed for the Bougainville Strait, and the *Wahoo* was in good position to intercept her. But this promising opportunity was again missed, due to a simple error. The sound operator cried out, "Echo ranging on our starboard quarter!" He had read the wrong bearing. Morton shouted, "Reciprocal!" but it was too late: Kennedy had ordered, "Flood negative and take her deep."[28] From several hundred feet below, the crew listened to the tanker's screws pass overhead. The target continued out of range.

After another run of missed opportunities, the *Wahoo* apparently scored one extremely valuable kill. On December 14, shortly after noon, Forest Sterling was operating the sonar gear. He detected propeller noises. A quick periscope observation revealed a large enemy submarine 3,000 yards away, heading directly toward them. The *Wahoo* had just enough time to swing around and fire three torpedoes from her stern tubes. They were only 800 yards from the enemy's track. Kennedy raised the scope ten seconds ahead of the expected hit. As he described what he was looking at, a deep explosion was heard throughout the ship. The first torpedo appeared to hit just forward of the conning tower and threw up a spout of water and debris. Kennedy attested that he saw "I-2" painted on her tower, and men on her bridge leaping into the sea as she went down. The *Wahoo* crash-dived, though no other enemy ship had been seen. Several members of the *Wahoo*'s crew believed they heard sounds of the enemy sub's compartments crumpling and breaking up as they reached crush depth. Being submariners themselves, the sounds made their blood run cold.

Postwar analysis did not find any evidence of a Japanese submarine sinking at this location and date. "I-2" was sunk a year and a half later, in the Bismarck Sea. It is possible that the torpedo had exploded prematurely, and Kennedy had misunderstood what he saw in the scope. As for the sounds heard by the crew, the mystery will never be solved.

Two more missed opportunities followed in the final week of the patrol. A large ship was observed through the periscope two days later, within a radar range of 10,000 yards. The angle on the bow was large, but O'Kane strongly believed the *Wahoo* could have overtaken the target with four hours of running fast on the surface. The captain refused and retorted, "Don't be stupid; you can't attack a ship from here!"[29] That response left O'Kane infuriated and speechless. The exchange was made within earshot of several members of the crew.

On December 21, while the *Wahoo* was en route out of her patrol area and headed "for the barn" in Brisbane, the lookouts sighted smoke on the horizon. O'Kane wanted to go after it, but Kennedy refused on the grounds that the *Wahoo* was passing into another submarine's assigned patrol area.

ON THE DAY AFTER CHRISTMAS, a smell of vegetation advertised the loom of Australia off the starboard bow. The lookouts caught sight of the Cape Moreton Light, which sat high on a bluff and could be seen as far as fifty miles out to sea. After passing through a controlled minefield and antisubmarine nets, the *Wahoo* lay to in Moreton Bay and took a local pilot aboard. No member of the crew could fail to take in this man's unforgettable getup— he wore a black suit and a bowler hat, and carried a folded umbrella under his arm. The chain-smoking pilot conned the *Wahoo* up the brown, muddy, dramatically serpentine Brisbane River. A bucolic Queensland landscape unfolded on either bank, and oystermen and swimmers waved at the passing submarine.

Gradually the outskirts of the city came into view—graceful neighborhoods of small, close-built homes with red tile roofs—until a last bend to the left revealed a steel bridge ahead and brought the office buildings of downtown Brisbane into view on the right bank. The *Wahoo* slid into its berth at New Farm Wharf, adjacent to the sub tender *Sperry*. A gangway was pushed across and officers and sailors of the relief crew came aboard. Among the visitors was Admiral James Fife Jr., the new commander of Task Force 42.

New Farm Wharf was undergoing rapid expansion and would soon rival Pearl Harbor as the largest submarine base in the Pacific. Squadrons Eight and Ten were serviced by the tenders *Fulton* and *Sperry*, each of 9,734 tons' displacement, and each fitted with cranes, machine shops, and enough spare parts to act as a self-contained repair facility for a large squadron of submarines. The base had taken over the waterfront facilities of the Bris-bane Stevedoring Company, and its wool sheds, once stacked to the rafters with Australia's prime export, had been converted into warehouses. A bar-racks and a new headquarters building were under construction.

Tensions in the city, climaxing in the "Battle of Brisbane" the previous month, had prompted the local American commanders to seek rest and recreation quarters elsewhere. The small beach communities of the Gold Coast provided plenty of towns suitable for the purpose. For the time being, however, submarine crews were still being quartered in and near the city. Houses and apartments were rented in Brisbane for visiting officers, and most of the enlisted men checked into the downtown Hotel Canberra. The majority of the crew was off the boat within two hours of berthing. They were to enjoy the perks of liberty—ice cream, mail call, sun, and fresh air.

Most of the officers, not including Kennedy, crowded into a small but comfortable beach cottage about fifteen miles outside the city. There would be no mess attendants, so they were to do their own cooking, and were con-tent to do so. On the second night they endured O'Kane's "tuna delight," with good humor. Off the ship, and in Kennedy's absence, conversation about the recent patrol loosened up and the men aired their criticisms. With two credited sinkings, including an enemy submarine, the *Wahoo* had turned in the best results of any boat returning to Brisbane in months. Kennedy would receive a Silver Star. But the good results and plaudits tended to obscure the disappointments of the patrol—the numerous errors, missed prospects, and aborted attacks. Grider noted in his memoir, "The *Wahoo* . . . was not making much of a record, and we knew it. We . . . had waited in the wrong places at the wrong time like unlucky fishermen. . . . We still felt really discouraged."[30]

On a long walk into the countryside on the second day, Morton and O'Kane plunged into a long conversation about submarine tactics. They found themselves in agreement: Kennedy had to go. O'Kane primly avoids the subject in his memoir, but it seems likely that he communicated his criticisms to Fife, either directly or through other officers. Morton, in a loose remark that may or may not have been made in earnest, had vowed to report Kennedy for cowardice. Several officers and enlisted men had filed requests for transfer off the *Wahoo*. Whatever Fife was told about Kennedy's performance, he apparently gleaned enough information to make his decision. In his brief endorsement of the *Wahoo*'s patrol report, Fife noted that the ship had had eight enemy contacts but made only two attacks, and "at least" three more of those contacts should have developed into attacks.[31] He relieved Kennedy and sent him back to the States.

Kennedy took the news bitterly but later attested that he realized the decision was correct. Like many peacetime skippers, he was slow to adjust to the more audacious and hazardous tactics required of a wartime submarine. Nor was he a coward, however—he would receive a second Silver Star later in the war, for his performance as a destroyer skipper in the Battle of Leyte Gulf.

On the last day of the year, Mush Morton took command of the *Wahoo*. When the crew gathered on the ship the day before she was to sail, he spoke to them briefly. "*Wahoo* is expendable," he said. "We will take every reasonable precaution, but our mission is to sink enemy shipping." The next patrol, accordingly, would be much more dangerous. Any man who did not care to risk his life was invited to see the yeoman and ask for a transfer—it would be granted automatically, and "nothing will ever be said about your remaining in Brisbane."[32] Sterling waited in his yeoman's shack, but there were no takers. Instead, the crew felt a surge in confidence. Morton told the men to pull down every Japanese ship silhouette that had been mounted on bulkheads by Kennedy's order. They were replaced by the new captain's collection of pinup girls, which he had obtained at a Hollywood studio. He had Sterling type up a stack of placards with the message "Shoot the Sons of Bitches."[33] These were likewise mounted throughout the interior of the ship. Morton reduced the number of lookouts from four to two, both to be stationed on the shears. In order to make the watches less monotonous, and keep the men on their toes, the watches would rotate every hour—from lookout, to radar, to sound, to the helm, to messenger duty in the control room. Any lookout who spotted a ship, if that ship was subsequently sunk, would receive a spot promotion. Morton quietly requisitioned extra supplies of medicinal brandy and grain alcohol for the ostensible purpose of "cleaning periscope lenses." He believed in the morale-building ritual of an occasional round of shots, particularly after a depth-charge attack.

Morton also pioneered a radical innovation. It had always been the skip-per's duty and prerogative to make periscope observations while directing attacks. Morton instead chose to make O'Kane his "co-approach officer," and to keep the executive officer on the periscope while Morton employed all the other data at his fingertips to maneuver the *Wahoo* into an optimal attack position. The captain would need a heavy dose of self-discipline to keep his hands off the periscope. In a moment of high tension, his natural instinct would be to shove the XO aside and seize the handles. The most critical input, in setting up a torpedo attack, was the target's "angle on the bow." Under Morton's scheme, O'Kane would be trusted to make the all-important observation accurately.

Some of the crew continued to worry that their new skipper was reckless and would throw their lives away in an unwise attack. According to Ster-ling, the sailors often asked one another, only half in jest, "Do you think he's crazy?"[34] He was an eccentric character. Even as captain he continued to roam around the boat in his red bathrobe and slippers. He told lurid stories in his glutinous Kentucky accent, and roared at his own jokes with almost maniacal laughter. Grider worried that the new skipper would find the transition from "camaraderie to authority" to be awkward and difficult, but that was never the case—Morton's authority was "built in, and never depended on sudden stiffening of tone and attitude."[35]

THE *WAHOO* COMMENCED HER THIRD PATROL on January 16. After sound tests and practice torpedo runs on her escorting destroyer, she set course at two-engine speed for the eastern end of New Guinea. Her orders would send her up the north coast of New Guinea, through the Vitiaz Strait between that island and New Britain. She was to reconnoiter a little-known Japa-nese seaport known as Wewak.

With the brown hills and green mountains of New Guinea slipping by on her port beam, the *Wahoo* ran on the surface as long as her skipper dared—not only at night, but for an hour each morning after dawn and each evening before dusk. Morton and O'Kane agreed that the risk of being sighted from the air in those hours was worth the added forty miles or so of daily mileage. Morton even refused to dive when one of the lookouts on the bridge spotted a distant plane. He chose instead to wait, a decision that was vindicated when the unidentified aircraft turned away, its aircrew apparently having failed to notice the *Wahoo*. The new captain also took a more audacious approach to using the periscope. Whereas Kennedy had favored only quick daylight periscope sightings with the scope raised just three feet above the surface, Morton was content to make long midday sightings with the scope raised to high elevation, and even employed a second scope on several occasions.

The navy still lacked decent charts for the Solomons, and nothing in the *Wahoo*'s inventory identified the location of the mysterious Wewak. The solution was found, by chance, in a "two-bit" Australian school atlas purchased in Brisbane as a souvenir by a member of the crew. A map in the atlas identified Wewak as an otherwise uncharted indentation about midway up New Guinea's northern coast. By comparing the coastline to an existing aerial photo, and matching the shape of the shoreline and the islands lying close offshore, Grider and O'Kane managed to pinpoint the location. Without reliable information about the position of reefs or shoals, the *Wahoo* would have to tread lightly. But Morton surprised his shipmates by announcing that he intended to take the submarine into Wewak's inner anchorage, rather than simply observe it from the offing. The operation order had directed *Wahoo* merely to "adjust speed, if possible, to permit daylight reconnaissance vicinity Wewak Harbor."[36] Morton chose to interpret "daylight reconnaissance" as "enter and attack enemy shipping."

In Grider's opinion, the captain had "advanced from mere rashness to outright foolhardiness."[37] Penetrating into the uncharted enemy harbor seemed pure madness, a gambit that would risk collective suicide. But Morton was nonchalant, and kept the men in the conning tower entertained with a steady run of wisecracks.

As dawn broke, the *Wahoo* crept around the islands guarding the entrance to the harbor. O'Kane spotted the top of a large tripod radio mast that might belong to an enemy warship, but the submarine could not enter the channel because a patrol craft or tugboat appeared to be crossing directly ahead. Morton probed the shore of some of the other outer islands, hoping to find a gap that would provide a direct view of the anchorage. But the area was dense with interlocking reefs, and the *Wahoo* had to take care not to run aground.

After several hours of cautious probing, the submarine entered the main channel and began the nine-mile run into the inner harbor, creeping along at 3 knots. O'Kane took several quick, low-elevation periscope observations, with water lapping up the lens. At 1:18 p.m., he made out the bridge structure of a large ship, which he first took to be a freighter or seaplane tender. Upon closer inspection it proved to be a *Fubuki*-class destroyer. Several small Japanese submarines were moored alongside her. There were good reasons for the *Wahoo* to turn around and make an escape. The crew were not sure of the position of reefs or the depth of the water, and the tidal currents were unpredictable. But Morton announced that the *Wahoo* would launch a surprise torpedo attack on the anchored destroyer: "We'll take him by complete surprise. He won't be expecting an enemy submarine in here."[38]

The *Wahoo* went to battle stations and continued advancing into the harbor at 3 knots. The forward torpedo-tube doors were opened in preparation for firing. The intended range was to be 3,000 yards. O'Kane took one last sighting and whispered urgently, "Captain, she's gotten under way, headed out of the harbor. Angle on the bow ten port."[39] A 10-degree angle on the bow meant that the destroyer was bearing almost directly down on the *Wahoo*. Morton altered his plan immediately: "Right full rudder." He would pass under the enemy ship and maneuver for a shot with the *Wahoo*'s stern tubes. Another quick periscope sighting revealed that the destroyer had zigged, and the angle on bow had opened to 40 degrees starboard. But O'Kane did not have time to make an accurate estimate of her speed. Morton guessed 15 knots, and that figure was entered into the Torpedo Data Computer (TDC), which provided an automatic gyro angle.

The *Wahoo* shuddered as three torpedoes were fired from her bow tubes. All ran hot, straight, and normal, but when O'Kane took another quick sighting, he saw that all had missed astern. They had underestimated the destroyer's speed. A speed of 18 knots was entered into the TDC, and a fourth torpedo fired. But the Japanese lookouts had evidently spotted the torpedo wakes and possibly the periscope. Fully alerted, the enemy turned sharply away and evaded the fourth shot. She held the turn through 270 degrees and bore down on the spot that marked the apex of the fan of torpedo tracks.

Peering through the scope, O'Kane now beheld that most dreaded of all images—a towering bow, looking huge in the circular field, with a surging bow wave indicating high speed. Forest Sterling felt "an almost uncontrollable urge to urinate."[40] But Morton seemed unfazed. "That's all right," he said, "keep your scope up and we'll shoot that SOB down the throat."[41]

The "down the throat" shot was the boldest and most desperate tactic available to any submarine. It had been discussed in theory but never attempted in practice. "Down the throat is certainly not a tactic to be sought," O'Kane wrote later. "It is rather a desperation shot."[42] The Wahoo's circumstances were certainly desperate. She was trapped in a harbor without reliable charts, and a well-armed destroyer would very soon be in position to depth charge her into oblivion. She had only two torpedoes left in her bow tubes and little hope of maneuvering to bring her stern tubes to bear.

O'Kane watched the enemy ship come on, growing larger in the circular field. He could see the faces of Japanese sailors looking straight back at him through the periscope lens. Her bow wave climbed up her hull to the height of her anchors. O'Kane shifted the scope to lower power—that view, he said, had the advantage of being "much less disturbing."[43]

The Wahoo did not have a torpedo to waste. If she fired too soon, the target would have time to turn away and evade. If she fired too late, the weapon would not run far enough to arm itself and would bounce harmlessly off the enemy's hull. The effective firing window fell within a range of approximately 1,200 to 700 yards. The destroyer, traveling near her top speed of about 30 knots, would travel that distance in about thirty seconds.

As the range closed to 1,250 yards, Morton said, "Any time, Dick." With the crosshairs centered on the bow, O'Kane said, "Fire!"[44] Keeping the scope up, O'Kane watched the track stretch away. The destroyer turned and evaded. Sterling later recalled being "calm with the cool certainty that he was going to die."[45]

O'Kane fired his fifth and last-available torpedo at a range of 750 yards, and Morton ordered a crash dive. The crew braced for depth charges, but another sound filled the submarine instead—an immense tearing sound, almost like a bolt of thunder. "Great cracking became crackling," O'Kane recalled, "and every old salt aboard knew the sound—that of the steam hitting a bucket of water, but here amplified one million times. The destroyer's boilers were belching steam into the sea."[46] From bow to stern, the Wahoo's crew erupted in cheers.

Morton brought the ship back to periscope depth and ordered up the scope. O'Kane looked first and then yielded to the captain. The destroyer's bow had been torn off just forward of the stack. She was foundering rapidly. Sailors were climbing the masts or diving into the sea. Several photos were taken with the ship's camera, a Kodak Medalist. Then the captain described what he was seeing through the ship's loudspeaker: "There must be hundreds of those slant-eyed devils in the rigging . . . anybody not on watch wanting a look, get to the conning tower on the double."[47] Dozens of men crowded into the little space and took turns at the scope, and several brought their own cameras to take souvenir snapshots.

Now Morton was willing to beat a retreat from the harbor. The channel allowed a submerged retreat at the relatively safe depth of 100 feet, navigating by dead reckoning and sonar. The *Wahoo* crept away at 3 knots, slow enough to preserve the batteries and avoid a disastrous hard grounding. The sonar operator listened for "beach noises"—the play of surf on beaches and reefs—and small steering adjustments were made to keep these warning sounds at roughly equal distances to port and starboard. When the noises were all abaft her beam, Morton and his crew knew they were safely away.

At dusk, the *Wahoo* came back to periscope depth. There was nothing to see but some distant lights ashore, far behind. The *Wahoo* surfaced, and clean air circulated through her length. She ran dead north on four engines for thirty minutes, until it was clear no one was in pursuit.

The crew was giddy, but also exhausted and on edge. O'Kane now realized that he had not slept in thirty-five hours; only adrenaline had sustained him through the long hours in and around Wewak. Morton permitted any man who wanted one to take a shower (a rare privilege on a submarine, due to the power required to run the distillers). Later, the skipper allowed the pharmacist's mate to dispense a ration of "depth charge medicine"—that is, a shot of three-star Hennessy brandy.

Morton's buccaneering spirit had been rewarded, but would the success at Wewak embolden the skipper to take even more unconventional risks, and would the *Wahoo*'s luck persist? As the crewmen not on watch turned into their bunks, clean and mildly intoxicated, some worried that Mush Morton was not entirely sane. The taciturn O'Kane put it this way: "Understandably some might be wondering just what was coming next."[48]

MORTON PUT THE SUB ON A NORTHWESTERLY COURSE, into waters that offered the likely prospect of spotting Japanese ships headed southeast from Palau. While the *Wahoo* crisscrossed her base course, and lookouts scrutinized the horizon for any sign of a mast or a column of smoke, the captain tinkered with drafts of his report on the Wewak engagement. It was radioed to Fife in Brisbane at 11:45 p.m. The following morning at ten, the *Wahoo* passed back into Nimitz's domain, and would forward all future reports to the Pacific Submarine Force headquarters in Pearl Harbor.

That afternoon, the boat crossed the equator (crossed under it, as she was running submerged), and Morton insisted on a proper observance of the ancient line-crossing rites. Naval tradition of many centuries required all "polliwogs," those officers and enlisted men who had not previously crossed the line, to be inducted into the "Court of King Neptune." A riotous ceremony was held in the forward battery. Pappy Rau, chief of the boat and a veteran of more than twenty years, was done up as King Neptune. He wore Morton's red bathrobe, a gold cardboard crown, and a fake beard, and he held a trident fashioned from a wooden broom handle. Another sailor played the role of the "royal baby," wearing only a large "diaper"—actually a towel held together by safety pins. The inductees, beginning with Lieutenant Grider, were required to answer a series of preposterous and insulting questions, then forced to choke down a disgusting potion scrounged from the gallery, and given an electric shock. Grider's head was shaved, much to his chagrin. He was forced to bow low and kiss Rau's belly, which had previously been greased with lard and lampblack. At the end of all that, he could call himself a "shellback" and be placated by the knowledge that no man ever had to suffer those indignities twice.

The newly bald third officer, while standing watch on the bridge at 7:57 the following morning, spotted a plume of smoke over the horizon about two points off the port bow. Morton came up to have a look, and then put the *Wahoo* on a course to intercept. Gradually she drew into a profitable attack position, ahead of the convoy. Morton took the *Wahoo* down as soon as the topmasts of two freighters peeked over the horizon. Looking through the periscope, O'Kane studied the ships as their hulls came into view, and estimated their angle on the bow as a manageable 50 degrees. Soon two more ships came "over the hill." The convoy was steaming at 10 knots on a course of 95 degrees, and there was no sign of an escort. It was an excellent setup. The attack angles were entered into the TDC, and as the range closed to 1,300 yards, the *Wahoo* fired four torpedoes from her stern tubes at the nearest two ships. All were "hot, straight, normal," and three of four struck home, hitting both targets.

Morton brought the ship around to align her bow tubes with a third ship, significantly larger than the two wounded freighters. She turned directly toward the *Wahoo*, apparently with the intention of ramming. "We'll shoot the SOB down the throat," Morton declared. O'Kane winced: "I had hoped never to hear those words again, much less in just three days."[49] The next torpedo missed badly, but the freighter yawed and presented her broadside. Watching through the periscope, O'Kane saw that she was a large troop transport. *Wahoo* fired two more torpedoes and went deep; as she was descending through 200 feet, the crew heard explosions indicating two hits.

Returning to periscope depth eight minutes later, a quick periscope sweep revealed that the transport was dead in the water. Another torpedo, fired at leisure, hit between her stack and her bridge. O'Kane, observing through the periscope, saw a "tremendous explosion blow the structures aft of her bridge higher than a kite. Momentarily we saw a gigantic hole in her size bigger than a Mack truck, until she listed toward us."[50] Troops began leaping into the sea, and her boats were lowered as she went down.

At 1:10 in the afternoon, Morton ordered *Wahoo* to the surface. Since there was no destroyer in the vicinity, the submarine could run on the surface with impunity. Morton took the *Wahoo* into the wreckage of the sunken troopship, where about 1,000 castaways had piled into boats, rafts, and small craft. Morton ordered, in an even voice, "Battle stations, man both guns."[51] This brought a quizzical glance from O'Kane, and Morton solemnly justified what he was about to do. "Dick," he said in O'Kane's version of the exchange, "the army bombards strategic areas and the air corps uses area-bombing so the ground forces can advance. Both bring civilian casualties. Now without other casualties, I will prevent these soldiers from getting ashore, for every one who does can mean an American life."[52] O'Kane accepted this reasoning, and the *Wahoo* moved in to complete the ghastly business.

Did Morton intend an outright massacre? The accounts vary slightly in some critical details. In O'Kane's telling, Morton ordered the gunners to "chase the troops out of their boats"—in other words, the boats were to be destroyed, but no swimmers were to be deliberately shot unless they fired back at the *Wahoo*. Grider's account was short on details and long on insinuation. He wrote of the skipper's "overwhelming biological hatred of the enemy," and offered no details of the incident other than to say it took place over several "nightmarish minutes."[53] Forest Sterling recalled seeing several hundred men. Some were swimming, some on lifeboats, and others "hanging onto planks or other items of floating wreckage. . . . They all stared without expression at *Wahoo*'s hull."[54] O'Kane wrote that the deck gunner's fire "was methodical, small guns sweeping from abeam forward like fire hoses cleaning a street."[55] Morton's patrol report stated that the gunners shot at the boats until "our fire was returned by small caliber machine guns. We then opened fire with everything we had."[56]

Wahoo now set off on a course of 85 degrees in pursuit of the two remaining ships, one of which had been damaged. The *Wahoo* ran on the surface at flank speed, with all four engines roaring. She tracked her quarry using the standard tactic of an "end-around" pursuit. The surfaced submarine ran on a parallel course at high speed, distant enough that she remained "hull down" under the horizon and thus unseen, but able to track the enemy's topmasts or stack smoke with periodic high-elevation periscope observations. Despite some radical zigzagging by the two ships, the *Wahoo* gradually overtook them and attained a favorable attack angle. Morton finally took her under at 5:21 p.m. As the fourth ship's hull rose above the horizon, periscope observations revealed that she was an oil tanker, a valuable and high-priority target. At 6:29, with the range at 2,300 yards, *Wahoo* fired a spread of three bow torpedoes at her. One hit and slowed her. Another two hours of maneuvering set up a stern tube shot, which scored a single hit amidships. She sank in minutes.

Pursuing the convoy's last surviving freighter into the night, hoping for a clean sweep, Morton bent on all-ahead full. The crippled freighter shot back with her deck guns. Most of the shots were wild, but when one splashed dead ahead and ricocheted directly over the *Wahoo*'s shears, Morton took her down again. For fifteen minutes they ran at a depth of 90 feet, tracking the ship by sonar alone; when the shellfire splashes grew more distant, the submarine came back to the surface.

Almost immediately, a lookout shouted, "Searchlight broad on our port bow!"[57] The beam was projecting from a ship over the horizon, just emerging. Morton correctly deduced that this was an escort ship, probably a destroyer, sent to collect the ships of this convoy. He maneuvered the *Wahoo* into position to torpedo the freighter as she closed on the beckoning searchlight. At 9:10 p.m., when the range was 2,900 yards by radar, the *Wahoo* fired her last two torpedoes. It was a long shot, fired without spread, a low-percentage attempt. Minutes ticked by. The torpedoes ran about a mile and a half. Improbably, they both hit with a colossal detonation that shook the *Wahoo*'s bridge. Fifteen minutes later, this 9,500-ton *Arizona Maru*-class freighter sank, leaving only a blank horizon for the destroyer's questing searchlight.

First Three Patrols of the *Wahoo* (SS-238)
1942–1943

Sea of Japan

KOREA

JAPAN

East China Sea

FORMOSA

North Pacific Ocean

1,000 Miles

MIDWAY ISLAND

KAUAI

OAHU

HAWAIIAN ISLANDS

HAWAII

Pearl Harbor

Manila

Philippine Sea

MARIANAS ISLANDS

WAKE

Fais

PHILIPPINES

Truk

MARSHALL ISLANDS

MINDANAO

Bougainville

Wewak

NEW GUINEA

TIMOR

Port Moresby

GUADALCANAL

Coral Sea

Townsville

AUSTRALIA

Brisbane

Tasman Sea

NEW ZEALAND

GILBERT ISLANDS

Solomon Islands

SANTA CRUZ ISLANDS

South Pacific Ocean

FIJI

NEW HEBRIDES

NEW CALEDONIA

Nouméa

SOCIETY ISLANDS

EQUATOR

1. August–October 1942
2. November–December 1942
3. January–February 1943

The officers and crew were amazed at what they had achieved. O'Kane remembers that "none of us had heard of any other submarine sinking her first ship before reaching her patrol area, to say nothing of a convoy of four more ships. These were the things submariners daydreamed about but never expected to happen."[58] Morton radioed Pearl Harbor to report the news, and *Wahoo*, her torpedoes gone, "headed for the barn."

The return should have been uneventful, but when the *Wahoo* crossed paths with another convoy on the following morning, Morton changed course to intercept. The periscope had shown a small freighter trailing behind the other ships. Morton conceived a plan. "Dick," he said to O'Kane, "we're the only ones who know we don't have any torpedoes; the enemy

doesn't know that. Supposing we were to battle surface and make a run at
them. Wouldn't they likely run off leaving the small freighter behind for our
deck gun?"[59] Having not seen any guns mounted on the trailing freighter,
O'Kane agreed that it was worth a try.

The *Wahoo* surfaced and took off after the convoy. The Japanese ships
rang up more speed and began a radical zigzagging pattern. These maneuvers
gave O'Kane the "impression of general confusion."[60] Just beyond a tanker,
the middle ship in the convoy, another set of masts began to appear. The
previously unseen ship was soon identified as a destroyer, and she was bearing directly down on the *Wahoo*. Morton ordered a retreat on the surface,
at four-engine flank speed, and gradually opened the range to 14,000 yards.

Morton assumed the destroyer would promptly give up the chase, not
wanting to leave her convoy far behind. That supposition turned out to be
wrong. On the bridge, the lookouts studied her through binoculars. Her
bow wave—"bone in the teeth"—had a white "V" pattern. As that "V"
began to fill in, to grow perceptibly deeper, the lookouts knew the enemy
was gaining. Then she turned her broadside toward the *Wahoo* and fired.
Morton expected the shells to fall wild, but about three seconds later there
was a "mighty clap of thunder" and geysers rose on both sides of the *Wahoo*,
just 150 feet away. Too close.

The crash dive was *Wahoo*'s fastest yet, according to O'Kane, and when
the boat passed through a depth of 250 feet, Morton told the planesmen
to keep her headed down. She went below test depth and waited for the
inevitable depth charges. "Now we're going to catch it," said Morton, as the
destroyer's screws were heard overhead. She dropped six depth charges, and
O'Kane remembers them as "tooth crackers" that "cracked and whacked,
dumping seeming tons of bolts into our superstructure."[61] The destroyer did
not stay for long, however. She had to get back to her flock of transports,
freighters, and tankers, now forty miles behind. Morton ordered a round of
"depth charge medicine" served out to the crew.

Returning to the surface two hours later, Morton radioed Pearl Harbor:
"Another running gun battle today. . . . *Wahoo* runnin' destroyer gunnin'."[62]

ON FEBRUARY 7, 1943, *Wahoo* entered Pearl with eight Rising Sun flags
on one of her signal halyards and a broom lashed to the periscope shears,
bristles up, to signify a "clean sweep." Hers had been, by a long margin, the

most remarkable submarine cruise of the war. As she came around Ten Ten
Dock, she was hailed by a large crowd of officers, personnel, and (oddly) news
reporters. The "Silent Service" had not promoted itself and received almost
no press coverage at all. But someone in the Pacific Fleet had decided that it
was time to publicize the submarine war, and much of the content of *Wahoo's*
reports had been passed by the censors for public release. Admiral Charlie
Lockwood had nicknamed Morton a "One-Man Wolfpack." A cavalcade of
photographers caught the *Wahoo's* inverted broom on film, and the picture
would run in newspapers throughout the United States. Upon going ashore,
the crew of the *Wahoo* was delighted to see an edition of that day's *Hawaiian
Advertiser*. The headline shouted, "*Wahoo* Running Japs A' Gunning."[63]

All five of the sinkings claimed by Morton were credited—five ships
totaling 32,000 tons. But the significance of *Wahoo's* third cruise tran-
scended the material damage done to the enemy. Morton's tactics had
turned a new page. They would be studied by all of his colleagues in the
submarine service. Hereafter, their performance was to be measured against
his. Skippers were to emulate his bold tactics or be pushed out of the service. Morton, O'Kane later said, had "cast aside unproven prewar concepts
and bugaboos."[64] In the future, submarines would be employed on the surface, diving only when absolutely necessary. They would be expected to
fight a much more persistent and audacious war against Japanese shipping.

THE WAHOO'S TRIUMPH, rousing as it was, could not sweep away the lingering frustration and disenchantment in the Pacific submarine force. Submarines had sunk 180 enemy ships totaling 725,000 tons in 1942, more
aggregate tonnage than Japan was able to build that year, but a pervasive
feeling remained that the fleet was falling short of its potential. Too many
skippers had clung to diffident prewar tactics. Evidence was gradually accumulating that the Mark 14 torpedo was a lemon, but the navy's Bureau of
Ordnance had closed ranks against its critics and implacably refused suggestions that a comprehensive and unbiased reevaluation was needed.

In the latter half of 1942, Admiral English had sent sixty-one war patrols
out of Pearl Harbor. Twenty-seven had returned empty-handed. Patrols off
Truk (Japan's major southern naval base) had been far less productive than
patrols into Japan's home waters. For all the glory of sinking a major enemy
fleet unit, chasing capital ships (battleships, cruisers, and carriers) was a

low-percentage enterprise. The enemy's freighters and oil tankers offered a better return on investment—they were slower and less well defended, and thus easier to stalk and sink. In the Atlantic, German wolf packs were demonstrating that a relatively small number of submarines could menace a vital economic and military lifeline. Japan was at least as vulnerable to a war of commerce as was Britain, and it was evident that the most profitable use of the Pacific submarine force was in attacking the sea links to Japan's major resource areas. But the submarine leadership had not yet made the case that all other priorities should be subordinated to a policy of cutting Japan's interior supply lines. Submarine admirals—English, Fife, Withers, Lockwood—had allowed their boats to be pulled here and sent there, to provide marginally important reconnaissance services or to support various campaigns in ill-conceived roles.

Among active-duty submarine officers, resentment was building against Bob English and his staff, who were free-handed with criticism even when it seemed undeserved. Not all skippers came back empty-handed because they had been timorous. Some were merely unlucky; some had been deployed to unpromising patrol areas; and some had watched their torpedoes explode prematurely, or fail to explode, or run under their targets, or run in a circle, or bounce innocuously off an enemy's hull. English, like Admiral Ralph Christie (Fife's predecessor in Brisbane), gave the back of his hand to reports of malfunctioning torpedoes. To one returning skipper he ludicrously claimed, "SUBPAC has never had a premature explosion."[65]

The Bureau of Ordnance was intolerant of criticism and sought to turn it back on the fleet by blaming reports of malfunctions on skippers, crews, and torpedo handlers. According to Clay Blair, an even-handed and even-tempered scholar who produced the most exhaustive history of the Pacific submarine campaign, "The torpedo scandal of the U.S. submarine force in World War II was one of the worst in the history of any kind of warfare."[66] Ned Beach, a submarine commander who later became a novelist and historian, remarked that the torpedoes "performed so poorly that had they been the subject of deliberate sabotage they hardly could have been worse," and added that every submariner he knew agreed that the men responsible should have faced court-martial.[67]

In the long run, it might have been better had the torpedoes failed absolutely in 1942. Complete failure would have compelled immediate and decisive action to identify and correct the various mechanical flaws. Instead, the weapons sometimes functioned properly, while in many other instances they appeared to do the job when they had actually exploded prematurely and harmlessly. Intermittent and apparent success perversely guaranteed that the deficiencies would not be discovered all at once. The torpedo problem was solved in fits and starts, over a period of two years, against the obdurate resistance of bureaucrats and engineers in Washington and Newport, Rhode Island. Meanwhile the submarine crews risked and sometimes gave their lives to carry unreliable weapons into enemy waters, all the time wondering whether their suspicions were justified. On October 20, 1942, the *Trigger*, while submerged at a depth of about 100 feet, fired a torpedo at an unescorted tanker. The weapon's rudder jammed and it ran in a circle, a failure that should have destroyed the *Trigger*. But the boat was saved by a second defect in the boomeranging torpedo. The detonator, which should have detected the *Trigger*'s magnetic field and activated the warhead upon reaching its strongest point, instead exploded at a distance great enough to leave the boat intact. The weapon had suffered two unrelated failures, the second providentially neutralizing the first. Meanwhile the enemy tanker went on her way, probably unaware that she had been fired on. The incident would have been laughable were it not so potentially deadly.

The first problem to be isolated and solved was the Mark 14's tendency to run about 10 feet deeper than set. It had required initiative on the part of Charlie Lockwood in Freemantle, Western Australia. His correspondence with the bureau in Washington brought a high-handed dismissal, replete with technical data purporting to show that the complaints were unwarranted. In June 1942, Lockwood took matters into his own hands by designing a series of tests. These conclusively demonstrated that the weapons were running about 11 feet deeper than their settings. With additional pressure from Admiral King, the engineers in Newport finally conducted their own tests and concluded that the Mark 14 was running *10* feet deeper than set. That was easily corrected by changing the depth setting, in most cases to zero.

ON THE STORMY MORNING OF JANUARY 21, 1943, a flying boat named the *Philippine Clipper* descended to 2,500 feet over mountainous terrain in Mendocino County, California. The big aircraft was a former Pan Am airliner, pressed into service by the navy to fly high-ranking officers between

Hawaii and the mainland. The pilot had lost his way in the impenetrable white murk. Aiming for San Francisco Bay, he was more than sixty miles off course to the north. He flew directly into the side of a mountain. No one survived. Among the dead was Admiral Robert English.

Nimitz tapped Charlie Lockwood as the new commander of the Pacific submarine force. It was a fortunate choice. Lockwood, more than any flag officer in the submarine fleet, had recognized and advocated a reconsideration of prewar doctrines and tactics. Arriving in Pearl Harbor to take up his new command in early 1943, he discovered to his satisfaction that the submarine base had been expanded and improved. New construction was apparent everywhere. Nimitz's CINCPAC staff had moved out of the submarine base and into a new headquarters building, freeing up space for Lockwood's operation. The new COMSUBPAC moved into a large white house on Makalapa Hill.

In December 1942, Admiral Christie had been relieved of command of Task Force 42 in Brisbane and sent to Newport to take command of the Naval Torpedo Station. Bitterly opposed to the assignment, Christie could do nothing to stop it. He had defended the torpedoes and obstinately dismissed the rising chorus of complaints against them. Now he would come under pressure to reform the obstruction at its source. Arriving in Newport, he had hardly unpacked his bags before receiving orders sending him back to Australia to take command of all submarines in the Southwest Pacific Area. He would serve in that position, subordinate to Lockwood, until November 1944.

Continued reports of premature explosions of torpedoes prompted Lockwood to wonder whether the Japanese had developed some countermeasure. Had the enemy devised some means to trick the torpedoes into exploding early? Many skippers became so distrustful of the device that they advocated disabling it in favor of the contact detonator. Lockwood, though sympathetic, was reluctant to allow such a drastic measure. The magnetic detonator was one of the navy's most prized technological innovations in the interwar period. It had influential proponents, including Mush Morton. Though it might not be entirely reliable, it also did not fail in every instance. The unreliable detonator was not disabled in favor of the contact detonator until late 1943 (except on the initiative of individual captains). In any case, the contact exploder was also unreliable.

In Australia, Christie refused to entertain grievances about the torpedoes. In his view, skippers who blamed their weapons were blowing smoke to obscure their own faults. Airing complaints about the torpedoes, he said, would jeopardize the collective morale and self-confidence of the submarine force. He was not entirely unbiased. For more than twenty years, dating back to a postgraduate program at MIT in the early 1920s, Christie had been personally involved in the development of the magnetic detonator and other torpedo technologies. In the mid-1930s, he had run the torpedo section of the Bureau of Ordnance. His fingerprints were all over the Mark 14. After the war, he told Samuel Eliot Morison that torpedo failures were "largely a question of upkeep on the part of repair and operating personnel. . . . I have always contended that, given a conscientious and experienced torpedo gang, much of the poor performances in 1942 would have been eliminated."[68] When William J. Millican of the *Thresher* reported that he had fired on a Japanese submarine and "clinked 'em with a clunk" (that is, the torpedo was a dud), Christie ordered that no written mention of the incident should appear in patrol reports or endorsements.[69] The discussion boiled over into a full-scale shouting match.

Writing to Lockwood that fall, Christie avowed that "torpedo performance here is steadily improving" and doubted the credibility of reported prematures and duds. Commanding officers, he added, had in some cases recounted torpedo failures "under conditions where it was impossible that he could see it."[70] The suggestion that captains were deliberately lying was too much for Lockwood. He slapped Christie down in a letter laced with sarcasm. "Thank you for your letter," he wrote. "From the amount of bellyaching it contains, I assume that the breakfast coffee was scorched or perhaps it was a bad egg. . . . [T]he facts remain that we have now lost six valuable targets due to prematures so close that the skippers thought they were hits. . . . Sorry to note that you believe the operating personnel is usually wrong about what they see, or think they see. Your Bureau training has not been wasted."[71] A shaken Christie lost no time in apologizing, but he would never fully acknowledge the egregious flaws of the Mark 14.

On a quick trip to Washington in early 1943, Lockwood threw down the gauntlet. He spread his criticisms widely through the Navy Department, presenting his case with pungent sarcasm. To a senior member of King's staff he said, "If the Bureau of Ordnance can't provide us with torpedoes that will hit and explode, then for God's sake get the Bureau of Ships to design a boat hook with which we can rip the plates off the target's side."[72] That salvo touched off a heated exchange with Admiral William H. P. "Spike" Blandy, chief of the Bureau of Ordnance. Blandy admitted that engineers at the Naval Torpedo Station had been slow to identify and correct the problems, but complained in turn that the fleet had resisted assigning good men to work in weapons development programs. "We sadly lack submarine officers in the bureau," wrote Blandy, "and you won't get the best results from your torpedoes until you let me have some. . . . As you know yourself, every time I try to get some submarine officers who also know torpedoes, I am usually offered somebody who hasn't made good in the boats themselves, and my efforts to get a good man are usually met with the objection that he is too valuable as a commanding officer."[73]

JAPAN'S DECISION TO LAUNCH A WAR in the Pacific had been motivated, above all, by the desire to possess the oil fields of Borneo and Sumatra, as well as the rubber plantations and tin mines of Malaya and other territories under Dutch or British control. Control of those prizes would avail nothing if Japan could not command the sea-lanes linking them to the home islands. Impoverished in natural resources, Japan's economy and war-making potential were perilously dependent on imported iron ore, bauxite, rubber, copper, zinc, and especially oil. Japanese fighting forces throughout the region required massive and sustained logistical backing, which could be supplied only by sea. The entire system could be held hostage by a fleet of aggressive and well-equipped submarines operating against Japan's critical interior sea routes. The freighters and tankers that would ply the sea routes would need to be protected at all costs; otherwise Japan's entire imperialist project would collapse like a sand castle in the surf. That is in fact what happened in 1944 and 1945.

All of this was clearly foreseen prior to the war, but Japanese naval leaders never made any real study of this problem, nor did they develop more than rudimentary capabilities in antisubmarine warfare (ASW). The nation's previous naval wars had been relatively short and decisive affairs in which commerce protection had never become a vital consideration. The samurai warrior culture esteemed offensive warfare more than defensive considerations, and no ambitious officer would waste his time specializing in the dreary and unglamorous business of protecting *marus*. There was no percentage in it; no hope of promotion or influence. Japan's fine destroyer fleet trained intensely for night torpedo attacks against enemy warships, but escorting convoys of merchantmen was never more than an afterthought. Antisubmarine warfare never gained a strong voice at the Navy Ministry or the Naval General Staff, and no unit was tasked with full-time convoy duties until months after the war began. As shipping losses mounted in 1944, the manifest necessity of convoys ran up against the need to keep the remaining ships circulating briskly. Even as entire convoys were slaughtered at sea, the Japanese navy was reluctant to put talented officers to the problem. The leadership could not bring itself to admit that antisubmarine warfare was a professional subspecialty requiring staff analysis, weapons development, and training. Atsushi Oi, one of a handful of staff officers assigned responsibility for antisubmarine warfare, was often told by skeptical colleagues that "escort-of-convoy was common sense to a navy officer."[74]

Effective convoying required, at a minimum, a scheme of cooperation between escorts and cargo ships. But Japanese naval personnel insisted on treating merchantmen with contempt. In the navy's hierarchy, recalled one veteran merchant mariner, he and his shipmates "were lower than military horses, less important than military dogs, even lower than military carrier pigeons."[75] On one ship with a mixed crew, all merchant mariners were confined below, while only Etajima (naval academy) graduates were allowed to take in the sun and sea air on deck. "That was their attitude. There was no sense you were all fighting together. You can't win with such an attitude."[76] In the second half of 1943, Japan brought heavy cargo ships to Truk under escort, and then dispersed cargos into small, cheaply built wooden barges called "sea trucks" for distribution to island garrisons. As the toll of Japanese shipping mounted in 1944 and 1945, decades-old vessels were hauled out of mothballs. Many were in such disrepair that their crews thought them unseaworthy even if they were not attacked. Ignobly, the Japanese employed Red Cross relief ships to carry troops and war materiel.[77] American submarines let them pass unmolested, as required by treaty law.

In late 1943, the Japanese detected a disturbing improvement in the performance of American torpedoes. Sinkings mounted rapidly, surpassing 300,000 aggregate tons in the month of November 1943.[78] A dependable Mark 14 torpedo was the single most important factor in the mid-war surge, but there were several others. Audacious and seasoned executive officers and third officers were promoted to command their own boats. The submarine fleet was equipped with better surface-search radar systems, better sonar, a better periscope, and eventually the Mark 18 electric torpedo, which left no wake. The code-breaking fruits of Pearl Harbor's communications intelligence hub (Fleet Radio Unit Pacific or "FRUPAC") were employed to guide submarines, by long-range radio broadcast, directly into the track of oncoming convoys. FRUPAC's Merchant Marine Unit charted Japanese shipping movements daily, and could provide timely and reliable intelligence of departures, destinations, noon positions, and the whereabouts of enemy minefields. In December 1943, the U.S. Navy's intelligence division could confidently report that "the enemy's sea lanes are under constant and forceful attack. . . . Our submarines range unhindered through the maritime vitals of 'Great East Asia,' and for more than a year and a half they have been exacting a much heavier toll in merchant tonnage than Japan's shipyards can possibly replace."[79] That was true in spite of the numerous disappointments of the early submarine campaign, and sinkings were on the verge of rising dramatically. In early 1944, Japanese shipping losses consistently surpassed 200,000 gross tons per month.

In the last eighteen months of the war, the American submarine force was finally deployed in a thorough campaign to blockade the home islands of Japan. American skippers came to know every bay and inlet of the Japanese coast, better even than they knew their own home shores. The *marus* were reduced to making desperate port-to-port dashes, with balsa logs and rafts triced down on deck to provide flotation when their ships went down. They took increasingly circuitous routes to avoid the most infested waters. Rather than cross the Yellow Sea, the *marus* crept along the coast of Korea and down the coast of China, seeking refuge in shallow waters or behind coastal islands. A dark night no longer offered asylum. Equipped with steadily improving radar systems, American submarines could identify and stalk unseen enemy ships to a radius of forty miles. Running on the surface at four-engine speed, at a pace nearing or exceeding 20 knots, and safe from aerial observation, the submarines attacked even the most strongly escorted convoys with impunity. With new sonar detection systems, submarines penetrated minefields to enter the Sea of Japan and severed the last remaining tendons connecting the home islands to the resource-rich territories of Korea and Manchuria.

The asphyxiation of Japan's sea communications was in itself sufficient to destroy the nation's capacity to wage war, a point laid bare by a few statistics on the oil situation. With negligible domestic oil production, Japan's imperialist project could not survive without a stable supply from the conquered territories of Borneo and Sumatra. Japanese naval planners had predicted self-sufficiency as soon as the captured oilfields were brought up to full production. But the vital artery was to be sustained by a handful of slow (and thus vulnerable) oil tankers. In 1942 (a frustrating year for the American submarine force, as we have seen), the Japanese lost just four tankers. In 1943, the figure rose to 23; in 1944, it was 132; and in the first eight months of 1945, the Allies destroyed 103 Japanese tankers. In 1942, 40 percent of East Indies crude oil production safely reached Japan. In 1943, that proportion declined to 15 percent; in 1944, it fell to 5 percent; and after March 1945, not a single drop arrived on Japanese shores. Crude oil reserves, having peaked at twenty million barrels in early 1941, diminished to fewer than a million in the fourth quarter of 1944.[80] The Japanese met the crisis with a crash tanker-building program, and by converting ordinary merchant ships to carry oil. But shipbuilding required steel, while the reverse was equally true—the steel mills required coking coal and iron ore that must be imported by sea. From a 1943 peak of 7.8 million tons, ingot steel production plummeted to a per-annum production rate of about 1.5 million tons in 1945, or about 15 percent of the industry's production capacity. As the aerial bombing campaign reached its zenith in 1945, devastating Japan's transport system and industrial areas, the nation's war production had already been hollowed out by the interdiction and destruction of its sea communications.

By the war's end, the Pacific submarine force would sink more than 1,100 *marus*, amounting to more aggregate tonnage than Japan had possessed on December 7, 1941. With fewer than 2 percent of all naval personnel, the submariners could claim credit for more than half of all Japanese ships sunk during the war, and 60 percent of the aggregate tonnage. Although their primary strategic purpose was to destroy the enemy's seaborne commerce, the submarines also sent 201 Japanese warships to the bottom, with a combined tonnage of 540,192.[81]

These triumphs were not achieved cheaply. Fifty-two World War II submarines "remain on patrol," to borrow the submariners' poignant euphemism. Forty-one boats are known to have been destroyed by enemy attack. The submarine force was very small when compared to the rest of the navy—the submarine service had a wartime average personnel strength of just 14,750 officers and enlisted men. About 16,000 men altogether made at least one war patrol. Of these, 375 officers and 3,131 men gave their lives—a mortality rate of 22 percent, higher than that for any branch of the armed services. It is perhaps understandable, then, that the submarine force demanded and received recognition of its tremendous contribution to the defeat of Japan. Charlie Lockwood, after the war, told a former skipper who had accepted a post on the faculty of the Naval Academy, "Now don't teach those midshipmen that the submariners won the war. We know there were other forces fighting there, too. But if they kept the surface forces and the flyboys out of our patrol areas we would have won the war six months earlier."[82]

Chapter Ten

F ROM THE DECK OF A SHIP INBOUND FOR PEARL HARBOR, THE FIRST
glimpse of Oahu offered a satisfying contrast to the flat tedium of the
Pacific. Dramatically steep greenish-brown slopes, alternately sunlit and
cast in the shadow of clouds, soared above the horizon. Diamond Head, a
jagged headland with the color and texture of corrugated cardboard, rose
out of the sea and gradually marched eastward to uncover the long arc of
Waikiki Beach and the city of Honolulu. The quartermasters called the
bearings as they passed to starboard: the pink edifice of the Royal Hawaiian
Hotel, the Aloha Tower (painted in wartime camouflage), the Punchbowl
Crater, Ahua Point. Patrol planes flew low overhead and picket boats drew
in close, giving each incoming ship a wary look. The signal tower at Fort
Kamehameha demanded and received recognition signals. A tugboat drew
aside the antisubmarine nets at the outer entrance to the Pearl Harbor
channel, then drew them back across the arriving ship's wake. The channel
was long, straight, and narrow, with surf breaking over coral reefs close
aboard to port and starboard, but it was safely dredged to a depth of 40 feet
and well marked by buoys.

Around Hospital Point, the entire panorama opened up: the central
basin, Ford Island, the teeming dock complexes and administrative buildings along the East Loch. First-timers who had sailed from the mainland were surprised to find that Pearl Harbor was rather small and snug.
The homeport of the mighty Pacific Fleet was nothing to compare with
San Diego or San Francisco Bay. The visual effect was heightened by
the scale and grandeur of the natural backdrop. To the north and west,
scrub growth and palm groves gave way to graceful, undulating sugarcane

fields and pasturelands stretching up into green foothills, and the towering ridgelines of the Waianae and Koolau ranges enclosed the horizon in
every inland direction.

Pearl Harbor had seemed somewhat more spacious earlier in the war, but
by the summer of 1943 the expanding fleet threatened to fill every available
berth and mooring zone, and newly arrived ships inched into an impossibly
congested harbor. Destroyers and other smaller vessels were often moored
two or three abeam, with gangplanks laid between them. All the seaman's
arts were needed to maneuver a battleship or carrier through the overcrowded channels and roadsteads, around other ships (whether underway
or moored), repair and fueling barges, floating dry docks, sunken battleships, and the ubiquitous whaleboats that crossed the channels with bells
clanging insistently. Tides, fogs, shoals, wind, and wakes were confounding
factors. Collisions or groundings were to be reported immediately, and they
could cripple a skipper's career prospects.

In mid-1943, following eighteen months of phenomenal exertions, Pearl
Harbor had largely recovered from the surprise air raid that had launched
the war. Veterans noted that the land around the harbor was noticeably less
green than it had been in 1941, because so much native foliage had been
uprooted and paved over to make way for new piers, shops, foundries, warehouses, hangars, barracks, tank farms, ammunition depots, antiaircraft batteries, administrative buildings, and windowless bombproof power plants.
The clang and rattle of machinery sang out from dawn to dusk, seven days a
week. Two new dry docks were under construction at the navy yard, including the enormous Drydock No. 4, more than 1,000 feet long and serviced
by a towering 50-ton gantry crane that traveled up and down the neighboring pier on a wide-gauge track. Dredging barges were constantly at work to
widen and deepen the channels and anchorages around Ford Island and
West Loch. Between 1941 and 1945, thirteen million cubic yards of mud,
silt, and sand was excavated from the harbor bottom.

To the west, construction teams were erecting long warehouses, a railroad spur, and a modern waterfront terminal on the Pearl City Peninsula.
Most of Pearl Harbor's fuel oil and diesel reserves had been pumped into
subterranean concrete vaults north of the base, which were linked by
pipelines to a huge new concrete fueling pier. Transportation around the
base was provided by fifty-eight miles of roads and a narrow-gauge marine
railway. Tractors pulled passenger wagons on regular routes, much like a

municipal bus system; they were usually crammed to capacity with servicemen and civilian workers.

Five of the eight battleships damaged in the Japanese attack had been repaired and returned to service. Salvage work continued on the *Arizona*, *Oklahoma*, and *Utah*. The reclamation of those wrecked leviathans had been one of the most stupendous challenges ever encountered by engineers, comparable in scale or complexity to the construction of great bridges, dams, or canals. With their hulls ripped open by Japanese aerial torpedoes, several of the great steel ships had come to rest on the harbor floor. To raise and maneuver them into dry docks, where they could be repaired and rebuilt, the salvage teams first had to patch the submerged holes in their sunken hulls, then pump enough water out to raise them to a draft of 35 feet. Thousands of tons of ordnance, weaponry, equipment, and debris had to be removed before the ships could be raised. Noxious and explosive gases built up in the enclosed compartments, posing the constant threat of fire or poisoning.

Workers who descended into the interiors of the damaged ships wore rubber boots and coveralls and carried portable breathing gear. They lit their way with heavy battle lanterns and communicated with the surface by telephone lines connected to air hoses. Powerful suction blowers ventilated the ships, but as new hatches were opened, hydrogen sulfide gas often rushed out with enough force to blow men off their feet. The ships were flooded with an unspeakable black sludge made up of seawater and fuel oil. Badly decomposed corpses were floated into canvas bags, hoisted to the surface, and transferred into boats by medics wearing facemasks. In the once-refrigerated storerooms, salvage teams found tons of decaying ham hocks and sides of beef that disintegrated when handled. One officer on the salvage detail recalled that removing the rancid meat was "one of the meanest jobs" in the entire enterprise. Eventually they found that high-pressure water hoses shredded the rotten meat into small fragments, and these could be pumped overboard by gasoline-powered suction pumps, "no doubt to the great relish of Hawaiian sea life."[1] Returning to the surface after an expedition into the ship, the salvage workers found themselves swathed head to foot in a black slime that could not be removed except by bathing in diesel fuel.

As the ships were pumped out, the interior decks and bulkheads remained coated with a greasy film. Scrubbing them clean was a Herculean challenge. High-pressure hoses, run from barges alongside, bombarded the surfaces with saltwater and various hot caustic solutions. The procedure was repeated again and again, sometimes for weeks at a time, until the surfaces felt and appeared clean. Inevitably, the water in Pearl Harbor was so badly polluted by these operations that it could no longer be used in the desalination plants, and water had to be pumped in from other parts of Oahu.

Salvage operations required immense manpower, and civilian reinforcements were brought in to supplement the Navy Yard's ranks. The workers were almost all young, unmarried men, drawn to Hawaii by high wages and a desire to be close to the war front. Many were crowded into apartments hastily erected in the Navy Yard. "Civilian Housing Area III" offered all the essential trappings of a small city, including a police force, post office, newspaper, baseball diamonds, movie theaters, and retail services. With a peak wartime population of 12,000, it was Hawaii's third-largest city (after Honolulu and Hilo).[2]

Professional divers, including both naval personnel and civilian contractors, did the difficult and dangerous job of inspecting, measuring, and patching the underwater damage. They mapped the flooded interiors, opened and closed watertight doors, disarmed unexploded ordnance, and removed debris and bodies. They worked in perfect darkness, feeling their way through the sludge-flooded innards of the sunken ships, where electric light was useless because it would only reflect back into the small glass ports on their heavy copper helmets. It was grisly work. Edward C. Raymer, a navy diver who wrote a vivid memoir of his work in the sunken battleships, dreaded colliding with the dead sailors who floated through the flooded compartments. He claims to have sensed the proximity of bodies before coming into contact with them, describing the intuition as a "strange feeling that I was not alone."[3] In early 1942, while searching for an unexploded Japanese torpedo warhead in the sunken *Arizona*:

> I reached out to feel my way and touched what seemed to be a large inflated bag floating on the overhead. As I pushed it away, my bare hand plunged through what felt like a mass of rotted sponge. I realized with horror that the "bag" was a body without a head. Gritting my teeth, I shoved the corpse as hard as I could. As it drifted away, its fleshless fingers raked across my rubberized suit, almost as if the dead sailor were reaching out to me in a silent cry for help.[4]

Divers took precise measurements of the underwater breaches in the hulls. Timber patches were constructed to fit those dimensions, and the divers returned to mount them over the holes. The patches were never quite watertight, but they were supplemented by sawdust, oakum, wooden plugs, and whatever other suitable materials could be found in the sunken ships, such as mattresses, pillows, and clothing. Water was then pumped out of the patched hull by gasoline-powered suction pumps. Because water always continued to leak into the ship through the makeshift patches, it was necessary to employ hundreds of pumps simultaneously just to keep the water from rising.

In the case of more seriously damaged ships, such as the *West Virginia* and *California*, it was deemed necessary to construct a "cofferdam," or watertight fencelike structure, all the way around the ship. A wall of 8-inch plank was reinforced with steel pilings driven deep into concrete foundations on the harbor floor. According to Homer Wallin, an officer who oversaw the work, the effort amounted to building a "makeshift drydock" on the site of the sunken battleships. It was "a stupendous and hazardous job."[5] Hundreds of tons of concrete was poured into the bottom of the harbor. The cofferdams were erected close aboard the sides of the ships, leaving a gap of about 2 to 3 feet. The hull damage was patched, the ship pumped out and raised, the cofferdam cast free of the pilings, and the entire unwieldy structure coaxed across East Loch into dry dock.

Presenting an even greater problem was the *Oklahoma*, which had rolled 150 degrees off the vertical and planted her superstructure into the mud at the bottom of the harbor. Only a portion of her keel and starboard bilge was visible above the surface. Workers and divers entered the ship through airlocks cut into her bottom, and descended into a Stygian labyrinth in which up was down and down was up, the decks overhead and the overheads underfoot. In December 1942, *New York Times* correspondent Robert Trumbull put on breathing gear and toured the "pitch black fetid boiler room of the capsized battlewagon."[6] The *Oklahoma* was judged a total loss, apart from her scrap value—but it was necessary to raise and relocate the 29,000-ton ship so that her valuable berthing position could be reclaimed for the fleet. Before she could be floated, she had to be rolled back to an upright position, a process that would require tremendous turning force. Twenty-one high-geared hauling winches were anchored to huge concrete foundations on Ford Island and rigged with high leverage. Heavy steel cables were run from the winches through hauling blocks to pads welded to the bottom of the ship. Each winch supplied 20 tons of pulling power, but even that was not enough. Submarine salvage pontoons were attached to the sunken topside, and compressed air was used to dig the superstructure out of the mud. The winches began taking up strain on the cables on the morning of March 8, 1943. The *Oklahoma* groaned, creaked, and gradually began to turn. The winches pulled her over at the rate of 3 feet per hour. They pulled for more than two months, until June 16, 1943, when she was upright with a 3-degree list. Another five months of work was needed to patch her hull and float her; finally she was maneuvered into the newly completed Drydock No. 4 on December 28.[7]

Rear Admiral William R. Furlong, commandant of the Pearl Harbor Navy Yard, enjoyed telling visitors that the battleships *West Virginia*, *California*, *Tennessee*, and *Nevada* had not just been repaired; they had been rebuilt from the keel up. They were modernized and newly equipped, superior in every respect to the ships that had been blasted, torpedoed, and sunk on December 7, 1941. Of the *West Virginia*, Admiral Furlong proudly concluded, "We built her new from the inside out. We went right to the bottom, like a dentist drilling out a rotten tooth."[8]

By the second anniversary of Pearl Harbor, only the *Arizona* remained on the harbor floor. Divers had confirmed that her keel was broken, and the engineers had concluded that the great hull could not be raised intact. Bringing her up in sections was theoretically possible, but the job would be immensely difficult and the cost would far exceed her scrap value. It was decided to leave her where she lay. She lies there still.

ON AN AVERAGE DAY IN 1943, Honolulu's honky-tonk Hotel Street district was overrun by 30,000 servicemen and civilian defense workers. Hawaiian traditions of charity and hospitality were strained to the breaking point. After the Battle of Midway, when the little sun-drenched city began to feel itself safe from the enemy, Honolulans grew increasingly annoyed by blackout procedures and other military regulations. Air-raid wardens stopped making their nightly rounds, coils of barbed wire rusted on the beaches, and national guardsmen slept at their posts.

Not many visiting servicemen had a good word to say about the city. "The men, almost without exception, detested Honolulu," wrote the sailor and memoirist Theodore C. Mason.[9] It was jaded, expensive, and desperately overcrowded. Samuel Hynes, a marine aviator, called it "another crowded Navy town, much like Pensacola or San Diego, full of sunlight and sailors and bad liquor." One of his fellow pilots, a Texan, pronounced it "Nothin' but Amarillo with a beach."[10] Oahu was nicknamed the "Rock," and the consensus verdict (according to *Paradise of the Pacific*, a popular local monthly magazine) was that there were "just too damn many people of all descriptions on this damn rock, and something ought to be done."[11]

Overcrowded buses and overpriced taxis brought the crowds of white-and-khaki-clad men to the Army-Navy YMCA, where they poured out onto the street and went looking for any kind of amusement. The heart of the vice district ran along Hotel Street from the "Y" to the river, a neighborhood of brash neon, booming jukeboxes, and peeling paint, where dirty sidewalks were lined with dismal bars, brightly lit penny arcades, and tawdry souvenir shops. An odor of stale beer and rotten fish wafted through the street. The beer was cold, but cocktails were watered down and overpriced, and insolent bartenders pestered the men to drink up and order another or else make space for the next paying customer. Burly Hawaiian bouncers kept the peace, but at the first sign of real trouble the shore patrol and military police were called in to knock heads and haul the malefactors away. Men stood in long lines for hot dogs, popcorn, ice cream, Coca-Cola, tattoos, massages, haircuts, pinball machines, shooting galleries, baseball batting cages, pool tables, and photos with a hula dancer. Fifteen cents would buy a bowl of *sai min*—pork and noodles—but a customer had to eat on his feet while being jostled on the crowded sidewalk, and some maintained that the "pork" was actually dog meat. Barefoot Asian boys aged six to twelve offered shoeshines for a quarter, shouting, "Hi, Pal!" and "Shine, Mac!"[12] On a typical afternoon, one officer remembered, Hotel Street was filled with "white hats of sailors on leave as far as you could see."[13]

For Hawaii's retail and business sector, the war was a gold rush. Between 1941 and 1943, 8,000 new businesses were established in the islands, and retail trade increased by $22 million, more than 75 percent. Rents skyrocketed, real estate prices surged, and bank deposits increased by fivefold. The editors of *Paradise of the Pacific* noted in May 1944 that "there were 288 restaurants here in 1939, and there are now 630, but it's still practically impossible to get a meal without standing in line."[14] The territorial economy had long been dominated by a *haole* (Caucasian) elite, but the war was especially kind to owners of retail businesses and restaurants, many of whom were ethnically Chinese, Japanese, Korean, or Filipino.

Local civilian and military authorities had agreed to tolerate a regulated sex trade for the duration of the war. In 1943, fifteen brothels employed 260 prostitutes in Honolulu's red light district.[15] Known as "cathouses" or "bell rooms" ("Give the bell a ring"), the establishments were scattered along Hotel, River, and North Beretania Streets, with discreetly lettered signs identifying them as (for example) the "Bungalow," the "Rex," the "Ritz," the "Anchor," the "Bronx," or the "Rainbow Hotel." On a typical afternoon when the fleet was in port, long lines of servicemen stretched down the stairways and out onto the sidewalks; the wait was often an hour or more. Each customer paid three dollars and was ushered into a small cubicle with a single cot. "Chop-chop," one such man recalls being told by the Chinese madam; he had better undress quickly because his three dollars had bought him only three minutes with "Missie Fuck-Fuck." As the woman entered, a timer was set. When it rang three minutes later, the encounter had ended whether the man had ejaculated or not, and the woman stood up and left the room.

The experience was altogether cheerless and degrading—"A guy might as well use a dead fish," one marine remarked afterward[16]—but the Honolulu brothels never lacked for customers. By one estimate, they sustained a war-time average of 250,000 customers per month. Each woman saw between fifty and a hundred men per day and earned about $25,000 per year. The madams earned as much as $150,000 each year. Local officialdom took a close interest in the enterprise, for reasons both venal and hygienic. The Honolulu Police Department registered each prostitute as an "entertainer" and expected to collect a share of her earnings; the standard bribe was reportedly fifty dollars per woman per month.[17] In turn, the vice squad acted as enforcers for the madams by intimidating, beating, or deporting their dis-obedient girls. Army and navy doctors examined each woman weekly, and outgoing customers were required to visit adjacent "prophylactic stations" for examination and treatment.[18]

The USO, with fifty-one clubs in the islands, provided more wholesome entertainment. A-list celebrities such as Bob Hope and Artie Shaw hosted lavish musical variety shows, with a big band fronted by guest singers, and the songs interspersed with stand-up routines or dance performances. The USO hosted huge dances in which men typically outnumbered women by a ratio of twenty-five to one. The "USO girls" were "respectable"—many were daughters of socially prominent Hawaiian families—and each was under the watchful eye of a chaperone. With a hardy sense of duty and patriotism, they bestowed their smiles and good cheer to all men equally, regardless of rank, looks, or dancing proficiency. They danced for three to four hours a night, with short breaks. Cutting in was permitted every two and a half minutes, when a whistle blew through the loudspeaker.

Left out of the USO events, and denied other perks available only to men in uniform, were the civilian defense workers. Young, unattached males, whose numbers swelled to 82,000 in 1944, were crowded into substandard housing complexes and stuck fast to the bottom of Oahu's social pecking order. Their wages were about 30 percent higher than those paid on the mainland for similar jobs, but they found that the cost of living in Hawaii was about 60 percent higher. Many made themselves conspicuous by wearing garish Hawaiian "aloha" shirts untucked over trousers, a fashion traditionally disdained by other *haole*. Fairly or unfairly, the war workers earned a reputation as "Okies, interlopers, and draft dodgers"[19]—notorious miscreants, gamblers, and drunks, unsuitable for civilized society. Servicemen generally despised them, landlords refused to rent to them, policemen harassed them, and women of all races would not give them the time of day. A territorial health department report concluded that "groups of war workers in this community apparently contain a rather notable number of unstable, alcoholic, psychoneurotic or psychopathic individuals."[20]

Many newly arrived mainland whites, particularly those from the American South, were nonplussed by the tolerant racial attitudes prevailing in Hawaii. The islands' many Asian and Pacific racial and ethnic groups coexisted on harmonious terms. Off-base housing, mass transit, and most retail establishments were largely desegregated (though African American servicemen still endured segregated barracks). Japanese Hawaiians, representing the single largest ethnic group in the territory, had feared persecution or worse after the attack on Pearl Harbor—but by mid-1943 it was evident that the overwhelming majority were loyal to the American cause. The extraordinary heroism in Italy of the all-*nisei* (second-generation Japanese American) 442nd Regimental Combat Team was publicized and celebrated in the Hawaiian press.

Mainland whites who expected to be treated with deference and respect were amazed when it was not automatically forthcoming. "The defense worker received the jolt of his life," observed a columnist in *Paradise of the Pacific*, "when he found that the other races had turned the tables on him and were eyeing him appraisingly, were calculating his probable social status, and were often 'looking down their noses' at him when he moved into their community."[21]

Given the radical gender imbalance in wartime Hawaii, interracial dating and marriage gained a social acceptance that would not reach the mainland until two or three generations later. In 1943 and 1944, according to territorial statistics, 32 percent of all marriages in Hawaii were between spouses of different races. Marriages between Chinese, Koreans, Japanese, Hawaiians, Puerto Ricans, and Filipinos were common. Almost one-half of all white men married a woman of another race, and 9 percent of all white women married a man of a different race. There were 189 marriages between a white man and an ethnic Japanese woman.[22] Then again, Hawaii's wartime divorce rate was 48 percent, almost three times higher than the rate on the mainland.[23]

For thousands of American servicemen, a long interval in wartime Hawaii left them impatient to get on with the war. Bill Davis, a navy fighter pilot stranded on Maui for months on end, remarked that the period seemed like an extended vacation. His days were full of tennis, leisurely training flights, and lunches at an officers' club. "This was all wonderful, but we were beginning to think our motto was that of John Paul Jones, when he said, 'I have not yet begun to fight.'"[24] Even Hawaii's extraordinary natural beauty assumed a monotonous and oppressive aspect. Men who had been too long in the islands were said to be "rock happy" or "pineapple crazy." The best remedy was to send them west, into battle. A reserve naval lieutenant, writing in a local paper, joked that "after three trips on a Honolulu bus, a 97-pound yeoman second class, armed with nothing weightier than a rolled copy of the Honolulu *Advertiser*, would joyously leap into a Jap pillbox."[25]

ADMIRAL NIMITZ, who ran the whole show in Hawaii, and whose monumental Allied theater command took in about a fifth of the earth's surface, lived in a stately white house at the top of Makalapa Hill. The hill, actually the cone of an extinct volcano, was a serene district of green lawns and recently erected homes. Japanese gardeners tended to the newly planted trees and native vegetation, which had not yet grown to maturity and thus did not obstruct the panoramic western views of Pearl Harbor. Makalapa Hill provided quarters for the navy and marine brass—houses for admirals and generals, bungalows for captains and colonels. The prefabricated structures were evenly spaced and built to cookie-cutter architectural plans. Streets bore the names of historic American naval battles, including earlier battles of the war in progress. Lest the enemy attempt to decapitate the high command at one stroke, the neighborhood's existence was held in strict secrecy: the name "Makalapa" was never permitted to appear in any public document or press communiqué.

CINCPAC headquarters was about a quarter mile from Nimitz's house. It was a plain two-story office building, built heavily of steel-reinforced concrete, purposely designed to draw no attention to itself. On a typical morning, Nimitz and his chief of staff, Raymond Ames Spruance, walked to work and arrived at their adjacent offices at the southwest corner of the second "deck" before 0800.

At 0900, the staff section heads crowded into Nimitz's office and sat in folding chairs for a daily morning conference. They received an intelligence briefing and reviewed incoming overnight communications. Discussions of forthcoming operations or other important subjects followed. As the fleet grew in 1943, the crowd at Nimitz's daily "open house" for commanding officers of ships newly arrived at Pearl Harbor grew steadily larger. Nimitz seemed to enjoy these encounters, and he drew much useful information from his freewheeling interviews with the skippers. His flag lieutenant, Arthur Lamar, commented that Nimitz "enjoyed visiting just as much with a young lieutenant (jg) commanding an LST as with a senior captain with a brand new battleship. He loved people!"[26]

In that respect Nimitz was similar to FDR, who had come to know the admiral well in 1940 and 1941, when he had served as the navy's personnel chief in Washington, and who had handpicked Nimitz for command of the Pacific Fleet. The white-haired Texan was cheered and energized in his interactions with subordinates of all ranks, and led with a distinctively warm and personal touch. After returning a salute, he customarily extended his hand and introduced himself: "My name's Nimitz." He kept a fund of slightly off-color stories, funny but never profane; he often used them as a means to dispel tension after men had aired disagreements. Others were astonished by Nimitz's capacity to remember old acquaintances and shipmates, officers and enlisted men—he rarely forgot faces and could often produce a man's name and cite details of his subsequent service. It was not just a matter of keen memory. From early in his career, Nimitz had kept a file of index cards with names and other pertinent information. His staff was always expected to keep those files updated. "In making inspections of ships and islands," recalled Lieutenant Lamar, "he always liked to call officers by name. We did this by means of cards which I made up before each visit, and I often coached the Admiral behind his back. All hands enjoyed this personal touch."[27]

The chief's working day, recalled Ralph Parker, another member of the CINCPAC staff, was "just one conference after another, in varying degree and in varying scope."[28] It might be with one man, just returned from the theater of operations, or with a group that filled the room and occupied every chair so that junior officers were obliged to stand with their backs against the wall. Nimitz was content to listen at length and was tolerant of dissent. He did not emulate King's iron-fist management style or MacArthur's bad habit of surrounding himself with flatterers. Even when discussions grew heated, Nimitz remained imperturbable. He did not sign off on a decision until all objections had been aired and registered. As Ralph Parker observed, "The old idea of Napoleonic command, of being so far superior to all your subordinates that none of them dares say anything but 'Aye Aye, Sir'—that idea no longer holds. It's absolutely necessary to get the opinion of subordinates, particularly those who have to carry out an order."[29]

Nimitz and Spruance often left the office together when the sun was still high in the sky. The two shared a compulsive need for strenuous outdoor exercise, and they often hiked to the top of Makalapa Crater, easily outpacing the much younger officers who joined them. Nimitz's competitive streak came out on the tennis court, where he ran Lamar around and never let the younger man take a set, and on the horseshoe court outside his quarters, where he could beat Spruance pitching with either hand. When the fleet surgeon told him that target shooting was an effective therapy for stress, Nimitz had a shooting range constructed outside his office and invited officers to join him in firing .22 and .45 target pistols, with wagers limited to a dime. "He quickly became an enthusiastic marksman," said Lamar, "and every day we used to fire several hundred rounds. I suppose by the time the surrender took place at Tokyo Bay, we must have fired at least half a million shots!"[30]

On Sunday afternoons, Nimitz, Spruance, and a party of other officers might head over the mountains to a secluded beach on Oahu's north coast, a place they nicknamed "Prostate Rest." Their regular routine was a two-mile hike down the beach, followed by a long swim. One weekend in the summer of 1943, Nimitz invited a few key intelligence officers to join the expedition. Tom Dyer, one of the cryptanalysts who had broken the Japanese naval codes before the Battle of Midway, was surprised to be invited. He borrowed a swimsuit to make the trip and rode in the back-seat, wedged between the two admirals. Nimitz, having sustained an injury, announced that he would sit on the beach rather than hike and swim, as was his usual custom. "I was perfectly willing to sit in the sun with him," said Dyer, who was no athlete and worked long hours in a windowless base-ment, "but Spruance suggested we take a walk down the beach. . . . It wasn't a walk, it was practically a marathon. He was putting one foot in front of the other at a very rapid pace." On the return swim, Dyer lasted about a quarter of a mile. He staggered back down the beach, badly sunburned and with the swimsuit chafing his thighs, and declared that he had "been injured in the line of duty."[31]

Nimitz did not relish publicity, but as wartime CINCPAC he was a pub-lic figure with duties akin to those of a civilian elected official. He often appeared at public functions and receptions, in white uniform and gloves. He dined regularly at the governor's palace. Newspaper photographers caught him touring ships, pinning medals to chests, dancing with a hula girl at an enlisted men's recreation center, or inspecting carrots at a Victory Garden Show in Honolulu while wearing a lei "made of tiny vegetables."[32] He attended dinner parties given by Hawaii's civilian upper crust, where women wore evening gowns and white-clad stewards served drinks on trays. Nimitz was always accompanied by his marine guards, men selected for height and appearance who dressed in rigidly starched uniforms. His car, a large gray sedan, flew a four-star flag and was always waxed to a gleaming luster. In January 1944, he was the guest of honor at a "Texas Round-Up" picnic in Moana Park, an event attended by 40,000 Texan servicemen. The smiling admiral was photographed pitching horseshoes with sailors and holding the corner of a Texas flag.[33]

At home in the evenings, he and Spruance relaxed over weak cocktails—an old-fashioned or a scotch and soda mixed in a tall glass, with a thimble of liquor and lots of ice. The two admirals often ended the evening sitting in armchairs at 37 Makalapa Drive, listening to a classical symphony on a phonograph. Their Filipino steward turned off the lights, opened the blackout shades, and let the night air into the house. Occasionally they discussed the war, but more often they sat in silence. By the summer of 1943, near the end of Spruance's fourteen-month stint as CINCPAC chief of staff—a period in which the two men had lived in the same house, worked in adjoining offices, and hiked for miles together most afternoons—each usually knew what was in the other's mind. They carried the weight of responsibility for hundreds of thousands of lives, and for the casualties that would inevitably escalate as the war moved closer to the enemy's homeland. As Nimitz's most trusted subordinate, Spruance would soon be rewarded with the navy's top seagoing command and would lead the bloody campaign westward across the heart of the Pacific.

Two decades later, following Nimitz's death, Spruance told a reporter that fear was a near-universal human trait, a condition that even the bravest men labored to keep in check. But Nimitz was out of the ordinary: "He was one of the few people I knew who never knew what it meant to be afraid of anything."[34]

ON JUNE 1, 1943, the first of a new class of 27,100-ton aircraft carriers crept into Pearl Harbor and inched into a berth north of Ford Island, directly flanking the still-capsized hull of the battleship *Utah*. The arrival of the *Essex* (CV-9) had been keenly anticipated. A navy band and a larger-than-usual complement of hula dancers waited on the pier. Up on Makalapa Hill, on the top "deck" of the CINCPAC headquarters, a crowd of officers passed around a pair of binoculars.

The *Essex* was much easier to handle than the older fleet carriers, but Captain Donald Duncan was relieved to have a pilot aboard to conn the big ship into the congested harbor.[35] The *Essex* was 872 feet long, and her beam at the flight deck was 147 feet. She had been designed to squeeze through the Panama Canal, but only just—in order to accommodate her passage two weeks earlier, several lighting towers and pilothouses along the top of the locks had been removed or cut down to size. "It was a very necessary thing," said Duncan, "because I well remember in going through the locks of the Canal, if you stretched a little bit, you could reach out and touch the edge of the roof from the wing of the navigation bridge, which was right along the same line as the side of the ship."[36]

Duncan had last seen Pearl Harbor in March 1942, when the devastation of the Japanese attack had been evident throughout the area. Fifteen months later, it appeared "that some tremendous effort had been made to get it straightened out and cleaned up and rebuilt. . . . [T]he Navy Yard was going strong, all damages being repaired; and the appearance of the place was one of being busy and confident and very much on the job."[37]

Many more aircraft carriers, large and small, would steam down the Pearl Harbor entrance channel in the ensuing six months. The new *Yorktown* and *Lexington*, named for the flattops lost at Coral Sea and Midway the previous year, were built on identical lines to the *Essex*. They arrived from the mainland in July and August. The fourth-in-class, the new *Hornet*, would follow by the end of the year. The navy planned to build and commission twenty-four of these huge first-line carriers by 1945. The 11,000-ton light carrier *Independence* (CVL-22), converted from a hull originally intended as a light cruiser, arrived in July and was soon followed by her sisters *Princeton* and *Belleau Wood*. Several diminutive escort or "jeep" carriers (CVEs) joined the fleet that fall. Though too slow to operate with the new fast carrier task forces, CVEs were valuable in transporting and resupplying aircraft and in providing air cover to amphibious operations.

The new fast battleships of the *Iowa* class would not reach the Pacific until 1944, but the *Colorado* and *Maryland* (*Colorado*-class battleships armed with 16-inch guns) were in port to be outfitted with new radar systems and additional antiaircraft mounts. Cruisers, destroyers, destroyer escorts, transports, fleet oilers, minesweepers, minelayers, mobile dry docks, hospital ships, and many other types of combatant and auxiliary ships squeezed into the harbor. A billion-dollar crash-building program in 1942 had produced more than a quarter of a million tons of amphibious landing craft, in a variety of types ranging from small Higgins boats to 300-foot-long tank-landing ships (LSTs). As the fleet grew, it became evident to anyone with a view of Pearl Harbor that a big offensive was in preparation.

The *Essex*-class carriers had been designed with all of the shortcomings of the earlier fleet carriers in mind, and were superior in every respect to their predecessors. They carried a complement of ninety-six planes and tore through the sea at 33 knots. Much of the design work had been coordinated by veteran aviator Jim Russell (who would eventually achieve four-star rank) during a tour of duty in the Bureau of Aeronautics before the war. Russell, who had served in carriers in many capacities for many years, pushed for new catapults and arresting gear, more and better firefighting equipment, and new maintenance and storage facilities. He placed the three aircraft elevators as far as practicable from the centerline of the ship, to create more elbow room in the hangar and allow for more rapid and flexible cycling of aircraft. More controversially, Russell designed a very large flight deck that retained its width and rectangular shape all the way to the forecastle. Engineers warned that the overhanging forward corners of the flight deck, weakly supported by two steel I-beams, would be vulnerable to collapse in heavy weather. Russell acknowledged the point but maintained that it was worth risking storm damage in order to construct "a proper flying field."[38] (Both were right: some of the *Essex*-class flight decks did suffer in extreme weather, but the damage was easily repaired and the trade-off deemed satisfactory.)

The *Essex* carriers were designed to be as light as possible within the necessary strength tolerances. As a result, said Captain Duncan, they were much more responsive to their helms: "When you gave [them] the gun, those ships really jumped. It was quite different than some of the older, heavier ships. That I think was an indication of what can be done with very detailed care to things of that kind."[39]

Russell offered "very strong representations" to his superiors about the importance of the pilot ready rooms, which he thought ought to be far more comfortable than those on the older aircraft carriers. They should be air-conditioned, well lighted, and placed as near as possible to the deck spots for each squadron's aircraft. Russell wanted large leather reclining chairs, arranged to face toward a blackboard and a teleprinter linked to Air Plot, so that each pilot could remain seated comfortably while working at his navigation board. He argued that men would be better rested and more effective if they could prepare for their flights in "peace and comfort . . . instead of standing up and getting on each others' toes, with very poor lighting and poor ventilation as in the ready rooms on the old carriers."[40] The point was brilliantly vindicated when the *Essex* and her sisters went into service.

The new carriers were matched with a new generation of carrier fighters and bombers. By June 1943, the Grumman F6F Hellcat had replaced the obsolete F4F Wildcat. The Hellcat was a very large aircraft, weighing 1,200 pounds unloaded, but it was powered by a monstrous 2,000-horsepower Pratt & Whitney engine and climbed at 3,500 feet per minute. Its flying range was just short of 1,000 miles. The cockpit, slickly faired into the fuselage, was heavily armored. The F6F carried six electrically charged .50-caliber guns and about twice the ammunition of the F4F.

The Wildcat had lagged behind the Japanese Zero fighter in climbing speed and maneuverability. The Hellcat would match the Zero's climbing speed below 14,000 feet and outpace it in a climb at higher altitudes. Its speed on the level or in a dive was superior to that of the Zero at any altitude.

On first impression, many assumed that the massive blue aircraft must be a bomber. Indeed, the new Grumman could be configured to carry 4,000 pounds of bombs or rockets, and it was sometimes used in the role of a fighter-bomber. "The plane was a monster," wrote Bill Davis, who first encountered it in August 1943. His squadron, VF-19, checked out in the F6F at Los Alamitos Naval Air Station in California. From the moment the engine fired, Davis was thrilled and amazed. "There was a thunderous backfire as flames shot out of the exhaust pipe. A sailor with a fire extinguisher moved toward the plane, but the engine quickly caught and the flames disappeared as the engine started to purr with a mighty roar. I could feel the power through the throttle as well as my ears and every quaking fiber of my body." Davis taxied to the end of the runway, checked the magnetos, and paused for a moment. He was a bit apprehensive, and had to summon his nerve before opening up the throttle. His description of that first check-out flight is worth quoting in its entirety:

The noise was fantastic. The response was instantaneous. Correcting for the torque of the giant engine, I started straight down the runway. I glanced at the instruments and couldn't believe that I had only applied half the engine's power. I pushed the throttle against the stop; the surge of power and speed was incredible.

The tail came up immediately as I eased the stick forward. A slight pull back and I was in the air. Instantly I hit the switch and pulled the wheels up so that anyone watching would know I was a hot pilot. Crossing the end of the field, I was already at five hundred feet. This thing really sang the song of the birds. I was really flying, and I had six .50-caliber machine guns, unloaded at the moment, but I knew I was ready for those Japs. Revenge would be mine.

I put the plane through every maneuver I knew, and a few more. It was amazingly responsive for a plane its size. It flew like a small fighter. Approaching the field, I made a tight turn into final approach, I knew everyone would be watching. Rolling out of the turn, I stalled it at the beginning of the runway. Pulling the flaps up as I taxied to the flight line, I knew I was home. This is what I'd been training for; I was ready.[41]

In order to retire the Wildcat and supply the rapidly expanding carrier fleet with new fighters, the Bureau of Aeronautics had pressed Grumman for a terrific ramp-up in production. In the month of July 1943, the Grumman plant in Bethpage, Long Island, turned out 250 Hellcats, and it was on pace to turn out 500 per month by 1944.[42] But Grumman fell behind in its production of spare parts, and when the shortages grew critical in the fall of 1943, the bureau took the drastic step of refusing to accept delivery of new planes until the backlog was filled.[43]

The venerable Douglas SBD Dauntless dive-bomber, which had destroyed four enemy carriers at the Battle of Midway and served as a vital workhorse in the air battle for Guadalcanal, was overdue for retirement. With a top speed of 260 miles per hour, the much-loved Dauntless could not keep pace with the TBF Avenger and the new Hellcat, and its bomb load capacity (1,200 pounds in most configurations) was insufficient. But its heir, the Curtiss SB2C Helldiver (an acronym for "Scout Bomber, Design Number 2, Curtiss"), had been plagued with problems from the start of its career, and its introduction into the fleet was delayed by more than a year. Early prototype SB2Cs suffered from longitudinal instability and structural weaknesses, especially in the tail and main wing beam, and several early test flights ended in crashes. Design modifications addressed some of these problems while creating others. In carrier trials, the SB2C's landing gear often collapsed and its tailhook often missed the arresting cables (or worse, snagged the cable and was wrenched out of the fuselage). The plane was prone to stalls, leaks, hydraulic failures, electrical shorts, and flat tires.

It was a demanding airplane to fly, with high stick forces and a weak aileron response. Pilots did not trust it in a dive and tended to release their bombs high, at the expense of accuracy. The Helldiver was especially balky at low airspeeds, as on a carrier landing approach. The aviators saddled the new plane with various unflattering nicknames: the "Bladder," the "Big-Tailed Beast," the "Ensign Exterminator," the "Son of a Bitch 2nd Class." The Dauntless pilot Samuel Hynes hated everything about the

SB2C, even its name, which he supposed had been chosen by some "public relations man." The Helldiver, wrote Hynes, "was as showy and as phony as the name, like a beach athlete, all muscle and no guts. It was a long, slab-sided, ugly machine, with a big round tailfin. . . . We were all afraid of the SB2Cs, and we flew them as though they were booby-trapped."[44]

Harold Buell, a veteran dive-bomber pilot who had recently taken command of VB-2, checked the Helldiver out in early 1944. He liked the large bomb load and faster airspeed and was not concerned about his own ability to handle the plane. But Buell worried about his squadron's less experienced pilots: "My first reaction was that the Beast, as this Curtiss monster was called, would be trouble for the squadron. Compared to the steady, forgiving SBD, this aircraft required much more pilot ability to fly both operationally and as a dive-bombing weapon."[45]

But in late 1943, after long delays, the Bureau of Aeronautics was determined to force the SB2C into service despite the risks, and began pressuring carrier and squadron commanders to cooperate. The plane was justly unloved and no fun to fly, but it did offer essential benefits over the Dauntless, notably its 295-mile-per-hour maximum airspeed (which would allow it to fly coordinated strikes with the other carrier planes), and its much higher bomb load (an internal bomb bay held 2,000 pounds of bombs, and a 500-pound bomb could be carried under each wing). The Helldiver, unlike the SBD, had folding wings, a feature considered indispensable in the new-generation carriers. For all its early problems, the SB2C could be produced rapidly and in the needed quantities. "It was a very complex plane, a very difficult plane to maintain, but there was the capability of 'cranking them out,'" said Lieutenant Commander Herbert D. Riley, a planner with the Bureau of Aeronautics. "That's what we had to have, building capacity. It was never a question of money; we could always get the money in those days. It was a question of the capacity of American industry to produce airplanes."[46]

By early 1944, the Curtiss plant in Columbus, Ohio, was turning out more than 300 Helldivers per month, and a Goodyear plant in Akron began producing them from Curtiss blueprints later in 1944.[47] Eventually, 7,140 Helldivers were built. As dive-bombing squadrons became more accustomed to the aircraft, they grew to tolerate its idiosyncrasies and even began to resent criticism directed against their aircraft. Despite its shortcomings, the SB2C would inflict plenty of punishment on the enemy in 1944 and 1945.

FOR NEARLY FOUR DECADES, since the presidential administration of Theodore Roosevelt, analysts at the Naval War College in Newport had studied
and planned for a prospective war against Japan. In successive iterations
of the "Orange" and "Rainbow" war plans, the navy had contemplated
a westward naval-amphibious offensive through the heart of the Pacific.
The American fleet would sortie from Pearl Harbor and hop from island to
island through the Marshall, Caroline, and Mariana groups. When it penetrated Japan's "outer defense" ring, it would meet and destroy Japan's main
battle line. That decisive naval victory would trigger the war's endgame.
Japan would be cut off from its territories on the Asian mainland and in
the South Pacific. Starved of imported raw materials, the Japanese economy
would collapse. An invasion of Japan might or might not be necessary, but
in either case victory would follow as a matter of course.

Several related versions of this blueprint sat on the shelves at Navy
Headquarters in Washington. It had been evident, following the Japanese
strike on Pearl Harbor, that the navy and its sister services lacked the necessary sea, air, or ground forces to undertake such a massive operation in 1942,
and would not be able to assemble them until 1943 or 1944, if even then.
But it always remained the navy's view—that is to say, the view of Ernest J.
King—that the Pacific War would eventually be won by executing the strategy outlined in War Plan Orange. There would be a direct westward assault
from Hawaii on Japanese-held islands in the central Pacific. It would be carried out by the Pacific Fleet and the Marine Corps, with the U.S. Army and
U.S. Army Air Forces in subsidiary roles. Nimitz and his admirals would be
in charge; MacArthur would have no part of it. The only issue to be decided
was *when* such a campaign should begin.

Characteristically, King wanted to get the show on the road as early
as possible, and he had exerted all his influence to send the needed forces
to Nimitz. As usual, his efforts were doggedly opposed by the British, who
wanted a concentration of all available Allied forces for the defeat of Germany, and by MacArthur, whose preferred road to Tokyo ran through the
Philippines, and who wanted no competing offensive to the north. But
King eventually succeeded in bringing his colleagues on the Joint Chiefs
around to his way of thinking and gradually won their undivided backing.
William Leahy, who had taken a direct hand in developing the Orange and
Rainbow plans during his long naval career, was an instinctive ally. George

Marshall was anxious about the state of the South Pacific and determined to keep Japan on the defensive. Throughout late 1942, King worked behind the scenes to persuade Marshall of the strategic importance of the Marianas, which lay directly astride sea routes linking Japan's home islands to the resource-rich East Indies. The Marianas would provide suitable airfields for the army's B-29 "Superfortresses," which would enter service in 1944 and could carry 10,000 pounds of bombs to a radius of 1,600 miles. From Guam and Tinian in the Marianas, the heavy bombers could strike major Japanese population centers and industrial areas. "I finally got General Marshall to understand," King wrote after the war.[48]

In the Allied conferences of early and mid-1942, the British military chiefs had hoped to win Marshall and the U.S. Army leadership over to their concept of a minimalist and purely defensive war in the Pacific, pending the final defeat of Germany. But when the high command met in Casablanca, French Morocco, in January 1943, it was immediately clear that Marshall and King had reached an understanding, and were in agreement that the Pacific required more reinforcements.

In the first meeting of the Combined Chiefs of Staff (CCOS), at Anfa Camp on the morning of January 14, Marshall proposed to allocate Allied troops, shipping, and munitions by a formula of " 70 percent in the Atlantic theater and 30 percent in the Pacific theater."[49] King spoke immediately after Marshall, leaving little doubt that the two Americans were reading from the same playbook. According to his estimates, said King, the Allies were engaging "only 15 percent of our total resources against the Japanese in the Pacific theater," a proportion that "was not sufficient to prevent Japan consolidating herself and thereby presenting ultimately too difficult a problem."[50]

General Sir Alan Brooke, chief of the British Imperial General Staff, was knocked back on his heels. He had long since marked King as an irredeemable Anglophobe and a "Pacific-firster," and now the ruthless admiral had apparently cast a spell over George Marshall. Brooke asked, Upon what basis had the Americans computed the 30 percent formula? King replied, somewhat lamely, that it "was a concept rather than an arithmetical computation," but in any case 15 percent was insufficient to do more than hold the lines in the Pacific. Brooke held his tongue but later told his diary that the proposed figure was "hardly a scientific way" of fixing allocation between theaters.[51]

The official minutes of the Combined Chiefs meetings, recorded in strictly anodyne terms, tended to disguise the heated subtext of the debate. The British had lost much of their Asia-Pacific empire and wanted it back. In Malaya, especially, they had been disgraced; in order to retrieve their prestige in the region, they must have a role in the defeat of Japan. But until Germany was knocked out of the war, Britain could offer no meaningful contribution to the Pacific theater. If the Americans closed in on Japan too early, British military power might be rendered strategically irrelevant in the Pacific, with portentous consequences for the future of the empire. But Ernest King was not at all interested in the future of the British empire, and he even appeared to take an unseemly relish in the humbling of British seapower.

In his diary, General Brooke confided a sour loathing for the "shrewd and somewhat swollen headed" admiral, whose objective seemed to be "an 'all-out' war against Japan instead of holding operations."[52] At dinner that night, Brooke watched in amusement as King drained one glass too many and became "nicely lit up." "With a thick voice and many gesticulations," the admiral remonstrated stridently with Churchill, to the prime minister's evident embarrassment.[53] Two days later, after another round of punishing negotiations, Brooke concluded wearily, "It is a slow and tiring business which requires a lot of patience. They can't be pushed and hurried, and must be made gradually to assimilate our proposed policy."[54]

The scale of the Pacific effort was only one dimension of their quarrel. Marshall's view, shared by Secretary of War Henry Stimson and to varying degrees by the other American service chiefs, was that Germany could be defeated only by a direct invasion across the English Channel, the operation code-named ROUNDUP. The British feared a debacle in northern France and preferred new operations in the Mediterranean. In 1942, Churchill and his generals had persuaded FDR to back their proposed invasion of North Africa (TORCH), over the sharp objections of Marshall and Stimson. Marshall, still smarting from that reversal, now wanted a firm commitment to execute ROUNDUP in the summer of 1943. The British refused to commit to a date for ROUNDUP, and were dubious that such an operation was feasible before 1944. But still, they asked for an immediate buildup of forces in England so that ROUNDUP could be launched if and when opportunity offered—that is, if and when the Red Army gained the upper hand on the eastern front, and a German collapse appeared imminent. Meanwhile, they favored further efforts in the Mediterranean, perhaps an invasion of Italy. Marshall did not much like this proposed southern line of attack, regarding it as a diversion from the "main plot" and a "suction pump" that would draw strength away from ROUNDUP.[55]

Selected excerpts of minutes of the Combined Chiefs meeting at Casablanca put across the substance of the opposing arguments, and show the degree to which King and Marshall now spoke with one voice on the importance of the Pacific:

ADMIRAL KING stated that the Japanese are now replenishing Japan with raw materials and also fortifying an inner defense ring along the line of the Netherlands East Indies and the Philippines.

SIR ALAN BROOKE inquired how far forward the U. S. Chiefs of Staff envisaged it would be necessary to go in order to prevent the Japanese from digging themselves in. He feared that if operations were too extended it would inevitably lead to an all-out war against Japan and it was certain that we had not sufficient resources to undertake this at the same time as a major effort against Germany.

GENERAL MARSHALL explained that it had been essential to act offensively in order to stop the Japanese advancing. For example, in New Guinea it had been necessary to push the Japanese back to prevent them capturing Port Moresby. In order to do this, every device for reinforcing the troops on the island had had to be employed. The same considerations applied in Guadalcanal. It had been essential to take offensive action to seize the island. Short of offensive action of this nature, the only way of stopping the Japanese was by complete exhaustion through attrition. It was very difficult to pause: the process of whittling away Japan had to be continuous.

SIR CHARLES PORTAL [RAF chief] asked whether it was not possible to stand on a line and inflict heavy losses on the Japanese when they tried to break through it. From the very fact that the Japanese continued to attack, it was clear that they had already been pushed back further than they cared to go.

GENERAL MARSHALL spoke of our commitments in the Pacific, of our responsibilities, with particular reference to the number of garrisons we have on small islands and the impossibility of letting any of them down. He insisted that the United States could not stand for another Bataan.

SIR ALAN BROOKE stated that we have reached a stage in the war where we must review the correctness of our basic strategic concept which calls for the defeat of Germany first. He was convinced that we cannot defeat Germany and Japan simultaneously. The British Chiefs of Staff have arrived at the conclusion that it will be better to concentrate on Germany. Because of the distances involved, the British Chiefs of Staff believe that the defeat of Japan first is impossible and that if we attempt to do so, we shall lose the war.

GENERAL MARSHALL stated that, in his opinion, the British Chiefs of Staff wished to be certain that we keep the enemy engaged in the Mediterranean and that at the same time maintain a sufficient force in the United Kingdom to take advantage of a crack in the German strength either from the withdrawal of their forces in France or because of lowered morale. He inferred that the British Chiefs of Staff would prefer to maintain such a force in the United Kingdom dormant and awaiting an opportunity rather than have it utilized in a sustained attack elsewhere. The United States Chiefs of Staff know that they can use these forces offensively in the Pacific Theater.

SIR ALAN BROOKE said that the British Chiefs of Staff certainly did not want to keep forces tied up in Europe doing nothing. During the build-up period, however, the first forces to arrive from America could not be used actively against the enemy; a certain minimum concentration had to be effected before they could be employed. His point was that we should direct our resources to the defeat of Germany first. This conception was focused in paragraph 2(c) of the British Joint Planning Staff's paper (C.C.S. 153/1) in which it was stated that we agreed in principle with the U. S. strategy in the Pacific "provided always that its application does not prejudice the earliest possible defeat of Germany."

ADMIRAL KING pointed out that this expression might be read as meaning that anything which was done in the Pacific interfered with the earliest possible defeat of Germany and that the Pacific theater should therefore remain totally inactive.

SIR CHARLES PORTAL said that this was certainly not the understanding of the British Chiefs of Staff, who had always accepted that pressure should be maintained on Japan. They had, perhaps, misunderstood the U. S. Chiefs of Staff and thought that the point at issue was whether the main effort should be in the Pacific or in the United Kingdom. The British view was that for getting at Germany in the immediate future, the Mediterranean offered better prospects than Northern France.

GENERAL MARSHALL said that he was most anxious not to become committed to interminable operations in the Mediterranean. He wished Northern France to be the scene of the main effort against Germany—that had always been his conception.

ADMIRAL KING said that we had on many occasions been close to a disaster in the Pacific. The real point at issue was to determine the balance between the effort to be put against Germany and against Japan, but we must have enough in the Pacific to maintain the initiative against the Japanese. . . . He felt very strongly . . . that the details of such operations must be left to the U. S. Chiefs of Staff, who were strategically responsible for the Pacific theater. He did not feel this was a question for a decision of the Combined Chiefs of Staff.

Brooke wanted to check the westward momentum of the Pacific offensive, for fear that it would divert shipping and other resources away from the Mediterranean. He asked that any decision to push past Rabaul to Truk be "deferred." In the event that Rabaul fell into Allied hands, Brooke wanted surplus forces in the South Pacific transferred to the Mediterranean. King replied that whatever forces became available in MacArthur's theater would be needed by Nimitz for the conquest of the Marshalls. Moreover, he added, "on logistic grounds alone it would be impossible to bring forces from the Pacific theater to the European theater."

The committee's final recommendations to Churchill and FDR represented a compromise skewed toward the American view. The Allies would aim to seize Burma and Rabaul by the end of 1943, with the proviso that "these operations must be kept within such limits as will not . . . jeopardize the capacity of the United Nations to take advantage of any favorable opportunity that may present itself for the decisive defeat of Germany in 1943." The Americans could launch further operations against the Marshalls and Carolines only after the capture of Rabaul, using forces already allocated to the Pacific theater.

At the Trident conference in Washington the following May, the Allies remained largely divided over the same issues and along the same lines. While en route to Washington, Brooke confided to his diary that he dreaded the renewal of old arguments: "Casablanca has taught me too much. Agreement after agreement may be secured on paper but if their hearts are not in it they soon drift away again!"[56]

In fact, the Joint Chiefs did not intend to offer any concessions at all concerning the scale of the Pacific campaign. When the Combined Chiefs of Staff convened in the ornate marble Board of Governors Room at the Federal Reserve Building on May 13, the Americans took a brusque tone from the outset. Admiral Leahy, now serving as *de facto* chairman of the Joint Chiefs, flatly informed the British that any provision limiting freedom of action in the Pacific "would not be acceptable to the United States Chiefs of Staff." He added that if the Americans suffered an unexpected reversal in the war against Japan, they would shift forces to the Pacific "even at the expense of the early defeat of Germany."[57]

On the morning of Friday, May 21, King provided a long briefing on the progress of the Pacific War, ending with an analysis of possibilities for the latter half of 1943 and 1944. "Regardless of which route might be taken," he concluded, "the Marianas are the key to the situation because of their location on the Japanese lines of communication."[58]

Brooke, in restrained exasperation, reiterated his familiar arguments. He later complained to his diary that King had tried "to find every loophole he possibly can to divert troops to the Pacific!"[59] But with few forces actively engaged against the Japanese, the British lacked standing to shape strategy in the theater. Without quite saying it, Leahy, King, and Marshall intimated that the Pacific was now an American responsibility, and left no doubt that they would fight it on their own terms and according to their own schedule. In Trident's final conference documents, the American strategic proposals were enacted wholesale, including "Seizure of the Marshall and Caroline Islands" without reference to the timing of MacArthur's assault on Rabaul.[60]

Two PARALLEL PACIFIC CAMPAIGNS, north and south of the equator, now had the imprimatur of the Allied high command. But Nimitz did not yet possess the sea or carrier air forces needed to wage a central Pacific offensive, and the troops in his theater required months of additional amphibious training. From his South Pacific headquarters, Halsey was calling for rein-forcements to carry his fight into the central Solomons. Nonetheless, King wanted hard deadlines for the central Pacific campaign. "In order that effec-tive momentum of offensive operations can be attained and maintained," he told his fellow chiefs on June 10, "firm timing must be set up for all areas."[61] Four days later, the Joint Chiefs of Staff instructed Nimitz to prepare to invade the Marshall Islands with a tentative sailing date of November 15, 1943. MacArthur was to release the 1st Marine Division in time to par-ticipate in the operation, and most of Halsey's naval and amphibious forces would be shifted to Pearl Harbor as well. With unusual candor the chiefs acknowledged that the date was somewhat arbitrary—but in the absence of deadlines "it is not repeat not practicable to provide able structure for our operations throughout the Pacific and Far East."[62]

Predictably outraged, MacArthur objected that the demands of his CARTWHEEL campaign precluded any transfers of troops or ships from his theater to Nimitz's. Indeed, MacArthur wanted (and would receive) cov-ering support from the Pacific Fleet's new fast carrier task forces in raids against Rabaul, Truk, and other Japanese bases on the southern route. Like-wise, Halsey was anxious about the withdrawal of aircraft from the SOPAC region for support of operations north of the equator. Diverting airpower from the drive on Rabaul, he warned Nimitz on June 25, "would seriously jeopardize our chances of success at what appears to be the most critical stage of the campaign."[63]

Without borrowing forces from the South Pacific, Nimitz could not realis-tically tackle the Marshalls until early 1944, and some on the CINCPAC plan-ning staff counseled patience. They argued, not unreasonably, that the new offensive should await the arrival of a large fleet of *Essex* carriers, which could spearhead long leaps across ocean wastes and beat back enemy land-based air attacks. By February or March 1944, a much-expanded Fifth Fleet could sim-ply steam into the Marshalls and seize the four or five largest Japanese bases in the group simultaneously. If the Japanese fleet came out to fight, the fast carrier task forces would willingly and confidently give battle.

But King wanted action in 1943. He insisted that the northern line of attack be opened *before* the final assault on Rabaul, so that the enemy could not concentrate his defenses against either prong of the westward advance. Enemy territory had to be taken, somewhere in the central Pacific, before the end of the year. Two competing suggestions were debated at CINCPAC

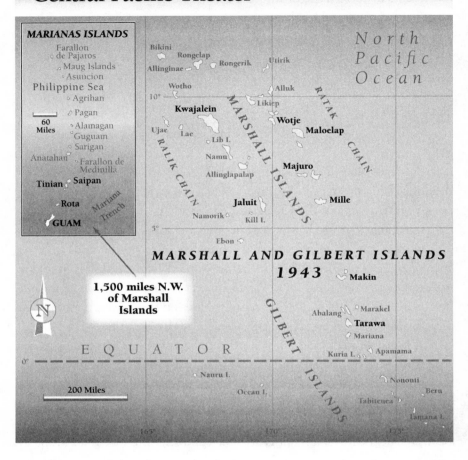

Central Pacific Theater

MARIANAS ISLANDS

Farallon de Pajaros
Maug Islands
Asuncion
Philippine Sea
Agrihan
Pagan
Alamagan
Guguam
Sarigan
Anatahan
Farallon de Medinilla
Tinian
Saipan
Rota
Mariana Trench
GUAM

60 Miles

Bikini
Rongelap
Allinginae
Rongerik
Utirik
Wotho
Alluk
Kwajalein
Likiep
Ujae
Lae
Wotje
Maloelap
Lib I.
Namu
Majuro
Allinglapalap
Jaluit
Mille
Namorik
Kill I.
Ebon

RALIK CHAIN
RATAK CHAIN
MARSHALL ISLANDS

North Pacific Ocean

10°

5°

1,500 miles N.W. of Marshall Islands

MARSHALL AND GILBERT ISLANDS
1943   Makin

Abalang
Marakel
Tarawa
Mariana

GILBERT

E   Q   U   A   T   O   R
Kuria I.
Apamama

0°

Nauru I.
Nonouti
Ocean I.
Beru
Tabiteuea
Tamana I.

ISLANDS

200 Miles

163°   170°   175°

headquarters. Captain Forrest P. Sherman, the influential chief of staff to Vice Admiral John Henry Towers (Commander Air Forces, Pacific, or "COMAIRPAC"), circulated a plan to recapture Wake Island and employ it as a springboard for a later assault on the Marshalls, which lay about 500 miles south. Spruance favored opening the new campaign much farther south and east, where the fleet could count on greater land-based air support from rear bases in the South Pacific. He wanted to launch the new offensive in the Gilbert Islands, some 600 miles southeast of the Marshalls. Nimitz was swayed by his chief of staff's reasoning, and persuaded King in turn. COMINCH arranged the necessary Joint Chiefs of Staff directive on

July 20, 1943. The operation, code-named GALVANIC, called for the simultaneous capture of objectives in the Ellice Islands, the Gilbert Islands, and Nauru by November 15 of that year.

SINCE HIS VICTORIOUS RETURN from Midway a year earlier, Raymond Spruance had privately hoped for another major command at sea. But it was not the taciturn admiral's way to lobby for a job, and he was neither surprised nor disconcerted when Nimitz told him, as the two men walked to CINCPAC headquarters one morning in May 1943, "There are going to be some changes in the high command of the fleet. I would like to let you go, but unfortunately for you I need you here."

In his version of the conversation, recalled years later, Spruance replied, "Well, the war is an important thing. I personally would like to have another crack at the Japs, but if you need me here, this is where I should be."

The next morning, as the two went again on foot from house to office, Nimitz brought the subject up again. "I have been thinking this over during the night," he said. "Spruance, you are lucky. I've decided that I am going to let you go, after all."[64]

Nimitz sold King on the assignment during their meeting in San Francisco later that month. On May 30, a dispatch from Navy Headquarters in Washington lifted Spruance to the rank of vice admiral. Shortly afterward, he was detached from the CINCPAC staff and placed in command of the Central Pacific Force, later designated the Fifth Fleet. It was the largest seagoing command in the history of the U.S. Navy.

Time was short. Spruance had little more than four months to plan the largest and most complex amphibious operation yet attempted. Naval forces and landing troops had to be collected from far-flung parts of the South Pacific and the mainland. His key commanders had not yet been named to their posts, nor had they even been identified. Writing the plan would be an immensely complicated and demanding job. Spruance moved quickly to recruit a chief of staff with the requisite experience and initiative. He chose an old friend and shipmate, Captain Charles J. "Carl" Moore, who was then serving in Washington as a member of Admiral King's war-planning staff. Spruance asked Moore to select the other key staff officers, poaching them from navy headquarters if he wished, but asked him to keep the headcount to a manageable minimum. Moore arrived in Pearl Harbor on August 5 and moved into a spare bedroom in Nimitz and Spruance's house atop Maka-lapa Hill.[65]

Spruance's command philosophy was to delegate any task that he did not absolutely have to do himself. He later observed, with worthy candor, "Looking at myself objectively, I think I am a good judge of men; and I know that I tend to be lazy about many things, so I do not try to do any-thing that I can pass down the line to someone more competent than I am to do it."[66] Carl Moore would have agreed with the entirety of that judgment. Spruance did not micromanage; he picked good men, gave them authority, and held them accountable. He never failed to grasp the data he needed to render major decisions, but once those decisions were made, he dismissed from his mind the details of their execution. By refusing to absorb himself in such particulars, he kept his mind clear to consider the broadest problems of strategy and organization. Plausibly, Spruance did not need to work as hard as others because he possessed the sort of mind that took in and processed information more rapidly. Ernest King, who was no simple-ton, attested that Spruance "was in intellectual ability unsurpassed among the flag officers of the United States Navy."[67] His distinction as a seagoing commander, at the Battle of Midway in 1942 and with the Fifth Fleet later in the war, would seem to vindicate his hands-off approach.

It was also true, at least in a limited sense, that Spruance was lazy. He seemed to bore easily, and often resisted talking about the war. He was a compulsive walker, and tended to walk out of the office at all hours of the day, whether or not work remained to be done. He often took members of his staff along with him. Moore wrote about one such instance in a letter to his wife, composed three days after his arrival in Hawaii: "Raymond is up to his tricks already, and yesterday took me on an eight mile hike in the foothills. It was hot and a hard pull at times, and particularly so as we carried on a lively conversation all the way which kept me completely winded."[68] Moore tried to engage the boss about the coming operation, but Spruance steered the conversation toward unrelated subjects and held forth on the virtues of physical fitness. A few days later Moore wrote his wife again: "Yesterday Raymond stepped up the pace and the distance and we covered over 10 miles in three hours. My right leg caught up with my left and both were wrecked by the time I got back. . . . If he can get me burned to a crisp or crippled from walking he will be completely happy."[69]

Spruance wanted Kelly Turner to command the amphibious fleet. It was not necessary to give the issue much thought. With a year of hard-earned experience in the South Pacific, Turner was the navy's preeminent amphibious specialist. Spruance knew him well, having served with him at sea and at the Naval War College. "I would like to get Admiral Kelly Turner from Admiral Halsey, if I can steal him," he told Nimitz in June.[70] With the northern Solomons island-hopping campaign in high gear, Halsey was not keen to release Turner, so Nimitz made it simple. In a personal "Dear Bill" dated June 26, the CINCPAC explained that he had been ordered to wage a new offensive in the central Pacific: "This means I must have Turner report to me as soon as possible."[71] When Turner came north, he brought several of his best staff officers with him, causing Halsey further heartburn.

Marine Major General Holland M. Smith would command the invasion troops, designated the Fifth Amphibious Corps (or "VAC"). Smith was one of the pioneers of amphibious warfare. He had persuaded the navy to adopt Andrew Higgins's shallow-draft boats as landing craft, and had successfully trained several divisions in amphibious operations at Camps Elliott and Pendleton in southern California. He had lobbied for a combat command in the Pacific, and was backed for the job by Secretary Knox and Admiral King. Nimitz did not know him well, but Spruance had worked with him in the mid-1930s, when both officers were stationed in the Caribbean. Nimitz offered him the job during an inspection tour of the South Pacific, and Smith readily accepted it.

Turner and Smith made a combustible pair. Both men were aggressive, ambitious, and overbearing. Both were respected authorities in the field of amphibious warfare, but had become accustomed to running things without competition or interference. Both were prone to fits of rage, and had earned nicknames as a result: "Terrible Turner" and "Howlin' Mad" Smith. Smith was exceptionally touchy about command relations between the navy and the Marine Corps. At Guadalcanal, Turner had offended General Vandegrift by infringing upon the latter's command prerogatives. During the planning of GALVANIC, Spruance sometimes wondered "whether we could get the operation planned out before there was an explosion between them."[72]

Arriving in Pearl Harbor the first week of September, Holland Smith was assigned quarters in a bungalow at the base of Makalapa Hill. The little house was beneath his rank, and he knew it. Always sensitive to any trace of an insult to the Marine Corps, he coldly reminded the responsible naval officer that he was a major general, senior to most admirals at Pearl, and demanded more suitable quarters. The assignment was explained as an oversight, though Smith did not believe it had been; apologies were offered and the general was lodged in a grander house higher on the hill.

Smith had previously met Kelly Turner in Washington, when the latter was the navy's war plans chief. He found the admiral precise and courteous, like "an exacting schoolmaster," and "affable in an academic manner,"[73] but he had also encountered Turner's famous temper. "He could be plain ornery. He wasn't called 'Terrible Turner' without reason."[74]

For Operation GALVANIC, Turner expected to stand above Smith in the chain of command. That would be consistent with the model employed in Operation WATCHTOWER. But Smith wanted direct command of all amphibious troops throughout the operation—prior to, during, and after the landing—and wished to report directly to Spruance.

To Turner the issue was simple. A precedent had been set in the South Pacific; the existing model was proven. By what right did Smith, a newcomer to the Pacific, propose to change it? To Smith the issue was one of principle, and concerned the status and honor of the Marine Corps. Smith suspected that the navy would take care of its own, and that he would not get a fair hearing in Pearl Harbor. The issue reverberated in Washington, and was even appealed to the secretary of the navy, who would not rule on the question directly but expected it to be resolved in such a way as to secure effective cooperation between the navy and the Marine Corps.

Spruance wanted no part of the dispute, and simply ignored it. "Oh, Carl, don't worry about it," he told Moore. "They know what I want to do, and they're not going to make any trouble." That was not so. When no compromise emerged after prolonged argument, Moore put the question to Spruance again, and was told, "Fix it up to suit yourself."[75]

The fleet commander's laissez-faire attitude placed Moore, a navy captain, in the unenviable role of refereeing a stand-up fight between an admiral and a general. "They both complained to me about the other," he recalled:

Holland Smith particularly complained about Kelly Turner. He was a whining, complaining type. He loved to complain. He loved to talk and loved to complain, and he would come and sit on my desk and growl about Turner. 'All I want to do is kill some Japs. Just give me a rifle. I don't want to be a commanding general. Just give me a rifle, I'll go out there and shoot some Japs. . . . I'm not worried about anything else around here.' See, that kind of a line. I was trying to soothe him down, and Turner would come and complain about that blankety-blank Smith, couldn't get any cooperation out of him, and so forth.[76]

At last a compromise emerged. Moore crafted an operational order that left Turner in command of the landing forces until the shore commander went ashore and assumed command of the troops. When Turner was so informed, all troops ashore would fall under command of the Fifth Amphibious Corps and thus report to Holland Smith. The model was accepted, and would remain in force throughout the remainder of the war.

Turner and Smith readily agreed on one point. Neither man wanted to capture the isolated phosphate rock island of Nauru, which had been included among the objectives assigned in the Joint Chiefs of Staff directive. Nauru's mountainous terrain presented difficulties, and it lay 380 miles south of Tarawa, the atoll that was GALVANIC's main objective. Nauru was of little value either to the enemy or to the Allies, and its small airfield could be kept "pounded down" by regular air raids.

On September 24, Admiral King flew into Pearl Harbor for his regular bimonthly conference with Nimitz. At CINCPAC headquarters the next morning, Spruance circulated a letter written by Holland Smith that laid out the case to scratch Nauru from GALVANIC. King asked, "What do you propose to take instead of Nauru?" Spruance proposed Makin, an atoll north of Tarawa, on the grounds that it was more strategically located and could be more easily stormed. "Admiral King gave me the fish eye," Spruance recalled, "but agreed to recommend the change of objectives to the JCS."[77]

The Gilbert Islands were sixteen palm-crowned atolls, straddling the equator about 400 miles west of the International Date Line. Each atoll was formed by an oblong ring of long, narrow, sandy islands enclosing a brilliant sapphire lagoon. Peak elevation was about 10 feet above sea level. Though they were near the equator, the islands were swept by a steady ocean breeze, and the air was pleasingly dry and fresh. Robert Louis Stevenson, who had visited the Gilberts in the 1880s, found "a superb ocean climate, days of blinding sun and bracing wind, nights of a heavenly brightness."[78]

Makin Atoll was three-sided, with a lagoon measuring eight by sixteen miles. Butaritari, a ribbon of sand thirteen miles long, was the only island in the atoll that could accommodate an airfield. Makin had been employed by the Japanese as a seaplane base, but little else. It was not strongly defended. Aerial photos had detected no large-caliber shore guns and few coastal fortifications, and the garrison was thought to number 500 to 800, of whom a proportion would be laborers rather than trained fighters.

Tarawa, eighty-three miles south of Makin and about 2,500 miles southwest of Hawaii, looked to be a considerably tougher nut to crack. The largest and southernmost island in the atoll was Betio, slightly more than two miles long and about half a mile wide, with an axis favorably oriented toward the prevailing winds. Betio, the Americans knew, was one of the most heavily fortified islands in the Pacific. A 4,000-foot airstrip lay behind a network of trenches, bunkers, and pillboxes constructed of concrete and overlaid with sand and palm logs. Shore guns ranging in size from 5 to 8 inches faced north, west, and south. On its lagoon shore, Betio was protected by coral reefs to a distance of about 1,200 yards. Based on aerial reconnaissance, the garrison appeared to number between 2,500 and 3,100 men.

The assault on Tarawa was assigned to the 2nd Marine Division, which had fought in the later stages of the Guadalcanal campaign and then had withdrawn to New Zealand for rest, recuperation, and additional training. The division was under the command of Major General Julian C. Smith, who first caught wind of the coming operation in mid-August, when he learned that Admiral Spruance was flying into Wellington and wanted to see him. Spruance, with Captain Moore in tow, walked into Smith's office and dropped a pile of documents on the desk. Did the general think his division could take Tarawa? Smith had not heard of Tarawa: "Never knew there was such an island."[79] He would review the documents, he said. When did Spruance need an answer? "I'm leaving tomorrow morning," said Spruance. Smith said his division would do the job.

Admiral King had envisioned GALVANIC as a navy and marine show, but George Marshall was keen to get the army into action in the central Pacific, and offered the 27th Infantry Division, then located in Hawaii. Nimitz assigned the assault on Makin to one of the division's regimental combat teams, the 165th Infantry. Major General Ralph C. Smith was to command these troops, completing a triumvirate of three (unrelated) Smiths in charge of the GALVANIC invasion forces. The command arrangement placing the marine Holland Smith above the soldier Ralph Smith was a source of predictable unpleasantness. The army's top man in the Pacific, General Robert C. Richardson, questioned the need for the army troops to be folded into the Fifth Amphibious Corps, and proposed that Ralph Smith report directly to Admiral Turner. Nimitz declined the suggestion. Operation GAL-VANIC required cooperation between the services on an unprecedented scale, and the CINCPAC was intolerant of infighting. But the interservice sensitivities inherent in this mixed command hierarchy would erupt into a public imbroglio the following year, in the Marianas.

The army assault regiment required intensive amphibious training, and Holland Smith oversaw landing exercises at several remote bays in the lesser Hawaiian Islands. Poor weather conditions forced the cancellation of several exercises, and beach conditions did not perfectly match those of the actual objective. Holland Smith was concerned about the regiment's readiness and even its morale. But he took some consolation in the mounting evidence, based on air and submarine reconnaissance, that Makin would be a walkover, at least when compared to Tarawa.

As in the Solomons, the Americans were short of accurate charts or hydrographic tables covering the Gilberts. They relied, in part, on information dating back to the nineteenth and even the eighteenth centuries. Summing up the state of the charts, Turner told Nimitz, "The land contours are inaccurate, soundings are few and unreliable, the orientation of land areas is frequently in error and even the location of the island is often questionable."[80] Putting reconnaissance teams ashore in advance of the operation was considered, but then ruled out, as it might alert the Japanese to the coming invasion. The submarine *Nautilus*, fitted with special equipment for periscope photography, brought valuable data back to Pearl Harbor in August. Aerial photographic reconnaissance, conducted in September and October by carrier planes and B-24s, provided more information on the state of Betio's coastal fortifications. The photos plainly revealed the locations of the big guns, which were mounted in strong concrete emplacements. The photos also revealed that the entire island was ringed with obstacles: coconut log seawalls, barbed wire aprons, antitank ditches, and concrete tetrahedrons in the surf.

Analysts estimated the size of the enemy garrison by counting the latrines and reckoning how many troops each latrine would serve. (They were constructed on pilings over the beach, so that the surf would carry away excrement, and therefore were readily identifiable in aerial photographs.) Low-altitude oblique shots of the beach defenses would have proved valuable in determining the precise locations of covered pillboxes and bunkers, but the rushed preinvasion schedule did not permit for such flights.[81]

Several dozen British residents of the Gilberts had fled to New Zealand and Australia at the outset of the war. Sixteen of these dislocated British colonialists, whom the Americans collectively nicknamed the "foreign legion," were questioned closely about conditions in Tarawa lagoon. A vital concern was the depth of water over the reefs that lay between the entrance to the lagoon and the north side of Betio. Some were confident that the reefs would be at least 5 feet deep at high water. If that was so, the American landing craft could pass over them with no danger of grounding. But the intended date of the invasion coincided with a neap tide, when the tidal range would be reduced to a minimum. Major F. L. G. Holland of New Zealand, who seemed to know Tarawa better than anyone else, warned that the depth over the reefs could be less than 3 feet. Moreover, the neap tide would cause irregular "dodging currents" that might carry the landing craft off their courses. After interrogating Major Holland at length, Julian Smith concluded that the man knew what he was talking about, and warned Admiral Turner and Holland Smith that the marines might have to disembark and wade ashore from the fringing reef, perhaps half a mile from Betio's north beach.

For twenty years the Marine Corps had planned and trained for a direct assault on a heavily defended beach. The Corps had developed and acquired the specialized landing craft required to mount such an operation, and had refined the specialized tactics of coordinating naval fire support, air support, and logistics. But the marines had not yet proved to themselves, or to the enemy, that a small fortress-island could be taken by frontal amphibious assault. Tarawa posed formidable problems. There would be no immediate means of achieving depth of deployment; the landing forces would initially be pinned down on a long, narrow beach. The flat little island would offer scant room for maneuvering onto the enemy's flanks. The battlefield was so contracted, it seemed doubtful that direct naval gunfire or air support could be provided without posing danger to the marines ashore. All understood in advance that the assault on Tarawa was unprecedented and might prove appallingly costly.

SINCE THE 1920S, NAVAL AVIATORS had been authorized to wear brown leather shoes with khaki uniforms, while surface naval officers were obliged to wear black. This negligible uniform distinction acquired symbolic importance when the flyers began calling themselves "brownshoes," and their more tradition-bound colleagues "blackshoes." The flyers made a point of bending the uniform code by scuffing their shoes and refusing to polish them, by growing their hair just a little longer than regulations allowed, and by wearing weather-beaten caps, including the distinctive "duck-billed" cap made famous by Marc Mitscher. The brownshoes liked to test the limits of naval discipline and decorum. "When you're in a battleship, you're in the Annapolis Navy," wrote Joseph Bryan III, who served as an intelligence officer on the *Yorktown*:

> But when you're in a carrier, you're in the fighting Navy. Your ship is being run by and for a bunch of barn-storming youngsters who don't tie their shoes at all, if they don't feel like it, and who would just as soon address Admiral King as "Ernie," unless it meant he'd ground them and keep them out of the next scrap.[82]

Vice Admiral Towers, who had headed the Aeronautics Bureau in Washington before taking up his billet as COMAIRPAC in October 1942, was the navy's senior aviator in active service and the acknowledged leader of the brownshoe navy. He had graduated from the Naval Academy in 1906, the same year as Raymond Spruance and one year after Nimitz. His remarkable career had advanced in close step with the evolution of naval aviation. He had learned to fly in 1911, in a primitive biplane with a wooden frame, fabric-covered wings, wire struts, and a top airspeed of 60 knots. Towers was a protégé of the pilot and aircraft designer Glenn Curtiss. He achieved various distance and endurance records; he set up the first flight-training program in Pensacola; he completed the first air crossing (in stages) of the Atlantic; he commanded the navy's first aircraft carrier, the *Langley* (CV-1). He had survived several plane crashes. Many of his contemporaries had not been so fortunate. For more than twenty years, he had battled King and Nimitz over such questions as funding for the carrier navy and promotions for career aviators. He had earned a somewhat begrudging respect from both colleagues, and reached reasonable compromises concerning the training, selection, and promotion of officers involved in naval aviation and aircraft carriers. But he was never personally close to any of the officers he regarded as "battleship-oriented," and he argued that the attack on Pearl Harbor and the sinking of the British battleships *Prince of Wales* and *Repulse* by Japanese air attack off Malaya in December 1941 had transformed naval warfare into something fundamentally new.

The brownshoes were simultaneously elites and insurgents. They disdained old naval dogmas and were resolved to subvert them. They wanted more of everything—more commands, promotions, decorations, publicity, and resources, and a more dominant voice in strategic planning. It was not enough, they argued, to rely on the leadership of traditional line officers who were "air-minded." The new fast carrier task forces were the vanguard of the fleet that would carry the war into the western Pacific. Therefore, the fleet ought to be led by men who had come up through the brownshoe ranks. Not even Ernest King or Bill Halsey, who had passed through flight training as captains on the wrong side of forty, were bona fide members of the flying fraternity—they were latecomers who had earned their wings in order to qualify for carrier command. Most of the "real" brownshoes were younger men, including a group of ambitious and talented "Young Turks" who had earned their wings in the 1920s, led air squadrons, skippered carriers, participated in the development of new aircraft, and were approaching the threshold for flag rank.

The emerging generation of aviators was uncomfortably mindful that their rivals in the Army Air Forces had climbed the promotion ladder more rapidly. The army flyers had also enjoyed the benefits of a more open-handed policy in awarding medals and other honors. Naval leaders correctly suspected that Hap Arnold's USAAF aspired to consolidate the functions of military aviation under its own aegis. With a political brawl over service unification looming in the postwar future, the danger to the navy's institutional interests was evident. Towers told a colleague in Washington that there had been a "failure of the high commands to give senior aviation officers, of long experience and proven professional ability, a real voice in strategic plans."[83]

As plans for GALVANIC took shape, Towers advised Nimitz to send the new carrier task forces on far-ranging missions to attack Japanese airfields and (if opportunity offered) the Japanese fleet. He warned against limiting their freedom of movement by keeping them corralled in defensive sectors. Spruance and Turner wanted the carriers to provide air cover to the fleet while troops were landed at Tarawa and Makin; Towers preferred to send them 600 miles northwest, into the Marshalls, where they could rain bombs down on the enemy's airfields and cut off his air response at the source. Towers, echoing his chief of staff, Forrest Sherman, thought the Gilberts a waste of time and balked at the scale of GALVANIC. The outspoken COMAIRPAC complained that "Spruance wants a sledgehammer to drive a tack."[84]

Towers went around Nimitz to make his case to King and others in Washington. On August 18, he wrote James Forrestal, undersecretary of the navy: "I must confess that those of us out here who are in a position to have a reasonably good idea of not only what is going on but also what is planned, have a feeling approaching utter hopelessness, and when I say this I'm referring to major plans and major policies."[85] Towers privately criticized the elevation of the blackshoe Spruance to command of the Fifth Fleet, and when certain remarks reached Spruance's ears, a rift opened between them. Spruance later told Admiral Charles M. "Savvy" Cooke Jr. that "if you were not an admirer of Towers, your path was not made smooth if he could help it. . . . Towers was a very ambitious man."[86] That was perhaps the most damning indictment Spruance ever aimed at a fellow officer.

From their high perch, Nimitz and Spruance believed they saw the big picture more clearly than did the brownshoe insurrectionists. The carriers could strike the enemy hard and across great distances, but they could not win the transpacific campaign outright. Whatever their capabilities or aspirations, the aviators and their machines must fit coherently into the grand scheme of amphibious invasions supported by finely choreographed logistics. The force that would take the Gilberts included 191 ships, 35,000 troops, and 117,000 tons of cargo. Coordination and protection of such an enormous force was an overriding concern, and no single component of the fleet should be let off the leash without considering the consequences to the whole. Nimitz, patient and forbearing as he was, eventually grew weary of the protests and grievances, and instructed Towers to lower his tone. In a heated meeting that fall, Towers recalled, Nimitz's "reaction was to the effect that I did not know what I was talking about."[87]

Prominent among the "Young Turks" was Captain Joseph J. Clark, known to friends and shipmates as "Jock" or "Jocko." At the war's outset, he had been executive officer of the old *Yorktown* (CV-5). Promoted captain in February 1942, he had returned to Washington to await reassignment. There he made a name for himself by proposing a plan, seemingly absurd on its face, to build 150 new aircraft carriers. By his own account, there was nothing scientific in the figure: he thought it obvious, after Pearl Harbor, that the navy would need a vast fleet of carriers to crush Japan, and he had simply plucked a big, round number "out of the air." Kelly Turner, still head of the navy's war plans unit, brushed the idea off, saying, "You can't get that many." But Admiral Towers thought Clark was "absolutely right" and arranged to send the young captain on a multi-city speaking tour to promote the idea.*[88]

Born and raised on a farm in northeast Oklahoma, Clark was of mixed Scotch-Irish and Cherokee Indian descent. He was a registered member of the Cherokee Nation, and the first Native American to graduate from the Naval Academy (class of 1917). By his own lights Clark was a typical "Oklahoma cowboy," but he was proud of his partial Cherokee lineage and even played it up. He had been registered (by his parents) as one-eighth Cherokee.† Clark willingly tolerated, or perhaps encouraged, physical descriptions referring to "the deep tan and high cheek bones of an Indian" (*Honolulu Star-Bulletin*, 1944), or his "hump-bridged nose and short-clipped, sparse hair which resembles a scalp lock and waves like prairie grass" (*Life* magazine, 1945).[89] He grinned broadly for photographers while wearing a majestic feathered headdress. Cartoons published in his ships' newspapers and cruise books depicted him wielding a tomahawk to scalp the Japanese prime minister Hideki Tojo or the emperor Hirohito. Clark invited the chief of the Cherokee Nation to attend the commissioning of the new *Yorktown* (CV-10).

Clark was a leader in the mold of Bill Halsey—a colorful and exuberant character who wore his heart on his sleeve and did not mind making

---

* The U.S. Navy had 119 aircraft carriers in commission at war's end. Had the conflict lasted until 1947 or 1948, a reasonable prognosis in the early days, Clark's figure might have been surpassed.

† Later genealogical research revealed that Clark's Cherokee ancestry was considerably more diluted. He had a single Cherokee great-great-great-grandmother, making him one-thirty-second Cherokee.

himself slightly ridiculous in the eyes of his men. He battled his weight and carried an impressive paunch. The shirt flaps of his khaki uniform did not stay tucked. In otherwise glowing fitness reports, superiors drew attention to his lack of personal tidiness and to his physical bearing. Clark allowed himself to be made an object of fun, or deliberately seemed to undercut his own authority. When a navigator grounded his ship in an impossibly crowded Bermuda anchorage, the captain took the conn and barked, "Goddamn you, now it's my turn to run it aground!"[90] A chief petty officer who served under him on the *Hornet* (CV-12) left this fond description:

> Jocko Clark was part American Indian; his lower lip stuck way out, and was always sunburned. Finally, the doctor on the *Hornet* gave him no choice but to wear a gauze 4x4 with a string over his ears so the pad protected his lip. Jocko did it, but it made him madder than hell. I've seen him snatch three or four of those things off in the course of a couple of hours. He'd tear it off and throw it down. And here would come the doctor and make him a new one. . . . Whenever he came on the bridge—GQ or any other time—he often wore sick bay pajamas that he slept in. Sometimes his hairy stomach would be sticking out, but he was oblivious to his appearance. He was just universally loved, respected, and admired on the *Hornet*. He had a great feeling for the pilots. More than once, when a pilot landed aboard, shot up or whatever, the doctor, the emergency crew, and Jocko would get to him all about the same time. Jocko would bend over the stokes litter and pin a medal on the guy right there on the stretcher. You know pilots appreciated that. He was really and truly a great man.[91]

Earning his gold wings in 1925, Clark had ascended rapidly through the ranks. He had flown several types of aircraft, eventually specializing in the Boeing F3B biplane fighter. He had skippered a carrier fighter squadron on the *Lexington* in 1933–34, when Ernest J. King was her captain. Clark had got on well with King, a history that stood him in good stead when the latter rose to COMINCH-CNO. Clark's first carrier command was the *Suwannee*, an 18,000-ton escort or "jeep carrier" converted from the hull of an oil tanker. While overseeing the commissioning of the ship in Newport News, Virginia, Clark drove the civilian yard workers and ship's crew to meet a seemingly impossible deadline, and managed to get the ship com-

missioned in time to take part in Operation TORCH, the invasion of North
Africa, in November 1942. He circulated a motto during this period of
breakneck effort: "Get things done yesterday; tomorrow may be too late!"[92]
The *Suwannee* distinguished herself during TORCH, and Clark received high
praise in his fitness reports.

In January 1943, he received orders sending him back to Newport News
as prospective captain of the new *Yorktown* (CV-10), second-in-class of the
Essex carriers. Clark subsequently learned that Admiral King had personally selected him for the prestigious new command.

The *Yorktown* had been launched on January 21, 1943, three weeks
before Clark's arrival, with Eleanor Roosevelt acting as sponsor. Several
minutes before the scheduled launch, while speeches were still underway,
the great carrier had shifted, groaned, and begun creeping down the launch
ways. The first lady, a seasoned veteran of ship-christening ceremonies,
seized the waiting bottle with both hands and bashed it against the moving
hull, shattering the bottle and splattering herself with champagne. All present agreed that the event was auspicious; the *Yorktown* was evidently in a
hurry to get into the war. The crew gave her the first of several nicknames:
"Ship in a Hurry."[93]

The unfinished *Yorktown* was moored at a Newport News Shipbuilding
& Drydock Company pier, where she would spend the next several months
being outfitted and commissioned. When Clark arrived on February 15, he
walked down the dock to have a look. Her wide flight deck towered over
him. He had come a long way from Alluwe, Oklahoma. "This was a proud
moment in my lifetime, and I knew it as I stood there."[94]

The race to get the *Yorktown* into service drove the new crew to the
edge of exhaustion. Clark was a slave driver, and he did not mind admitting
it. Three other *Essex* carriers were in advanced construction, and Clark
liked the idea of getting the *Yorktown* out to Pearl Harbor ahead of them
all. That was a long shot, however, because the first-in-class *Essex* had been
commissioned on the last day of 1942, and would soon depart on her shakedown cruise. Clark also had his eye on the *Lexington* (CV-16), another sister,
which was being commissioned in Boston at the Fall River Company under
the supervision of Captain Felix B. Stump. The fourth, *Bunker Hill* (CV-17),
Captain John J. Ballentine, was at the Bethlehem Steel shipyard in Quincy,
Massachusetts. Clark frankly avowed that he wanted to beat the *Essex* to
the Pacific, and "Beat the *Essex*" was adopted as the ship's motto.

Captain Donald Duncan of the *Essex* was a friend and academy classmate, and the two captains conferred closely and learned from one another's experiences. By mutual agreement they made copies of all outgoing correspondence concerning the outfitting of the ships, and shared it among themselves and with Stump and Ballentine.[95] Clark was glad to share information, but his natural competitive instincts were never far from the surface; he expected the *Yorktown* to be superior to her sisters in every measurable respect.

The yard set a commission date of April 15, but warned that the schedule was likely to slip. Clark declared that he intended to meet it. Four thousand of the 31,000 workers at the yard were put on the job, and Clark lobbied to have needed building materials diverted from other ships under construction. He avowed that he would not "cut corners," at least insofar as care and quality of equipment were concerned. But he was more than willing to finagle materials by underhanded means and to fudge safety regulations. An air officer on the rival *Essex* suspected that "a lot of dishonest things were done to get things provided for the *Yorktown* which should have come to the *Essex* just so we wouldn't get finished in time, but we never were able to prove anything."[96] Clark had ammunition loaded directly from flatcars, a prohibited procedure. When the yard could not meet his schedule for painting the hull, he put the crew on the job. He even assigned junior officers to join in the chipping and painting, upending an ancient naval taboo and prompting at least one young lieutenant to put in for a transfer. "Jocko had tremendous drive," recalled George W. Anderson, the new ship's navigator (and a future chief of naval operations). "He always wanted to be first. He was very competitive. . . . It was drive, drive, drive all the time."[97]

Much of Clark's time was apportioned to recruiting officers, and for this purpose he traveled frequently to Washington to look in on "BUPERS" (the Bureau of Naval Personnel). He wanted certain men in certain jobs, notably Raoul Waller as his executive officer. But he was also cognizant of the danger of bringing too many of his "friends" along, and he liked to use reservists in important roles—an attitude less common among many of his contemporary Annapolites.[98] The commissioning period also involved intensive training. Clark purposely cut short the "Abandon ship" drill, telling the crew that he preferred to use the time for the "Don't give up the ship" drill. He instead stressed damage-control and firefighting procedures.

Before she could be commissioned, the *Yorktown* was required to pass a stem to stern inspection by the Board of Inspection and Survey, whose members arrived the second week of April. They tested all of the ship's machinery, her major propulsion systems, auxiliary machinery, arresting gear, launching gear, catapult, magazines, and ammunition hoists. The ship's charts and other required documents and publications were turned out and cataloged. The board found that all was in order and released the ship for commissioning on April 15, as scheduled. At 0700 on the appointed morning, the ship inched out of her berth and got underway. It was a short voyage across Hampton Roads and into a new berth at the Norfolk Navy Yard, where the *Yorktown* was formally entered into the service of the U.S. Navy.

April and May comprised a period of strenuous training, fitting out, and shaking down. The ship performed sea trials, cruising up and down the Chesapeake Bay. Her gunners shot at target sleeves towed by planes. On May 5, the *Yorktown* landed her first plane, a new F6F flown by the legendary fighter pilot Jimmy Flatley, who reported aboard as commander of the new Air Group Five. Among the newcomers were thirty-six of the troublesome SB2C Helldivers, with freshly trained aircrews and a group of engineers and mechanics from the Curtiss plant in Columbus, Ohio. The *Yorktown* was the first carrier to take the unpopular "Beasts" aboard.

On May 21, the *Yorktown* put to sea with an escort of three destroyers and turned south. Her destination was the Gulf of Paria, a shallow inland sea enclosed by Trinidad and the coast of Venezuela. A major naval supply depot and air station had been established on Trinidad. The gulf was more than seventy miles long, offering ample space for high-speed exercises and air operations. A single deepwater entrance channel was blocked by antisubmarine nets. The gulf was thus protected against German U-boats, and for that reason it was prized by the navy as a shakedown cruising area.

Air Group Five landed at the air station on Trinidad and flew out to the carrier each day. Clark was particularly irascible during this stressful period, often bellowing at the crew through a handheld bullhorn. He was quick to place men "in hack" (confine them to quarters), but he did not hesitate to make spot promotions when a man showed exceptional ability or initiative. Clark was especially concerned with the speed and efficiency of plane-handling procedures during flight operations. He was relentless in timing the airedales, who brought the planes up from the hangars and spotted them (positioned them for launch) on the flight deck. Clark demanded that planes be spotted as tightly as possible to leave a maximum amount of deck run available on the forward flight deck. Getting armed and fueled-up planes aloft quickly was the prime objective of any aircraft carrier. The interval between recovering (landing) planes and respotting the next group for launch was the period when the ship was most vulnerable to attack. Contacts with the enemy, he told the crew, were likely to be rare and ephemeral: "Not only must we seek them out but we must be ready to make the most of [contacts] when they do come and to hit, both night and day, on those occasions when suitable targets are found."[99]

The arrival of larger and heavier planes taxed the strength and endurance of the deck crews, but Lieutenant Joe Tucker of the Air Department had a solution in hand. At the navy yard in Norfolk he had spotted two jeeps and two small tractors parked near the pier, and decided to commandeer them. He had them lifted onto the *Yorktown* by a crane and stowed in the hangar. (Marine guards had been bribed with bottles of spirits to look the other way.) Tucker's mechanics devised a makeshift towbar that hooked around the forward wheels of the aircraft. Constant repetition and practice using the vehicles to move the airplanes led to much more rapid cycling and respotting. The jeeps and tractors, which Tucker called "mules," proved to be an effective innovation and were adopted on all carriers of the class.[100]

Clark had previously been billeted as a plane inspector at the Curtiss plant in Columbus, Ohio, so he was well acquainted with the new SB2C Helldiver and its tribulations. During operations in the Gulf of Paria, the Curtiss machines suffered chronic mechanical failures. One abruptly lost power after launch, and its pilot was forced to execute a water landing ahead of the ship. Another made a hard landing, and its tail wheel collapsed. Tail hooks were yanked out of more than a dozen planes. *Yorktown*'s mechanics and the visiting Curtiss engineers attempted to repair the accumulating damage, but spare parts were not always available and there was only so much that could be done on the hangar deck of a ship at sea. By mid-June, more than half had to be grounded, and Lieutenant Tucker estimated that the Helldiver needed about 200 modifications before it would be ready for service. He recommended returning the entire squadron to Curtiss and asking to draw a squadron of SBDs for the *Yorktown*'s first cruise to the Pacific. After lengthy discussion, Captain Clark agreed, and ordered the damaged SB2Cs put ashore at Trinidad. He wrote a seven-page memorandum detailing their defects. When the *Yorktown* returned to Norfolk a week later, Clark drove up to Washington and explained the problem to Admiral King. King agreed to let the ship take aboard a squadron of thirty-six new SBD-5s.

"The war was won largely by Grumman and Douglas," Clark wrote; "that was the Navy's war, Grumman and Douglas." By 1943, the SBDs were too slow to fly in a coordinated strike with the TBFs and F6Fs, so they "were actually a handicap in wartime. But we had to live with them, because they were the only dive bombers that we could rely on in the navy, the only ones that were in stock with enough of them on hand to do the job. So for a long time, before the bugs were worked out of this SB2C, that was the navy's dive bomber."[101]

On July 6, *Yorktown* sailed for the Pacific with a destroyer screen in company. After a quick run to Panama, zigzagging at 30 knots through the Windward Passage to thwart U-boats, she dropped anchor in Colón on the morning of the tenth. On the following morning, with the captain and much of the crew recovering from a riotous liberty, the *Yorktown* inched into Gatun Locks with less than a foot of clearance on either side. There was not even space enough for bumpers. The concrete sides of the lock scraped sickeningly against the hull. Clark screamed constantly at the helmsman. The executive officer, Raoul Waller, dashed starboard and port across the flight deck "like a fussy old maid about her cat."[102]

The *Yorktown* raised Oahu at dawn on July 24 and eased down the entrance channel at midday. A welcome message from Admiral Nimitz was sent by blinker light: "The *Yorktown* carries a name already famous in the Pacific, and in welcoming you we anticipate that you will maintain the high reputation of your predecessor." Clark replied: "Many thanks for your message. That's what we came here to do."[103]

As the Pacific War moved west, and drew closer to the enemy's main bases of support, the Americans would inherit the same disadvantages of distance that had undone the Japanese in the lower Solomons. Forces assigned to galvanic included 116 combatant ships and 75 auxiliary vessels. They would sortie directly from ports throughout the Pacific, including New Zealand, Samoa, Efate, the Solomons, Fiji, Hawaii, and the American West Coast. A supreme logistics effort was required to push such a fleet across the Pacific. A supply train of auxiliaries (including fifteen fleet oilers) would provide underway refueling and replenishment from bases at Funafuti, Espiritu Santo, the Fijis, and Pearl Harbor. Looking beyond the Gilberts, into the Marshalls and Marianas, the service and supply forces would be obliged to move quickly into newly conquered territories and convert them into advanced rear bases to support the next westward leap. Timing must be meticulous and exact. Admiral Spruance, when interviewed by historians after the war, often remarked that strategy and tactics never approached the importance of logistics in the transpacific campaign.

Logistics was the realm of the Service Forces, Pacific Fleet (SERVPAC), commanded by Vice Admiral William L. Calhoun. In September 1943, SERVPAC listed 324 vessels, but the central Pacific offensive required a tripling of that figure in six months, to 990 vessels in March 1944. Since early 1942, Calhoun's command had been run out of CINCPAC headquarters on Makalapa Hill, but inexorable expansion soon forced the commander of SERVPAC (COMSERVPAC) into a new, dedicated headquarters next door. In October 1943, Calhoun commissioned a new Service Squadron Four to provide logistical support for GALVANIC. The squadron operated from Funafuti atoll in the Ellice Islands, south of the Gilberts—the nearest Allied-held territory to the atolls that were to be conquered. Funafuti was well matched to its role as a forward mobile supply and repair base. Its large lagoon could comfortably accommodate several hundred ships, but its single narrow entrance could easily be shielded against incursion by enemy submarines. Funafuti was also the headquarters of land-based air forces assigned to GALVANIC, under the command of Rear Admiral John H. Hoover (commander of Aircraft Central Pacific), whose flagship was the seaplane tender *Curtiss.*

The planning of GALVANIC was not quite so truncated as that of WATCH-TOWER the previous year, but the schedule seemed oppressive to leading participants and commanders, many of whom were not assigned to their roles until August or September. Admiral Harry W. Hill would command the Southern Amphibious Group, the force assigned to take Tarawa. Admiral Turner, who stood above him as commander of the Fifth Amphibious Force, would sail with the Northern Amphibious Group against Makin. Hill was not briefed on his duties until September 18, when he met with Turner in Efate. With the target date five weeks away, Turner could not yet say which transports would be assigned to Tarawa, or even what Hill's flagship would be.[104] The circumstances, Hill recalled, were "hectic, if not confused."[105] He never had the opportunity to meet his air support commander, and did not meet most of his primary commanders until the live rehearsals on the eve of sailing for the operation. The communications plan was late arriving in Efate. He moved aboard his flagship, the battleship *Maryland*, less than a week before the fleet sortied.

General Julian C. Smith intended to land three battalions on Betio's northern beaches—one each on the beaches designated Red 1, Red 2, and Red 3. He held no illusions about the strength of the enemy's defensive fortifications. The log seawall revealed by reconnaissance photos stood about 20 feet above the high-tide mark, and varied from about 3 to 6 feet tall. Directly behind it was a complex of rifle pits and covered pillboxes, connected by trenches and positioned to provide interlocking fields of fire on the beach and lagoon. Coral sand and rocks were piled between the seawall and the pillboxes to obscure visibility from the beach. Concrete obstacles and iron spikes were positioned to stop armored vehicles, and tank traps had been dug to a depth of about 6 feet.[106]

Admiral Turner chose to hold one regiment (the 6th) of the 2nd Marines in reserve, a decision hotly opposed by Julian Smith. Turner alone would decide whether to commit the reserve force, though he was expected to consult with Holland Smith, who would be present on his flagship. As in the Guadalcanal campaign the previous year, Turner's decision to hold ground forces in reserve forced the marine commanders to alter their plan of attack. After being curtly overruled, General Julian Smith insisted that the orders be spelled out in writing, "as I did not feel that the plan should be my responsibility."[107]

The most worrisome aspect of the assault on Tarawa atoll remained the coral reef in the lagoon. Thanks to a titanic construction ramp-up spurred by Admiral King, new landing craft and amphibious vehicles were available in much greater numbers. There was a confounding array of different types, all designated by acronyms beginning with "L" (landing): LCVPs, LCVs, LCMs, LCIs, LSTs, LVTs, LCTs, and so on. Not all were equally suited to the task at hand. Training exercises often resulted in significant damage and mechanical failures, and a chronic dearth of spare parts kept damaged craft on the beach.[108] Well-trained crews were needed to operate the landing craft, but training programs on the mainland were strained to the breaking point. Prior to GALVANIC, one amphibious officer recalled, "Several LCTs and LCIs had no officers or men who had ever been to sea prior to their trans-Pacific voyage."[109]

The answer to Tarawa's reefs was the LVT (landing vehicle, tracked), an amphibious tractor often called the "amtrac" or "alligator." These clever little vehicles could clamber up and over shallow coral heads and drive up a beach. In tests overseen by General Holland Smith, an amtrac charged up a Hawaiian beach, crushed a log barricade under its treads, and "walked clean through seven lines of barbed wire."[110] They could be transported in LSTs and launched directly into the sea about two to three miles offshore.

The 2nd Marine Division, in September 1943, could muster a hundred amtracs, but many had been hard run in the Guadalcanal operation and were in a sad state of disrepair. General Julian Smith estimated that he could make seventy-five of the craft seaworthy by cannibalizing parts from the remaining twenty-five, which would then be junked. Fifty new LVTs were found in Samoa, and they were fetched by LSTs after the division had already sailed from Wellington. Each amtrac could carry about one platoon, and would be required to make several return trips back to the transport group. Some would inevitably be disabled or destroyed. The trouble would arise with the second and third waves, as the supply of available amtracs diminished. Most of the marines in those later waves would likely be obliged to land in ordinary Higgins boats (LCVPs), which might not manage to cross the reefs. If they could not, the men would have to wade in to the island under heavy enemy fire.

Each of the three Red beaches would be seized, initially, by one battalion. Estimates of Japanese troop strength ranged as high as 4,000, so the attackers would be at approximate parity with the defenders. Early planning for Tarawa had contemplated the possibility of seizing an island adjacent to Betio and converting it into an artillery platform. The option was discarded as it could lead to a lengthy stalemate in the shallows separating the two islands. If the marines on the three Red beaches were unable to penetrate directly inland, Julian Smith would move forces down to the west end of the island, "secure that and then attack from the flank."[111]

Without overwhelming superiority in numbers (at least initially), the marines would trust in airpower and heavy naval fire support to gain the upper hand. For about two and a half hours before the initial landings, the island would be worked over by carrier planes and raked by battleships, cruisers, and destroyers offshore. The fire support group would draw in as close as 1,000 yards from the beach. In the first phase, they would concentrate their fire on the 8-inch artillery emplacements and knock them out. In the second phase, they would simply blanket the entire 300-acre island with high-explosive shells. General Julian Smith and his fellow marines were not nearly as sanguine as were the admirals concerning the potential of the preinvasion bombardment. Having suffered under repeated naval barrages on Guadalcanal, the marines understood that troops could hunker down in well-covered bunkers or trenches and withstand such punishment.

After the marines had taken the beaches, naval fire support would become a considerably thornier subject. The island was very small, so friendly and enemy forces would necessarily be engaged at eyeball-to-eyeball range. But the marines must have the ability to call in naval shelling and air attacks, even on targets very near their own positions. Phase III of the fire support plan was triggered when the assault forces had an initial foothold on the beach. At that point, targeting and firing decisions would shift into the hands of shore parties. Marines ashore, the GALVANIC plan took pains to emphasize, "are not merely spotting agencies, but also control firing."[112] They would select the targets, call fire down on those targets, and order firing to end. The same was true of air support. The marines were to set up reflective panels or smoke pots marking their forward positions. The pilots were warned that these markers "must be scrupulously observed, and direct support attacks executed without endangering our ground forces."[113]

Carl Moore worked fifteen-hour days to complete the operational plans for GALVANIC in time to meet the sailing date. The basic plan could fit into three pages, but no fewer than seventeen "planning annexes" were appended. There was a communication plan, an intelligence plan, a meteorological plan, an air search plan, a logistics plan, and contingency plans for major action. Plans directed the movement and rendezvous of various fleet elements.[114] Minor changes in any one annex often compelled a run of corresponding changes to others. On October 13, three weeks before the sailing date, Moore warned Spruance that the planning process was in chaos, and that many important decisions remained to be rendered. He gently implied that the boss ought to spend more time in the office and involve himself more closely in the vital work. But Spruance remained as serene and aloof as always, often disappearing for hours into the hills above headquarters. "Raymond is so funny," Moore wrote his wife:

When he feels the urge for exercise, nothing can stop him. He won't stop for anything but goes tearing off, usually with me grabbing at his coattails trying to get him to sign something or give me some decision that will let me proceed until he gets back. Invariably he begs me to come along, knowing darn well that I won't, and if I did the work would stop. When he gets back, it's hard to make him pay attention long enough to read and sign before he flops into bed. What a life I have.[115]

On October 29, Moore and the Fifth Fleet staff worked late into the night to complete the final product. The GALVANIC operations plan ran to 324 pages and weighed three pounds. A platoon of marines was rounded up to perform the careful work of mimeographing, collating, and binding 300 copies. At 5:00 a.m. they were finished. Couriers began distributing copies to commands and ships throughout the Navy Yard. Copies were boarded on planes to be flown to New Zealand, Noumea, Efate, Funafuti, and Samoa. Moore, dog-tired and mentally shattered, wrote his wife on the morning of the thirtieth: "The heartbreaking struggle is over."[116] But the real heartbreak, as he was to reflect many years later, awaited in Tarawa lagoon.

Chapter Eleven

FOR THE SAKE OF SECRECY, AS WAS CUSTOMARY, THE RANK AND FILE were left in ignorance of their destination until the ships were well underway. As the 2nd Division transport fleet left Wellington Harbour on the morning of November 7, most marines assumed they were headed to Hawke's Bay, on the east coast of North Island, for more landing exercises. It was even supposed that they might march back down the gangways to the Wellington wharves later the same day, in time for a dance previously scheduled for that evening.

That rumor was toppled in midmorning when an announcement cleared by General Julian Smith told them that they were en route to a major operation. The destination was not yet disclosed. Speculation favored Wake Island or perhaps even the Japanese bastion at Truk. Several days later, after training maneuvers with Admiral Harry Hill's Southern Attack Group off the New Hebrides, the marines and the ships' crews were told that they were headed to Tarawa, a name that very few had ever heard. They learned more about the objective while underway. Aerial photographs and contour maps were laid out on wardroom tables. On the transport *Sheridan*, a plaster model of Betio Island was placed on deck, and the men were briefed on the planned landing. Lieutenant Frank W. J. Plant recalled listening to a Radio Tokyo broadcast in the *Sheridan's* boardroom. "Salute to the men of the 2nd Marine Division," said Tokyo Rose; "Say goodbye to land: you'll never see it again. We know where you are going—to the Gilberts!"[1]

The transports were hot and overcrowded. Men slept whenever and wherever they could. They read dog-eared magazines, played cards, smoked cigarettes, cleaned their rifles, and sharpened their bayonets. Even for young marines in peak physical condition, the voyage was exhausting. Lieutenant G. D. Lillibridge shared a cabin with eight or nine other officers. Each had a cot, but the cots took up every square foot of floor space, so men had to walk over them to enter and exit. Each time someone went out to use the head, everyone in the cabin was inevitably roused. In any case, it was usually too hot to sleep in the ship's interior. Lillibridge bedded down on deck, where the air was much cooler, but he was stirred awake by men creeping around him and by the frequent rain showers that swept over the ship. Sleep deprivation and cumulative exhaustion settled in as the fleet approached the equator.

The greater part of the Fifth Fleet sortied from Pearl Harbor on the morning of November 10. A parade of ships filed down the channel all morning—destroyers and cruisers first, at five-minute intervals; then carriers and battleships, at fifteen-minute intervals; finally the transports and auxiliaries. It was a stirring sight. Gray ships dotted the horizon in every direction, too many to count. Ray Gard of the *Yorktown* recalled the "marvelous sight" and wondered, "Are there any other ships anywhere?"[2] Admiral Spruance, who had hoisted his flag on the cruiser *Indianapolis*, took his daily exercise by pacing the deck for hours each day. With no immediate decisions to make, the admiral slept in his cabin, read paperbacks, and listened to music. Carl Moore began to gather his thoughts about the next step on the road to Tokyo: the conquest of the Marshall Island group, which lay northwest of the Gilberts. From recent experience he knew that it would fall to him to write the plan of operations—his friend and boss would take a bare minimum of interest in the details.

Operational control of the fleet was in the hands of Kelly Turner, whose flagship was the battleship *Pennsylvania*. His erstwhile nemesis, Holland Smith, was quartered on the same ship, and the two men spent most of their waking hours together. They had evidently decided to put their previous acrimony behind them, and surprised everyone by becoming fast friends. An early draft plan for GALVANIC had specified that Smith would remain at Pearl Harbor, shorebound at his Fifth Amphibious Corps headquarters. Smith, fuming, prepared to appeal the decision to Washington—but Turner intervened to have the decision reversed, and invited Smith and his staff to share his flagship. "They were just the best buddies you've ever seen in your life," Moore recalled, "and they clicked perfectly in everything they did. They just got along perfectly fine. They messed together. They just loved each other. And as long as the operation was underway there couldn't have been a closer-knit group."[3]

The approach to the Gilberts was largely uneventful. Radar screens occasionally picked up enemy planes, but none appeared in visual range. American carrier planes patrolled overhead and occasionally made simulated dive- and torpedo-bombing runs on the friendly warships and transports below. Strict radio silence enjoined any use of short-range TBS (talk-between-ships) except in case of emergency, so ships communicated by blinker light. On the seventeenth, recalled a journalist on one of the transports, "we wrapped ourselves around the International Date Line, so that no one was ever quite certain what day it was; often it was Monday and Tuesday within the same twenty-four hour period."[4] The fleet grew steadily as new units appeared at predetermined coordinates, and the overwhelming display of naval power was a thrill to all who witnessed it. Roger Bond, a quartermaster on the Saratoga, counted thirteen aircraft carriers in a single day. Less than a year earlier, the Saratoga and Enterprise had been the sole remaining American carriers left in the Pacific. To lay eyes on thirteen friendly flattops between sunrise and sunset, said Bond, made it "an awesome, awesome day."[5]

The American carrier task forces were awesome indeed. Seventeen carriers of various types participated in GALVANIC. Frank Plant recalled being "stunned" by the sight of so many ships, especially the giant battleships and carriers: "I was amazed that the fleet was there to protect one little Marine division. That gave me a very proud feeling."[6]

Intelligence had indicated that the Japanese might launch an air attack against the Fifth Fleet from bases in the Marshalls. On November 15, Nimitz's headquarters diary noted "extensive movement of aircraft in the Marshall-Gilbert Islands."[7] An air officer on the Yorktown estimated that the Japanese had 250 land-based aircraft within reach of the Gilberts, and he predicted that the ship would suffer at least one bomb or torpedo hit during the operation.[8] The American carriers were spread far and wide in the week before D-Day. Halsey had requested support in the upper Solomons, where the Japanese navy was threatening to interfere with his amphibious landings at Empress Augusta Bay on Bougainville. Nimitz had detached two of four carrier task groups to detour south and raid Rabaul, with the stipulation that they hurry back north and fall in with the GALVANIC forces by November 12.

Task Force 50, comprising six large and five light carriers divided into
four task groups, was commanded by Rear Admiral Charles A. Pownall.
The bald-headed Pownall, affectionately called "Baldy," flew his flag in the
Yorktown. He had come under criticism for a perceived tentativeness in
carrier raids against Marcus and Wake Islands earlier in the fall. One of
his most strident critics was his own flag captain, Jocko Clark. "I had felt
that our admiral was not up to snuff," Clark later said, framing his criticism more tactfully than he did at the time. "He was a very fine gentleman and a good leader in peacetime, but I think the war was too much for
him."[9] Pownall was unsettled by Clark's aggressive "seaman's eye" handling
of the ship in tight task-force formations. During the raid against Marcus
Island, little more than 1,000 miles from Tokyo, Clark had recommended
flying several follow-on strikes against the Japanese airfield to be sure it was
entirely smashed. Pownall had demurred, preferring to get out of the hot
zone in a hurry. He had refused Clark's emotional appeal to risk extensive
search-and-rescue efforts to recover the aircrew of a downed TBF Avenger.
(The men were subsequently captured by the Japanese.) On all of these
counts, Clark thought Pownall too timid, and many of his fellow captains
apparently shared that opinion.[10]

The carriers were new, many of their screening ships were new, and most
of their airplanes were new. An entirely new set of doctrines was taking
shape. The manuals were being rewritten. Captain Truman J. Hedding,
Pownall's very able chief of staff, had headed a committee of air officers
responsible for developing new tactical instructions for the carrier task
forces. Hedding liked a circular formation with one or two carriers in the
center, surrounded by two inner rings of alternating battleships and cruisers
and an outer ring of destroyers. The battleships and cruisers were primarily
responsible for antiaircraft defense, and the destroyers for antisubmarine
defense.[11] When it was time to launch or recover aircraft, all vessels turned
into the wind simultaneously. The concept of a circular formation was not
new, but the execution became considerably more difficult at the higher
speeds possible with the new carriers and battleships, and as the task forces
grew larger. Spruance later wrote that the "problems . . . were many, but
they were solved as we went along."[12] (He could have said the same of the
entire war.)

The aviators were not reconciled to Spruance's decision to keep the carriers penned in defensive positions off the Gilberts. The controversy had

remained very much alive right up to eve of the GALVANIC operation, with Admiral Towers arguing that the carrier raids against Wake and Marcus in August and September had provided fresh evidence in favor of mobility and aggressive tactics. In an October 9 meeting in CINCPAC headquarters, Towers distributed color photos of the results of those carrier strikes. If the carriers were permitted to go west, he argued, they could unload even greater devastation on Japanese bases in the Marshalls, cutting off the Japanese air threat at its source. Spruance met these arguments by citing the orders of the Joint Chiefs of Staff, which required the capture of atolls in the Gilbert Islands. He had not been ordered to knock out enemy airbases in the Marshalls or to seek out and destroy elements of the Japanese fleet. Those objectives, as important as they were, were secondary. The role of carrier airpower in the coming operation was to protect the fleet, the transports, and the invasion beaches. That would change in an instant, however, if the Japanese fleet rushed east to offer battle: "If a major portion of the Jap fleet was to attempt to interfere with GALVANIC," Spruance wrote his subordinate commanders, "it is obvious that the defeat of the enemy fleet would at once become paramount."[13]

In preparation for GALVANIC, Japanese bases throughout the region had come under a regular schedule of heavy aerial bombardment. American carrier bombers had visited Tarawa and Makin since mid-September, as well as the secondary airfields at Apamama and Nauru. In preparation for the invasion, American forces had developed new airfields at several islands south of the Gilberts—in the Ellice group (Funafuti, Nanomea, Nukufetau) and at Baker Island. All were within air-striking range of the Gilberts. B-24 Liberators of the Seventh Air Force flew a daily "milk run" between fields at Canton Island and Funafuti and enemy airfields throughout the central Pacific. Pownall's carriers would eventually fly more than 2,200 sorties, including bombing raids, fighter sweeps, photographic reconnaissance flights, and close support of the amphibious landings.

GIVEN THE GREAT SIZE OF THE FLEET advancing on the Gilberts, it seemed likely that Japanese air patrols or submarines would discover it and raise an alarm. But on the night of November 19, as the American fleet crept over the eastern horizon and lookouts first glimpsed Tarawa's moonlit palm groves, they detected no sign of life. Could the enemy be entirely ignorant of their presence? At 10:45 p.m., a searchlight cut across the sky, apparently attempting to signal friendly aircraft. The beam did not sweep across the sea horizon. If it had, it probably would have revealed the invasion fleet. To their surprise and gratification, the Americans had evidently achieved tactical surprise.

All remained serene as the warships and transports maneuvered into their assigned stations south and west of the atoll. The marines awakened shortly after 3:00 a.m. and bolted down their traditional Dog-Day breakfast of steak and eggs. (On one of the troop transports, a corpsman callously remarked that the hearty meal would make a ghastly mess of the abdominal wounds he expected to treat later in the day.) The men gathered up their gear and prepared to descend into landing boats. Having been assured that the big guns of the battleships and cruisers would lay waste to Betio prior to the invasion, they awaited the spectacle with keen interest.

The island remained quiet until 4:41 a.m., when a star shell burst above the airfield, backlighting palm trees in searing red light. Several minutes later, an 8-inch battery on the southwest point of the island opened fire on the battleship *Maryland*. The *Maryland*'s 16-inch guns replied immediately, and with five salvos silenced the opposing gun. But the Japanese had three more 8-inch Vickers guns emplaced on different parts of Betio, and towers of whitewater soon erupted near and around the transport group. The crowded troopships lost no time in getting underway and heading west, out of range.

The artillery duel continued for an hour. The *Maryland* and *Colorado*, about two miles offshore, raked the entire length of the island with their massive 16-inch high-fragmentation shells. Admiral Hill took the *Maryland* close inshore in hopes of drawing fire that would unmask the location of the larger batteries. The *Indianapolis*, Spruance's flagship, ran down the eastern and southern coasts of the atoll, firing on lookout towers, gun emplacements, and barges moored in the lagoon. The big shore guns repeatedly fell silent for short periods, only to begin firing anew some minutes later.[14] Julian Smith speculated that these pauses occurred when gun crews were killed or wounded in the naval barrage and were subsequently replaced by new personnel. It was relatively easy to disable the big guns, he said, because the 16-inch shells could be aimed right into the open emplacements.[15] Keeping them out of action proved more difficult, and some were still firing on the American fleet on the morning of D-Day plus one.

Two minesweepers led the way into Tarawa lagoon. They swept the entrance channel of mines (finding none) and laid down markers for the destroyers and transports. Two destroyers, *Ringgold* and *Dashiell*, followed close behind and engaged the smaller shore batteries. *Ringgold* was struck, probably by a 5-inch shell. The damage was contained.

From the decks of the American ships, the bombardment of Betio presented a dazzling spectacle. Orange-red muzzle flashes lit up the sea in a quarter circle to the south and west of the island. The shells whistled like freight trains and drew incandescent arcs across the night sky. The entire length of Betio blazed like a funeral pyre. Sheets of flame ascended hundreds of feet into the air. Robert Sherrod, a *Time* magazine correspondent, watched from the deck of one of the transports. "The sky at times was brighter than noontime on the equator," he wrote. "The arching, glowing cinders that were high-explosive shells sailed through the air as though buckshot were being fired out of many shotguns from all sides of the island."[16] The marines cheered wildly at each successive blast. Even William Rogal, a hard-boiled Guadalcanal veteran who knew from personal experience that sheltered troops could withstand such punishment, regarded the display as "awesome."[17]

A few minutes after six, with dawn breaking in the east, the naval barrage lifted abruptly and the first wave of carrier planes droned in from the south. For the next twenty minutes, more than a hundred TBFs, SBDs, and SB2C bombers pounded the island with high-explosive and incendiary bombs. The Japanese antiaircraft batteries remained largely silent, suggesting that their crews had been killed or driven into bomb shelters. A long procession of Hellcats flew low over the lagoon side of the island and strafed the beach defenses. Tremendous columns of smoke coiled up from the fires and carried away to the east. The rising light revealed that the bombing and bombardment had torn the tops off most of the island's coconut palms, leaving a landscape of naked, blackened, blasted stumps. Sherrod was encouraged. "Surely, we all thought, no mortal men could live through such destroying power. Surely, I thought, if there were actually any Japs left on the island (which I doubted strongly), they would all be dead by now."[18] Watching the island through field glasses from the bridge of the *Indianapolis*, Carl Moore thought that "it seemed that no living soul could be on the island. . . . [I]t looked like the whole affair would be a walkover."[19]

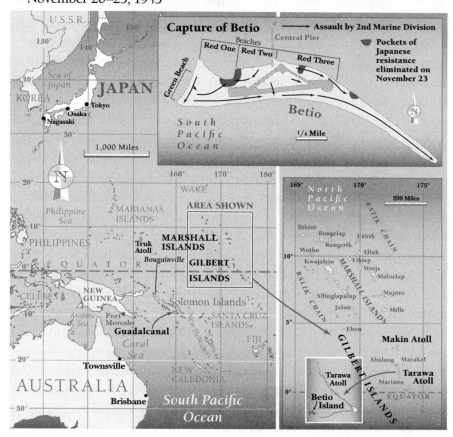

Operation GALVANIC
November 20–23, 1943

Appearances were deceiving. The island's redoubtable defenses were manned by 2,600 highly trained veterans of the Imperial Navy's Special Naval Landing Force (*Kaigun Tokubetsu Rikusentai*), sometimes called "Japanese marines." These elite troops had been drawn from two units ranked among the navy's best—the Third Special Base Defense Force (formerly the Sixth Yokosuka Special Naval Landing Force) and the Seventh Sasebo Special Naval Landing Force. Man for man, they were among the finest in the Japanese armed forces. They were picked men, physically larger than the average Japanese; many were taller than six feet. There were, in addition, another 2,200 labor troops, mostly Koreans. The commanding officer,

Rear Admiral Keiji Shibasaki, had overseen construction of fortifications on an unprecedented scale. He had reportedly told his troops that "a million men cannot take Tarawa in a hundred years."[20]

During the worst of the morning's naval and air bombardment, the defenders remained concealed in subterranean bunkers and bomb shelters. Constructed of coconut logs and reinforced concrete, buried under tons of sand, these structures were impervious even to direct hits overhead by large naval shells, and provided sufficient capacity to protect nearly the entire garrison at once. These large underground shelters were linked by an elaborate network of trenches and tunnels, allowing the Japanese to move rapidly and under cover into firing positions. When Japanese lookouts spotted the minesweepers and destroyers entering Tarawa lagoon, Shibasaki began transferring men from the southern (ocean-facing) shore to the northern (lagoon-facing) positions. He had resolved to meet any attack on the beaches, whether north or south. He had little choice in the matter, as the airfield occupied almost all of the territory in the middle of the island. Strong redoubts stood at fixed intervals along the beach, with enfilading fields of fire on either side. Between them were infantry trenches, machine-gun nests, barbed wire, minefields, and gun emplacements. Some forty artillery pieces of varying calibers defended the island. Should the Americans gain a foothold, they would be limited initially to a narrow strip of beach between the surf and the log seawall. In that case, Shibasaki would rally his forces to a punishing counterattack. He had fourteen light tanks in reserve for that purpose.

The Imperial General Headquarters had earlier promulgated a "Plan Z" that envisioned sending most of the Combined Fleet east to intercept any Allied attack on the Gilbert-Marshalls area. Relentless pressure in the Solomons and New Guinea had forced Admiral Koga to abandon those preparations. There would be no pitched naval battle in the central Pacific. The Japanese response to GALVANIC would be limited to submarine patrols and airstrikes launched from bases in the Marshalls. Betio had been strongly armed and generously supplied with ammunition and other necessities, but there would be no rescue. Shibasaki and his garrison were cut off and alone, and they knew it.

"H-HOUR," THE LANDING OF THE FIRST WAVE, had been scheduled for 8:00 a.m. But a combination of relatively minor problems prompted Admiral Hill to order a one-hour postponement. The transports, forced to retreat from the enemy's artillery fire, required time to maneuver back into their designated positions off the lagoon's entrance channel. Once there, they labored to maintain their stations against a stronger-than-expected southerly current. To aggravate matters, Hill's radio communications were in a sorry state. The blast force of the *Maryland*'s big guns had played havoc with his communication center, which was located on an exposed wing of the flag bridge. With the flagship's first predawn salvo, the electrical circuits had shorted out and radio communications were lost. Throughout most of the ensuing morning, Hill's signalmen were forced to send orders by blinker light. Delays and disorder inevitably followed.

Most of the marines scheduled to land in the first wave had been "boated" (transferred into the Higgins boats and LVTs) before dawn, and had passed several tense and uncomfortable hours in the small, cramped, sea-tossed craft. Sea spray leapt over the bows and soaked the men and their weapons. Miserably seasick men vomited into buckets. Japanese 8-inch shells occasionally landed nearby and sent cascades of seawater down on their heads. The boats were first ordered to pull back, then summoned to return. Hours passed; uncertainty reigned. "We floated all night going up and down those darn waves," Lieutenant Plant recalled. "I tried to snatch a little sleep using the Chaplain's shoulder for a pillow."[21]

When the first wave of boats left the line of departure at 9:00 a.m., they were promptly taken under fire by well-hidden guns emplaced on Betio's lagoon shore. At about half a mile from the beach, the boats began running hard aground on shallow coral heads. Most of the amtracs, having been designed to cope with exactly this contingency, managed to cross the reefs without trouble. Their treads dug into the coral, their engines raced, their bows tilted up toward the sky, and they trundled stolidly over the obstruction. The marines were bounced from their benches and had to seize the handholds and one another to avoid sprawling to the deck. Where there was enough depth on the inshore side of the reef, the amtracs slid back into the sea and began behaving like boats again.

The volume and intensity of fire grew as the boats motored in toward the landing beaches. Shibasaki's defenses included 75mm field artillery pieces and 37mm antitank guns, both positioned to fire on the most likely lanes of approach. Neither the amtracs nor the Higgins boats carried enough armor to stop the shells. A man in William Rogal's boat peered over the bow to look ahead, but his timing was very bad. A 37mm shell struck the bow, Rogal recalled, and "the force of the explosion threw his body to the rear of the amtrac, showering everyone on the port side with blood and brains."[22] Lieutenant Lillibridge's boat came under heavy fire, and shells pierced the starboard and port sides simultaneously. The men threw themselves down flat on the bottom.[23] Light mortars burst around and over the craft, including one that exploded directly overhead and inflicted shrapnel wounds on several marines.

Most of the first-wave boats headed toward Beach Red 1, in a cove tucked between the pier and the northwestern point of the island. Because of the indented shoreline, the approach lanes to Beach Red 1 came under a concentrated crossfire by weapons of many different types and calibers. Within about 150 yards' range of the beach, machine gunners and riflemen in pits and pillboxes opened up and peppered the sides of the amtracs. The captains of the leading boats instinctively veered away from the lethal hailstorm—either right, toward Beach Green on the western end of the island, or left, toward Beach Red 2 and the long pier. Many boats put ashore near the point separating Beach Red 1 from Beach Green, which had been designated only as a contingency landing zone but would prove important on the second day of the battle.

As Rogal's amtrac headed toward Beach Red 2, mortars burst overhead and showered his platoon with shrapnel. When the boat grounded on the sand, Rogal shouted, "Let's go!" and went over the side, the surviving men close behind him. Above the seawall to the left, he saw a machine-gun emplacement—one of the major "strong points" on the lagoon beach that would kill about 300 marines that day.

The amtracs drove directly onto the beaches and lowered their ramps. Most first-wave units made it to the seawall, which shielded them against a direct line of fire, but found that they could go no farther without attracting heavy fire from enemy positions immediately inland. In those early stages, the few brave souls who went over the top were either shot dead or wounded and forced back to the beach. Small, isolated units crouched against the wall, kept their heads down, and waited for tanks, air support, and reinforcements.

The volume of Japanese mortar, artillery, and automatic-weapons fire seemed to swell as the morning progressed. The first assault wave had come in amtracs, but a greater proportion of the following waves came in Higgins boats, which could not traverse the reefs. A boat carrying Frank Plant grounded hard on the reef and flung the men forward against the bow. The platoon leader shouted, "Men, debark!" The ramp went down with a clatter and the marines lined up to step into the sea. Several men were shot immediately, and the crew pulled them back into the boat to be evacuated. Plant had been near the stern, and was one of the last in his boat to reach the ramp: "By the time we reached the front of the boat, the water all around was colored purple with blood."[24] Their boots could touch bottom, but the water came up to their shoulders. Machine-gun and rifle fire mottled the sea around them. Mortars sent up towers of spray. Hellcats flew strafing runs less than 100 feet overhead, and for a terrible moment Plant thought there must have been some mistake, because the planes seemed to be aiming directly at him. Then he realized that they were strafing Japanese positions just inland of the beach.

The first combat correspondents had been scheduled to go in with the fifth wave, but by ten that morning it was no longer accurate to describe the action as a sequence of organized "waves." There was one continuous wave, constant movements of Higgins boats headed in both directions between the line of departure and Beaches Red 1 and 2. As grounded boats piled up on the reefs, a diminishing number of functional amtracs attempted to ferry troops to the beaches. Most marines in those later waves were forced to wade into the face of concentrated enemy fire. Bob Sherrod, accompanying a platoon, was dropped into neck-deep water about 700 yards from the beach. Heavy fire continued while the men in his group approached the shore. As they waded into the shallows, they were forced to expose more of their bodies to the murderous fire. In the space of five minutes he saw six marines cut down. "The remarkable thing," observed Sherrod, "was that no man turned back, though each became a larger target as he trudged slowly through the shallow water. It was a ghastly, yet splendid picture, and no man who ever saw it will ever forget." The journalist was surprised to reach the base of the pier without being hit—rounds had seemed to strike immediately to his left and right, and "I could have sworn that I could have reached out and touched a hundred bullets."[25] Gradually, enough marines managed to get ashore to consolidate a fragile toehold between the seawall and the surf.

At 11:00 a.m., Colonel David M. Shoup staggered ashore at the same spot. He had been hit by shrapnel in both legs, and a bullet had grazed his neck, but the wounds seemed manageable and he resolved to carry on. Shoup, a former 2nd Division operations and training officer who had taken an important part in planning GALVANIC, had no prior experience with combat. He had been given command of the 2nd Marines after the transports had sailed from Wellington, when the regiment's previous commander had succumbed to nervous exhaustion.

As the senior American officer on Betio, Shoup now took command of all troops ashore. He set up his first command post directly under the pier, with the sea awash around his knees. A radio strapped to a sergeant's back provided a tenuous communications link to other units on the beach. The news was not good. Nowhere had the marines penetrated beyond the seawall. Shoup rallied his men to clean out the pier, and then moved his command post up the beach to a protected spot snug up against the seaward side of a Japanese blockhouse. Enemy soldiers were directly on the other side of a double-tiered coconut log wall. "There were still Japanese inside," the colonel later said, "but to get them out my men would have to blow me up along with them. So we posted sentries at all the openings to keep them inside."[26] One of Shoup's leg wounds was bleeding freely, and was bandaged by a corpsman.

His communications were terrible. Combat radio "manpacks," soaked in seawater during the long wade, were disabled or unreliable. He had to shout to be heard over the roar of rifle and artillery fire. Message runners carried dispatches up and down the beach, but many were cut down while dashing across exposed positions. When Shoup got through by radio to the third battalion commander, still in a transport in the lagoon, he urged that additional reinforcements be landed east of the pier, where the volume of enemy fire was more moderate. From there, they could work their way west along the beach or attack directly inland.

When Lieutenant Plant stumbled up the beach, Shoup ordered him to stay at the command post and act as air coordinator. Plant, with the help of a skilled radioman, got through to the *Maryland* and asked for "everything you can bring." The air officer on the *Maryland* was concerned about the risk of friendly fire. "Those targets are only a few hundred yards from the beach," he said. "Where are your front lines?" Plant reported, "Front line is on the beach." There was a pause as the meaning sank in, and the voice replied, "Wilco."[27]

By training and instinct, the marines were predisposed toward aggressive infantry tactics. Enemy positions should be taken quickly, by frontal or flanking attacks. Forward momentum was imperative, and it must be sustained even at the cost of heavy early casualties because a stalled advance might deteriorate into a dangerous stalemate. But on Betio, in those early hours of the battle, the marines could not gain an initial foothold above the seawall. The coral "no-man's-land" between the wall and the Japanese firing positions was strewn with dead marines. Corpsmen exposed themselves to deadly fire to pull the wounded to safety. Armored vehicles were urgently needed to spearhead the drive inland. A few LVTs roared up the beach, ramps up, and tried to climb the seawall. They succeeded only in exposing themselves to point-blank antitank fire. By midmorning, dozens of wrecked and burning amtracs lay on the beach or in the shallows. By the end of the day, half the amtracs that had been hurled against Betio were out of action.

When tank lighters put seven medium Sherman tanks ashore on Beach Red 3 at about noon, they led the first effective direct assault on heavily fortified enemy positions. Many of the machines were disabled by enemy fire, or fell into tank traps or drove over mines. But even an immobilized Sherman provided cover for the flamethrower teams and riflemen who followed close behind, and the disabled tanks themselves could be employed as makeshift pillboxes. In the early afternoon, above Red 3, the marines finally began the slow, murderous process of pushing into the island's interior. They flanked and wiped out the pillboxes, though it was often necessary to revisit the same positions more than once as enemy soldiers entered them through covered trenches. A lieutenant reported, after the battle, "The combination of tanks, flamethrowers, and riflemen proved effective in destroying the enemy with minimum losses."[28]

Sherrod, following close on the heels of the advancing infantry and jotting down notes whenever he could take cover, recorded what he saw: "A Jap ran out of a coconut-log blockhouse into which Marines were tossing dynamite. As he emerged a Marine flamethrower engulfed him. The Jap flared like a piece of celluloid. He died before the bullets in his cartridge belt finished exploding 60 seconds later."[29]

Lieutenant Lillibridge and his platoon joined a group of marines huddled against the seawall on Beach Red 2. "The scene was utterly weird, out of some very bad John Wayne movie," he wrote. "I ducked up to the captain with my men bunched up behind me and I blurted out, 'Do you know where A company is?' He pointed out over the wall and said 'I think they're out there somewhere.' Without thinking I jumped up and said 'Let's go,' and without even looking back I went over the seawall and just ran straight ahead. Everybody followed me. It was absolutely insane, not asking if this was impossible, but I wasn't thinking clearly."[30]

On the *Maryland*, cruising about a mile offshore, General Smith and Admiral Hill were frustrated by unreliable radio links with Shoup and other unit commanders. The reports from the beachhead were fragmentary and perplexing. The marines were asking for more of everything—reinforcements, ammunition, air support, half-tracks and tanks, drinking water, medical corpsmen and supplies. The commanders and their staffs struggled to form an accurate picture of the situation ashore. Their most reliable source of information was provided by one of the *Maryland's* Kingfisher spotter planes, which circled above the island for much of the day. Lieutenant Commander Robert McPherson, the pilot, made detailed observations of the Japanese positions, and even strafed or dropped grenades when opportunity offered. General Julian Smith sent a staff officer along on one of the floatplane's several flights on the afternoon of D-Day.[31]

Smith had committed his reserve troops, the first and third battalions of the 8th Marines, but by midafternoon, the beachheads remained precarious. He radioed Holland Smith: "Successful landings on Beaches Red 2 and 3. Toehold on Red 1. Am committing one LT [Landing Team] from division reserve. Still encountering strong resistance." The marines had suffered heavy casualties, he added. "The situation is in doubt."[32]

The assault on Makin (eighty-three miles north of Tarawa) was well in hand, but Holland Smith was irked by the slow advance of the army troops on that island. He now realized that the fight on Betio (in the Tarawa atoll) was shaping up to be a bloodbath. After conferring briefly with Admiral Turner, he agreed to release the Corps reserve regiment, the 6th Marines, to be landed on Betio.

The marines now had a tenuous hold on the western part of Betio and on a small salient directly inland of Shoup's command headquarters. The close coordination of naval gunfire and air support was critical to maintaining these positions. Two destroyers drew in close to the island and dropped 5-inch shells on targets as directed by radio.

Hours of unremitting bombardment made a mess of Shibasaki's telephone communications. The wiring had been buried in shallow trenches or even left out on the sand, and much of it was shredded and useless. Frustrated at his inability to make contact with various units via field telephone, the admiral decided to move his command post to the south side of the island.

He would yield up the large concrete blockhouse that had been his headquarters to be employed as a field hospital for the wounded. But as Shibasaki and a group of staff officers left the blockhouse on foot, one of the destroyers managed a lucky shot. A 5-inch shell detonated directly among them, killing the admiral and several other senior officers. That sudden beheading of the Japanese command threw the defenders into confusion and may have accounted for their failure to coordinate an early *banzai* charge. It was a momentous development that probably saved many American lives. Without sufficient depth of deployment, a massed counterattack against any one point of the marine lines would have been difficult to beat back.

As darkness fell, the firing quieted down and the marines prepared for the night. Rogal recalls that first night on Betio as being strangely subdued, "almost uneventful."[33] Neither side wanted to divulge their positions by firing their weapons. A Japanese plane circled overhead, unseen. Guadalcanal veterans promptly designated it "Washing Machine Charlie," and joked that the same persistent nocturnal visitor they had come to know so well at Henderson Field had trailed them north. The specter of a bayonet charge kept them on edge. For every one man who slept, two were ordered to remain awake and alert. The marines had landed more than 5,000 men on the island, but they were corralled into three narrow beaches and two salients, neither of which penetrated more than seventy yards inshore. Their ammunition dumps were exposed and vulnerable to a single well-aimed grenade. Frank Plant could not sleep at all: "Our vulnerability and the value of darkness to the Japanese method of fighting, especially a massive banzai attack using in effect suicide tactics, became so real and so terrorizing."[34]

D-Day plus one dawned at low tide, and the retreating sea revealed a macabre scene. Dead marines were strewn along the beach or floating on the water. The blackened, gnarled shapes of more than fifty wrecked amtracs and Higgins boats were half awash in the shallows or grounded on the coral flats. A sweet stench of decaying flesh wafted over the island; it would worsen steadily as the sun rose. Marines foraged through the packs and pockets of their dead friends for ammunition, canteens, cigarettes, and rations.

The three assault battalions, pinned down on their three narrow beachheads, shared a sense of relief and even surprise at having survived the night. The dreaded enemy bayonet charge had never materialized. But their circumstances remained perilous. They were scattered in small, largely isolated units. Unless they took more territory, they were likely to be driven back into the sea. It was impossible to obtain an accurate tally of their casualties, but it seemed likely that more than a third of the troops who landed on D-Day had been killed or wounded. Losses were proportionally higher among officers and noncommissioned officers. "We're in a mighty tight spot," said Colonel Shoup. "We've got to have more men."[35] The marines needed more of everything, in fact—more men, more ammunition, more armored vehicles, more artillery. To fight in the heat they would need more freshwater and salt tablets. The doctors and corpsmen had worked all night to treat the wounded and evacuate them to the fleet, but first aid supplies of every category were running low. Marshall Ralph Doak, a chief pharmacist's mate, worked to evacuate wounded marines to an LST that had been converted into a temporary hospital ship. Near the beach, he recalled, the surf was tinted visibly red.[36]

General Julian Smith, from his headquarters on the *Maryland*, had notified Shoup that he intended to land the diversion reserve, the first and third battalions of the 8th Marines, at 6:00 a.m. The reserves had loaded into Higgins boats well before dawn, and many had been circling in the lagoon for half the night. As the first waves churned in toward Beach Red 2, Japanese machine guns and light artillery opened up, and it was soon evident that the landing would be no less bloody than those of the previous day. The Japanese had apparently set up additional weapons in their strong pocket at the junction of Red 1 and 2. The LCVPs hung up on the reef, and marines waded into enemy fire in waist-deep water. Men took refuge behind the concrete obstacles placed offshore by the Japanese, or behind disabled landing craft. From there, however, it was a long dash across open beach. "The carnage was terrible!" Rogal wrote. "The water to my front was soon dotted with the floating bodies of the dead and wounded. Most of [that battalion] had been eliminated—more than 300 casualties."[37]

Japanese soldiers had apparently swum out to a small wrecked freighter on the reef. From that position, their rifles and machine guns could reach marines disembarking from grounded landing craft 400 yards offshore. Carrier dive-bombers attempted to destroy the vessel, but missed repeatedly.[38] "From the beachhead it was a sickening sight," Bob Sherrod recorded. "Even before they climbed out of their Higgins boats, the reserves were under machine-gun fire. Many were cut down as they waded in, others drowned. Men screamed and moaned. Of twenty-four in one boat only three reached shore."[39]

The awful scene on the beach helped to spur the marines already on the island to attack with renewed energy. The morning's plan was simple. Shoup intended to cut the island in two by driving directly south, across the airfield, to the ocean shore. Major Henry P. Crowe's forces at Red 3 were to overrun the network of formidable defenses that stood between him and the airfield. Major Michael P. Ryan, who held a small salient at the northwestern point of the island, was to attack south, along Beach Green, and attempt to secure it as a bridgehead for further troop landings.

Marines brought their 75mm pack howitzers up the beach and began pummeling enemy firing positions farther inland; naval fire support was called down on the enemy's strong points; Hellcats flew low overhead and strafed; dive-bombers hit assigned targets based on radioed coordinates. Cumulatively, this onslaught began to break down the enemy's defenses, but the Japanese were resilient. The enemy's pillboxes could be cleaned out only by direct infantry assault.

It was the proudest and the most terrible day in the history of the Marine Corps. Men fought with extraordinary courage, returning to the line of fire even after having been wounded several times. "They'd fight with broken arms, gunshot wounds, shrapnel wounds," recalled Vern Garrett, a *Yorktown* pharmacist's mate. "I'd patch them up and tell them to go back to the ship and they'd say, 'I'm all right,' and they would just keep on fighting."[40] Lieutenant William D. Hawkins, a Texan, was one of those rare men who seemed entirely indifferent to danger. He dashed across exposed firing fields with wild-eyed, manic courage; he personally attacked one enemy pillbox or machine-gun nest after another, throwing grenades into firing ports; he refused to be evacuated even after suffering serious shrapnel wounds. Hawkins commandeered an amtrac, loaded the remains of his platoon into it, and charged into concentrated machine-gun fire. A witness told Sherrod, "I'll never forget the picture of him standing on that amtrac, riding around with a million bullets a minute whistling by his ears, just shooting Japs. I've never seen such a man in my life."[41] Shortly after noon a bullet caught him in the shoulder and severed an artery. He died in minutes. Later, Betio's captured airfield would be named Hawkins Field, and the lieutenant's mother would accept a posthumous Medal of Honor from President Roosevelt.

Not all men were equally courageous. Some quailed and stuck fast in their foxholes and had to be prodded into action. Finding a corporal hiding under a pile of rubble, Shoup smacked the man's legs until he came out. He asked the corporal to tell him his mother's first name. "Well," said Shoup, "do you think she'd be proud of you, curled up in a hole like that, no damn use to anybody?" The corporal admitted that she would not be proud, but said that the rest of his squad was dead and he had no orders. Shoup pointed to several marines crouched below the seawall and said, "Pick out a man, then another and another. Just say, 'Follow me.' When you've got a squad, report to me."[42] The corporal did it, and took his new squad into battle. Shoup never learned what became of him.

Fear was instinctive and omnipresent. Even Shoup, who earned a Medal of Honor for his performance at Tarawa, struggled to keep his nerves under control. He was not the Hollywood archetype of a battlefield commander, said Frank Plant, who was by his side throughout the battle—"not the typical hero type or even the typical Marine officer; he was rotund and physically rather clumsy. I remember thinking at times when he had to get somewhere by crawling that that was pretty tough on an old fellow; actually he was only in his late 30s." The colonel occasionally revealed signs of "fear which approached despair."[43] Sherrod observed that Shoup's hands shook as he held a field telephone. His voice grew hoarse from shouting over the din of battle. "God!" he exclaimed to a group of officers at the command post. "How can a man think with all this noise going on?"[44] When a young major complained that his men would not follow him to the airstrip, Shoup reduced the problem to a simple formula: "You've got to say, 'Who'll follow me?' And if only ten follow you, that's the best you can do, but it's better than nothing."[45]

American carrier planes operated above the island from dawn to dusk, and Plant continued to call down airstrikes on enemy targets. Battalion commanders radioed their requests to Shoup, using keyed block numbers on a map, and Shoup relayed them to Plant. "Air liaison officer!" the colonel might say; "Tell them to drop some bombs on the southwest edge of 229 and the southeast edge of 231. There's some Japs in there giving us hell."[46] Plant would radio the request, and about ten minutes later the dive-bombers would hurtle down from overhead and drop 1,000-pounders on or near the targets.

All agreed that there was room for improvement in ground-air coordination. At times it seemed that there were too many planes over Betio. When a long file of Hellcats strafed enemy positions, their propellers kicked up sand and dust and obscured visibility. Plant asked that the attacks "be spaced more apart to allow the air to clear in between attacking planes."[47] There were no midair collisions, but several near misses. "We thought we were pretty doggone good with our bombs and bullets," said Alex Vraciu, veteran of the Guadalcanal campaign, "but it didn't turn out that way."[48] Bombs that struck near fortified positions did little or no damage: only a direct hit had any real chance of killing the men inside. In most cases, said another pilot, "you couldn't really see what you were shooting at or bombing."[49]

Naval gunfire or "call-fire" proved especially valuable against Japanese firing positions and pillboxes above Beach Green, on the western side of the island. A gunfire spotter made radio contact with the fleet and called 5-inch fire down on the enemy's strong points. The shelling came as close as fifty yards to the forward American lines. Immediately after the ships ceased fire, tanks and infantrymen attacked. In many cases, the naval shellfire provided the margin of victory; in others, it was credited with reducing marine casualties. By noon, Major Ryan's forces had taken control of the entire western end of the island, to a depth of 200 yards above Green. Reinforcements could now be landed without opposition. General Smith, receiving the news by semaphore signal, ordered the first battalion of the 6th Marines ashore. They would land before dark, take cover in foxholes for the night, then move through Ryan's forces and roll up the southern shore at daybreak. Additional reserves were put ashore on Bairiki, the adjoining island to the east, in order to prevent Japanese troops from fleeing up the atoll.

From Red 2, Lieutenant Wayne Sanford led F Company across heavily contested ground to the southern side of the airstrip. Machine gunners and riflemen covered one another in turn. The men tumbled into an antitank ditch some yards back from the southern beach. The advance completed Shoup's goal of cutting the island in half, but there were many enemy soldiers remaining in the now-enlarged interior of the American lines, and much more hard fighting was needed to finish them off. Snipers fired constantly— from pillboxes, from trenches, and from the tops of the few palm trees that still had fronds to conceal a man. Ammunition resupply was a constant worry, and ammunition carriers dashed back through heavy fire to carry the belts from the north to the south side of the island.

A strong pocket remained in the area just inland of the juncture of Red 1 and 2. Here the Japanese had set up additional machine guns on the first night of the battle, and commanded a sweeping field of fire over both land-ing beaches. The pocket would not be fully reduced until the third day of the fight.

Robert McPherson, circling over the island in his floatplane as he had all day on November 20, provided invaluable information about the progress of the battle. Lieutenant Plant communicated directly with him by radio and relayed updates to Shoup, who was plainly relieved to have those firsthand accounts from a bird's-eye perspective.[50] As on the previous day, McPherson occasionally found occasion to strafe Japanese positions or drop grenades from the cockpit.

Fortifications behind Red 3 were among the most stubborn on the island. Again and again, pillboxes that had been cleaned out with grenades or flamethrowers became a renewed threat. They were divided into com-partments by strong interior walls, so a grenade thrown into a firing port might kill just one or two men, leaving others unharmed. Reinforcements entered through tunnels or covered trenches. Major Crowe wondered aloud, "Do they have a tunnel to Tokyo or something?"[51] Marines entered some of these subterranean spaces and fought their enemies with bayonets and knives. Tanks advanced and fired into slots at point-blank range. Bulldoz-ers pushed coral and sand up against the firing ports, covering them and smothering the occupants.

By early afternoon on the second day, November 21, it was evident that the Americans would prevail. It was not yet clear how long it would take to secure the island, or how many more lives would be lost in the effort. High tide was at 12:18 p.m., and for several midday hours the navigability of the lagoon was much improved. Higgins boats and tank lighters brought a steady flood of supplies, ammunition, tanks, half-tracks, and heavy con-struction equipment to the pier. Wounded men on stretchers were carried back to the fleet, where they would be transferred to hospital ships. The sight of a jeep hauling a 37mm gun up the pier seemed significant to Bob Sherrod, who noted, "If a sign of certain victory were needed, this is it. The jeeps have arrived."[52]

Japanese snipers remained active everywhere on the island. The sound of bullets whizzing past their ears became so familiar that many marines ignored it. Men made a point of walking upright in studied nonchalance. "Walking along the shore with bullets all around should have been ter-rifying," one lieutenant later remarked, "but after a while you figured there was nothing you could do about it, and you just quit worrying."[53] Refusing to acknowledge the Japanese snipers, whose fire was usually inaccurate at longer ranges, offered a way to broadcast one's disdain for the enemy. "Shoot me down, you son of a bitch," barked a private, as he ambled down Beach Red 2 and a bullet cut through the air nearby.[54] Another marine was shot in the hand and lost part of his thumb; he "just laughed and kept going."[55] A lieutenant was "nicked in the rear" as he stood talking at Shoup's headquarters. "I'll be damned," he remarked. "I stay out front four hours, then I come back to the command post and get shot."[56]

Colonel Shoup, who wore a mask of dust and dirt like every other marine on the island, summed up the situation that afternoon: "Well, I think we're winning, but the bastards have got a lot of bullets left. I think we'll clean up tomorrow."[57] He was plainly exhausted, having slept not at all the previous night. He was still bleeding through his bandage. His report to General Julian Smith would enter Marine Corps lore: "Casualties many; percentage of dead not known; combat efficiency: We are winning."[58] At 8:30 p.m., Colonel Merritt Edson, the 2nd Division chief of staff and a veteran of many hard battles on Guadalcanal, stepped on the beach and relieved Shoup of command.

On the third day of the battle, Japanese resistance buckled and collapsed. The 6th Marines rolled up the southern shore and joined with other units to overrun the airfield. The last axis of organized resistance in central Betio was in a two-story steel-reinforced concrete blockhouse that had withstood all direct hits by shells or bombs. The hard-run bulldozers were called into service to finish the job. They approached with blades raised as armor against fire, and shoved a small mountain of sand and coral up to cover the entrance and firing slots. A few marines climbed to the top of the structure and poured gasoline down the air vents. A single hand grenade was enough to convert the blockhouse into a kiln. The remains of 300 Japanese were later excavated from the interior.

Except for a few isolated snipers and stragglers, all remaining Japanese forces were now corralled into the long narrow eastern tail of the island. Marines cautiously entered the pillboxes and dugouts and discovered that many Japanese had taken their own lives. The war correspondent Jim Lucas found a bunker filled with Japanese soldiers who had removed their shoes, put their rifles in their mouths, and pulled the triggers with their toes. The forces penned in the eastern end of the island, about 300 men, staged a *banzai* attack at dusk. The marines held their positions and mowed them down.

Mopping up actions continued in the next three days, but seventy-six hours after the initial landing, Betio was declared secured. General Julian Smith went ashore with his staff and took command at noon on November 23.

Even before the fighting was concluded, the marines had begun the sad and grisly work of burying their dead. There was no time to lose. Bodies decayed rapidly in the tropical sun, and a fetid stench had settled over the island. The living worked instinctively, without being ordered to do it—they waded into the shallows and retrieved their floating comrades, dragged the bodies up the beach and lined them up in rows, collected their dog tags. Bulldozers dug long trenches. Chaplains presided over the burial ceremonies. White crosses were planted in long rows. About 1,000 marines were killed, and twice that number wounded. The abnormally high ratio of dead to wounded was explained by the fact that so many men who died had been struck in the lagoon or on the beaches, where they could not be safely rescued and were often hit by additional fire.

Nearly the entire Japanese garrison was killed, more than 4,000 troops and laborers. The marines had taken 146 prisoners, mostly Korean laborers. Just seventeen Japanese combatants had allowed themselves to be taken alive, and only one officer—an ensign. The Koreans were quick to let their captors know that they were not Japanese, and many pitched in willingly to assist in burying the American dead. The marines attached less urgency to the task of getting the enemy dead under the ground, but that was necessary on grounds of sanitation alone. Clouds of big green tropical flies were abuzz over the burial sites. "The stench of death hung over Betio," wrote Lucas. "We had slaughtered more than 4,000 Japanese. Their grotesquely burned, blackened corpses littered every foot of the atoll, many of them dead for three days. They were bloated and swollen. For weeks we were to taste and smell corruption."[59] Burial details heaved the enemy dead into bomb craters, and bulldozers shoved coral over them.

The hospital ship *Solace* entered the lagoon on the morning of the battle's climactic day. As soon as she had dropped her anchor, landing craft and launches came alongside. Normally, casualties were brought aboard on only one side at a time, but now the gangplanks were lowered on both sides of the ship simultaneously. At midday, corpsmen held up sheets in an attempt to shield the wounded from the tropical sun. The *Solace*'s doctors and nurses were on their feet for the ensuing twenty-four hours.[60]

A transport, the *President Polk*, brought heavy equipment and supplies needed to begin the work of restoring the airfield and converting the shattered island into a modern naval and air base. The unloading of massive machines in the shallow lagoon presented familiar problems. Admiral Hill had hoped to have the transports out of the area in twenty-four hours, but a week after D-Day the navy was still struggling to get needed cargo out of the ships and onto the beach. Only the LCTs were large enough to move the heaviest units, such as steam shovels and cranes, but only three LCTs were in working order. "Speaking in the words of the poets, this is a hell of a place to unload," Hill told Spruance, "and I am afraid we can't report as much progress as I had hoped." Turner reported the same sorts of frustrations at Makin. "As is almost always the case with the Army, and often with the Marines, it was very difficult to get enough men to unload boats, even slowly," he told Spruance on November 30. "As soon as the troops debarked from the LSTs and APs, they simply evaporated. Boats would lie at the pier for hours on end without a pound moving, while those garrison troops were out sightseeing."[61]

Bulldozers, landed on Betio while the fighting was still hot, cleared the airstrip of corpses and debris. Bomb and shell craters were filled and paved over with coral cement. Four days after the invasion, the first American fighter planes landed on Betio. Construction teams cleared the roads and began assembling a water purification plant. Amid the mountains of wreckage shoved to the edges of the roads and taxiways were uprooted palm trees, smashed tanks and armored vehicles, lengths of sheet iron ejected from blasted pillboxes, and the contorted remains of hundreds of bicycles.

Holland Smith had monitored the progress of the fight on Betio from his flagship off Makin Atoll, eighty-three miles north of Tarawa. The general was losing patience with the 165th Infantry Regiment's methodical, go-slow approach to reducing Makin's modest enemy garrison (which numbered just 600 men, only half of whom were fighting troops). The job, in Smith's view, should have been accomplished on D-Day. But after landing on the east shore of Makin's main island of Butaritari, the army troops held fast in defensive positions against discontinuous mortar and machine-gun fire. A second landing on the north (lagoon) side of Butaritari followed later that morning. Casualties were light, but as darkness fell on the night of November 20, only about half the island was in American hands.

The army's tactical concept of a gradual advance may have limited its casualties from hour to hour, but it extended the duration of the battle for

Butaritari. Receiving reports of the carnage on Betio, Smith badly wanted to take his flagship south, but plans had specified that he and Turner (on the *Pennsylvania*) would remain off Makin until Butaritari was captured. General Ralph Smith did not declare the island secure until 1:40 a.m. on November 23.[62] Throughout and after GALVANIC, the marine-army antagonism inherent in the "Smith over Smith" command setup was kept under a lid. But the same two generals would reprise their dispute on Saipan eight months later, with more public repercussions.

Holland Smith flew down to Tarawa in a PBY patrol plane on the morning of November 24. Looking down at Betio as the seaplane circled above the lagoon, he was shocked and saddened: "The sight of our dead floating in the waters of the lagoon and lying along the blood-soaked beaches is one I will never forget. Over the pitted, blasted island hung a miasma of coral dust and death, nauseating and horrifying."[63] He went ashore that afternoon. The island was swarming with marines wearing three-day beards and layers of grime and coral dust. They were hungry, thirsty, and exhausted. Many sat alone, seemingly dazed, wearing the expression called the "thousand yard stare." Smith and a number of other senior officers presided over a simple flag-raising ceremony near the airstrip. As the islands had been a British protectorate, a Union Jack was hoisted alongside the Stars and Stripes.

With rare exceptions, the flag officers of the U.S. Navy had no direct experience of combat prior to the war. The assault on Tarawa had been a case study in amphibious operations—and it was necessary, from a professional view, for all senior officers who had participated in planning the invasion to see the results firsthand. In the two weeks after the battle, a stream of high-ranking visitors toured the devastated island. Admiral Hill went ashore on November 25 and wrote Spruance the next day, urging him to do the same. Examining the formidable Japanese defenses, he said, was "a liberal education for all of us."[64] Admiral Nimitz and a party of CINCPAC staff officers flew into Tarawa on a DC-3 about a week after the initial assault. Nimitz had never seen anything like it, and he told his flag lieutenant, Arthur Lamar, that it was "the first time I've smelled death."[65] General Julian Smith hosted an incongruously lavish dinner in his mess tent, complete with a white tablecloth and hearts of palm salad. Lamar noted that dead marines were still washing up on the beach.

As Holland Smith inspected the remains of the Japanese defenses, he concluded that the aerial bombing and naval gunfire had been ineffective. In some places, pillboxes were entirely intact, appearing as if they had not been touched at all. Many of the subterranean works were covered with alternating layers of concrete, palm logs, steel beams, and coral sand. One bunker was later found to be covered with "six feet of reinforced concrete, on top of which were two layers of crisscrossed iron rails, covered by three more feet of sand, two rows of coconut logs topped by a final six feet of sand."[66] In his postwar memoir, Smith recorded the cutting view that "the Navy was inclined to exaggerate the destructive effect of gunfire and this failing really amounted to a job imperfectly done."[67] He told the admirals that Tarawa should have been subjected to three full days of uninterrupted naval bombardment. As for the carnage inflicted as the marines waded to shore, the navy should have moved heaven and earth to get more LVT tractors to the Pacific in time for GALVANIC.

Admiral Turner answered these criticisms at the time and again after the war. No one who had seen Tarawa could fail to be moved by the scale of the carnage; all resolved to learn from the operation and apply those lessons in future amphibious invasions. But it would not be tactically wise to station a fleet off an atoll such as Tarawa for a week or more prior to an operation. The risk of submarine incursion was too great. As if to prove his point, the navy lost a jeep carrier in an especially horrific submarine attack on November 24.

The *Liscome Bay* (CVE-56) was operating as part of Task Group 50.2, about twenty miles southeast of Makin. Her air group had conducted air searches, artillery-spotting missions, and strafing and bombardment runs over the atoll. Before dawn on the twenty-fourth, the ship was at flight and general quarters, on a course of 270 degrees, at a speed of 15 knots. Frequent sonar contacts had been reported that night, and extra lookouts had been posted. At 5:09 a.m., an officer on the starboard gallery walkway spotted an inbound torpedo wake. He alerted the bridge by telephone, but there was no time to evade. It struck amidships at 5:10, at the most vulnerable part of the hull. The blast immediately detonated the carrier's principal magazine, and all of her aircraft bombs went up at once.

The blast ascended to 1,000 feet. A witness stationed in Fly Control described it as "a huge ball of bright orange-colored flame, with some white spots in it like white-hot metal."[68] Debris fell on ships nearly two miles away.

Michael Bak, a sailor on the destroyer *Franks*, remembers watching in horror as the cosmic orb rose into the predawn sky. "We watched the whole thing," he said. "We were just dumbfounded that the ship was blowing up."[69]

The after half of the *Liscome Bay* was simply no longer there. There were no survivors from any part of the ship aft of frame 118. Fires raged in the hangar, and power cut out to the remaining sections of the bow. The ship sank in twenty-three minutes. "It was dark out there, but I remember it was just like putting a candle out," said Bak. "The ball of fire was knocked out as the ship sank."[70] Destroyers moved in to pick up survivors, and aircraft patrolled overhead. By midmorning there was nothing left to be seen but "wreckage and empty life rafts."[71]

The *Liscome Bay* took 687 of her crew with her into the deep. Among the slain was Rear Admiral Henry M. Mullinnix, commander of the Escort Carrier Group. The carrier's loss accounted for about a third of all American lives lost in Operation GALVANIC. If Ralph Smith's troops had moved faster to overrun Makin, perhaps the fleet could have withdrawn a day or two earlier, sparing the *Liscome Bay* her fate. Taking the number of casualties from all services into account, the Marine Corps doctrine of aggressive offense was to be preferred to the army's stolid pace. Nimitz later concluded, "Nowhere has the Navy's insistence upon speed in amphibious assault been more sharply vindicated."[72]

THE LESSONS OF TARAWA were carefully studied and applied in plans for future amphibious landings. With benefit of hindsight, the marines concluded that the assault forces had carried too much equipment to the beaches. When landing on a very small island such as Betio, it was better to go in light and rely on a steady resupply by sea. Many officers recommended leaving the packs on the transports and carrying only a belt. The landing forces should take fewer rations, less water, but more grenades, and leave behind bedding rolls, sandbags, gas masks, barbed wire, and mess kits. Radios should be waterproofed and perhaps brought in on flotation trays. Ammunition should likewise be wrapped to keep it dry. In any future operation in which landing craft would have to cross a coral reef, it was essential to supply an adequate number of LVTs. There was room for improvement of ship-to-shore coordination of air and naval fire support.

Most later agreed that navy leaders had exaggerated the destructive potential of naval bombardment. Rear Admiral Howard F. Kingman, commander of the fire support group, had reportedly pledged in a briefing, "It is not our intention to wreck the island. We do not intend to destroy it. Gentlemen, we will obliterate it."[73] Remarks in the same vein were attributed to Admiral Hill. It is conceivable that these sentiments were more inspirational than predictive, intended to lift the spirits of the young marines who would launch an unprecedented assault on a heavily defended beach. (Many marines later attested that the tremendous barrage was a boost to morale, if nothing else.) The U.S. Navy had studied the effects of bombardment on strong fortifications, and the limitations were well understood. The battleships' 16-inch high-explosive shells would strike Betio with a terminal velocity of 1,500 feet per second. They would demolish structures above ground, but according to Admiral Hill it was always understood that they would have "doubtful penetrating power."[74] Indeed, during the first morning's bombardment, many of the naval projectiles hit the island at too shallow an angle—some were observed to ricochet and bound off into the sea.

That was not to say that the naval barrage had done no good at all. At a stateside lecture in January 1944, General Edson (newly promoted) enumerated the results: "They did take out the coast defense guns during that two and a half hours before H-hour," he said. "They did take out the antiaircraft guns. They took out or neutralized a certain percentage of the anti-boat guns, but they took out practically none of the beach defenses, emplacements which have your machine guns, some of the 37mm, anti-boat guns and rifles. The bombardment also completely disrupted the communications set-up on the island."[75]

News of the losses suffered at Tarawa caused a minor public imbroglio at home. General Vandegrift, newly appointed commandant of the Marine Corps, made the controversial decision to allow publication of photographs depicting dead marines strewn along Beach Red 2. No such photographs had previously appeared in the American press. Compared to the carnage occurring elsewhere in the world, 3,000 casualties in three days was not an inordinate loss. But the American people received the news with some shock. Pointed questions were raised in the press and in Congress. What was the strategic importance of Tarawa? Was the toll worth it? Had the marines or the navy botched the job? Holland Smith stoked the controversy by offering some pointed on-the-record observations to reporters. The navy had failed to provide adequate numbers of amtracs, he said, and the prein-vasion naval bombardment had been deficient. He compared the assault at Tarawa to Pickett's charge at the Battle of Gettysburg. MacArthur, always attuned to stateside politics, offered oblique comments to the effect that good commanders do not allow their forces to suffer needlessly high casual-ties. As usual, these criticisms were echoed and amplified in William Ran-dolph Hearst's national newspaper chain.

The commotion quickly reverberated from Washington back to Pearl Harbor. On December 14, King penned an angry memo to Nimitz, dressing the CINCPAC down for failing to release timely information in conjunc-tion with his reports. King had been obliged to reply to "editorial com-ment, radio broadcasts, and remarks in Congress" concerning the navy's lack of support for the marines. The COMINCH was vexed by Holland Smith's public claim that he had not received as many landing craft as he had requested. Likening Tarawa to Pickett's charge was foolish, not least because one was a victory and the other a debacle. In that vein, King com-plained that Nimitz's censors were passing stories that reported heavy casu-alties "without even mentioning the fact that it was victory."[76]

Nimitz also heard directly from parents and wives of some of the slain marines. "You killed my son on Tarawa," a mother wrote from Arkansas. The CINCPAC insisted on reading and answering all such letters. He told Lamar, "This is one of the responsibilities of command. You have to send some people to their deaths."[77]

With the prominent exception of Holland Smith, navy and marine leaders closed ranks in support of one another and defended the overall conduct of Operation GALVANIC. General Vandegrift insisted that the American people must be "steeled" to the inevitable costs of war. Tarawa, he said, had been "the first true amphibious assault of all time," an operation that "validated the principle of the amphibious assault, a tactic proclaimed impossible by many military experts." As for the casualties: "Of course it was costly—we all knew it would be, for war is costly."[78] The real lesson of Tarawa was that the Japanese were doomed, for they could no longer feel secure on any island, no matter how strongly fortified and defended.

Julian Smith emphatically denied that the losses could be attributed to any clearly avoidable deficiency or tactical error. "It was a grand scrap, well-planned and hard-fought. If I had to do it over again, there's no single thing that I could do better."[79] Writing to a friend back in the States, Smith judged that "our naval gunfire was magnificent as well as our air support. Our intelligence was far better than we can expect in most attacks. So far as I'm concerned there were no surprises in the whole operation."[80] Writing to another friend on Christmas Day, Smith opined that the casualties suffered on Tarawa were in fact "very light."[81] Admiral Spruance, who had personally argued for taking the Gilberts, always insisted that the conquest of Tarawa was absolutely necessary despite the costs.[82] As the picture became clearer, influential voices in the American press endorsed that view. Tarawa was only the first of several such island battles to come, warned a *New York Times* editorial on December 27, 1943: "We must steel ourselves now to pay that price."[83]

Holland Smith, alone among the major commanders of GALVANIC, concluded that Tarawa had been a misadventure and that the Gilberts should have been bypassed altogether. He said it plainly, and was the only one to do so: "Tarawa was a mistake."[84] With this, Smith breached a powerful taboo. No one wanted to hear that young American lives had been thrown away to no good purpose. But the retroactive case against GALVANIC, iconoclastic though it was, did not and does not warrant a back-of-the-hand dismissal. With a further buildup of forces, the Pacific Fleet could have penetrated directly into the Marshalls, bypassing the Gilberts. Such an operation would have become feasible by February 1944, just three months after GALVANIC. Whether Betio's airfield would remain a threat to sea communications is arguable, but without possession of the Marshalls the Japanese would have encountered great difficulties in keeping the island supplied with aircraft, parts, fuel, and other needed supplies. Ernest King's determination to get the central Pacific offensive underway before the end of 1943 had certainly carried weight in the decision to go through the Gilberts.

When the question was put to him many years later, Julian Smith was philosophical: "Well, I think it was just one of those things. War is war." Whether Tarawa could have been safely bypassed or not, it was a victory. The navy and marines had learned valuable lessons that would be put to profitable use in future operations. If the Americans had not made those mistakes at Tarawa, they would have made them in the Marshalls, suffering proportionally higher casualties in the latter as a result. And the bloody conquest of Tarawa had proved an important point to both sides in the conflict. Japan's grand strategy rested on the supposition that the American people would not stand for the losses required in a long war. But Tarawa served notice to the enemy that no price was too high, "and every one of those islands that they were fortifying became a base for us to bomb Japan and to carry the war farther on."[85]

IN ACCORDANCE WITH SPRUANCE'S PLAN, Baldy Pownall had stationed his aircraft carriers (Task Force 50) in defensive zones northwest of the Gilberts. Remarkably, the sprawling armada of flattops and screening vessels managed to steal into these enemy-dominated waters undetected by either submarine or air patrols.[86] Beginning at dawn on November 19, airstrikes rained destruction down on Japanese airfields and installations throughout the region. Fighter and bombing squadrons returned from Tarawa and Makin with inflated estimates of the damage inflicted on Japanese defenses, and were later chagrined to learn of the bloodbath on Betio. Their impressions, they realized, had been far too optimistic.

Pownall's flagship, the *Yorktown*, was skippered by his erstwhile detractor Jocko Clark. She was at the center of Task Group 50.1, which included her sister the *Lexington* and the light carrier *Cowpens*. On the morning of the landings at Tarawa and Makin, the three air groups concentrated their attention on the two largest airfields in the eastern Marshalls, on the atolls of Jaluit and Mille. TBF Avengers were employed as glide-bombers, armed with 1,000-pound bombs. One scored a direct hit on an ammunition dump at Mille, sending an awe-inspiring mushroom cloud up through the cloud ceiling. "We demolished the place," said Ralph Hanks of VF-16, the *Lexington*'s fighter squadron. "There was little or no aircraft opposition."[87] *Yorktown*'s hardworking Hellcat squadron (VF-5) flew combat air patrols and antisubmarine patrols over the carriers. Many pilots completed three or four flights before nightfall on D-Day.

Admiral Koga's Operation Z had envisioned hard-hitting naval and air counterattacks on just such an offensive as GALVANIC, but the situation in the South Pacific did not permit committing any major part of the Combined Fleet to defend the Gilberts. Koga was still mainly concerned with the two-headed threat to Rabaul. American intelligence indications of a fleet moving out of Truk turned out to be a red herring. But the big airfields in Kwajalein Atoll were plentifully supplied with medium bombers, and the submarine threat remained a source of serious concern. On the afternoon of D-Day, radio eavesdroppers on the *Yorktown* intercepted a Japanese transmission ordering more submarines into the area, and (as a *Yorktown* air officer noted in his diary) "for land-based bombers on Kwajalein to find us and attack as soon as possible."[88] Mitsubishi G4M (Allied code name "Betty") units promptly began leapfrogging east and south, down the archipelago of Japan's island airbases. Pownall and his commanders expected night attacks by G4Ms armed with aerial torpedoes, and knew also that the enemy bombers would approach at wave-top altitude in order to avoid early radar detection. As anticipated, blips began appearing on radar screens shortly after sunset.

From the start of the war, the Japanese had proved to be more adept in fighting at night, whether on the sea or in the air. Few American aviators had even attempted to land aboard a carrier after nightfall. Defending ships against night air attacks was a relatively new problem, and the Americans were groping toward tactical innovations to meet the threat. Each of Pownall's task groups stationed a single destroyer about fifteen to twenty miles west of the center of the formation to act as a radar picket. Aboard each task group's flag carrier, the Combat Information Center (CIC) tracked bogeys and vectored fighters to intercept them. But it was immensely difficult to see the darkened enemy planes, and the Hellcats did not often get an opportunity to engage them. Later, as radar-directed antiaircraft fire grew more sophisticated, ships learned to shoot down night attackers sight unseen. In November 1943, that technology remained in its infancy. "At that time we didn't have night fighters," said Truman Hedding. "The Japanese Betties would come in just at evening dusk, just as it was getting dark, and we couldn't do anything about it. They would fly around and drop torpedoes at us, and they were getting us too, now and then."[89]

The G4Ms approached low over the sea, typically flying "down the moon path," as Hedding recalled, so that the target ships were silhouetted in moonlight.[90] Under such conditions, the rectangular profile of an aircraft carrier was instantly recognized. If the ships were traveling at speeds above 10 knots, they left long fluorescent wakes that were as good as illuminated arrows pointing to their locations. On the night of November 20, Pownall ordered Task Group 50.1 to slow to 8 knots in hopes of rendering it invisible from the air. That ruse involved a dangerous trade-off—if the enemy pilots spotted the slow-moving fleet, the carriers would make easy targets.

Task Group 50.3, about forty miles south, bore the worst of the night's attack. About fourteen torpedo-armed G4Ms got through the screening ships and dropped their fish at close range. One struck the starboard quarter of the light carrier *Independence*. She suffered heavy casualties and major damage and had to withdraw for repairs. The crew managed to make her seaworthy enough to limp back to Funafuti. From there she was sent back to San Francisco for extensive repairs. She did not get back into the war until the following July.

At dawn on the twenty-first, the *Yorktown* and *Lexington* air groups returned to Mille, where they bombed the airstrips and other installations as they had the previous day. Japanese air units were staging through the island, and each time the Americans returned, it seemed that the Japanese had more planes on the ground and circling overhead. In the afternoon, Captain Hedding (Pownall's chief of staff) ordered the *Yorktown*'s fighter squadron to fly a reconnaissance mission over Mille to determine how many bombers remained. Commander Charlie Crommelin, VF-5's skipper, volunteered to lead a group of eight Hellcats on the flight.

Hedding's orders were to observe and report, not to attack—but Crommelin elected to fly low over the Japanese airfield on the pretense of taking a closer look. He strafed a G4M as it taxied toward the runway, and set it afire. He banked and came around for another strafing run. Before he reached the edge of the field, Crommelin's cockpit was hit directly by a 20mm anti-aircraft shell. The blast destroyed most of his instruments and shattered his Plexiglas canopy. Crommelin suffered severe shrapnel wounds in his face, neck, chest, and right arm. He lost all vision in his left eye and could barely see through his right. The windshield was intact, but a spider-web pattern of cracks obscured visibility. Crommelin, barely able to see through the blood, managed to open his canopy so that he could look out of the right side of the cockpit. He leveled off at 300 feet. A wingman flew alongside and escorted the skipper 120 miles back to the *Yorktown*. The chances of a successful recovery seemed dubious, but Crommelin made a perfect approach, snagged an arresting cable, and then taxied forward to the parking area and shut his engine down. While trying to hoist himself out of the cockpit, he collapsed. Jocko Clark's action report noted, "He was lifted from the cockpit in a semiconscious condition, suffering from severe shock and loss of blood."[91] Crommelin was carried down to sickbay on a stretcher. His left eye was saved. After a lengthy recuperation in the United States, he was reassigned and flew again.

Aerial torpedo attacks continued almost every night, depriving the crews of rest. On the *Yorktown*, Clark told the officers on duty to awaken him each time a strange plane appeared on radar. Depending on its location, course, and speed, Clark would decide whether to arise and return to the bridge in pajamas to take the conn.

During these frequent night attacks on Task Force 50, the Combat Information Centers on the various carriers were scenes of intense activity and nervous tension. Green blips moved across the radar screens, sometimes turning and approaching the center of the screen. A plane making a torpedo run would approach at high speed and then bank sharply away. At that moment the operators could assume that a torpedo was in the water. "Those minutes seemed like years, when you are sitting there waiting to see whether you're going to get hit," recalled Fitzhugh Lee, an officer on the *Lexington*. "CIC was not a happy place to be." Most of the young radar operators did their jobs with icy skill. Now and again a man would break down under the strain. "We had a few who lost control of themselves and started weeping, crying, praying, and things like that."[92] Whenever it happened, Lee relieved the man at once, lest his hysteria spread and cause a general contagion.

Despite having suffered two consecutive days of heavy air losses, the Japanese doggedly hurled their remaining land-based bombers against Task Force 50. November 23 was another long day of furious air combat. The *Lexington*'s fighters (VF-16), flying combat air patrol, intercepted an inbound airstrike and shot down seventeen of the nineteen intruders. The next day, the same squadron claimed another dozen enemy planes. Lieutenant (jg) Ralph Hanks, an Iowa pig farmer before the war, became an "ace in a day" by shooting down five Zeros in a single skirmish. In a fifteen-minute air engagement, his throttle never left the firewall and his Hellcat surpassed 400 knots in a diving attack. Hanks had to stand on his rudder pedals and use his entire upper-body strength to keep his stick under control. Intense g-forces caused him to black out several times. This first massed encounter of Zeros and Hellcats did not bode well for the future of the now-obsolete Japanese fighter plane.

The instinctive rivalry between the *Yorktown* and *Lexington* air groups was stoked by the former's perception that the *Lexington*'s fighters were always lucky to be aloft when the enemy appeared. VF-5, gloated the pilots of VF-16, had been "skunked." Captain Clark, competitive as he was, sent a genial signal to the *Lexington*'s skipper, Felix Stump: "Well, you've beat us out so far. I hope we have better luck next time."[93]

Late-afternoon sorties often required night recoveries, and in these situations returning airmen tended to look for any friendly flight deck. Cases of mistaken identity were endemic among the *Essex*-class carrier air groups because the ships were built on identical lines and were difficult to tell apart even in daylight. *Yorktown* planes landed on the *Lexington* on the evenings of November 22 and 23, and in each case the pilots were not aware of the mismatch until they climbed out of their cockpits.

Heavy thunderheads moved into the area late that afternoon, and Pownall ordered all planes aloft to recover and secure. Five FM-1 Wildcat fighters from the *Liscome Bay* (which would be destroyed the following morning) lost their way in the squall and could not pick up their ship's YE homing beacon. They flew west and radioed the *Yorktown* to ask permission to land aboard and return to their carrier the next day. Clark, after consulting with Pownall, assented.

The planes entered the landing circle as the last light drained out of the western sky. The first three FM-1s landed without mishap. The pilot of the fourth forgot to lower his tailhook and was given a wave-off by the landing signal officer. The pilot ignored or did not see the wave-off, came down hard, bounced, gunned his throttle in an apparent bid to get airborne and come around for another try, then came down again and somersaulted over the crash barrier. Several parked planes were destroyed, and four plane pushers were killed immediately. The crashed plane burst into fire, and the flames quickly spread to engulf most of the flight deck amidships. Within twenty seconds the crew had foam hoses on the fire, but the parked planes had been gassed up and armed for morning launch, and their tanks and ammunition went up in a chain of explosions. Magnesium flares ignited and lit up the ship and the sea all around her with an intense yellow light. The wing gun magazines of the parked F6Fs began firing their .50-caliber rounds, forcing the fire brigade to duck and take cover.[94]

Clark kept the ship headed into the wind to prevent the fire from spreading to as-yet-undamaged planes parked farther forward. "The intense heat was almost unbearable on the island superstructure," he later wrote. "If the island caught fire, navigation and ship control would be nearly impossible."[95] Clark shouted over the noise to direct the firefighting efforts. "I remember Captain Clark leaning over the navigation bridge, directing the firefighters doing a remarkable job to save the ship," Truman Hedding later recalled.[96] Men in asbestos suits dragged hoses directly into the heart of the conflagration and spread a 3-inch layer of Foamite throughout the stricken area. Tractors towed burning planes to the edge of the flight deck, where they were shoved overboard. The fire burned for half an hour before it was entirely extinguished at 7:05 p.m. Remarkably, the *Yorktown* had suffered no serious damage and resumed normal flight operations the next morning.[97] Several firefighters received commendations for their courage and initiative.

Task Force 50 had done plenty of damage to Japanese airpower in the eastern Marshalls, but the aviators agreed that more could have been accomplished. The brownshoes shared a growing conviction that the carriers were not being properly deployed. With newer and better airplanes and ships, the carrier forces could and should accept more risks. Hedding, years later, offered tactfully measured criticism: "I think there was a tendency to be rather conservative and a little careful of what might happen. We didn't want to have our ships damaged."[98] Clark was blunter: "The fallacy of confining carriers to defense sectors had cost us one carrier sunk, another put out of action, and many lives lost."[99] The blackshoe admirals at the top of the command chain, in Clark's view, had been slow to understand the capabilities of the new fast carrier forces, and the only remedy was to promote aviators into senior policy-making jobs in Washington and Pearl Harbor.

On November 26, with Tarawa firmly in American hands and most of the Fifth Fleet bound for Pearl Harbor, Nimitz released the carriers from their defensive positions and recommended that they raid Kwajalein (where about sixty torpedo planes were thought to be) and other enemy bases in the northern Marshalls. Four heavy cruisers joined up with Pownall's force, and new planes flew over from the departing escort carriers and landed aboard to replace losses. Rear Admiral J. L. "Reggie" Kauffman was sent aboard the *Yorktown* as an observer; his assignment was to watch Pownall and report to Nimitz on his performance.

Shortly after sunset that evening, another round of air attacks fell on the northbound task force. Two G4Ms approached to within a mile of the *Yorktown* and dropped flares onto the sea, apparently as a guidepost for other attackers. Pownall again slowed the task group to reduce the visibility of its wakes. The main attack instead fell on the *Enterprise* and her consorts (Task Group 50.2), some twenty miles west.

The *Enterprise* Air Group commander was Butch O'Hare, the famed fighter pilot who had become the navy's first flying ace in February 1942 by destroying five Japanese planes in a single flight. The deed had earned him the Medal of Honor. O'Hare and colleagues had improvised a night fighting "Bat Team" consisting of two Hellcats and a single TBF Avenger equipped with an airborne radar system. Their tactic was to send the three planes out on a vector provided by the fighter director officer (FDO). The Avenger would follow its radar bearings to the intruders. The fighter pilots would fly wing on the larger plane, peering through the darkness in hopes of glimpsing the enemy's exhaust flames. If the fighters made visual contact, they would break off and attack.

As a solution to the threat of night attacks, the Bat Team concept was makeshift and provisional. Better tactics would have to await improved technology and much more training. In November 1943, however, it was the only solution at hand.

When radar screens in the *Enterprise's* Combat Information Center discovered inbound bogeys, just before 6:00 p.m. on November 26, the carrier launched two Hellcats (one piloted by O'Hare, the other by Ensign Andy Skon) and sent them on a heading to intercept. The radar-equipped TBF Avenger, launched a few minutes later, would follow and rendezvous with the two fighters, or so it was hoped, nearer to the approaching enemy formation. This was to be the first combat trial of Bat Team tactics. The TBF was piloted by Lieutenant Commander John C. Phillips, skipper of the carrier's torpedo bombing squadron (VT-6). The bomber also carried a radar specialist, Lieutenant Hazen Rand, and a third man, ordnanceman and gunner Alvin B. Kernan, who would describe the flight in his postwar memoir, *Crossing the Line*.

The venture was anarchic from start to finish. The *Enterprise's* FDO did his level best not only to guide the three planes toward a rendezvous, but also to give new bearings directing them toward the targets that showed up intermittently on the ship's radar. About an hour after O'Hare left the ship, the FDO radioed to say that he appeared to be directly among "many bogeys," but neither O'Hare nor Skon could see anything at all. The *Enterprise* radar also showed Phillips within a mile of the two Hellcats, but neither the fighter pilots nor the crew of the Avenger could see any sign of the other. They and the Japanese were all adrift in a deadly game of blind man's buff.

Kernan, peering out of the TBF's gun turret, lost all sense of the horizon. "You stare out into the dark night, and after a time you don't know up from down. The first few turns are okay, but then disorientation begins. A flicker of light could be a star in the sky or a ship on the ocean or another plane coming at you on a fast angle."[100] Occasionally he saw a flare burning in the distance, presumably dropped by enemy planes, or a burst of antiaircraft fire from one of the American ships. The FDO continued to relay headings to Phillips, and Rand obtained intermittent returns on his radar scope. A few minutes after 7:00 p.m., Rand reported a large cluster of six blips about three miles ahead. Phillips gave chase and Rand called out the diminishing range—three miles, two miles, one mile, a thousand yards. At 400 yards, Phillips saw the telltale blue exhaust flames, and radioed, "I have them in sight. Attacking."[101]

Phillips's decision to attack was not in line with Bat Team doctrine. The TBF did not possess either the maneuverability or the firepower to take on a large formation of heavily armed bombers. But Phillips did enjoy the advantage of complete surprise—the Japanese had never been challenged by carrier planes at night, and had no reason to anticipate such an attack. As the TBF overtook the formation, Phillips could make out the long cigar-shaped outline of the darkened planes. He opened fire on the rightmost G4M with his two fixed .50-caliber machine guns and apparently struck the gas tanks at the vulnerable wing root, because the plane immediately caught fire. Phillips pulled up and left, mindful that the other planes would return fire promptly; as Kernan's turret gun came to bear, he opened fire in turn, aiming at the flames. "He blew up all at once," wrote Kernan. "A long trail of fire went down and down into the blackness of the ocean below, where it kept on burning, a red smear on the black water."[102] The Japanese, surprised and flustered, apparently began exchanging fire among themselves. Their tracer lines struck out at one another, but they did not come near the Avenger as it pulled away to safety.

O'Hare and Skon saw the G4M go down and turned toward the melee. This brought them within visual range of the TBF and the remaining enemy bombers. O'Hare, wary of firing on the wrong aircraft, asked Phillips to turn on his recognition light. Phillips flashed it, briefly. The Japanese planes apparently saw the light and opened fire, striking the Avenger's underbelly and wounding Rand; at the same time, Phillips fired back. Again, he scored; and again, Kernan poured more fire into the burning wing. The G4M went down in a long controlled dive, apparently attempting a water landing. It left an extended trail of burning fuel on the ocean.

In the melee the Hellcats and the TBF again lost contact, but they were coached into a rendezvous by the *Enterprise* FDO. All three planes turned on their recognition lights long enough to slide into formation, the two fighters above and behind either wing of the Avenger. For the first and last time that night, the three American planes were flying in formation as planned. Kernan caught a glimpse of Butch O'Hare's face, lit up by his canopy light. His canopy was open and his goggles pushed back on his head.

About a minute after the three American aircraft had lit themselves up, a fourth aircraft closed in from behind on the starboard side. It was a wayward Mitsubishi that had become separated from its formation and had mistaken the American planes for friends. Realizing his mistake, he opened fire and struck O'Hare's plane. Kernan fired back and may or may not have hit the enemy plane, which veered sharply away to port.

O'Hare's plane was gone, and he did not respond to radio hails. "Something whitish-gray appeared in the distance," wrote Kernan, "his parachute or the splash of the plane going in."[103] Skon rejoined with difficulty, and the two American planes circled the area at low altitude. There was no sign of O'Hare. At about 9:00 they headed back toward the *Enterprise*, tracking the ship by following its long fluorescent wake. The carrier turned on the hooded flight deck lights that could be seen only from aft and above. Remarkably, both Phillips and Skon recovered safely, without damage to their planes. Dawn searches by carrier planes, a PBY seaplane, and a destroyer turned up no sign of O'Hare or his aircraft.

O'Hare's loss was headline news in the United States. He was one of the most famous flyers in the American armed forces, a singular hero to Irish Americans, and one of the most respected and best-liked men in the carrier navy. A Solemn Pontifical Mass of Requiem was held at the Basilica of Saint Louis in Missouri. O'Hare received a posthumous Navy Cross and gave his name to the busiest commercial airport in the world.

Sorrow tended to obscure the fact that this first attempt to use carrier fighters against a nighttime air attack had been a success. The Americans had shot down two and possibly three twin-engine medium bombers at the cost of one fighter. Phillips was credited with destroying two G4Ms, and it is likely that Kernan shot down a third. (No one saw what happened to the Betty that shot down O'Hare, but the Japanese recorded three planes lost.) No American ship had been struck by a torpedo.

Two task groups, 50.1 and 50.2, now churned north through squalls and scud to attack the source of the persistent night attackers—the enemy's huge airfields on the atoll of Kwajalein. Jocko Clark met with Truman Hedding and the *Yorktown* squadron leaders to devise new procedures for defense against night attacks, and promised his fighter pilots that if they were unable to land on the ship at night he would pick them up at sea. Two new Bat Teams drilled for hours in daylight.

Launching and recovering the three-plane sections tended to derange the task force's cruising formation, and getting the ship back into its assigned position at the center of the screen gave Clark (and Pownall) plenty of heartburn. Clark reluctantly concluded that his air group was not ready to operate at night. If attacked, the *Yorktown* would have to rely on her anti-aircraft guns and her helm.

The endless series of attacks, day and night, threatened to exhaust the crews of the several carriers and their cruising ships. Airedales curled up on deck in the passageways around the hangar and caught an hour of sleep whenever they could.

The two task groups rendezvoused on December 1, several hundred miles northeast of the Marshalls. At a shipboard conference on the *Yorktown*, Pownall declined suggestions that he launch a fighter sweep over Kwajalein on December 3, returning with a full airstrike on December 4; he chose the less risky option of sending everything in his arsenal against the atoll at dawn on December 4, and beating a quick retreat that afternoon. The task force commenced a high-speed approach toward the heart of the Marshalls, and against expectations arrived at its launch point at dawn on December 4 without any sign of being detected by enemy air patrols.

The six carriers began launching their fighters and bombers at 6:30 a.m. Lieutenant Commander Edgar E. Stebbins, who had been tapped by Clark to replace the slain O'Hare as *Yorktown*'s air group commander, was first over the atoll about ninety minutes later. He counted thirty ships in the lagoon, including two cruisers. The strike had caught the Japanese by complete surprise. Only a handful of Zeros were at altitude, and all were quickly destroyed by the F6F squadrons. John C. Phillips, piloting the same TBF Avenger that he had flown in the successful night action a week earlier, soared above the atoll at 20,000 feet. From that commanding height, Kernan recalled, the atoll "spread out before us in an enormous boomerang of narrow white-beached islands, with a big lagoon in the center, dark blue here, light there."[104] Phillips took inventory of targets ashore or in the lagoon and directed the bombers in his squadron to attack them in turn. "Black antiaircraft bursts rocked the plane," wrote Kernan, "and the fighter planes taking off from Roi-Namur far below seemed more interesting than ominous."[105]

TBF Avengers glide-bombed the anchored ships and sank three transports. Heavy flak perforated many of the sturdy planes, but none were destroyed. Hellcats strafed a seaplane base at Ebeye, setting more than a dozen Kawanishis afire. At least two dozen Zeros scrambled as the initial strike was underway, and chased the retreating bombers into the north. Tail-gunners took down several more Zeros during the flight back to the carriers.

The morning strike returned to the task force singly or in isolated groups of two or three. For more than an hour Pownall's ships steamed into the wind and recovered planes. Nearly the entire American strike returned safely to the task force. The exceptions were few. Just two F6Fs were shot down in the morning's action. A gang of about ten Zeros pounced on VF-5 commander Ed Owen, whose plane was thoroughly shot up as it dived to escape. Owen pointed his nose north, but his instruments had shorted out and he began losing altitude. His engine conked out, and he deadsticked down toward the sea, intending to try a water landing. But the sea below was rutted with daunting waves, and Owen thought it unlikely that he could ditch safely. He unbuckled, pushed himself out of the cockpit, pulled his chute, and hit the water. Floating alone on the sea, he wondered whether he was finished, but a destroyer presently came over the horizon and picked him up. He was back aboard the *Yorktown* in time for lunch.

The Japanese air groups on Kwajalein had been badly roughed up, but they had fought with their familiar determination and persistence, and there was every reason to expect a fierce counterstrike on Task Force 50. Ed Stebbins reconnoitered and photographed a large airfield on Roi that appeared to have been left completely unmolested. He counted about sixty apparently undamaged G4Ms parked on the field. These long-legged bombers could be expected to attack the task force, either that afternoon or after dark. Stebbins radioed the *Yorktown* to urge that another strike be launched against the field in hopes of destroying the planes on the ground. A Combat Information Center officer hand-carried the message up to Pownall on the flag bridge.

After conferring with Admiral Kauffman, Pownall rendered his decision—he would not order another strike on Kwajalein. The plan of operations, agreed several days earlier, had called for an afternoon strike against Wotje, which lay about 150 miles east. That strike would be recovered as the task force ran north at its highest effective cruising speed. Adding another strike on Kwajalein would keep the carriers within that atoll's air-striking range for another twenty-four hours. Pownall did not want to push his luck, and saw no reason to upend the existing plan.

By his own account, Jocko Clark was "dumbfounded" and could barely contain his fury. As the *Yorktown*'s air squadron leaders landed aboard and reported to the bridge, all pleaded to lead their planes in another attack on Kwajalein. Clark beseeched Pownall: "You'd better get back there and knock out those Bettys, or they'll come and get you!"[106] Pownall listened with diminishing patience. The strike on Kwajalein was to have been a hit-and-run raid. Clark and his aviators put emphasis on the "hit," while Pownall was more concerned with the "run." The admiral summarily ordered his flag captain to prepare the strike on Wotje as planned. The task force was going to clear out, and it would defend against the inevitable counterstrikes as they came.

The first wave of intruders arrived shortly before noon—a group of single-engine Nakajima B5N torpedo planes ("Kates"). They approached at low altitude in order to stay off the American radar screens and avoid the F6Fs orbiting high above. The screening ships opened fire as they came into range, and the sky was mottled with black flak bursts. One went down just off the *Yorktown*'s starboard quarter. *Lexington* skipper Felix Stump steered sharply to starboard to avoid a torpedo, which very nearly clipped the ship's port bow. The surviving bombers turned away and ran for home, and the antiaircraft guns fell silent. Less than an hour later, another wave of Kates came skimming in from the south. The antiaircraft fire started up again, and the F6Fs, having come down from altitude to repel the first wave, now shot down all but four of the attackers. One dropped a torpedo on the *Lexington*, missing widely. The three others flew over and around the cruiser *San Francisco* and bored in toward the *Yorktown*. The carriers' short-range antiaircraft guns opened fire, narrowly missing the cruiser. One Nakajima went down, then another; a third flew on toward the carrier, its wing guns strafing the flight deck and its rear guns firing back at the *San Francisco*. Clark stood on the bridge and shouted to his gunners to destroy the plane. They did not need to be coaxed. Three different calibers of fire (40mm,

20mm, and 5 inch) converged on the lone plane as it came level with the catwalk of the *Yorktown*. As the line of fire passed across the *San Francisco*, Admiral Pownall leaned out and shouted from the flag bridge: "Cease fire! Cease fire! You are firing at that cruiser!"[107]

Once again, Clark was speechless. Did the admiral not see that an enemy torpedo plane was bearing down on the *Yorktown*? He pretended not to have heard the order. "I heard it all right but I didn't obey it, because I wasn't about to let that plane hit me."[108] When the Nakajima was less than 150 yards away, a 40mm shell connected with its left wing root and tore the wing off. The plane crashed into the sea just astern of the *Yorktown*. The landing signal officer, who had flung himself prone to avoid a strafing attack, stood up and mockingly raised his paddles to make the signal for a "perfect landing."

Photographer's Mate Al Cooperman, stationed in the catwalk, had captured the moment that the enemy plane was struck by 40mm fire. The photograph, one of the most famous of the Pacific War, depicted the aircraft disintegrating in midair. Clark ordered a copy distributed to each member of the crew. *Life* magazine later featured the photo as its "Picture of the Week."[109]

Task Force 50 had needed more than a little luck to escape serious damage, and all were unnerved by the sudden appearance of two waves of attackers in broad daylight. The *Yorktown*'s gunners had peppered the *San Francisco* badly, killing one man and injuring twenty-two. Her skipper, A. Finley France Jr., knew that the friendly fire was unavoidable and deliberately did not report the incident out of consideration for Clark's chances of promotion to flag rank. Pownall apparently drew the same conclusion, because he never raised the issue of Clark's failure to obey his order to cease fire.

The task force launched a large combat air patrol and braced itself for more attacks. Clark would have liked to turn the formation around and launch another strike against Kwajalein, but Pownall was definitively committed to getting his ships out of there. At three in the afternoon, the Wotje strike returned and landed aboard. The task force rang up 25 knots and raced north. The weather was now working against the Americans. The destroyers labored heavily in rough seas, forcing Pownall to slow the entire task force to 18 knots. In addition, the sky was clear and visibility unimpeded, offering the fleeing ships no opportunity to hide from aerial snoopers.

Clark was thoroughly disgusted with Pownall's decision to run. The midday air attack, in his view, had proved his point that the task force should have remained off Kwajalein and slugged it out with the Japanese. He repeatedly smashed his fist down on the chart table and exclaimed, "Goddamn it, you can't run away from airplanes with ships!"[110]

Those sixty-odd G4Ms on Roi had not yet appeared, but they could be expected to attack in darkness. Sure enough, the radar screens began to light up shortly before sunset. They depicted a large number of blips flying in expanding search squares. At 7:45 p.m., Bettys and Kates first made contact with the *Essex* group. For the next several hours, wave after wave of enemy planes tracked the ships, dropped parachute flares, and launched torpedoes. What followed, as recorded in the *Essex* cruise book, was "the longest sustained night torpedo attack of the war to date. For seven and a half hours, enemy planes were continually pressing attacks, and *Essex* personnel remained at battle stations until two o'clock the next morning—almost 24 hours after starting the attack on the atoll."[111] Antiaircraft fire repeatedly lit up the sky in a fantastic spectacle and took down dozens of attackers. A three-quarter moon rose in the east and illuminated the task force and its long white wakes. Many torpedoes missed narrowly; no ship in the group was hit.

The cruisers *New Orleans* and *Oakland* steamed directly ahead and astern of the *Yorktown*. The formation turned sharply and in unison, starboard and port, as the attackers bored in toward the center, always aiming for the high rectangular shape of the big carriers. Two torpedoes missed the *Yorktown* narrowly—one astern and the other across the bow. When radar tracked a very large wave approaching from the south, Captain Sol Phillips of the *Oakland* asked permission to drop back, light up the ship, and draw off the attackers. The request was granted, and the *Oakland* doggedly shot down perhaps a dozen G4Ms with her formidable antiaircraft weaponry. At a few minutes after 11:23 p.m., several flares appeared to port, and another G4M penetrated the outer screen to the northeastward. As the plane roared in, just 15 feet above the sea, the big antiaircraft guns held fire for fear of hitting American ships. Clark ordered a hard right turn into the teeth of the attack. The plane released its torpedo at about 1,000 yards off the starboard bow, then zoomed low over the *Yorktown*'s flight deck. The torpedo ran straight but Clark had time to steer away, and it crossed the bow with ample room to spare. The retreating plane was taken down by the carrier's port-side guns. Another followed, also flying over the *Yorktown*, its machine-gun tracers cutting a path across the flight deck, and flew on toward the *Lexington*. The plane made a good drop and veered away. About twenty seconds later, a powerful blast sent a tower of flame up the *Lexington*'s stern. She lost steering control and was forced to reduce speed. Pownall immediately ordered the entire task force to slow, and the screening ships closed around the wounded ship.

The attackers continued to come on, singly or in pairs, and pierced the outer destroyer screen every few minutes. A wall of flak met any plane that approached within 2,000 yards of the *Lexington*. The volume and accuracy of the antiaircraft fire apparently dampened the pilots' spirits, because many G4Ms seemed to turn away early, or made premature and poorly aimed torpedo drops. The *Lexington*'s crew rigged emergency steering gear and had her underway shortly after midnight.

The moon set at 1:27 a.m., and the attacks petered out. By two, there was no sign of enemy planes in sight or on the radar screens. The task force secured from quarters and continued north at high speed. The gunners curled up on deck and slept next to their weapons. A large combat air patrol launched at dawn, and the task force braced itself for another air attack, but none came. At last they were out of range.

Clark was exhausted and on edge. He was relieved to have avoided a crippling torpedo hit, but deeply disappointed by the task force's failure to destroy enemy airpower in the Marshalls, a goal he believed might have been achieved with more vigorous tactics.

During the three-day run back to Pearl Harbor, Clark hatched a strategy to oust Baldy Pownall from his job as commander of the fast carrier task force. He and several members of his staff penned a memorandum laying out the case against Pownall, citing several specific decisions that had betrayed a lack of aggressiveness. This paper, which was not signed, would be circulated among senior officers on the CINCPAC staff. Clark also collected aerial photographs of the G4Ms parked on the airfield at Roi. Even after having seen the photos, Pownall had ruled against urgent bids to return and pulverize the planes before they could attack the fleet. The memorandum did not directly address the issue of Pownall's nerve, but in conversations with colleagues Clark denounced the admiral as a "yellow son of a bitch."[112]

Clark went even further. An air intelligence officer on his staff, Lieutenant Herman Rosenblatt, was well-connected in Washington. Rosenblatt had been an attorney in his civilian life prior to joining the navy, and had done legal work for the Roosevelt family. He knew the president and first lady and was personally close to two of their sons. Sam Rosenman, one of FDR's most trusted aides and speechwriters, was Rosenblatt's uncle. With Clark's approval, Rosenblatt phoned the White House from Pearl Harbor and urged that Pownall be transferred out of his command. He then flew back to Washington and spread the complaints about Pownall throughout official Washington.

The campaign verged perilously close to mutiny. It might have easily boomeranged on Clark, perhaps even ruining his hopes of promotion to flag rank. Criticizing one's superior officer behind the scenes was contrary to the "navy way," but opening a back channel to the commander in chief was beyond the pale. In a postwar interview, however, Clark was unrepentant. "I was very fortunate in having a pipeline to the president," he said. "[Pownall] had a chance to score a victory, and he passed it up. I think many commanders make mistakes, and I guess maybe I made some myself, but if you don't have the will to win, you have no business in the war."[113]

Clark's attack on Pownall was probably moot. Nimitz had monitored the admiral's performance closely. Rear Admiral Kauffman, who had been sent along on the mission to observe Pownall firsthand, provided his confidential recommendation that Pownall be relieved. Leading brownshoe admirals in Pearl Harbor, notably John Towers and Forrest Sherman, had already concluded that another man should command the fast carrier task force. Pownall was relieved on January 3, 1944, and replaced by Rear Admiral Marc "Pete" Mitscher, one of the best-liked and most respected senior aviators in the navy.

Nor did Jocko Clark's high jinks do any damage to his career. He received a Silver Star for his performance as captain of the *Yorktown*. On the first day of 1944 he was promoted to rear admiral. A week later he was given command of one of Mitscher's carrier divisions. His flagship was to be the new *Hornet*.

Chapter Twelve

CHESTER NIMITZ WAS NOT ONE TO FLAUNT THE POWER OF HIS towering rank. In presiding over discussions at his headquarters, the CINCPAC was usually content to listen more than he spoke. He elicited the reasoned opinions of planners and commanders; he allowed a full airing of objections and criticisms, unimpeded by a stifling deference to rank or seniority; he shepherded his subordinates toward consensus before fixing his signature to operational orders. Rarely had he overruled his leading advisers, and never over their unanimous opposition.

But on December 7, 1943—the second anniversary of the attack on Pearl Harbor—when the commanders who had recently returned from GALVANIC convened at the conference table in his headquarters, Nimitz announced that he had chosen a daring bypass strategy for the next phase of the central Pacific campaign. The Fifth Fleet would steam directly into the heart of the Marshalls and land amphibious forces on the giant atoll of Kwajalein. Japanese-held atolls and airfields to the south and east—Maloelap, Wotje, Mille, and Jaluit—would be bombed and shelled into oblivion, but they would not be seized until later, if at all.

It was a more ambitious gambit than Ray Spruance, Kelly Turner, or Holland Smith had envisioned, and the three united in resisting it. Spruance was concerned that the islands bypassed to his rear would threaten sea communications from Hawaii and the Gilberts. The Japanese would fly planes into the bypassed airfields and use them to harass the transports and auxiliaries as they attempted to supply the fleet and its new advanced bases. Moreover, the fast carriers had already been assigned to raid Japanese bases to the south, and once they were gone, Spruance would not have enough airpower to maintain pressure on the bypassed airfields. Holland Smith, having returned from the devastation of Tarawa with sharp opinions, wanted to concentrate the entire Amphibious Corps on a single objective in the southeastern Marshalls. He would have two divisions for the next invasion, and did not want them divided.

But Nimitz was paying close attention to intelligence derived from reconnaissance flights and radio intercepts. The Japanese had poured reinforcements into the outer (eastern) Marshalls at the expense of Kwajalein. The latter would be a much easier nut to crack, and the bypassed islands could be tolerably neutralized with steady air pressure and local control of the sea. "We're going into Kwajalein," said Nimitz. "The Japanese aren't expecting us there."[1] The CINCPAC held firm against the objections of his subordinates. When the issues had been fully aired, he implied that if the existing fleet and amphibious commanders didn't want to go into Kwajalein, he would assign the task to others who did.

Nimitz's bold approach was to be vindicated by subsequent events. The Japanese navy did not anticipate the move against Kwajalein. Commander Chikataka Nakajima of the Combined Fleet staff told American interrogators after the war, "There was divided opinion as to whether you would land at Jaluit or Mille. Some thought you would land on Wotje but there were few who thought you would go right to the heart of the Marshalls and take Kwajalein. There were so many possible points of invasion in the Marshalls that we could not consider any one a strong point and consequently dispersed our strength."[2]

Forward fleet bases were to be had in the Marshalls. The region's capacious atolls offered protected anchorages large enough to accommodate the entire Pacific Fleet. Hawaii was thousands of miles behind the front lines and growing steadily more distant with each new westward thrust. The fast carrier task force had extraordinary mobility and reach, but the long voyage back to Pearl Harbor for provisions and repairs cut short its forays and inhibited its seakeeping potential. When operating far to the west of Pearl, Jocko Clark recalled, "you would hit three days at most and go back, so you couldn't hit more than once a month or once every six weeks."[3] With these considerations in mind, Spruance asked for permission to take the atoll of Majuro, 270 miles southeast of Kwajalein. Majuro's large, placid lagoon would offer a protected fueling area and a superb advanced base for the mobile floating logistical forces of Service Squadron Ten. Nimitz assented.

Holland Smith, wary of Japanese defenses on Majuro, was determined not to disperse his landing forces. But the latest and best intelligence indicated that the Japanese had pulled most of their troops out of the atoll. In a December conference at CINCPAC headquarters, Nimitz turned to Ed Layton, the fleet intelligence officer, and said, "Tell General Smith how many Japanese are there, the number you told me this morning."

"Six," Layton replied.

"Six?" Smith said. "You mean six thousand."

"No, six," insisted Layton. Radio eavesdroppers had intercepted a ration report indicating that the remaining garrison on Majuro was consuming six rations per day. Based on that and other intelligence, General Smith was persuaded that a single battalion would be more than sufficient to overrun Majuro.[4]

Nimitz advised Admiral King of his plans on December 14. The operation was given the code name FLINTLOCK, with D-Day on both Kwajalein and Majuro set for January 31, 1944. Spruance would remain as commander of the Fifth Fleet, Turner as commander of Amphibious Forces, and Holland Smith in charge of the assault corps. Task Force 58, which now consisted of twelve carriers embarking more than 700 planes, would establish temporary air supremacy over the entire region. Beginning two days before D-Day, the carrier planes would rain devastation down on the airfields on Kwajalein and those in the southeastern Marshalls.

THE TASK FORCE 58 that put to sea for FLINTLOCK was nearly twice the size of the force that had struck the same atolls less than two months earlier. The armada of flattops and screening ships, 217 vessels in all, had expanded so suddenly and spectacularly that it seemed a different entity altogether, as indeed it was. Veteran dive-bomber pilot Harold Buell, circling above in his SB2C, "could not look over the huge fleet, stretching as far as eye could see, without a shiver going up my spine."[5]

Task Force 58 was now separated into four task groups. Each was a small fleet in itself, steaming in a semi-autonomous circular cruising formation, and commanded by a rear admiral. The task groups remained adjacent to one another, near enough to provide mutual support but far enough apart to avoiding running afoul when conducting flight operations or maneuvering against air attack. As the Iowa-class battleships entered service, they were deployed fore and aft of the carriers at the center of the formations, adding their formidable antiaircraft firepower to the defense of the vulnerable flattops. Most of the battleship admirals were senior to the aviation admirals, and under traditional concepts of seniority they should have run the show—but Nimitz and King had long since decreed that a brownshoe admiral must command each carrier task group, and the rule was adopted without fuss.

"I think that for anyone that participated in the war, there were actually two wars," said Roger Bond, a veteran quartermaster on the *Saratoga*. "If you went out to the Pacific after, let's say, January of 1944, you had a completely different experience and viewpoint than those before, because it really was two different operations."[6] The carrier duels of 1942 had been tense fencing matches in which the fortunes of war had often turned in unexpected directions. Opposing task-force commanders had played cat and mouse with weather fronts, always maneuvering to gain the most tactically favorable position with respect to the enemy. The impulse had always been to stay on the move, to get in and get out, to hit and run. In 1944, Task Force 58 could simply take station off an enemy-held island and batter its airfields into oblivion, brushing off the risk of counterstrikes. The immense size of the task force ensured its omnipotence in whatever part of the ocean it occupied. Hundreds of F6Fs won and maintained complete air superiority through the daylight hours. Improved radar systems and increasingly efficient Combat Information Centers provided ample warning of incoming enemy planes. Screening ships carried more and better antiaircraft weapons, and the introduction of the proximity fuse (which detonated the shell upon detecting the enemy aircraft in proximity) rendered those weapons much more lethal. Destroyers, steaming at the outer edges of the task groups, employed better sonar systems and had refined their tactics against enemy submarines. The remarkable logistical capabilities of Service Squadron Ten permitted the carrier forces to remain at sea for six to eight weeks without putting into any port or anchorage, which in turn expanded their range and mobility. The big ships fueled at sea, took on ammunition at sea, and replenished provisions at sea. Replacement aircraft were ferried out to the western Pacific on jeep carriers and flown aboard whenever they were needed. C. S. King, a chief yeoman on the *Hornet*, spent more than a year and a half on the ship without ever once setting foot on shore. He could have taken liberty at a recreation area on any number of atolls, but never felt the need: "I spent an ungodly amount of time out there in the Pacific without ever leaving the ship. I didn't really notice it. . . . I just felt at home at sea. I really did. I felt like that's what the Navy's all about."[7]

Airstrikes on enemy airfields always commenced with a fighter sweep. Elements of several different Hellcat squadrons coalesced into a tremendous air formation, typically numbering sixty or seventy aircraft. The pilots flew in compact formations, often with little more than 3 or 4 feet between wingtips. They arrived over the target at high altitude and dove on any Japanese fighters that rose to meet them. With decisive advantages in speed, defensive armor, and firepower, the F6Fs made short work of their adversaries. David S. McCampbell, the most prolific navy ace of the Second World War, led his *Essex* Hellcats into several major air battles in 1944. He always made a point of targeting the enemy leaders first—"it may throw the rest of the pilots off a little bit, disrupt the formation." According to McCampbell, the Hellcat squadrons had no use for the "Thatch Weave," a tactic designed to compensate for the F4F Wildcat's inferior speed and maneuverability against the Zero. The F6F was a better aircraft than the Zero in every respect, and therefore suited to more aggressive tactics. One quick burst of .50-caliber fire, aimed into the Zero's vulnerable wing-root, and "they would explode right in your face."[8] By early 1944, these initial fighter sweeps usually wiped the sky clean of Japanese fighters, and when the dive-bombers and torpedo bombers arrived some minutes later, they encountered little or no remaining air opposition.

Rear Admiral Mitscher, who flew his flag in the *Yorktown*, emphasized that the entire carrier task force was just a sophisticated support system for its aviators. "Pilots are the weapon of this force," he told his staff. "Pilots are the things you have to nurture. Pilots are people you have to train, and you have to train other people to support the pilots."[9] He was a small, wiry man with a gaunt and weathered face. There was barely a hair left on his head, and he used the call sign "Bald Eagle." Rarely did Mitscher ever leave the *Yorktown's* flag bridge. He was usually perched on a stool, dressed in wrinkled khakis and a faded duck-billed cap, with a pair of binoculars on a strap around his neck. He normally had very little to say, but he listened carefully and absorbed everything his pilots told him. When he did speak, it was in a wan, raspy voice, and he was not always successful in making himself understood. Jocko Clark, his first flagship captain, said he had to teach himself to read lips in order to decipher the admiral's words.

Arleigh Burke, Mitscher's longtime chief of staff in Task Force 58, observed that the admiral often had an uncanny sense of what the enemy was about to do, and he was usually right. He was not clairvoyant, said Burke—he simply had the intuition of a veteran aviator who had been flying from carriers as long as any pilot in the navy. His expectations were high, and he did not hesitate to relieve a man who failed to meet them. "He was a little bit of a fellow, a sandblower, who was a magnificent commander," Burke said. "He knew his pilots; he knew his job; he was skillful himself. . . . He was wise, he was simple, he was direct, and he was ruthless."[10]

THE INEXORABLE ATTRITION of Japanese airpower in the central Pacific had been underway since long before FLINTLOCK. At the end of December 1943, the Americans had four working airfields in the Gilberts, including three that could accommodate heavy bombers. Rear Admiral John H. Hoover's land-based air command sent USAAF bombers against the eastern Marshalls from rear bases at Canton and Ellice Islands and new bases at Makin and Tarawa. The workhorse of this campaign was the Consolidated B-24 Liberator, often escorted by F6Fs or P-39 Airacobras. The raiders noted a steady decline in the number of enemy fighters that rose to meet them. Navy PB4Ys, a naval version of the B-24, flew reconnaissance missions over the islands and laid mines in the channels. Nimitz's headquarters diary recorded the near-daily "milk runs" that preceded the FLINTLOCK landings. On January 21, fifteen B-24s dropped 30 tons of bombs on Roi-Namur and Kwajalein islands. The next day, ten B-24s dropped 20 tons of bombs on Roi; on January 29, five B-24s left 13 tons; on January 30, seven B-24s added another 21 tons. Mille, Jaluit, Malelop, Taroa, and Wotje were all bombed heavily on the same day.[11]

On the morning of January 28 (D-Day minus three), Admiral Frederick C. Sherman's Task Group 58.3 landed a knockout blow on the airfield at Kwajalein Island. The dawn F6F sweep encountered no Japanese fighters at all, and the bomber squadrons that followed ensured that the airfield would not return to action before the amphibious fleet arrived. The next day, Sherman's group struck Eniwetok, the westernmost of Japan's fortified Marshalls atolls, and gave it the same kind of treatment. Sherman's carriers remained off Eniwetok for three days while their air groups pulverized the airfields and ground installations. On the third day, not much was left but heaps of rubble and a few palm trees that had been completely stripped of their foliage. The airmen reported that they could not find any targets on the ground or in the lagoon that seemed worth bombing, and "the island looked like a desert waste."[12]

The warships assigned to bombard the landing beaches came over the eastern horizon before dawn on January 31. Off Roi, at 6:51 a.m., Admiral Richard L. Conolly maneuvered his flagship *Maryland* to a position 2,000 yards off the northern beaches. That amounted to point-blank range for 16-inch guns—or as Holland Smith put it, "So close that his guns almost poked their muzzles into Japanese positions."[13] At precisely 7:15 a.m., the naval guns fell silent all at once, and the drone of carrier planes immediately filled the void. A precise airstrike followed, and as the planes flew away, the guns opened up again. A 127mm artillery emplacement on Roi fired gamely at the cruisers and destroyers offshore, but quickly attracted return fire that knocked it out of action. Truman Hedding recalled, "We learned a lot about softening up these islands before we sent the Marines in. We really worked that place over. They developed a tactic called the 'Spruance haircut.' We just knocked everything down; there wasn't even a palm tree left."[14] The islands in Kwajalein Atoll were struck by about 15,000 tons of bombs and naval shells in the seventy-two hours before H-Hour, amounting to more than a ton of ordnance for each man in the Japanese garrison. A wag on Turner's command ship adapted Winston Churchill's verdict on the Battle of Britain: "Never in the history of human conflict has so much been thrown by so many at so few."[15]

Transports carried nearly 64,000 troops of the 4th Marine Division and the Army's 7th Infantry Division. The first troop landings were to occur on several small islands adjoining Roi-Namur, designated IVAN, JACOB, ALLEN, ANDREW, ALBERT, and ABRAHAM. Aerial photos had shown that they were either deserted or very lightly garrisoned, but if they contained any enemy artillery pieces, they might pose a threat to the landing boats. Once they had been secured, the marines would set up artillery batteries to direct fire onto the fortified beaches of Roi-Namur.

H-Hour for the landings on IVAN and JACOB had been set for 9:00 a.m., but choppy seas and a stiff breeze made for a difficult transfer into the amtracs. Once in the boats, marines were tossed cruelly on the swells and soaked to the skin by heavy salt spray. The inexperienced navy crews struggled to keep the boats in formation. With their radios drenched and unusable, orders had to be passed verbally from boat to boat. Delays inevitably followed. At 9:30, the first boats churned in toward the beaches. Carrier planes dived low to bomb and strafe the Japanese firing positions. The boats destined for IVAN, battling heavy waves and winds, had to slow their speed to navigate through uncharted reefs. Several of the first-wave amtracs turned away from their assigned landing beaches on the ocean-facing side, and instead went around the island and put ashore on the lagoon beaches. This improvised landing succeeded, as the handful of Japanese defenders could not move into new positions quickly enough to counter it. From their beachhead, small groups of marines quickly overran the island and declared it secure at 11:00.

In the early afternoon, troops went ashore on the little islands ALLEN, ALBERT, and ABRAHAM, all to the east of Roi-Namur. As they raced into the beaches, the Higgins boats and LVTs fired bow-mounted machine guns and rockets and destroyed many of the Japanese guns. Having circled offshore for hours, many wet and seasick marines were relieved to stagger ashore, even if greeted with a hail of enemy fire. In most cases, on these secondary islands, effective fire support, air support, and the not-inconsiderable firepower mounted on the landing craft forced the small Japanese garrisons to keep their heads down, facilitating a bloodless landing. ALBERT was secured at 3:42, ALLEN by 4:28, and ANDREW (where there were no defenders at all) by 3:45. ABRAHAM, where only six Japanese soldiers were found, was secured by nightfall. American casualties had been minimal. That night, howitzers were hauled ashore and positioned to lay down fire on the fortified beaches of Roi and Namur.

The snafus encountered on D-Day were manageable, and none had been entirely unanticipated. "The Commanding General and Staff of the Northern Landing Force were well aware that things might not go as planned on D-Day," General Schmidt's chief of staff later observed.[16] But the morning had witnessed a general breakdown in the command and control of landing craft. Admiral Conolly attributed the problem to the inexperience of the boat crews and a dearth of pre-landing rehearsals, exacerbated by rough weather and the loss of radios to water damage. For all of that, the admiral proudly concluded, "the plans were made to work and that is the final test of a command and its organization."[17]

The bulk of the 4th Marine Division was to storm the lagoon-side beaches of Roi and Namur at dawn on February 1. All would land in amtracs.

In order to avoid the confusion and disorder of Tarawa, the first two waves would climb into the amtracs while the vehicles were still embarked on the LST tank carriers. According to the operations plan, the amtracs would roll down the ramps and launch some miles offshore. Then they would enter the lagoon by the channel east of Namur and rendezvous off the landing beaches. But the little landing craft had labored mightily in the heavy seas offshore on D-Day, so Admiral Conolly decided to take the LSTs into the lagoon before dawn and launch the boats much closer to the beaches.

Covered by the big guns of the battleship *Tennessee* and other fire support ships, the tank carriers entered the lagoon at dawn. Carrier airstrikes and marine artillery on the adjoining islands added to the toll of misery inflicted on the defenders. The volume of fire from Japanese positions on both Roi and Namur had slackened considerably since the previous day. The bombardment of Roi, delayed by the passage of LSTs between the support units and the island, began at 7:10 a.m. The scheduled landing, designated "W-Hour," was set for 10:00.

Getting the amtracs off the LSTs was not nearly as straightforward as had been anticipated. Those on the upper decks had to be lowered by elevators to the tank decks, but in a nasty twist, it turned out that the second-generation amtracs ("LVT-2s") were too long to fit in the elevators. They had to be moved onto an inclined ramp, and even then they fit by just inches. Each machine had to be maneuvered just so, and delays unavoidably ensued. A malfunctioning elevator on one LST stranded nine amtracs on the weather deck. At 8:53 p.m., bowing to the inevitable, Conolly pushed W-Hour back to 11:00 a.m.

At 11:12, a signal dropped from the destroyer *Phelps*, sending the first waves of landing boats toward Roi. It was a thirty-minute run into the Red beaches. The naval barrage rose to a crescendo, and the air coordinator held the Avengers and Hellcats to above 2,000 feet so they could continue to bomb the islands while the naval guns were pouring shells into it. The simultaneous air and naval bombardment during the approach of the first wave was judged a great success, and similar tactics were to be employed in later amphibious operations.

The planes and naval guns desisted with exact timing as the first boats scraped ashore. The treads of the LVTs bit into the sand and drove up the beaches, firing their machine guns and rockets at enemy positions. The

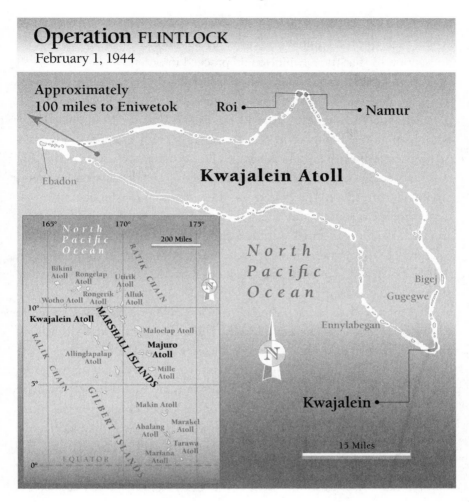

Operation FLINTLOCK
February 1, 1944

Approximately 100 miles to Eniwetok

Roi • Namur

Ebadon

Kwajalein Atoll

North Pacific Ocean

Bigej

Gugegwe

Ennylabegan

Kwajalein •

15 Miles

165° 170° 175°

North Pacific Ocean

200 Miles

RATIK CHAIN

Bikini Atoll
Rongelap Atoll
Utirik Atoll
Rongerik Atoll
Alluk Atoll
Wotho Atoll

MARSHALL ISLANDS

10°

Kwajalein Atoll

Maloelap Atoll

RATIK CHAIN

Allinglapalap Atoll

Majuro Atoll

Mille Atoll

5°

GILBERT ISLANDS

Makin Atoll

Abalang Atoll
Marakel Atoll

Tarawa Atoll

Mariana Atoll

0° EQUATOR

first waves hit Namur about fifteen minutes later. Four battalions were put ashore on the two connected islands before noon.

Roi was a relative cakewalk. Wendy Point, the island's western extremity, was swiftly overrun by armored amtracs. The marines found that many of the pillboxes and defensive entrenchments had been blasted to rubble by the heavy bombing and bombardment. Japanese defenders seemed stupefied by the mighty shelling and did not fight with their usual ferocity. The landscape had been so drastically chewed up by naval shelling and bombing that many landmarks identified on the maps were no longer there. Infantry units could not be sure exactly where they were, relative to their assigned targets, so they instinctively kept advancing toward the northern beaches. A few high-spirited companies had to be summoned back to the island's midsection so that the advance could proceed in order.

When the first tanks came ashore at midday, all remaining resistance was crumbling. Roi's level terrain was well suited to these machines, which punched directly into the heart of the island and fired on pillboxes at point-blank range. By three in the afternoon, friendly fire posed more danger to the marines than did enemy fire. From the air, observers noted that marines were walking upright, without bothering to take cover from enemy fire. By late afternoon, the only remaining organized resistance on Roi was in a complex of bunkers at the northeastern end of the island. A large and well-coordinated attack on this section pushed the remaining defenders back to the beach, where they perished under artillery fire or took their own lives. At 6:02 p.m., Colonel Louis R. Jones reported that the northern side of the island was secured.

The marines had a much rougher time on Namur, which was joined to Roi by a sand spit on the lagoon side. There the terrain was less accommodating to the tanks and armored vehicles. Most of the heavy armor was stopped at the top of Beach Green, and could only provide fire support from behind the attacking infantrymen. Tanks became mired in soft sand, or drove into shell craters and tank traps, or could not climb over the heaps of rubble that were the remains of bombed-out defensive emplacements. As on Roi, the naval barrage had thoroughly altered the landscape, so the advancing marines could not identify the landmarks they found on their maps. Thick underbrush and heavy palls of smoke obscured visibility. At the center of the island, Japanese snipers concealed themselves in a brush field and shot several marines as they came within range. There seemed little danger of a counterattack in force, but the nests of Japanese riflemen would have to be cleaned out by direct infantry assault.

A large concrete blockhouse stood near the geographic center of the island. Heavily reinforced with steel, it had withstood the bombing and shelling of the past seventy-two hours, and now gave cover to several dozen Japanese soldiers. At 1:05 p.m., a platoon of marines surrounded and prepared to destroy it. They tossed charges and grenades into several apertures. The structure went up in an earth-shattering explosion, and debris rained down on the heads of men all over the island. An officer on the lagoon beach reported that "trunks of palm trees and chunks of concrete as large as packing crates were flying through the air like match sticks. . . . The hole left where the blockhouse stood was as large as a fair-sized swimming pool." [18] The titanic blast claimed the lives of about twenty marines and wounded about a hundred more. Upon later examination, officers concluded that the grenades and demolition charges had touched off a magazine stocked with torpedo warheads. Reinforcements were summoned from the beach to plug the gap in the marine lines.

In the mid-afternoon, marines cleared lanes for the tanks so that they could be brought up to the edge of the field of underbrush, from which Japanese snipers continued to fire. The tanks poured 37mm canister shot into the field until no one fired back. As night fell on February 1, about two-thirds of the island was firmly in American hands. A pocket of resistance remained in the northeast corner, but the final attack would have to wait until daylight on February 2.

The morning's attack was led by medium Sherman tanks advancing through lanes cleared by the marines. Infantrymen followed with grenades and flamethrowers. The last sustained resistance was offered by a small group of Japanese soldiers firing from an antitank ditch behind the ocean beach. Tanks flanked the trench and poured canister fire into it.

Sporadic firing continued through midday, but the island was declared secured at 2:18 p.m. An American flag was raised above a scorched wasteland. Peace reigned over Roi-Namur as night fell on February 2.

The army's 7th Infantry Division was assigned the job of taking banana-shaped Kwajalein Island, at the southeastern corner of the atoll. As at Roi-Namur, assault troops first landed on smaller adjacent islands and set up batteries of 105mm and 155mm howitzers. Minesweepers swept the best deepwater entrance to the lagoon. The fire support ships of the Southern Attack Force closed to within 2,000 yards and leveled a seawall above the assault beaches. Two regiments (the 32nd and 184th) landed on the lagoon side of Kwajalein at 9:30 a.m. on February 1. At first, the attackers encountered only feeble and intermittent resistance and quickly secured the eastern half of the island. The heavy punishment inflicted on the garrison from air and sea had apparently done its work. But the army troops moved slowly and methodically, advancing cautiously against the enemy's fixed positions in line with their doctrine and training. On D-Day plus one, opposing lines were drawn across the western third of the island. The remains of the Japanese garrison was given time to dig into new positions. Major General Charles H. Corlett's forces called in heavy airstrikes and naval fire support, which steadily reduced the enemy's bunkers and pillboxes to piles of rubble.

As on Makin three months earlier, General Holland Smith was not satisfied with the army's stolid pace: "I could see no reason why this division, with ample forces ashore, well covered by land-based artillery and receiving tremendous naval and air support, could not take the island quicker."[19]

The fight for Kwajalein dragged out for four days. Prodded repeatedly to finish the job, and reminded of the ever-growing risk of enemy air and submarine incursion against the fleet waiting offshore, General Corlett ordered a decisive westward push on the fourth day of the battle. Tanks led the way, firing point-blank into one pillbox after another; troops followed with hand grenades and flamethrowers. "Every now and then, gas, oil, and ammunition dumps would be blown up," recalled Ken Dodson, a naval officer on one of the transports offshore. "The explosions and the gunfire shook the ship. The roar was never-ending. Then came the smoke and the stench, getting worse every day, until we were heartily glad to leave the place."[20] As in every other such fight, Japanese stragglers infiltrated the American lines through tunnels and overlooked bunkers, and the assault troops quickly learned to watch their backs. *Nisei* interpreters (second-generation Japanese Americans) broadcast surrender appeals through loudspeakers, but there were only a few dozen takers, and most of the men who gave themselves up were Korean laborers.

Kwajalein Island was declared secure at 7:20 p.m. on February 4. Ken Dodson went ashore the next morning. Writing to his wife, he described a desolate landscape of "shell craters and hillocks of upturned coral." Dodson was sickened by the sight of the enemy dead, and was surprised to find that he pitied them:

Some of the Japanese had been dead from the first bombardment, the day before we landed. Their bodies were seared and bloated, and the stench was sickening. I saw one half buried in a pillbox. You could not tell whether he had on any clothes or not. The skin was burned off his back and his head lay a few feet from his body. Another looked like a bronze statue in Golden Gate Park. He lay forward in a crouch, helmet still on, both hands holding on to a coconut log of his pillbox. There were many, many others. I lie in bed at night remembering how they looked, and that awful sweetish sickening stench of powder, and kerosene and decaying human flesh, and I wonder, after all, what war is all about. I feel sorry for those Japs in a way. They died courageously after a stubborn, last-ditch, hopeless fight. They fought for the things they had been taught to believe in, with their poor little bundles with pictures of their wives and kiddies tied to their belts. . . . They can't tell me war is a fine and noble thing.[21]

In the week after the end of Operation FLINTLOCK, a deluge of high-ranking visitors descended on the battle-scarred islands of Kwajalein Atoll. Nimitz flew out from Pearl Harbor with an entourage of officers. On February 5, when fires were still burning on Kwajalein Island, he toured the blackened wastes with Spruance, Turner, Smith, and several other major commanders of the fleet and Amphibious Corps.

Three weeks earlier Nimitz had been the guest of honor at a huge "Texas Picnic" in a Honolulu park. Walking among 40,000 sailors, soldiers, and civilians, the CINCPAC had pitched horseshoes, posed for photographs, and signed autographs. Afterward, the park looked as if it had been hit by a hurricane—clean-up crews had to cart away more than fifty truckloads of garbage and debris. An estimated 120,000 beer bottles had been left strewn across the grass. Now, upon setting foot on the lagoon beach at Kwajalein, Nimitz was waylaid by a mob of correspondents.

"What do you think of the island?" one asked.

The admiral drew a cheerful laugh by replying, "Gentlemen, it's the worst scene of devastation I have ever witnessed—except for the Texas picnic."[22]

A destroyer carried the party across the enormous lagoon to Roi-Namur. Steaming at 20 knots, the ship still took more than two hours to complete the passage. The officers were conducted on a brief tour of the devastated pair of islands. None who saw the scene could fail to appreciate the combat efficiency of the "Spruance haircut" and the "Mitscher shampoo." Looking down at Roi and Namur from an F6F circling overhead, one navy pilot thought it looked like "the moon," or "plowed ground." The beach and roads were strewn with the charred and misshapen remains of equipment, tanks, and armored vehicles. "I don't think there was a stick of anything standing," he said. "It looked just completely beaten up."[23] A sailor who visited one of the captured atolls observed that the "palms were shredded where shells and bomb fragments had made direct hits, leaving stumps that looked like old-fashioned shaving brushes stuck, bristles up, in the sand."[24]

Holland Smith did not appreciate the parade of sightseers. Kwajalein Atoll, he said, had become a "regular tourist haunt. . . . The big army and navy brass from Pearl Harbor descended on us like flies." Undersecretary of the Navy James V. Forrestal, dressed in a plain khaki shirt and trousers without insignia, rode shotgun in a jeep through the ruins of Roi and Namur. Admiral Spruance and General Schmidt sat in back. The garrison was taxed with hosting tours at a time when they should have been occupied in clearing the airfield, setting up barracks, burying their dead, and erecting new antiaircraft batteries. On Smith's orders, no more marine drivers were supplied to the jeep pool, a decision that led to the unusual sight of generals driving their own vehicles. "The photographers had a gala day snapping pictures against the background of shelled buildings," he recalled, "while visiting brass hunted for samurai swords and other souvenirs."[25]

The single battalion assigned to take Majuro had walked up the beaches unopposed. The Japanese garrison had pulled out a week earlier. Admiral Hill declared the atoll secure scarcely more than two hours after the initial landing. The huge anchorage would accommodate all the mobile floating logistical assets of Service Squadron Ten, and become (for the time being) the principal advanced base for the Fifth Fleet.

Mitscher's carriers began filing into the lagoon on February 4. On each ship, lookouts leaned out on either side of the bridge to identify the locations of shoals and reefs, which were easy to spot in the shallow pastel-colored sea. Except for a few ships requiring major repairs, none needed to cross the Pacific to return to Pearl Harbor. They were able to refuel, rearm, and reprovision in the lagoon from supply ships, oilers, and barges. These assets dramatically enlarged the operating range of the fleet and allowed for previously unknown feats of seakeeping.

As Nimitz and his commanders considered the repercussions of the rapid and relatively low-cost victory, they elected to accelerate the schedule of future operations in the region. Eniwetok, the next major atoll on the program, had been slated for capture in May. But Japanese military power in the Marshalls was obviously crumbling more quickly than anticipated.

Sherman's Task Group 58.3 had made a shambles of the airfield on Eniwetok's Engebi Island. According to the CINCPAC headquarters diary, aerial photos had "disclosed that the defenses were minor and in general the atoll undeveloped. The airstrip is in use but at present appears to be used as a staging base."[26] According to plans agreed to earlier with MacArthur's SWPA headquarters, the fast carriers of Task Force 58 were to sweep south to support Halsey's assault on Kavieng. When MacArthur agreed to allow Halsey to bypass Kavieng, the carriers were unburdened of that mission, and could therefore be employed in the central Pacific. Finally, a mother lode of valuable maps, charts, and documents related to Eniwetok were discovered in Japanese bunkers at Roi-Namur. These suggested that the Japanese garrison there ranged between 2,700 and 4,000 men, and they were racing against the clock to erect stronger fortifications on the main island of Engebi. Time was of the essence. For the moment, Eniwetok was low-hanging fruit; it could be captured with existing naval forces and amphibious troops. No intervening return to Pearl Harbor seemed necessary. Why not just take it right away?

Credit for the proposal to pounce on Eniwetok in February, rather than waiting until May as earlier planned, was afterward claimed by a long roster of commanders, including Smith, Sherman, Turner, Hill, and Spruance. It appears that the idea presented itself to all of them simultaneously. Nimitz gave the operation his blessing. It would be carried out by a hastily assembled task force commanded by Admiral Hill. The 22nd Marines and two battalions of the 106th Infantry would provide the assault troops. Task Force 58 would strike the Japanese fleet and air base at Truk Atoll in the Caroline Islands, to coincide with the landings. The date for both operations was set for February 17. The capture of Eniwetok was designated CATCHPOLE; the carrier strike on Truk was named HAILSTONE.

Reporting to Spruance at Kwajalein on February 5, Hill learned that he would command the Eniwetok Expeditionary Group (designated Task Group 51.11) and must complete the major operation in less than two weeks. The marine-army expeditionary troops, drawn from a floating reserve of 9,300 men that had not been needed at Majuro or Kwajalein, would be commanded by Marine Brigadier General Thomas E. Watson. Task Group 58.4, commanded by Rear Admiral Samuel P. Ginder and built around the carriers *Saratoga*, *Princeton*, and *Langley*, would continue to pummel the remaining defenses at Engebi and cover the landings from the air. High-

and low-angle aerial photographs were combined with the captured Japanese charts and documents to provide an accurate picture of the objective. Importantly, the Japanese charts provided accurate information about the best deepwater channel into the lagoon at Eniwetok.

Moving up the invasion of Eniwetok required stripping the new garrisons of Kwajalein Island and Roi-Namur of manpower and supplies. The landing boat crews were green and had not trained with the troops. General Watson reported that "the infantry, amphibian tractors, amphibian tanks, tanks, aircraft, supporting naval ships, and most of the staffs concerned had never worked together before."[27] Nevertheless, the forces available for the operation were plentiful and well equipped. Having presided over the bloody assault on Tarawa, Admiral Hill was relieved to have adequate numbers of amtracs. The Army's 708th Provisional Amphibian Tractor Battalion sailed with 119 LVTs, most of which were the heavily armored newer models. "At Eniwetok, I felt like a millionaire," Hill later remarked, "but at Tarawa, I was a pauper."[28]

As in FLINTLOCK, the CATCHPOLE plan of operations called for capturing nearby islands and using them as artillery platforms to sweep the beaches of Engebi. At 6:59 a.m. on February 17, the cruisers and destroyers of the naval fire support group began bombarding the island's defenses. Marine artillerymen landed on smaller adjacent islands and set up field batteries that could hit Engebi's beaches. After twenty-four hours of this treatment, the first boatloads of marines landed on the island and quickly overran it. The flag was raised on the following morning. The islands of Eniwetok and Parry were seized in the following three days.

The marines lost 254 killed and 555 wounded; the army, 94 killed and 311 wounded. Of the 2,700 troops of the Japanese garrison, only 66 were taken prisoner. With the huge lagoon of Eniwetok as its westernmost fleet anchorage, the Fifth Fleet now had a well-situated springboard to strike at the Marianas, which lay scarcely more than a thousand miles away.

As THE AMERICAN COMMANDERS took stock of what they had achieved in the Marshalls, their confidence and self-assurance rose to new heights. In less than three months' time, the costly lessons of Tarawa had been refined and integrated into amphibious planning and doctrine, and the results had been more than satisfactory. To the extent that further improvement was needed, it was in the details of execution rather than any deficiency in the plans themselves. Holland Smith concluded in his final report, "In the attack of coral atolls, very few recommendations can be made to improve upon the basic techniques previously recommended and utilized in FLINTLOCK."[29]

Nowhere in the Pacific had the preinvasion bombardment and aerial bombing of islands been more effective. General Schmidt estimated that 50 to 75 percent of the Japanese garrison on Roi-Namur had been killed before the first marine set foot on the island. Those who had survived the barrage were apparently dazed, and patently less ferocious than their counterparts on Betio and other Pacific battlefields. Carrier airstrikes in the three days before the landings managed to knock out nearly every Japanese airplane in the entire archipelago. Upon departing from the targets, pilots noted that "ground installations were reduced to mounds of rubble; hardly a tree was left standing and those remaining were completely stripped of their foliage by the terrific bombardment."[30]

Most of the marine and army assault troops had never experienced combat before FLINTLOCK or CATCHPOLE, but their training had produced a first-rate performance. The only lapse in discipline had been on Roi, when several units had charged across the airfield and surged ahead to the north shore. The lines had been reassembled before the enemy could attack the exposed flanks. In any event, no ground commander could find much fault in troops who showed too much spirit on the attack. As in other such operations, Japanese stragglers and infiltrators remained a threat behind the advancing American lines, and infantrymen were obliged to do the grim work of cleaning out the bunkers, tunnels, and emplacements one by one with demolition charges, flamethrowers, and hand grenades. By 1944, however, not even the newcomers had any illusions about the enemy's way of waging war.

Nimitz's decision to spring past the fortified outer islands and aim the main attack at Kwajalein had been vindicated. The Japanese, surprised by the landings, had been robbed of time to strengthen their defenses on the beaches. Japanese garrisons had been left in possession of several atolls in the southeastern Marshalls, but Nimitz was in no hurry to clean them out. The airfields were pressured by daily air raids, and whenever new planes were flown in from Truk or Rabaul, they were destroyed in short order. Daily "milk runs," staging from the Gilberts or the Ellice Islands, continued until the end of the war. The routine bombing raids were conducted largely by F4U Corsair fighters escorting army medium bombers. Rarely did the raiders encounter any air opposition at all. The garrisons wasted away for lack of supplies and provisions. Many were killed in the relentless air bombardments; many others took their lives in desperation.

Tokyo had staked its defense of the "unsinkable aircraft carriers" of the Gilberts and Marshalls on the concept of a network of mutually supporting terrestrial airfields. Within the overlapping radii of the nodes of that network lay a vast zone of ocean wastes and low-lying coral atolls. Over the breadth and width of that zone, so it was hoped, Japanese naval fighters and bombers would sustain local control of the skies. Any concerted naval or amphibious attack would be repelled with the help of air reinforcements moving freely and quickly between the nodes. That entire strategic concept, so vital to Japan's hopes, had been exposed as a chimera by the concurrent expansion and qualitative upgrade of American carrier airpower. Impotently dispersed across dozens of atolls, subjected to a rain of ruin from the air and sea, the defenders could barely even delay the American advance. In less than three months and with relative ease, FLINTLOCK and CATCHPOLE had kicked down Japan's mid-Pacific barricade.

For the victors, possession of the western Marshalls brought a windfall of strategic rewards. Control of the spacious lagoon anchorages and fine coral airfields allowed American naval and air forces to stage from bases on the threshold of Japan's new "absolute defense line," which ran through the nearby Marianas. Admiral Lockwood's submarines could be circulated back into their patrol areas more rapidly, with the effect of increasing the number of submarine patrol days in the sea-lanes south of Japan by approximately one-third. Admiral Koga had not yet committed his main fleet to a decisive stand, but he could not afford to hold it back indefinitely. The mighty Fifth Fleet was now poised to strike into Japan's inner ring of defenses, and could be confident of forcing a major naval confrontation in the next stage of its westward drive. With overwhelming superiority in carrier aviation, the Americans stood a reasonable hope of scoring a victory on the scale of the great fleet battles of Tsushima or Trafalgar, an event that would guarantee the eventual defeat of Japan.

OPERATION HAILSTONE, the carrier air attack on Truk, had been long on the drawing board. On December 26, 1943, Nimitz had informed King that he thought the operation would become feasible by the following April, but he pledged to do it earlier if circumstances allowed: "Much depends on extent of damage inflicted on enemy in all areas in next 2 months."[31] The crumbling of Japanese airpower in the Marshalls was just such a favorable development. CINCPAC headquarters had also been mulling over plans for an invasion of Truk, an operation that would have required five divisions plus an additional regiment, making it the largest amphibious operation yet attempted in the Pacific. HAILSTONE might or might not obviate the need to capture Truk—the raid's outcome would do much to reveal whether the big atoll was a suitable candidate for bypass.

Located 669 miles southwest of Eniwetok, Truk was another colossal atoll with a fringing reef enclosing a lagoon roughly thirty by forty miles in size. Its topography and appearance were different from those of the Gilberts and Marshalls. A cluster of about a dozen islands near the center of the lagoon ascended to 1,500-foot volcanic peaks, their soaring slopes alternately rocky and heavily forested. About 2,000 Micronesian natives lived on the islands, most in thatched-hut villages on the grassy plains above the beaches. Since mid-1942, Truk's enormous lagoon had served as the Combined Fleet's major southern fleet anchorage. It was so large, in fact, that high-speed fleet exercises had been held within its reef-protected confines. For most of the war, the superbattleships *Yamato* and *Musashi* had ridden at anchor behind torpedo nets, immobilized for the sake of fuel economy. The fleet's administrative headquarters was located in a modest complex of wood-frame buildings on the island of Tonoas, south of Weno.

The aviators and crewmen of Task Force 58 shared a sense of dread about the impending raid. The enemy's "mystery base" at Truk had acquired the reputation of an unassailable fortress. In the past, carrier task force commanders had been wary of attacking major terrestrial airfields because the enemy's long-range bombers could deliver devastating counterstrikes on the vulnerable flattops. Such raids had always been brief, followed by a speedy withdrawal. But HAILSTONE was to be a sustained foray deep into enemy waters. Task Force 58 would lie off Truk for two full days, well within range of aerial counterattack. The operation seemed considerably more dangerous than any previously attempted by the fast carrier forces.

A dearth of intelligence about Truk had enhanced its mystique. The atoll's distance from Allied bases had rendered aerial reconnaissance impractical before 1944. It was thought to be a major hub of Japanese airpower, defended by hundreds of crack airmen in Zero fighters. Its soaring peaks were supposed to bristle with antiaircraft guns. Its channels were reportedly treacherous to navigate, heavily mined, and amply defended by coastal artillery. Newspapers had nicknamed Truk "Japan's Gibraltar" or the "Japanese Pearl Harbor."

Lieutenant James D. Ramage, a Bombing Squadron 10 pilot on the *Enterprise*, recalled his slack-jawed reaction to the news that his ship was bound for Truk: "Wow!" Ramage's radio-gunner, David Cawley, added that the squadron was "tense and concerned" as Task Force 58 steamed into enemy waters—"For the previous two years of the war," he said, "the very thought of approaching Truk seemed fatal."[32] Admiral Mitscher, according to a story that circulated through the crew of the *Yorktown*, had remarked, "The only thing we knew about Truk was in the *National Geographic*."[33] A mordant cartoon published in the *Essex* cruise book depicts the skipper speaking through a bullhorn from the bridge. He announces that the *Essex* is headed to Truk. In the next moment he is struck speechless by the sight of his entire crew diving into the sea.

The fearsome reputation was undeserved. Truk Lagoon offered a well-protected anchorage for the Combined Fleet, and was suitably located on the sea route between Japan's southern territories and its home islands— but the Imperial Japanese Navy had never poured much effort or resources into developing its airfields, port facilities, shore fortifications, or repair shops. The comparison to Pearl Harbor was absurd. In 1944 the atoll had a single midsize floating dry dock. There were no major power stations, no piers capable of accommodating large ships, and no underground fuel storage. Damaged ships usually had to make the long passage north to Japan for repairs. Ship-to-shore transfers of supplies and troops were carried out by lighters and other small craft. Truk's four airfields lacked advanced ground installations and were too small to allow proper dispersal of parked planes. Only in late 1943 did the Japanese navy begin a crash program to expand and extend the airfields. Labor was in short supply, so working parties were drafted from the crews of the warships in the anchorage. "The sailors actually enjoyed the work because it allowed them to go ashore," recalled an air officer on the carrier *Zuikaku*.[34]

In February 1944, the atoll was garrisoned by about 7,500 army troops and another 3,000 sailors and support personnel. Fixed antiaircraft defenses were limited to about forty batteries. Admiral Shigeru Fukudome, who held several important jobs on the Combined Fleet staff, told interrogators after the war that Truk had been little more than a staging area, a way station for ships and aircraft traveling between Japan and the South Pacific. Not until the end of 1943 had there been any concerted attempt to fortify it against attack. In his judgment, the atoll would have fallen easy prey to the sort of amphibious invasion the Americans had just completed in the Gilberts and Marshalls.

Admiral Koga had evidently understood as much, because he pulled most of his major combatant ships out of Truk after the fall of Kwajalein and Majuro. He was forewarned by a reconnaissance overflight on February 4, when two marine PB4Ys flew high over the atoll, and by radio intercepts in the following week, which his staff interpreted as evidence that the American carrier task force was on the move. The planes were sighted and identified, and easily outran the floatplane Zeros that rose to intercept them. Koga gave orders to move most of his larger warships to Palau and thence to Tawi Tawi in the Sulu Archipelago of the southern Philippines. Ships began heaving up their anchors and speeding for the exit channels. Koga, in his flagship *Musashi*, departed for Tokyo Bay with a fleet of cruisers and destroyers on February 10. He was resolved to keep his main fleet intact to fight a decisive battle at some future date. Left in the lagoon anchorages were a handful of light cruisers, destroyers, auxiliary naval vessels, about twenty *marus* (cargo ships), and five oil tankers. Including small craft, there were approximately fifty vessels in mid-February.

After rendezvousing in Majuro atoll for refueling and replenishment, the American fleet had sortied and taken a westward course on February 12. The striking force included most of the fast carrier task forces under Vice Admiral Mitscher—the greater part of Task Force 58, including five fleet carriers (*Enterprise, Yorktown, Essex, Intrepid,* and *Bunker Hill*) and four light carriers (*Belleau Wood, Cabot, Monterey,* and *Cowpens*). The nine carriers held an armada of more than 560 planes. The HAILSTONE force also included a powerful surface fleet, including seven battleships. Admiral Spruance, the big boss afloat, was embarked on the *New Jersey*. Nine submarines had been assigned to take station off the main channels out of the atoll; they would sink targets of opportunity and stand by to rescue downed aviators.

No Japanese snoopers bothered the fleet on its approach to its launch point, less than a hundred miles east-northeast of Truk. The Americans had again achieved an improbable surprise. Before dawn on February 17, five carriers turned into the wind and launched seventy-two Hellcats. Coalescing into a single tremendous formation, the fighters climbed into the west. Less than thirty minutes later they flew over the atoll's outer eastern cays at altitudes between 16,000 and 22,000 feet. The morning was "clear, cool and beautiful."[35] The air battle for Truk was very nearly over before it began. With an advantage in both numbers and altitude, the Hellcats easily destroyed nearly all the Japanese fighters that rose to intercept them. The fighter sweep shot fifty-six Japanese planes out of the sky and then destroyed another seventy-two on the ground in bombing or strafing runs. Antiaircraft fire was spirited but inaccurate; the American pilots, with several such carrier strikes under their belts, had learned to fly through heavy flak without losing nerve.

Four F6Fs went down in the initial melee, and at least one (according to VF-6 pilot Alex Vraciu) was a victim of friendly fire. "There were dog fights all over the place," he later said. "I even saw one of our Hellcats shoot another Hellcat down. It was a great deflection shot but . . . one of our guys just shot first before being sure and this other poor pilot was forced to parachute out. In the course of the action, I saw a number of Japanese parachutes in the air."[36]

The American airmen had anticipated a much hotter response. They had been told that they might encounter as many as 200 enemy fighters over Truk. As it turned out, there were fewer than 200 aircraft of all types in flyable condition on the atoll's four airfields. According to estimates given in postwar interrogations, the Japanese had 68 operational airplanes on the Moen field, 27 on the Dublon field, 20 on Eten, and 46 on Param, for a total of 161. Parked on the big field at Eten were some 180 aircraft that were damaged, grounded for lack of spare parts, or immobilized for lack of aircrews. Most would be destroyed on the ground.

Though Admiral Koga had correctly anticipated the enemy's move against Truk, air and naval forces were not on the alert when the American planes suddenly appeared overhead. According to Masataka Chihaya, a staff officer with the Fourth Fleet, the pilots, ground personnel, and ships' crews had been kept in twenty-four-hour readiness since the over-flight of the two marine PB4Ys two weeks earlier, and had reached a state of collective exhaustion.[37] Worse, morale and even discipline had eroded since the withdrawal of the heavy warships. Pilots had refused to climb into their cockpits when so ordered, and many men had gone absent with-out leave. The atoll's commander, Vice Admiral Masami Kobayashi, had apparently concluded that the American fleet was still engaged in the Marshalls, and authorized a downgrade in the alert level. On February 16, many pilots and other personnel had left their barracks for R&R. The morning of the American raid found a large proportion of Truk's aviators asleep in the atoll's largest town, on the island of Dublon, having partied late into the night at local drinking establishments. Their only means of returning to their airfield on the island of Eten was by ferry, and the ferry could not accommodate all of them at once. Many aircraft, both on Eten and on the airfields of Moen and Param islands, had been disarmed and drained of fuel. Kobayashi's ignominious failure to keep his forces on alert put an end to his naval career; he was relieved of command and then forced to retire from active service.

The first American dive-bombers and torpedo bombers arrived over the target area while the Hellcats were still engaged in strafing runs. Radio chat-ter and instructions from the task force directed the dive-bombers' atten-tion to about thirty ships anchored in the lagoon. James D. Ramage, flying a VB-10 Dauntless, noted that several Zeros flew by him without offering combat. He assumed that they were dispirited by the one-sided results of the air fight and were determined to survive it. It was a syndrome that had become increasingly common during the later stages of the South Pacific air campaign.

The *Enterprise* dive-bombers dropped 1,000-pound armor-piercing bombs on targets chosen from the aerial photos taken earlier. Ramage's division was assigned to attack ships anchored in the lee of Dublon Island, one of Truk's major anchorage areas. The planes hurtled down through flak bursts and smashed the stationary ships. Ramage planted a bomb on the stern of the 13,000-ton *Hoyo Maru*. Another SBD division targeted the 7,000-ton aviation stores ship *Kiyozumi Maru* and lit her up; she began foundering immediately. A VT-6 Avenger flew low over an ammunition ship, the *Aikoku Maru*, and landed a bomb dead-center amidships. The tar-get went up in a huge, rolling ball of flame that engulfed the plane and destroyed it. The shockwave was powerful enough to rock Lieutenant Ramage's aircraft, more than 2,000 feet overhead. "It was, I think, the biggest explosion I've ever seen, other than the atomic bombs," said Ramage. "It was just an enormous blast."[38]

Major Gregory "Pappy" Boyington, the famed marine fighter ace of the Black Sheep squadron (VMF-214), had been shot down and captured off Rabaul a week earlier. He and several other prisoners of war were flown into Truk while the raid was developing. As the G4M bomber carrying them rolled to a stop, Boyington and his fellow prisoners were thrown out onto the airstrip. They looked up and were surprised to see an F6F Hellcat flying low over the airfield, walking .50-caliber fire across the parked planes. The bomber from which they had just been ejected went up in a sheet of flame. The Americans were shoved into a pit by the side of the airfield, and from this relatively protected vantage point they watched the action overhead and cheered for the attackers. Boyington:

There was so much excitement I couldn't do any differently. I just
had to see those Nip planes, some of the light planes like the Zeros,
jump off the ground from the explosion of our bombs and come down
"cl-l-l-lang," just like a sack of bolts and nuts. The planes caught on fire
and the ammunition in them began going off. There were 20-mm cannon shells and 7.7's bouncing and ricocheting all around this pit. Some
of these hot pieces we tossed back out of the pit with our hands.[39]

Later, during a lull in the action, the prisoners were collected from the pit and escorted to another part of the island. Boyington observed, "There were huge pieces of concrete upended, plane parts scattered all over, and the place was a shambles."[40]

Wave after wave of American carrier planes arrived over the atoll. Air group leaders circled above and directed attacks. Destruction rained down on airfields, buildings, hangars, and machine shops. Squadrons assigned to attack shipping were armed with armor-piercing bombs; those intended to work over the airfields and shore installations carried incendiary and fragmentation clusters. Torpedoes tore into ships anchored in the lagoons and ships running for the exit channels. Parked planes were wiped out on the ground. By midday, several of the afternoon strikes encountered no air opposition at all.

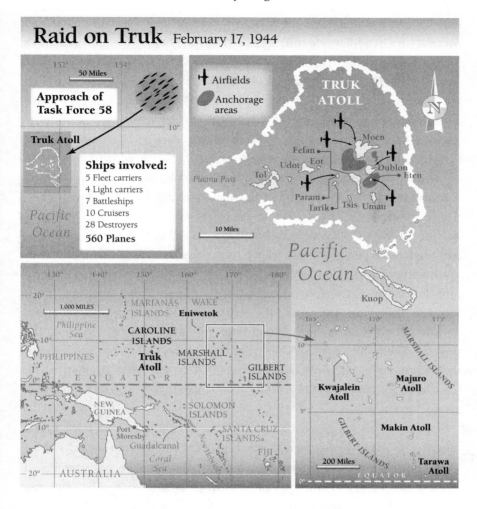

Raid on Truk February 17, 1944

Approach of Task Force 58

Truk Atoll

Ships involved:
5 Fleet carriers
4 Light carriers
7 Battleships
10 Cruisers
28 Destroyers
560 Planes

† Airfields

Anchorage areas

TRUK ATOLL

Moen
Fefan
Udot Eot
Tol
Piaanu Pass
Param
Tarik Isis Uman
Dublon
Eten

Pacific Ocean

Kuop

1,000 MILES
Philippine Sea
PHILIPPINES
MARIANAS ISLANDS WAKE Eniwetok
CAROLINE ISLANDS
Truk Atoll
MARSHALL ISLANDS
GILBERT ISLANDS
EQUATOR
NEW GUINEA
SOLOMON ISLANDS
Port Moresby
Guadalcanal
SANTA CRUZ ISLANDS
Coral Sea
FIJI
AUSTRALIA

MARSHALL ISLANDS
Kwajalein Atoll
Majuro Atoll
Makin Atoll
Tarawa Atoll
200 Miles
EQUATOR

Japanese fighters orbiting to the east of the lagoon pounced on a few Hellcats as they flew back toward the task force. The rudder section of Woodward M. Hampton's F6F was shot away during a strafing run over one of the airfields. When he flew over the northeastern reefs, his Hellcat was ambushed by two Zeroes. He attempted to escape by steering into a cloud. "I was heading now in a northerly direction and continued on the same course while being attacked, unable to turn or counteract the moves of the enemy," he wrote in his action report. "The plane was continuously hit by enemy fire and was slowly being shot to pieces."[41] Hampton's cockpit was riddled with 20mm rounds, destroying most of his instruments. His flight goggles were shot off his head. He concluded his cause was hopeless, but he resolved to take at least another enemy fighter with him. When one of his assailants overran him in a high side run, "I pulled the nose of my plane up until I was on him and gave him a sharp burst from which he burst into flame." The second plane then turned away, and Hampton flew on to the east. Spotting the outer screening ships of the American task force, he made a violent water landing and managed to get free of the cockpit "after submerging for what seemed like a great depth." As he broke the surface and filled his lungs, Hampton was relieved to see a friendly destroyer bearing down on him.[42]

Several downed pilots were rescued in similar fashion. Destroyers and submarines had been stationed as lifeguards around the atoll. The submarine *Searaven* rescued three *Yorktown* aviators several miles north. An *Essex* F6F pilot, George M. Blair, parachuted into Truk Lagoon. Since no American ships could penetrate the channel entrances (which were mined), Blair assumed he was as good as captured. A Japanese destroyer bore down on him, but it was driven off by several other planes of his squadron. Blair was rescued by an OS2U Kingfisher catapulted from the cruiser *Baltimore*. The floatplane made a daring landing on the lagoon and flew back to the task force without mishap. More than half of all American aircrewmen shot down during the two-day action were safely recovered. In many cases, friendly airplanes circled low over the life rafts until a floatplane or destroyer arrived on the scene.

Under relentless air attack, several Japanese ships cast off their moorings and got underway at high speed. The light cruiser *Katori* and destroyer *Maikaze* fled the lagoon through the north passage, but the pair was chased by a division of TBFs and struck by several 500-pound bombs. By noon the *Katori* was down by the stern and the *Maikaze* was ablaze. Circling above, with his bombs expended, Lieutenant Ramage attempted to direct newly arriving bombers to deliver the killing blow on the two cripples. But Admiral Mitscher, identifying himself by his call-sign "Bald Eagle," got on the circuit and ordered all planes to stay clear. "Do not, repeat do not, sink that ship. Acknowledge."[43] The flight leaders were perplexed. Why should they leave the crippled enemy ships alone?

The reason was soon evident. Admiral Spruance had chosen to bring a column of surface ships into the waters immediately north of the atoll. This force included the battleships *New Jersey* and *Iowa*, the cruisers *Minneapolis* and *New Orleans*, and four destroyers. Mitscher was anxious to avoid a misidentification that might result in friendly fire. Moreover, Spruance was evidently keen to have his big guns finish off any cripples they found in their path. The *Minneapolis* and *New Orleans* sank the two immobilized ships with three or four salvos. The *New Jersey* narrowly avoided two torpedoes launched by the sinking destroyer. The American ships closed and offered to pick up survivors, but almost all the Japanese sailors took their own lives rather than submit to capture. The warships continued in a full counterclockwise circuit of the atoll and retired to the eastward after nightfall. They fell in with Mitscher's carriers at dawn the following morning.

Spruance's decision to bring a surface task group into the combat area was not popular with the aviators. In their view, the surface units were not needed at Truk and only got in their way. Mitscher was obliged to provide ten F6Fs from the *Cowpens* to fly combat air patrol over Spruance's column. Those Hellcats could have been more profitably employed in strafing runs, and their obligation to cover the slow withdrawal of the warships forced several pilots to make dangerous night recoveries. The *Iowa* was bombed by a Japanese plane, but suffered little damage. Her gunners fired on and destroyed another plane, which proved to be an American SBD; both the pilot and his back-seater were killed. With an ugly turn of luck, one or more of the ships in Spruance's column might have run into a torpedo, an event that could have cost him his command. The ordinarily conservative fleet commander had behaved with impulsive bravado, and for no better reason than a blackshoe's inborn desire to claim a piece of the action for the big guns. Admiral Sherman's tactful conclusion was that "this expedition accomplished little and only complicated the attacks by the carrier planes."[44] Lieutenant Ramage was less gentle: "So the big battleships finally drew blood against a cruiser that was almost dead in the water. It must have been a great victory."[45]

Carl Moore, the Fifth Fleet chief of staff, was later asked to explain Spruance's reasoning. As always, Moore was candid. The boss was on a sightseeing expedition. "Well, I think it was a matter of curiosity. . . . I think Admiral Spruance was as much interested in taking a look at Truk as he was in hunting for Japanese ships."[46] Moore also speculated that the chief may have been motivated to taunt the Japanese by operating the flagship within plain sight of their largest naval base outside the home islands.

That night, a flight of Nakajima B5N "Kate" torpedo planes stalked the American task force. The intruders had not flown from Truk—their origin has never been conclusively determined, but it is likely they launched from either Rabaul or Saipan. Night fighters attempted to intercept them but could not find them in the darkness. A few minutes after midnight, one of the prowlers roared low over the flight deck of the carrier *Intrepid*. The incident spooked the crew, and Admiral Alfred E. Montgomery of Task Group 58.2 ordered a hard port turn to throw off the attackers. But the B5N had already dropped its torpedo, and while the *Intrepid* was still in its turn, an explosion astern sent a powerful shockwave through the hull. The torpedo had struck the carrier's vulnerable starboard quarter. Eleven of her crew were killed and another seventeen wounded in the explosion. Damage-control parties sealed off the flooded compartments, and the ship could make way under her own power, but her rudder jammed and kept her in a helpless turn. She nearly collided with the *Essex*. She was in no danger of sinking but could not keep pace with the task force; she withdrew to Majuro and thence to Pearl Harbor and San Francisco for repairs.

At 2:00 a.m. on the eighteenth, the *Enterprise* launched a flight of twelve radar-equipped TBF Avengers to attack the surviving Japanese ships in Truk Lagoon. Each aircraft was armed with four 500-pound bombs. The concept of a low-altitude night attack, with the planes guided to the targets by radar alone, had been studied and discussed but never attempted. It required the pilots to navigate to Truk on instruments. Once over the lagoon, they circled over the anchorages until radar echoes provided an image of the targets. The mission was a tactical breakthrough, unprecedented in the annals of aviation or naval history. Lieutenant Commander William I. Martin, who had trained the airmen, called it "a real classic." He recalled:

> Radar displays at that time required an operator to do a great deal of
> interpreting. It was like learning a new language. Instead of it being
> a polar plot, looking down on it like a map, the cathode ray tube just
> gave indications that there was an object out there. After considerable
> practice, a radar operator could determine that there was a ship there
> and its approximate size. You related the blip on the radar scope to the
> image of the ship.[47]

The pilots approached the targets at an altitude of 250 feet or even lower, and released their bombs based on radar readings alone. At masthead altitude, with a slow airspeed, this method of bombing proved devastatingly accurate. The Avengers scored thirteen direct hits and sank eight Japanese ships. The antiaircraft fire was thick but wild; only one of the twelve planes was shot down.

As February 18 dawned, Task Force 58 put another 200 planes into the sky. They met negligible air opposition over the atoll and worked over the remaining targets at their leisure. Hundreds of incendiaries were dropped on smoking airfields, airplane parking areas, and hangars. The bombers paid special attention to the fuel tank farms, which had been spared on the first day in order to prevent smoke from obscuring visibility.

Two days earlier, the Japanese cruiser *Agano* had been sunk north of Truk by the American submarine *Skate*. A destroyer, the *Oite*, had been dispatched to pick up the survivors, numbering about 400 officers and sailors. The destroyer had set course for Saipan but was ordered back to Truk after the raid began. Crammed with the rescued crewmen of the sunken *Agano*, the star-crossed *Oite* entered the lagoon on the morning of February 18 and was quickly set upon by a flight of TBF Avengers from the *Bunker Hill*. Struck amidships by a torpedo, the *Oite* broke in half and went down. She took more than 500 men down with her; only 20 survived.

Flight leaders reported that they were having trouble locating worthy targets. Spruance, aware that he might be flogging a dead horse, ordered all planes back to their carriers, and Task Force 58 retired toward Majuro.

For the Americans, Truk's extravagant reputation inflated the symbolic importance of the victory. Even so, judging by the material results, HAIL-STONE had been one of the most smashing carrier raids of the war. Though most of Japan's heavy naval units had previously fled the lagoon, the attackers had sunk three light cruisers, four destroyers, three auxiliary or training cruisers, and six other naval auxiliaries. They had, in addition, sent about thirty merchant ships to the bottom of the lagoon, including five precious oil tankers. In aggregate, the total shipping losses approached 200,000 tons. Many of those vessels had been laden with munitions and other supplies that could not be recovered. Seventeen thousand tons of fuel went up in the attack, at a time when fuel was running very short.[48] The Japanese had lost 249 aircraft, most destroyed on the ground. All of that was accomplished at negligible cost to the striking force. Mitscher's carriers lost twenty-five aircraft, including those destroyed in accidents; all but nine pilots and aircrewmen were recovered safely and would fly again. The only ship to suffer any significant damage was the *Intrepid*, but she would return to service later in the year.

A navy communiqué announced that "the Pacific fleet has returned in Truk the visit made by the Japanese fleet on Dec. 7, 1941, and effected a partial settlement of the debt."[49] *Time* magazine's verdict was accurate: "The overfeared power of land-based air power had been set aside by greater air power from the sea."[50]

Truk was thereafter useless as a fleet base; it would not serve in that function again. Its airfields were cleared and repaired, and when Koga ordered Rabaul's air units evacuated, most flew to Truk. But if the atoll was vulnerable to Mitscher's attention in February 1944, it would be no less so later in the spring. Task Force 58 would revisit Truk in April, when no shipping remained in the lagoon. During this repeat performance, the air groups concentrated their attentions on the airfields and aircraft of the erstwhile Japanese bastion, and left it a smoking ruin.

A Hellcat prepares to launch from the *Yorktown* during Operation GALVANIC, November 1943. *Official U.S. Navy Photograph.*

A Hellcat crash-lands on the *Enterprise* during Operation GALVANIC, November 1943.
U.S. National Archives.

Combat Information Center (CIC) of the *Lexington* (CV-16) during a carrier raid on Japanese bases in the central Pacific, November 1943.
Official U.S. Navy Photograph.

Lexington Hellcat pilots (VF-16) are briefed by the squadron's commanding officer, Lieutenant Commander Paul D. Buie, during Operation GALVANIC, November 1943.
Official U.S. Navy Photograph.

VF-16 pilots exult after massacring a formation of enemy planes headed for Tarawa, November 23, 1943. Fourth from right is Lieutenant (jg) Ralph Hanks, who has just become an "ace in a day" by shooting down five Zeros in one flight.
U.S. National Archives.

Crewmen catch up on their sleep during a lull in the action. Photo taken on the flight deck of the *Lexington* during Operation GALVANIC, November 1943.
U.S. National Archives.

A wounded aviator is lifted from his aircraft after returning to the *Saratoga* (CV-3) from a raid on Rabaul, November 1943.
U.S. National Archives.

Soldiers of the army's 7th Infantry Division attack a Japanese blockhouse on Kwajalein Island, February 4, 1944.
U.S. National Archives.

Vice Admiral Raymond A. Spruance (center) and Admiral Nimitz (right) tour Kwajalein on February 5, 1944. They are accompanied by a brigadier general (left).
Official U.S. Navy Photograph.

"The thousand-yard stare." A combat-weary marine is hoisted aboard a transport in Eniwetok Lagoon in the Marshall Islands.
U.S. National Archives.

Troops of the 163rd Infantry Regiment storm the beach on Wadke Island, Dutch New Guinea. *U.S. National Archives.*

Vice Admiral Marc A. Mitscher, Commander Task Force 58, with his chief of staff, Commodore Arleigh A. Burke. Photo taken in spring 1945. *Official U.S. Navy Photograph.*

A basketball game in the forward elevator well of the USS *Monterey* (CVL-26). The jumper on the left is Lieutenant Gerald R. Ford, an athletics officer and future president of the United States. Circa June–July 1944.

U.S. National Archives.

Battle of the Philippine Sea, June 19, 1944. A Hellcat recovers aboard the *Lexington*.
Official U.S. Navy Photograph.

A Curtiss SB2C Helldiver enters the *Yorktown*'s landing pattern, circa June–July 1944. *U.S. National Archives.*

Army reinforcements wade ashore on Saipan, June or July 1944.
U.S. National Archives.

A marine discovers a Japanese family hiding in a cave on Saipan, June 21, 1944.
U.S. National Archives.

SB2C Helldivers return to the *Yorktown* after a raid in the Marianas in early July 1944.
U.S. National Archives.

Admiral Spruance and Lieutenant General Holland M. Smith, USMC, at a flag-raising ceremony at Smith's headquarters on Saipan, marking the end of organized Japanese resistance on the island, July 10, 1944. *Official U.S. Navy Photograph.*

Chapter Thirteen

ADMIRAL MINEICHI KOGA, THE TACITURN COMMANDER IN CHIEF OF the Combined Fleet, had been a close personal friend of his predecessor Isoroku Yamamoto. But Koga lacked his late friend's strategic and political audacity. He never dared to challenge the suzerainty of the Tokyo-based Naval General Staff (NGS) or the leadership's single-minded fixation on the all-important "decisive fleet battle"—a concept that dominated Japanese naval planning and strategic thinking before and during the war. This climactic clash of fleets was to occur somewhere in the western Pacific. It would involve substantially all of the capital ships in both the American and the Japanese navy. It would occur (it was hoped) in tactical circumstances favoring the Japanese side. It might begin with punishing land- and carrier-based air attacks on the American fleet, perhaps while the Americans were tied down in support of some major amphibious operation. But the big guns of the Japanese battleships would deliver the *coup de grace*. The thrashing would be so complete, so shocking, and so devastating that the government of Franklin D. Roosevelt would be moved to ask for a truce. Diplomatic negotiations would follow, and Japan would secure a peace that preserved its sovereignty, its honor, and some portion of its empire.

It would be no exaggeration to say that bringing about a single, all-deciding naval battle amounted to an obsession among the Tokyo admirals. The idea had been inculcated into generations of students at the Japanese Naval Academy at Etajima through the writings of the American strategist Alfred Thayer Mahan. The annals of history provided many convincing examples of such battles, none better than Admiral Heihachiro Togo's wipeout of a Russian fleet in Tsushima Strait in 1905. Intensive Naval Staff College

study of the Anglo-German Battle of Jutland (1916) had further hammered
the principle home—though in that instance, it was agreed, the British had
grasped the chance of a decisive victory but let it slip through their fingers.
Teikichi Hori, a "treaty faction" admiral purged from the Imperial Japanese
Navy in 1933, observed that Japanese naval planning had ossified perilously
in those years of ultranationalist ferment: "This kind of creeping formalism
spread until it became a kind of strategic orthodoxy and [the navy] ended
up as a smug little society which insisted that all ideas on strategy should
conform to this orthodoxy."[1]

Literally from the first minutes of the Pacific War, events proved that
airpower and submarine warfare had unseated the battle line as the ultimate arbiter of naval power. But the admirals had refused to relinquish their
trust in the big guns. Though Isoroku Yamamoto had been one of the most
air-minded officers to reach the top rungs of the Japanese navy, his move
against Midway had been a bid to force a decisive battle early in the war. He
had intended a critical role in that battle for the surface warships, including
his flagship *Yamato*. Aviators were not fast-tracked to promotions, nor were
they placed into important sea commands and planning jobs as they had
been in the U.S. Navy. Not until 1944 was the carrier task force integrated
into the heart of the Combined Fleet. War planning proceeded under the
orthodox assumption that the battleships (especially the leviathans *Yamato*
and *Musashi*) would play a leading part in the war's final act.

So Koga never doubted that he must sooner or later hurl the Combined
Fleet into the path of the advancing enemy. But when and where? Since
1942, the heavy ships (battleships and carriers) had been kept in reserve,
well out of the enemy's reach. The Japanese carriers had not come out to
fight since the Battle of the Santa Cruz Islands in October 1942. After losing the battleships *Hiei* and *Kirishima* off Guadalcanal a month later, the
navy had largely relied on its destroyers and land-based airpower to wage its
campaign in the South Pacific. Koga would prefer to make his stand within
range of friendly terrestrial air bases. He needed time to rebuild his carrier
air groups, and as the fuel supply became critical, he had good reason to
hope that the battle would be fought as near as possible to the oilfields of
Borneo and Sumatra.

On the other side of the ledger, Koga had to acknowledge that time was
not on his side. Month by month, the titanic output of the enemy's industrial plant was arriving in the advanced war zones of the Pacific. American

scientific and technical expertise was opening an ever-widening mismatch in air combat efficiency, especially in the vital categories of radar, radio communications, and antiaircraft defenses. The submarine campaign was obliterating 200,000 tons of Japanese shipping per month, and it would soon cripple the nation's war industries. The enemy's twin advances in the south and central Pacific were swallowing up strategically vital territories. All such considerations weighed in favor of committing the Combined Fleet as soon as tactical circumstances permitted.

Nor could any military commander ignore the increasingly strident demands emanating directly from the throne. The god-king Hirohito was pressuring his liaison conference to wage the war more aggressively, to confront the American fleet and crush it. As a young crown prince, Hirohito's education had been largely entrusted to the leading army and navy heroes of the Russo-Japanese War, Admiral Togo and General Maresuke Nogi. The boy had been steeped in Mahanian doctrine, and apparently never doubted that the war must be won by a decisive fleet engagement in the pattern of Tsushima. He let it be known that he was sorely disappointed by the loss of Guadalcanal. After the fall of Attu in May 1943, he sternly rebuked his army and navy chiefs of staff. The emperor expressed anxiety over the waning prestige of Japanese military power and its consequences for the future of his Asian-Pacific empire. His queries became increasingly pointed, shrill, and even sarcastic. He demanded to be briefed in detail, whereas he had previously been satisfied with knowing only the broad strokes, and took a direct part in deciding major questions of strategy. On August 5, as Allied forces drove into the central Solomons, the emperor dressed down the chief of the Army General Staff, General Hajime Sugiyama:

> If we continue fighting in this manner, it will be like Guadalcanal. It will only raise the fighting spirit of the enemy, and then the neutral countries will start to waver, China will get big-headed, and the impact on the countries in the Greater East Asian Co-Prosperity Sphere will be enormous. Can't you somehow beat down the American forces head on at some front? All the battle fronts look bad. Can't you give the American forces a walloping? If we continue to get pushed back steadily this way, it will have a significant impact on other countries, not just on the enemy. Now, just where are you going to show some success? Where are you going to stage a decisive battle?[2]

In mid-September, the emperor convened a series of meetings with military leaders at the Imperial Palace. On the agenda was a fundamental overhaul in war strategy. With the support of General Hideki Tojo, who simultaneously held the offices of prime minister and army minister, leaders at the liaison conference agreed to a "New Operational Policy" calling for a significant contraction in Japan's western defense perimeter to islands far behind the front lines. The new "absolute defense line" would run from the Kurile Islands south through the Marianas, Truk, Palau, New Britain, western New Guinea, the East Indies, and Burma. Positions on that inner perimeter would be heavily reinforced with land-based air units and army troops to be transferred from Manchuria. Garrisons outside the perimeter, including those in the Gilbert and Marshall island groups, would receive no further reinforcement. If attacked, they must exact a bloody toll on the enemy before perishing in combat to the last man.

The buildup of strength on the inner perimeter would take time—time to move troops from the mainland, to erect new shore fortifications, to build aircraft, and to train new air groups—so the policy designated "mid-1944" as "our approximate target for full readiness."[3] But the new policy did not rule out an early confrontation with the American fleet, if opportunity offered: "Whenever the occasion presents, we shall capture and destroy the enemy's offensive forces."[4]

Koga was keen to fight his Tsushima sooner rather than later. Since May 1943, the commander in chief and his staff had been studying and revising plans for Operation Z, which envisioned a grand sortie of the Combined Fleet to confront the American fleet in the central Pacific, if possible while the enemy was pinned down in support of an amphibious invasion. Admiral Pownall's carrier raids of September and October 1943 had twice coaxed a powerful Japanese fleet out of Truk. Koga personally commanded the second of these sorties, and anchored his ships in Eniwetok Atoll for four days in October. In both instances it was soon understood that the American movements had been hit-and-run carrier raids rather than sustained operations, and the fleet returned to Truk.

Relentless shipping losses and the MacArthur-Halsey drive on Rabaul prompted successive revisions to Operation Z. In late October it was decided that the fleet would not come out to fight in Micronesia or in defense of the Bismarcks. The decisive confrontation would be postponed until the enemy attempted to pierce the inner perimeter. Koga would make his stand in the

Philippine Sea, in defense of either the Marianas or Palau, depending on the movements of the American fleet. Pursuant to those decisions, when the Fifth Fleet launched its offensive into the central Pacific, Japanese garrisons in the Gilberts and Marshalls received diffident air support and no naval support at all, except as provided by submarine patrols.

After suffering heavy air losses at the Battle of the Santa Cruz Islands (October 1942), the Japanese carrier task force had retired to the Inland Sea for repairs, for refitting, and for the rebuilding of its decimated air groups. Incumbent commander Chuichi Nagumo (who had led the carrier striking force in the attack on Pearl Harbor, the Battle of Midway, and the carrier duels off Guadalcanal) was relieved and sent back to the homeland to command the Sasebo Naval District. His successor was Vice Admiral Jisaburo Ozawa, a tall, gruff, unsightly man nicknamed "the Gargoyle."* Ozawa took the fleet carrier *Zuikaku* as his flagship. The force was reorganized and designated the Third Fleet, consisting of three carrier divisions, two battleships, six cruisers, and more than a dozen destroyers. Most of the Third Fleet's air strength was concentrated in Carrier Division 1 (the veteran fleet carriers *Zuikaku* and *Shokaku* and the light carrier *Zuiho*) and Carrier Division 2 (the heavy sisters *Hiyo* and *Junyo*, both built on converted passenger-liner hulls and commissioned in mid-1942).

Throughout most of 1943, the Japanese carriers remained idle at Truk or in home waters. The same was not true of the air groups. Ozawa's carrier planes were repeatedly sent south to bolster the deteriorating fortunes of the land-based naval air forces at Rabaul and satellite airfields in the Solomons and New Guinea. In July 1943, most of Carrier Division 2's aircraft (about 150) flew into Rabaul to be integrated into the Twenty-Sixth Air Flotilla. The Zero pilots, trained at great expense to fly from aircraft carriers, suffered disastrous losses in pitched daily air battles against relentless waves of well-armed B-24s and B-25s.

In August and September, several Japanese fighter units were ordered to fly down to the primitive airstrip at Buin, on southern Bougainville, where conditions on the ground and in the air were even worse than at Rabaul. Halsey's heavily reinforced Guadalcanal-based air forces (AIRSOLS) bat-

---

* The nickname was *Oni Gawara* in Japanese. Ozawa had suffered a facial injury while serving on a destroyer early in his career. The injury had immobilized his facial muscles, making it impossible for him to smile or show other emotions through facial expressions.

420 IAN W. TOLL

tered the hard-pressed dirt airstrip day by day, and many of the Japanese carrier pilots who survived longer than a week succumbed to exhaustion and disease. In October 1943, the flyable remnants of Japan's badly mauled air forces at Buin began pulling back to Rabaul.

The following month, Koga ordered nearly 200 planes of Carrier Division 1 into Rabaul from Truk (Operation RO). Among them were many of the Third Fleet's most skilled and experienced airmen, including all of the squadron leaders. More than half of those planes were shot down within a week, and virtually none of the downed aviators were recovered. One of Admiral Ozawa's staff officers recalled the scene at the Spring Island airfield in Truk as the survivors arrived on November 13:

> I was astonished by the small number of planes that had returned. There were hardly any fighters to be seen. But it was worse with torpedo planes and fighter bombers. None of them had come back. . . . On the field Ozawa was giving the commander's speech of instruction that customarily followed an operation. Afterward I heard from some fliers about the speech. Ozawa had climbed the platform to address them and, being overcome with dismay at how few of his men had survived, was unable to utter a word. He stood there on the platform in silence for a very long time, weeping bitterly.[5]

On January 25, 1944, as the combined AIRSOLS and Fifth Air Force campaign against Rabaul reached its overpowering culmination, Koga fed another 150 planes from Carrier Division 2 into the meat grinder. Few of the Zero pilots had flown in combat prior to the deployment. They were instructed to avoid engaging the American bombers and fighters except when "battle circumstances appear particularly favorable to you."[6] For the sake of morale more than anything else, Nakajima torpedo planes from Carrier Division 2 were dispatched on risky night missions against Halsey's ships off Bougainville and MacArthur's transports off New Guinea. Those flights scored no hits on American shipping, but dozens of the valuable bombers were lost to antiaircraft fire and operational accidents. Masatake Okumiya, an air staff officer, recalled the dreadful last days at Rabaul:

> The days passed in a blur. Every day we sent the Zeros up on frantic interception flights. The young and inexperienced student pilots had

become battle-hardened veterans, their faces showing the sudden realization of death all about them. Not for a moment did the Americans ease their relentless pressure. Day and night the bombers came to pound Rabaul, to smash at the airfield and shipping in the harbor, while the fighters screamed low on daring strafing passes, shooting up anything they considered a worth-while target. So intense were the enemy attacks that we were unable to find time to attack their bases. Our losses mounted steadily, and the list of dead and missing pilots grew visibly.[7]

The losses from Carrier Division 2 in this last operation at Rabaul amounted to about ninety planes. Among those few aviators who returned to Truk in late February, many had been laid low by malaria and other tropical diseases. They also brought with them the incubus of defeatism and despair, which inevitably spread through the remaining Third Fleet air groups.

IN JAPAN, NEWS OF THE FEBRUARY 1944 raid on Truk was reported with unusual candor. Some news reports falsely asserted that the Americans had attempted an amphibious landing and been repulsed, but on February 18 the Imperial General Headquarters released an accurate and unsparing account:

A powerful American task force suddenly advanced to our Caroline Islands Wednesday morning and repeatedly attacked our important strategic base, Truk, with a great number of ship-based planes. The enemy is constantly repeating powerfully persistent raids with several hundred fighters and bombers, attacking us intermittently. The war situation has increased with unprecedented seriousness—nay, furiousness. The tempo of enemy operations indicates that the attacking force is already pressing upon our mainland.[8]

As always, the dire tone of this release was intended to arouse the Japanese people to greater efforts and sacrifices. But the regime could not countenance any admission that Japan might be in danger of losing the war. The editors of the widely circulated *Mainichi Shinbun* must have failed to appre-

ciate the subtle distinction. A front-page opinion piece, published on February 23, warned, "The decisive battles of offense and defense in the Pacific
will not be carried out on the homeland shores of America and Japan. They
will be fought out . . . on island bases several thousands of miles distant. If
the point is reached when the enemy advances to the shores of our homeland, already there is nothing more that can be done."[9]

The article included some pointed criticism of the training of civilians
to fight with bamboo spears, and added that the only real hope of repelling
the American advance was to build more warplanes and aircraft carriers.
When the newspaper landed on the desk of Prime Minister Hideki Tojo, he
blew his stack. Orders went out from the Information Board to suppress the
article, but since more than 100,000 copies had already been distributed,
the damage (such as it was) could not be undone. The Army Ministry issued
a reprimand to the paper, forced the editor in chief to resign, and summoned other leading editors to be admonished against such commentary.
The army drafted the journalist who had written the article, a common
method of disciplining wayward writers.

Tojo was unpopular with the Japanese people and despised by most of
the leading figures in the navy. He was pompous, shrill, and demonstra-
tive, and tended to silence reasoned discussion with outlandish flights of
rhetoric and sloganeering. He was always leaping to his feet, even in closed
meetings of senior cabinet and military officers. In October 1943, when a
minister referred to a disappointing harvest, Tojo stood and bellowed, "Even
if we eat nothing, we members of the cabinet intend to give our lives for
the nation!"[10] His antics sometimes seemed to ape those of Hitler and Mussolini, but Japanese culture was unsympathetic to the notion of concentrating power in the hands of one man. The emperor was the nation's singular
figurehead, and his ministers were expected to govern with an attitude of
humility and reticence.

The emperor was the ultimate underwriter of Tojo's long ascendancy
in the ruling circle. For nearly three years Hirohito trusted and listened to
Tojo, and even after the war the emperor defended the general's conduct
and leadership. Immediately after the Truk raid, Tojo moved to consolidate his grip on the military planning and command functions of both the
army and the navy. Since the Meiji era, authority in each service had been
divided between a ministry and a general staff. But now, with the emperor's
support, Tojo forced the resignation of General Sugiyama, the army chief of

staff, and named himself to that post while retaining his positions as army minister and prime minister. Navy chief of staff Admiral Nagano resigned and was replaced by the navy minister, Admiral Shigetaro Shimada, who also kept his existing job. The shake-up brought the planning staffs of both services under the control of the ministries. Because Tojo had always found Shimada a pliable colleague, it also brought the entire regime more firmly under the control of Tojo. Opposition within the general staffs melted away when the emperor let it be known that he had backed the plan.

BETWEEN NOVEMBER AND FEBRUARY, most of the aircraft carriers were again pulled back to Japan for repairs and to take on replacement airplanes and aircrews. The *Zuikaku* went into dry dock at Kure; the *Shokaku*, at Yokosuka in Tokyo Bay. The carriers were fitted with new radar systems and antiaircraft weaponry. New aircraft were embarked from Iwakuni Naval Air Station in Hiroshima Bay. Because the newly trained aircrews had not yet been cleared for carrier landings, it was decided to lift the planes aboard by crane rather than fly them aboard after the fleet had put to sea.

Six months was needed to train the new air groups. But the Americans could not be expected to oblige that timetable, so all understood that the Third Fleet might be thrust into battle before it was ready. Ozawa's air staff fixed an optimistic deadline of April 1 to have the new carrier air force fully trained, equipped, and ready to confront the enemy. The Third Fleet was to have 500 aircraft on nine carriers (five heavy, four light). Another 400 to 500 land-based fighters and bombers would be positioned on island airfields within easy range of the Marianas and Palau.

Japanese war planners had hoped to produce 40,000 new military aircraft in 1944, but the production rate was barely half that level in the fall of 1943. Aviation plants were straining under the pressure of material shortages, maladroit logistics, and a paucity of trained machinists and engineers. Shipping losses bit deeply into deliveries of Malaysian and Jakartan bauxite, the industry's chief source of aluminum alloys. The Mitsubishi complex in Nagoya had expanded steadily, employing 43,000 workers by the end of 1943, but it had turned out only 1,029 new Zeros in 1943, fewer than half the number demanded by the military services. The Japanese aircraft industry had relied to a disproportionate extent on a small, overworked coterie of talented craftsmen and technicians, and was never optimized for mass production. Belated efforts to introduce standard production-line techniques brought some improvement, but neither Mitsubishi nor the other major aircraft suppliers (Nakajima, Aichi, Kawasaki, Tachikawa, Yokosuka) managed to ramp up output fast enough to fill the military's ballooning wartime orders.

When a government inspector passed through the Nagoya works in late 1943, he was surprised to learn that newly manufactured Zeros were still being hauled away from the plant by teams of oxen. There was no airfield adjoining the Mitsubishi plant. The new units had to be transported overland to Kagamigahara, twenty-four miles away, where the navy would accept delivery. The aircraft were too delicate to transport on trucks, and the railheads were not convenient. Twenty oxen had died, and the remaining thirty were verging on complete exhaustion. Feed had been obtained on the black market, but the supply was not reliable. Essential wartime deliveries of replacement aircraft thus hung on the fate of a diminishing herd of underfed beasts. Mitsubishi engineers at length discovered that Percheron horses could haul the aircraft to Kagamigahara faster and required less to eat. These ludicrous exertions, when compared at a glance to the arrangements at Boeing, Douglas, or Grumman, tell most of the story of Japan's defeat.

Recent encounters with the new-generation American fighters—the Hellcat, the Corsair, and the Lightning—had settled any remaining doubts that the Zero was overmatched and obsolete. Jiro Horikoshi's airplane had been a feat of pioneering ingenuity, and it will always be a milestone in the history of aviation. From the start of its remarkable career, however, the Zero had always embodied a set of design compromises. Horikoshi's team had wrung every last ounce of surplus weight out of the aircraft, and given it a very large wingspan and control surfaces in proportion to its size. These traits gave the Zero long range, a fast climbing speed, and supreme agility, but they also made it sluggish at altitude, slow in a dive, and disastrously vulnerable to enemy fire. Mitsubishi had invested its limited design and development resources into two new interceptors, the J2M *Raiden* and the A7M *Reppu*. Both airplanes offered performance improvements over the Zero, but the early prototypes were plagued with mechanical failures and design flaws. Given enough time and engineering manpower, all of those problems might have been overcome (just as, for example, the assorted defects of the Curtiss SB2C and the B-29 Superfortress were corrected as those machines entered service). But time was short, and engineering manpower was sorely limited. Only small numbers of the Zero's successors were placed into service, and they were never popular with the airmen or air staff.

Without a viable alternative, the Japanese navy instead committed itself to improving the Zero. Mitsubishi tinkered with successive alterations throughout the war, generally adding horsepower, firepower, and armor plating while reducing wingspan—the Model II, the Model 21, the Model 22, and the Model 52 "Hei," of which more were built than any other version. Performance improvements were generally too slight to be noticed by the American pilots who engaged the planes. Lieutenant Commander Iyozo Fujita, one of the few veteran Zero pilots who survived the war, found that Model 52 lacked the speed and agility of its predecessors. It was "simply aggravating to fly," he said. "The aircraft's nose did not rise quickly enough, so it was hard to aim my machine guns well. Because of this, I felt that I lost a lot of opportunities to get hits on enemy aircraft."[11] The navy also experimented with configuring the Zero as a fighter-bomber, fixing a 550-pound bomb under its fuselage, but an airplane powered by a 1,000-horsepower engine was not well suited to such a role. In all its versions, the Zero was still packaged in the same light airframe, which could not absorb much punishment without blowing apart or bursting into flame. Design alterations consumed an exorbitant amount of the Mitsubishi engineers' time and energy, diverting their attention from the next-generation planes. They also clogged up the company's manufacturing operations. Output at the Nagoya works fell short of the navy's targets every year from 1940 through 1945.

In the 1930s, Japanese firms had imported American and European precision machine tools, needed to polish, grind, and mill high-performance metals. Prewar embargos had cut off those critical imports. By 1942, the plants were equipped with aging equipment that could not be replaced or upgraded. As a nation destitute of natural resources and mining deposits, Japan lacked access to the high-performance lightweight metals found in the 2,000-horsepower engines that powered the big American fighters. The Japanese aviation industry consistently struggled to produce reliable new aircraft engines that achieved high power ratings within desired weight limits. Atsushi Oi, an officer at the Naval Personnel Bureau, pointed to the small scale of Japan's "so-called shadow industries such as the automobile industry which can be easily converted to produce aircraft engines."[12]

Critical deficiencies at home were exacerbated by retrograde conditions in the advanced combat theaters. The Japanese had nothing to rival the civil engineering capability of the U.S. Seabees. Island airstrips were built with light construction equipment and backbreaking manual labor. In the early phase of the war, the Japanese had captured many of the best Allied airfields in the South Pacific and Southeast Asia. As they were wrested back by the enemy, the Japanese were forced to retreat to bases in which ground support facilities were inadequate and living conditions abysmal. Pilots and mechanics were quartered in tents, cooked over open fires, and bathed in fuel drums. Latrines were built over vile open-pit cesspools. Medical facilities were undermanned and undersupplied, and surgery was often performed without anesthesia. There was always a need for replacement airplanes and airmen, but that was only one facet of the logistics problem. Airfields in forward combat areas required a constant resupply of aviation fuel, spare parts, lubricants, ordnance, and ammunition. Fresh ground crews had to be flown in to replace those who succumbed to illness, injury, or death by bombing. Newly trained mechanics were less skilled than the veterans. Japanese air cargo transports were limited in number, and many were lost to operational accidents and enemy attacks. The throttling of Japanese maritime transportation was well underway and growing worse month by month.

Under such conditions, aircraft on the front lines fell into poor repair. Saburo Sakai, the fighter ace, told his superiors that every Zero fighter should receive a complete overhaul after 150 flight hours. In the South Pacific, however, most Zeros in service surpassed 200 hours and began running very rough.[13] By 1944, most front-line fighters were shot down before they ever had a chance for a maintenance overhaul.

Writing years after the war, Jiro Horikoshi observed that his country could not draw from the deep wellsprings of engineering and technical expertise that existed in the United States. There was nothing in Japan to compare with America's sprawling complex of universities, research laboratories, design firms, and heavy industries. Japan had a small circle of gifted engineers employed by the navy, the army, and about a dozen industrial firms. Owing to rivalries between the army and the navy and between rival companies and cartels (zaibatsu), much of their work was duplicative and wasteful. All too often their talents were squandered on impractical, profligate, stop-and-start projects that never got off the ground (in some cases, literally). They were resourceful and dedicated, but there were not enough of them. Horikoshi and his colleagues drove themselves to the verge of complete exhaustion and collapse, until the doctors and bosses ordered them to rest. "Such poor management of technical policy created the situation where we had no other choice but to rely on the Zeros from the beginning of the war until its end," Horikoshi wrote, "and this, in turn accelerated Japan's defeat."[14]

THE NEWEST ADJUNCT TO OZAWA'S FORCE was the *Taiho* ("Great Phoenix"), a 29,300-ton fleet carrier with an armored flight deck designed to withstand the sort of dive-bombing attack that had destroyed four carriers at the Battle of Midway. This was the first Japanese carrier to have such armor. The heavy steel deck required costly trade-offs, with the result that the ship's two hangars were small in proportion to her great size, and were serviced by just two elevators. She would carry only seventy-five aircraft, twenty fewer than the new American carriers. *Taiho* entered service in March 1944 and sailed that month to Singapore, where Ozawa took her as his flagship.

Two new carrier bombers were gradually replacing their obsolete predecessors. A new torpedo plane, the Nakajima B6N *Tenzan* ("Heavenly Mountain"), was faster and had a longer range than its predecessor, B5N ("Kate"). Its service introduction had been delayed by a balky in-house engine produced by Nakajima, and the navy had eventually insisted on a more reliable Mitsubishi power plant. The *Tenzan*, which the Allies designated the "Jill," seated a three-man aircrew and could carry a torpedo or a 1,754-pound bomb load for a distance of 2,000 nautical miles. It had gone into production in 1943; by early 1944 Nakajima was turning out about a hundred new planes per month.

The long-serving Aichi D3A dive-bomber ("Val") was giving way to the Yokosuka D4Y *Suisei* ("Comet"), a fast and maneuverable aircraft derived from a design by the German manufacturer Henkel, and powered by a 1,400-horsepower radial piston engine built by Aichi under license from Daimler-Benz. The Allies named her "Judy." Like the Jill, the Judy's service introduction had been delayed by various problems with early prototypes, notably a tendency for the wings to flutter while in a dive. The issue was eventually corrected with stronger wing spars and revamped dive brakes. With a maximum speed of 342 nautical miles per hour in level flight, the *Suisei* was the fastest carrier dive-bomber to be placed in general service by any combatant nation during the Second World War. It had been developed by engineers at the Yokosuka Naval Air Technical Arsenal, an Imperial Navy facility, but most of the units that went into service were built in Nagoya by Aichi. Its chief drawbacks were a lack of armor and self-sealing fuel tanks and its high speed in flight deck takeoffs and recoveries. Like all Japanese carrier planes, it was relatively easy to shoot down. The *Suisei* also lacked folding wings, a feature that had become *de rigueur* in the American carrier planes. Planes with fixed wings required more storage space, reducing the potential size of the air groups, and they required more time to cycle between the hangars and the flight decks. While the *Essex* carriers and their "airedales" had achieved quantum leaps in plane-handling efficiency, Ozawa's crews were hard-pressed even to meet the standards set by Nagumo's *Kido Butai* (carrier striking force) in 1941 and 1942.

If well-handled, the *Tenzan* and *Suisei* offered considerably better performance than their predecessor airplanes. They flew faster, higher, longer, and farther. Their introduction into the fleet had been rocky, but the same was true of carrier planes produced by other nations. If wartime Japan had possessed the resources to build a new fleet of larger and more sophisticated aircraft carriers to compare with the *Essex* class, and had simultaneously trained a new generation of pilots with the skill to measure up to 1942's "first team," the *Tenzan* and *Suisei* might have posed a deadly threat to the American fleet. But most of Ozawa's aging Third Fleet carriers (the *Taiho* excepted) were too small to comfortably handle the hot new machines. The heavy sisters *Hiyo* and *Junyo*, whose top speed was about 24 knots, could not launch or recover them at all unless the wind was blowing hard. Because it needed a full deck run to achieve its takeoff speed, the *Suisei* had to be spotted well aft. That limited the number of bombers that could be launched in a single cycle. Air staffs experimented with new catapults and even fuselage-mounted rockets to get the new dive-bombers safely aloft.

Carrier recoveries were always a white-knuckle performance. The *Suisei* approached fast and low, often failing to snag the arresting cables. When the new dive-bombers entered the landing circle, recalled an air officer on the *Zuikaku*, "there was always great tension on the bridge. We had special respect for the crews of these planes."[15]

The Japanese navy had been slow to acknowledge that its flight-training pipeline was inadequate. Most of the replacement aircrews who went aboard Ozawa's carriers that spring of 1944 had spent fewer than 150 hours in the cockpit and had acquired only rudimentary flying skills. Virtually none had practiced gunnery or qualified for carrier landings. The projected flight-training shortfall had been anticipated and discussed among Japanese aviators prior to the war, but no concerted effort to expand the pool of qualified flyers had come until 1941, when it was too late. Ruinous air losses in the Rabaul campaign had left the Japanese with no choice but to rush their cadet pilots through truncated programs and send them out to the fleet. Ozawa now faced the daunting task of preparing those undertrained young men to fight the decisive naval battle that loomed in the immediate future.

The elite Japanese naval air corps that launched the Pacific War had been trained in a small, super-exclusive program at the Kasumigaura Naval Air Training Center, the "Japanese Pensacola," near the city of Tsuchiura, about fifty miles north of Tokyo. The trainees had received two years of classroom instruction, flight training, and gunnery training, followed by an additional year of training in a forward operational unit. Recruits were selected from among recent graduates of Etajima (the naval academy), noncommissioned officers in the fleet, and civilian students between the ages of sixteen and nineteen. Screening criteria were extremely and even excessively rigorous. Even so, fewer than half those accepted survived to the end of the training program. When naval warrant officer Saburo Sakai applied for flight training in 1937, he was one of seventy chosen from a pool of 1,500 applicants. In primary flight training, each instructor was responsible for just three students. Lesser performers were pared from the program at every stage. Of the seventy men in Sakai's class, forty-five washed out before receiving their wings.[16] Most cadet pilots accumulated more than 500 cockpit hours before they were permitted to attempt a carrier landing.

The small and selective program produced some of the best aviators in the world, but it did not generate enough of them. In the mid-1930s, the Imperial Navy was producing only about a hundred new pilots per year. That figure grew after the China Incident (1937), but not rapidly enough to fulfill the navy's internal goals. Even in the early stages of the Pacific War, when the Japanese naval air squadrons ruled the skies throughout the theater, senior aviation officers were concerned about the supply of replacement aircrews. The navy had about 3,500 trained pilots in front-line service at the start of the Pacific War. Reserves were thin, and attrition would immediately begin to strain the system. Three months before Pearl Harbor, the Imperial Navy optimistically adopted a plan to train 15,000 new pilots. Masatake Okumiya, serving as an air staff officer at Kasumigaura, pointed

out that the navy did not have enough combat airplanes to continue training pilots like they did in peacetime—that is, by sending the Kasumigaura
graduates to advanced units to perform an additional year of "on-the-job"
training. Moreover, even if the funnel was opened to a much larger training
pipeline, "We would not feel the effect of the mass-training program for at
least another two to four years."[17]

Japan's flight-training system was simply not designed to expand. The
small size of the aviation industry and the existing pool of flyers were inflexible constraints. Ninety percent of Japanese pilots were enlisted personnel or warrant officers. A navy-sponsored civilian flight-training program
had been founded in 1934, drawing from the ranks of university students,
but it was too small to matter until 1943. The sensitivities and prerogatives
of the naval officer corps were a barrier to new recruitment avenues—the
Etajima clique stalwartly resisted the influx of reservist pilots and treated
them poorly when they were assigned to front-line units. The Yokaren program, which recruited adolescents directly out of secondary schools, was
expanded rapidly, and new training centers established throughout the
Japanese islands. But these young men often had little education in the
sciences and no prior experience handling machinery, and they needed as
much as two and a half years of ground instruction before starting primary
flight training.

The dearth of qualified and experienced instructors was a bottleneck.
The prewar student-instructor ratio of three to one was obviously unsus-
tainable. In 1941, each instructor took on eight students; in 1942, twelve.
More than twelve was deemed impracticable. The navy's veteran aviators
were desperately needed in front-line units, and they were rarely sent back
to Japan for assignment as instructors. The Imperial Navy did not acknowledge the existence of such a syndrome as "pilot exhaustion," preferring to
believe that all such frailties could be solved by an appeal to the purified
warrior spirit (Senshin), and never adopted a general policy of rotating pilots
out of the combat zone. "They won't let you go home unless you die" was the
Japanese aviator's mordant lament. But if veterans were not reassigned as
flight instructors, men in the training pipeline could not benefit from their
hard-won expertise.

Saburo Sakai, one of the few aces to be brought back to Japan as a wartime instructor (he had been wounded over Guadalcanal), was disgusted by
the attitude of the young ensigns and lieutenants under his charge. Sakai

and other noncommissioned officers were required to address the Etajima graduates as "Honorable Ensign" or "Honorable Lieutenant." The officers behaved with self-aggrandizing disdain toward enlisted combat veterans, including wounded heroes and aces who had shot down dozens of enemy planes. "Hey, you!" they shouted rudely. "How's my skill coming along?"[18] Enlisted pilots were assigned menial tasks after hours, such as mess cooking and peeling potatoes, while the officers partied at restaurants and tea houses and got drunk on high-shelf liquor. Even in advanced combat squadrons, officers treated their more skilled and experienced enlisted wingmen like members of a lesser caste. The effect on unit cohesion was predictable. Long after the war, Sakai remained bitter:

> I never learned anything from those officers who graduated from the Naval Academy about how to search out and spot the enemy, or how to outmaneuver and shoot them down. Instead, we learned from fellow noncoms, and the noncoms learned from the old noncoms, and the old noncoms learned from the warrant officers who were themselves learning from the special-service officers at the bottom of the officer heap. We became like brothers, looking after each other. Yet those officers, graduates of the Naval Academy, unskilled, lacking in any technique, *they* were officially our leaders. The nation does not know this. How many of their precious men were killed because of the misjudgments and lack of military acumen of those men! It was horrific, let me tell you![19]

In 1943, as the Japanese naval air corps was macerated in the South Pacific, the Imperial Japanese Navy made a despairing bid to expand all its flight-training recruitment channels simultaneously. Selection standards for the *Yokaren* program were relaxed, and about a dozen new regional training centers were established. For example, *Otsu Yokaren* Class No. 19 admitted 1,500 recruits in December 1942. The following class, No. 20, admitted 2,951 young men in May 1943.[20] The brightest and most capable candidates were put into an accelerated track and rushed into primary flight training. Inevitably, the duration and quality of their training deteriorated. The amount of flight time required to graduate declined steadily. By early 1944, the average was fewer than 150 hours. Gunnery training and target shooting were dropped from the program; the cadet pilots would have to learn how to shoot after arriving in forward units. In retrospect, it was suddenly clear that the navy's unduly restrictive prewar recruiting standards, and its practice of ousting so many apparently competent students from Kasumigaura, had been shortsighted and self-defeating. Sakai was undoubtedly right when he judged that the "forty-five pilots expelled from my own student class at Tsuchiura were superior to those men who completed wartime training."[21]

The navy also began recruiting large numbers of university students into flight schools. The students were enthusiastic; the navy received 20,000 such applications by mid-1943. It seemed as if all the young men at the top universities (Tokyo, Keio, Waseda) were clamoring to become naval aviators. The scholar and diarist Kiyoshi Kiyosawa worried that the naval air war would devour the nation's future leadership. "Japan was expecting great future contributions from these young people. These youths will be destroyed. . . . In the present war this is of the greatest concern."[22]

Kiyosawa was disturbed to hear that many of the young men were severely beaten and abused after enlisting in the navy. Inductees were forced to stand on tip-toe for an hour or more. If they failed, they were beaten savagely with bamboo rods, shoes, and leather sword straps. In May 1944, he recorded "reports that in the navy the thrashing of young recruits is widespread. It is particularly extreme toward student conscripts. I hear that they thrash them with clubs and a great many suffer broken hip bones."[23] Later that year, he lamented the fate of new inductees at Yokosuka Naval Base: "According to friends, the recruits are cruelly beaten with clubs and other things, and because of this many become deformed. When one man said things in the wrong way, the entire squad was beaten and knocked down. Is there anywhere in the world a place as barbaric as this?"[24]

AS A FORMER CHIEF OF NAVAL PERSONNEL, Admiral Nimitz held decided views about administration and staffing. Decades of experience had taught him that headquarters staffs, if allowed to drift unchecked, would grow inexorably until they were bloated, listless, and unwieldy. New branches and subdepartments would sprout like mushrooms after a hard rain. Growth in one department would elicit demands for more manpower from the others. New administrative strata would creep into the organizational charts. Departments would burst out of their appointed office spaces and surge into building annexes. Fiefdoms would arise and rivals would fall on one another in bitter internal disputes. Nimitz had seen it all before, and he was determined not to see it happen in Pearl Harbor. He let it be known that headcount was to be kept to a manageable minimum. He enforced the edict himself, if necessary, by hauling his department heads into his office and compelling them to explain and justify the addition of officers or enlisted men to the headquarters roster.

But Nimitz's theater command was expanding rapidly as new ships, hardware, and personnel flooded into the theater from the mainland. A small staff, desirable as it was, could not handle the immense complexities of planning, command, and administration. A CINCPAC annex housed the staff functions for the management of logistics and the maintenance of the fleet. An ever-expanding array of subordinate commands built up their staffs. Whenever possible, those organizations took in members of all branches of the armed services.

Among Nimitz's greatest priorities was to manage and contain the internal tensions and astringent personal rivalries inherent in the multiservice theater command. In this respect he was about as successful as any leader could have been. He frowned on open bickering between the services, and was scrupulously even-handed in hearing every man's point of view. Even the stormiest discussion was guided to a constructive conclusion. No matter how virulently they argued, men left his office on cordial terms. Many who worked with Nimitz later recalled his shrewd use of the well-applied joke. While winding down a testy planning session in the spring of 1944, the admiral said he was reminded of history's "first amphibious operation," conducted by Noah. "When they were unloading from the Ark, he saw a pair of cats come out followed by six kittens. 'What's this?' he asked. 'Ha, ha,' said the tabby cat, 'and all the time you thought we were fighting.'"[25]

The antagonisms could be soothed, but they could not be banished altogether. Several individual relationships were strained to the breaking point. Kelly Turner and Holland Smith occasionally behaved like the best of friends, but when they were forced to commit themselves to the details of planning an operation, there was always the risk of a new eruption. In February 1944, Turner was promoted to the three-star rank of vice admiral, and Raymond Spruance was promoted to full admiral with four stars, but Holland Smith was left behind in the two-star rank of major general. They had all worked together in the successful Gilbert and Marshalls operations. Smith had suspected that the navy would take care of its own while keeping the marines in their place, and here was stark confirmation. "You people ought to be proud of making stars," he spat at Turner. "You people going around and getting a star. . . . Every time the marines go into battle, you're liable to get a star." Turner replied, "Yes, and I'm proud to get stars for my command of the marines."[26] In Washington, General Vandegrift pushed Admiral King to approve the well-deserved promotion. Smith received his third star in May 1944.

The army continued to chafe under the setup that placed Smith in command of the Fifth Amphibious Corps (VAC). Before Operation GALVANIC, General Robert C. Richardson had tried and failed to extract his amphibious 27th Infantry Division from Holland Smith's command. Now he returned to the theme with redoubled determination. Saipan and Guam, next stop on the road to Tokyo, were not mere ribbons of coral sand, like the central Pacific atolls—they were large and ruggedly mountainous islands. The marines, according to the army view, were specialized assault troops trained to seize a beachhead. Warfare on larger landmasses was the army's area of special expertise. Thus an army general should command the VAC, or at least the army troops therein. Nimitz gave Richardson a respectful hearing, but then he rejected his proposals on the grounds that one does not fix what is not broken. But the CINCPAC had to keep Admiral King closely advised of these disputes, because there was always the possibility that they would be appealed to General Marshall, Secretary of War Henry Stimson, or even President Roosevelt.

Nor was the Army Air Forces pleased with its lot in Nimitz's theater, which was to be stuck fast under Rear Admiral John H. Hoover, Nimitz's commander of shore-based aircraft. Hoover was at loggerheads with his principal USAAF subordinate, General Willis Hale, over various issues related to procedures on airbases with mixed army, navy, and marine air units. Richardson had inserted himself into that dispute as well, and the reverberations had reached the Joint Chiefs of Staff through the Army Air Forces chief Hap Arnold. Hoover and Hale were said to cordially hate one another, though both denied it when queried by Nimitz. Hale had even failed to call on Hoover when passing through Funafuti, where Hoover had his headquarters—a serious breach of decorum. General Arnold would later demand local command of the islands serving chiefly as USAAF bases, and Nimitz would refuse. Arnold felt strongly enough to take the issue up with his fellow joint chiefs, who had little inclination to intervene in a local issue of command relationships. Stimson bluntly advised Arnold to stop rocking the boat.

The relationship between Nimitz and his deputy, the aviator John Towers, remained strained. Towers and the brownshoes had continued to press their case for greater recognition of the ascendancy of carrier aviation. Towers wanted action to rectify the disparity in decorations awarded to army and navy pilots, he wanted more real power for aviators on all planning staffs, and he wanted to permit more press coverage of the American carrier raids deep into enemy waters. War correspondents in Pearl Harbor did what they could to stoke the flames. Wartime censorship limited what they could actually write about the discord, but they liked to goad the aviators into complaining about the surface officers. When Admiral Nimitz learned that one of his staff officers had been asked, "What camp do you belong to?" he realized that the aviators had been airing the navy's dirty laundry in the presence of newsmen. Not for the first time, or the last, the CINCPAC read Towers the riot act.

But the issues raised by Towers were substantive, and they demanded to be addressed. Admiral King (himself an aviator) had asked retired Vice Admiral Harry E. Yarnell, something of a legend in the navy, to conduct a thorough survey and submit recommendations for future personnel policies. Yarnell had solicited the written and oral testimony of most of the navy's major commanders in the Pacific, and produced a report, which was delivered to King in the fall of 1943. His chief recommendation, that the commander in chief of the Pacific Fleet should be an aviator, was deemed unacceptable inasmuch as it would require relieving Nimitz of command. But the collected views of the admirals did lend strength to the aviators' case. A few ambitious brownshoes demanded sweeping all of the non-aviators, including Nimitz and Spruance, out of their jobs. But most leading figures (including Halsey, Spruance, Kinkaid, Turner, Calhoun, and Fitch) stressed that aviation must be welded into an effective component of the fleet and naval commands. Aviators should be strongly represented on all planning staffs and in every major command, and take a leading role in planning deployment of the carrier task forces. But the situation in the Pacific did not call for a general purge of blackshoe officers. Indeed, some senior line officers worried that the navy had been too hasty in moving young aviators up the career ladder. They could not suddenly acquire the skills and experience needed to command a big ship at sea. Time and again, remarked the blackshoe Carl Moore, aviators had been rushed through seagoing commands with the sole purpose of making them eligible to skipper a carrier.

"So they put them in a tanker for a year and then they give them command of a 50,000-ton carrier, and they terrify everybody else in the same ocean."[27]

On April 28, 1944, Navy Secretary Frank Knox died of a heart attack. He was succeeded by his undersecretary, James Forrestal, the former bond salesman who had been recruited out of the Wall Street firm Dillon Read in 1940. Forrestal had championed the cause of the aviators. He had often run afoul of Ernest King, who resented the civilian's aggressive interest in policy-making. The two men did not get along at all. But before Knox's death, Forrestal and King had agreed on a significant new personnel policy. All non-aviation officers in important commands must take an aviator as chief of staff, and all aviators in important commands must take a black-shoe as chief of staff. It was a compromise intended to spread the aviators' views and expertise into every command, but without forgoing the contrasting perspective of surface officers.

The announcement brought protests from many who were content with the status quo. Among the two most prominent duos broken up by the new policy were Raymond Spruance and Carl Moore (Fifth Fleet), and Marc Mitscher and Truman Hedding (Task Force 58). Neither Spruance nor Mitscher wanted to lose their incumbent chiefs of staff, and both asked that an exception be granted. Both were refused, though Moore was not forced out until the summer of 1944. Mitscher's new chief of staff was Arleigh Burke, who made his name commanding a destroyer squadron in the Solomons. Burke reported aboard Mitscher's flagship, the Lexington, in March 1944.

THE MARIANAS HAD NOT FIGURED PROMINENTLY in prewar American planning for a war against Japan (War Plans Orange and Rainbow), chiefly because the islands lay well north of the direct sea route between Hawaii and the Philippines. But Admiral King was convinced that the Marianas represented the war's strategic keystone because they were well situated on the sea routes linking Japan to its resource territories in the South Pacific and its fleet base at Truk. They also would offer a satisfactory base of operations for the Pacific submarine fleet, as they were located on the threshold of the fleet's hunting grounds. And the island of Tinian offered suitable territory for airfields that would allow the new B-29 bomber to reach the Japanese home islands.

In successive Allied conferences in Washington (May 1943) and Quebec (August 1943), the Combined Chiefs of Staff had deliberately chosen to defer final decisions concerning Pacific operations in 1944, with the understanding that the direction and timing of the next thrusts would be guided by events and opportunities. King had managed to insert references to the Marianas in Allied conference documents, but the Combined Chiefs did not formally order the capture of these islands until the Cairo conference in November 1943. Cairo's final conference documents endorsed a series of "Specific Operations for the Defeat of Japan, 1944," including the stipulation that "a strategic bombing force will be established in Guam, Tinian and Saipan for strategic bombing of Japan proper."[28]

For all the agitation between the navy and the USAAF, King and Arnold were now wary allies. Arnold believed that airfields on these islands offered the best hope of fulfilling the promise of the B-29 Superfortress. This huge airplane could carry twice the bomb load of the B-17 to a range of some 1,600 miles. Its pressurized cabin allowed it to operate at high altitudes, safely above the reach of enemy fighters. The B-29's introduction into service had been repeatedly delayed by defects large and small, most notably in its 2,200-horsepower Wright Duplex Cyclone engines. Arnold had been a voluble champion of the B-29, repeatedly assuring Marshall, Stimson, Congress, and the president that it would be ready for service by the beginning of 1944, and that several hundred of the giant machines could begin regular bombing runs over Japan from airfields in China. The Congress had kept faith with the B-29, pouring more than $1 billion into it by the end of 1943. But only ninety-seven B-29s had been produced, and only sixteen of those could be flown. Arnold told the president, "I regret exceedingly to have to inform you that there has been a holdup in production of engines. It looks now as if it will be impossible to get the required number of B-29s together in China to start bombing before the first of March, and with the possibility of not getting them there before the first of April. At this writing I expect to have 150 B-29s in China by March 1st, of which 100 can be used against Japan."[29]

FDR had personally assured the Chinese government that the B-29s were coming and would bomb Japan from Chinese airfields. It was a mainstay in his strategy to keep China in the war against Japan. He feared the consequences if the Army Air Forces was unable to make good on the repeated pledges. Meanwhile, Arnold was growing increasingly skeptical that China offered the best location for B-29 airbases. Chiang Kai-Shek had agreed to convert and enlarge existing airfields to receive the big bombers, but construction had lagged behind schedule, and there was no assurance that the Chinese could protect the bases against the ever-enterprising Japanese army. In early 1944, it appeared that the B-29s would have to begin operations from bases deep in the country's interior, at Chengtu and Chungking. Smaller airfields nearer the coast might be used for refueling stops, but they were not secure enough to serve as major operating bases. In April 1944, the first B-29s were flown into China from India, with the pilots taking them "over the hump"—a route that was both dangerous and resource-inefficient because of the immense amount of fuel required.

With all of those considerations in mind, USAAF planners had taken an increasing interest in the Marianas. Guam, Saipan, and Tinian offered the best prospects of big airfields within range of Japan. They were large enough to accommodate a fleet of 1,000 B-29s. The bomber's effective radius of 1,600 miles would bring Tokyo and the industrial regions of the Kanto Plain within reach. Once captured, bases on the Marianas would be secure against the enemy and could be amply supplied by sea. In October 1943, USAAF planners formally recommended that the Fifth Fleet and the amphibious forces of the central Pacific extend their offensive to the Marianas. That recommendation was accepted and adopted by the Combined Chiefs of Staff in Cairo two months later.

With its breathtaking range and tremendous weight-carrying capacity, the B-29 was a weapon without precedent, and it was coveted by commanders all over the Pacific. MacArthur expected a major allocation of the new planes to General Kenney's Fifth Air Force. Nimitz and his subordinates were interested in their capabilities for long-range antisubmarine patrols and mine-laying missions. But Hap Arnold had long preached the gospel of concentrated airpower and had often expressed his grief and indignation at the tendency to disperse bombers all over the globe. He was determined to deploy virtually all available B-29s in bombing raids against Japan and to keep them under his direct control. With Marshall's support, he convinced the Joint Chiefs of Staff to create the Twentieth Air Force, comprising the 20th and 21st Bomber Commands, to be controlled directly by the JCS. This was presented as a *fait accompli* to MacArthur and Kenney, who raged against the decision but could do nothing to reverse it.

Once the Japanese were ousted from the Marshalls, MacArthur was determined to bend Nimitz's line of advance southward. Indeed, MacArthur hoped to consolidate all available forces for his planned invasion of Mindanao, the southernmost major island of the Philippines. The Pacific Fleet might cover his northern flank by seizing Truk and Palau. Even better, the Allies might seize this opportunity to exorcise the demon of a divided command, and anoint MacArthur the Pacific Supremo. The Pacific Fleet and the formidable Fifth Amphibious Corps would then come under his direct command. An invasion of the Marianas did not fit into this master design.

MacArthur's chief of staff, Major General Richard Sutherland, formally presented the case against the Marianas in Washington. He observed that 1,000 miles of ocean lay between the Marshalls and the Marianas. To mount a major amphibious invasion across such a distance would drain Allied shipping resources and require many months of preparation. The invasion could not be supported by any land-based aircraft, and the carriers of Task Force 58 would not be able to establish complete dominion in the skies above the landing beaches while simultaneously fighting off the Japanese fleet, should it come out to fight.

Nor did MacArthur hesitate to bypass the Joint Chiefs of Staff by appealing directly to Secretary Stimson and even to Roosevelt. He predicted that the bloodbath at Tarawa would be repeated, but on a far greater scale. MacArthur would contain American casualties by bypassing strong positions and moving quickly to seize territory where the enemy was not strongly entrenched. This last argument, as MacArthur and his acolytes knew well, would be endorsed and trumpeted by the general's supporters in Congress and in the Hearst press. In mid-January 1944, MacArthur sent a statement of his views on the subject to Stimson (via Brigadier General Frederick H. Osborn):

These frontal attacks by the Navy, as at Tarawa, are tragic and unnecessary massacres of American lives. . . . The Navy fails to understand the strategy of the Pacific, fails to recognize that the first phase is an Army phase to establish land-based air protection so the Navy can move in. . . . Mr. Roosevelt is Navy-minded. Mr. Stimson must speak to him, must persuade him. Give me central direction of the war in the Pacific, and I will be in the Philippines in ten months. . . . Don't let the Navy's pride of position and ignorance continue this great tragedy to our country.[30]

While the relatively bloodless conquest of the Marshalls still lay in the future, trepidation about the potential costs and risks of taking the Marianas found a foothold even in Nimitz's CINCPAC headquarters. On January 27, 1944, a conference of senior officers from throughout the Pacific convened in Pearl Harbor. MacArthur was represented by Sutherland and his air and naval chiefs, General Kenney and Admiral Kinkaid. Halsey remained in the South Pacific but sent his chief of staff, Admiral Carney. All leading players on Nimitz's staff were there, as were the naval air chief John Towers, the logistics chief William L. Calhoun, and General Richardson of the army.

From the outset, it was apparent that few were inclined to invade the Marianas. According to Kenney, the sole voice in favor of the operation was that of "Soc" McMorris, Nimitz's chief of staff. The inevitable absence of land-based air support for the fleet and amphibious forces was deemed a serious obstacle. Many were wary of infantry combat losses on a scale much greater than those of Tarawa. Towers was concerned that the Japanese would stage punishing airstrikes through bases on Iwo Jima and Chichi Jima. Kinkaid pointed to a lack of good natural harbors in the Marianas, remarking that "any talk of the Marianas for a base leaves me entirely cold."[31] Calhoun agreed that it would be simpler to move the supporting train of auxiliaries and support vessels along the northern coast of New Guinea. Kenney, with Towers's emphatic support, cast doubt on the entire enterprise of using B-29s against Japan from bases in the Marianas. Fighters would lack the range to accompany the bombers on the long missions, and without fighter support the Superfortresses would be obliged to bomb from a very high altitude, where accuracy would be poor. Such bombing raids, he said, would be "a stunt" and nothing more. Their consensus recommendation against invading the Marianas was recorded in a memorandum, which Nimitz endorsed and sent on to King. General Kenney later wrote, "The meeting finished with everyone feeling good and ready to work together to get the war over."[32] At a closing luncheon on the twenty-eighth, Nimitz told the assembled group that victory was in sight.

Informed by Sutherland of the result, MacArthur assumed all was settled. All opposition to his proposed line of attack had apparently evaporated, and Nimitz had at last agreed to commit his powerful fleet to the thrust toward the Philippines. MacArthur contacted Marshall and asked for follow-up directives from the Joint Chiefs. His proposed strategy significantly exceeded what the conferees in Pearl Harbor had discussed. He should have the bulk of all Pacific naval forces placed under his command, with Halsey as his new fleet chief, and he wanted the B-29s.

Startled by the sudden uprising, King moved quickly to stamp it out. He wrote Nimitz: "I read your conference notes with much interest, and I must add with indignant dismay."[33] He rebutted the major arguments against the Marianas and closed with the blunt observation that the proposal to join forces with MacArthur in the south "is not in accordance with the decisions of the Joint Chiefs of Staff."[34] Marshall and Arnold were similarly unmoved.

In any case, subsequent events in the Pacific undermined the case against invading the Marianas. Prewar ideas concerning major amphibious operations had been rendered moot by the immense power of the Pacific Fleet to sweep away opposition in the air and on the beaches. In Operations FLINT-LOCK, CATCHPOLE, and HAILSTONE, Task Force 58 began to reveal the scale of its overwhelming strength. In the four months to come, Mitscher's rampages deep into enemy waters would demonstrate that land-based air cover was no longer the *sine qua non* of amphibious invasions and other major naval operations. Truk was neutralized and could be safely bypassed. A precipitous decline in the quantity and quality of Japanese airpower permitted more ambitious offensives across the Pacific. Many American officers felt a special obligation to liberate the people of Guam, a U.S. territory under occupation since the start of the war. New doubts were raised against MacArthur's proposed alternative in the south. The fast carriers could not be deployed to their best advantage in the confined waters between the Dutch East Indies and the southern Philippines. Asked to review the competing views emerging from the Pacific, the Joint Chiefs of Staff planners came down squarely on the side of continuing two parallel offensives, and stressed that the northern line of attack offered the shorter route to Tokyo. Nimitz and his officers reconsidered their objections and finally accepted that the Marianas operation was feasible. On February 29, the operation was designated FORAGER, and planning got underway at CINCPAC headquarters.

On March 11, the Joint Chiefs published a new schedule of operations against Japan. MacArthur's long jump to Hollandia, on the north central coast of New Guinea, would be completed on April 15. Truk would be kept under pressure by regular air raids and bypassed. The Marianas would be taken by June 15, Palau by September 15. The deadline for the invasion of

Mindanao was set for November 15, though that date was merely a place-holder. The return to the Philippines might become feasible earlier, depending on the course of events. That took care of the entire program against Japan for the calendar year 1944.

Nimitz and MacArthur had not yet met in a face-to-face command summit. The latter had routinely declined every invitation to travel outside his theater. The admiral, sensitive to protocols, could not invite himself to Australia. MacArthur was senior to him by a long stretch. (The general had received his first star when Nimitz was a commander.) When the CINCPAC asked for permission to tour naval commands in the Southwest Pacific area, the request was quickly granted, and Nimitz was invited to visit Brisbane. He arrived by seaplane on March 25 and found MacArthur and a retinue of staff officers waiting at the dock.

Nimitz and his flag lieutenant, Arthur Lamar, socialized pleasantly with the MacArthur family. They brought candy and orchids from Pearl Harbor and a silk outfit for the general's six-year-old son. Their meetings the next day, Admiral Kinkaid recalled, were stiffly formal but largely constructive. There was only one strained moment, when Nimitz called MacArthur's attention to a clause in the latest directive from the Joint Chiefs. The two theater commanders were to consider a contingency plan, to be activated in case Japanese resistance suddenly weakened, to move directly toward Formosa and the China coast. MacArthur, who never tolerated any talk of circumventing the Philippines, let loose a gale of indignant rhetoric. In a private report to King, Nimitz recapitulated the exchange that followed:

Then he blew up and made an oration of some length on the impossibility of bypassing the Philippines, his sacred obligations there—redemption of the 17 million people—blood on his soul—deserted by American people—etc. etc.—and then a criticism of "those gentlemen in Washington, who, far from the scene, and having never heard the whistle of pellets, etc., endeavor to set the strategy of the Pacific war"—etc. When I could break in I replied that, while I believed I understood his point of view, I could not go along with him, and then—believe it or not—I launched forth in a defense of "those gentlemen in Washington" and told him that the JCS were people like himself and myself, who, with more information, were trying to do their best for the country, and, to my mind, were succeeding admirably.[35]

MANY ORDINARY JAPANESE BEGAN to suspect that they had been misled, and that the tide of war had turned against their forces in the Pacific. The pattern of official news releases defied logic and common sense. Imperial announcements referred confusingly to glorious victories and strategic withdrawals. New "defense lines," always closer to the homeland, must be held at all costs. Military experts, writing in the newspapers or speaking on the radio, soberly explained that Japan's grand strategy was to "draw the enemy in"—to allow him to come closer to the homeland, where at last he could be crushed with one blow. Courageous Japanese troops defended advanced positions to the last man, perishing all together like *gyokusai*— "smashed jewels." Whenever a new position was captured by the enemy, it was confidently explained that defeat had been expected, and preparations had been laid in place for it. Official reporting about the war situation, wrote a Japanese American woman who spent the war years in Japan, "involved such obvious contradictions that even the more simple-minded listeners became doubtful."

> Everyone who could think at all realized that the country was in a more and more desperate state, its back to the wall. When it became impossible to hide the truth longer, the broadcasters would announce a battle or an island lost, and each time they did so the program was ended with music. It was always the same—the sad, sweet strains of *Umi Yukaba*, a well-loved old song. All over the nation people would bow their heads while someone quietly turned off the radio. The conviction of ultimate defeat had become widespread but everyone was careful not to speak his opinion; each carried on silently lest his doubts prevent another from doing his best.[36]

But they wondered, and worried. Aiko Takahashi, a young woman living in Tokyo, mused in her diary, "What exactly is happening? It's like picking colors in the dark, and for better or worse, there is no criticism of the government. It simply makes us uneasy."[37] The regime generally permitted accurate reporting of the progress of the war in Europe, and it was evident that Japan's Axis partners were not faring well against the Allies. The surrender of a quarter of a million German troops at Stalingrad was reported in Tokyo the same week that the Japanese people learned that their army had abandoned Guadalcanal. The straightforward accounts from Europe were contrasted with the vague, shifting, and often contradictory narrative about the war in the Pacific. In September 1943 came news that the Italian government of General Pietro Badoglio had capitulated to the Allies. Since the previous July, when the dictator Benito Mussolini had been deposed and arrested, press reports had assured the Japanese people that the new government would carry on fighting for the Axis. Now Allied forces were pouring into southern Italy, and the German army was in retreat. At a newsstand in downtown Tokyo, observed the diarist Kiyoshi Kiyosawa, "people are standing in long, long lines, and they are eager to buy newspapers. It appears they received a considerable shock."[38] Japanese military authorities took to the airwaves and editorial pages and confidently asserted that the fall of Italy was a piece of good fortune, for the Third Reich had finally "thrown off the burden called Italy and an indestructible resistance would now be possible."[39] Kiyosawa lamented the stupidity and shortsightedness of official propaganda. The state-controlled news media was playing fast and loose with whatever remained of its authority and credibility. "It appears that the Japanese newspapers do not even have the common sense and logic of elementary school students."[40]

Regime-sanctioned slogans and themes extolled the indomitable power of *Yamato Damashii*—the collective Japanese fighting spirit. Even if the enemy possessed material superiority—and in 1943, hints of America's enormous industrial output were seeping into news accounts—Japanese workers and warriors were capable of arousing themselves to new peaks of devotion and self-sacrifice. In the end, no matter what the cost, the transcendent spirit of the Japanese must prevail. When American forces stormed the Aleutian island of Attu in May 1943, a Japanese garrison of 2,650 soldiers fought a savage battle and died almost to the last man. Their cause had been hopeless—General John L. DeWitt's 7th Infantry Division assault troops had outnumbered the defenders by five to one—but they chose collective death over the ignominy of surrender. In Japan, the annihilation of the Attu garrison was inscribed as an important moral victory. It had proved that the Japanese warrior was willing to give everything for his country. The term *gyokusai*, first coined to describe the mass combat deaths and suicides at Attu, became increasingly familiar as one Japanese island garrison after another perished in similar fashion. Leading Japanese newspapers reported that "the heroic spirits of Attu" literally rose from the dead, took corporeal form, and renewed the fight against American forces when they landed on Kiska island three months later. "Foreign reports reveal that the American forces fought intensely and bitterly against this army of spirits over a period of three weeks," the *Japan Times and Advertiser* reported on August 24, 1943. "In the South Pacific sector, too, spirits of the Japanese troops have tangled with the enemy, causing many of them mental derangements and others to kill themselves as a result of nervous breakdown and morbid fear."[41]

By contrast, noted the Japanese commentators, the individualistic and luxury-loving Americans could never hope to emulate Japan's feverish devotion to victory in the Pacific. They wanted only to survive and go home alive. Long before they reached Japanese shores, the Americans would tire of the war and ask for terms of peace. So it was said. The chief of the Board of Information made the case at a speech in Yokohama in May 1943: "Soldiers are not tools but spirit! They are souls! American soldiers are crudely made and over-produced."[42] When General George S. Patton slapped an American soldier in Sicily in August 1943, the incident prompted excited commentary in the Japanese press. Here was incontrovertible proof that the enemy's fighting spirit was flagging! Since the United States was a democracy, its people would sooner or later bring pressure to bear on their leaders to seek a peaceful accommodation with Japan. Time was on Japan's side, because "conditions within America do not allow for a long drawn-out war."[43]

Homefront civilians were forever being exhorted to arouse themselves to greater efforts, to unite and summon their collective spiritual strength for an impending decisive confrontation with the enemy. "The present situation is truly grave," the *Showa* emperor told them, in an Imperial Rescript opening a special session of the Diet on October 26, 1943. "The Japanese people must fully display their total strength and thereby destroy the evil ambition of the enemy nations."[44] The people replied with exceptional fervor. That fall, apparently without a word of complaint, the Japanese government abolished holidays and weekends. There would be no more days of rest; the people would "return their holidays to the emperor."[45] Labor drafts were steadily expanded into new categories. Unmarried women and university students were conscripted into civil defense work and war industries. Progressively younger children were drafted into the workforce: in September 1943, all girls over the age of fourteen; the following April, all children of both genders over the age of ten. Although the American air raids were still more than a year away, measures to evacuate children from the cities

were initiated in October 1943. Military conscription was expanded. In the
fall of 1943, college students aged nineteen or older (except those majoring
in science or engineering) were called to service. Middle-aged men as old as
forty-five were inducted. The send-off ceremonies were every bit as elaborate
and well attended as those of 1941, but the mood had turned perceptibly
darker. People had seen too many wooden boxes wrapped in white cloth,
containing the cremated remains of dead soldiers and sailors repatriated
from the war zones. Aiko Takahashi, the young woman in Tokyo, told her
diary that the send-off processions had become "rather pathetic affairs. . . .
As I look at them, I have the wrenching thought that today once again, a
funeral of living people is passing and youngsters with their sleeves rolled
up are being sent off to die."[46]

ALMOST EXACTLY A YEAR after Isoroku Yamamoto's aircraft was shot down
over Bougainville, his successor as commander in chief of the Combined
Fleet met a similar fate. Wary of Mitscher's rampaging carrier task force,
Admiral Koga had made up his mind to transfer his headquarters ashore,
from the battleship *Musashi* (then at Palau) to the town of Davao on Mindanao. On the night of March 31, Koga and most of his senior staff officers
and cryptographers boarded three Kawanishi flying boats off Babelthuap
and took off for the 650-mile flight. The big four-engine planes flew into
a tropical witches' brew off Cebu, and two of the three went down. Koga's
plane simply disappeared, and none of the aircrew or passengers was ever
seen again. A plane carrying Vice Admiral Shigeru Fukudome, Koga's chief
of staff, ditched at sea about six miles off the coast. The vice admiral survived and managed to get ashore, where he was promptly taken prisoner by
Filipino guerrillas. His captors found a cache of highly classified documents
on his person. These included a signal book, an updated codebook, and a
copy of "Plan Z," the Combined Fleet's master operational plan for a fleet
action in the western Pacific. Fukudome was returned unharmed to local
Japanese army forces under circumstances that remain obscure, but the captured documents were handed over to the Americans. A submarine spirited
the precious intelligence to MacArthur's general headquarters in Brisbane.
    Realizing that the crown jewels had fallen into the enemy's hands, the
Imperial Japanese Navy moved quickly to promulgate a new edition of
the codebook and to write a new operational plan for the looming battle.

Koga's death was hushed up until May, when a new commander in chief was appointed. This was Admiral Soemu Toyoda, a torpedo specialist who had graduated from Etajima in 1905. Toyoda established his headquarters in an anchored flagship (the light cruiser *Oyodo*) in Tokyo Bay. A new plan of battle, designated "A-Go," was prepared in Tokyo by the Navy General Staff and distributed the same week.

A month earlier, Tokyo had ordered another major fleet reorganization, the fourth since the attack on Pearl Harbor. The main striking force of the Japanese navy was redesignated the "First Mobile Fleet" (*Dai Ichi Kido-Kantai*). Its two principal elements were the Third Fleet, which included nine aircraft carriers arrayed in three task groups; and the Second Fleet, consisting of most of the navy's major surface warships, including the battleships and heavy cruisers. Vice Admiral Ozawa was "fleeted up" to command the entire force, while simultaneously retaining direct command of the Third Fleet, with *Taiho* as his flagship. The Second Fleet, commanded by Vice Admiral Takeo Kurita, was to function as a subordinate screening force, although Ozawa might send it to engage the enemy in a conventional naval gunnery battle if and when opportunity offered. The Combined Fleet had been reshuffled several times before, but the creation of the First Mobile Fleet took the unprecedented step of placing the carriers at the nucleus of the force, with the battleships relegated to a subsidiary role. For the first time in the history of the Imperial Navy, a carrier admiral would exercise tactical command over the battleships.

Traditions, dogmas, and cultural norms had long stood in the way of this necessary reform. Apart from the fixed ideas of the battleship adherents, it was simply not the way of the Imperial Navy to place a junior admiral over a senior admiral in the command chain. Before August 1943, when Kurita relieved Vice Admiral Nobutake Kondo in command of the Second Fleet, Ozawa (Etajima class of 1909) could not be placed above Kondo (class of 1907) without causing severe loss to the latter's "face." It was necessary that Kondo be retired or transferred to other duties before Ozawa took command of the mixed force. Kondo was given command of the China Area Fleet, and he held that position until May 1945.

Throughout the spring of 1944, Ozawa's fleet moved between Singapore and anchorages in the southwestern part of the Sulu Sea (between the Philippines and Borneo). His movements were largely dictated by three considerations, all markers of the Japanese navy's deteriorating fortunes. First, he needed to keep his flight decks in close proximity to terrestrial airfields, because his inexperienced pilots could not always be trusted to land safely on the carriers. Second, the fuel shortage, which had been exacerbated by the sinking of tankers, forced the fleet to operate near its sources of oil in Borneo and Sumatra. Third, the escalating threat posed by Pacific Fleet submarines kept Ozawa's fleet besieged in shallow and enclosed waters.

In early March, the Japanese carriers anchored off Singapore and their air groups dispersed to the region's various airfields for training exercises. The early results were not encouraging. Many of the new pilots had first climbed into the cockpit of a trainer aircraft less than six months earlier. The powerful new *Suisei* and *Tenzan* bombers were a bit too hot for many of the green pilots to handle, even from terrestrial airfields. They had received little or no gunnery or navigational training, and were obligated to follow a squadron or division leader who knew where he was going. "The training was intense, and almost every day there was an accident," said maintenance officer Hiroshi Suzuki of the *Zuikaku*. "There were a lot of crashes because the pilots and mechanics were mostly rookies, and they were flying new aircraft. Besides that, the weather in Singapore was usually very bad, and we had a lot of rain."[47]

In the second half of March, Carrier Division 1 and two divisions of the Second Fleet moved about a hundred miles south to Lingga Roads, off the coast of Sumatra. This anchorage, near the Palembang oilfields, was spacious enough for the carriers to conduct basic flight operations. Its narrow entrance channels could be policed against submarine infiltration. Here the rookie pilots would practice their carrier landings, but when the planes moved from airfields to flight decks, operational losses rose to fearsome proportions. Minoru Nomura, air officer on the *Zuikaku*, recalled watching as a *Tenzan* dropped a dummy torpedo and roared low over the carrier's bow, just clearing it. As the crew heaved a sigh of relief, "the pilot began to bank for a right turn. At that instant his right wingtip made contact with the water. Plane and crew disintegrated instantly. It was over in a moment."[48] The powerful new torpedo bombers and dive-bombers were unforgiving when flown at low speeds. Many dropped into the sea astern of the carriers as they made the final turn in the landing approach. Planes failed to snag an arresting wire and went careening into the island or over the side. Midair collisions occurred directly overhead. "This is self-destruction air warfare," a *Junyo* pilot ruefully commented.[49]

Admiral Shimada issued the revised Plan A ("A-Go") in Directive No. 373 on May 3. The plan envisioned a fleet battle in one of two "decisive battle" zones—in waters off Palau or the western Caroline Islands. The First Mobile Fleet would be supported by nearby elements of the shore-based First Air Fleet. If the Americans attacked the Marianas, Ozawa would remain in local waters in the hope of "luring" the enemy fleet south. Thus the plan depended on the Americans' accepting the proffered bait. "The decisive battle," Shimada wrote, "will be fought as close as possible to the forward base of our mobile fleet."[50]

The battle *must* be fought in those southern waters because the fuel situation required Ozawa to stay within easy reach of Dutch East Indian oilfields. The relentless attrition of oil tankers, chiefly credited to the American submarines and their now-reliable torpedoes, had chained the fleet to the refineries at Tarakan, Balikpapan, and Palembang. The immediate fueling situation could be alleviated by allowing the ships to take on unrefined Borneo petroleum, which was pure enough to drive the engines, but volatile and dirty. Ship's engineers detested the stuff because it left layers of filthy sediment in the boilers, and it greatly increased the risk of explosions and fires.

Until mid-May 1944, therefore, orders issued by Admiral Toyoda pursuant to A-Go did not admit the possibility of a fleet battle off the Marianas. If the Americans attacked Saipan and its neighbors, land-based naval air forces on the islands must attack and destroy the enemy fleet. These air units could be reinforced from the homeland, by sending planes to stage through the "Jimas" (the Bonin Islands, including Iwo and Chichi). Meanwhile, ground forces on Saipan were being strengthened and reinforced, and the local army commander, Lieutenant General Yoshitsugu Saito, had confidently pledged to repel any amphibious invasion. Still, uneasy questions remained: What if the Fifth Fleet declined to chase the enemy into the southwest? Could Japan risk the loss of territory so near the homeland without committing its fleet to make a stand?

The answer was given on May 11, when the Naval General Staff rescinded its prohibition against pumping crude oil directly into Japanese ships. In the third week of May, most of the First Mobile Fleet anchored at Tawi Tawi in the Sulu Archipelago, between Mindanao and Borneo, and shuttle tankers from Tarakan filled every ship to capacity. But Tawi Tawi was no good for flight training because there were no suitable airfields in the area. Ozawa, appalled by the deadly losses incurred during carrier flight operations, had decided not to continue such training exercises: "I cannot bear to lose the lives of any more of my men in these accidents."[51] Though urgently in need of more preparation, the air groups were largely idled in the last month before the Japanese fleet was compelled to give battle. According to Lieutenant Commander Zenji Abe, air group leader on the *Junyo*, the prevailing breeze was not strong enough to get the *Suisei* carrier bombers aloft even at the ship's maximum speed. "So we couldn't take off," said Abe, "and had no training after we left Japan from early May until 19 June, when the big American task force came over to the Marianas to attack Guam and Saipan. . . . So for forty or fifty days, we had no training flights at all."[52]

Admiral Matome Ugaki, the erstwhile Combined Fleet chief of staff, who had functioned as Yamamoto's right hand and had survived the aerial ambush that killed the former commander in chief in April 1943, had recovered from his wounds and was back in the fleet. He had been appointed commander of the First Battleship Division of the Second Fleet, a command that included both the *Yamato* and the *Musashi*. He was glad to be back at sea but was discouraged by the state of training, both in his own battleships and throughout the fleet. In the privacy of his diary, Ugaki wavered between despondency and mystic appeals to *bushido*, the warrior spirit. He regarded the strategic plans to be basically sound, but doubted that the First Mobile Fleet possessed the means to execute them. Meeting the enemy at sea seemed a daunting prospect because "the only possible consequence is to become easy prey to enemy planes and submarines. The further we venture out, the more we shall be beaten. It's like one can't help getting soaked if one goes out in the rain without a coat or umbrella."[53] But the fleet could not afford to procrastinate, he observed a few days later, because the Americans were gaining strength all the time.[54] On April 27, he went aboard Ozawa's flagship, the *Taiho*, to participate in tabletop war-gaming exercises. In Ugaki's judgment, the game supervisors allowed assumptions that were unrealistically favorable to the Japanese side. He judged that the navy's fixation on a decisive battle amounted to an irrational obsession, and wondered why "they don't give enough consideration to attacking enemy elements easy to destroy."[55]

Ugaki's entries in April and May 1944 are filled with conflicting judgments and sentiments. The tone leaves no doubt that he knows his country is defeated, but he will not say so outright, even in his diary. On April 24: "The enemy's present strength is just like a raging fire, so irresistible that a small amount of water can hardly put it out."[56] His pessimistic insights ring true, while his efforts to arouse his own spirits are feeble and half-hearted: "However, at the same time the enemy, too, may not be as good as we think. It may turn out all right, if and when we fight with them."[57]

If the decisive battle was to be fought off the Marianas, a scenario made feasible by the Tarakan crude, Ozawa would launch his strike at very long range, 300 miles or more to the westward of the enemy. The Japanese planes would attack the American fleet and then land on airfields in Guam. There they would replenish fuel and ammunition and continue flying sorties until the enemy fleet was annihilated. This use of "shuttle-bombing" from shore bases was at the heart of A-Go. Successive aerial hammer blows would fall on the American fleet from Ozawa's carriers and the Marianas airfields. Ozawa would then unleash all his forces, including the battleships and other surface warships, to pursue the cripples and wipe them out. Shimada's directive put across Tokyo's absolute conviction in the plan: "Complete success is anticipated."[58]

Keeping the First Mobile Fleet out of the enemy's reach appealed to the logic of "outranging," a guiding tactical principle in Japanese planning and weapons systems. Outranging was a theme found in the design of the Imperial Navy's many long-ranged aircraft, including the Zero and the G3M and G4M medium bombers. For all the problems and challenges of the Japanese aircraft industry in wartime, the new-generation carrier dive-bombers and torpedo bombers had significantly greater range than their American counterparts. (The *Suisei* flew so far that it was often configured as a reconnaissance plane, and had been employed on ultra-long-range missions since 1942.) Outranging had been employed to good effect in surface naval actions by the Type 93 (Long Lance) torpedo. The superbattleships, with their 18.1-inch guns, were designed to strike an enemy from beyond his effective range. Outranging and shuttle-bombing offered some theoretical promise of rectifying the disparity in force between the two opposing fleets. The Japanese were well aware that they were outnumbered. A May 9 intelligence estimate distributed by the Naval General Staff predicted that the U.S. fleet would sail with sixteen battleships, including eight of the fast new types. As for carriers, the estimate was eight large fleet types, ten light carriers, and approximately twenty jeep carriers.[59] Those figures were close enough to the mark.

The shuttle-bombing tactic embodied in A-Go was sound in theory, but it was an expediency chosen to spare the pilots the ordeal of landing on the carrier flight decks. It was a tactical concept selected, in part, to mitigate the deficiencies in the carrier pilots' skills, and therefore pointed to the larger problem that would inevitably decide the outcome of the impending battle. The Japanese aviators were simply not ready to meet their adversaries on anything approaching equal terms.

The officers and pilots told one another that A-Go was a good plan that would deliver a badly needed victory for Japan. By some reports, the Japanese officers and crews were confident in the week before sailing for battle. High hopes were invested in the land-based First Air Fleet, also called the Base Air Force, commanded by Vice Admiral Kakuji Kakuta and headquartered on Tinian. Shore-based naval air had always been closely integrated into the Imperial Navy's fleet command structure. Naval leaders had retained a lingering belief, despite plenty of contrary evidence, that their land-based bombers could deal devastating blows to enemy fleets at sea.

On paper, the First Air Fleet had a huge complement of about 1,750 planes, but that figure overstated Kakuta's actual strength in the Marianas by more than threefold. His command suffered from poor ground support facilities, a shortage of qualified mechanics and aircrews, and scarcities of spare parts, ammunition, and fuel. The submarine threat in waters between the home islands and the Marianas had rendered it impractical to crate the planes and send them by sea. Most were flown in from Japan by unseasoned and undertrained pilots through airfields in the Bonin and Volcano archipelagoes. Operational accidents, including crashes and navigation failures, accounted for crippling losses of both aircraft and aviators. On the eve of the American attacks, Kakuta was thought to have about 435 aircraft in flyable condition.

Quite apart from the amphibious campaign and the ubiquitous depredations of the fast carriers, American submarines were cutting the internal tendons of the Japanese war effort. The undersea campaign had grown steadily more potent since mid-1943. On June 7, the Naval General Staff announced that 210,000 tons of shipping had been lost in May. Since the beginning of April, the Japanese had lost five destroyers, six tankers, four troopships, and fourteen freighters. The Japanese fleet was constantly stalked, reconnoitered, harassed, and hunted by submarines operating from Pearl Harbor and Australia. Each of Japan's superbattleships had caught a torpedo fired from an American submarine. The *Yamato* had taken a hit from the *Skate* on Christmas Day, 1943; the *Musashi* was torpedoed by the *Tunny* while departing Palau on March 29. Though the huge ships could easily withstand single torpedo hits, the damage had to be repaired in Japanese home waters, requiring long voyages and absences that consumed scarce fuel and deranged the formations and plans of the Japanese commanders.

In April and May 1944, every major movement of Ozawa's fleet was tracked and reported by submarines. American boats skulked off Lingga Roads near Singapore, observing and reporting as Japanese ships entered and exited. They assailed tankers shuttling between Tarakan and Tawi Tawi, off the northeast coast of Borneo. Freighters and troop transports carrying reinforcements from China went down between Shanghai and Manila. The veteran light cruiser *Yubari* was destroyed in an attack by the *Bluegill* off Halmahera on April 26. On May 6, the *Crevalle* sank the big tanker *Nisshin Maru* off Borneo.

As the First Mobile Fleet gathered in Tawi Tawi in mid-May, it was reconnoitered by the submarines *Lapon* and *Bonefish*. On May 15, the *Bone-fish* (Commander Thomas W. Hogan) damaged a tanker and sank one of its escorting destroyers, the *Inazuma*. His sighting reports confirmed that a major fleet rendezvous was in progress at Tawi Tawi, and two more sub-marines, the *Puffer* and *Bluefish*, shadowed the approaches during the fol-lowing week. The *Puffer*'s attack on the seaplane tender *Chitose* on May 22 resulted in two hits, both apparent duds. On June 5, she sank two valu-able cargo ships, the *Takasaki* and the *Ashizuri*. In a three-day rampage off Tawi Tawi between June 6 and 9, the submarine *Harder* (Commander Sam-uel D. Dealey) ran up one of the most extraordinary scores in the history of submarine warfare. On the sixth, just south of Tawi Tawi, the *Harder* sank a charging destroyer, the *Minazuki*, with a down-the-throat shot. She repeated the performance the following day with another down-the-throat shot, sinking the destroyer *Hayanami*. On the eighth, Dealey found the vet-eran destroyer *Tanikaze* in his sights and sank her with a four-torpedo salvo.

Destroyers, having been conceived and designed as submarine hunters, were the submariner's natural enemy. The destruction of so many such ves-sels was a source of singular satisfaction to the American submarine crews. It also weakened Ozawa's antisubmarine screening force, a factor that would prove decisive in the impending carrier battle.

While fretting over the location and intentions of the Fifth Fleet, the Japanese army and navy were also forced to react to MacArthur's offensive up the northern coast of Dutch New Guinea. In a finely choreographed series of sealifts, Admiral Kinkaid's naval forces had put army amphibious troops ashore on Hollandia (April 21) and Wakde Island (May 17). In each case the invaders had secured airstrips in a matter of days, and USAAF planes had begun exerting pressure on points farther west. In May, MacArthur was driving toward the "Bird's Head" peninsula of northwestern New Guinea. On May 20, naval and amphibious forces began maneuvering into position to attack Biak Island. About 10,000 Japanese troops held the island, including an elite 222nd Regiment that had been battle-tested in China. The initial landings caught the defenders by surprise, but in the drive to capture Biak's three airfields, the fighting bogged down and both sides suffered heavy losses.

The Japanese deemed Biak a critical outpost in the defense of the southern inner perimeter. The island's airfields were an important node in the forthcoming battle envisioned in A-Go. If they were lost, they would be turned against the Japanese. USAAF B-24 bombers would launch a lethal bombing campaign against western New Guinea, Palau, and the southern Philippines. They would command the sea-lanes east of Mindanao. Therefore, Admiral Ugaki wrote in his diary, "Biak Island is the most critical crossroad of the war."[60] He suspected that the Japanese army was less than sanguine about its prospects on Biak and therefore was inclined to abandon the garrison as it had on so many other islands. But the navy could not countenance such a retreat, and Ugaki urged Ozawa to pressure Tokyo to send all available air and troop reinforcements into the area.

On May 29, Admiral Toyoda of the Combined Fleet ordered "Operation KON" to commence. KON involved the massing of land-based air units and troops behind the lines, and plans to move troops quickly into disputed areas to respond at the point of attack. It was thought that the U.S. Fifth Fleet might even be lured south to intervene in the campaign, an event that would activate A-Go and perhaps lead to a war-altering decisive naval victory. Kakuta was ordered to fly some 480 planes into airfields at Sorong and Halmahera island, from which they could attack the American amphibious fleet off Biak. Encouraged by reports from the island, where the Japanese garrison had repeatedly driven American forces back in counterattacks, the Imperial General Headquarters resolved to send in land reinforcements. Short of transports, the navy resorted to the old tactic of using destroyers and cruisers as makeshift troopships, which staged at Sorong. The flotilla, committed by Vice Admiral Naomasa Sakonju, would fetch 2,500 troops of the Second Amphibious Brigade from Zamboanga, Mindanao, on May 31 and land them on Biak three days later. Much of their weaponry and supplies would be towed in by barges.

Sakonju's approach was detected on June 3 by Allied reconnaissance planes, and the flotilla was intercepted by a cruiser-destroyer force under Admiral Victor A. C. Crutchley. Heavy air attacks on June 8 sank one of Sakonju's ships and damaged another. The Japanese warships, crowded with troops and in no condition to fight, withdrew in a running battle.

The failure of the first reinforcement mission only redoubled Ozawa's determination to hold Biak. At Tawi Tawi, where divisions of ships were arriving from Lingga Roads, the staff pored over maps of Biak and western New Guinea and contemplated their options. Their prevailing view remained that the U.S. fleet would sail through the Palau islands to force a diversionary fight. Ugaki was keen to bring his heavy ships into action but reluctant to risk them to force the troop reinforcements through to Biak. On June 10, Admiral Toyoda ordered the battleships *Yamato* and *Musashi*, with the light cruiser *Noshiro* and six destroyers, to attempt another troop landing. Admiral Ugaki, who had admitted in his diary the previous morning that "I thought we had no choice but to give up Biak," would command the combined force. He sailed from Tawi Tawi that afternoon and rendezvoused with additional forces in Batjan on June 11.[61]

With nothing to compare to the Americans' sophisticated amphibious equipment and landing craft, the Japanese warships were forced to the expedient of carrying army landing craft on their decks—one each on the destroyers, two each on the cruiser and battleships. With the decks awkwardly burdened in this way, the ships could not come to action or use their guns to bombard shore positions. The troops would have to be landed before the squadron went into action; if the Americans interfered, this reinforcement mission was likely to end in another failure. En route, Ugaki admitted in his diary that he was "worried" about his anemic air cover, and considered that his ships were likely to come under punishing air attack before they could get troops ashore or bring their naval guns to bear on any enemy target: "I think that to reach the front line itself without air cover is awfully difficult, but I won't grumble about it now. I shall do all that is humanly possible."[62]

The Biak operation was complicated by a series of indications that the Americans were staging a major operation north of the equator, probably aimed at the Marianas. Long-range scouting flights launched from Nauru had photographed a powerful American fleet anchored at Kwajalein and Majuro. A few days later, on June 9, another flight confirmed that the carriers and battleships seen earlier were gone. Where were they? Where were they going? On Toyoda's flagship, still anchored in Tokyo Bay, the staff officers continued to believe that the Pacific Fleet's next thrust would be aimed toward Palau and the southern Philippines. Only the staff intelligence officer, Commander Chikataka Nakajima, predicted that the enemy was headed to Saipan. On June 10, American carrier planes were sighted about 300 miles east of Guam. The next day came a powerful fighter sweep over Saipan and Guam. On the night of June 12, Kakuta's headquarters radioed its best estimates of the situation off the Marianas, judging that the enemy force consisted of eleven carriers.[63]

Kakuta's early reports on the air fight over the Marianas were largely upbeat. Though he was losing a great many planes, he believed (or said he believed) his forces were inflicting proportionate damage on the American carrier forces. Air scouts had not yet detected Turner's amphibious fleet, so the Japanese surmised that the action in the Marianas might be nothing more than a raid or a feint. Other air scouts had seen MacArthur's transports passing through the Admiralties, indicating that a major landing might be at hand in the south.

At this moment, the strategic merit of the Americans' double-headed offensive was plainly in view. The Japanese high command found itself frozen in place, awaiting clarity on the location and objective of the Fifth Fleet.

On June 13, with minesweepers working off Saipan's leeward beaches and battleships bombarding the coast, it seemed clear that an invasion of that island was imminent. Without waiting for orders, Ugaki suspended the Biak operation and began clearing his decks of the landing craft. Impatient for orders to fall in with Ozawa, he weighed the pros and cons of rushing north on his own initiative. Two hours later, Admiral Toyoda suspended Operation KON and gave new orders: "Set Op A in motion for the decisive battle."[64] The First Mobile Fleet filed out of the channel at Tawi Tawi. Ozawa set course at high speed for the Guimaras Strait in the Western Visayas region of the Philippines, where the fleet would take on 10,800 tons of fuel before sailing for the San Bernardino Strait. Ugaki's force of battleships, cruisers, and destroyers broke off the attack on Biak and sped north at 20 knots, keeping Mindanao to port, intending to rendezvous with Ozawa in the Philippine Sea. The Biak garrison was left to make the now-customary last stand, and die to the last man.

Chapter Fourteen

O N JUNE 6, 1944, AS ALLIED TROOPS STORMED THE BEACHES OF northern France, President Roosevelt offered a simple prayer over the radio: "Almighty God: Our sons, pride of our Nation, this day have set upon a mighty endeavor, a struggle to preserve our Republic, our religion, and our civilization, and to set free a suffering humanity. . . . With Thy blessing, we shall prevail over the unholy force of our enemy."[1]

The president knew, but could not yet disclose, that another great amphibious flotilla was underway in the Pacific. If not for the invasion of northern France (OVERLORD), the Pacific operation (FORAGER) would have surpassed all previous amphibious landings in scale and sophistication. That two such colossal assaults could be launched against fortified enemy shores, in the same month and at opposite ends of the Eurasian landmass, was a supreme demonstration of American military-industrial hegemony. The force that sailed against the Marianas included more than 600 ships carrying more than 300,000 men. Admiral Marc Mitscher's Task Force 58 now included fifteen aircraft carriers divided into four task groups. Task Force 51, the Joint Expeditionary Force, carried 127,000 amphibious assault troops, including the 2nd, 3rd, and 4th Marine Divisions and the army's 27th Infantry Division. Records enumerated 40,000 discrete categories of supplies and munitions in the holds of the transports. These had been combat-loaded so that they could be removed and transferred to the beach-head quickly and in exactly the quantities requested by the troops ashore. For every one marine or soldier in the landing force, the transport fleet carried more than a ton of supplies and equipment. A single supply ship brought rations to feed 90,000 men for a month. Mitscher's task force carried eight million gallons of aviation fuel, and would burn more than four million barrels of bunker oil during the operation.[2]

An F6F pilot, flying above Task Force 58 during the five-day passage from Eniwetok to Saipan, was impressed by the sight of the fleet as it turned into the wind to launch aircraft. Carriers, battleships, cruisers, and destroyers turned together and steadied on the same course. "The wakes from all of those ships were perfectly symmetrical with each other, like a perfect corps de ballet, but some of these ships weighed thirty-five thousand tons. I looked down on this power and wondered what kind of fools these Japanese were. They had made one of the greatest miscalculations of all time, and boy, were they going to pay a price."[3]

The top echelon of the command roster was unchanged from previous operations. Spruance would command the entire fleet from his flagship, the cruiser *Indianapolis*, but he would leave tactical command of the carriers to Mitscher. Kelly Turner commanded Task Force 51, consisting of 486 vessels ranging in size from battleships (the older, slower class, optimized for shore bombardment) to landing craft. The marine Holland Smith retained his job as commander of the Fifth Amphibious Corps. General Ralph Smith of the U.S. Army remained his subordinate as commander of the 27th Infantry Division. Task Force 51 was subdivided into a Northern Attack Force, which would take Saipan (and which Turner commanded directly), and a Southern Attack Force, which would tackle Guam. The southern group was commanded by Admiral Richard L. Conolly, and the assault troops of that group were commanded by General Roy Geiger, the marine who had very adeptly run the Cactus Air Force during the Guadalcanal campaign.

Two weeks earlier, a massive explosion had ripped through a row of moored LSTs in the West Loch of Pearl Harbor. Its cause could never be established with certainty because all direct witnesses vanished in an instant. A subsequent investigation concluded that it was likely an ammunition-loading accident, perhaps caused by a dropped mortar round. The blast quickly touched off the magazines of adjoining vessels. Debris and bodies rained down across Ford Island and onto the decks of ships moored as far as half a mile away. Fires raged throughout the day and were not brought fully under control until the following morning. The disaster destroyed six LSTs slated for FORAGER. Casualties were heavy: 163 killed and 396 wounded. No reference to the incident was permitted to appear in the press.

If the West Loch disaster had occurred six months earlier, in the prelude to FLINTLOCK, it would have forced Nimitz to postpone the operation. But in the late spring of 1944, the Pacific Fleet was so abundantly outfitted that it could shrug off the loss of six LSTs. Two days after the accident, Nimitz assured King that salvage and clean-up operations were underway and "FORAGER target date will be delayed but little if at all."[4]

The Marianas were nothing like the low-lying coral atolls of the Gilberts and Marshalls. They were big, rugged islands, dominated by steep peaks, yawning gorges, undulating tablelands, and fields of sugarcane. The lowlands were overgrown with thick vegetation. Saipan, Guam, and Tinian, the three principal islands in the southern Marianas and FORAGER's main objectives, took in almost 300 square miles altogether. Saipan, twelve miles long, was dominated by a ridge of volcanic mountains running down the middle of most of its length. Its highest peak, Mount Tapotchau, rose to 1,554 feet. The western (or leeward) side of the island descended through terraced hills and sugarcane fields to a populated coastal plain. Three towns were situated on the west coast. Saipan was home to about 30,000 civilians, of whom about five-sixths were Japanese or Okinawans, the remainder mostly Chamorros and Koreans. The marines and soldiers of the Fifth Amphibious Corps had previously fought in flat, constricted terrain. In Saipan they would fight a wide campaign through towns, canefields, and mountainous backcountry. They would assume all the responsibilities and risks inherent in fighting among a civilian population.

Working with aerial photographs and radio intercepts, American intelligence analysts had estimated that the Japanese garrison numbered between 15,000 and 17,000 troops. That estimate was far short of the mark. Reinforcements shipped from Japan and China in April and May had brought the island's troop strength to almost 30,000. The garrison included 22,702 army troops (the Forty-Third Division and a mixed brigade, the Forty-Seventh Independent) and 6,690 naval personnel, including more of the elite Special Naval Landing Forces ("Japanese marines") who had fought at Tarawa. Overall command of the Marianas and Palau was entrusted to Vice Admiral Chuichi Nagumo, whom the Americans remembered well as the commander of *Kido Butai*, the carrier strike force that had attacked Pearl Harbor and been smashed six months later at Midway. Nagumo's command center was on Saipan. Tactical command of ground forces, and the preparation of the island's fixed fortifications, was left in the hands of Lieutenant General Yoshitsugu Saito.

The Saipan garrison would have been even larger if not for the effective depredations of Pacific Fleet submarines. The Japanese army's Forty-Third Division had sailed from Japan in two transport groups. The first, a half-dozen dilapidated freighters escorted by a small cruiser-destroyer force, had left Tokyo Bay on May 14. During the miserable five-day voyage, a sergeant recalled, the men had been crammed into a stifling hold, "laid out on shelves like broiler chickens."

> You had your pack, rifle, all your equipment with you. You crouched there, your body bent. You kept your rubber-soled work shoes on continually, so your feet got damp and sweaty. Water dripped on you, condensation caused by human breathing. The hold stank with humanity. A few rope ladders and one narrow, hurriedly improvised stairway were the only ways out. We expected the ship to sink at any moment.[5]

That first convoy reached Saipan without incident on May 19. But the second convoy, seven transports carrying 7,000 troops and most of the Forty-Third Division's heavy weaponry, supplies, and provisions, was attacked by American submarines. Five of the seven transports were torpedoed and destroyed. Most of the troops were rescued, but the sinkings deprived Saito's forces of armaments, provisions, and other important supplies. A rushed construction program was to have rendered Saipan "impregnable," but in May the general complained to Imperial General Headquarters that a lack of needed construction materials and equipment had kept his men "standing around with their arms folded." Coastal defenses and antiaircraft batteries had been erected hastily, and in many cases the work was incomplete. Defensive works were built of earth and wood, rather than heavy reinforced concrete as on Tarawa. Crates of ammunition, artillery, barbed wire, and other munitions were stored in naval depots near the western beachheads. American forces would seize much of this material intact. A report later submitted by Pacific Fleet headquarters estimated that just one-third of the heavy artillery on the island had been mounted in gun emplacements. Fortifications and firing positions above the landing beaches were "in much smaller quantities than had been heretofore encountered, with surprisingly few concrete pillboxes and blockhouses along the beaches."[6]

More than 1,000 miles lay between Saipan and Eniwetok, the western-most atoll in American hands. Turner's amphibious fleet would be required to operate at sea, within easy reach of the invasion beaches, possibly for many weeks. Reaching a safe anchorage would require a voyage of several days. Turner's vulnerable transports would depend entirely on the air protection provided by Task Force 58. Japanese airfields on Saipan, Guam, and Rota were thought to be abundantly supplied with land-based fighters and bombers, and they could be reinforced quickly by aircraft staged through airfields in the Bonin and Volcano island groups to the north. Given the record of Mitscher's recent carrier raids against enemy territory throughout the theater, the Americans could confidently rely on Task Force 58 to win control of the skies above the southern Marianas. But what happened if Ozawa's First Mobile Fleet appeared on the scene? Would Mitscher be cut loose to go after it? Or must he remain near the beachheads and the invasion fleet? Therein lay a worrying ambiguity that had not been directly addressed in Spruance's orders, or in FORAGER's operational plans.

The problem had been on Ernest King's mind throughout the spring. Though his instincts were always aggressive, the COMINCH had misgivings about the looming confrontation with the Japanese fleet. Earlier in his career, war games at the Naval War College had exposed the logistical strains that would develop as the Pacific Fleet moved deep into enemy waters. King assumed that the Imperial Navy had conserved an elite cadre of aviators. The Americans had underestimated the Japanese in the past. Might they be on the verge of repeating the error? In an off-the-record interview with reporters in February 1944, the COMINCH confided his anxieties: "We know the Japs are a very patient people, and will spend years, if necessary, laying a trap for us to walk into, and we fear we may wake up one of these bright mornings with a very bloody nose."[7] From Tokyo's point of view, King said, "it is better strategy for them to let us come to the very end of our long lines of communications and then attack us. Why should they come to meet us on some middle ground and away from their bases? We have to come to them, and they know it. Therefore they will make it as difficult as possible."[8]

Nimitz assured the COMINCH that Spruance was prepared for the contingency of a major fleet battle. Task Force 58 possessed a formidable numerical advantage: fifteen carriers to Ozawa's nine, seven battleships to Ozawa's five, and 950 carrier planes to Ozawa's 450. But Spruance was convinced that the Japanese would not risk their fleet to oppose the invasion of the Marianas. He assumed that the enemy would wait for the most advantageous tactical circumstances. Since the main body of the Japanese fleet had not contested MacArthur's landings on Biak, where it would have enjoyed a clear margin of naval superiority, Spruance assumed it would not travel more than 2,000 miles to the Marianas: "I was of the opinion that the Japanese fleet was waiting for a time when they could count on strong shore-based air to help them. Outlying groups of islands, such as the Marianas, could not be counted on for this, as we had demonstrated our ability to smother them with our superior carrier air strength."[9]

TASK FORCE 58, STEAMING in the vanguard of the American fleet, completed fueling on June 8 and 9. The weather was clear and the sea mild. A steady light breeze blew from the east. Radar periodically registered "bogies" to the west, but none made contact with the task force or its aircraft until the afternoon of June 10, when F6Fs were vectored ahead to intercept and destroy two Japanese patrol planes. On the following morning, a flight of G4M bombers approached from the northwest. They were also intercepted and destroyed. It seemed likely that the Japanese were now alerted to the approach of a powerful carrier force.

The task force was now less than 200 miles from Saipan, well within air-striking range. With his presence unmasked, Mitscher knew he could expect another long, tense night dodging low-flying G4Ms armed with torpedoes. Even if the intruders did not score, they would keep the American ships on the defensive, maneuvering evasively, all night long. The effort would exhaust the crews on the eve of a long and demanding operation. Better to launch the customary fighter sweep now, he reasoned, rather than wait until dawn.[10] At 1:00 p.m., ships in Task Force 58 turned into the wind and began launching planes—sixteen Hellcats from each *Essex*-class carrier, twelve from each light carrier, 208 fighters altogether. All were fitted with belly tanks, and about half were armed with 500-pound bombs.

Arriving over Saipan, Guam, and Rota shortly before 3:00 p.m., they caught the Japanese unprepared. The Hellcats shot down about thirty Zeros and damaged some additional (unknown) number of aircraft on the ground. The attackers were met by intense antiaircraft fire, especially around the Japanese airfield on Orote Peninsula, Guam. Eleven F6Fs sustained fatal damage as a result of antiaircraft fire (three of the eleven downed pilots were later recovered). Alex Vraciu, now with the *Lexington*'s VF-16, flew a strafing run over a seaplane ramp on Saipan. A flak burst nearly took his plane down, but he stabilized and flew back to the *Lexington*, his engine running rough: "This is where the F6F Hellcat's ruggedness is really appreciated."[11]

That night, Mitscher launched small "Bat Team" fighters to "heckle" the Japanese airfields—that is, to circle above them and strafe them intermittently, a tactic intended to keep the Japanese awake and leave them exhausted and on edge the following morning.

Kakuta's First Air Fleet had begun the day with approximately 435 aircraft manned and operable. The initial daylight fighter sweep on June 11 had destroyed as many as a third while also cratering the runways and demolishing many of the vital ground support facilities. At the end of the first week of aerial combat and carrier strikes, Kakuta's flyable inventory was reduced to about a hundred planes. The remaining aircraft had survived only because they had been camouflaged under palm fronds and brush and dispersed to locations far from the airfields. Air reinforcements arrived in small numbers from the home islands and from Truk. But the First Air Fleet, upon which so much hope had rested, never posed more than a nuisance to American forces.

Spruance ordered two task groups, half of Mitscher's force, to divert north and raid the airfields on Iwo Jima and Chichi Jima. Mitscher assigned the job to Task Groups 58.1 and 58.4, commanded by Rear Admirals Jocko Clark and William K. Harrill, respectively. Task Group 58.1 reached its point option on the afternoon of June 15 and launched a large composite strike against Iwo and Chichi Jima. Hellcats shot down about two dozen Japanese fighters while the accompanying bombers worked over the airfields, ammunition dumps, fuel tanks, and ground complexes. F6Fs armed with small fragmentation bombs cratered the runways and then banked around for low-altitude strafing runs. Again, the sturdy construction of the American planes worked to their advantage, and many damaged or shot-up aircraft returned safely to the carriers.

A small typhoon was brewing in the area. Late afternoon brought towering seas, and green water broke over the flight decks. On the *Belleau Wood*, a plane hurtled over a crash barrier and started a raging fire. Winds and sea rose steadily through the night. Flight operations were impossible in those tempestuous conditions, so Clark maneuvered his carriers well to the east, into calmer waters. By midday on June 16, the storm had abated enough to allow for another large strike. VB-2 pilot Harold Buell, flying a SB2C Hell-

diver from the *Hornet*, was assigned to attack shipping in the small harbor
of Chichi Jima, a place nicknamed the "punch bowl." It was a technically
difficult dive into a snug harbor surrounded by steep hills, with only a single
exit to the west. Antiaircraft fire was intense. Buell, who returned to strike
this same harbor several more times in the course of the war, later wrote,
"Chichi Jima was a tough, dirty target that always scared the hell out of me
and left me feeling like I hadn't accomplished anything except to stay alive
when I got safely outside the bowl again." [12]

ON THE MORNING OF JUNE 13, forty-eight hours before the first scheduled landings, the first bombardment group arrived off Saipan and Tinian. It included seven new "fast" battleships under the command of Vice
Admiral Willis A. "Ching" Lee, detached from Task Force 58 to make an
early start of working over Saipan's beach defenses, accompanied by about
a dozen destroyers. The group rained 16- and 5-inch high-explosive shells
down on the zones immediately inland of the landing beaches, and for all
appearances the entire area was left a smoking ruin. For fear of mines on
the ocean shelf, Lee's battleships remained at long range, 10,000 to 16,000
yards. The destroyers drew in close to shore and concentrated their guns
on both islands' barracks and bivouac areas. [13] Under the cover provided by
the barrage, six minesweepers swept the waters off the landing beaches. No
mines were found. On June 14, two 96-man Underwater Demolition Teams
(UDTs) were transported to the edge of the fringing reef. Frogmen swam in
close under the Japanese shore artillery, charted the reef, and determined
the lanes that the landing craft should take the following day. The divers
found no artificial beach obstructions. They blasted out coral heads to clear
paths for the landing craft. Under fire by artillery on shore, the demolition
teams lost four men killed and five wounded.

The weather was beautiful, very sunny and bright, almost blindingly so—
but the breeze was constant and the air was pleasantly dry. On the transport
fleet, approaching from the east, the landing troops found that they were able
to sleep far better than they had in the South Pacific. Men dozed on deck,
some in sun and some in shade; men wrote letters, played cards and checkers, tossed a medicine ball for exercise. Carrier planes patrolled overhead
throughout the daylight hours. The sheer size of the fleet was a balm to their
spirits. On many ships, the radio chatter between the planes above Saipan

and the battleships offshore was piped through the ships' loudspeakers, allowing the men aboard to form a mental picture of the action. Scale plaster models of Saipan were laid out on wardroom tables, with the locations of landing beaches, airfields, towns, and known shore batteries marked in colored ink.

On the night before D-Day, the 2nd Division marines scrubbed themselves and their dungarees. They arose well before dawn and ate a hearty breakfast. The island now loomed off the starboard bow. The flat snub cone of Mount Tapotchau was barely discernible against the slightly lighter sky, but patches of the island were now and again illuminated by muzzle flashes or star shells. The fire support group, commanded by Rear Admiral Kingman, rendezvoused with the amphibious assault group under Admiral Turner. At first light the enormous fleet, numbering several hundred vessels, moved into assigned stations. The big guns put on a typically majestic show as they blasted the shore defenses. Sailors began lowering the landing craft. The marines, noted combat correspondent Pete Zurlinden, seemed relaxed and even bored as they watched the naval guns and carrier bombers spread destruction along the shore. They sorted through their gear one last time and sighted along their rifles. Virtually all of the noncommissioned officers were veterans of previous amphibious assaults. "To most of them," wrote Zurlinden, "this is an old story. . . . They are quiet, laconic in their conversation."[14] They had seen and done it before.

From his flagship *Rocky Mount*, Admiral Turner raised the signal "Land the Landing Force." At 8:13 a.m., the force control officer signaled the first-wave landing boats to gather behind the line of departure, 4,000 yards offshore. The assault beaches were spread along a four-mile front to the north and south of Charan Kanoa, a sugar refinery and village on the southern part of the leeward coast. The boats motored toward shore in a line abreast, LVTs crammed with troops and accompanied by armed and armored amtracs, gunboats, and army DUKWs (amphibious trucks). Those first boats got ashore with few casualties, and within eight minutes marines had a foothold on every landing beach. The second and third waves followed close behind. Machine-gun fire was heavy above the southernmost landing beaches, designated Yellow 1 and Yellow 2. There the marines were pinned down for more than an hour, and could do nothing but dig into the sand. A larger-than-expected western swell broke over the reef and overturned boats loaded with ammunition, machine guns, light artillery pieces, and drinking water.

As they reached the reef, about 1,000 yards from shore, the fourth and fifth waves were under intense artillery and mortar fire. The weapons, positioned on ridges above the beaches, had been registered to hit the reefs, and when they opened up, the entire reef line seemed to erupt in a barricade of whitewater and flames. This first salvo was so closely timed that witnesses offshore assumed a series of mines must have been detonated by one signal. A few craft took direct hits and suffered 100 percent casualties. But the American fleet was very generously supplied with landing craft, more than 800 altogether, and enough got through to deliver 8,000 men to the beaches in the first twenty minutes.

For the remainder of that critical first day, the marines concentrated on holding the beaches and getting more men, equipment, and weaponry ashore. Seven battalions of artillery (75mm and 105mm howitzers) and two tank companies landed in the afternoon. Twenty thousand marines were ashore by the end of the day. Japanese artillery and mortar fire remained unrelenting throughout. Marines employed shell craters as makeshift foxholes and continually deepened them as the barrage continued and intensified. Direct hits claimed many lives. Five battalion commanders were wounded and evacuated; one battalion lost three commanders in quick succession. Lieutenant Robert B. Sheeks was crawling up the beach when a mortar shell hit two marines immediately to his left. "There was an explosion and these two guys just evaporated. We couldn't see any sign of them. They were disintegrated, just mixed in with the sand and vegetation and scattered all over the place."[15]

The naval bombardment had succeeded in knocking out most of the big coastal guns and in pulverizing some of the larger fixed fortifications that were easily seen from the offing or from planes overhead. But General Saito's forces had effectively concealed smaller mobile artillery pieces and mortars in the high ground inland of the beaches. Holland Smith gradually ascertained that Japanese troop strength on the island was about 40 to 50 percent higher than anticipated by intelligence estimates. By nightfall the marines had penetrated about 1,500 yards inland at the deepest point in their perimeter. Their artillery could not yet effectively reach the enemy, who was tucked behind the ridgeline, but the carrier bombers aimed their bombs and machine guns at the muzzle flashes, and the naval guns began to find the range, helped by aerial spotting floatplanes. On the morning of June 16, heavy fighting continued all along the perimeter. American casual-

Invasion of Saipan June 15, 1944

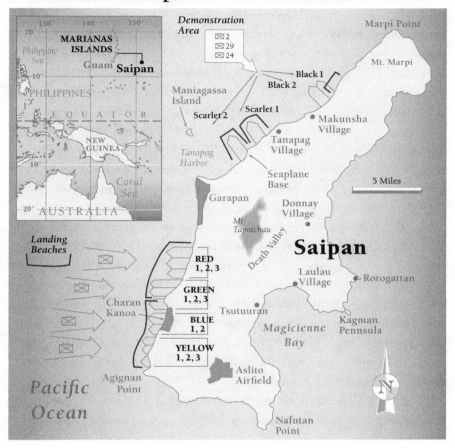

ties surpassed 2,500. Smith requested all available reinforcements and recommended that the invasion of Guam, previously scheduled for June 18, be indefinitely postponed.

Smith pressured his division and battalion commanders to move inland, but the terrain above the beach impeded most of the tanks and armored vehicles, and there were few suitable footpaths allowing for rapid infantry movements. On the afternoon of June 16, most of the 27th Division was landed. Smith intended to send the soldiers across relatively accessible terrain toward the southeastern part of the island, where they would capture Aslito Airfield.

On June 16, Saito decided to commit his reserves to a night counterattack on the northern flank of the 2nd Marine Division, near the northern limit of the American perimeter. The Japanese made no special effort to conceal their intentions. On the fleet offshore, sailors watched as Japanese troops rallied in the town of Garipan and aroused their sprits with "parades, patriotic speeches and much flag waving."[16] At 8:00 p.m., about forty light tanks and two columns of infantry advanced south along the coast road. Their approach was easily tracked by ships offshore. Star shells kept them brightly illuminated. Naval gunfire caught the tanks at an exposed point and destroyed about twenty of the machines. Marines took the attackers under fire with machine guns and 75mm howitzers, and a close melee ensued, with heavy losses on both sides, but especially to the attackers. The Japanese army rallied and attempted several more attacks in the early morning hours, but the marines held their positions and destroyed the remaining tanks with field artillery, infantry antitank weapons, and bazookas.

Corpsmen set up stations on the beach to treat the wounded. It proved impossible to shield them from the relentless mortar fire. Private Richard King described the macabre scene in a letter to his parents: "All along the beach, men were dying of wounds. Maybe you will think this is cruel, but I want you to know what it was like. Mortar shells dropping in on heads, and ripping bodies. Faces blown apart by flying lead and coral. It wasn't a pretty sight, and I will never forget the death and hell along that beach. It rained all the night and mud was ankle deep."[17]

The failure of Saito's all-out counterattack shifted the momentum to the invaders. On June 17, marines pushed inland and overran many of the artillery batteries that had inflicted such misery for three days. The 4th Division marines and the 27th Division soldiers broke through in the south and pushed all the way to Magicienne Bay, bisecting the island and cutting off the remaining Japanese in the south. Aslito Airfield was secured on June 18. The 4th Division was now poised to swing north and begin driving the remaining Japanese forces back into the northern half of the island.

On June 18 at 10:00 a.m., Smith went ashore and established his Fifth Amphibious Corps headquarters in the ruins of Charan Kanoa. The big sugar refinery that dominated the town was a smoking ruin, except for its blacked smokestack, which had somehow survived. Railroad cars had been scattered across the tracks. Japanese resistance was weakening, at least on the ridges behind the position, but the remaining forces were pulling back into the northern half of the island. From his new vantage point ashore, Smith looked out at the fleet and noted that it was considerably smaller than it had been. Spruance had detached most of the warships, including two cruiser divisions and several destroyer divisions, to rendezvous with Mitscher and Task Force 58 in anticipation of a major fleet battle west of the Marianas. The transports had withdrawn to the east, to avoid losses by air attack.

Smith knew that the enemy fleet must be met and destroyed, and that the warships were protecting his beachhead even if they lay beyond the horizon. But the sight of a powerful fleet offshore weighed in the psychological attitudes of the contending forces. Smith frankly told his staff officers that he was concerned that its sudden disappearance would prompt a surge in the morale of enemy ground forces.

THE FIRST MOBILE FLEET HAD PAUSED in Guimaras Strait to take on 10,800 tons of fuel. It passed through the Visayan Sea and into the San Bernardino Strait (between Luzon and Samar). As night fell on June 15, the great fleet emerged into the Philippine Sea.

Ozawa correctly surmised that his movements had been tracked by American submarines since his departure from Tawi Tawi. He had intercepted coded radio transmissions likely alerting Pearl Harbor to his whereabouts. Large signal fires were seen on the peaks along the coast south of San Bernardino Strait, where pro-American guerrillas regularly reported ship movements to the enemy. Ugaki's force of battleships and cruisers, having broken off the attack on Biak and sailed north past Halmahera, had been shadowed by enemy long-range bombers. The Japanese fleet was not going to take the enemy by surprise.

Fuel was a stringent consideration. The navy had allocated seven precious oilers to get the First Mobile Fleet this far. They were filled with the crude Borneo petroleum that degraded the performance of the ship's boilers and was volatile and potentially dangerous to handle. Given the constraints, Ozawa had managed his fueling situation exceptionally well, but he had little margin for unexpected developments. He could bring his carriers within striking range of the Marianas, but would have to withdraw to the Inland Sea immediately after the battle.

Ugaki's warships fell in with Ozawa's force on June 16. Refueling continued throughout the following night. With tanks topped off, the fleet steamed east. The officers and men of the First Mobile Fleet sensed that they were on the verge of making history. "This operation has an immense bearing on the fate of the Empire," Ozawa signaled the fleet. "It is hoped that all forces will do their utmost and attain results as magnificent as those achieved in the Battle of Tsushima."[18]

The first part of the message was incontrovertible; the second was merely a hope, and a forlorn one. Postwar interrogations and Ugaki's contemporary diary entries leave no doubt that senior commanders were concerned about the fleet's readiness for battle, and that the aviators were badly overmatched. They fastened their hopes to their tactical advantages, of which there were more than a few. For all the wartime tribulations of the Japanese aircraft industry, the new-generation carrier bombers could fly some 200 miles farther than their American counterparts. Because the Japanese still possessed airfields on Guam and other islands, their carrier planes could (in theory) strike the American fleet, refuel and rearm at the airfields, and then give the Americans another working-over before returning to their carriers. If all went as planned, this "shuttle-bombing" tactic might enable Ozawa to strike the enemy twice while his carriers remained out of range. The Japanese now possessed accurate knowledge of the composition and location of the American fleet, so there would be no unpleasant surprises as at Midway. The trade wind from the east worked in favor of the Japanese, as it would require the Americans to move east into the wind to conduct flight operations. Possession of the "lee-gauge" gave Ozawa the power to control the timing of events, and would severely constrain the Americans' ability to give chase to the west. Turner's amphibious fleet, tethered to the Saipan beachhead, lacked tactical mobility. The land-based air forces of the Marianas might yet mete out retribution to the American fleet, or so it was hoped—Ozawa had not yet learned how badly Kakuta's air units had been mauled, perhaps because the latter was reluctant to admit it. Insofar as Ozawa knew, Kakuta's airmen had delivered a week's worth of hard knocks on the American fleet and its carrier air groups. He assumed that the airfields on Guam and Rota were prepared to receive and turn around his carrier planes as planned.

On any terms other than a direct comparison with the resources of the Fifth Fleet, the First Mobile Fleet was an awesome force. It was the largest concentration of carrier airpower the Imperial Navy had ever amassed, about 50 percent larger than the force that had attacked Pearl Harbor in

1941. *Taiho*, with its armored flight deck and newly constructed torpedo blister, was thought to be the toughest and most impervious carrier in either of the opposing fleets. The behemoths *Yamato* and *Musashi* were the world's two mightiest surface warships. Spirits among the Japanese rank and file were seemingly buoyant. Masatake Okumiya recorded that many of his fellow officers believed that victory was ensured, and "our pilots were convinced that they would shatter the attacking American fleet."[19] Ugaki, after surveying the great armada from his bridge, mused in his diary, "Can it be that we'll fail to win with this mighty force? No! It can't be!"[20]

As always, Admiral Spruance walked for hours around the forecastle of the *Indianapolis*, often accompanied by Gil Slonim, an intelligence officer detailed to the Fifth Fleet. A series of contact reports had tracked the Japanese fleet from Tawi Tawi, and Filipino coastwatchers had reported a "large carrier and battleship force" traversing the San Bernardino Strait on June 15. Some hours later, the submarine *Flying Fish* sighted a large enemy task force consisting of "at least three battleships, three carriers and a number of cruisers and destroyers."[21] Well to the south, a short time later, the submarine *Seahorse* reported another large group of enemy warships traveling northward in a location about 200 miles east of Surigao Strait. This was Ugaki's surface warship group.

Spruance summoned a squadron of long-range, radar-equipped PBM seaplanes from Eniwetok. They would begin long-range search flights to the west to locate the Japanese fleet. That these two widely separated elements or task forces might be headed to a rendezvous was an obvious possibility, but there was no proof of it. Spruance was vigilant to the danger of an end-run attack on the amphibious fleet off Saipan. Divided forces and flanking attacks had been a hallmark of Japanese naval strategy in many previous engagements.

Early on the morning of June 16, the submarine *Cavalla*, on her first war patrol, discovered several tankers and supply ships that previously had not been located. At 9:15 p.m. the same day, at a point about 800 miles west-southwest of Saipan, *Cavalla*'s radar detected many large ships headed east at 19 knots. Captain Herman J. Kossler radioed Admiral Lockwood in Pearl Harbor with the contact report: "fifteen or more large combatant ships."[22]

When this information was received several hours later on the *Indianapolis*, Carl Moore woke Spruance. Reviewing all the reports received in the past twelve hours, they concluded that the enemy fleet was deliberately

hovering beyond the striking range of the American carriers. It appeared
to Spruance that Ozawa was merely probing, and perhaps hoping to lure
the Americans west. Upon learning that the Japanese fleet had departed
its anchorage in Tawi Tawi, Spruance had assumed it would come directly
toward him and attempt a pitched surface battle. "For a second time it
turned out wrong," he told Nimitz. "Their attitude about risking their fleet
had not changed. Their methods of operation had changed, in that they
were using carriers again. They intended to use their fleet to exploit advantages that their carrier air might gain. They had no intention of throwing
everything at us by coming in to Saipan at high speed to fight it out."[23]

Spruance's bottom line was that he would not leave the amphibious
fleet, the transports, and the beachhead unprotected until he knew the
location of every element of the Japanese fleet. The easterly wind would
always limit the potential westward progress of Task Force 58 during daylight, but Spruance would not allow the flight decks to stray farther than
near air-striking range from the Marianas. In the Battle of Tsushima, which
Spruance and his colleagues had studied at the Naval War College, Admiral Togo had waited for the Russian Fleet to come to him. That "waiting"
strategy was always on his mind, as he would write later: "We had somewhat
the same situation, only it was modified by the long-range striking power
of the carriers."[24] Now he was inclined to wait and let Ozawa come east.
He summoned the two carrier groups (commanded by Clark and Harrill)
back from the Bonins. Mitscher asked for confirmation that he remained in
tactical command of Task Force 58, and Spruance confirmed that Mitscher
was indeed, but with the proviso that he would "issue general directives
when necessary."[25] He also asked to be informed in advance of Mitscher's
plans. Spruance had the carriers on a short leash.

As Clark took his task force south on June 17, he sent long-range search
flights to the southwest. Results were negative. Knowing that the Japanese
fleet was out there, probably not far beyond the maximum 350-mile search
radius of his planes, he considered racing west through the night and inter-
posing his ships between Ozawa and the home islands of Japan. It was a
historic opportunity, and Clark knew it. He proposed the venture to Harrill
via TBS, but the latter firmly declined. They had been ordered to return to
Task Force 58. Clark considered taking Task Group 58.1 and going it alone,
but he realized that would entail great risk: "I did not wish to find myself

on a windy corner with so many Japanese airplanes that I could not shoot them all down."[26] Both Clark and Harrill returned south and fell in with Mitscher midday on June 18.

OZAWA ARRAYED HIS FLEET IN TWO LARGE GROUPINGS. A van force, consisting of Carrier Division 3 and the First Battleship Division under Ugaki, was positioned about a hundred miles in advance (east) of the main body. The van force was under the command of Vice Admiral Takeo Kurita. The rear group was divided into two carrier divisions, of which the strongest, representing about half the air strength of the Mobile Fleet, was Carrier Division 1, which included the *Taiho, Shokaku*, and *Zuikaku*. Ozawa retained direct command of the division from his flagship *Taiho*.

Upon receiving *Cavalla's* updated contact report on the morning of June 18, Mitscher and his staff officers considered the possibilities from Ozawa's point of view. He was likely on a tight fuel budget. He would attempt to employ the greater range of his carrier planes to advantage by striking the Americans with massed carrier airpower from beyond 300 miles west. Therefore he would steam east and launch his planes either late that afternoon or before dawn on the nineteenth. Events would soon confirm that these deductions were on the mark. (Mitscher and his staff also considered that Ozawa might send his surface forces ahead to attempt a night attack, but that scenario was less certain.) To close the range on the enemy, and orient Task Force 58 favorably to the prevailing easterly winds, Mitscher asked Spruance for permission to take the carriers farther west. Spruance, still eyeing the risk of a flanking attack on Turner's amphibious fleet, answered in the negative. As logged in the Fifth Fleet war diary, Spruance "informed CTF-58 that in his opinion the main enemy attack would come from the westward but might be diverted to come from the southwestward and that diversionary attacks might come from either flank or reinforcement might come from the Empire."[27] If morning searches were negative, Spruance instead proposed that Mitscher launch another round of bombing raids on airfields at Guam and Rota.

Mitscher was nonplussed by these directives. Like every other aviator in the fleet, he was keen to get at the enemy carriers. He was ill at ease with the likelihood that Task Force 58 might have to fight off a huge carrier airstrike without any means of hitting back. The suggested raids against Guam and Rota were not entirely sensible because the operations of the previous week had nearly exhausted the aerial ordnance suitable to such a mission (contact-fused land bombs); what was left in ample supply were armor-piercing bombs designed to punch holes in ships. Mitscher launched his search, but he had no expectation of finding enemy ships within the limited radius of his planes. They did not, although in a few instances the American scouts brushed elbows with their Japanese counterparts at or near the limit of their outbound flights. An Aichi reconnaissance float-plane ("Jake") was shot down at the end of one of these searches. Afternoon patrols (on bearings between 195 degrees and 315 degrees to a distance of 325 miles) were also negative. Ozawa was plainly keeping the Americans at arm's length. The pattern fit Mitscher's expectations: Ozawa would launch planes at dawn on the nineteenth while keeping his flight decks carefully beyond the range of counterstrikes.

Mitscher respected Spruance, and was not inclined to pester his commander for a different decision. The task group commanders and their air staffs were freer in disparaging their blackshoe chief and his overcautious attitude. As Jocko Clark returned from his northern foray that morning, he was flabbergasted to learn that Spruance had chained Task Force 58 to the Saipan beachhead. The end-run scenario was a chimera, he insisted—even from a position 250 miles farther west, the task force could have readily covered Saipan "with our radar, our search planes, and our submarines keeping us informed of the movements of the enemy fleet."[28] Like most of the carrier admirals, Clark chalked up Spruance's decision to the characteristic blackshoe officer's ignorance of "the full capabilities of the fast carriers."[29] Ted Sherman, the veteran carrier admiral, wrote that Spruance was a career surface naval warrior who "still was thinking in terms of a surface action. . . . There were no 'ends' in aerial warfare."[30]

Certainly Spruance chose conservative tactics in Operation FORAGER. He admitted it at the time and never regretted it afterward. He knew Nimitz's mind and priorities better than any other man in the fleet. His orders were to cover the beachhead and transport fleet at all costs. Kelly Turner had advised that he could not withdraw the transports on June 18 and 19 without placing the troops ashore in jeopardy. Seventy thousand Americans were on Saipan, fighting an unexpectedly bloody campaign—1,500 men had already been killed and 4,000 wounded, and those figures were expanding rapidly. Holland Smith had observed that the presence of a powerful fleet offshore weighed heavily in the morale of the contending forces. His soldiers and marines relied on a continual flow of supplies, reinforcements, and ammunition over the beachhead. He needed to evacuate his growing numbers of wounded. Japanese air attacks had fallen on the fleet offshore every evening, at or shortly after dusk. Smith and Turner knew and accepted that Task Force 58 must contend with the enemy fleet, but they had every right to expect that the fleet would guard their precarious sea-to-land operation against disagreeable surprises from any quarter. The navy had offered solemn commitments to the army and marines; issues of interservice unity were at stake.

As night fell on June 18, a dispatch from Pearl Harbor brought news that a radio transmission had been picked up in the enemy's presumed vicinity. (Ozawa had broken radio silence to make contact with airbases in the Marianas.) Direction-finding (DF) devices had fixed the point of origin in a zone 355 miles west-southwest of the American fleet. That location was consistent with the contact provided by the *Cavalla* earlier in the day. At Flag Plot on the *Lexington*, it seemed to settle the issue, or at least added enough evidence to merit an aggressive move to engage the enemy. At about 11:30 p.m., Mitscher made his last appeal. By TBS to the *Indianapolis*, he informed Spruance that he intended to turn west at 1:30 a.m., in order to put Task Force 58 in a position to launch airstrikes against Ozawa the following dawn. That would provide space for the carriers to head east throughout June 19, keeping bows pointed into the wind for continuous flight operations.

The proposal languished for an hour as Spruance considered the situation and discussed it with Moore and his other staff officers. The waters were further muddied by a partially jammed transmission from the submarine *Stingray*, radioed from a location farther south and east. It might have been a contact report that had been jammed by a flanking force underway for the dreaded end run on Saipan. Moreover, Spruance reasoned, the DF fix was an approximation and might be off by a considerable distance. It might have been sent by any Japanese ship, not necessarily the main body; it might be a ruse, transmitted by a lone destroyer sent away for just that purpose. It proved nothing. Spruance replied at 12:30 p.m.: "Change proposed does not appear advisable. . . . End run by other carrier groups remains possibility and should not be overlooked."[31] As his fleet diary put it, somewhat defensively, "It was of highest importance that our troops and transport forces on and in the vicinity of Saipan be protected and a circling movement by enemy fast forces be guarded against."[32]

Alfred Thayer Mahan had lectured that a naval commander with a clear advantage must pursue, attack, and destroy the enemy, and "nothing can excuse his losing a point which by exertion he might have scored."[33] To a colleague who remarked that the British had done "well enough" in a recent battle, Horatio Nelson had famously replied, "If ten ships out of eleven were taken, I would never call it well enough, if we were able to get at the eleventh."[34] Throughout the (admittedly brief) history of carrier warfare, the cardinal rule had been to strike first. Spruance's decision to jerk the leash, against which Task Force 58 was straining so fervently, amounted to a coldly considered choice to allow Ozawa to strike the first blow. It might even let Ozawa strike the *only* blow, because there was no assurance that Task Force 58 would get far enough west to launch a counterstrike. Spruance's decision was unprecedented, and it seemed to defy elementary doctrine. The aviators were incredulous. Had the victor of Midway lost his mind, or merely his nerve?

The verdict was received on the *Lexington* with disappointment and no small amount of out-and-out disgust. According to Truman Hedding, Mitscher was "very upset." Hedding and Burke made a pact that they would forevermore commemorate the anniversary of June 19 by getting together and "crying in our beer."[35] A *Yorktown* officer complained to his diary: "The Navy brass turned yellow—no fight—no guts. . . . Spruance branded every Navy man in TF-58 a coward tonight. I hope historians fry him in oil."[36] Mitscher was immediately beset with proposals that he appeal the decision, that he point out in detail all of the advantages of going west and the potential hazards of remaining yoked to Saipan, but Mitscher refused all such entreaties and insisted on supporting the chief's decision. The operations officer of Task Force 58 was Jimmy Thach, the legendary fighter pilot who had developed air tactics to defeat the Zero with the slow-climbing F4F Wildcat. "I talked to Arleigh Burke very urgently to tell him that we would never catch those people if we didn't run toward them."[37] The staff tinkered with various drafts of messages that Mitscher might send to Spruance in hopes of reversing the decision. According to Thach, he and Burke even proposed that the task force commander threaten to resign his command. Mitscher seemed to take offense at the insubordinate chatter he heard on his bridge, and when Admiral John W. "Black Jack" Reeves of Task Group 58.3 radioed to urge going west, Mitscher slapped him down in uncommonly vehement terms: "Your suggestions are good but irritating. I have no intention of passing them higher up. They certainly know the situation better than we do. Our primary mission is to stay here to await W-Day [Guam landing] and assist the ground forces. . . . I hope in your message you are not recommending abandonment of our primary objective."[38]

Carl Moore predicted that the decision would provoke "a lot of kibitzing in Pearl Harbor and Washington about what we should have done, by people who don't know the circumstances and won't wait to find out."[39] He was not wrong. The double guessing occurred in real time, as the CINCPAC staff in Pearl Harbor monitored dispatches and plotted the positions of the contending forces on a chart spread out on a table. John Towers, who wanted Spruance's job for himself, urged Nimitz to order Spruance west. Nimitz refused, according to a member of his staff, not because he disagreed with Towers's reasoning but because "it will be the beginning of my trying to run the tactical side of operations of the fleet from ashore."[40]

Spruance, characteristically, betrayed no signs of self-doubt. Having given his orders, he went to bed. But Mitscher and his staff, a quarter of a mile away aboard the *Lexington*, did not rest. They prepared their plans for the next day. Without need of the bombers, they would stow them in the hangars or fly them off to attack Guam and Rota. The flight decks would be kept clear for the fighters. "The die had been cast," Burke said. "We knew we were going to have hell slugged out of us in the morning. We knew we couldn't reach them. We knew they could reach us."[41]

DAWN ON JUNE 19 REVEALED ANOTHER FAIR DAY, with a steady easterly breeze and mild seas. The clear blue sky overhead was not entirely welcome, as it offered no hope of concealment against the expected waves of Japanese warplanes. General quarters had sounded at 3:00 a.m., and the ships were buttoned up for action—hatches dogged down, battle shutters secured over port holes, life vests and steel helmets served out to all crew.

Task Force 58 was about 150 miles west-southwest of Saipan. Three task groups (commanded by Reeves, Montgomery, and Clark) were arrayed in a line running north to south. Ching Lee's battleships and cruisers (Task Group 58.7) were positioned thirty-five miles west, in the direction of the enemy, to function as an antiaircraft screen. Harrill's Task Group 58.4, the weakest of the four task groups, was placed immediately north of Lee. Paul Backus, an officer on the *South Dakota*, recalled that the battleship's crew was thrilled to be placed in this advanced position, and sailors eagerly scanned the western horizon in hopes of spotting the Japanese fleet. The prospect of a naval gunfight prompted a "tremendous uplift in the morale of the ship. . . . [M]aybe the Japs were going to get a taste of five or six or seven new battleships all together for a change, and we would really go after their battle line. We even put our big colors up at the foretop."[42]

Search flights continued to come up negative. Radar-equipped planes from the *Enterprise*, launched at 2:00 a.m., had found nothing. A much larger air search departed at 5:30, covering nearly half the compass rose to a distance of 325 miles; still nothing. Longer-ranged Mariner seaplanes launched from waters off Saipan had found radar blips at 1:15 a.m., probably the van force under Admiral Kurita. The reported position placed the enemy ships about 330 miles away at a bearing of 258 degrees. But the report did not reach Spruance and Mitscher until 8:50 a.m., and the distance was beyond effective air-striking range.

With the first combat air patrol and antisubmarine patrols airborne, the task force turned west to gain sea room for the next round of flight operations. A few enemy "snoopers" intruded onto the southeastern fringes of the fleet, and were shot down or chased away. A lone Zero was taken down by antiaircraft fire. The combat air patrol fighters were ordered to climb to 25,000 feet.

At 7:30 a.m., radar operators noted a cluster of blips over nearby Guam. Hellcats from the *Belleau Wood* hurried over to Orote Airfield and tore into a group of Japanese planes. They were soon joined by reinforcements from the *Yorktown*, *Hornet*, and *Cabot*. In an hour-long air battle, about thirty Japanese planes went down in flames; only one F6F was lost. The morning massacre over Guam was followed by several more throughout the day, as planes launched from Ozawa's carriers sought refuge at Orote.

At 10:05 a.m., the *Alabama*'s radar screens registered many bogeys about 125 miles west, altitude 24,000 feet or higher. This was the leading edge of Ozawa's first airstrike, arriving precisely when and where it was expected.

Arleigh Burke, on behalf of Mitscher, ordered all carriers to launch all Hell-cats spotted on their decks—"so we launched all our fighters, the whole blooming works."[43] Fighter directors summoned the planes over Guam back to protect the task force with a two-word call: "Hey Rube!"

Throughout the task force, bombers and torpedo planes were launched and told to fly away to the east. For the moment they were superfluous, and if kept aboard they would only clog the decks, hangars, and elevators. The aircraft were to circle over the southern Marianas, well away from the incoming enemy planes, so that they would not clutter the radar screens or risk being misidentified.

In the rush to scramble, the Hellcat pilots did not bother to find an assigned plane. Each man simply slid into the first vacant cockpit and awaited the signal to launch in turn. Without pausing to rendezvous into group formations, the planes simply banked around their carriers and climbed into the west. Lieutenant Don McKinley of Fighting Squadron 25 (of the *Cowpens*) did not recall receiving any specific vector or altitude instructions. Knowing that the Japanese planes were coming from the west, he pointed his nose in that direction and hung on his propeller. Alex Vraciu took off from the *Lexington* and followed the instructions given by the fighter director officer (FDO) to climb at full power on vector 250. The steep ascent tested the limits of the F6F's Pratt & Whitney R-2800 engine, and some of the older and more hard-run planes fell behind. Vraciu's engine spat oil onto his windshield, obscuring his vision. His formation was a mess, and he could not make contact with his squadron because the radio circuits were congested with pilot chatter. (In written comments submitted after the battle, another squadron leader complained that "some squadrons still persist in 'hogging the air' with instructions and idle chatter that should have been clarified and settled before their flight.")[44]

Peering through the oil-smeared windshield, Vraciu spied many enemy planes on an opposite heading, several thousand feet beneath him. Visibility conditions were almost freakishly good—a rare atmospheric condition caused contrails to form at 20,000 feet or even lower. When the air melee was at its height, the sky was interwoven with a web of stark white lines. "We could see vapor trails of planes coming in with tiny black specks at the head," said Ernest Snowden, head of the *Lexington* air group. "It was just like the sky writing we all used to see before the war."[45]

McKinley was climbing through 7,500 feet when he saw a three-plane section of Nakajima "Jill" torpedo planes, painted brownish gray with the circular red *hinomaru* on their wings and fuselages, about 1,500 feet beneath him. He executed a wingover and slid in behind them. He fired a quick burst as the first plane swam into his sights. The plane entered a shallow dive, trailing smoke. McKinley chased a second Jill all the way down to sea level. Before he could overtake it and shoot it down, both planes reached the outer edge of Lee's battleship-cruiser task group, and antiaircraft bursts mottled the sky around them. McKinley fired a last burst and pulled away as the Japanese plane hit the sea and exploded.

This first wave of sixty-nine Japanese planes had been launched from the light carriers of Kurita's van force. About half a dozen were lost at sea during the long overwater flight. Others had drifted off to the south and made a run for friendly airfields on Guam. Those that remained on course for the American fleet were assailed by a swarm of Hellcats, and most went down in flames in the first minutes of combat. A handful of the intruders traded altitude for speed and made torpedo runs or diving attacks on Lee's battle line. One planted a 250-kilogram bomb on the *South Dakota*, doing little damage to the ship but killing or wounding fifty of her crew. Another crash-dived into the side of the *Indiana*, causing only trifling damage. The cruiser *Minneapolis* reported minor damage from a near miss.

The diarist and sailor James Fahey had witnessed plenty of naval action in the South Pacific, but he had never seen an air battle at close range. He was awed by the spectacle: "Jap planes were falling all around us and the sky was full of bursting shells, big puffs of smoke could be seen everywhere. . . . Bombs were falling very close to the ships, big sprays of water could be seen and Jap planes were splashing into the water."[46] Lee's battle line had perfectly executed the role assigned to it by Spruance. It had provided an early warning radar "tripwire"; it had diverted and absorbed the brunt of aerial attacks; it had chewed up the enemy planes with antiaircraft fire. None of the first-wave attackers had reached striking range of the American carriers.

In the cramped and dimly lit Combat Information Centers (CICs), confidence surged. The combination of radar and fighter direction had come a long way since the relative dark ages of 1942. The morning's interception had been nearly flawless. On most carriers, the Combat Information Center was housed in a single large windowless compartment, one level below the flight deck amidships. The pilots' radio chatter was piped into the room through a loudspeaker. In one corner stood a vertical screen of transparent

The Turkey Shoot
Battle of the Philippine Sea, Phase 1, June 19, 1944

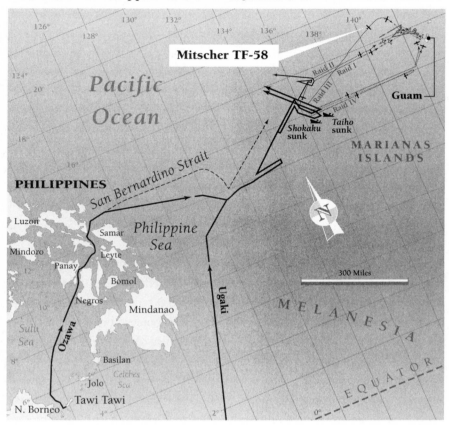

Plexiglas. The ship's position was fixed at the center; a series of concentric rings measured distance in all directions. A bank of radar screens was positioned on one side of the screen. The fighter director officer and his assistants sat at a table on the opposite side, facing the screen. As the radar operators called out their readings, sailors armed with grease pencils marked up the screen with red and white "X's." Red X's denoted bogeys, or planes not identified by IFF ("identification-friend-or-foe") transmitters; white X's represented the American aircraft. With each radar sweep, the sailors wiped the screen clean with a wet cloth and drew new X's. As the minutes passed, the red markings marched steadily toward the center of the screen, and the white ones crept outward as they flew a course to intercept. The CIC personnel watched the converging groups of red and white until the voices on the radio confirmed visual contact: "Tally Ho!"

During an air melee the radar screens provided little actionable data. Red and white X's were clustered together on the same corner of the screen. The radio circuits rang with confusing chatter. On June 19, however, the giddy tone of the voices on the radio left no doubt that the Americans were massacring their opponents. With each new sweep of the radar, there were fewer red markings. One or two red X's might continue toward the center of the screen, with the white ones following close behind. Each sequence ended with the screen wiped clean of all red X's, and a sailor made a small notation indicating the time and the number of enemy planes "splashed." Sam Sommers of the *Cowpens* peeked into his ship's Combat Information Center on the afternoon of June 19 and noted a "foot-long smear of red at the end of lines of white 'X's' coming from near the center of the panel."[47]

ADMIRAL OZAWA'S SECOND BIG COMPOSITE AIRSTRIKE of the day, consisting of thirty-five dive-bombers, twenty-seven torpedo planes, and forty-eight fighters, left Carrier Division 1 shortly after 8:00 a.m. The ill-fated flight encountered setbacks and reversals from the outset. Eight planes were forced to turn back immediately, either because their engines were not performing or because they could not retract their landing gear. As the eastbound planes flew over Kurita's van force, jumpy antiaircraft gunners wrongly assumed they were enemy and opened fire. Two were shot down, and eight more were damaged and forced to turn back. As the different plane types flew at varying cruising speeds, the squadrons gradually drifted apart into smaller groups, and many planes lost contact with their leaders, whom they were attempting to follow because they lacked experience in overwater navigation.

Lieutenant Commander Zenji Abe, one of the few veterans in that wave, was flying one of the older model Aichi D3A "Val" dive-bombers. It was a long flight, and he was physically and mentally exhausted. "I was suffering from a very unusual physical condition caused by prolonged fatigue," he recalled, "and felt I was in a plane being flown by somebody else." Each time he looked around, he noticed that fewer planes remained in his formation. Abe assumed they had either turned back or "dived into the sea from mental confusion."[48]

At 11:07 a.m., American radar screens picked up the first enemy planes as they approached from the southwest. A dozen *Essex* Hellcats led by Commander David McCampbell were among the first to engage the intruders. Visibility remained superb, and McCampbell could easily pick out the contrails several thousand feet below. Attacking from above in a shallow dive, the defenders tore into the attackers. The brief encounter was possibly the greatest slaughter in the history of combat aviation. About sixty Japanese aircraft went down in fifteen minutes.

Alex Vraciu of the *Lexington*, who had scrambled to intercept the first wave and whose plane was still well supplied with fuel and ammunition, followed the fighter director officer's vectors to a position about thirty-five miles west of the task force. "Spot-gazing intently, I suddenly picked out a large, rambling mass of at least fifty enemy planes 2,000 feet below, portside and closing," he recalled. "My adrenaline flow hit 'high C.' I remember thinking, 'This could develop into a once-in-a-lifetime fighter pilot's dream.'"[49] Vraciu could see no Zeros flying cover over the bombers and torpedo planes. He banked into a high-side run on a "Judy" dive-bomber, evaded the tail-gunner's tracers, and fired a short burst. The target rolled over and dived toward the sea, flame billowing out of the wing tank. Vraciu bored in behind two more planes, trading altitude for speed to keep them in his sights, and gave each one a burst from a range of about 1,000 yards. As usual, a few rounds of .50-caliber fire were enough to take down the lightly built Japanese machines. Trailing fire and smoke, they headed down toward the blue sea below.

Flying east now, stalking the enemy bombers as they raced toward the American carriers, Vraciu destroyed two more. As he emerged over the outermost screening ships, antiaircraft fire began to rock his F6F. In seven minutes he had shot down five Japanese planes, and he could have let the antiaircraft fire take care of the remaining "bandits," but he had a sixth plane in his sights and did not want to let it go. He overtook it, lined it up, pressed the trigger, and was amazed at the results. "Number six blew up with a tremendous explosion right in front of my face. I must have hit his bomb. I had seen planes blow up before but never like this! I yanked the stick up sharply to avoid the scattered pieces and flying hot stuff, then radioed, 'Splash number six!'"[50]

Zenji Abe's Aichi was one of a few Japanese planes to run the gauntlet of fighters and penetrate into the heart of the American fleet. At 13,000 feet, he saw white wakes on the sea ahead, below, and to the left of his engine cowling. He knew a swarm of Hellcats was behind and above him. His wingmen were gone. Without time to set up a proper dive-bombing attack, Abe simply lowered his nose and flew toward the nearest carrier. The plane wobbled and shuddered as it flew into a barrage of antiaircraft fire. He released his bomb over the *Wasp*. It missed, but detonated close enough to the ship to cause light damage and injure two men. Against the odds, Abe escaped and returned to the Japanese task force, where he recovered on the carrier *Junyo*. He was the only Japanese pilot to drop a bomb on an American carrier that day and live to tell the tale.

Four Japanese torpedo planes made runs on the *Enterprise* and the *Princeton*. All were taken down by antiaircraft fire. "On at least one occasion," wrote a lieutenant stationed on the bridge of one of the big carriers, "so many Japanese planes were being shot down—great balls of fire, which, in spite of intense sunlight showed brilliantly red against the sky, or long plummets of black smoke plunging to the sea—that it was impossible to make an accurate count of them. For minutes on end there were beautiful vapor streams forming crisscrossing white arcs against the azure sky as planes dived and climbed."[51]

Running low on gas, Alex Vraciu entered the *Lexington*'s landing circle and made a clean recovery. As his Hellcat came abeam of the island, he looked up at the Flag Bridge and held up both gloved hands with six fingers extended. Several war correspondents (stationed on the *Lexington* because she was Mitscher's flagship) witnessed the gesture and described it in their newspapers, making Vraciu's six gloved fingers one of the enduring iconic images of the Battle of the Philippine Sea.

WHILE LAUNCHING THE LAST OF HIS SECOND WAVE, Ozawa's flagship had come under attack by an American submarine, the *Albacore*. From a range of 5,300 yards, Skipper J. W. Blanchard had fired a six-fish spread at the *Taiho*. Warrant Officer Sakio Komatsu, piloting one of the just-launched planes, caught sight of an incoming wake and reacted with extraordinary dexterity and valor. He banked hard and dived into its path. The aircraft, pilot, and torpedo were consumed in the explosion. Four more torpedoes missed astern, but the sixth struck a particularly vulnerable part of the *Tai-*

ho's hull, near her aviation gasoline tanks. *Albacore* went deep and endured a long period of depth-charging, but the crew heard the explosion and correctly reckoned that they had scored at least one hit.

The *Taiho's* crew was initially confident of containing the damage, and Ozawa appeared to be in high spirits after the attack. The carrier, Japan's newest, had been engineered to absorb one torpedo hit and more, so there was no reason to believe she was in danger. But when the damaged avgas tanks spread combustible fumes throughout the lower deck, a damage-control officer made the fatal decision to attempt to ventilate the ship. The *Taiho's* air ducts and blowers spread the gases through her interior, and a chain of spectacular explosions tore through the ship. Her armored flight deck heaved and finally ruptured. Flames roared up from the hangar. Shortly after 11:00 a.m., Ozawa removed the emperor's portrait from his stateroom and transferred his flag from the stricken ship. He descended first into the destroyer *Wakatsuki*, then moved to the cruiser *Haguro*, and finally to the *Zuikaku*.

The *Taiho* was obviously finished, but her captain hesitated to order the crew off the ship. That evening, shortly after six, the blazing wreck finally went down, taking more than 1,500 men with her. That concluded the maiden combat cruise of the *Taiho*.

Albacore's sister *Cavalla* had been stalking the Japanese fleet and faithfully reporting its movements for a week. Skipper Herman Kossler's persistence was rewarded with a prime opportunity to attack the *Shokaku* at point-blank range. Raising his periscope a few minutes before noon, he saw the ship looming on the near horizon. He could make out a fantastic degree of detail, including her "bedspring" radar, her enormous "sun and rays" ensign, and even the faces of individual crewmen on the flight deck. The *Cavalla* fired six torpedoes at a range of 1,200 yards. Three of the six connected, and the ship immediately began settling by the head.

The *Cavalla* went deep to evade the inevitable depth-charge treatment. Her main induction system was flooded, rendering her dangerously heavy. She went more than a hundred feet below test depth. The crew counted 106 depth charges in a three-hour ordeal. Half were uncomfortably close, but the *Cavalla* escaped with only superficial damage.

Shokaku's engine rooms quickly flooded, cutting all power to the ship. Dead in the water, she burned helplessly. Without power the firefighters could not get water pressure to the hoses. Bucket brigades threw water on the flames, but that did little good. Explosions in the lower decks and hangar began to tear the carrier apart. The captain ordered the crew off the ship. At 2:10 p.m., her magazine detonated in a mighty thunderclap. The big ship rolled onto her starboard beam ends, her bow lifted from the sea, and she slid under.

Of the six carriers that had attacked Pearl Harbor in December 1941, the *Shokaku* was the fifth to go into the abyss. Now only the *Zuikaku* remained.

While the two stricken carriers were still fighting their losing battles for survival, Ozawa committed most of his remaining airpower to a third strike: thirty fighters, forty-six Zero fighter-bombers, and six torpedo planes from Carrier Division 2. The admiral had not yet learned that his first two strikes had been obliterated in air combat without seriously damaging any American ship. Had he known of those results, he might have hesitated to commit everything he had to another attempt on the American fleet.

The outbound formation cleaved into three widely separated elements soon after departing the Japanese carriers. The largest group diverted off course to the north, then course-corrected to the south and approached the American fleet from the northwest. At a few minutes before one, American fighter director officers directed Hellcats to intercept bogeys on a bearing of 338 degrees at a distance of seventy miles. All the intruders, numbering about forty-seven planes, were either driven away or downed in a nine-minute melee. Several of the attackers were seen to veer off, evidently not eager to risk flying into antiaircraft fire. Another group of bogeys was picked up on radar a few minutes after 2:00 p.m., on a bearing of 205 degrees at a distance of a hundred miles. Outbound search planes skirmished with the newcomers, until the ubiquitous radar-guided F6Fs arrived in force. As in the earlier waves, a few Japanese planes got through the Hellcats and made spirited runs into the heart of the American task force, where they were incinerated in a storm of antiaircraft fire.

Other elements of the last waves took a southerly heading and failed to find the American fleet at all (or perhaps evaded battle) and flew toward airfields on Guam or Rota. They were tracked on radar. Fighter director officers began vectoring Hellcats toward the islands, setting up the day's climactic aerial massacre. A dozen F6Fs from the carrier *Cowpens* arrived over Orote Airfield as a group of about forty Japanese planes were in landing approach. Another seven F6Fs from the *Essex* and eight from the *Hornet* converged on the same location and joined the attack.

The Americans enjoyed insuperable tactical advantages over Orote Peninsula. The Japanese planes were in a low-altitude, low-speed landing approach. With their fuel tanks running dry, they had no alternative but to land. Most of the Japanese antiaircraft batteries around Orote had been silenced by a week of bombing and strafing attacks. The runway was pockmarked and cratered. F6Fs stalked the approaching Japanese planes down to treetop altitude. Ensign W. B. "Spider" Webb of VF-2 slipped into the traffic circle as if he were intending to land, positioning his Hellcat directly behind a division of three Japanese planes. Holding his thumb down on the trigger, he swept them with .50-caliber fire. All three went down. Webb banked port and shot down another; the Japanese pilot managed to get free of his cockpit and pull his chute. Webb had lost altitude in the turn. When he pulled up, he found another Japanese plane in his sights, blew it apart with another short burst, and then flew through the debris. That brought his score to five. Webb now found himself in a head-on run with an aggressive Zero. When it closed to 1,000 yards, optimal range for the F6F's guns, he fired and cut the plane in half. Running low on ammunition, he destroyed two more bombers with short bursts and then pulled away to return to his carrier. Webb's remarkable run of kills was confirmed by his gun camera.

The afternoon slaughter at Orote Airfield wiped out approximately thirty of the forty-nine planes that attempted to land. About nineteen managed to put down on the badly pockmarked airfield, but most of these would never fly again.

Throughout the day, as the air groups made their reports to Mitscher, the number of claimed kills climbed to extravagant proportions. Even accounting for the usual exaggerations and double counting, it was evident that Task Force 58 had scored a victory on a magnitude that no one had expected or foreseen. Of the 373 aircraft launched by Ozawa's carrier force, only 130 had returned intact. Approximately 50 more had been destroyed after taking off from Guam or Rota. The Americans had lost just twenty-five Hellcats, four by operational accidents.[52] The ratio of kills had been about eleven to one. In the Task Force 58 ready rooms, the pilots were celebrating as if they had won the war. "Medicinal" brandy was served and glasses were raised in toasts. On the *Lexington*, a euphoric fighter pilot remarked, "Hell, this is like an old time turkey-shoot."[53] The remark was often repeated, and the name stuck. Historians would call it the first day of the Battle of the Philippine Sea, but to the aviators it was always the "Marianas Turkey Shoot."

THROUGHOUT THE LONG DAY OF AIR OPERATIONS, a steady 15-knot easterly wind had required the Americans to move east, toward Guam and away from the enemy.[54] For the moment, the Japanese fleet lay well beyond the reach of a counterstrike. Spruance knew that one or two Japanese carriers had been torpedoed, but he did not yet know that they were gone. If they were crippled and afloat, as seemed likely, it should be possible to finish them off. With those considerations in mind, Spruance approved Mitscher's plan to chase the enemy into the west.

Ozawa had only intermittent radio contact with the commander in chief of the Combined Fleet during the chaotic afternoon of June 19. Toyoda had issued orders for a temporary withdrawal to the northwest. The fleet would refuel and then "advance and attack enemy task force in cooperation with Base Air Force."[55]

Though he had only 102 operational planes remaining on his carriers, including about forty on the *Zuikaku*, Ozawa believed that many of his missing airplanes must have landed on Guam. He also assumed, or perhaps hoped, that the Americans must have suffered grave losses in both ships and aircraft. Ozawa remained under the mistaken impression that Kakuta's land-based planes had taken a generous bite out of the American task force. His few returned pilots had reported that they had "succeeded in causing four carriers to emit black smoke."[56]

But on Toyoda's flagship *Oyodo*, at anchor in Japan's home waters, the Combined Fleet staff was gradually facing up to the magnitude of the Japanese defeat. It was time to get the surviving ships to safety. At 9:00 p.m., Admiral Toyoda signaled: "Task force will make a timely withdrawal depending upon the local situation, and move as its commander considers fit."[57]

On the twentieth, American air searches failed to find any sign of Ozawa's retreating fleet until 3:42 p.m., when an *Enterprise* TBF Avenger piloted by Lieutenant R. S. Nelson radioed a garbled contact report. The time and imputed distance put the enemy fleet about 270 miles northwest. Mitscher signaled the task force: "Expect to launch everything we have, probably have to recover at night." [58]

Low whistles were heard in the squadron ready rooms as the pilots studied the charts and entered data into their plotting boards. Laden with fuel, bombs, and torpedoes, the American warplanes would fly to the edge of their maximum fuel radius. The afternoon was getting on, so they would return to the task force after nightfall. It was a dicey proposition. Very few American pilots had qualified for night carrier landings. Many would be forced to ditch at sea. But this was to be Mitscher's last opportunity to strike Ozawa, at least in this round, because the Task Force 58 destroyers did not have the fuel for another day's pursuit. He gave his order: "Launch the deckload strikes and prepare a second load." Truman Hedding questioned it, alluding to the distance and risks, but Mitscher only replied, "I understand, but launch the deckload strikes." [59]

Mitscher put the word out: "The primary mission is to get the carriers." On the ready room chalkboards, the three-word directive was written and underlined: "Get the carriers." [60]

At 4:21 p.m., Task Force 58 turned east, away from the enemy and into the wind, and began launching planes. Just eleven minutes were needed to get 216 planes aloft—eighty-five Hellcats, some to fly high cover and some carrying 500-pound bombs; fifty-four TBF Avengers, all but a few armed with bombs rather than the heavy aerial torpedoes; fifty-one SB2C Helldivers with 1,500-pound composite bomb loads; and twenty-six SBD Dauntless dive-bombers. (The SBDs were soon to be replaced; this was to be the last carrier combat mission in the aircraft's storied career.)

As the planes were launching, Nelson sent a corrected contact report. The enemy fleet, widely separated into three groups, was actually sixty miles farther west than Mitscher had assumed. Mitscher considered and rejected the option to cancel the attack and recall the planes. He decided to hold the second deckload strike in reserve for the following morning.

By 4:36 p.m., the 216-plane formation was on its way. Fuel limitations did not allow for a rendezvous into standard squadron or section formations. Planes joined up when and if opportunity offered in what James Ramage called "a running rendezvous." [61] Fuel mixtures were leaned and engines throttled back to minimum power for level flight. According to Ensign Don Lewis of VB-10, stretching an aircraft's fuel reserve was as much art as science. It was a matter of flying "gently," of climbing little by little to altitude, of keeping the aircraft balanced by switching between auxiliary fuel tanks.[62]

The outgoing formations droned along at about 130 to 140 knots. Many of the aviators later confessed that they were physically exhausted after a week and a half of intensive combat flight operations. The dive-bombers climbed to 20,000 feet, where the physical strain on the aircrew was severe—the cockpits were arctic, men clapped their gloved hands to keep them warm, and ice crystals accumulated in their oxygen masks.

No one had any illusions. They all knew that they were going beyond normal fuel range and might be getting wet at the end of the day. Mitscher and the other task force commanders had proved that they would go to great lengths to rescue downed aviators. That bond of trust now paid dividends.

The leading planes overtook the trailing edge of the Japanese fleet at about 6:25 p.m., less than an hour before sunset. The pilots saw long white wakes, indicating that the enemy ships were moving at high speed. In the first (westernmost) group were six large fleet oilers and six destroyers. Flight leaders told their squadrons to ignore the tempting targets and continue flying northwest because their orders were to attack the "Charlie Victors" (carriers). About ten minutes later, the leading wave of planes reported many ships ahead, including carriers.

Ozawa had managed to get about eighty planes aloft, mostly Zero fighters—no small feat considering the beating his air groups had suffered the previous day. F6Fs, flying high cover over the bomber squadrons, moved ahead to engage the enemy fighters. About twenty Zeros went down in the first few minutes of air combat. Commander Jackson D. Arnold of the *Hornet* Air Group directed all planes to attack the *Zuikaku*. Sinking the big flattop, Arnold told his pilots, "was their ticket home."[63] There was neither time nor fuel to set up coordinated attacks—they would just drop their noses and go straight into the heart of the enemy fleet.

Hal Buell led the *Hornet* Helldivers in a shallow dive toward the target, hoping to achieve surprise. Antiaircraft fire reached up toward them, but the first bursts were low. The Helldivers pushed over into a steep dive and flew through an intense, multicolored barrage. It was the heaviest antiaircraft fire that the veteran Buell had ever encountered. "In the lead plane I was a focal point, and with the mass of shells passing all about me, I felt like I was diving into an Iowa plains hailstorm. . . . Some threw out long tentacles of flaming white phosphorus unlike anything I had ever seen before."[64] The *Yorktown*'s VB-1 Helldivers followed behind the *Hornet* planes and rained a dozen bombs down on the big carrier. Towers of whitewater rose on either side of the ship as bombs missed her narrowly, but two or three found the mark. *Zuikaku* burned fiercely and coasted to rest as her power cut out. F6Fs roared low over her flight deck in strafing runs and killed dozens of her crew.

The SBDs of VB-10 arrived over the fleet at 15,500 feet and began a high-speed breakup into their dives. In a shallow dive, with 200 knots airspeed, Don Lewis went over his checklist, shifted to low blower, and pushed over. He attacked the *Hiyo*. She went into a radical turn, and Lewis corkscrewed several times to keep the target in his sights. The dive, said Lewis, "seemed to take an eternity. Never had a dive taken so long." Flying through a massive volume of antiaircraft fire, the flight deck looking "tremendous" beneath him, he released his bomb at 1,500 feet and pulled out and up. [65]

A group of *Wasp* dive-bombers had paused to attack the fleet oilers, thirty or forty miles east of the main action. Two were so badly damaged that they had to be abandoned and scuttled. Other attackers planted bombs on the light carrier *Junyo*, the stern of the *Chiyoda*, a former seaplane tender, and the battleship *Haruna*. Four *Belleau Wood* Avengers armed with torpedoes dropped out of a cloud and made a high-speed run on the heavy carrier *Hiyo*, scoring at least one and possibly two torpedo hits. The *Hiyo*'s crew lost control of the resulting fires and had to abandon her later that night. She went down by the bow a few minutes before 10:00 p.m., bringing to three the number of Japanese carriers destroyed in the two-day battle. *Zuikaku* suffered badly enough that her skipper ordered the crew to abandon ship, but the fires were finally brought under control and the order countermanded. For once, Japanese damage-control efforts were successful, and the badly damaged carrier managed to limp back to the Inland Sea.

Lightened by the absence of their bombs, the escaping planes flew through a deadly gauntlet of antiaircraft fire. The Japanese formation was spread very wide across the sea, so it was a long flight to exit the screen. Fleeing planes were rocked hard by nearby bursts, and columns of water shot up ahead and among them as the destroyers and cruisers fired their main batteries into their paths. Pilots flew down to wave-top level, pulled up, and kicked their rudders right and left, hoping to prevent the gunners from finding the range.

Buell's plane took a direct hit and almost went down. An antiaircraft shell blew a hole through the middle of his starboard wing, and a piece of shrapnel penetrated the cockpit and cut a gash across his back. The wing trailed a tail of fire, which began burning through the wing's aluminum skin, exposing the frame beneath. The wounded Buell forced the stick as far left as it would go in order to keep his unwieldy dive-bomber in level flight. (That the wounded Helldiver could fly at all, let alone fly all the way back to Task Force 58, was proof of its rugged construction.)

Admiral Ugaki recorded that the antiaircraft fire was so heavy, it took on a life of its own. Even after the American planes had left the scene, it continued sporadically into the night. "Most of the fire was aimed at stars," he wrote. "Even within a single ship, orders were hard to deliver. Firing couldn't be stopped easily."[66]

On the long return flight, in gathering darkness, American warplanes coalesced into small groups. Adjusting their engine settings to "slow cruise," they tried to coax every possible mile out of each gallon of remaining gasoline. One pilot, battling fatigue, breathed pure oxygen through his mask even though he was at just 2,000 feet altitude, hoping that it would give him energy to complete the mission. The radio circuits remained busy as pilots discussed their predicament. Hours passed. Fuel needles dipped toward empty. Entire sections or squadrons decided to ditch their planes in one location, reasoning that several rafts lashed together were easier to spot than a single one. Most of the aviators kept their cool, Vraciu recalled, but "some of them were breaking down—sobbing—on the air. It was a dark and black ocean out there. I could empathize with them, but it got so bad that I had to turn my radio off for a while."[67]

Even for those pilots with enough fuel to get home, it was no easy task to find the American fleet. Flying in darkness was a new experience for all but a few. Some were drawn off course by lightning flashes on the southern horizon. Those who flew long enough picked up a homing beacon—a faint signal through the earphones—and followed it back to the fleet.

Admiral Mitscher had previously informed all Task Force 58 ships that they should, when ordered, point their searchlights vertically into the sky. Lighting up ships in enemy waters defied prevailing doctrine, and might have been fatal had there been Japanese submarines in the vicinity, but Mitscher felt obligated to accept the risks. The decision to turn on the

Mitscher in Pursuit
Battle of the Philippine Sea, Phase II, June 20, 1944

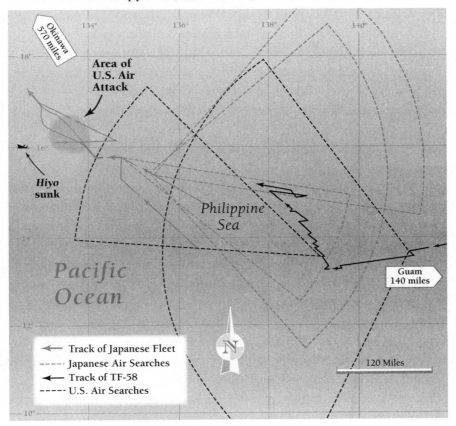

lights became an important part of Mitscher's legacy, a badge of his personal regard for his pilots. But the decision was not unprecedented, nor was it deemed especially controversial at the time. The prior week's action had allayed fears about the enemy air threat, and the enemy submarine threat had been reduced by the hunter-killer groups, which had destroyed six or seven Japanese boats in the previous ten days. During the Battle of Midway two years earlier, Spruance had ordered the *Enterprise* and *Hornet* lit up to recover aircraft returning from a late-day strike against the retreating Japanese fleet. To a historian who congratulated him for his courage in rendering that decision, Spruance later offered this comment:

I think you are greatly overemphasizing the importance of turning on the lights at night to bring planes back to the carriers and to get them safely on board. A carrier without its air group is a disarmed ship, a liability and not an asset. The time to consider the risk in turning on the lights for a night recovery is before launching the attack. If the planes are to be launched so late in the day that a night recovery is probable, and if the tactical situation is such that you are not willing to do what is required to get the planes back safely, then you have no business launching the attack in the first place.[68]

In the historical literature, Mitscher is often quoted as giving a terse, cinematic order: "Turn on the lights." But that order is almost certainly apocryphal. According to Arleigh Burke, the Task Force 58 staff had earlier prepared a detailed plan to light up the task force. Nor was "Turn on the lights" an order that a seasoned carrier task force commander would have given. It was too unspecific. Which lights? The red and green running lights? The signal lights? The truck lights at the masthead? The glow lights on the flight deck? The hooded lights that could be seen only from astern, by a plane on final landing approach?

In prewar exercises, it had been discovered that a searchlight pointed vertically into the sky rendered a ship visible from a long way off. At about 8:30 p.m., when the radar screens lit up with planes approaching from the northwest, and the task force turned into the wind to begin recovery operations, vertical shafts of light appeared all across the task force. Most of the carriers turned on their other exterior lights as well, and a few had rigged floodlights on the island superstructures to illuminate their flight decks. Many of the battleships and cruisers also lit up, and destroyers fired star shells from their 5-inch guns.

It was a scene no witness would ever forget. The great fleet, spread across the horizon as far as the eye could see, made a phantasmagoric spectacle. Lieutenant John A. Harper, landing signal officer on the *Belleau Wood*, thought it looked like "a big city at night."[69] Hal Buell, approaching from the westward in his damaged SB2C, was reminded of "Coney Island on the Fourth of July."[70] E. J. Lawton, flying an *Enterprise* Avenger, compared it to a "Mardi Gras setting, fantastically out of place here, midway between the Marianas and the Philippines."[71] The screening ships lit up alongside the carriers—a well-intended gesture of solidarity that probably did more harm than good. Paul Backus, an officer on the *South Dakota*, recalled that one or two planes made passes on the battleship as if to land, before realizing the error at the last moment and zooming off into the darkness.[72]

Mitscher had ordered pilots short of fuel to land on any available carrier, and had told the carriers to take any airplane that entered her landing circle. In the anarchic recovery, nearly half of the planes that landed on a carrier did so on the wrong one. Planes approached in disorderly groups, without sufficient intervals. "It was kind of every man for himself," said Ramage.[73] Pilots played chicken with one another. Many "took their own cuts" (landed even when waved off by the landing signal officers). Some ran out of fuel as they were directly astern of the flight decks, and crashed in the carriers' wakes. Desperate pilots refused to give way to one another. One landing signal officer waved off two planes approaching simultaneously, and then threw himself flat on deck as they flew "over us so low it seemed they almost grazed us, flat as we were."[74] Exhausted, confused, or wounded pilots forgot to run through their pre-landing checklists, failed to lower their landing gear or tailhooks, and belly-crashed. Buell ignored a late wave-off and dropped his damaged Helldiver onto the *Lexington*. The plane bounced, failed to catch a wire, and catapulted over the crash barriers. Wreckage skidded toward the airplanes parked on the bow. Two sailors were killed, and six parked aircraft destroyed.

When a wrecked plane fouled a flight deck, the crew worked quickly to extract the aviators from their cockpits and shove the wreckage over the side. Keeping the decks clear for the dozens of planes circling above was the overriding concern. By a lucky stroke, the *Enterprise* managed to recover two aircraft simultaneously, an unprecedented feat—two aircraft approached abreast, wingtip to wingtip, and each snagged a different arresting wire. Sam Sommers marveled at the approach of a badly damaged Hellcat to his carrier, the *Cowpens*. Half the aircraft's rudder had been shot away, and the pilot could make only gradual and tentative turns. Eschewing the normal circular landing approach, he came in directly from astern, giving up altitude little by little, and landed flawlessly, "like a dragonfly on a lily pad. . . . He didn't bounce. No tire screeched. There were about four inches of surface at the top and bottom of where his rudder had been."[75]

The light show attracted at least one confused Japanese pilot, who very nearly landed his Aichi dive-bomber on the *Belleau Wood*. It flew down the crossleg at suitable speed and altitude, wheels down and flaps set for land-

ing. Lieutenant Harper, assuming it was American, signaled "too high" with
his paddles. The plane went higher, suggesting that the pilot was reading
the signals improperly. It was banking away when a spotlight revealed the
red "meatballs" on the fuselage. The *Belleau Wood* suddenly darkened, but
the antiaircraft gunners did not have time to react. (In retrospect, Harper
regretted that he was unable to coax the plane aboard: had he done so, it
would have been the most dramatic capture in the history of aviation.) The
cruiser *Oakland* later reported that a Japanese plane had made an apparent
landing pass before turning away and disappearing into the darkness.

For lack of fuel or available flight decks, planes were forced to make
water landings all around the task force. Gas-starved engines began to
cough and catch; the acrid smell of burning hydraulic fluid seeped into the
cockpit; the stick went dead in the pilot's gloved hand. Because a deadstick
water landing was riskier than a powered landing, many pilots chose to
ditch even though they had fuel to spare. If a pilot was on top of his emergency landing checklist, he remembered to unhook the radio cord from his
helmet, tighten his shoulder straps, confirm that his canopy was retracted
and locked, bank into the wind, open his flaps, put the plane into a nose-up
landing attitude, and drop slowly until he was just 10 or 15 feet above the
sea. Then he chopped the throttle and braced for impact. In calm seas—
and the sea was mercifully tranquil that night—the impact might be no
greater than that of a hard carrier landing. He had a minute or perhaps
even two minutes to unbuckle and climb out onto the wing. His parachute
would keep buoyant for several minutes; when it got heavy, the pilot could
inflate his Mae West.

From the Task Force 58 ships, men could look around and see downed
planes and pilots and crewmen all around them. Passing carriers dropped
light buoys. Floating airmen shined their waterproof pack lights and blew
their whistles. Some fired flares. Destroyers scanned the sea with searchlights. Coming alongside a floating man, they lowered cargo nets and hauled
him aboard.

The last planes were recovered and brought aboard by 10:15 p.m. The
task force turned northwest and proceeded at 16 knots. Searchlights scanned
the sea ahead. Each task group left a single destroyer behind to search for
and pick up downed aviators. At first light, the sky would fill with search
planes to cover the zone in which many aviators were expected to be found.

Of the 216 planes that had participated in the strike, eighty ditched at sea or deck-crashed on recovery. Another twenty went missing and were presumed destroyed in air combat over the Japanese fleet. The number of personnel in the missing planes totaled 209 (100 pilots, 109 aircrew), but 100 men were fished out of the water that night and another 60 picked up in the ensuing days. That cut losses to 16 pilots and 33 aircrewmen. Task Force 58 could readily afford to lose a hundred planes, especially since the losses could be made good by drawing reserve aircraft from the jeep carriers stationed near Saipan.

For the Japanese, another round of grievous air combat losses was exacerbated by a night recovery that was proportionally even more disastrous than Task Force 58's. By Ozawa's count, he had only thirty-five flyable carrier aircraft remaining in his arsenal at the end of June 20. His losses since departing Tawi Tawi a week earlier exceeded 400 planes. If there was any cold consolation at all, it was that none of his ships was crippled—in two days of battle, every Japanese ship that had been struck by a bomb or torpedo had either sunk or managed to contain the damage, so that the First Mobile Fleet could make way at a brisk 20 knots. Ozawa had a 300-mile lead in his homeward dash. Task Force 58's fuel limitations (the destroyers were low) and the delays involved in recovering downed American airmen precluded a vigorous chase. The defeated fleet refueled at Nakagusuku Bay, Okinawa, and then returned to the Inland Sea.

RETURNING TO THE WATERS OFF SAIPAN on June 23, Admiral Spruance was obliged to answer anxious queries from Pearl Harbor. Most urgently, Nimitz wanted a firm date fixed for W-Day, the invasion of Guam. (Plans for Operation FORAGER had named that date as June 18, just three days after the Saipan landings, but that schedule was never realistic and had been suspended on June 16.) The ground campaign on Saipan, now in its ninth day, had stalled in the island's interior highlands, where Japanese troops were taking full advantage of the onerous terrain. After conferring with Smith and Turner on the *Indianapolis*, Spruance reluctantly admitted that he was unable to promise a date for Guam. No troops could be withdrawn from Saipan until the Americans had broken the deadlock in that island's mountainous spine, and all floating reserve forces needed to be kept in place until the issue was decided. That was the unanimous opinion of Smith, Turner, and General Roy Geiger (who was to command American troops in the Guam operation). "I did not, and do not, like the delay involved," he told Nimitz, "but I felt that I had to accept the judgment of the generals who have to do the job as to the tools they require." [76]

American forces controlled about a third of the island, including almost all of the territory south of a line bisecting the island between the eastern landing beaches and Magicienne Bay. Approximately 1,500 Japanese troops had been surrounded within a strong position at Nafutan Point on the island's southern coast. (The Nafutan pocket had attempted several break-outs, including a ferocious *banzai* charge on June 26 that won the Japanese soldiers temporary possession of the adjacent Aslito Airfield, but they were now securely bottled up and running short of ammunition.) On June 22, the first American planes flew into Aslito—a squadron of USAAF P-47s that had catapulted from jeep carriers offshore. Seventy-four P-47s were operating from the airfield by June 24. On Saipan's eastern shore, the 2nd Marine Division was pushing against obdurate resistance north toward the town of Garapan and Tanapag Harbor. The 4th Marine Division tidied up the zone between the mountainous ridge and the western shore. Holland Smith ordered the 27th Infantry Division into the middle section of the front, the high ground between the two marine divisions.

On June 23, the three divisions launched a coordinated attack all along the fighting front. Holland Smith had intended his mixed marine-army forces to drive north in a line abreast, advancing simultaneously and relatively quickly. But Ralph Smith's army division was slow off the mark, launching its attack about an hour late. Running up against guerrilla-type opposition in the island's steep, rocky, treacherous midsection, the soldiers took cover in foxholes and awaited massed artillery support to clear the ground before them. But that gave the enemy time to move reinforcements into the cliffs and caves around Mount Tapotchau, the highest point on the island. There they set up machine guns and mortars in well-sheltered high-ground positions.

Positioned on the right and left flanks of the stalled 27th Division, where the coastal terrain was flatter and more forgiving, the marines sustained their forward momentum. They flanked and overran strong positions, or simply cut them off and bypassed them, leaving them to be cleaned out by reserve units. The discrepant pace of advance created a shallow U-shape in the American lines, an arrangement that threatened to expose the interior flanks of the two marine divisions to punishing counterattacks. The army would have to pick up the pace or the entire front might degenerate into a bloody stalemate.

Once again, as during GALVANIC and FLINTLOCK, the performance of the 27th Infantry Division was unfavorably compared to that of the marines. In this instance, however, the disparity seemed to threaten the success of the entire operation. Holland Smith was well attuned to the interservice sensitivities at stake on Saipan and their potential to make trouble in Washington. But he was under intense pressure from higher-ups to complete the pacification of Saipan, and he needed every part of the line to move. In a series of dispatches to Ralph Smith's command post, Holland Smith urged a more spirited attack. But on June 24, the "U" deepened. Smith sent Major General Sanderford Jarman forward to the 27th Infantry Division headquarters to discuss the problem. Jarman, who was slated to command Saipan's garrison once the island was secured, returned to the Fifth Amphibious Corps headquarters at Charan Kanoa to report that Ralph Smith had pledged to achieve further advances the following day. If he could not get the division moving, Ralph Smith had told Jarman, "he should be relieved."[77]

At the heart of the issue were differing tactical concepts and doctrines. By instinct and training, the marines relied on energetic, aggressive, rapid attacks. They would endure higher casualties in order to decide the issue more rapidly. The army concept was to take ground gradually, with attacks supported by massed artillery bombardment. Entire battalions moved together on a broad front, taking up flanking positions whenever possible. At night, they tended to withdraw to secure positions some distance behind the front lines. Those principles were suited to the clash of large armies on continental battlefields, but they were less effective against small enemy units dug into irregular positions in the rock-strewn heights of a coral island. In an amphibious operation, with a large fleet lying offshore, potentially exposed to enemy attacks or the vagaries of weather, time was an oppressive factor and haste was paramount. The army's stolid tempo granted the enemy time to improve his defensive arrangements, both on Saipan and on the adjoining islands where the battle had not yet been joined. Moreover, the awful conditions in those bald coral hills threatened to deteriorate into a general crisis of morale. The rear echelons were hard-pressed to carry sufficient food, water, or ammunition up to the front lines. In a letter to his parents, Private Richard King described pernicious depredations of heat and thirst: "It was 120 degrees and we stayed on the coral, all day in the hot sun, and were slowly going crazy. I couldn't open my mouth at all, my tongue was swollen five times its normal size, my throat burned to a crisp, and blood coming out of my nose and mouth."[78]

On June 24, Holland Smith took a boat to the *Indianapolis* and asked Spruance for authorization to relieve Ralph Smith of his command. Turner emphatically supported the request. Carl Moore warned against it, referring to the risk of an open breach between the U.S. Army and the Marine Corps, but Spruance felt that he must endorse his ground commander's wishes. Moore wrote out the order and Spruance signed it. Ralph Smith was relieved of command and sent back to Pearl Harbor, a disgrace from which his career never recovered, and General Jarman took command of the division. Spruance told Nimitz that Smith's relief "was regrettable but necessary. He has been in command of that division for a long time and cannot avoid being held responsible for its fighting efficiency or lack thereof."[79]

Within another week of hard fighting, the army broke through the strong pockets that had held it up. But it fell to the 2nd Division to stage the decisive attack on Mount Tapotchau, which they did after beating back several tank attacks in sugarcane fields west of the ridgeline. At last the peak was seized by a combined effort of the 2nd Battalion, 8th Marines and the 1st Battalion, 29th Marines. On the west coast, other elements of the 2nd Division fought a bitter action among the charred ruins of Garapan and broke through to capture Tanapag Harbor on July 3.

Now commenced the final stage of the battle for Saipan, when remaining Japanese units and stragglers fell back into the northern heights of the island, and the fighting deteriorated into "isolated, sporadic, and desperate resistance by the enemy. There was little semblance of organized opposition."[80] Small groups of enemy fighters took shelter in limestone caves. The positions were often bypassed, until special units came along and cleaned them out with flamethrowers and hand grenades. Often the Japanese emerged in one final, screaming charge, and had to be cut down with rifle fire or even bayonets.

Of the great naval battle that had taken place offshore, the infantrymen knew nothing. If they had, they would have thought little of it. "Our vision of the war was largely tunnel-vision," wrote William Manchester, a marine private who fought on Saipan and later became a renowned biographer. "To each of us the most important place in the world was his foxhole. The impact of MacArthur's and Nimitz's twin offensives was lost on us. Most

Marines were as ignorant of Pacific geography as their families at home."[81] After a week on Saipan, Manchester and his fellow marines looked very much like the men who had conquered Guadalcanal two years earlier— gaunt, bearded, caked with mud and soot, habitually staring into the middle distance with a vacant, weary expression. They marched in long columns, hugging the roadside ditches into which they would dive at the first indica- tion of enemy fire. They did not salute an officer because to do so would mark him as a preferred target for enemy snipers. At dusk they dug a deep foxhole and did not stop to rest or eat until it was completed. The nights were neither dark nor quiet. The scarred landscape was lit by star shells and long-burning parachute flares. The stillness was disturbed by the engines of tanks on the move, by the rattle of machine guns and the whistle-blast of artillery shells. Veterans learned to identify each caliber of incoming shell by its sound: "There were shells that fizzled like sparklers, or whinnied, or squealed, or whickered, or whistled, or whuffed like a winter gale slamming a barn door," wrote Manchester. "The same principle governed all these sounds: the projectile's blast created a vacuum into which air rushed."[82]

For the remaining Japanese fighters, penned into a shrinking perimeter in northern Saipan, the barrage was relentless and deadly. The marines kept up constant pressure with their field artillery and truck-mounted rocket launchers. With complete air supremacy, the American land-based fighters and carrier planes rained down bombs, rockets, and strafing fire on the Japa- nese lines. To all of that was added the big guns of the warships operating offshore, which kept at it throughout the daylight hours and often contin- ued into the night. The diarist James Fahey (whose ship, the *Montpelier*, operated off Saipan for several weeks) noted the uncanny contrast between the ship's commonplace routines and the carnage unfolding in plain sight ashore. "It was funny to see some of the fellows fishing from the side of the ship, others laying in the sun getting a tan, and up forward on the bow some of the officers are boxing, while on the beach men are killing each other, some are in agony from wounds. Our planes are strafing and bombing and our ships are bombarding the Japs. The two scenes are so close to each other and yet it is from one extreme to another or two different worlds."[83]

Lieutenant Ben Bradlee, future editor in chief of the *Washington Post*, served off Saipan on the destroyer *Philip*. For several days Bradlee commu- nicated by radio with a "call-fire" coordinator ashore. This man, a marine lieutenant whom Bradlee never met, was so close to enemy lines that he often wanted shells planted on targets immediately adjacent to his own position. During some of these radio transmissions, Bradlee swore he could hear Japanese soldiers yelling in the background:

> I've lost his name, unfortunately, but this guy was one brave son of a bitch. He would ask for gunfire in such-and-such a place—often within a few yards of his foxhole—and I would relay the coordinates he gave me to the gunnery officer. First "Fire," then deafening explosion. Then pause, while the 57-pound shells streaked toward their target, followed by comments from our unseen buddy. "Fan-fucking-tastic"; "Bullseye" maybe. Often, even. And sometimes: "That was a little close, friends. Back off a blond one."[84]

Some 140,000 rounds of 5-inch ammunition were fired on targets ashore during the month-long campaign for Saipan. That remarkable figure did not include the larger-caliber weapons of the cruisers and battleships. All told, according to records later submitted to the Navy Department, 11,000 tons of naval ordnance fell on Saipan. With such a superabundance of firepower in the offing, the call-fire coordinators did not always limit their targets to known enemy locations. "It was often employed," Nimitz told King in his report on FORAGER, "against an area where enemy installations were only suspected rather than known to exist."[85] And why not, so long as the ammunition resupply train, staging from Eniwetok, continually replenished the fleet's magazines?

As on Tarawa and other Pacific islands, the shells persistently failed to penetrate fortified bunkers or caves, but heavy bombardment provided an effective neutralizing effect immediately before tank or infantry attacks. Men ashore sometimes requested night illumination of the enemy lines, then closed the radio link and bedded down for the night. Ships offshore, in compliance with the most recent request, kept the area brightly lit with an uninterrupted sequence of star shells and other illumination rounds. Piercing nightlong radiance over "no-man's-land" deterred the night attacks and infiltration tactics that the Japanese infantry had employed to lethal effect in earlier campaigns.

Suffering under cumulative punishment from land, air, and sea, the Japanese garrison was driven to desperation. Caves and entrenchments provided some measure of bodily protection, but any movement of supplies or troops across open ground drew prompt, accurate, and powerful salvos. Even when it did not kill or maim the defenders, incessant bombardment drove them to the end of their wits. Sergeant Takeo Yamauchi, one of a relative handful of Japanese soldiers to survive the battle for Saipan, later described the ordeal:

> The extreme intensity of those flashes and boiling clouds of smoke still remain in my mind today. They went sixty meters straight up! Huge guns! From battleships. A total bombardment from all the ships. The area I was in was pitted like the craters of the moon. We just clung to the earth in our shallow trenches. We were half buried. Soil filled my mouth many times. Blinded me. The fumes and flying dirt almost choked you. The next moment I might get it![86]

Small and isolated outfits went to ground in caves or heavily vegetated ravines. Stragglers, having lost contact with their officers, joined up with other groups and awaited orders that never came. Internal communications broke down. Food and water ran low. They struggled up into the northern hills, retreating haphazardly from the advancing enemy forces. Pitiable civilian refugees, including entire starving families, fell in with the soldiers and begged for food, water, and protection. For a few days in early July, Yamauchi and a handful of survivors from his platoon took shelter in a deep ravine. Their officers had gone missing. They concealed themselves in the underbrush, avoided the low-flying Hellcats, and waited for orders. All around them were the putrefying bodies of fallen comrades: "Corpses burned black. Hanging from the branches of trees, tumbled onto the ground. Corpses crawling with maggots." When Yamauchi proposed that they attempt to surrender, he was firmly rebuked: "Squad Leader, you're talking like a traitor. Behave like a military man!"[87]

In a fortified cave near the island's northwest coast, General Saito found it increasingly difficult to maintain contact with his remaining forces. He had been obliged to move his field headquarters five times; his sixth and final command post was in a place the Japanese called the "Valley of Hell." His field telephone network was of no use because the ground cables had been chewed up in the weeks-long barrage. Message runners appointed to carry dispatches to commanders in the field were often cut down in their tracks. On the morning of July 6, he radioed the Imperial General Headquarters in Tokyo and reported that the cause was lost. He issued one final order to all Japanese army forces remaining on the island:

Heaven has not given us an opportunity. We have not been able to utilize fully the terrain. We have fought in unison up to the present time, but now we have no materials with which to fight, and our artillery for attack has been completely destroyed. Our comrades have fallen one after another. Despite the bitterness of defeat, we pledge "Seven lives to repay our country." . . .

Whether we attack or whether we stay where we are, there is only death. However, in death there is life. We must utilize this opportunity to exalt true Japanese manhood. I will advance with those who remain to deliver still another blow to the American devils. I will leave my bones on Saipan as a bulwark of the Pacific.[88]

Saito's declaration that he would "advance with those who remain" was evidently to be understood as an allegory. The general was exhausted and badly strained; he wore a long beard and was (according to one of his officers) "a pitiable sight."[89] He held a last banquet with his officers, a meal of canned crabmeat washed down with sake. Then he left the cave, sat on a rock, faced the east, gripped a ritual dagger with both hands, and plunged it into his abdomen. In its fullest expression, ritual *seppuku*, or suicide, required the dying samurai to carve out his bowels by slicing across and then diagonally upward. It is not known how far Saito's knife traveled before his aide-de-camp fired a shot into his right temple. As for Admiral Nagumo, whose command post was in another bunker, he is said to have followed Saito's example. But no eyewitness report of Nagumo's suicide survived, presumably because all who saw it took their own lives in turn, or were slain in battle. According to secondhand reports, the bodies of both commanders were cremated and their ashes scattered.

"Seven lives to repay our country" was the slogan often employed to rally Japanese soldiers to a suicidal attack, usually in the form of a massed *banzai* charge. Each son of heaven was to do his utmost to slay seven devils before he was taken down in turn. A Japanese warrior ablaze with the *Yamato* spirit (so it was said and even at times believed) would go on fighting even after he had received mortal wounds. According to an ancient samurai myth, a swordsman beheaded by an adversary could (if he possessed sufficient power of will) muster the dying strength for one more mighty swing of the sword, thus taking his slayer down with him. An American marine nearly shot dead by a blinded Japanese soldier in Garapan marveled at the man's "fighting resolution": "Instead of seeking aid for his terrible injury he determined to go out fighting, killing one last enemy."[90]

Saito's final orders summoned all remaining Japanese soldiers (included all walking wounded) to a rendezvous at the village of Makunsha, on the Tanapag Plain near the northwest coast, after nightfall on July 6. From there they would launch an all-out "general attack" or *banzai* charge into the American lines. The immobilized wounded were to take their own lives or be killed in their cots. Runners spread out to disseminate the orders, and soldiers from all through the shrinking perimeter did their best to converge on the little town. Private Taro Kawaguchi answered the call, though he no longer had a weapon. He left one final entry in his diary. Noting that he had faced north, bowed to the emperor, and bid a silent good-bye to his parents and relatives, Kawaguchi pledged to do his best in the climactic attack. "Looking back through the years, I am only 26 years old. Thanks to the Emperor, both my parents, and my aunt I have lived to this day and I am deeply gratified. At the same time it is deeply regrettable that I have nothing to report at this time when my life is fluttering away like a flower petal to become a part of the soil. . . . I, with my sacrificed body, will become the whitecaps of the Pacific and will stay on this island until the friendly forces come to reclaim the soil of the Emperor."[91]

About 3,000 Japanese troops answered the call, or managed to get to the staging point without being immolated in the ongoing artillery bombardment. The uninjured and best-armed men were positioned at the head of the column, four men abreast. Those who still carried rifles fixed their bayonets; others armed themselves with makeshift spears fashioned from knives or bayonets attached to the end of long wooden poles. At the end of the column was placed a pathetic cavalcade of sick and wounded men, bleeding and bandaged, some hobbling along on crutches, many with no weapons at all.

At 4:45 a.m., shortly before dawn, the head of the column charged down the track of the narrow-gauge coastal railway line and crashed into a sector of the American line held by the two battalions of the 27th Infantry Division. They screamed as they came on, as always: "*Banzai!*"

By sheer weight of numbers, they burst through a seam between the 1st and 3rd battalions of the 106th Infantry. The two battalions were quickly cut off and then further divided into isolated pockets. The mass of charging men raced southward, overrunning more American positions, until they ran into several marine artillery batteries about a mile down the coastal road. The gunners kept up a steady fire as the attackers closed the range, claiming heavy casualties—but the Japanese continued on, climbing over the heaps of their fallen friends, until the marines were firing at nearly flat trajectories with fuses cut to four-tenths of a second. Forced to abandon their guns, the artillerymen took their fire locks to render them useless and staged a fighting retreat to the southward.

The Americans who witnessed the extraordinary and desperate charge regarded it with a mixture of horror, amazement, contempt, and admiration. It was, said William Manchester, "the most spectacular banzai of the war."[92] About 400 American soldiers and marines were killed in the melee, many by stabbing wounds. As the stampede thinned out and spent its remaining energy, small pockets of marines and soldiers fought at close quarters with their adversaries until tanks and infantry reinforcements were rushed in to join a punishing counterattack. Manchester remembered "wading through the slime and detritus of entrails, gore, splintered bones, mangled flesh, and brains."[93] By 9:00 a.m., the counterattack had restored the lines. Small parties of marines and soldiers systematically destroyed the many isolated pockets of enemy fighters left in the rear areas. After a body count, the American commanders estimated that 4,311 Japanese were killed in the morning's action. As the afternoon heat settled over the island, bulldozers shoved the bodies into mass graves. But a thin layer of soil could not stifle the rank miasma or tame the clouds of plump black flies that rose from the killing grounds and spread like a plague over the entire island.

SAIPAN WAS HOME TO ABOUT 25,000 JAPANESE or Okinawan civilians, many of whom had emigrated from Japan or Okinawa shortly after 1919, when the Marianas (except Guam, an American territory wrested from Spain in the Spanish-American War) were mandated to Japan by the Treaty of Versailles. In the latter stages of the campaign on Saipan, many followed the retreating remnants of the Japanese army into the northern hills. On July 8, as American forces began their final offensive, approximately 8,000 civilians were scattered within the Japanese lines. Before his ritual disembowelment, General Saito had declared that it was their duty to avoiding falling into captivity—that is, to take the same way out as General Saito. Families were bound by the *oyaku-shinju* (parent-child death pact). They were obligated to take their lives and those of their kin by any means at hand. Cyanide capsules were given out until there were no more. Soldiers offered to shoot civilians in turn, and did not always wait to be invited. In a crowded cave, one grenade might do the work of twenty bullets. Sword-wielding officers beheaded dozens of willing victims. There were reports of children forming into a circle and tossing a live hand grenade, one to another, until it exploded and killed them all. In a cave filled with Japanese soldiers and civilians, Yamauchi recalled, a sergeant ordered mothers to keep their infants quiet, and when they were unable to do so, he told them, "Kill them yourself or I'll order my men to do it." Several mothers obeyed.[94] As the Japanese perimeter receded toward the island's northern terminus at Marpi Point, civilians who had thus far resisted the suicide order were forced back to the edge of a cliff that dropped several hundred feet onto a rocky shore. In a harrowing finale, many thousands of Japanese men, women, and children took that fateful last step.

The self-destructive paroxysm could not be explained by deference to orders, or by obeisance to the death cult of imperial *bushido*. Suicide, the Japanese of Saipan earnestly believed, was the sole alternative to a fate worse than death. The Americans were not human beings—they were something akin to demons or beasts. They were the "hairy ones," or the "Anglo-American Demons." They would rape the women and girls. They would crush captured civilians under the treads of their tanks. The marines were especially dreaded. According to a story circulated widely among the Japanese of Saipan, all Marine Corps recruits were compelled to murder their own parents before being inducted into service. It was said that Japanese soldiers taken prisoner would suffer hideous tortures—their ears, noses, and limbs would be cut off; they would be blinded and castrated; they would be cooked and fed to dogs. Truths and half-truths were shrewdly wedded to the more outrageous and far-fetched claims. Japanese newspapers reproduced photographs of Japanese skulls mounted on American tanks. A cartoon appearing in an American servicemen's magazine, later reproduced and translated in the Japanese press, had suggested that marine enlistees would receive a "Japanese hunting license," promising "open season" on the enemy, complete with "free ammunition and equipment—with pay!"[95] Other cartoons, also reproduced in Japan, characterized the Japanese as monkeys, rats, cockroaches, or lice. John Dower's study *War Without Mercy* explored the means by which both American and Japanese propaganda tended to dehumanize the enemy.

Among the Japanese, who could not read or hear any dissenting views, the
excesses of American wartime rhetoric and imagery lent credibility to the
implication that a quick suicide was the path of least suffering.

Saipan was the first Pacific battlefield in which Americans had encountered a large civilian population. No one had known what to expect. Would
women and children take up weapons and hurl themselves at the Americans? A pamphlet distributed to the 2nd Marine Division prior to the landing warned that the men would come into contact with a large population
of enemy civilians: "We do not know how many of the Japanese *civilians* will
actively fight us. . . . The women and children will be no more or less dangerous than our own mothers, sisters, or small brothers would be under similar circumstances." The presence of civilians required close attention to the
rules of war, the pamphlet warned:

> We must . . . be absolutely sure in our own minds that a civilian is
> fighting us or harming our installations before we shoot him. Interna-
> tional law clearly demands that civilians who do not fight back at us—
> whether they are Japanese or Korean civilians working as laborers or
> specialists for the military, or noncombatants in the armed forces, like
> doctors and nurses, or ordinary civilians with no connection with the
> military—must, whenever possible, be taken alive, and must not be
> injured or have their possessions taken from them except after a due
> trial by competent authority. Neither such a person nor his property
> are the property of any one of us who captures him. It is one thing to
> kill a Japanese soldier in battle; it is an entirely different thing to kill
> civilians who have not fought against us, whether they are Japanese or
> not. The latter is murder, nothing more nor less.[96]

Even the most hardened veteran American island-fighters had no wish
to kill women and children in cold blood, and were distressed when civilians
were caught in the crossfire. On D-Day plus two, William Rogal's platoon
was cleaning out bunkers and covered emplacements in the hills behind the
landing beaches. When someone dropped a grenade into one such fortifica-
tion, "to our horror the explosions produced screams and crying of children.
Six or seven little Chamorro girls in school uniforms had taken shelter in
the hole. Our corpsmen did what they could for their wounds but some of

them looked pretty far gone. This was the only time I saw combat Marines with tears in their eyes."[97]

In the waters off Marpi Point, cruisers and destroyers continued to provide call-fire on Japanese targets. The crews watched as hundreds of civilians leapt from the sheer face of "Banzai cliff" and plummeted into the rocks and surf below. The tide carried the bodies out to sea. James Fahey noted in his diary that the sea was so thick with bodies that his ship could not avoid running over them. "I never saw anything like it for bodies floating around," he wrote on July 13. "The water is full of them, the fish will eat good."[98] Bodies sometimes fouled the ships' screws, and divers had to drop over the stern to pull them free. On Sunday, July 16, 1944, Fahey attended a mass on deck, but he could not pull his eyes away from the scene. "The ships just run over them. You can't miss them all, the water is full of dead Japs. . . . [Y]ou could see them floating by, men, women, and children. The north section was loaded with floating bodies."[99]

Special Japanese-speaking units were sent to the front lines to broadcast surrender appeals to enemy soldiers and civilians. Loudspeakers were mounted on jeeps and on vessels offshore, and Japanese-speaking personnel (including Hawaiian *Nisei*) broadcast a series of set phrases toward the enemy enclave around Marpi Point. "*Shimpai shinaide!*" (Don't be afraid!) and "*te o age!*" (put your hands up).[100] The messages promised food and water, asserted that many others had already surrendered, and assured the Japanese soldiers that they had fought gallantly and could surrender with their honor intact. American floatplanes dropped leaflets marked "Surrender Pass," which provided instructions for how to approach American forces—with arms up and a white cloth grasped in one hand.

According to Marine Lieutenant Robert B. Sheeks, a Japanese-language officer who organized such appeals, it was not always easy to persuade his fellow marines that the effort was worthwhile. "The whole idea at the time seemed outlandish to most Marines," he recalled, "as everyone was convinced that no Japanese would ever surrender." His superiors had at first provided little encouragement or funding for the program. A Hawaiian newspaper had absorbed the cost of printing the surrender leaflets, as the military would not allocate funds for the purpose. Sheeks's unit had even diverted its own recreation funds to buy loudspeaker equipment. Only after repeated petitions were they permitted to land the loudspeakers on the beach. On Saipan, Sheeks toured the island and proselytized to the various unit commanders. Their skepticism gradually gave way as it became apparent that the appeals were working, at least in some cases. No one liked the sight of women and children leaping to their deaths from the northern cliffs. In the end, both commissioned and noncommissioned officers gave full priority to the surrender broadcasts, and provided the manpower and protection needed to get the loudspeaker-jeeps up to the front lines. "In spite of tough talk, a lot of Marines were quite cooperative and even kindly toward prisoners, both civilian and military," said Sheeks. "When they saw the miserable condition of refugees they tried to help them, gave them water, and bandaged them up. Most Marines were kind guys, basically."[101]

THE FINAL ATTACK ON MARPI POINT was something of a footrace, as various units of the 2nd and 4th Marine Divisions competed to be the first to overrun this last morsel of contested territory on the island. Holland Smith pulled the 27th Infantry Division back and employed it as a reserve force. At 4:15 p.m. on July 9, the 4th Marine Division reported that they had seized the point, and Admiral Turner declared the island secured. An official flag-raising ceremony was held at Holland Smith's headquarters in the village of Charan Kanoa. The announcement came as a surprise to the many marine units on the island that were still engaged in fierce firefights. To call Saipan secure was to say only that no portion of the island remained under the control of organized enemy forces. Thousands of Japanese soldiers were still hidden in caves or heavily vegetated ravines throughout the island's hilly north—and every so often, for weeks afterward, a small group of desperate and isolated enemy fighters rushed out at the Americans in a climactic suicidal *banzai* charge.

The conquest of Saipan was the most costly operation to date of the Pacific campaign. Of the American ground forces, 2,949 men were killed and 10,464 wounded. In the final tally, about 27,000 Japanese fighters, virtually the entire garrison, were killed in action or took their own lives. The Americans captured 736 military prisoners of war, most of whom were Korean labor troops. Even before the island was declared secure, construction teams had begun the work of converting Tanapag Harbor into a modern depot. Mines and wrecked small craft were cleared to open a

150-foot channel to the waterfront, and heavy earth-moving equipment began the work of improving and extending the piers and building new seaplane ramps.

In Tokyo, senior officers of the Imperial General Headquarters had already written off Guam and Tinian. No naval interference was possible after Ozawa's overwhelming defeat at sea, and if the Americans had conquered Saipan, they would not be thwarted by the smaller garrisons on the islands farther south. The tenacious defense of Saipan had forced the Americans reluctantly to postpone the capture of Tinian and Guam, originally scheduled to occur within a week after the landing on Saipan. Nimitz, troubled by the long delay, had pressured Spruance and Turner to fix a date for these latter operations. But Holland Smith had insisted on holding the Guam troops in reserve for possible deployment on Saipan, and in light of the tougher-than-expected fight on that island, it was decided that another reserve force, the army's 77th Infantry Division, should be brought up from Hawaii to join the Third Marine Amphibious Corps (the 3rd Marine Division and the 1st Provisional Marine Brigade) under General Roy Geiger. On July 7, with the battle for Saipan entering its final phase, Admiral Spruance finally felt confident enough to fix the landing dates for Guam (July 21) and Tinian (July 24).

Both islands had been subjected to intermittent aerial bombing since the Saipan landing, and Japanese airpower on the islands had been virtually snuffed out. Rear Admiral Dick Conolly's Southern Attack Force began continuous daily naval bombardment of Guam on July 8. For the thirteen days prior to the first assault, Japanese defenses on the western beaches suffered under a rain of projectiles ranging in caliber from 5 to 16 inches. It was the most sustained preinvasion naval bombardment of the war.

Thirty miles long and 210 square miles in area, Guam was the largest island in the Marianas and offered the most potential as a forward operating base. It had the archipelago's best deepwater harbor at Apra. Its large airfield at Orote was the best in the region, and its expansive rolling tablelands and hard coral soil would provide good sites for more. It was unique in having been American territory for more than four decades before the Japanese invasion in December 1941. A large proportion of all U.S. Navy stewards and messboys were Chamorro natives of Guam, contributing to a feeling that Guamians were members of the extended "navy family." Under the Japanese regime, the island's people had suffered from forced labor, crop confiscations, compulsory education in Japanese, and summary punishment for suspected disloyalty.

Ringed by coral reefs and rocky cliffs, Guam was a tough prospect for any amphibious attacker. The island's most indispensable military assets were Apra Harbor and Orote Airfield, which directly adjoined one another on the midsection of the west coast. Beaches to the immediate north and south of this area presented the least difficulties for an amphibious landing. Conolly's battleships, cruisers, and destroyers had concentrated their guns on those beaches and the ground above them, around Asan Point and Agana to the north, and Gann Point and Agat to the south. For all of these reasons, there was never any doubt in the minds of the Japanese about where the Americans would put their forces ashore. Lieutenant General Takeshi Takashina, the island commander, had superintended the construction of formidable entrenchments and fixed fortifications above the beaches; on the other hand, those same defenses had been shelled heavily and at length in the two weeks before the revised W-Day.

On the morning of July 21, the 3rd Marine Division and the 1st Provisional Marine Brigade landed simultaneously on the Asan and Agat beaches, respectively. Shore artillery opposed the landings and inflicted heavy punishment, particularly on the southern force. The southern beachhead was quickly expanded to swallow up Agat Village; the marines in this sector then pushed north through furious opposition to sever Orote Peninsula from the rest of the island. In the north, the 3rd Marine Division stood up to a counterattack at dawn on July 22, then drove up into the hills behind their tanks, suffering heavy casualties, until they controlled all of the area between Chonito Cliff and Adelup Point to Asan Point, to a depth of about a mile inland. The Japanese employed night infiltration tactics and mass bayonet charges, but as on Saipan the attackers lost many men in these gambits. On the night of July 25, a ferocious counterattack fell on the 3rd Battalion, 22nd Marines—a mass of drunken soldiers led by sword-wielding officers emerged from the edge of a mangrove swamp and penetrated through the lines to a command post and field hospital. The attack was broken up by heavy machine-gun, artillery, and mortar fire. The Japanese army suffered heavily in this sequence, losing many of its senior officers. On July 25, the U.S. Army's 77th Division, less one regiment to be held in reserve, came ashore at Agat and took over defense of the beachhead.

The 4th Marines overran Orote Peninsula in five days of hard fighting between the morning of July 26 and July 30. On July 28, the 3rd Division joined up with the 77th Infantry Division on Mount Tenjo, fusing the two separated beachheads into one continuous line. Once the Orote Peninsula and Apra Harbor were overrun on July 30, things got much easier for the Americans. Within six hours after it was captured, the Orote airstrip was repaired, and the first American aircraft (a Navy TBF) came in to land.

General Takashina was felled by machine-gun fire as he retreated from his command post on the night of July 28. His successor, Lieutenant General Hideyoshi Obata, ordered a tactical retreat, under relentless artillery and naval fire, into the jungle hills of the island's north. Without resupply, his troops soon began to starve. The last push northward came on August 8 and 9, when General Geiger ordered, "Push all Japanese from Guam." The last organized resistance was stamped out on August 10, although thousands of enemy soldiers remained at large in the hills, either singly or in small groups. Spruance and the USS *Indianapolis* anchored in Apra Harbor, and Admiral Nimitz and General Vandegrift landed at Orote Airfield. Obata followed Saito and Nagumo and died by his own hand. American casualties in the conquest of Guam included 1,214 men killed and nearly 6,000 wounded.

Tinian, lying just three and a half miles from Saipan, was a relatively uncomplicated operation. A sham landing near Tinian town was followed quickly by an invasion in force by the 2nd and 4th Marine Divisions on the northern beaches. Supplies and reinforcements could be landed promptly from nearby Saipan. Flat and forgiving terrain allowed the attackers to move quickly. Taken by surprise, Japanese defensive arrangements were thrown into turmoil. In nine days of fighting, the Japanese forces were forced into a shrinking pocket in the south. A last *banzai* charge was broken up on the night of July 31, and the island was declared secured. Holland Smith rated the battle for Tinian as "a model of its kind," in which "the result brilliantly consummated the planning and performance." [102] The island was to be the major airbase of the Twentieth Air Force, which would eventually operate more than 1,000 B-29 Superfortresses from the Marianas.

THOUGH AMERICANS WERE SLOW TO APPRECIATE IT, they had just won the decisive victory of the Pacific War. Capture of the Marianas and the accompanying ruin of Japanese carrier airpower were final and irreversible blows to the hopes of the Japanese imperial project. For another year the Tokyo junta would clutch at the absurd hope that further exhibitions of fanatical resistance might force the conqueror to the negotiating table. But FORAGER had provided airfields from which the big new bombers could strike the population and industrial centers of the Kanto Plain, including Tokyo. It had provided a base of submarine operations at the crossroads of the Pacific, bringing the enemy's critical sea-lanes within immediate reach. The Americans had demonstrated that they could win dominion of the skies anywhere in the Pacific, with carrier airpower alone; that they could leap across long ocean distances to invade well-defended continental land-masses; and that the naval-air-amphibious juggernaut could move faster and farther than the enemy had imagined possible. The Imperial Japanese Navy had staked its hopes on winning a decisive naval battle in the west-ern Pacific, but that contest had been forced on Ozawa before his aviators were ready, with the result that Japan's carrier air force was permanently and irreversibly demolished. Loss of the Marianas brought down the Japa-nese government and ushered into power a new prime minister and cabinet with a putative goal of finding a way out of the war (though they would fail in this regard).

Two years earlier, Ernest J. King had insisted on launching an early Pacific counteroffensive in the Solomon Islands. Relying on his influ-ence with the navy-minded Roosevelt and his tense rapport with General Marshall, King had secured approval from the Joint Chiefs for Operation WATCHTOWER. He had rebuffed the objections of Admiral Ghormley and General Vandegrift, the local navy and marine commanders to whom it fell to carry out the precarious operation, and had ridden roughshod over Gen-eral MacArthur, who wanted the Pacific campaign consolidated under his singular authority. Warned that the Americans did not yet have sufficient naval power, airpower, or logistics capability to begin a major amphibious operation in the South Pacific, King trusted his aggressive instincts. He pointed out that the Japanese were at a similar disadvantage. More time might allow the navy and marines to improve their margin of superiority, but time would also strengthen the defenders, who were gradually digging themselves into the territory they had seized.

Had the Americans been pushed off Guadalcanal, as had seemed likely in September and October of 1942, King might have lost his command and the Pacific War might have taken a different course. But Operation "Shoe-string," as WATCHTOWER was ruefully nicknamed by the men who carried it out, vindicated King's philosophy of the early counterattack. In subsequent operations of 1942 and 1943, north and south of the equator, planners had been forced to work against oppressive deadlines and commanders had been forced to rely on deficient or awkward logistics. But the Americans had always appeared before they were anticipated, and the Japanese had been obliged to fight earlier than they would have liked. "Everywhere, I think, you attacked before the defense was ready," Admiral Kichisaburo Nomura told interrogators after the war. "You came far more quickly than we expected."[103] On many other islands where the defenses were mature, the Americans merely leaped past them and let the defenders "wither on the vine."

By early 1944, the fully mobilized American war economy had put an end to the era of shortfalls. Amphibious operations of previously unimaginable scale were now possible. On Saipan, American ground forces occasionally complained that specific items were needed but unavailable. For example, their portable radio packs were often inoperable for lack of spare batteries. The batteries were there, in the holds of Turner's transports and in sufficient numbers. Delays in getting them into the hands of the radiomen could be blamed on the customary and inevitable snafus. An intricate choreography was required to move materials from the ships offshore to the beachhead supply dumps to infantry units in advanced positions. In some cases it was a matter of better paperwork and record-keeping—if the beachmasters did not know exactly what they had on the beach, and where to find it, they could not very well get it to the front lines. Inefficiencies were being identified and corrected; procedures steadily improved as all personnel learned from experience.

Raymond Spruance, when discussing the war after it was over, often returned to the point that tactical decisions in major battles were less important than the superior logistics of American forces.[104] A sea of ink has been spilled on Spruance's controversial determination to keep his carriers near Saipan on the night of June 18–19, 1944. Another small ocean has been spilled on Halsey's even more controversial decision to chase the Japanese carriers north on the night of October 24–25, 1944, during the Battle of Leyte Gulf. In each case, different tactics might have altered the result of the battle at hand, but neither could have had a lasting influence on the course of the war. The Americans had developed the capability to project overwhelming force into the distant frontiers of the western Pacific, and no tactical masterstroke or blunder could reverse the increasingly lopsided balance of power between the combatants.

On July 17, when Nimitz and King flew into newly pacified Saipan, both admirals took pains to assure Spruance that his performance in the Battle of the Philippine Sea had been entirely satisfactory. "Spruance, you did a damn fine job there," said King, upon stepping off his plane. "No matter what other people tell you, your decision was correct."[105] He had hewn closely to his orders, which were to protect the beachhead at all costs. With a wide margin of superiority—and that margin growing inexorably each passing month—the high command had no use for brash tactical gambits that might provide an opening for an improbable Japanese victory. Surveying grand strategy from a high perch, the COMINCH and CINCPAC instinctively understood that the last phase of the Pacific campaign would be won "by the numbers."

The capability of Service Squadron Ten to provide logistical support with no meaningful shore establishment had enabled the Fifth Fleet to operate from desolate central Pacific atolls. Now, in the Marianas, a sophisticated and permanent forward base of operations would backstop the final assault on the Philippines and Japan's home islands. Guam was at the end of a 5,800-mile supply line stretching from the American mainland through Oahu, Kwajalein, and Eniwetok. It was a continental island, 210 square miles in area, with ample territory for airfields, barracks, warehouses, port amenities, fuel storage, training ranges, recreation facilities, and a new Pacific Fleet headquarters. It lay astride the main sea routes linking east to west and north to south, and was thus well situated to support the next offensive thrusts. It had been and would remain a U.S. territory, with a friendly and loyal native population, and would serve as a keystone of American military power in the region long after the defeat of Japan.

The transformation began while the battle for Guam was still hot, when the garrison beach party and the port director came ashore under fire and began directing boat traffic onto the landing beaches. Several thousand tons of material was landed each day. Most supplies and equipment were left in open-air supply dumps, as few warehouses had survived the aerial and naval bombardment of the previous weeks. Lion Six, an advanced naval base-building unit commanded by Captain Adolph E. Becker Jr., began clearing Apra Harbor and preparing it to receive large cargo ships. The jetty was extended, a submarine net raised, and temporary pontoon piers linked to the shore by a coral-filled causeway. The first Seabees to arrive on the island, the 5th Naval Construction Brigade, upgraded and extended the airfields and paved and widened the roads. Vice Admiral John H. Hoover, the low-profile admiral who had been Nimitz's commander of shore-based air, assumed overall command of the Marianas. A new Island Command assumed authority on Guam. Most of the transport fleet and many of the warships pulled out and sailed for Pearl Harbor.

Working and living conditions were wretched in those early days of the base-building struggle. Men were quartered in tents, but their bivouac areas were prone to flooding in the frequent torrential rains, and it was essential to construct platform tents both for lodging and for office space. Canned rations fed the men until a makeshift galley was established in a Quonset hut. A reservoir in the island's interior provided water to the coastal towns, but the pipelines had been destroyed by naval bombardment, so all fresh-water had to be brought in from the fleet in five-gallon cans. Flies and an awful stench rose from the shallow graves of dead Japanese, so the dead had to be dug up and burned. Mosquitoes and the tropical diseases they carried caused a health and sanitation emergency; the construction teams had to drain swamps and other areas of standing water and spray them with dis-infectant. Fuel was brought ashore in fifty-five-gallon drums and stored in open-air dumps. Several of those dumps went up in flames, causing spectac-ular explosions and conflagrations that lasted days. Thousands of Japanese mines were scattered around the beaches and footpaths, and several men were killed by walking into an area not yet cleared by mine disposal units.

Tens of thousands of American combat and construction troops had to be fed. A naval reserve lieutenant who had worked in hotels and res-taurants organized the first large mess hall, in which the galley took up all of a small Quonset hut and the food was served directly into mess kits through small windows. Men often waited as long as two hours to be served. American forces had also assumed responsibility for feeding and sheltering the island's 24,000 native Chamorros. Many of their homes and villages had been destroyed or were not yet safe from the enemy. In early August, about 18,000 civilian inhabitants were living in three refugee camps near the coast.

The island's unpaved roads were churned up by tanks, jeeps, and trucks, and when the rainy season set in, they were transformed into impassable quagmires. Many vehicles were stranded in the mud and abandoned. The primitive oxcart tracks and footpaths had to be widened, extended, and paved over. But trucks were needed to haul coral rock to primitive cement-mixing areas, and there were never quite enough trucks, or enough mechanics and spare parts to maintain them. The trucks operated twenty-four hours a day, with their drivers working in shifts. Roads to the coral pits were given first priority for improvement, as no major construction could begin anywhere until vast quantities of coral cement became available. The roads were to be built to last, and the builders adhered to the same standards they would meet in building a road in the United States. Rocky outcroppings and ridges were blasted out and inclines were regraded. A four-lane road between Sumay and Agana was underway before the island was declared secure. Before the war's end, more than 103 miles of new paved roads were completed on Guam.

During the enemy's two-and-a-half-year occupation, labor troops had built a 4,500-foot coral surface airstrip at Orote Peninsula. Seabees cleared the wrecked planes away by shoving them into great mountains of dirt and debris on the sides of the runways. "They were wrecks of twisted aluminum and steel," wrote the sailor James Orvill Raines, who marveled at how high the wreckage towered over the working strip. "They had the appearance of piled junk."[106] The island's northern third was dominated by a limestone plateau, providing suitable terrain for B-29 fields, each 8,500 feet long and 200 feet wide. As 1945 began, construction teams began hacking the two big runways out of the jungle.

A base construction officer later recalled a predicament on Guam: "There were always too many men and too few men—too many for the housing that was finished, and too few for the work to be done."[107] Men living in tents were often felled by exhaustion and tropical diseases. The prefabricated Quonset hut provided the answer, and thousands of the corrugated steel kits were landed at the new pontoon piers in Apra Harbor. Because the construction units were overtaxed on larger projects, and the huts required no special machinery to build, many American marines and soldiers were told, "There are your homes—build them."[108] The sections were plainly labeled and easily screwed together. The quality of accommodations gradually improved. Showers and scrub racks were included in all barracks. By early 1945, the entire area around Apra Harbor and Orote Peninsula was covered with symmetrical rows of Quonset huts and larger prefabricated administrative buildings, warehouses, and hangars. Visiting officers and civilians were quartered in double-decked BOQs (bachelor officer quarters) that were comfortably furnished and attended by navy orderlies.

Within six months, the detritus of battle had been shunted to the sides of roads and the edges of the jungle, and Guam began to take on the look of an established base. A huge tank farm and pipeline system accommodated half a million barrels of fuel oil, and another 328,000 barrels of aviation gasoline.[109] Hundreds of big steel arch-rib warehouses were crammed to the rafters with munitions and equipment. Fresh provisions were stored in 68,000 cubic feet of refrigerated storage. Large passenger aircraft of the Naval Air Transport Service (NATS) arrived and departed by the hour, giving the airfield at Orote the look of a major commercial airport in the United States. Prior to Operation FORAGER, some had predicted that Apra Harbor could not handle more than ten or twenty large vessels, but after extensive improvements and the extension of a long jetty, it was found to accommodate as many as 231 commissioned ships.[110] A sophisticated water system provided twelve million gallons per day of fresh, potable water from sixty-seven springs and reservoirs. Five hospitals supplied beds for 9,000 patients. A Quonset hut housed an advanced infectious-disease research laboratory, staffed by leading doctors in the field. Blood and fecal samples were flown into Guam from other Pacific islands. The doctors reproduced the diseases in white mice, identified the viruses, and cultivated inoculations.

Ernie Pyle, a combat journalist who had made his name in the European theater, traveled to Guam in the spring of 1945. The island's old coastal towns remained in ruins, and the heaps of charred rubble reminded him of Western Europe. Just around a bend in the road, however, one found a sprawling landscape of blinding white concrete and long rows of Quonset huts, a scene that would not have looked out of place on Oahu. Pyle marveled at the quantity of provisions, supplies, and munitions stored in the warehouses of this remote Pacific outpost. "You could take your pick of K rations or lumber or bombs," he wrote, "and you'd find enough there to feed a city, build one, or blow it up."[111]

Nimitz and a small portion of his staff moved to Guam in January 1945. His new advanced headquarters and residence were built on CINCPAC Hill, a bluff overlooking the ruins of Agana. Arthur Lamar, the flag lieutenant, described the new CINCPAC residence as a "beautiful white clapboard cottage with four bedrooms and four baths opening onto a square court with grass and flowers in the middle. We had a large living room-dining room and a long screened porch right on the edge of a cliff overlooking the harbor."[112] As in Pearl Harbor, a horseshoe court and shooting range were built in the yard. A nucleus of the CINCPAC planning and operations staff accompanied the chief to Guam, but the bulk of the organization remained behind, in Pearl Harbor. Nimitz, who always preferred a small staff and had resisted the inexorable growth of his organization, was pleased with the new setting. He adopted the "no ties" policy that had prevailed at SOPAC headquarters in Noumea but never at Pearl Harbor. Khaki uniform shorts, never approved in Oahu, were deemed suitable in Guam; Nimitz often wore them himself, to the surprise and amusement of others.

Sprawling encampments eventually accommodated more than 165,000 troops, including several marine and army divisions. Before V-J Day, the total number of American personnel on Guam surpassed 200,000. For lack of transportation, most troops never left their own camps. They had no reason to do so—each camp was equipped with many of the comforts, conveniences, and entertainments of home. Civilian visitors from the United States were surprised to learn that more than 200 movies were screened on an average night. Nearly all were shown outside, often on the side of a hill where the terrain formed a natural amphitheater, and the men sat on crates, logs, or old fuel drums. Movie reels were traded from one camp to another, but inevitably men were obliged to watch the same films twenty or thirty times, and could recite the dialogue as it left the actors' lips. Baseball diamonds, football fields, and basketball courts sprouted up in recently cleared minefields, and an athletics office organized large and sophisticated sporting leagues. There were thirty-five boxing arenas, and one well-promoted fight attracted 18,000 spectators.

Thousands of radios were distributed to the camps. A "Pacific American Expeditionary Forces Station" provided news and entertainment, but many listeners still preferred the popular jazz and buffoonish propaganda of Radio Tokyo. There was a brisk trade in Japanese souvenirs, and prices of certain items (especially enemy battle flags and samurai swords) eventually rose to extravagant heights. Traveling USO camp-shows were performed on outdoor stages ringed with benches. The hardworking entertainers often put on four or five identical shows per day, moving from one camp to another on buses. The navy shipped forty pianos into Guam. Troops put on lavish in-house productions, which often poked fun at their own commanding officers. Several dozen stores or PXs offered cigarettes, candy bars, magazines, soda foundations, ice cream, toiletries, and native souvenirs. The shelves were swept clean each day, often before noon, and in some of the larger camps it was deemed necessary to establish two duplicate stores in one location so that one could be restocked while the other was open for business. Beer was rationed, two cans per man, in large recreation huts and beer gardens. Cash circulated, from paymasters to men to stores and back to paymasters. On an average day, $30,000 was sent back to the United States.[113]

In the densely vegetated hills overlooking these trappings of an ultramodern, omnipotent, and prosperous military civilization, Japanese stragglers watched, starved, and considered their alternatives. Now and again an American was ambushed or felled by sniper fire, but most surviving Japanese seemed preoccupied with food and survival. Recognizing that malnutrition and disease would gradually reduce the threat posed by enemy holdouts, the island commanders took a patient approach to rounding them up. Loudspeaker trucks lumbered over the dirt tracks in the northern hill country, broadcasting their rhythmic appeals for honorable surrender. Leaflets were dropped from airplanes. Japanese POWs were sent back into the jungle to persuade their comrades to give themselves up.

Driven to desperation by hunger, many Japanese drew in close to the American encampments and looked for opportunities to steal food. Sentries often killed or captured these emaciated intruders around the edges of ration dumps, warehouses, or mess halls. In one often-related incident, a Japanese soldier was found sitting among a company of marines watching an outdoor movie. When discovered, he grinned broadly and raised his hands. Another surrendered to a marine sitting on a privy, later explaining that those circumstances seemed to offer the best odds of not getting shot. When a Japanese straggler was spotted one night on CINCPAC Hill, Nimitz's marine guards chased the man back into the jungle and Nimitz, dressed in pajamas, emerged from the house with a pistol in hand.

Even long after the end of the war, hundreds of Japanese remained stubbornly at large in the jungles of Guam. Small groups lived in caves and survived by hunting lizards, toads, and rats, trapping fish, and stealing food from local farms and villages. Chamorros, embittered by the Japanese occupation of 1941–44, tended to attack them on sight. The Japanese government sent emissaries, and a steady trickle of holdouts came out of the jungle each year throughout the late 1940s and early 1950s.

The last Japanese straggler on Guam was Sergeant Shoichi Yokoi,

a native of Aichi Prefecture, who lived in a remote section of the Talo-
fofo river valley until 1972. This latter-day Robinson Crusoe survived in
the jungle for almost twenty-eight years by eating fruit, nuts, snails, rats,
pigeons, shrimp, eels, and native plants. His story remains an extraordinary
example of what can be achieved with advanced wilderness survival skills.
Yokoi built traps of wild reeds and wove clothing of pago fibers. He avoided
disease by bathing frequently and boiling water before drinking it. He dug
an underground shelter and installed bamboo walls and floors. Until 1964,
he had remained in occasional contact with other Japanese holdouts, but
for the last eight years of his ordeal he was alone. When captured by two
Chamorro natives in January 1972, Yokoi accurately identified the month
and year. Doctors judged the fifty-six-year-old man to be in excellent health
and in full possession of his mental faculties.

His return to Japan caused a national sensation. Yokoi said that he had
known the war was over since 1952, but had dreaded the disgrace of surrender. "I am ashamed that I have returned alive," he told reporters. In a visit to
the grounds of the Imperial Palace, he addressed himself to the emperor and
empress: "Your Majesties, I have returned home. I deeply regret that I could
not serve you well. The world has certainly changed, but my determination
to serve you will never change."[114]

Such sentiments could not fail to ignite the Japanese imagination.
Many of his countrymen hailed Yokoi as an authentic samurai, a paragon of
bushido and *chukin* ("zealous devotion"). Others found his story as tragic as
it was poignant. Only a fanatic chooses to live alone in a jungle for twenty
years after he knows his war is lost. And was it not precisely that sort of
fanaticism that had dragged Japan down to a calamitous defeat in 1945?

Epilogue

D URING THE WAR, WHENEVER POSSIBLE, THE JAPANESE ARMY arranged to repatriate the cremated remains of fallen soldiers. Burial details dug a pit, filled it with brushwood, piled the bodies on top of the wood, poured gasoline onto the bodies, and set them on fire. Teishin Nohara, a soldier from Tochigi Prefecture who fought in China, recalled that the job had to be done quickly and was not always done well. "It was like baking sardines," he recalled:

> You just set fire to it and let the flames consume the wood. Then you took up bones from the parts that burned, put them in a bag, and filled out a tag with the dead man's name. You said a silent prayer, sure, but there wasn't any "ceremony." It was war, so you couldn't help it. When it rained you couldn't even really burn them, so say the battalion commander had died, you'd burn just his body and distribute bits of his bones to the rest. You can't tell this kind of truth to the families of the deceased! So you burn what you can quickly. You just do it, keep going. Ten. Twenty. You have to move fast.[1]

Transported to the homeland by ship, the bags were forwarded to regional distribution centers. Each man's ashes were transferred into a small wooden box, and the box was wrapped carefully in clean white cotton cloth. The boxes were sorted according to the dead man's home district and village, and loaded onto special funeral trains for delivery to the family. A local military affairs office was notified of the train's scheduled arrival so that a ceremony to honor the "spirits of the returning war dead" could be duly performed.

As the train pulled up to the platform, a representative of the family stepped forward and bowed. A window was raised. A soldier wearing a mask lifted the box in white-gloved hands and offered it through the window. When it was accepted, he bowed and closed the window. Fumio Kimura, a soldier who performed this duty in Shiga Prefecture, recalled the familiar scene: "Elderly parents and young wives holding children's hands or carrying babies clung to the box and wept. 'This is your father.' Thinking, *This will be us tomorrow*, we soldiers cried also and could only stand silently at the window."[2]

The box was carried back to the village in a somber procession, with the family often accompanied by neighbors, friends, local officials, Buddhist priests, veterans, and representatives of local patriotic leagues. Schoolchildren were often led out of school to bow in unison as the procession passed.

When no remains were recovered, as in the case of sailors lost at sea, the family sometimes received an empty box. Hitoshi Anzai, a boy living in Tokyo, was curious to know why the box purportedly containing his brother's remains rattled when he shook it. Since his brother's ship had gone down at sea, what could be inside the box? He pried it open and found a small sliver of wood with his brother's name written on it. It had been nailed loosely to the bottom of the box in such a way as to "make it sound like there actually was a piece of the dead man's bone inside when the box was shaken."[3] The boy was offended at having been deceived. Worse, he noted that his brother's name had been misspelled.

Toru Izumi, a soldier posted in Matsuyama, was charged with receiving and distributing the remains of several hundred soldiers who had perished in the South Pacific. Izumi and his fellow soldiers pitied the families who were to receive empty boxes. More than forty years later he offered a pained confession:

> When we thought of the feelings of the members of the dead soldier's family, we couldn't bear to hand them an empty box. After discussion, we concluded that since the soldiers had died together, praying over another soldier's remains should be the same thing. Unable to face the greater sadness of families with no remains inside the boxes and believing that the heroic war dead would rest in peace better, we decided to take a few fragments of remains from other boxes. All the while fearing that it was wrong to deceive the bereaved families, we

divided the fragments of bones into different boxes, our hands trembling as we did this. I have yet to determine whether what we did was right. It has remained a hurt inside me that will never ease.[4]

Entire sections of Japanese newspapers were devoted to stories about the war dead. As soon as a military affairs office released the name of a man killed in action, local reporters and photographers rushed to the family's home. Often it was the journalists who broke the news to the dead man's next of kin. "You assumed that they knew, but often they hadn't heard anything," said Uichiro Kawachi of the *Yomiuri Shinbun*. "They'd wail and cry. It was awful."[5] The reporters always asked for a photograph of the fallen man—if they brought a photo back to the newsroom, said Kawachi, the story "always made the paper. . . . Every paper competed for a picture."[6]

Editors and military censors frowned on stories that played up a family's grief. Rather, the reporters should emphasize the dead man's "laudable virtues" and the family's pride in a son, husband, or father who had given his life for his country and his emperor. As the casualties mounted in the middle years of the Pacific War, reporters began recycling fixed phrases: "They spoke without shedding a tear." (Kawachi said that he often used that phrase "no matter how much they'd cried.") Over time, editors and reporters developed several story archetypes that could be recycled *ad infinitum*:

When a series of ten articles was planned for the paper, all the participating reporters would discuss themes and the style each would use. "I'll use the 'small mother' voice." "I'll use the 'struggling, yet gallant mother' type." Like this we'd establish a theme for the series. There were lots of styles. You could write the story any way you wanted. You'd have a mother who had been weeping, mourning for her son, crying so hard and long that her face was swollen and her voice was choked. Her dead son would appear before her and beg her, "Don't cry, Ma. When you cry, it only hurts me to see you so sad." Then she'd stop. That's what we'd write. We couldn't repeat the same thing every time, so we'd have to change it around.[7]

Censorship was practiced in all the major combatant nations of the Second World War, but in no other nation was the control of wartime reporting so Orwellian in its ambition and extent as in Japan. The morning after the attack on Pearl Harbor, leading editors were summoned to a meeting at the cabinet's Board of Information. They were told that the cause of the war was "the enemy's egotistic ambition to control the world," and it was the duty of the Japanese press to "instill a deep hatred for America and Britain in the minds of the people."[8] Apart from the ordinary control of battle-field reporting, media representatives were to attend mandatory meetings in which they were instructed on how to shape the attitudes and perceptions of the Japanese people. The papers were to assist in promulgating official slogans: "We must advance to increased war power,"[9] "We must carry out the responsibilities of the homefront," "Luxury is the enemy," "Be frugal and save," "Serve the nation with one death." Editors were required to par-ticipate in humiliating group sessions in which passages from their recent issues were read aloud and either praised or singled out for criticism. The distinction between reporting and editorial commentary faded. Stories that intoned solemnly about the *kokutai*—the "imperial way," a political order founded on reverence for the *Showa* emperor—were lavished with praise and held up as examples to be imitated.

The administrative apparatus of censorship was never consolidated into any one agency of government. An article that did not offend the army might raise hackles in the Navy Ministry, and editors sometimes found themselves wedged helplessly between the opposing requirements of the two services. A ranking officer in a local police station might summon an offending editor or reporter to be upbraided and threatened with imprison-ment. The army press section began holding regular monthly meetings at a Tokyo restaurant, to which all leading editors were "invited." (Attendance was recorded.) Officers commented on each publication's recent stories and made "requests" (issued orders) concerning the content and themes of upcoming editions.

Guidelines were often arbitrary and seemingly meaningless. A word or phrase might be declared out of bounds with no coherent justification pro-vided. An independent writer who fell out of favor found that editors no longer took his calls or acknowledged his submissions. Recidivist offenders were hauled away to prison to be beaten, tortured, starved, and incarcer-ated indefinitely. A reporter whose byline appeared above an imperti-nent article might find himself drafted into the army and shipped to the front lines, without military training, the following day. A paper might be ordered to suspend publication for several days or weeks, long enough to drive it into bankruptcy. On occasion, an article would be "recalled," requiring that drivers be sent out to tear the objectionable pages from copies still on the newsstands, and to affix a seal to the cover identifying it as a "Revised Edition."

As commodities of every kind grew scarce, the junta discovered another useful lever to reward compliance and punish insubordination—raw newsprint. In December 1942, the vice chief of the Board of Information told editors in chief that the supply of newsprint would be "negligible" in the following year, and that allocations would be decided according to how closely their publications adhered to government direction. The editors were pressured to make their leading reporters available to "tour the provinces making speeches on the realization of the Holy War for the Information Board."[10]

In Japan, where the literacy rate was among the highest in the world, newspapers were a large and lucrative business. Enterprising owners quickly grasped that the war and its pressures offered an opportunity to expand circulation at the expense of less jingoistic competitors. The prime beneficiary of the new regime was the ultranationalist *Asahi Shinbun*, the largest daily newspaper in Japan with a circulation exceeding two million. *Asahi* had the scale to build a sophisticated internal "inspection division," an in-house layer of censorship that minimized the danger that any article would run afoul of the regime. The leading papers competed fiercely for readers—but not, as *Asahi* correspondent Shoryu Hata later admitted, "over the quality and accuracy of the reports that would be left to history, but rather over how most effectively to rouse the public. Because of this pressure and competition, there were reporters who wrote total lies."[11]

Star reporters were assigned to cover the Imperial General Headquarters (IGHQ) in Tokyo. Being headquarters correspondent was one of the most prestigious postings in Japanese journalism—but the job, Uichiro Kawachi recalled, was little more than that of a glorified stenographer. All headquarters correspondents labored under the tyrannical eye of the *Kempeitai* (the domestic state security service). They were required to wear a plain army uniform without insignia. Correspondents regularly and falsely published under bylines placing them at the front, even though they had never left the Tokyo headquarters building. When an official announcement was released, the correspondents were required to copy down each word verbatim, taking care to avoid errors or typos. Any deviation from the exact wording of the announcement, however trivial, was grounds for revocation of press credentials. To guard against such errors, each correspondent first called his newsroom and read the statement over the phone, then delivered by hand a printed copy to a courier waiting outside on a motorbike. The courier sped to the newsroom and rushed the document into the hands of the editors, so that the text could be double- and triple-checked before it was published in the late edition.

Kawachi, who covered the headquarters for *Yomiuri*, explained that announcements from the Imperial General Headquarters held near-sacred status because they were issued in the name of the *Showa* emperor and were accompanied by the imperial seal. Any error in transcription was tanta-mount to blasphemy. Any reference to the emperor in the pages of a newspa-per was required to comply with exacting guidelines. The *kanji* (characters) for "*Showa Tenno*" must be separated from the preceding and following *kanji* by an extra space. "*Showa Tenno*" must not appear at the bottom of a line of text—instead, a space was to be left blank and the name carried to the top of the next line. Reverence for the emperor, said Kawachi, was behind the tendency of the Imperial Headquarters to disseminate increasingly blatant falsehoods in the later stages of the war. Since the emperor was infallible, no past declaration could have been inaccurate. It logically followed that all new announcements must confirm the truth of what had been reported previously. "Back then it was inconceivable that the Emperor could make a mistake," said Kawachi. "He was a god. You couldn't change what he'd said and explain that it was in error."[12] Instead, new lies were offered to prop up past fabrications and errors, until the entire edifice of the regime's authority and credibility began to buckle under the strain.

Among the losers in wartime Japan's media industry were smaller weekly and monthly magazines with an audience of scholars and other intellec-tual elites. Many such publications had been associated with "liberal" or pro-democratic views in the years before the war, when a more indulgent political atmosphere had put up with some degree of dissent. *Chuo Koran* (The Central Review) had been published continuously since the nineteenth century, and was one of the nation's most esteemed public affairs journals, with a long record of opposing militarist influence in domestic politics and imperialist adventures abroad. Its past was enough to place *Chuo Koran* and its staff under harsh scrutiny, but the magazine managed to remain in print, with a circulation of 100,000, by repositioning itself to the right. Shigeo

Hatanaka, *Chuo Koran's* editor in chief until he was forced out in 1943, hired military officers to write articles in line with favored themes. He called such contributors his "magic shields." Meanwhile, said Hatanaka, the magazine did what it could to carry the torch of liberalism by writing "paradoxically"— that is, "sounding as if we were going along, but only on the surface in an editorial or in a style which might have appeared to be right-wing."[13]

At regular monthly meetings with the army, the editors bravely declared that *Chuo Koran's* mission was to persuade intellectuals to support the war. Their readers, they argued, were too sophisticated to be moved by unbridled jingoism and mechanical sloganeering. They needed reason and persuasion. But that line of argument found no purchase with the authorities. "At one meeting," Hatanaka recalled, "we at *Chuo Koran* were practically told to slit our bellies open."

> They said our way of thinking was wrong. "Everyone must put their
> minds to war," was their slogan. To them, that meant run up the flag,
> sing military songs, and cheer loudly! Even a nihilistic attitude toward
> war was wrong. They said they could tell if we were sincere just by
> looking at the color in our faces.[14]

If Hatanaka had hoped for support among his fellow editors, he hoped in vain. His colleagues watched in stony disapproval as *Chuo Koran* was chastised. He imagined that they were thinking, "It serves them right!"[15] If the authorities wanted to knock a competitor out of print, so much the better. In any case, an editor who defended a rival might find his own publication singled out for added scrutiny. In March 1943, when all Japanese magazines were ordered to print the slogan "We'll never cease fire till our enemies cease to be," *Chuo Koran* printed it inside the magazine, following the editorial, rather than on the cover as specified. This small act of defiance sealed its fate. A shutdown order followed within days. Hatanaka was branded a communist and hauled off to prison, where he was beaten and tortured almost daily for nine months.

In November 1943, all new newspaper subscriptions were banned. Thereafter, only existing subscribers would receive deliveries. Smaller newspapers were merged into larger ones. The giants *Asahi* and *Yomiuri*, both militantly nationalistic, swallowed up many of their smaller competitors. By 1944, many more once-flourishing magazines and newspapers had suspended publication and shuttered their doors. With a handful of compliant titans dominating the news-gathering and -reporting business, official censorship was greatly simplified. Readers furtively complained that indistinguishable government-sanctioned piffle ran in every paper on the newsstand.

ON THE AFTERNOON OF JUNE 20, 1944, as the defeated First Mobile Fleet retired north toward Japan, the staff at the Imperial General Headquarters had struggled to form a clear picture of Ozawa's situation. Communications were fragmentary and confusing, but what little information got through was distressing. Two fleet carriers were definitely gone, and only a handful of planes had returned from the strikes of June 19. But there remained some hope that the enemy's fleet had been bloodied in the previous day's action, and that a proportion of Ozawa's planes had flown on to Guam. An intercepted American radio transmission mentioned "survivors" of the *Bunker Hill*, raising hopes that the carrier had been sunk—but subsequent intercepts referred to downed aviators, not to the ship's crew.[16] When the American carrier planes attacked Ozawa on the evening of June 20, sinking a third Japanese carrier (the *Hiyo*), the staff at the Imperial General Headquarters could read the writing on the wall. If Spruance had chased Ozawa halfway across the Philippine Sea, his fleet must be intact. The scale of the naval defeat thus presented itself in unambiguous terms. On the same evening, messages from General Saito's headquarters on Saipan indicated that the Americans had secured the southern half of the island. Without naval or air support, Saito's position was tactically hopeless; it was only a matter of time before Saipan would fall to the Americans.

Senior military officers privately admitted, "We can no longer direct the war with any hope of success."[17] In Europe, the Allies were driving east from their Normandy beachhead while the Russians were advancing west into Poland. Hirohito's military advisers privately told the emperor that the loss of Saipan was inevitable. But the emperor was in no mood to accept that verdict, and he pushed his chiefs to renew the fight by any means possible. "If we ever lose Saipan, repeated air attacks on Tokyo will follow," Hirohito told Tojo. "No matter what it takes, we have to hold there."[18] In a late-afternoon meeting at the Imperial Palace on June 20, he directed Tojo and Shimada to muster all available naval and air forces for another desperate attack on the American fleet, to be followed by troop landings on the contested island.

Knowing full well that the sovereign's proposal was tactically daft, the Naval General Staff worked through the night and circulated a draft plan on June 21. The Fifth Fleet, under Vice Admiral Kiyohide Shima, would be summoned from Ominato Naval Base in northern Honshu. Admiral Shima would rendezvous with two fleet oilers and a troopship carrying one regiment, then sortie from Yokosuka for the Marianas on July 2. Another army division would embark on transports totaling 80,000 tons and put to sea in the first week of July. The surviving elements of Ozawa's fleet would be reinforced with the escort carriers *Kaiyo*, *Taiyo*, and *Shinyo*. Having lost nearly all of his aircraft in the recent battle, Ozawa would embark new air groups consisting of naval air-training squadrons and army fighters. Admiral Kurita's Second Fleet, having previously been ordered to sail for the Singapore area, would refuel and rearm in the western part of the Inland Sea and then return directly to the Marianas. All available land-based aircraft would stage through Iwo Jima and renew the air battle against the American carrier force. The American fleet would be destroyed in time for the troop reinforcements to put ashore on Saipan.

Conceived at the man-god's command and in the depths of despair, the plan to recapture Saipan was preposterous on its face. It was not even clear that enough fuel could be provided to put the various fleet elements into position to renew the battle. The American submarines would likely claim many more victims. American seaplanes would discover the incoming forces early. The army leadership was implacably opposed to putting their fighter squadrons aboard aircraft carriers, and it was not clear that the army airmen could even take off from the flight decks. The troopships would need a stroke of good fortune to get anywhere close to Saipan, and even if the troops could be landed, they would likely be wiped out on the beaches. But the *Showa* emperor had lost faith in his military leaders and did not want to hear their objections. For three days the services scrambled to launch an operation they knew to be suicidal. On June 24, Admiral Toyoda of the Combined Fleet weighed in with his formal opposition. That same day, Tojo and Shimada informed the emperor that there was no hope of recovering the island, and that they had cancelled the operation on their own authority. Even then, Hirohito refused to accept that judgment as final, and he convened a larger board of military advisers on June 25. When they confirmed that Saipan was a lost cause, Hirohito told them to put their conclusions in writing and left the room.

As usual, the Japanese people could only guess at the full truth. For several weeks in June and July, news reporting on the battle for Saipan was perplexing and contradictory. The Board of Information was evidently undecided. When and how should the public be informed that the island was to be yielded to the enemy? The July 1 issue of *Toyo Keizai* ventured to declare, "It can be acknowledged that this one island has such value that we will expend all our power to protect it."[19] Prior to the invasion, that opinion had been unimpeachable, but now it elicited an "advisory warning" from the police. Lacking clear guidance from the government, the newspapers generally resorted to hollow sloganeering in stories headlined "The Fighting Will of 100 Million Seethes" or "The Establishment of an Impenetrable Defense Cordon and Total Tenacity."[*][20]

Even without reliable news reports, ordinary Japanese could deduce that the loss of Saipan would open a desperate new phase of the war. Maps were unrolled and studied. Saipan was not far south. It had been Japanese territory for more than twenty years. It was home to a large population of Japanese civilians. If the Americans could land an invasion force on Saipan, within bombing range of the homeland, then the regime's past claims of fantastic and annihilating victories must have been fabrications. Aiko Takahashi told her diary on July 18, 1944, that Japan had obviously suffered another crushing defeat, but "reports in newspapers and magazines boast that giving up these islands is a tactic for drawing in the enemy and the enemy is doing what we want."[21] She did not believe it, nor did many other ordinary Japanese. But it was not safe to air such opinions within earshot of others. Sachi Ariyama, a boy in Kawagoe, recalled that his father was arrested after expressing a casual opinion that the fall of Saipan meant "things were serious." After many hours of interrogation he was released, but the entire family remained under surveillance until the end of the war.[22]

Disaster in the Marianas inevitably loosened Tojo's grip on power. In February the general had fortified his control of the cabinet by adding the job of army chief of staff to his concurrent offices of prime minister and army minister, and by arranging for the malleable Admiral Shimada to serve simultaneously as navy minister and navy chief of staff. Controlling

* Wartime propaganda often referred to the Japanese people as the "100 Million." The figure was overstated by about 30 million.

such an all-encompassing portfolio of political and military offices, Tojo could scarcely duck responsibility for the Saipan debacle. In late June he issued a public statement referring to his "great shame" before the emperor. He had never used such language in the past.

Since the fall of Guadalcanal in early 1943, an anti-Tojo coalition had been maneuvering behind the scenes to oust the general from power. The group included several former prime ministers, military leaders, diplomats, elected members of the Diet (parliament), and various members of the imperial family. The prime mover was Prince Fumimaro Konoye, who had twice served as prime minister in the prewar years and whom Tojo had pushed out of office six weeks before the attack on Pearl Harbor. Konoye worked with a navy group around Admiral Mitsumasa Yonai, another former prime minister who had been Yamamoto's chief ally in opposition to the Tripartite Pact. Konoye and Yonai built support among a working group of former prime ministers called the *jushin* (senior statesmen). Konoye expressed his views to Marquis Koichi Kido, lord keeper of the privy seal and chief adviser on the emperor's personal staff.

Tojo did not go willingly. For several weeks in late June and early July 1944, the opposing factions grappled for ascendancy. According to rumors, Tojo wanted to have his adversaries arrested by the *Kempeitai*, but he could not turn up sufficient grounds to bring charges against figures as influential as Konoye and Yonai. He proposed another cabinet reshuffling in which he would retain at least one of his accumulated jobs, perhaps that of army minister. The Combined Fleet chief, Admiral Toyoda, threatened to resign if Shimada was permitted to remain simultaneously as the head of the Navy Ministry and the Naval General Staff. The *jushin* collectively declined to accept any offices in a cabinet that retained Tojo.

Konoye feared that the war and its disruptions would prompt a socialist upheaval, as in Russia during the Great War. His greatest concern was the survival of the *kokutai*. In the 1930s, the army's *kodo* (imperial way) faction had often advocated collectivist values in the guise of right-wing ideology—for example, by urging a "restoration" of all industry and private property to the throne, or threatening to rectify economic inequality by direct force of arms. Konoye reportedly went so far as to tell his fellow *jushin* that he feared revolution more than defeat: "Even if defeated, we could maintain the national structure and the imperial family, but in case of a leftist revolution, we could not."[23] The mayhem prompted by aerial bombing and foreign invasion might bring another breakdown in army discipline, a return of factionalism and assassinations, and a complete disintegration of Japan's fragile political order.

The *jushin* were determined to be rid of Tojo, and Kido was persuaded to throw his considerable influence behind the cause. But who would take Tojo's place? Existing power-sharing arrangements could not be easily unscrambled. For all his manifest flaws, Tojo had managed to unify the army. He had brought the *kodo* faction to heel, and neutralized many of its leading figures by sending them to forward posts. During his premiership, the rebellious young officers had not broken out in open defiance, as they so often had in the past. The struggle for primacy and influence between the army and the navy remained as bitter as ever, but Tojo had kept the rivalry from boiling over into open conflict. For two and a half years, he had maintained a brittle consensus within the ruling circle. It was not clear that a successor could prolong the intricate balancing act.

Konoye urged Yonai to serve again as prime minister, but the admiral declined, insisting that the army would only accept one of its own. On the same grounds, the *jushin* agreed that no civilian should be proposed for the post. A general was needed. Several names were considered and rejected. The man selected by default was Kuniaki Koiso, a retired general who had served throughout the war years as governor of Korea. He was to be little more than a figurehead, chosen only to mollify the army. Yonai would serve as vice premier as well as navy minister, and the new cabinet would be presented to the nation as a unity government with power to be shared by the army and navy.

Tojo's position became untenable on July 15, when Shimada was ousted from his dual posts. Tojo's last hope of a reconstituted cabinet was defeated on July 17, when the *jushin* signed a joint memorandum stating that "a partial shuffling of the cabinet will not do."[24] He resigned on July 18. In a nationwide radio address that evening, Tojo told his countrymen that "Japan has come to face an unprecedented great national crisis. Our enemies, the United States and Britain, have gradually increased the intensity of their counter-offensive and have at last advanced into the Marianas." In the same breath he prophesied the elusive triumph that would save Japan: "The situation now approaches when opportunity will occur to crack the enemy and to win victory."[25]

That same day, the Japanese public learned of the previous week's mass civilian suicides on Saipan. The *Asahi Shinbun* printed a translated *New York Times* story on the deaths. Accompanying commentary in *Asahi* and other papers commixed sorrow with pride. The suicides were lauded as a beacon of hope and inspiration. The mothers who had killed their children and themselves were "the pride of Japanese women." Kiyosawa collected other such examples of overwrought and lachrymose sentiments: "Courage springs forth a hundred, a thousand-fold more, a blaze of glory, for the first time in history. . . . The essence of a great race shines brightly at the last moment. . . . And thus we are strengthened by this, the true form of Japan."[26] Admiral Ugaki felt a deep sense of "shame," but also thought the civilians had set a good example for their countrymen: "No people but the Yamato nation could do a thing like this. I think that if one hundred million Japanese people could have the same resolution as these facing this crisis, it wouldn't be difficult to find a way to victory."[27] Like Kiyosawa, the Tokyo diarist Aiko Takahashi was disgusted by the harrowing account and refused even to call it bravery: "We should have the courage, come hell or high water, to give up the fight."[28]

The "imperial mandate" was conferred upon Koiso and Yonai on July 22, 1944. Together, they released statements emphasizing their determination to foster close cooperation between the army and the navy. Behind closed doors, they had discussed the need to take steps toward peace, but in their public communications they steadfastly resolved to carry on the war with undiminished intensity. "The Government will firmly adhere to the nation's established foreign policy," said Koiso on taking office, "and work for a thorough-going realization of the principles of the Greater East Asia, thereby carrying the Holy War to a complete victory and thus setting the Imperial mind at ease."[29]

The Koiso government was hobbled from the beginning. Its every move was carefully calibrated to reassure army hardliners. Insiders would compare the Koiso cabinet to a "charcoal-burning car"—like the retrofitted vehicles on the streets of wartime Tokyo, it moved haltingly and often broke down.[30] Koiso was refused a seat on the Supreme Council, and thus was denied a voice in war strategy. Admiral Yonai found himself marginalized. Tojo's allies retained control of the *Kempeitai* and manipulated politics through the mechanisms of internal repression. Koiso dutifully mouthed the same bellicose avowals and victory forecasts that had been Tojo's trademark. On September 16, the new leader assured a national radio audience:

"Japan is preparing to launch a great offensive in the near future to crush Britain and America."[31]

Many senior figures in the ruling circle (including Konoye, Kido, Yonai, and perhaps the emperor) evidently regarded the Koiso cabinet as a transitional government. Getting rid of Tojo was a first step toward peace, but no further maneuvers in that direction could be safely attempted until conditions had ripened. What was needed, according to various opinions, was either a smashing victory or a catastrophic defeat. In late June, Kido had asked Foreign Minister Mamoru Shigemitsu to prepare a plan to seek a diplomatic settlement with the United States. The most likely route was to ask Stalin's government to act as a mediator. To this end, Kido warned Koiso to be scrupulous in avoiding any action likely to antagonize Russia. But all the senior government figures agreed that the rank and file of the army would not countenance a peace initiative until it was obvious that Japan was utterly defeated. When and if such a moment came, the emperor must be persuaded to end the war on the strength of an outright imperial decree.[32]

Hirohito clearly wanted to find a way out of the war, but he remained convinced that an acceptable peace could be negotiated only in the aftermath of a major victory. "I wanted to grasp the chance to quickly conclude a negotiated peace after striking a crushing blow on the enemy someplace," he said in his postwar *Soliloquy*. "Then, with America staggering, we would have been able to find room for a compromise."[33] Steeped in the history of the Russo-Japanese War, determined at all costs to win his Battle of Tsushima, the emperor could not bring himself to admit that his nation was already defeated.

Critics have faulted Hirohito for failing to intervene sooner to stop the war, but there was never any realistic prospect of a negotiated peace. Terms short of unconditional surrender would not have enticed the Allies, while even the most dovish Japanese leaders assumed a diplomatic settlement must maintain some version of Japan's Asian empire. As for the militarist junta, terms of "peace" had been offered by two military "experts" in a broadcast by *Domei* News Service three weeks before the invasion of Saipan:

Complete destruction of American naval power and maritime trade; abolition of private banking institutions and trade unions; restriction of American steel and oil production; destruction of all shipyards except those building river and coastal vessels; creation of a political authority, free from "influences wielded by economic interests" and modeled after the "pure sovereignty of Japan," to maintain strict surveillance over the United States for ten or more years, or perhaps indefinitely.[34]

That offer was evidently tongue in cheek. It had not been presented by the foreign ministry or any other qualified representative of the Japanese government. But Kido's more earnest diary musings on the subject suggest that he had yet to face up to his country's dire predicament. He imagined that Japan might cling to some portion of its Asian empire by pitting the Allies against one another. In a March 31 entry, he surmised that Japan might approach the government of Great Britain and offer to mediate a truce with the Nazis. With peace restored in Europe, London might then be willing to assist Japan in negotiating a settlement with the United States. The British leadership, Kido presumed, would maneuver to prevent the Americans from becoming the supreme power in the Pacific. In the same vein, the Russians might choose to bolster Japan's regional standing as a bulwark against the Anglo-American nations.[35]

In early 1944, with the defeat of Germany and Japan already foreseeable, Kido sketched out terms of peace that would involve "considerable concessions." He envisioned a five-nation commission involving the United States, Britain, the Soviet Union, China, and Japan. All other independent nations in the region would be made "permanent neutral powers, similar to Switzerland." Japan would undertake not to fortify its occupied territories and islands. The five powers would agree to guarantee freedom of trade throughout the region. Japan would remain sovereign in Manchuria and Korea.

Such a proposal would have been rejected by the Allies at any time after December 7, 1941. By 1944, the United States and Britain were implacably committed to forcing Japan's unconditional surrender. Even so, Kido worried that his plan "may, at a glance, be considered too conciliatory and weak-kneed" by Japanese hardliners.[36]

Insofar as the Japanese people were permitted to know, a truce was unthinkable. Right-wing scholars took to the airwaves to extol the virtues of an ancient suicide cult, embodied in the legend of the 47 Ronin who resolved to take their lives in obeisance to a slain master. For the first time the public heard talk of "body crashing" and "sure hit" weapons—the

early euphemisms for suicide tactics to be employed by aircraft, submarines, and speedboats. A new slogan, "One hundred million smashed jewels," carried the implication that the entire nation was to share the fate of
Saipan's civilians. In the July issue of *Daijo Zen*, a Buddhist priest authored
an article entitled "Be Prepared, One Hundred Million, for Death with
Honor!"[37] Historians lectured on the quasi-religious *kamikaze* ("divine
wind") that had defeated a Mongol invasion fleet seven and a half centuries earlier. One of the Koiso government's early initiatives was to arm
and train civilians, including women, in the use of bamboo spears against
enemy invaders.

In the mass media, Americans were increasingly depicted as "beasts,"
"devils," or "butchers." It was categorically reported that they intended
to slaughter every last Japanese man, woman, and child. The authorities
warned that the enemy had already amassed thousands of canisters of poi-
son gas to be released over the homeland. The newspapers were filled with
descriptions of American battlefield atrocities and the mutilation or des-
ecration of Japanese corpses. (Not all such reports were fabrications. A *Life*
magazine photograph depicting an American woman admiring a Japanese
skull was seen by millions of Japanese that summer.) When the Diet convened in September, Hirohito issued a rescript: "Today our imperial state is
indeed challenged to reach powerfully for a decisive victory. You who are
the leaders of our people must now renew your tenacity and, uniting in your
resolve, smash our enemies' evil purposes, thereby furthering forever our
imperial destiny."[38]

The samurai philosopher Miyamoto Musashi had written about the
challenge posed by an adversary who "while appearing to be beaten still
inwardly refuses to acknowledge defeat." In such cases, a swordsman must
adopt a tactic called "knocking the heart out."

> This means that you suddenly change your attitude to stop the enemy
> from entertaining any such ideas, so the main thing is to see enemies
> feel defeated from the bottom of their hearts.
> You can knock the heart out of people with weapons, or with your
> body, or with your mind. It is not to be understood in just one way.
> When your enemies have completely lost heart, you don't have to
> pay attention to them anymore. Otherwise, you remain mindful. If
> enemies still have ambitions, they will hardly collapse.[39]

The Pacific War had entered its endgame. But another 1.5 million Japanese servicemen and civilians would die before the heart was knocked out of the men who ruled Japan.

As OVERSEAS SHIPPING FELL PREY to American air attacks and submarines, the Japanese economy fell to pieces. Rationing grew more stringent; skyrocketing inflation led to price controls and a burgeoning underground economy; shortages of food and household goods grew critical. Everyone went hungry except farmers, who prospered by selling food on the black market. White rice was the immemorial emblem of Japanese prosperity and bliss, but now urbanites could rarely get any of it, and had to make do with unhulled brown rice or other inferior substitutes such as sweet potatoes and barley. Women bartered their wedding kimonos for food and wore the rustic khaki trousers called *monpe*. Trees were cut down on streets and public parks; streetlamps and iron railings were removed for scrap metal; bells were taken away from temples and shrines. The public water supply was often interrupted, and the public bathhouses were usually closed. Ordinary Japanese, who had always valued their personal cleanliness, now bathed just two or three times per month. People despaired of getting rid of lice, and tried to ignore it. Outbreaks of tuberculosis claimed hundreds of thousands of lives.

People were expected to work harder while eating less. Malnourishment and exhaustion comprised a nationwide syndrome, but the regime's answer—always the same answer—was that the people must arouse themselves to greater efforts and sacrifices. If tired, people should practice group calisthenics; the exercise would help lift their spirits, and never mind if it burned scarce calories. Military authority insinuated itself into commonplace domestic routines, as when an army colonel delivered a five-part radio lecture entitled "While You Are Eating Breakfast." Every problem, deficiency, or impasse was put down to an "inadequacy of regulations"—but as new regulations proliferated, they took on an inflexible logic of their own. Kiyosawa, who read widely and kept detailed notes of the drift of official propaganda, detected an increasing tendency to blame civilians for Japan's production shortfalls: "Gradually there are emerging from the government arguments that attribute war responsibility to the productive inadequacy of the homefront."[40]

Open dissent was seldom heard in wartime Japan. But undercurrents of resentment and unrest grew steadily more conspicuous as the conflict wore on. Local officials and representatives of community councils often behaved like petty tyrants, and ordinary citizens suspected that they were diverting extra quantities of rationed food to their own kin. Aiko Takahashi told her diary that she was fed up with the endless mandatory civil defense meetings: "The community council big shots put on their pompous clothes and their pompous faces and strutted about with a pompous number of people."[41] Officers of the *Kempeitai*, looking for evidence of foreign influences or leftist sympathies, barged into private homes in the dead of night. They pulled books off shelves, upended desk drawers, tore down pictures, and did not even deign to remove their shoes before entering a *tatami* room. One often-heard wartime rumor referred to an old man who was determined to obey all rules and regulations. He ate only his official rations, refusing all food obtained by his relatives on the black market. For his scruples he starved to death.

Ordinary people were prepared to suffer hardships and deprivations, but they expected their fellow citizens to bear the same load. Many commented bitterly on wealthy families whose domestic servants were engaged in work that did not advance the war effort. Affluent women escaped participation in the despised air-defense drills by sending maids in their place. Class antagonisms were channeled into acts of vandalism. Tires of private automobiles were slashed; rocks were thrown through windows; intruders broke into upscale homes and wantonly destroyed the furniture and housewares. Rumors of official corruption or special privileges for the wealthy and well-connected evoked a cold fury. It was widely known that the military was active behind the scenes in running the black market. Policemen and military authorities penalized ordinary citizens who traded illegally for food and other goods, but protected malefactors in their own ranks. Law courts and prosecutors were intimidated into backing off. Expensive restaurants were shut down by decree, ostensibly because of food shortages, but then reopened as military "clubs" where officers ate and drank heartily while being entertained by geishas. Hiroyo Arakawa, whose family ran a bakery in Tokyo's Fukagawa district, recalled that soldiers and policemen often helped themselves to goods from the local shops and refused to pay.[42] This saying circulated in wartime Japan: "In this society there is nothing but the army, the navy, the big shots, and the black market. It is only fools who stand in line."[43]

Anonymous gestures of defiance triggered paroxysms of repression.

Sumio Ishida, a local policeman in Shizuoka Prefecture, recalled that someone in his district began mailing unsigned letters to prominent political
figures. The letters were filled with sentiments such as "Please stop this war
as soon as possible. . . . Japan will lose this war for certain. . . . Aren't you
aware of how difficult the lives of the Japanese people have become?"[44] Ishida's entire precinct was mobilized to catch the perpetrator. Plainclothesmen
staked out mailboxes twenty-four hours per day. The police took handwrit-
ing samples from hundreds of citizens. A months-long investigation finally
led to an arrest. The perpetrator was a fifty-three-year-old woman whose
son had died in the South Pacific. The war ended before she was brought
to trial.

To many, the war seemed to tear at the seams of an ancient and sacred
social contract. Whatever super-familial bonds had once held Japan together
threatened to rupture. The nation had always taken justifiable pride in a
low crime rate, but the war brought a sharp increase in petty property theft.
Handbags and briefcases were snatched on overcrowded trains. Shoes left
in the entrance halls of restaurants or the vestibules of private homes disappeared. Thieves reached in through kitchen windows and took food off the
stove as it was cooking. "Foremost Thief Nation of the Whole World," complained an April 1944 headline in the *Mainichi Shinbun*.[45] Authorities wrung
their hands about juvenile delinquency, diminishing respect for elders, and
a breakdown in Confucian ideals of filial piety. Farmers, observed Aiko
Takahashi in January 1944, seemed to take malicious pleasure in their new
power over the city dwellers—they "hold the key to our lives—food—and
sit in the kingly position of lords of production. By selling on the black
market, they are enjoying extraordinary prosperity."[46] Urban evacuees were
treated harshly by rural families. Children from the cities were forced to live
in sheds and survive on scraps from the host family's table. After observing
these patterns of behavior, a young girl in Niigata "became disillusioned
with the disgraceful qualities in our people. They had become a herd whose
humanity had been shorn from them by war."[47]

Direct defiance of authority was impossible. Spies were everywhere, and
the *Kempeitai* was quick to arrest anyone suspected of holding left-wing or
"anti-*kokutai*" views. Children were encouraged to inform on their parents
and teachers. Libraries were compelled to produce lists of titles loaned to
every patron, and the police combed those lists for clues of who might harbor foreign sympathies or unacceptably liberal tendencies. The regime cre-

ated an atmosphere of omnipresent paranoia. Traitors and infiltrators were said to be everywhere. "During those years everything happened behind heavy doors, out of our sight," wrote the novelist Michio Takeyama (author of *Harp of Burma*) after the war. "What's become clear now was wholly unclear then. Day after day we simply trembled in fear, struck dumb with astonishment at incomprehensible developments."[48] Malnourished and overworked, driven like a herd of beasts, instructed how to act and what to think, deprived of any sound basis for rational judgment, threatened with torture and prison at the first divergence from enforced norms, the Japanese people were powerless to alter the doomed course chosen by their leaders. Having long since surrendered whatever rights and freedoms they had once possessed, they were fated to share in the coming Götterdämmerung of 1945.

NOTES

Prologue

1. Clemens, *Alone on Guadalcanal*, p. 57.
2. Read, "Report by Lieut. W. J. Read on Coastwatching Activity," p. 59.
3. Clemens, *Alone on Guadalcanal*, p. 149.
4. Ibid., p. 32.
5. Rhoades, "Secret Diary," p. 1.
6. Ibid., p. 4.
7. Clemens, *Alone on Guadalcanal*, p. 106.
8. Ibid., p. 110.
9. Entry dated May 4, 1942, in Rhoades, "Secret Diary," p. 4.
10. Clemens, *Alone on Guadalcanal*, p. 105.
11. Ibid., p. 147.
12. Rhoades, "Secret Diary," p. 7.
13. Clemens, *Alone on Guadalcanal*, p. 187.
14. Ibid., p. 188.

Chapter One

1. The phrase may have been Bundy's. Stimson and Bundy, *On Active Service in Peace and War*, p. 506.
2. Karsten, *Naval Aristocracy*, p. xiv.
3. See the trenchant comments on this subject by Ruthven E. Libby, in Vice Admiral Ruthven E. Libby, USN (ret.), USNI Oral History Program, 1984, pp. 56–62.
4. Twining and Carey, *No Bended Knee*, p. 29.
5. MacArthur to Army Chief of Staff, May 23, 1942, in NARA, RG 38, "CNO Zero-Zero Files," Box 38.
6. Trumbull, "Big Bombers Won."
7. Mears, *Carrier Combat*, p. 78.
8. Smith and Finch, *Coral and Brass*, p. 18.
9. Tom Lea, "Peleliu Landing," in *Reporting World War II*, Vol. 2: *Part II*, p. 500.

10. Churchill to Roosevelt, June 13, 1942, in Loewenheim, Langley, and Jonas, eds., *Roosevelt and Churchill*, p. 220.

11. "Sacrifice Will Win, Says Admiral King."

12. Walter Muir Whitehill, "A Note on the Making of This Book," in King and Whitehill, *Fleet Admiral King*, pp. 649–50.

13. Stoler, *Allies and Adversaries*, p. 69.

14. Ambrose, *Eisenhower*, p. 141.

15. Entry dated January 20, 1943, in Alanbrooke, *War Diaries*, p. 364.

16. Admiral Ernest J. King to Joint Chiefs of Staff, "J.C.S.—Defense of Island Bases in the Pacific," April 6, 1942, FDR Safe Files, Box 4, George C. Marshall file.

17. "Memorandum for the President," January 18, 1942, Ernest J. King Papers, Box 9, FDR correspondence file.

18. "Situation in South Pacific and Southwest Pacific Areas as of the end of May, 1942," Commander in Chief, U.S. Fleet to Chief of Staff, U.S. Army, memorandum dated May 12, 1942, in NARA, RG 38, "CNO Zero-Zero Files," Box 60.

19. King, "Memorandum for the President," March 5, 1942, Ernest J. King Papers, Box 9, FDR correspondence file.

20. COMINCH to CINCPAC 2303-2306, June 24, 1942, in CINCPAC War Diary, Book 1, pp. 602–3.

21. COMINCH to CINCPAC 1840, June 25, 1942, in ibid., p. 603.

22. COMSOPAC to CINCPAC 0015, June 26, 1942, in ibid., p. 604.

23. PESTILENCE Operation Plan, COMSOPAC File No. A 4-3/A16-3, Serial 0017, in NARA, RG 38, "SOPAC Amphibious Force Diary, July 1942," Box 173; and COMSOPAC dispatches in CINCPAC War Diary, Book 1, pp. 487–596.

24. "Interview of Captain M. B. Gardner, USN, Chief of Staff, ComAirSoPac," January 13, 1943, Bureau of Aeronautics, pp. 2–3, Samuel Eliot Morison Papers, Coll/606, Box 24.

25. D. J. Vellis, oral history, recorded in Olson, *Tales from a Tin Can*, p. 89; and Huie, *Can Do!*, pp. 93–95.

26. "Callaghan's Report of Conference" on *Saratoga*, July 28, 1942, Samuel Eliot Morison Papers, Coll/606, Box 24.

27. Vandegrift and Asprey, *Once a Marine*, p. 105.

28. "Division Commander's Final Report on Guadalcanal Operations," May 24, 1943, pp. 2–4, Samuel Eliot Morison Papers, Coll/606, Box 25.

29. Vandegrift and Asprey, *Once a Marine*, p. 111.

30. COMINCH to CINCPAC 2303-2306, June 24, 1942, in CINCPAC War Diary, Book 1, pp. 602–3.

31. "Joint Directive for Offensive Operations in the Southwest Pacific Area," July 2, 1942, in, NARA, RG 38, "CNO Zero-Zero Files," Box 38, folder labeled "Memos to Gen. Marshall, 15 Jan. 42–1 Sept. 44."

32. "COMSWPACFOR to COMINCH, etc., July 9, 1942," in COMSOPAC, "Top

Secret Incoming and Outgoing Dispatches, 1942–45," in NARA, RG 38: 0313, Container 1.

33. COMINCH to Chief of Staff, U.S. Army, July 10, 1942, in NARA, RG 38, "CNO Zero-Zero Files," Box 38, folder labeled "Memos to Gen. Marshall, 15 Jan. 42–1 Sept. 44."

34. COMINCH to COMSOPAC 2100, July 10, 1942, in CINCPAC War Diary, Book 1, p. 616.

35. Twining and Carey, *No Bended Knee*, p. 30.

36. Merillat, *Guadalcanal Remembered*, p. 21.

37. Twining and Carey, *No Bended Knee*, p. 27.

38. Lt. Chester M. Stearns, interview in November 1943 on board *Baltimore*, in Morison's Notebook, Pacific XII 1943, Samuel Eliot Morison Papers, Coll/606, Box 26.

39. Justice Chambers, Major, USMCR, oral history, in NARA, RG 38, "World War II Oral Histories and Interviews, 1942–1946."

40. Donald Dickson, Major, USMC, oral history, in ibid.

41. Mears, *Carrier Combat*, p. 100.

42. Vandegrift and Asprey, *Once a Marine*, p. 120.

43. Twining and Carey, *No Bended Knee*, p. 45.

44. Details to follow in NARA, RG 38, "SOPAC Amphibious Force Diary, August 1942," Box 173.

45. Roland N. Smoot, USNI Oral History Program, 1972, p. 92.

46. "Annex King to Operation Plan No. A3-42," p. 3, in NARA, RG 38, "SOPAC Amphibious Force Diary, July 1942," Box 173; also Rogal, *Guadalcanal, Tarawa and Beyond*, pp. 51–52.

47. "Vice Admiral Crutchley's Report on Operation Watchtower," September 3, 1942, Samuel Eliot Morison Papers, Coll/606, Box 26.

48. Merillat, *Island*, p. 28.

49. Roland N. Smoot, USNI Oral History Program, 1972, p. 93.

50. Tregaskis, *Guadalcanal Diary*, p. 15.

51. Rogal, *Guadalcanal, Tarawa and Beyond*, p. 52.

52. Manchester, *Goodbye, Darkness*, p. 162.

53. Tregaskis, *Guadalcanal Diary*, p. 31.

54. Twining and Carey, *No Bended Knee*, p. 63.

55. Justice Chambers, Major, USMCR, oral history, in NARA, RG 38, "World War II Oral Histories and Interviews, 1942–1946"; also Tregaskis, *Guadalcanal Diary*, p. 36.

56. Many histories have credited the *San Juan*'s guns with destroying the Kawanishis. Admiral Crutchley, who commanded the fire support groups, credits the F4Fs' strafing attack. "Vice Admiral Crutchley's Report on Operation Watchtower," September 3, 1942, pp. 9–10, Samuel Eliot Morison Papers, Coll/606, Box 26.

57. Photo negatives taken from the *Wasp* air group commander's plane confirmed that VF-71's claims were accurate. *Wasp* Action Report, "Capture of the Tulagi–Guadalcanal Area, 7–8 August 1942," dated August 14, 1942, FDR Map Room Papers, Box 178.

58. Donald Dickson, Major, USMCR, oral history, in NARA, RG 38, "World War II Oral Histories and Interviews, 1942–1946."

59. Pharmacist Frederick A. Moody, USN, oral history, recorded at the Navy Department, April 21, 1943, in NARA, RG 38, "World War II Oral Histories and Interviews, 1942–1946."

60. Tregaskis, *Guadalcanal Diary*, p. 44.

Chapter Two

1. Lundstrom, *First Team and the Guadalcanal Campaign*, p. 38.
2. Lindsay, *Coast Watchers*, p. 197.
3. Lundstrom, *First Team and the Guadalcanal Campaign*, p. 48.
4. Entry dated August 8, 1942, p. 6, Commander Amphibious Force, Task Force 62, War Diary, August 1942, in NARA, RG 38, "World War II War Diaries," Box 173.
5. Lundstrom, *First Team and the Guadalcanal Campaign*, p. 52.
6. Sakai, Caidin, and Saito, *Samurai!*, p. 151.
7. Ibid.
8. Ibid., p. 152.
9. Calhoun, *Tin Can Sailor*, p. 53.
10. Thomas C. Kinkaid, CCOH Naval History Project, No. 429, Vol. 1, p. 186.
11. *Wasp* Action Report, "Capture of the Tulagi-Guadalcanal Area, 7–8 August, 1942," p. 5, dated August 14, 1942, FDR Map Room Papers, Box, 178.
12. Merillat, *Island*, p. 33.
13. Vandegrift and Asprey, *Once a Marine*, p. 127.
14. Donald Dickson, Major, USMCR, oral history, p. 4, in NARA, RG 38, "World War II Oral Histories and Interviews, 1942–1946," Box 8.
15. "Division Commander's Final Report on Guadalcanal Operations," May 24, 1943, Phase II, pp. 2–5, Samuel Eliot Morison Papers, Coll/606, Box 25; also Vandegrift and Asprey, *Once a Marine*, p. 128.
16. Tregaskis, *Guadalcanal Diary*, p. 56.
17. Donald Dickson, Major, USMCR, oral history, pp. 4–5, in NARA, RG 38, "World War II Oral Histories and Interviews, 1942–1946," Box 8.
18. Twining and Carey, *No Bended Knee*, p. 73.
19. Justice Chambers, Major, USMCR, oral history, in NARA, RG 38, "World War II Oral Histories and Interviews, 1942–1946," p. 11.
20. Kittredge, "Savo Island."
21. Lord, *Lonely Vigil*, p. 41.
22. Read, "Report by Lieut. W. J. Read on Coastwatching Activity," p. 22.

23. Tregaskis, *Guadalcanal Diary*, p. 52.

24. Operation Plan No. A3-42, Annex KING, in NARA, RG 38, "SOPAC Amphibious Force Diary, July 1942," Box 173.

25. 1st Division Administrative Order 2a-42, July 22, 1942, in ibid.

26. Turner to Colonel James W. Webb, August 20, 1942, Richmond K. Turner Papers, Series I, correspondence, Box 1.

27. "CruDiv 16 War Diary," p. 1, extracted from WDC 60984, Samuel Eliot Morison Papers, Coll/606, Box 26.

28. Koda, "Doctrine and Strategy of IJN."

29. Ibid.

30. "CruDiv 16 War Diary," p. 1, extracted from WDC 60984, Samuel Eliot Morison Papers, Coll/606, Box 26.

31. Twining and Carey, *No Bended Knee*, p. 64.

32. Charles Clarke to Samuel Eliot Morison, January 13, 1947, Samuel Eliot Morison Papers, Coll/606, Box 27.

33. Smith, *Battle of Savo*, p. 118.

34. Dull, *Battle History of the Imperial Japanese Navy*, p. 187.

35. Morison, *History of United States Naval Operations in World War II*, Vol. 5, p. 37.

36. "To CTF-44, From Executive Officer, HMAS Canberra," CINCPAC File A16/ Solomon Serial 62636, in NARA, RG 38, "WWII Action and Operational Reports," Box 14.

37. Kittredge, "Savo Island."

38. Toshikazu Ohmae, "The Battle of Savo Island," in Evans, ed., *Japanese Navy in World War II*, p. 236.

39. Chief of the Bureau of Ships, U.S. Navy, "U.S.S. QUINCY, U.S.S. ASTORIA and U.S.S. VINCENNES, Report of Loss in Action."

40. Ibid.

41. Lt. Cmdr. Bion B. Bierer to Mary Bierer, October 16, 1942, letter in possession of Bob Begin, quoted here with his permission.

42. Chief of the Bureau of Ships, U.S. Navy, "U.S.S. QUINCY, U.S.S. ASTORIA and U.S.S. VINCENNES, Report of Loss in Action."

43. "To CTF-62, From Comdesron 4," TOR 0610z, appended to Crutchley's report to Turner, CINCPAC File A16/Solomon Serial 62636, in NARA, RG 38, "WWII Action and Operational Reports," Box 14.

44. Rogal, *Guadalcanal, Tarawa and Beyond*, p. 56.

45. Tregaskis, *Guadalcanal Diary*, p. 62.

46. Harry L. Vincent in "Veterans' Biographies," p. 52.

47. Pharmacist Frederick A. Moody, USN, p. 15, oral history, recorded at the Navy Department, April 21, 1943, in NARA, RG 38, "World War II Oral Histories and Interviews, 1942–1946," Box 20.

48. Mikawa's remarks are excerpted in Toshikazu Ohmae, "Battle of Savo Island," in Evans, ed., *Japanese Navy in World War II*, p. 244.

49. Chief of the Bureau of Ships, U.S. Navy, "U.S.S. QUINCY, U.S.S. ASTORIA and U.S.S. VINCENNES, Report of Loss in Action."

50. Twining and Carey, No Bended Knee, p. 69.

51. Office of Naval Intelligence, "Battle of Savo Island," pp. 43–44.

Chapter Three

1. Buell, Master of Seapower, p. 221.

2. Ibid.

3. Harry W. Hill, CCOH Naval History Project, No. 685, Vol. 2, p. 267.

4. John L. McCrea, USNI Oral History Program, 1990, pp. 169–70.

5. "Memorandum for the President, Via Admiral Leahy," August 13, 1942, COMINCH File A16-3(1), FDR Map Room Papers.

6. "Reinforcement of Hawaii and South Pacific Areas," Commander in Chief, U.S. Fleet to Chief of Staff, U.S. Army, memorandum dated August 13, 1942, in NARA, RG 38, "CNO Zero-Zero Files," Box 38.

7. Crutchley to Turner, August 10, 1942, letter enclosure in COMSOPAC to CINCPAC, "Preliminary Report Watchtown Operation," dated August 16, 1942, in NARA, RG 38, "WWII Action and Operational Reports," Box 14.

8. COMINCH to Secretary of the Navy, September 14, 1942, "Investigation of the Loss of the U.S.S. VINCENNES, U.S.S. QUINCY, U.S.S. ASTORIA, and HMAS CANBERRA," Richmond K. Turner Papers, Series 1, correspondence, Box 1.

9. Vandegrift and Asprey, Once a Marine, p. 129.

10. Fletcher to Hanson Baldwin, July 9, 1947, Samuel Eliot Morison Papers, Box 26.

11. Morison, History of United States Naval Operations in World War II, Vol. 5, pp. 29–30, including footnote on p. 30.

12. Lundstrom unpacks the subject at length, concluding with a measured defense of Fletcher. See Lundstrom, Black Shoe Carrier Admiral, pp. 368–83.

13. NARA, RG 38, "SOPAC Amphibious Force Diary," August 15, 1942, Box 173.

14. "War Diary, Amphibious Force SOPAC," August 16, 1942 entry, in ibid.

15. "War Diary, Amphibious Force SOPAC," August 9, 1942 entry, in ibid.

16. Vandegrift to Turner, 151015, COMSOPAC War Diary, quoted in Merillat, Guadalcanal Remembered, source note, p. 307.

17. Rogal, Guadalcanal, Tarawa and Beyond, p. 58.

18. "MR 203, Japanese Naval Activities," FDR Map Room Papers, Box 64.

19. Fletcher to COMSOPAC to CTF-61, 211120, in CINCPAC War Diary, Book 1, p. 807.

20. Merillat, Guadalcanal Remembered, p. 152.

21. Rogal, Guadalcanal, Tarawa and Beyond, p. 61.

22. "Division Commander's Final Report on Guadalcanal Operations," May 24, 1943, Phase III, p. 1, Samuel Eliot Morison Papers, Coll/606, Box 25.

23. Vandegrift and Asprey, Once a Marine, p. 132.

24. Ibid., p. 134.
25. Clemens, *Alone on Guadalcanal*, p. 196.
26. Vandegrift and Asprey, *Once a Marine*, p. 136.
27. "8th Fleet War Diary," p. 1, extracted from WDC 161259/397/901, Samuel Eliot Morison Papers, Coll/606, Box 26.
28. "Detailed Battle Report No. 6 of the Fifth Air Attack Force," issued at Rabaul, September 10, 1942, extracted from WDC 161012/399.901, Samuel Eliot Morison Papers, Coll/606, Box 26.
29. "Staggering Blow," *Domei* News Broadcast, Samuel Eliot Morison Papers, Coll/606, Box 26.
30. Hara, Saito, and Pineau, *Japanese Destroyer Captain*, p. 95.
31. "Diary, No. 25 Air Flotilla," pp. 3–4, extracted from WDC 161012/399.901, Samuel Eliot Morison Papers, Coll/606, Box 26.
32. "Military Value of British New Guinea," in Japanese Demobilization Bureau Records, *Reports of General MacArthur*, p. 24.
33. Hara, Saito, and Pineau, *Japanese Destroyer Captain*, p. 95.
34. "Diary, No. 25 Air Flotilla," p. 2, extracted from WDC 161012/399.901, Samuel Eliot Morison Papers, Coll/606, Box 26.
35. "Division Commander's Final Report on Guadalcanal Operations," May 24, 1943, Phase III, p. 6, Samuel Eliot Morison Papers, Coll/606, Box 25.
36. Miller, *Cactus Air Force*, p. 24.
37. "COMAIRSOPAC War Diary for August 1942," August 13, 1942, entry, Samuel Eliot Morison Papers, Coll/606, Box 27.
38. Entry dated August 13, 1942, in CINCPAC War Diary, Book 1, p. 825.
39. David Galvan quoted in Bergerud, *Fire in the Sky*, p. 79.
40. Brand, *Fighter Squadron at Guadalcanal*, p. 67.
41. Vandegrift and Asprey, *Once a Marine*, p. 139.
42. Clemens, *Alone on Guadalcanal*, p. 208.
43. Twining and Carey, *No Bended Knee*, p. 84.
44. Clemens, *Alone on Guadalcanal*, p. 209.
45. Vandegrift and Asprey, *Once a Marine*, p. 142.
46. Ibid.
47. Merillat, *Island*, p. 75.
48. Vandegrift and Asprey, *Once a Marine*, p. 144.
49. "Japanese Naval Operations; Estimate of," Intelligence Center, Pacific Ocean Areas, July 24, 1942, in CINCPAC War Diary, Book 1, pp. 841–43.
50. COMSOPAC to CTF-61, 220910, in ibid., p. 808.
51. "Diary, No. 25 Air Flotilla," extracted from WDC 161012/399.901, Samuel Eliot Morison Papers, Coll/606, Box 26.
52. Harry D. Felt, USNI Oral History Program, Vol. 2, p. 109.
53. Ibid., p. 110.
54. "COMAIRSOPAC War Diary for August 1942," August 24, 1942, entry, Samuel Eliot Morison Papers, Coll/606, Box 27.

55. Harry D. Felt, USNI Oral History Program, Vol. 2, p. 112.
56. "Narrative Report of Action with Enemy on August 24, 1942," Commander, *Saratoga* Air Group, enclosure (e) to *Saratoga* Action Report, September 10, 1942, in NARA, RG 38, "WWII Action and Operational Reports," Box 14.
57. Hara, Saito, and Pineau, *Japanese Destroyer Captain*, pp. 100–101.
58. Buell, *Dauntless Helldivers*, p. 122.
59. *Enterprise* Action Report, September 5, 1942, p. 3, in NARA, RG 38, "WWII Action and Operational Reports," Box 14.
60. Lt. Cmdr. Keiichi Arima, in Werneth, ed., *Beyond Pearl Harbor*, p. 30.
61. *Enterprise* Action Report, September 5, 1942, enclosure (b), "Report of Fighter Director," in NARA, RG 38, "WWII Action and Operational Reports," Box 14.
62. Ibid.
63. Ibid.
64. Ibid.
65. Mears, *Carrier Combat*, p. 117.
66. Thomas C. Kinkaid, CCOH Naval History Project, No. 429, Vol. 1, p. 198.
67. Mears, *Carrier Combat*, p. 121.

Chapter Four

1. Jackson, *That Man*, p. 111.
2. Ibid.
3. Harold Smith account in Rosenau, ed., *Roosevelt Treasury*, p. 323.
4. Lippmann, "Awkward Giant," p. 9.
5. Brinkley, *Washington Goes to War*, p. 202.
6. Childs, *I Write from Washington*, p. 242.
7. *Congressional Record*, 77th Cong., 2nd sess., Vol. 88, Part 6, pp. 5538–41.
8. Brinkley, *Washington Goes to War*, p. 111.
9. Childs, *I Write from Washington*, p. 312.
10. *Congressional Record*, 77th Cong., 2nd sess., Vol. 88, Part 6, p. 7691.
11. "Washington in Wartime."
12. Leahy, *I Was There*, p. 136.
13. Donald Duncan, CCOH Naval History Project, No. 678, Vol. 7, p. 380.
14. McIntire, *White House Physician*, p. 141.
15. John L. McCrea, "Setting Up Map Room in White House and Other Incidents in Connection with Service There," interview by W. W. Moss, March 19, 1973, p. 4, FDR Map Room Papers, Box 178.
16. Ibid., p. 6.
17. Dower, *War Without Mercy*, p. 161.
18. Leahy, *I Was There*, p. 122.
19. Entry dated April 15, 1942, in Alanbrooke, *War Diaries*, p. 249.
20. Ibid., p. 246.

21. Churchill to Roosevelt, July 9, 1942, in Loewenheim, Langley, and Jonas, eds., *Roosevelt and Churchill*, p. 222.

22. King and Whitehill, *Fleet Admiral King*, pp. 398–99.

23. Ibid.

24. Baldwin, "Solomons Action Develops into Battle for South Pacific."

25. Baldwin, "U.S. Hold in Solomons Bolstered."

26. Harold H. Larsen, interview in Navy Department Bureau of Aeronautics, January 18, 1943, p. 14, in NARA, RG 38, "World War II Oral Histories and Interviews, 1942–1946," Box 16.

27. Bergerud, *Fire in the Sky*, pp. 79–80.

28. Harold H. Larsen, interview in Navy Department Bureau of Aeronautics, January 18, 1943, p. 3, in NARA, RG 38, "World War II Oral Histories and Interviews, 1942–1946," Box 16.

29. Read, "Report by Lieut. W. J. Read on Coastwatching Activity," pp. 81–82.

30. Joseph J. Foss, USMCR, interview in Navy Department, April 28, 1943, in NARA, RG 38, "World War II Oral Histories and Interviews, 1942–1946," Box 9, p. 5.

31. Ibid., p. 6.

32. Astor, *Wings of Gold*, p. 155.

33. Joseph J. Foss, USMCR, interview in Navy Department, April 28, 1943, in NARA, RG 38, "World War II Oral Histories and Interviews, 1942–1946," Box 9, p. 5.

34. Brand, *Fighter Squadron at Guadalcanal*, pp. 95–96.

35. Bergerud, *Fire in the Sky*, p. 80.

36. Vandegrift and Asprey, *Once a Marine*, p. 147.

37. Twining and Carey, *No Bended Knee*, p. 89.

38. Vandegrift and Asprey, *Once a Marine*, p. 148.

39. Emphasis in the original. McCain to Vandegrift and Geiger, September 14, 1942, p. 1, Alexander Vandegrift Collection, Coll/3166, Box 2, folder "Correspondence Jan–Sept 1942."

40. McCain to Vandegrift, September 20, 1942, p. 1, ibid.

41. Harold H. Larsen, interview in Navy Department Bureau of Aeronautics, January 18, 1943, p. 3, in NARA, RG 38, "World War II Oral Histories and Interviews, 1942–1946," Box 16.

42. Buell, *Dauntless Helldivers*, p. 125.

43. Bergerud, *Fire in the Sky*, p. 81.

44. Buell, *Dauntless Helldivers*, p. 147.

45. Clemens, *Alone on Guadalcanal*, p. 230.

46. C.O. *Enterprise* to CINCPAC, "Action of August 24, 1942, Report of," September 5, 1942, CV6/A16-3/(10-My), Serial 008, p. 22, in NARA, RG 38, "WWII Action and Operational Reports," Box 14.

47. CINCPAC Report, "Solomons Island Campaign—Torpedoing of SARATOGA, WASP, and NORTH CAROLINA," Serial 03168, October 12, 1942, enclosure

"Hull Damage and Damage Control Measures," in NARA, RG 38, "WWII Action and Operational Reports," Box 17.

48. CINCPAC Report, "Solomons Island Campaign—Torpedoing of SARATOGA, WASP, and NORTH CAROLINA," Serial 03168, October 12, 1942, in ibid.

49. Wolfert, *Battle for the Solomons*, p. 40.

50. Cmdr. William C. Chambliss, USNR, oral history, in NARA, RG 38, "World War II Oral Histories and Interviews, 1942–1946," Box 6.

51. Ibid.

52. Lt. Chester M. Stearns, interview in November 1943 on board *Baltimore*, Morison's Notebook, Pacific XII 1943, Samuel Eliot Morison Papers, Coll/606, Box 26.

53. CINCPAC Report, "Solomons Island Campaign—Torpedoing of SARATOGA, WASP, and NORTH CAROLINA," Serial 03168, October 12, 1942, enclosure "Captain Forest Sherman to Secretary of the Navy," in NARA, RG 38, "WWII Action and Operational Reports," Box 17.

54. Hersey, "Sinking of the Wasp."

55. Cmdr. William C. Chambliss, USNR, oral history, in NARA, RG 38, "World War II Oral Histories and Interviews, 1942–1946," Box 6.

56. Ibid.

57. CINCPAC Report, "Solomons Island Campaign—Torpedoing of SARATOGA, WASP, and NORTH CAROLINA," Serial 03168, October 12, 1942, in NARA, RG 38, "WWII Action and Operational Reports," Box 17.

Chapter Five

1. *Kokusai Shashin Joho* (International Graphic Magazine), Vol. 21, No. 12, December 1, 2602 (1942).

2. Ibid., Vol. 21, No. 10, September 1, 2602 (1942).

3. Hideki Tojo, speech at the War Ministry, December 8, 1942, excerpted in Tolischus, *Through Japanese Eyes*, p. 155.

4. Admiral Kichisaburo Nomura, former ambassador to Washington, January 22, 1943, in ibid., p. 154.

5. Diary indicates that this occurred on December 17, 1942; see Kiyosawa, *Diary of Darkness*, p. 6.

6. Hiroyo Arakawa, oral history, in Cook and Cook, eds., *Japan at War*, p. 179.

7. Ibid.

8. Sakai, Caidin, and Saito, *Samurai!*, p. 184.

9. Asada, *From Mahan to Pearl Harbor*, p. 183.

10. Ibid., p. 281.

11. Ibid., p. 280.

12. Ibid., p. 279.

13. Junichiro Watanabe, "Isoroku Yamamoto and the Sword-smith Sadayoshi

Amada," Hisato Takeuchi, trans., Nihontocraft.com, online at http://www
.nihontocraft.com/Yamamoto NBTHK.html (accessed November 2014).

14. Reiji Masuda, oral history, in Cook and Cook, eds., *Japan at War*, p. 301.
15. Entry dated August 13, 1942, in Ugaki, *Fading Victory*, p. 183.
16. Entry dated August 20, 1942, in ibid., p. 186.
17. Entry dated August 24, 1942, in ibid., p. 193.
18. Entry dated September 1, 1942, in ibid., pp. 202–3.
19. Entry dated August 24, 1942, in ibid., p. 193.
20. Entry dated September 13, 1942, in ibid., p. 214.
21. Entry dated October 7, 1942, in ibid., p. 228.
22. Astor, *Wings of Gold*, p. 62.
23. Potter, *Nimitz*, p. 76.
24. Ibid., p. 236.
25. "CINCPAC Conference in *Argonne*," September 28, 1942, p. 1, Samuel Eliot Morison Papers, Coll/606, Box 24.
26. Ibid.
27. Ibid., pp. 1–3.
28. Arnold, *Global Mission*, pp. 360–61.
29. Arnold to Hopkins, "Plans for Operations Against the Enemy," September 3, 1942, Harry L. Hopkins Papers, Book 5: The Air Offensive, Box 313.
30. Ibid.
31. Arnold, *Global Mission*, p. 344.
32. Ibid., p. 342.
33. Vandegrift and Asprey, *Once a Marine*, pp. 171–72.
34. Entry dated September 30, 1942, excerpted in Merillat, *Guadalcanal Remembered*, p. 159.
35. Arthur Lamar, oral history, in *Recollections of Fleet Admiral Chester W. Nimitz*, p. 13.
36. Les Cleveland, "Soldiers' Songs: The Folklore of the Powerless," *New York Folklore*, Vol. 11, 1985, online at http://faculty.buffalostate.edu/fishlm/folksongs/les01 .htm.
37. Turner to Vandegrift, September 28, 1942, quoted in Vandegrift and Asprey, *Once a Marine*, p. 169.
38. Merillat, *Guadalcanal Remembered*, pp. 177–78.
39. Huie, *Can Do!*, p. 41.
40. Harold H. Larsen, interview in Navy Department Bureau of Aeronautics, January 18, 1943, p. 7, in NARA, RG 38, "World War II Oral Histories and Interviews, 1942–1946," Box 16.
41. Mears, *Carrier Combat*, p. 136.
42. Tregaskis, *Guadalcanal Diary*, p. 250.
43. Joseph J. Foss, USMCR, interview in Navy Department, April 28, 1943, in

NARA, RG 38, "World War II Oral Histories and Interviews, 1942–1946," Box 9, p. 11.

44. Harold H. Larsen, interview in Navy Department Bureau of Aeronautics, January 18, 1943, p. 7, in NARA, RG 38, "World War II Oral Histories and Interviews, 1942–1946," Box 16.

45. Ibid., p. 11.

46. Merillat, *Guadalcanal Remembered*, p. 180.

47. Action Report, U.S.S. *San Francisco*, night action, November 12–13, 1942, p. 60, item 300, in NARA, RG 38, "WWII Action and Operational Reports," Box 23. This report contains a detailed description of the same shells employed in the October 13–14 night bombardment. Also see Admiral T. Koyanagi, memorandum entitled "The Retreat from Guadalcanal," dated May 1, 1967, John Toland Papers, Box 3, "Guadalcanal."

48. Entry dated October 14, 1942, in Merillat, *Guadalcanal Remembered*, p. 179.

49. Mears, *Carrier Combat*, p. 145.

50. Huie, *Can Do!*, p. 46.

51. Vandegrift and Asprey, *Once a Marine*, p. 176.

52. Twining and Carey, *No Bended Knee*, p. 121.

53. Vandegrift and Asprey, *Once a Marine*, p. 176.

54. Merillat, *Guadalcanal Remembered*, p. 180.

55. Huie, *Can Do!*, p. 46.

56. Clemens, *Alone on Guadalcanal*, p. 257.

57. Mears, *Carrier Combat*, p. 146.

58. Twining and Carey, *No Bended Knee*, p. 157.

59. Bergerud, *Fire in the Sky*, p. 82.

60. Lt. Cmdr. John E. Lawrence's notes in Halsey and Bryan, *Admiral Halsey's Story*, p. 116.

61. COMSOPAC to CINCPAC, Info COMINCH, 160440, in CINCPAC War Diary, Book 2, p. 950.

62. John L. McCrea, USNI Oral History Program, 1990, pp. 170–71.

63. See Col. Brown's notes in Halsey and Bryan, *Admiral Halsey's Story*, p. 111.

64. Layton, Pineau, and Costello, *"And I Was There,"* pp. 461–62.

65. CINCPAC TO COMINCH, 160937, in CINCPAC War Diary, Book 2, p. 895.

66. COMINCH TO CINCPAC, 160245, in ibid.

67. Col. Julian Brown's notes in Halsey and Bryan, *Admiral Halsey's Story*, p. 109.

Chapter Six

1. Lt. Comdr. Roger Kent quoted in Halsey and Bryan, *Admiral Halsey's Story*, p. 116.

2. Wolfert, *Battle for the Solomons*, p. 99.

3. Vandegrift and Asprey, *Once a Marine*, p. 185.

4. Ibid.

5. Hara, *Japanese Destroyer Captain*, p. 116.

6. *Enterprise* Action Report, November 10, 1942, enclosure: Fighting Squadron 10 Report on Flight of October 25, 1942, in NARA, RG 38, "WWII Action and Operational Reports," Box 21.

7. Edward L. Feightner, "The *Enterprise* and Guadalcanal," in Wooldridge, ed., *Carrier Warfare in the Pacific*, p. 82.

8. C.O., *Enterprise* to CINCPAC (via etc.), November 10, 1942, in NARA, RG 38, "WWII Action and Operational Reports," Box 21.

9. Ibid.

10. "CO, Striking Fleet to CinC, Combined Fleet," October 27, 1942, item 7, p. 2, Samuel Eliot Morison Papers, Box 25, Folder "CruDiv 8 Combat Report."

11. *Enterprise* Action Report, November 10, 1942, enclosure B: "Comments, Action by the Task Force on October 26, 1942," by Lt. Cmdr. James H. Flatley, in NARA, RG 38, "WWII Action and Operational Reports," Box 21.

12. "CruDiv 8 Combat Report No. 5," WDC 161270, November, 18, 1942, item 3, Samuel Eliot Morison Papers, Box 25.

13. VS-8 and VB-8 Reports to CO, U.S.S. *Hornet*, November 2, 1942, in NARA, RG 38, "WWII Action and Operational Reports," Box 21.

14. Author's interview with Oral L. "Slim" Moore, Berkeley, CA, February 27, 2013.

15. "CO, Striking Fleet to CinC, Combined Fleet," October 27, 1942, item 7, p. 2, Samuel Eliot Morison Papers, Box 25, Folder "CruDiv 8 Combat Report."

16. Hara, *Japanese Destroyer Captain*, p. 121.

17. *Hornet* Action Report, *Hornet* CO to CINCPAC, et al., October 30, 1942, in NARA, RG 38, "WWII Action and Operational Reports," Box 21.

18. Kernan, *Crossing the Line*, p. 63.

19. Interview with Cmdr. F. Monroe, Morison's Notebook, Pacific XII 1943, p. 2, Samuel Eliot Morison Papers, Coll/606, Box 26.

20. *Hornet* Action Report, Executive Officer to CO, October 30, 1942, in NARA, RG 38, "WWII Action and Operational Reports," Box 21.

21. *Hornet* Action Report, *Hornet* CO to CINCPAC, et al., October 30, 1942, in ibid.

22. "War Damage Report," enclosure to *Enterprise* Action Report, November 10, 1942, in ibid.

23. Beaver, *Sailor from Oklahoma*, p. 184.

24. C.O. *Enterprise* to CINCPAC (via etc.), (*Enterprise* Action Report), November 10, 1942, in NARA, RG 38, "WWII Action and Operational Reports," Box 21.

25. Francis Foley, "The *Hornet* and the Santa Cruz Islands," in Wooldridge, ed., *Carrier Warfare in the Pacific*, p. 73.

26. *Hornet* CO to CINCPAC, et al., October 30, 1942, in NARA, RG 38, "WWII Action and Operational Reports," Box 21.

27. Report of Cmdr. E. P. Creehan, enclosure B, *Hornet* Action Report, October 30, 1942, in ibid.

28. Report of C. H. Dodson, Communications Officer, *Hornet* Action Report, October 30, 1942, in ibid.

29. "CO, Striking Fleet to CinC, Combined Fleet," October 27, 1942, item 4, Samuel Eliot Morison Papers, Box 25, Folder "CruDiv 8 Combat Report."

30. "CruDiv 8 Combat Report No. 5," WDC 161270, November 18, 1942, item 7, Samuel Eliot Morison Papers, Box 25.

31. Hara, *Japanese Destroyer Captain*, p. 125.

32. Halsey and Bryan, *Admiral Halsey's Story*, p. 122.

33. Clemens, *Alone on Guadalcanal*, p. 267.

34. Peattie, *Sunburst*, p. 184.

35. Lt. Cmdr. Iyozo Fujita, oral history, in Werneth, ed., *Beyond Pearl Harbor*, p. 241.

36. Read, "Report by Lieut. W. J. Read on Coastwatching Activity," p. 78.

37. Leahy, *I Was There*, p. 118.

38. FDR to Joint Chiefs, October 23, 1942, holograph of memorandum reproduced in Sherwood, *Roosevelt and Hopkins*, pp. 622–23.

39. Halsey to Nimitz, October 31, 1942, quoted in Lundstrom, *First Team and the Guadalcanal Campaign*, p. 337.

40. Cmdr. William J. Kitchell's notes, in Halsey and Bryan, *Admiral Halsey's Story*, p. 123.

41. Trumbull, "All Out with Halsey!"

42. Wolfert, *Battle for the Solomons*, p. 127.

43. Halsey and Bryan, *Admiral Halsey's Story*, p. 123.

44. C.O., U.S.S. *Enterprise*, "Action Against Japanese Forces Attempting the Recapture of Guadalcanal, November 13–14, 1942—Report of," November 19, 1942, in NARA, RG 38, "WWII Action and Operational Reports," Box 18.

45. C.O., U.S.S. *San Francisco*, "Air Attack, November 12, 1942," report dated November 16, 1942, in NARA, RG 38, "CINCPAC Action and Operational Reports," Box 19.

46. Entry dated November 18, 1942, "War Diary," 1942–44, Papers of Captain Flavius J. George, USNR.

47. C.O., U.S.S. *San Francisco*, "Air Attack, November 12, 1942," report dated November 16, 1942, in NARA, RG 38, "CINCPAC Action and Operational Reports," Box 19.

48. Sullivan, "Ship Ahead Just Disappeared."

49. Hornfischer, *Neptune's Inferno*, p. 254.

50. "Narrative by L. E. Zook, Signalman First Class, U.S. Navy," recorded May 27, 1943, in Samuel Eliot Morison Papers, Coll/606, Box 26.

51. Calhoun, *Tin Can Sailor*, p. 77.

52. Action Report, U.S.S. *San Francisco*, "Night Action of November 12–13, 1942," item 300 in "Chronological Log," in NARA, RG 38, "CINCPAC Action and Operational Reports," Box 19.

53. Entry dated November 18, 1942, "War Diary," 1942–44, Papers of Captain Flavius J. George, USNR.
54. Wolfert, *Battle for the Solomons*, p. 160.
55. Action Report, U.S.S. *San Francisco*, "Night Action of November 12–13, 1942," item 300 in "Chronological Log," in NARA, RG 38, "CINCPAC Action and Operational Reports," Box 19.
56. Entry dated November 18, 1942, "War Diary," 1942–44, Papers of Captain Flavius J. George, USNR.
57. Calhoun, *Tin Can Sailor*, p. 84.
58. "Narrative by L. E. Zook, Signalman First Class, U.S. Navy," recorded May 27, 1943, in Samuel Eliot Morison Papers, Coll/606, Box 26.
59. "Narrative by Lieut. Graham C. Bonnell, US Navy," recorded January 25, 1944, in NARA, RG 38, "World War II Oral Histories and Interviews, 1942–1946," Box 1.
60. Calhoun, *Tin Can Sailor*, p. 92.
61. "Narrative by Lieut. Graham C. Bonnell, US Navy," recorded January 25, 1944, in NARA, RG 38, "World War II Oral Histories and Interviews, 1942–1946," Box 1.
62. Cmdr., Torpedo Squadron 10, "Action of November 13–15, 1942," submitted to the CO, U.S.S. *Enterprise*, in NARA, RG 38, "WWII Action and Operational Reports," Box 18.
63. "Action Against Japanese Forces Attempting the Recapture of Guadalcanal, November 13–14, 1942—Report of," November 19, 1942, in NARA, RG 38, "WWII Action and Operational Reports," Box 18.
64. Buell, *Dauntless Helldivers*, p. 183.
65. Edward L. Feightner, "The *Enterprise* and Guadalcanal," in Wooldridge, ed., *Carrier Warfare in the Pacific*, p. 85.
66. Mears, *Carrier Combat*, p. 155.
67. Wolfert, *Battle for the Solomons*, p. 169.
68. "Action Against Japanese Forces Attempting the Recapture of Guadalcanal, November 13–14, 1942—Report of," November 19, 1942, in NARA, RG 38, "WWII Action and Operational Reports," Box 18.
69. Thomas C. Kinkaid, CCOH Naval History Project, No. 429, Vol. 1, p. 209.
70. Paul H. Backus, U.S. Navy (ret.), USNI Oral History Program, 1995, p. 195.
71. Earl Hicks quoted in Olson, *Tales from a Tin Can*, p. 102.
72. Entry dated Monday, November 16, 1942, in Ugaki, *Fading Victory*, p. 276.
73. Cmdr., Torpedo Squadron 10, "Action of November 13–15, 1942," submitted to the CO, U.S.S. *Enterprise*, in NARA, RG 38, "WWII Action and Operational Reports," Box 18.
74. Cmdr., Bombing Squadron 10, "Action of November 14–15, 1942," submitted to the CO, U.S.S. *Enterprise*, in ibid.

Chapter Seven

1. Masanobu Tsuji, "Guadalcanal," p. 28, unpublished memoir dated May 31, 1967, John Toland Papers, Series 1: The Rising Sun, Box 17.

2. Ibid., p. 46.

3. "Address or Message of Jap Detachment C.O. in Solomons," Samuel Eliot Morison Papers, Coll/606, Box 26.

4. "Diary Taken at Kokumbona," entries dated December 23 and 26, 1942, Samuel Eliot Morison Papers, Coll/606, Box 26.

5. Lt. Ko-o's diary excerpted in Masanobu Tsuji, "Guadalcanal," p. 51, unpublished memoir dated May 31, 1967, John Toland Papers, Series 1: The Rising Sun, Box 17.

6. Entry dated December 8, 1942, in Ugaki, Fading Victory, p. 301.

7. Entry dated Monday, November 16, 1942, in ibid., p. 276.

8. Raizo Tanaka, "The Struggle for Guadalcanal," in Evans, ed., Japanese Navy in World War II, pp. 198–99.

9. Ibid., p. 200.

10. CINCPAC to COMINCH, "Solomon Islands Campaign, Fifth Battle of Savo, 30 November 1942," in NARA, RG 38, "WWII Action and Operational Reports," Box 20.

11. CINCPAC to COMINCH, "Solomon Islands Campaign, Fifth Battle of Savo, 30 November 1942," in ibid.

12. Morison, History of United States Naval Operations in World War II, Vol. 5, p. 315.

13. CINCPAC to COMINCH, "Solomon Islands Campaign, Fifth Battle of Savo, 30 November 1942," in NARA, RG 38, "WWII Action and Operational Reports," Box 20.

14. Raizo Tanaka, "The Struggle for Guadalcanal," in Evans, ed., Japanese Navy in World War II, p. 204.

15. Ibid., p. 206.

16. Hitoshi Imamura, oral history, in Brawley, Dixon, and Trefalt, eds., Competing Voices from the Pacific War, p. 108.

17. Entry dated December 7, 1942, in Ugaki, Fading Victory, p. 297.

18. Entry dated December 8, 1942, in ibid., p. 299.

19. Kokusai Shashin Joho (International Graphic Magazine), Vol. 21, No. 12, December 1, 2602 (1942).

20. Foreign Minister Tani quoted in Tolischus, Through Japanese Eyes, p. 113.

21. Tojo speech excerpted in ibid., p. 155.

22. Entry dated November 4, 1942, in Ugaki, Fading Victory, p. 283.

23. Hara, Japanese Destroyer Captain, p. 157.

24. Joichiro Sanada, "Statement Concerning Particulars of Evacuation from Guadalcanal Island," January 20, 1950, John Toland Papers, Box 3, "Guadalcanal."

25. Gen. Kenryo Sato, "Dai Toa War Memoirs," p. 10, John Toland Papers, Box 16.

26. Joichiro Sanada, "Statement Concerning Particulars of Evacuation from Guadalcanal Island," January 20, 1950, John Toland Papers, Box 3, "Guadalcanal."

27. Ibid.
28. Masanobu Tsuji, "Guadalcanal," p. 57, unpublished memoir dated May 31, 1967, John Toland Papers, Series 1: The Rising Sun, Box 17.
29. Bix, *Hirohito and the Making of Modern Japan*, p. 461.
30. Joichiro Sanada, "Statement Concerning Particulars of Evacuation from Guadalcanal Island," January 20, 1950, John Toland Papers, Box 3, "Guadalcanal."
31. Adm. T. Koyanagi, memorandum entitled "The Retreat from Guadalcanal," dated May 1, 1967, John Toland Papers, Box 3, "Guadalcanal."
32. CINCPAC to COMINCH, "Solomon Islands Campaign—Fall of Guadalcanal, period 25 January to 10 February, 1943," April 17, 1943, in NARA, RG 38, "WWII Action and Operational Reports," Box 20, item 64, p. 13.
33. Adm. T. Koyanagi, memorandum entitled "The Retreat from Guadalcanal," dated May 1, 1967, pp. 6–8. John Toland Papers, Box 3, "Guadalcanal."
34. Yahachi Ishida letter (undated) in Gibney, ed., *Senso*, p. 132.
35. CINCPAC to COMINCH, "Solomon Islands Campaign—Fall of Guadalcanal, period 25 January to 10 February, 1943," April 17, 1943, in NARA, RG 38, "WWII Action and Operational Reports," Box 20, item 64, p. 14.
36. Adm. T. Koyanagi, memorandum entitled "The Retreat from Guadalcanal," dated May 1, 1967, p. 6, John Toland Papers, Box 3, "Guadalcanal."
37. CINCPAC to COMINCH, "Solomon Islands Campaign—Fall of Guadalcanal, period 25 January to 10 February, 1943," April 17, 1943, in NARA, RG 38, "WWII Action and Operational Reports," Box 20, item 81.
38. Glen C. H. Perry's notes, December 2, 1942, in Perry, *Dear Bart*, p. 114.
39. Agawa, *Reluctant Admiral*, p. 342.
40. Twining and Carey, *No Bended Knee*, p. ix.
41. Hara, *Japanese Destroyer Captain*, p. 93.
42. Nobutake Kondo, "Some Opinions Concerning the War," in Goldstein and Dillon, eds., *Pacific War Papers*, p. 313.
43. "Fire Scroll," *Book of Five Spheres*, quoted in Cleary, *Japanese Art of War*, p. 81.
44. Raizo Tanaka, "The Struggle for Guadalcanal," in Evans, ed., *Japanese Navy in World War II*, p. 209.
45. Hara, *Japanese Destroyer Captain*, p. 164.
46. Buell, *Dauntless Helldivers*, p. 208.
47. Vollinger, "World War II Memoirs of John Vollinger."
48. Robert Bostwick Carney, CCOH Naval History Project, No. 539, Vol. 1, p. 289.
49. Pyle, *Last Chapter*, p. 5.
50. Potter, *Bull Halsey*, p. 245.
51. Ibid., p. 247.
52. Capt. C. W. Fox, Supply Corps, USN, oral history, p. 10, recorded July 9, 1943, in NARA, RG 38, "World War II Oral Histories and Interviews, 1942–1946," Box 9.
53. Halsey and Bryan, *Admiral Halsey's Story*, p. 272.
54. Capt. C. W. Fox, Supply Corps, USN, oral history, p. 10, recorded July 9, 1943, in NARA, RG 38, "World War II Oral Histories and Interviews, 1942–1946," Box 9.

55. Entry dated November 4, 1943, in Fahey, *Pacific War Diary*, p. 71.
56. "Bull's-Eye."
57. Halsey to Nimitz, October 31, 1942, quoted in Hoyt, *How They Won the War in the Pacific*, pp. 172–73.
58. Dower, *War Without Mercy*, p. 79.
59. Solberg, *Decision and Dissent*, p. 37.
60. Lodge, "Halsey Predicts Victory This Year."
61. Fussell, *Wartime*, p. 117.
62. Lodge, "Halsey Predicts Victory This Year."
63. *New Zealand Herald*, January 7, 1943, excerpted in Halsey and Bryan, *Admiral Halsey's Story*, p. 143.
64. DeWitt Peck, CCOH Marine Corps Project, No. 701, p. 121.
65. Capt. Harold Hopkins, RN, to Edwin Hoyt, June 8, 1969, quoted in Hoyt, *How They Won the War in the Pacific*, p. 169.
66. Halsey to Nimitz, December 11, 1942, William Frederick Halsey Papers.
67. Spruance to Nimitz, February 18, 1960, Raymond A. Spruance Papers, MS Collection 12, Box 2, Folder 5.
68. Robert Bostwick Carney, CCOH Naval History Project, No. 539, Vol. 1, p. 293.
69. Entry dated November 4, 1943, in Fahey, *Pacific War Diary*, p. 71.
70. Halsey and Bryan, *Admiral Halsey's Story*, p. 139.
71. Vandegrift and Asprey, *Once a Marine*, p. 217.
72. Halsey and Bryan, *Admiral Halsey's Story*, p. 137.
73. Halsey to Nimitz, January 8, 1943, p. 6, William Frederick Halsey Papers.
74. Ibid.
75. Halsey to Nimitz, November 29, 1942, p. 1, William Frederick Halsey Papers.
76. Halsey and Bryan, *Admiral Halsey's Story*, p. 138.
77. Agawa, *Reluctant Admiral*, p. 331.
78. Ibid., p. 336.
79. Layton, Pineau, and Costello, *"And I Was There,"* p. 474.
80. Ibid., p. 475.
81. Edwin T. Layton, oral history, in Stillwell, *Air Raid, Pearl Harbor!*, p. 276.
82. Kenneth A. Boulier account in Russell, ed., *No Right to Win*, p. 236.
83. Entry dated April 18, 1944, in Ugaki, *Fading Victory*, pp. 330, 353.
84. Entry dated April 18, 1944, in ibid., p. 354.
85. Ibid., p. 355.
86. Entry dated May 22, 1943, in Kiyosawa, *Diary of Darkness*, p. 29.
87. Agawa, *Reluctant Admiral*, p. 392.

Chapter Eight

1. Special Service Division, *Instructions for American Servicemen in Australia*.
2. Leckie, *Helmet for My Pillow*, p. 140.

3. Ibid., p. 144.
4. Alex Haley, "The Most Unforgettable Character I've Ever Met," in Shenk, ed., *Authors at War*, p. 127.
5. Keresey, *PT 105*, p. 131.
6. Entry dated October 24, 1943, in Fahey, *Pacific War Diary*, p. 58.
7. Ralph, *They Passed This Way*, p. 158.
8. " 'Shocking' Street Scenes at Night."
9. Lake, "Desire for a Yank," p. 623.
10. *Courier-Mail*, October 29, 1942, p. 4.
11. "Hey! You Diggers! He Came, He Saw, He Conquered," Wolfson Collection of Decorative and Propaganda Arts.
12. *Truth* (Brisbane), June 14, 1942.
13. Manchester, *American Caesar*, p. 286.
14. Perry, *Most Dangerous Man in America*, p. 192.
15. Thomas C. Kinkaid, CCOH Naval History Project, No. 429, Vol. 1, pp. 250–51.
16. Ibid., p. 254.
17. Schaller, *Douglas MacArthur*, p. 72.
18. Childs, *I Write from Washington*, p. 251.
19. Manchester, *American Caesar*, p. 327.
20. COMINCH to CINCPAC, March 27, 1942, in CINCPAC War Diary, Book 1, p. 534.
21. "CINCPAC Conference in *Argonne*," September 28, 1942, p. 1, in Samuel Eliot Morison Papers, Coll/606, Box 24.
22. Halsey and Bryan, *Admiral Halsey's Story*, pp. 154–55.
23. MacArthur, *Reminiscences*, pp. 173–74.
24. Robert Bostwick Carney, CCOH Naval History Project, No. 539, Vol. 1, p. 329.
25. Manchester, *American Caesar*, p. 338.
26. Reiji Masuda, account in Cook and Cook, eds., *Japan at War*, p. 302.
27. Kenney, *General Kenney Reports*, p. 206.
28. Radike, *Across the Dark Islands*, p. 135.
29. MacArthur, *Reminiscences*, p. 169.
30. Robert Bostwick Carney, CCOH Naval History Project, No. 539, Vol. 1, p. 315.
31. U.S.S. *Dunlap* Action Report, August 18, 1943, enclosure (A), 18: DD384/A16-3 Serial 012, in NARA, RG 38.
32. Hara, *Japanese Destroyer Captain*, p. 179.
33. Mimeo Secret Outline Plan, pp. 241–43, "Outline Plan for Opns of the SWPA, 1944," Reno III: General Headquarters Southwest Pacific Area, October 20, 1943, online at http://www.ibiblio.org/hyperwar/USA/USA-P-Strategy/Strategy-W.html (accessed November 3, 2014).
34. Ibid.
35. Entry dated November 2, 1943, in Fahey, *Pacific War Diary*, p. 65.
36. Fitzhugh Lee, oral history, in Wooldbridge, ed., *Carrier Warfare in the Pacific*, p. 111.

37. Potter and Nimitz, *Great Sea War*, p. 301.
38. Okumiya, Horikoshi, and Caidin, *Zero!*, pp. 222–23.
39. Ibid., p. 225.
40. Ibid., p. 224.
41. Manchester, *American Caesar*, p. 338.
42. Robert Bostwick Carney, CCOH Naval History Project, No. 539, Vol. 1, p. 315.
43. Ibid., pp. 313–14.
44. "Narrative by Lieut. Graham C. Bonnell, US Navy," recorded January 25, 1944, in NARA, RG 38, "World War II Oral Histories and Interviews, 1942–1946," Box 1.
45. Ibid.

Chapter Nine

1. Beaver, *Sailor from Oklahoma*, p. 216.
2. Mason, *Rendezvous with Destiny*, p. 93.
3. Harris, Mitchell, and Schechter, eds., *Homefront*, p. 35.
4. Archibald, *Wartime Shipyard*, p. 17.
5. Ibid., p. 192.
6. Ibid., p. 193.
7. Russell, *Hell Above, Deep Water Below*, p. 39.
8. Grider and Sims, *War Fish*, p. 22.
9. Russell, *Hell Above, Deep Water Below*, p. 74.
10. COMINCH to CINCPAC, February 22, 1942, in CINCPAC War Diary, Book 1, p. 252.
11. Alan Polhemus, interview at the Independence Seaport Museum, Philadelphia, PA, October 17, 2000. Transcript in the museum archives.
12. Grider and Sims, *War Fish*, p. 43.
13. Ibid., p. 43.
14. U.S.S. *Wahoo*, "Report of First War Patrol," entry dated October 5, 1942, in McDaniel, ed., *U.S.S. Wahoo (SS-238)*, p. 9.
15. Grider and Sims, *War Fish*, p. 41.
16. O'Kane, *Wahoo*, p. 61.
17. Grider and Sims, *War Fish*, p. 45.
18. Russell, *Hell Above, Deep Water Below*, p. 185.
19. Grider and Sims, *War Fish*, p. 51.
20. Sterling, *Wake of the Wahoo*, p. 17.
21. U.S.S. *Wahoo*, "Report of First War Patrol," entry dated November 8, 1942, in McDaniel, ed., *U.S.S. Wahoo (SS-238)*, p. 27.
22. O'Kane, *Wahoo*, p. 76.
23. Sterling, *Wake of the Wahoo*, p. 17.
24. O'Kane, *Wahoo*, p. 81.
25. Grider and Sims, *War Fish*, p. 52.

26. Sterling, *Wake of the Wahoo*, p. 26.
27. O'Kane, *Wahoo*, p. 82.
28. Ibid., p. 83.
29. Ibid., p. 94.
30. Grider and Sims, *War Fish*, p. 49.
31. Admiral James Fife Jr., "U.S.S. *Wahoo*, Second War Patrol, Comments on," December 28, 1942, in McDaniel, ed., *U.S.S. Wahoo (SS-238)*, p. 43.
32. Sterling, *Wake of the Wahoo*, p. 72.
33. O'Kane, *Wahoo*, p. 117.
34. Sterling, *Wake of the Wahoo*, p. 76.
35. Grider and Sims, *War Fish*, p. 51.
36. Quoted in O'Kane, *Wahoo*, p. 121.
37. Grider and Sims, *War Fish*, p. 54.
38. Ibid., p. 59.
39. Ibid., p. 60.
40. Sterling, *Wake of the Wahoo*, p. 81.
41. O'Kane, *Wahoo*, p. 138.
42. Ibid., p. 177.
43. Ibid., p. 138.
44. Ibid., p. 139.
45. Sterling, *Wake of the Wahoo*, p. 81.
46. O'Kane, *Wahoo*, p. 139.
47. Sterling, *Wake of the Wahoo*, p. 82.
48. O'Kane, *Wahoo*, p. 143.
49. Ibid., p. 148.
50. Ibid., p. 150.
51. Ibid., p. 153.
52. Ibid.
53. Grider and Sims, *War Fish*, p. 73.
54. Sterling, *Wake of the Wahoo*, p. 100.
55. O'Kane, *Wahoo*, p. 154.
56. U.S.S. *Wahoo*, "Report of Third War Patrol," entry dated January 26, 1943, in McDaniel, ed., *U.S.S. Wahoo (SS-238)*, p. 51.
57. O'Kane, *Wahoo*, p. 160.
58. Ibid., pp. 161–62.
59. Ibid., p. 163.
60. Ibid., p. 164.
61. Ibid., p. 166.
62. Ibid., p. 168.
63. Sterling, *Wake of the Wahoo*, p. 119.
64. O'Kane, *Wahoo*, pp. 161–62.
65. Blair, *Silent Victory*, p. 341.
66. Ibid., p. 879.

67. Edward L. Beach, "Culpable Negligence," in Sears, ed., *Eyewitness to World War II*, p. 70.

68. R. W. Christie to Samuel Eliot Morison, February 11, 1949, Samuel Eliot Morison Papers, Coll/606, Box 24.

69. Blair, *Silent Victory*, p. 391.

70. Ibid, p. 414.

71. Ibid.

72. Ibid., p. 403.

73. Ibid., p. 404.

74. Atsushi Oi, "Why Japan's Antisubmarine Warfare Failed," in Evans, ed., *Japanese Navy in World War II*, p. 410.

75. Reiji Masuda account in Cook and Cook, eds., *Japan at War*, p. 304.

76. Ibid., p. 303.

77. For example, see Yuji Nishihama's letter (undated) to the editor of the *Asahi Shinbun*, in Gibney, ed., *Senso*, pp. 139–40.

78. JANAC, "Japanese Naval and Merchant Shipping Losses During World War II by All Causes," February 1947, Chronological List of Japanese Merchant Vessel Losses, pp. 29–99. The total in November 1943 was 70 ships with aggregate tonnage of 320,807, the great majority credited to submarines.

79. Navy Department Intelligence Report, "Japan Merchant Marine Losses," December 15, 1943, Serial P1 23–41, FDR Map Room Papers, Box 160, MR 400, "Jap Reference Folder, 1942–1945."

80. USSBS, *Effects of Strategic Bombing on Japan's War Economy*, Appendix Table C-50, "Japanese Imports, Production, and Inventories of Crude Oil," p. 135.

81. JANAC, "Japanese Naval and Merchant Shipping Losses During World War II by All Causes," February 1947, Table 1: "Summaries of Japanese Shipping Losses," p. vi.

82. Smith and Finch, *Coral and Brass*, p. 235.

Chapter Ten

1. Wallin, "Rejuvenation at Pearl Harbor," p. 1536.

2. Downes, "How a War Was Won and a City Vanished at Pearl Harbor."

3. Raymer, *Descent into Darkness*, p. 4.

4. Ibid., 4.

5. Wallin, "Rejuvenation at Pearl Harbor," p. 1535.

6. Trumbull, "Repair: VI."

7. Department of the Navy, *Building the Navy's Bases in World War II*, Vol. 2, p. 130.

8. Trumbull, "Repair: IV."

9. Mason, *Battleship Sailor*, p. 21.

10. Hynes, *Flights of Passage*, p. 160.

11. Wilson, "Soldier and a Jukebox."

12. Brown, *Hawaii Goes to War*, 92.
13. Richardson, *Reflections of Pearl Harbor*, p. 41.
14. "Honolulu: Island Boomtown."
15. Ibid.
16. Bailey and Farber, *First Strange Place*, p. 105.
17. Jean O'Hara's unpublished memoir, cited in ibid., p. 112.
18. Michael Bak Jr., USNI Oral History Program, 1988.
19. Bailey and Farber, *First Strange Place*, p. 55.
20. Ibid., p. 33.
21. Wilson, "War Workers as a Social Group."
22. "Interracial Marriage in Hawaii."
23. "Honolulu: Island Boomtown."
24. Davis, *Sinking the Rising Sun*, p. 149.
25. Lt. Robert C. Ruark, USNR, "Ho-Hum in Hawaii," *Liberty*, April 21, 1945, quoted in Bailey and Farber, *First Strange Place*, p. 59.
26. Lamar, "I Saw Stars," p. 16.
27. Ibid., p. 43.
28. Ralph C. Parker, CCOH Naval History Project, No. 507, p. 128.
29. Ibid., p. 131.
30. Lamar, "I Saw Stars," p. 11.
31. Thomas H. Dyer, USNI Oral History Program, 1986, pp. 282–84.
32. Brown, *Hawaii Goes to War*, p. 97.
33. Arlen, "Year in Retrospect."
34. Interview with Raymond A. Spruance by Philippe de Baussel for Paris *Match*, July 6, 1965, p. 1, Raymond A. Spruance Papers, MS Collection 12, Box 1, Folder 1.
35. Donald Duncan, CCOH Naval History Project, No. 678, Vol. 7, p. 415.
36. Ibid., p. 399.
37. Ibid., pp. 418–19.
38. James S. Russell, CCOH Aviation Project, 1960, Part 4, Part 1.
39. Donald Duncan, CCOH Naval History Project, No. 678, Vol. 7, p. 416.
40. James S. Russell, CCOH Aviation Project, 1960, Part 4, Part 1, p. 21.
41. Davis, *Sinking the Rising Sun*, pp. 107–8.
42. War Production Board, "Official Munitions Report of the U.S.," No. 21, December 1, 1943, "Airplanes by Plants," Harry L. Hopkins Papers.
43. Herbert D. Riley account in Wooldridge, ed., *Carrier Warfare in the Pacific*, p. 103.
44. Hynes, *Flights of Passage*, pp. 142–43.
45. Buell, *Dauntless Helldivers*, p. 215.
46. Herbert D. Riley account in Wooldridge, ed., *Carrier Warfare in the Pacific*, p. 102.
47. War Production Board, "Official Munitions Report of the U.S.," No. 21, December 1, 1943, "Airplanes by Plants," p. 28, Harry L. Hopkins Papers.
48. "Extract of Notes by Fleet Admiral Ernest J. King for the J.C.S. Historical Section," p. 2, Ernest J. King Papers.

49. U.S. Department of State, *Foreign Relations of the United States [FRUS]: The Conferences at Washington, 1941–1942, and Casablanca, 1943. III. The Casablanca Conference*, p. 549.

50. Ibid., p. 536.

51. Entry dated January 16, 1943, in Alanbrooke, *War Diaries*, p. 359.

52. Entry dated January 14, 1943, in ibid., p. 356.

53. Entry dated January 16, 1943, in ibid., p. 359.

54. Ibid., p. 360.

55. Excerpts to follow are drawn from Combined Chiefs of Staff minutes at Casablanca. U.S. Department of State, *FRUS: The Conferences at Washington, 1941–1942, and Casablanca, 1943. III. The Casablanca Conference*, pp. 560–775.

56. Entry dated May 4, 1943, in Alanbrooke, *War Diaries*, p. 398.

57. U.S. Department of State, *FRUS, 1943, Conferences at Washington and Quebec, 1943*, Vol. 1, p. 93.

58. Ibid., p. 146.

59. Entry dated May 17, 1943, in Alanbrooke, *War Diaries*, p. 405.

60. U.S. Department of State, *FRUS, 1943, Conferences at Washington and Quebec, 1943*, Vol. 1, p. 369.

61. "Memorandum for the Joint Chiefs of Staff," June 10, 1943, in NARA, RG 38, "CNO Zero-Zero Files," Box 38, in file "Memos to General Marshall, 1942–1944."

62. "War Department 4952-15," June 14, 1943, in CINCPAC War Diary, Book 3, p. 1604.

63. COMSOPAC to CINCPAC, June 25, 1943, in ibid., p. 1611.

64. Interview with Raymond A. Spruance by Philippe de Baussel for Paris *Match*, July 6, 1965, pp. 3–4, Raymond A. Spruance Papers, MS Collection 12, Box 1, Folder 1.

65. Charles Moore, CCOH Naval History Project, No. 655, Vol. 5, p. 803.

66. Spruance to RADM E. M. Eller, July 22, 1966, Raymond A. Spruance Papers, MS Collection 12, Box 2, Folder 7.

67. King and Whitehall, *Fleet Admiral King*, p. 491 (footnote).

68. Charles Moore, CCOH Naval History Project, No. 655, Vol. 5, p. 803.

69. Ibid., p. 805.

70. Interview with Raymond A. Spruance by Philippe de Baussel for Paris *Match*, July 6, 1965, p. 6, Raymond A. Spruance Papers, MS Collection 12, Box 1, Folder 1.

71. CINCPAC to COMSOPAC, June 26, 1943, William Frederick Halsey Papers, Box 15.

72. Interview with Raymond A. Spruance by Philippe de Baussel for Paris *Match*, July 6, 1965, pp. 6–7, Raymond A. Spruance Papers, MS Collection 12, Box 1, Folder 1.

73. Smith and Finch, *Coral and Brass*, p. 109.

74. Ibid., p. 110.

75. Charles Moore, CCOH Naval History Project, No. 655, Vol. 5, p. 827.

76. Ibid., pp. 825–26.

77. Dyer, *Amphibians Came to Conquer*, p. 618.

78. Stevenson and Calder, *Island Landfalls*, p. 47.
79. Julian C. Smith, Lt. Gen., US Marine Corps, (ret.); Mr. Benis M. Frank, interviewer, Historical Division, Headquarters, U.S. Marine Corps, Washington, DC, pp. 275–76.
80. "Report of Amphibious Operations for the Capture of the Gilbert Islands, from Cmdr. Fifth Amphibious Force to COMINCH," December 4, 1943, Serial 00165, enclosure C, in USMC Archives, "WWII, Tarawa and Makin, 1943," Box 6.
81. Ibid., p. 2.
82. Bryan, *Aircraft Carrier*, p. 109.
83. Hoyt, *How They Won the War in the Pacific*, p. 256.
84. Interview with Raymond A. Spruance by Philippe de Baussel for Paris *Match*, July 6, 1965, p. 5, Raymond A. Spruance Papers, MS Collection 12, Box 1, Folder 1.
85. Towers to Forrestal, August 18, 1943, Spruance Papers, quoted in Hoyt, *How They Won the War in the Pacific*, p. 255.
86. Spruance to Savvy Cooke, February 9, 1963, Raymond A. Spruance Papers, MS Collection 12, Box 2, Folder 6.
87. Hoyt, *How They Won the War in the Pacific*, p. 257.
88. Clark and Reynolds, *Carrier Admiral*, p. 90.
89. Reynolds, *On the Warpath in the Pacific*, p. 1.
90. Ibid., p. 163.
91. Chief Petty Officer C. S. King account in Wooldridge, ed., *Carrier Warfare in the Pacific*, p. 279.
92. Reynolds, *On the Warpath in the Pacific*, p. 161.
93. Joseph J. Clark, CCOH Naval History Project, Part 2, Vol. 2.
94. Clark, *Carrier Admiral*, p. 108.
95. Donald Duncan, CCOH Naval History Project, No. 678, Vol. 7.
96. Fitzhugh Lee account in Wooldridge, ed., *Carrier Warfare in the Pacific*, p. 107.
97. George W. Anderson Jr., USNI Oral History Program, 1983, pp. 112–13.
98. Ibid.
99. Reynolds, *On the Warpath in the Pacific*, p. 221.
100. Joseph J. Clark, CCOH Naval History Project, Part 2, Vol. 2, p. 417.
101. Ibid., pp. 412–13.
102. George W. Anderson Jr., USNI Oral History Program, 1983, p. 115.
103. Reynolds, *On the Warpath in the Pacific*, p. 223.
104. Harry W. Hill, CCOH Naval History Project, No. 685, Vol. 3, p. 290.
105. Ibid., p. 297.
106. "Report of Operations, Galvanic," Commanding General, 2nd MarDiv, from CO, CT-6. Ref: (a) Ltr CG, 2ndMarDiv, RMC CT/541, serial 002ND2 (Secret), dated November 11, 1943, in USMC Archives: "WWII, Tarawa and Makin, 1943," Box 6.
107. Julian C. Smith, Lt. Gen., US Marine Corps, (ret.), Mr. Benis M. Frank, inter-

viewer, Historical Division, Headquarters, U.S. Marine Corps, Washington, DC, p. 286.

108. CINCPAC to COMINCH, June 20, 1943, in CINCPAC War Diary, Book 3, p. 1607.

109. Dyer, *Amphibians Came to Conquer*, p. 608.

110. Smith and Finch, *Coral and Brass*, p. 120.

111. Julian C. Smith, Lt. Gen., US Marine Corps, (ret.), Mr. Benis M. Frank, interviewer, Historical Division, Headquarters, U.S. Marine Corps, Washington, DC, p. 287.

112. "Corps Operation Plan Number 1–43," Annex Baker, p. 14, Fifth Amphibious Corps files.

113. "Corps Operation Plan Number 1–43," Annex Able, p. 4, Fifth Amphibious Corps files.

114. Charles Moore, CCOH Naval History Project, No. 655, Vol. 5, p. 830.

115. Ibid., p. 836.

116. Ibid., p. 834.

Chapter Eleven

1. Frank W. J. Plant, personal account, No. 1024, USMC Archives.

2. Ray Gard quoted in Reynolds, *On the Warpath in the Pacific*, p. 274.

3. Charles Moore, CCOH Naval History Project, No. 655, Vol. 5, p. 831.

4. Lucas, *Combat Correspondent*, p. 175.

5. Roger Bond account in Wooldridge, ed., *Carrier Warfare in the Pacific*, p. 132.

6. Frank W. J. Plant, personal account, No. 1024, USMC Archives.

7. CINCPAC War Diary, November 15, 1943, Vol. 4, p. 1686.

8. Reynolds, *On the Warpath in the Pacific*, p. 274.

9. Joseph J. Clark, CCOH Naval History Project, Part 2, Vol. 2, p. 438.

10. For example, see Donald Duncan, CCOH Naval History Project, No. 678, Vol. 7, p. 426.

11. Truman J. Hedding account in Wooldridge, ed., *Carrier Warfare in the Pacific*, pp. 117–18.

12. Spruance to Professor Potter, March 3, 1955, on Naval Task Force organization in World War II, Raymond A. Spruance Papers, MS Collection 12, Box 2, Folder 4.

13. Hoyt, *How They Won the War in the Pacific*, p. 280.

14. "Colonel Weller's Report of NGF at Tarawa," (undated), Julian C. Smith Papers, COLL/202, Series 4, Tarawa.

15. Julian C. Smith, Lt. Gen., US Marine Corps, (ret.), Mr. Benis M. Frank, interviewer, Historical Division, Headquarters, U.S. Marine Corps, Washington, DC, p. 281.

16. Sherrod, *Tarawa*, p. 61.

17. Rogal, *Guadalcanal, Tarawa and Beyond*, p. 122.

18. Sherrod, *Tarawa*, p. 62.

19. Charles Moore, CCOH Naval History Project, No. 655, Vol. 5, p. 855.

20. Manchester, *Goodbye, Darkness*, p. 223.

21. Frank W. J. Plant, personal account, No. 1024, p. 22, USMC Archives.

22. Rogal, *Guadalcanal, Tarawa and Beyond*, p. 124.

23. Lt. G. D. Lillibridge, 1967, PC No. 1342, USMC Archives.

24. Frank W. J. Plant, personal account, No. 1024, p. 23, USMC Archives.

25. Sherrod, *Tarawa*, p. 68.

26. David M. Shoup, oral history, p. 2, Fifth Amphibious Corps files.

27. Frank W. J. Plant, personal account, No. 1024, USMC Archives.

28. CO, LT 1/6 to C.G., 2nd MarDiv, December, 6, 1943, "Report of Operations, GALVANIC," USMC Archives.

29. Sherrod, "Marines' Show."

30. Lt. G. D. Lillibridge, 1967, PC No. 1342, USMC Archives.

31. Julian C. Smith, oral history, p. 293, Historical Division, Headquarters, U.S. Marine Corps, Washington, DC.

32. Smith and Finch, *Coral and Brass*, p. 122.

33. Rogal, *Guadalcanal, Tarawa and Beyond*, p. 127.

34. Frank W. J. Plant, personal account, No. 1024, USMC Archives.

35. Sherrod, "Marines' Show."

36. Marshall Ralph Doak, *My Years in the Navy*, online at http://www.historycentral .com/Navy/Doak (accessed November 10, 2014).

37. Rogal, *Guadalcanal, Tarawa and Beyond*, p. 128.

38. Ibid., pp. 128–29.

39. Sherrod, "Marines' Show."

40. Vern Garrett, oral history, in Smith and Meehl, eds., *Pacific War Stories*, p. 159.

41. Sherrod, *Tarawa*, p. 96.

42. Wukovits, *One Square Mile of Hell*, p. 165.

43. Frank W. J. Plant, personal account, No. 1024, USMC Archives.

44. Robert B. Sheeks, oral history, in Smith and Meehl, eds., *Pacific War Stories*, p. 188.

45. Sherrod, *Tarawa*, p. 97.

46. Ibid., p. 93.

47. Frank W. J. Plant, personal account, No. 1024, USMC Archives.

48. Alex Vraciu quoted in Astor, *Wings of Gold*, p. 209.

49. Jim Pearce quoted in ibid.

50. Frank W. J. Plant, personal account, No. 1024, USMC Archives.

51. Wukovits, *One Square Mile of Hell*, p. 183.

52. Sherrod, *Tarawa*, p. 101.

53. Lt. Melvin A. Traylor Jr. quoted in Wukovits, *One Square Mile of Hell*, p. 187.

54. Sherrod, *Tarawa*, p. 95.

55. Ibid., p. 77.

56. Ibid., p. 96.

57. Sherrod, "Marines' Show."

58. Smith and Finch, *Coral and Brass*, p. 125.

59. Lucas, *Combat Correspondent*, p. 200.

60. Cooper, *Navy Nurse*, p. 87.

61. R. K. Turner to Spruance, November 30, 1943, Raymond A. Spruance Papers, MS Collection 12, Series I, correspondence.

62. "Commander of Central Pacific Force, War Diary," November 23, 1943, entry, p. 20, FDR Map Room Papers, Box 182.

63. Smith and Finch, *Coral and Brass*, p. 129.

64. H. W. Hill to Spruance, November 25, 1943, p. 2, Raymond A. Spruance Papers, MS Collection 12, Series I, correspondence.

65. Arthur Lamar, "Recollections of Fleet Admiral Nimitz," USNI Oral History Program, 1970, p. 40.

66. Vandegrift and Asprey, *Once a Marine*, p. 236.

67. Smith and Finch, *Coral and Brass*, p. 132.

68. Memorandum, King to Nimitz regarding the loss of U.S.S. *Liscome Bay* (CVE-56), December 30, 1943, Serial 002903, in NARA, RG 38, Records of the Office of the CNO, Box 36.

69. Michael Bak Jr., USNI Oral History Program, 1988.

70. Ibid.

71. Memorandum, King to Nimitz regarding the loss of U.S.S. *Liscome Bay* (CVE-56), December 30, 1943, Serial 002903, in NARA, RG 38, Records of the Office of the CNO, Box 36.

72. Potter and Nimitz, *Great Sea War*, p. 323.

73. Major J. F. Mills quoted by Lucas, *Combat Correspondent*, p. 170.

74. Harry W. Hill, CCOH Naval History Project, No. 685, Vol. 3, p. 305.

75. Edson's remarks excerpted in "Colonel Weller's Report of NGF at Tarawa" (undated), Julian C. Smith Papers, COLL/202, Series 4, Tarawa.

76. Memorandum King to Nimitz, December 16, 1943, Serial: 04258, Holland M. Smith Collection, COLL/2949, Box 1.

77. Lamar, "I Saw Stars," p. 16.

78. Vandegrift and Asprey, *Once a Marine*, p. 232.

79. Julian Smith to Willie Llew, December 20, 1943, Julian C. Smith Papers, COLL/202, Box 8, Series 7, Correspondence, December 1943.

80. Julian Smith to Warren W. Brown, December 25, 1943, ibid.

81. Julian Smith to Islar Simms, December 25, 1943, ibid.

82. For example, see Spruance to Samuel Eliot Morison, March 19, 1963, Raymond A. Spruance Papers, MS Collection 12, Box 2, Folder 6.

83. "Mid-Pacific Stronghold," p. 19.

84. Smith and Finch, *Coral and Brass*, p. 134.

85. Julian C. Smith, Lt. Gen., US Marine Corps, (ret.), Mr. Benis M. Frank, interviewer, Historical Division, Headquarters, U.S. Marine Corps, Washington, DC, p. 309.

86. C.O. *Yorktown*, "Report on Operation Galvanic, 19 November to 27 November, 1943," in NARA, RG 38, "WWII Action and Operational Reports," Box 14.

87. Lt. (jg) Ralph Hanks, oral history, in Hammel, ed., *Aces Against Japan*, p. 170.

88. Diary of Alexander Wilding Jr. quoted in Reynolds, *On the Warpath in the Pacific*, p. 276.

89. Truman J. Hedding (ret.), USNI Oral History Program, 1972.

90. Ibid.

91. C.O. *Yorktown*, "Report on Operation Galvanic, 19 November to 27 November, 1943," in NARA, RG 38, "WWII Action and Operational Reports," Box 14.

92. Fitzhugh Lee account in Wooldridge, ed., *Carrier Warfare in the Pacific*, p. 112.

93. Quoted in Reynolds, *On the Warpath in the Pacific*, p. 282.

94. C.O. *Yorktown*, "Report on Operation Galvanic, 19 November to 27 November, 1943," in NARA, RG 38, "WWII Action and Operational Reports," Box 14.

95. Clark and Reynolds, *Carrier Admiral*, p. 134.

96. Truman J. Hedding (ret.), USNI Oral History Program, 1972.

97. C.O. *Yorktown*, "Report on Operation Galvanic, 19 November to 27 November, 1943," in NARA, RG 38, "WWII Action and Operational Reports," Box 14.

98. Truman J. Hedding (ret.), USNI Oral History Program, 1972.

99. Clark and Reynolds, *Carrier Admiral*, pp. 136–37.

100. Kernan, *Crossing the Line*, p. 99.

101. Ibid.

102. Ibid., p. 100.

103. Ibid., p. 102.

104. Ibid., p. 106.

105. Ibid.

106. Clark and Reynolds, *Carrier Admiral*, p. 138.

107. Ibid., p. 139.

108. Joseph J. Clark, CCOH Naval History Project, Part 2, Vol. 2, p. 432.

109. Reynolds, *On the Warpath in the Pacific*, p. 292.

110. *Honolulu Star-Bulletin*, January 27, 1944, quoted in Clark and Reynolds, *Carrier Admiral*, p. 140.

111. *U.S.S. Essex* Cruise Book, 1944 (unpaginated).

112. George W. Anderson Jr., USNI Oral History Program, 1983, p. 120.

113. Joseph J. Clark, CCOH Naval History Project, Part 2, Vol. 2, p. 444.

Chapter Twelve

1. Edwin T. Layton, "Recollections of Fleet Admiral Nimitz," USNI Oral History Program, 1970, p. 90.

2. USSBS, *Interrogations of Japanese Officials*, No. 139, Interrogation Nav No. 34, Interrogation of Commander Nakajima, Chikataka, Imperial Japanese Navy, October 21, 1945, p. 143.

3. Joseph J. Clark, CCOH Naval History Project, Part 2, Vol. 2, p. 445.

4. Edwin T. Layton, "Recollections of Fleet Admiral Nimitz," USNI Oral History Program, 1970, p. 91.

5. Buell, *Dauntless Helldivers*, pp. 215–35.
6. Roger Bond account in Wooldridge, ed., *Carrier Warfare in the Pacific*, p. 132.
7. C. S. King account in ibid., p. 285.
8. David S. McCampbell account in ibid., p. 196.
9. Mitscher quoted by Arleigh A. Burke in ibid., p. 167.
10. Arleigh A. Burke account in ibid., pp. 167–68.
11. CINCPAC War Diary, Book 5, pp. 1834–47.
12. Sherman, *Combat Command*, p. 226.
13. Smith and Finch, *Coral and Brass*, p. 145.
14. Truman J. Hedding (ret.), USNI Oral History Program, 1972.
15. Smith and Finch, *Coral and Brass*, p. 144.
16. Shaw et al., *History of U.S. Marine Corps Operations in World War II*, p. 152.
17. Richard L. Conolly to Commandant of Marine Corps, November 26, 1952, in ibid.
18. 1st Lt. Samuel H. Zutty quoted in ibid., p. 171.
19. Smith and Finch, *Coral and Brass*, p. 146.
20. Kenneth Dodson letter dated February 9, 1944, in Shenk, ed., *Authors at Sea*, p. 293.
21. Ibid., pp. 294–96.
22. Potter, *Nimitz*, p. 334.
23. Astor, *Wings of Gold*, p. 224.
24. Beaver, *Sailor from Oklahoma*, p. 283.
25. Smith and Finch, *Coral and Brass*, p. 148.
26. Entry dated January 6, 1944, in CINCPAC War Diary, Book 5, p. 1833.
27. "Special Report of FLINTLOCK and CATCHPOLE Operations," March 1, 1944, p. 7, USMC Archives.
28. Harry W. Hill, CCOH Naval History Project, No. 685, Vol. 3, p. 297.
29. Shaw et al., *History of U.S. Marine Corps Operations in World War II*, p. 227.
30. Sherman, *Combat Command*, p. 226.
31. CINCPAC to COMINCH, December 26, 1943, in CINCPAC War Diary, Book 4, p. 1830.
32. Ramage, "Raid on Truk."
33. Astor, *Wings of Gold*, p. 227.
34. Minoru Nomura, "Ozawa in the Pacific," in Evans, ed., *Japanese Navy in World War II*, p. 291.
35. Ramage, "Raid on Truk."
36. Astor, *Wings of Gold*, p. 229.
37. Masataka Chihaya, "Account of the Fiasco of Truk," in Goldstein and Dillon, eds., *Pacific War Papers*, p. 279.
38. Astor, *Wings of Gold*, p. 223.
39. Boyington, *Baa Baa Black Sheep*, p. 250.
40. Ibid., p. 252.
41. Statement of Lt. (jg) Woodward M. Hampton, VF-1, Ernest J. King Papers, Box 9.

42. Ibid.
43. Ramage, "Raid on Truk."
44. Sherman, *Combat Command*, p. 230.
45. Astor, *Wings of Gold*, p. 235.
46. Charles Moore, CCOH Naval History Project, No. 655, Vol. 5, pp. 896–97.
47. William I. Martin account in Wooldridge, ed., *Carrier Warfare in the Pacific*, p. 149.
48. Masataka Chihaya, "Account of the Fiasco of Truk," in Goldstein and Dillon, eds., *Pacific War Papers*, p. 282.
49. "Return Visit."
50. Ibid.

Chapter Thirteen

1. Agawa, *Reluctant Admiral*, pp. 196–97.
2. Entry dated August 5, 1943, *Sugiyama Memo*, 2 vols. (Tokyo: Hara Shobso, 1967), quoted in Irokawa, *Age of Hirohito*, p. 91.
3. "New Operational Policy" document quoted in Bix, *Hirohito and the Making of Modern Japan*, p. 468.
4. Ibid.
5. Minoru Nomura, "Ozawa in the Pacific," in Evans, ed., *Japanese Navy in World War II*, p. 295.
6. Okumiya, Horikoshi, and Caidin, *Zero!*, p. 228.
7. Ibid., p. 227.
8. Morison, *History of United States Naval Operations in World War II*, Vol. 7, p. 331.
9. *Mainichi Shinbun*, February 23, 1944, quoted in entry dated March 16, 1944, in Kiyosawa, *Diary of Darkness*, p. 160.
10. Entry dated October 5, 1943, in ibid., p. 91.
11. Lt. Cmdr. Iyozo Fujita, oral history, in Werneth, ed., *Beyond Pearl Harbor*, p. 241.
12. Atsushi Oi, "The Japanese Navy in 1941," in Goldstein and Dillon, eds., *Pacific War Papers*, p. 23.
13. Sakai, Caidin, and Saito, *Samurai!*, p. 185.
14. Horikoshi, Shindo, and Wanteiz, *Eagles of Mitsubishi*, p. 141.
15. Minoru Nomura, "Ozawa in the Pacific," in Evans, ed., *Japanese Navy in World War II*, p. 300.
16. Sakai, Caidin, and Saito, *Samurai!*, p. 27.
17. Okumiya, Horikoshi, and Caidin, *Zero!*, pp. 36–37.
18. Saburo Sakai oral history, in Cook and Cook, eds., *Japan at War*, p. 139.
19. Ibid., p. 140.
20. Tagaya, *Imperial Japanese Naval Aviator*, p. 9.
21. Sakai, Caidin, and Saito, *Samurai!*, p. 27.
22. Entry dated March 12, 1944, in Kiyosawa, *Diary of Darkness*, p. 154.
23. Entry dated May 30, 1944, in ibid., p. 202.

24. Entry dated September 30, 1944, in ibid., p. 259.
25. Potter, *Nimitz*, p. 358.
26. Julian C. Smith, Lt. Gen., US Marine Corps, (ret.), Mr. Benis M. Frank, interviewer, Historical Division, Headquarters, U.S. Marine Corps, Washington, DC, p. 307.
27. Hoyt, *How They Won the War in the Pacific*, p. 371.
28. U.S. Department of State, *FRUS, 1943, The Conferences at Cairo and Tehran*, Vol. 4, p. 780.
29. Coffey, *Hap*, p. 334.
30. Potter, *Nimitz*, p. 340.
31. Ibid., p. 342.
32. Kenney, *General Kenney Reports*, p. 348.
33. Potter, *Nimitz*, p. 343.
34. Ibid., p. 344.
35. Ibid., p. 354.
36. Terasaki and Miller, *Bridge to the Sun*, p. 134.
37. Aiko Takahashi diary, entry dated April 21, 1943, in Yamashita, ed., *Leaves from an Autumn of Emergencies*, p. 169.
38. Entry dated September 9, 1943, in Kiyosawa, *Diary of Darkness*, p. 76.
39. Entry dated December 9, 1943, in ibid., p. 117.
40. Entry dated September 11, 1943, in ibid., p. 77.
41. "Battle of the Spirits," *Japan Times and Advertiser*, August 24, 1943.
42. Entry dated May 26, 1943, in Kiyosawa, *Diary of Darkness*, p. 31.
43. Entry dated September 5, 1943, in ibid., p. 75.
44. "Position Truly Grave," *Advertiser* (Adelaide, Australia), October 27, 1943, p. 1.
45. Cook and Cook, eds., *Japan at War*, p. 173.
46. Aiko Takahashi diary, entry dated June 10, 1943, in Yamashita, ed., *Leaves from an Autumn of Emergencies*, p. 170.
47. Maintenance Lt. Hiroshi Suzuki, oral history, in Werneth, ed., *Beyond Pearl Harbor*, p. 93.
48. Minoru Nomura, "Ozawa in the Pacific," in Evans, ed., *Japanese Navy in World War II*, p. 306.
49. Entry dated May 31, 1944, in Ugaki, *Fading Victory*, p. 380.
50. Navy Directive No. 373 quoted in Minoru Nomura, "Ozawa in the Pacific," in Evans, ed., *Japanese Navy in World War II*, p. 310.
51. Minoru Nomura, "Ozawa in the Pacific," in Evans, ed., *Japanese Navy in World War II*, p. 302.
52. Lt. Cmdr. Zenji Abe, oral history, in Werneth, ed., *Beyond Pearl Harbor*, p. 55.
53. Entry dated April 16, 1944, in Ugaki, *Fading Victory*, p. 349.
54. Entry dated April 18, 1944, in ibid., p. 361.
55. Entry dated April 27, 1944, in ibid., p. 365.
56. Entry dated April 24, 1944, in ibid., p. 363.
57. Entry dated May 9, 1944, in ibid., p. 368.

58. Morison, *History of United States Naval Operations in World War II*, Vol. 8, p. 215.
59. Entry dated May 8, 1944, in Ugaki, *Fading Victory*, p. 368.
60. Entry dated May 25, 1944, in ibid., p. 376.
61. Entry dated June 9, 1944, in ibid., p. 391.
62. Entry dated June 10, 1944, in ibid., p. 393.
63. Entry dated June 13, 1944, in ibid., pp. 395–96.
64. Minoru Nomura, "Ozawa in the Pacific," in Evans, ed., *Japanese Navy in World War II*, p. 313.

Chapter Fourteen

1. Rosenman, *Working with Roosevelt*, p. 434.
2. "Commander Joint Expeditionary Force, Marianas Operations, to CINCPAC," August 25, 1944, FDR Map Room Papers, "U.S. Navy Action Reports, August–September 1944," Box 185.
3. Davis, *Sinking the Rising Sun*, p. 197.
4. CINCPOA to COMINCH, May 23, 1944, in CINCPAC War Diary, Book 5, p. 220.
5. Takeo Yamauchi, oral history, in Cook and Cook, eds., *Japan at War*, p. 282.
6. CINCPAC to COMINCH, "Operations in the Pacific Ocean Areas—June 1944," dated November 7, 1944, A16-3/Sum, Serial 003623, FDR Map Room Papers, "U.S. Navy Action Reports, March to June 1944," Box 183, p. 9.
7. Notes by Glen C. H. Perry, King's meeting with reporters, February 18, 1944, in Perry, *"Dear Bart,"* p. 248.
8. Buell, *Master of Seapower*, p. 439.
9. Spruance to Samuel Eliot Morison, January 20, 1952, Raymond A. Spruance Papers, Coll/707, Box 1.
10. Narrative by Arleigh Burke, Office of Naval Records and Library, recorded August 20, 1945, in NARA, RG 38, "World War II Oral Histories and Interviews, 1942–1946," Box 4.
11. Astor, *Wings of Gold*, p. 257.
12. Buell, *Dauntless Helldivers*, p. 289.
13. CINCPAC to COMINCH, "Operations in the Pacific Ocean Areas—June 1944," dated November 7, 1944, A16-3/Sum, Serial 003623, FDR Map Room Papers, "U.S. Navy Action Reports, March to June 1944," Box 183, p. 30.
14. Zurlinden, "Prelude to Saipan, 15 June, 1944," p. 582.
15. Robert B. Sheeks, oral history, in Smith and Meehl, eds., *Pacific War Stories*, p. 192.
16. Sherman, *Combat Command*, p. 240.
17. Richard King, letter to his parents, September 8, 1945, in Carroll, ed., *War Letters*, pp. 300–2.
18. Hopkins, *Nice to Have You Aboard*, p. 138.
19. Okumiya, Horikoshi, and Caidin, *Zero!*, p. 234.
20. Entry dated June 17, 1944, in Ugaki, *Fading Victory*, p. 407.

21. Commander, Fifth Fleet, War Diary for June 1944, A12/1, Serial 00398, entry dated June 15, 1944, FDR Map Room Papers, "U.S. Navy Action Reports, July to August 1944," Box 184, p. 10.

22. Blair, *Silent Victory*, p. 653.

23. Spruance to Nimitz, July 4, 1944, Raymond A. Spruance Papers, MS Collection 12, Series I, correspondence, Box 2, Folder 1.

24. Spruance to E. B. Potter, February 21, 1955, Raymond A. Spruance Papers, Coll/707, Box 3.

25. CINCPAC to COMINCH, "Operations in the Pacific Ocean Areas—June 1944," dated November 7, 1944, A16-3/Sum, Serial 003623, FDR Map Room Papers, "U.S. Navy Action Reports, March to June 1944," Box 183, p. 80.

26. Clark, "Marianas Turkey Shoot," in Sears, ed., *Eyewitness to World War II*, p. 195.

27. Commander, Fifth Fleet, War Diary for June 1944, A12/1, Serial 00398, entry dated June 15, 1944, FDR Map Room Papers, "U.S. Navy Action Reports, July to August 1944," Box 184, p. 18.

28. Clark, "Marianas Turkey Shoot," in Sears, ed., *Eyewitness to World War II*, p. 197.

29. Ibid., p. 195.

30. Sherman, *Combat Command*, p. 243.

31. CINCPAC to COMINCH, "Operations in the Pacific Ocean Areas—June 1944," dated November 7, 1944, A16-3/Sum, Serial 003623, FDR Map Room Papers, "U.S. Navy Action Reports, March to June 1944," Box 183, p. 81.

32. Commander, Fifth Fleet, War Diary for June 1944, A12/1, Serial 00398, entry dated June 20, 1944, FDR Map Room Papers, "U.S. Navy Action Reports, July to August 1944," Box 184.

33. Westcott, ed., *Mahan on Naval Warfare*, p. 80.

34. Ibid., p. 82.

35. Truman J. Hedding (ret.), USNI Oral History Program, 1972, pp. 77–78.

36. Reynolds, *On the Warpath in the Pacific*, p. 354.

37. Thach quoted in Astor, *Wings of Gold*, p. 273.

38. Taylor, *Magnificent Mitscher*, p. 215.

39. Charles Moore, CCOH Naval History Project, No. 655, Vol. 5, p. 1021.

40. George W. Anderson Jr. (ret.), USNI Oral History Program, 1983, p. 140.

41. Narrative by Arleigh Burke, Office of Naval Records and Library, recorded August 20, 1945, in NARA, RG 38, "World War II Oral Histories and Interviews, 1942–1946," Box 4.

42. Paul H. Backus (ret.), USNI Oral History Program, 1995, p. 195.

43. Arleigh A. Burke account in Wooldridge, ed., *Carrier Warfare in the Pacific*, p. 163.

44. "Comments and Recommendations on Operations from 11 July 1944 to 3 July 1944," Commander, VF-15, p. 3, CINCPAC Serial 003607, in NARA, RG 38, "WWII Action and Operational Reports," Box 36.

45. Cmdr. Ernest Snowden quoted in Astor, *Wings of Gold*, p. 282.

46. Entry dated June 19, 1944, in Fahey, *Pacific War Diary*, p. 171.

47. Sommers, *Combat Carriers*, p. 91.

48. Lt. Cmdr. Zenji Abe, oral history, in Werneth, ed., *Beyond Pearl Harbor*, p. 55.

49. Alex Vraciu quoted in Astor, *Wings of Gold*, p. 277.

50. Ibid., p. 279.

51. Danton, "Battle of the Philippine Sea," p. 1025.

52. Commander, Fifth Fleet, War Diary for June 1944, A12/1, Serial 00398, entry dated June 19, FDR Map Room Papers, "U.S. Navy Action Reports, July to August 1944," Box 184, p. 23.

53. Taylor, *Magnificent Mitscher*, p. 227.

54. Commander, Fifth Fleet, War Diary for June 1944, A12/1, Serial 00398, entry dated June 19, FDR Map Room Papers, "U.S. Navy Action Reports, July to August 1944," Box 184, p. 23.

55. Entry dated June 19, 1944, in Ugaki, *Fading Victory*, p. 411.

56. Ibid., p. 409.

57. Telegram No. 2220, cited in ibid., p. 412.

58. Clark, "Marianas Turkey Shoot," reprinted in Sears, ed., *Eyewitness to World War II*, p. 200.

59. Truman J. Hedding (ret.), USNI Oral History Program, 1972, p. 79.

60. Clark, "Marianas Turkey Shoot," reprinted in Sears, ed., *Eyewitness to World War II*, p. 200.

61. James D. Ramage account in Wooldridge, ed., *Carrier Warfare in the Pacific*, p. 173.

62. Don Lewis account (excerpted in James D. Ramage account) in Wooldridge, ed., *Carrier Warfare in the Pacific*, p. 173.

63. Buell, *Dauntless Helldivers*, p. 297.

64. Ibid., p. 298.

65. Don Lewis account (excerpted in James D. Ramage account) in Wooldridge, ed., *Carrier Warfare in the Pacific*, p. 177.

66. Entry dated June 20, 1944, in Ugaki, *Fading Victory*, p. 414.

67. Alex Vraciu quoted in Astor, *Wings of Gold*, p. 307.

68. Spruance to E. B. Potter, January 2, 1960, Raymond A. Spruance Papers, Coll/707, Box 3.

69. Harper, *Paddles!*, p. 222.

70. Buell, *Dauntless Helldivers*, p. 305.

71. *Enterprise* Action Report, VT-10 enclosure. FDR Map Room Papers, "U.S. Navy Action Reports, March to June 1944," Box 183.

72. Paul H. Backus (ret.), USNI Oral History Program, 1995, p. 195.

73. James D. Ramage account in Wooldridge, ed., *Carrier Warfare in the Pacific*, p. 184.

74. Excerpt from the *Ottumwa Courier*, quoted in Buell, *Dauntless Helldivers*, p. 315.

75. Sommers, *Combat Carriers*, p. 90.

76. Spruance to Nimitz, July 4, 1944, Raymond A. Spruance Papers, Coll/707, Box 1.

77. "Extract of a letter from Maj. Gen. Jarmon, 23 June 1944," Holland M. Smith Collection, Coll/2949, Box 1.

78. Richard King, letter to his parents, September 8, 1945, in Carroll, ed., *War Letters*, pp. 300–2.

79. Spruance to Nimitz, July 4, 1944, Raymond A. Spruance Papers, Coll/707, Box 1.

80. CINCPAC to COMINCH, "Operations in the Pacific Ocean Areas—June 1944," dated November 7, 1944, A16-3/Sum, Serial 003623, FDR Map Room Papers, "U.S. Navy Action Reports, March to June 1944," Box 183.

81. Manchester, *Goodbye, Darkness*, p. 261.

82. Ibid.

83. Entry dated June 25, 1944, in Fahey, *Pacific War Diary*, p. 176.

84. Bradlee, *Good Life*, p. 78.

85. CINCPAC to COMINCH, "Operations in the Pacific Ocean Areas—June 1944," dated November 7, 1944, A16-3/Sum, Serial 003623, FDR Map Room Papers, "U.S. Navy Action Reports, March to June 1944," Box 183.

86. Takeo Yamauchi, oral history, in Cook and Cook, eds., *Japan at War*, p. 283.

87. Ibid., p. 289.

88. "Lieutenant General Saito's Last Message to Japanese Officers and Men Defending Saipan," translation of D-2 section of 4th Marine Division, captured July 9, 1944, Ernest J. King Papers.

89. From a captured Japanese officer's personal account, cited in Appendix IX, "Saipan: The Beginning of the End," by Major Carl W. Hoffman, USMC, Historical Branch, G-3 Division, Headquarters, U.S. Marine Corps, 1950, p. 284, USMC Archives.

90. Rogal, *Guadalcanal, Tarawa and Beyond*, p. 165.

91. Taro Kawaguchi diary excerpted in Brawley, Dixon, and Trefalt, eds., *Competing Voices from the Pacific War*, p. 126.

92. Manchester, *Goodbye, Darkness*, p. 269.

93. Ibid., p. 270.

94. Takeo Yamauchi, oral history, in Cook and Cook, eds., *Japan at War*, p. 289.

95. Dower, *War Without Mercy*, p. 249.

96. "Saipan," HM9-16, p. 6, published by the 2d Marine Division, 1944, USMC Archives.

97. Rogal, *Guadalcanal, Tarawa and Beyond*, p. 156.

98. Entry for Thursday, July 13, 1944, in Fahey, *Pacific War Diary*, p. 190.

99. Entry for Sunday, July 16, 1944, in ibid., p. 191.

100. Robert B. Sheeks account in Smith and Meehl, eds., *Pacific War Stories*, p. 193.

101. Ibid., p. 192.

102. Smith and Finch, *Coral and Brass*, p. 201.

103. USSBS, *Interrogations of Japanese Officials*, Vol. 2, p. 387.

104. See, for example, Spruance's commencement speech at Brown University, June 1946, Raymond A. Spruance Papers, MS Collection 12, Box 2, Folder 4.

105. Buell, *Quiet Warrior*, p. 320.

106. James Orvill Raines to Ray Ellen Raines, November 2, 1944, in Raines, *Good Night Officially*, p. 114.
107. Hammer, "Organized Confusion," p. 408.
108. Lewis Thomas account in Shenk, ed., *Authors at Sea*, p. 237.
109. Department of the Navy, *Building the Navy's Bases in World War II*, p. 353.
110. Hammer, "Organized Confusion," p. 407.
111. Pyle, *Last Chapter*, p. 19.
112. Lamar, "I Saw Stars," p. 26.
113. Hammer, "Organized Confusion," p. 417.
114. Kristof, "Shoichi Yokoi, 82, Is Dead."

Epilogue

1. Teishin Nohara, oral history, in Cook and Cook, eds., *Japan at War*, pp. 33–34.
2. Fumio Kimura account in Gibney, ed., *Senso*, p. 109.
3. Hitoshi Anzai account in ibid., p. 119.
4. Toru Izumi account in ibid., p. 34.
5. Uichiro Kawachi, oral history, in Cook and Cook, eds., *Japan at War*, p. 214.
6. Ibid.
7. Ibid., pp. 214–15.
8. Cook and Cook, eds., *Japan at War*, p. 66.
9. Entry dated December 11, 1943, in Kiyosawa, *Diary of Darkness*, p. 122; Cook and Cook, eds., *Japan at War*, p. 174.
10. Entry dated December 19, 1942, in Kiyosawa, *Diary of Darkness*, p. 5.
11. Shoryu Hata, oral history, in Cook and Cook, eds., *Japan at War*, p. 212.
12. Uichiro Kawachi, oral history, in ibid., p. 217.
13. Shigeo Hatanaka, oral history, in ibid., p. 64.
14. Ibid.
15. Ibid., p. 67.
16. Minoru Nomura, "Ozawa in the Pacific," in Evans, ed., *Japanese Navy in World War II*, p. 327.
17. Irokawa, *Age of Hirohito*, p. 92.
18. Bix, *Hirohito and the Making of Modern Japan*, p. 476.
19. Entry dated July 17, 1944, in Kiyosawa, *Diary of Darkness*, p. 226.
20. Ibid., p. 225.
21. Aiko Takahashi diary, entry dated July 18, 1944, in Yamashita, ed., *Leaves from an Autumn of Emergencies*, 174.
22. Sachi Ariyama letter, undated, in Gibney, ed., *Senso*, p. 178.
23. Entry dated July 18, 1944, in Kido, *Diary of Marquis Kido*, p. 394.
24. Entry dated July 17, 1944, in ibid., p. 389.
25. Tojo radio broadcast, July 18, 1944, in Tolischus, *Through Japanese Eyes*, p. 156.
26. Entry dated July 20, 1944, in Kiyosawa, *Diary of Darkness*, pp. 228–29.
27. Entry dated July 29, 1944, in Ugaki, *Fading Victory*, p. 437.

28. Aiko Takahashi diary, entry dated July 18, 1944, in Yamashita, ed., *Leaves from an Autumn of Emergencies*, p. 174.

29. Premier Kuniaki Koiso, July 22, 1944, in Tolischus, *Through Japanese Eyes*, p. 156.

30. Kase, *Journey to the Missouri*, p. 85.

31. Koiso address, September 16, 1944, in Tolischus, *Through Japanese Eyes*, p. 9.

32. Kase, *Journey to the Missouri*, p. 75.

33. Irokawa, *Age of Hirohito*, p. 92.

34. Japanese peace terms broadcast by Domei news agency, May 23, 1944, in Tolischus, *Through Japanese Eyes*, p. 9.

35. Entry dated March 31, 1944, in Kido, *Diary of Marquis Kido*, p. 382.

36. Entry dated January 6, 1944, in ibid., p. 374.

37. Victoria, *Zen at War*, p. 138.

38. Rescript dated September 7, 1944, in Bix, *Hirohito and the Making of Modern Japan*, pp. 472–80.

39. "Fire Scroll," *Book of Five Spheres*, quoted in Cleary, *Japanese Art of War*, p. 84.

40. Entries dated August 26, 1943, March 15, 1944, and April 7, 1944, in Kiyosawa, *Diary of Darkness*, pp. 69, 157, 174.

41. Aiko Takahashi diary, entry dated March 27, 1943, in Yamashita, ed., *Leaves from an Autumn of Emergencies*, p. 168.

42. Hiroyo Arakawa, oral history, in Cook and Cook, eds., *Japan at War*, p. 179.

43. Quoted in entry dated April 30, 1943, in Kiyosawa, *Diary of Darkness*, p. 25.

44. Sumio Ishida account in Gibney, ed., *Senso*, p. 176.

45. Entry dated April 24, 1944, in Kiyosawa, *Diary of Darkness*, p. 183.

46. Aiko Takahashi diary, entry dated January 4, 1944, in Yamashita, ed., *Leaves from an Autumn of Emergencies*, p. 173.

47. Kii Aoki account in Gibney, ed., *Senso*, p. 172.

48. Takeyama, *Scars of War*, p. 140.

BIBLIOGRAPHY

Archival Collections

Archives and Special Collections (USMC Archives), Library of the Marine Corps, Quantico, Virginia

Fifth Amphibious Corps files
Holland M. Smith Collection
Julian C. Smith Papers
Alexander Vandegrift Collection

Franklin D. Roosevelt (FDR) Library, Hyde Park, New York

FDR Safe Files
Harry L. Hopkins Papers
Map Room Papers, 1941–1945
John Toland Papers, 1949–1991

Naval Historical Foundation Collection, Manuscript Division, Library of Congress, Washington, DC

William Frederick Halsey Papers
Ernest J. King Papers

Operational Archives Branch, Naval History and Heritage Command (NHHC) Archives, Washington, DC

Papers of Captain Flavius J. George, USNR
Samuel Eliot Morison Papers
Raymond A. Spruance Papers
Richmond K. Turner Papers

Oral History Collections

Oral History Collection, Columbia Center for Oral History (CCOH), Columbia University, New York, NY

Robert Bostwick Carney   Charles Moore
Joseph J. Clark   Ralph C. Parker
Donald Duncan   DeWitt Peck
Harry W. Hill   James S. Russell
Thomas C. Kinkaid

Oral History Program, U.S. Naval Institute (USNI), Annapolis, MD, 1969–2005

George W. Anderson Jr.   Ruthven E. Libby
Paul H. Backus   John L. McCrea
Michael Bak Jr.   Henry L. Miller
Thomas H. Dyer   Joseph J. Rochefort
Harry D. Felt   Roland N. Smoot
Truman J. Hedding

Action Reports, Government and Military Publications, Documentary Collections, Unpublished Diaries and Correspondence

Bierer, Bion B. (Lt. Cmdr.), to Mary Bierer, October 16, 1942. Letter in the possession of Bob Begin.

Chief of the Bureau of Ships, U.S. Navy. "U.S.S. QUINCY, U.S.S. ASTORIA and U.S.S. VINCENNES, Report of Loss in Action," September 2, 1943. Online at http://blog.usni.org/wp-content/uploads/2009/03/savo-battle-damage-reports.pdf (accessed November 22, 2014).

Commander in Chief, U.S. Pacific Fleet. "CINCPAC Grey Book: Running Estimate of the Situation for the Pacific War." [Cited as CINCPAC War Diary.] Naval Historical Center, Washington, DC.

Department of the Navy, Bureau of Yards and Docks. *Building the Navy's Bases in World War II: History of the Bureau of Yards and Docks and the Civil Engineer Corps, 1940–1946.* Washington, DC: Government Printing Office, 1947.

Dyer, George C. *The Amphibians Came to Conquer: The Story of Admiral Richmond Kelly Turner.* Washington, DC: Department of the Navy, Government Printing Office, 1972.

Genda, Minoru. VR 519. "Tactical Planning in the Imperial Japanese Navy." Lecture delivered at the U.S. Naval War College, March 7, 1969.

Heimdahl, William C., and Edward J. Marolda, eds. *Guide to United States Naval Administrative Histories of World War II.* Washington, DC: Naval History Division, Department of the Navy, 1976.

Japanese Demobilization Bureau Records. *Reports of General MacArthur*, Vol. 2, Part 1. Washington, DC, 1966.

Joint Army Navy Assessment Committee (JANAC). "Japanese Naval and Merchant Shipping Losses During World War II by All Causes." Washington, DC: Government Printing Office, 1947.

Koda, Yoji, Vice Admiral, JMSDF (ret.). "Doctrine and Strategy of IJN." Remarks delivered at the US Naval War College, Newport, RI, January 6, 2011.

Matloff, Maurice, and Edwin M. Snell. *Strategic Planning for Coalition Warfare 1941–1942*. Washington, DC: Office of the Chief of Military History, Department of the Army, 1953–1959.

McDaniel, J. T., ed. *U.S.S. Wahoo (SS-238): American Submarine War Patrol Reports*. Riverdale, GA: Riverdale Books, 2005.

Morton, Louis. *Strategy and Command: The First Two Years / U.S. Army in World War II*. Washington, DC: Government Printing Office, 1962.

National Archives and Records Administration (NARA). Record Group (RG) 38: Records of the Office of the Chief of Naval Operations, 1875–2006: CNO Dispatches, 1942–1947. [Cited as "CNO Zero-Zero Files."]

———. Record Group 38: Records of the Office of the Chief of Naval Operations, 1875–2006: World War II Oral Histories, Interviews and Statements, ca. 04/1942–ca. 12/1946. [Cited as "World War II Oral Histories and Interviews, 1942–1946."]

———. Record Group 38: Records of the Office of the Chief of Naval Operations, 1875–2006: World War II War Diaries.

———. Record Group 38: Records of the Office of the Chief of Naval Operations, 1875–2006: WWII Action and Operational Reports.

Nimitz, Catherine Freeman, and John T. Mason. *Recollections of the Fleet Admiral Chester W. Nimitz*. Annapolis, MD: U.S. Naval Institute, 1970.

Office of Naval Intelligence, Combat Narratives. "The Battle of Savo Island." Washington, DC: Government Printing Office, 1943.

Read, W. J. "Report by Lieut. W. J. Read on Coastwatching Activity: Bougainville Island, 1942–43." Australian National Library, Canberra, ACT, Australia.

Recollections of Fleet Admiral Chester W. Nimitz. Annapolis, MD: U.S. Naval Institute, 1970.

Reminiscences of Admiral Spruance as related by Dr. David Willcutts, Fifth Fleet Medical Officer. Ms. Item 297, U.S. Naval War College Archives, Newport, RI.

Rhoades, Lt. Cmdr. F. A. "Secret Diary of a Coastwatcher in the Solomons." Fredericksburg, TX: Admiral Nimitz Foundation, 1985.

Rosenman, Samuel I., ed. *The Public Papers and Addresses of Franklin D. Roosevelt*. 13 vols. New York: Harper & Brothers, 1950 (1941–1945 vols.).

Shaw, Nalty, et al. *History of U.S. Marine Corps Operations in World War II: Central Pacific Drive*. Historical Branch, G-3 Division, Headquarters, U.S. Marine Corps, 1958.

Special Service Division, Services of Supply, U.S. Army. *Instructions for American Servicemen in Australia*. Washington, DC: War and Navy Departments, 1942.

Stimson, Henry L. *Henry Lewis Stimson Diaries*. (Microfilm edition, reel 3.) Manuscripts and Archives, Yale University Library, New Haven.

U.S. Army, Far East Command. *The Imperial Japanese Navy in World War II: A Graphic Presentation of the Japanese Naval Organization and List of Combatant and Non-Combatant Vessels Lost or Damaged in the War*. Japanese Operational Monograph Series, No. 116. Tokyo: Military History Section, Special Staff, General Headquarters, Far East Command, 1952.

U.S. Civilian Production Administration. *Industrial Mobilization for War: History of the War Production Board and Predecessor Agencies, 1940–1945*. Vol. 1: *Program and Administration*. Washington, DC: Government Printing Office, 1947.

U.S. Department of State. *Foreign Relations of the United States* [cited as *FRUS*]:
The Conferences at Cairo and Tehran, 1943. Washington, DC: Government Printing Office, 1961.
The Conferences at Washington, 1941–1942, and Casablanca, 1943. Washington, DC: Government Printing Office, 1968.
The Conferences at Washington and Quebec, 1943. Washington, DC: Government Printing Office, 1970.

U.S. Naval Administration in World War II. Washington, DC: Department of the Navy, Naval Historical Center, 1976.

U.S. Office of Naval Operations. *U.S. Naval Aviation in the Pacific*. Washington, DC: Government Printing Office, 1947.

U.S. Strategic Bombing Survey (USSBS). *Air Campaigns of the Pacific War*. Washington, DC: U.S. Strategic Bombing Survey, Military Analysis Division, 1947.

———. *The Campaigns of the Pacific War*. Washington: U.S. Strategic Bombing Survey (Pacific) Naval Analysis Division, 1946.

———. *The Effects of Strategic Bombing on Japan's War Economy*. Washington: Government Printing Office, 1945.

———. *Interrogations of Japanese Officials*. 2 vols. Washington, DC: Government Printing Office, 1947.

———. *Japanese Merchant Shipping*. Washington, DC: Government Printing Office, 1946.

———. *Summary Report (Pacific War)*. Washington, DC: Government Printing Office, 1946.

U.S.S. Essex Cruise Book, 1944. Navy Department Library, Naval History and Heritage Command, Washington, DC.

"Veterans' Biographies," published for the Battle of Midway Celebration. Marines' Memorial Club, San Francisco, 2009.

The War Reports of General of the Army George C. Marshall, Chief of Staff, General of the Army H. H. Arnold, Commanding General, Army Air Forces [and] Fleet Admiral Ernest J. King, Commander-in-Chief, United States Fleet and Chief of Naval Operations. Philadelphia: Lippincott, 1947.

Wolfson Collection of Decorative and Propaganda Arts. Wolfsonian Library, Miami Beach, FL.

Books

Agawa, Hiroyuki. *The Reluctant Admiral: Yamamoto and the Imperial Navy.* New York: Kodansha International, 1979.

Alanbrooke, Lord. *War Diaries, 1939–1945,* ed. Alex Danchev and Daniel Todman. Berkeley: University of California Press, 2001.

Ambrose, Stephen E. *Eisenhower: Soldier, General of the Army, President-Elect, 1890–1952.* New York: Simon & Schuster, 1983.

Archibald, Katherine. *Wartime Shipyard.* New York: Arno Press, 1977.

Arnold, Henry Harley. *Global Mission.* 1st ed. New York: Harper, 1949.

Asada, Sadao. *From Mahan to Pearl Harbor: The Imperial Japanese Navy and the United States.* Annapolis, MD: Naval Institute Press, 2006.

Astor, Gerald. *Wings of Gold: The U.S. Naval Air Campaign in World War II.* New York: Presidio Press/Ballantine Books, 2004.

Bailey, Beth, and David Farber. *The First Strange Place: Race and Sex in World War II Hawaii.* Baltimore: Johns Hopkins University Press, 1994.

Beach, Edward L. *The United States Navy: A 200 Year History.* Boston: Houghton Mifflin, 1986.

Beaver, Floyd. *Sailor from Oklahoma: One Man's Two-Ocean War.* Annapolis, MD: Naval Institute Press, 2009.

Benedict, Ruth. *The Chrysanthemum and the Sword: Patterns of Japanese Culture.* Tokyo: Charles E. Tuttle, 1954.

Bergerud, Eric M. *Fire in the Sky: The Air War in the South Pacific.* Boulder, CO: Westview Press, 2000.

Bix, Herbert P. *Hirohito and the Making of Modern Japan.* New York: HarperCollins, 2000.

Blair, Clay. *Silent Victory: The U.S. Submarine War Against Japan.* 1st ed. Philadelphia: Lippincott, 1975.

Boyington, Gregory. *Baa Baa, Black Sheep.* New York: Putnam, 1958.

Bradlee, Benjamin C. *A Good Life: Newspapering and Other Adventures.* New York: Simon & Schuster, 1995.

Brand, Max. *Fighter Squadron at Guadalcanal.* New York: Pocket Books, 1996.

Brawley, Sean, Chris Dixon, and Beatrice Trefalt. *Competing Voices from the Pacific War: Fighting Words.* Santa Barbara, CA: Greenwood/ABC-CLIO, 2009.

Brinkley, David. *Washington Goes to War: The Extraordinary Story of the Transformation of a City and a Nation.* New York: Alfred A. Knopf, 1988.

Brown, DeSoto. *Hawaii Goes to War: Life in Hawaii from Pearl Harbor to Peace.* Honolulu: Editions Limited, 1989.

Bryan, J. *Aircraft Carrier.* New York: Ballantine Books, 1954.

Buell, Harold L. *Dauntless Helldivers: A Dive-Bomber Pilot's Epic Story of the Carrier Battles*. New York: Orion, 1991.

Buell, Thomas B. *Master of Seapower: A Biography of Fleet Admiral Ernest J. King*. Boston: Little, Brown, 1980.

———. *The Quiet Warrior: A Biography of Admiral Raymond A. Spruance*. Annapolis, MD: Naval Institute Press, 1987.

Calhoun, C. Raymond. *Tin Can Sailor: Life Aboard the USS Sterett, 1939–1945*. Annapolis, MD: Naval Institute Press, 1993.

Carroll, Andrew, ed. *War Letters: Extraordinary Correspondence from American Wars*. New York: Scribner, 2001.

Carter, Worrall Reed. *Beans, Bullets, and Black Oil: The Story of Fleet Logistics Afloat in the Pacific During World War II*. Washington, DC: Department of the Navy, 1953.

Childs, Marquis W. *I Write from Washington*. New York: Harper, 1942.

Churchill, Winston, and Martin Gilbert. *The Churchill War Papers*. London: W. Heinemann, 1993.

Clark, J. J., and Clark G. Reynolds. *Carrier Admiral*. New York: D. McKay, 1967.

Cleary, Thomas. *The Japanese Art of War: Understanding the Culture of Strategy*. Boston: Shambhala Classics, 2005.

Clemens, Martin. *Alone on Guadalcanal: A Coastwatcher's Story*. Annapolis, MD: Naval Institute Press, 1998.

Coffey, Thomas M. *Hap: The Story of the U.S. Air Force and the Man Who Built It, General Henry H. "Hap" Arnold*. New York: Viking Press, 1982.

Coletta, Paolo E. *Admiral Marc A. Mitscher and U.S. Naval Aviation: Bald Eagle*. Lewiston, NY: Edwin Mellen Press, 1997.

Colman, Penny. *Rosie the Riveter: Women Working on the Home Front in World War II*. New York: Crown, 1995.

Cook, Haruko Taya, and Theodore F. Cook, eds. *Japan at War: An Oral History*. New York: New Press, 1992.

Cooke, Alistair. *The American Home Front, 1941–1942*. New York: Atlantic Monthly Press, 2006.

Cooper, Page. *Navy Nurse*. New York: Whittlesey House, McGraw-Hill, 1946.

Costello, John. *The Pacific War*. New York: Rawson, Wade, 1981.

Davis, William E. *Sinking the Rising Sun: Dog Fighting and Dive Bombing in World War II: A Navy Fighter Pilot's Story*. 1st ed. St. Paul, MN: Zenith Press, 2007.

Dower, John W. *Japan in War and Peace: Selected Essays*. New York: New Press; distributed by W. W. Norton, 1993.

———. *War Without Mercy: Race and Power in the Pacific War*. New York: Pantheon Books, 1986.

Dull, Paul S. *A Battle History of the Imperial Japanese Navy, 1941–1945*. Annapolis, MD: Naval Institute Press, 1978.

Dye, Bob, ed. *Hawaii Chronicles II: Contemporary Island History from the Pages of Honolulu Magazine*. Honolulu: University of Hawai'i Press, 1998.

Evans, David C., ed. *The Japanese Navy in World War II: In the Words of Former Japanese Naval Officers*. Annapolis, MD: Naval Institute Press, 1993.

Fahey, James J. *Pacific War Diary, 1942–1945*. Boston: Houghton Mifflin, 1963.

Forrestal, James. *The Forrestal Diaries*, ed. Walter Millis. New York: Viking Press, 1951.

Fussell, Paul. *Wartime: Understanding and Behavior in the Second World War*. Oxford: Oxford University Press, 1989.

Gibny, Frank, ed. *Senso: The Japanese Remember the Pacific War*. Armonk, NY: M. E. Sharpe, 1995.

Goldstein, Donald M., and Kathryn V. Dillon, eds. *The Pacific War Papers: Japanese Documents of World War II*. Washington, DC: Potomac Books, 2006.

Grider, George, and Lydel Sims. *War Fish*. New York: Little, Brown, 1958.

Halsey, William F., and J. Bryan. *Admiral Halsey's Story*. New York: Whittlesey House, 1947.

Hammel, Eric, ed. *Aces Against Japan: The American Aces Speak*. New York: Pocket Books, 1992.

Hara, Tameichi, with Fred Saito and Roger Pineau. *Japanese Destroyer Captain: Pearl Harbor, Guadalcanal, Midway—The Great Naval Battles as Seen Through Japanese Eyes*. Annapolis, MD: Naval Institute Press, 2011.

Harper, John A. *Paddles! The Foibles and Finesse of One World War II Landing Signal Officer*. Atglen, PA: Schiffer, 1996.

Harris, Mark Jonathan, Franklin D. Mitchell, and Steven J. Schechter, eds. *The Homefront: America During World War II*. New York: Putnam, 1984.

Hopkins, Harold. *Nice to Have You Aboard*. London: Allen & Unwin, 1964.

Horikoshi, Jiro, Shojiro Shindo, and Harold N. Wanteiz. *Eagles of Mitsubishi: The Story of the Zero Fighter*. Seattle: University of Washington Press, 1981.

Hornfischer, James D. *Neptune's Inferno: The U.S. Navy at Guadalcanal*. New York: Bantam Books, 2011.

Hoyt, Edwin. *How They Won the War in the Pacific: Nimitz and His Admirals*. New York: Weybright & Talley, 1970.

Huie, William Bradford. *Can Do! The Story of the Seabees*. New York: E. P. Dutton, 1944.

Hynes, Samuel. *Flights of Passage: Recollections of a World War II Aviator*. London: Bloomsbury, 2005.

Ickes, Harold. *The Secret Diary of Harold L. Ickes*. New York: Simon & Schuster, 1954.

Irokawa, Daikichi. *The Age of Hirohito: In Search of Modern Japan*. New York: Free Press, 1995.

Jackson, Robert H. *That Man: An Insider's Portrait of Franklin D. Roosevelt*. Oxford: Oxford University Press, 2003.

Karsten, Peter. *The Naval Aristocracy: The Golden Age of Annapolis and the Emergence of Modern American Navalism*. New York: Free Press, 1972.

Kase, Toshikazu. *Journey to the Missouri*. New Haven: Yale University Press, 1950.

Kennedy, David M. *The American People in World War II: Freedom from Fear, Part Two.* Oxford: Oxford University Press, 2003.

Kenney, George C. *General Kenney Reports: A Personal History of the Pacific War.* New York: Duell, Sloan, & Pearce, 1949.

Keresey, Dick. *PT 105.* Annapolis, MD: Naval Institute Press, 1996.

Kernan, Alvin B. *Crossing the Line: A Bluejacket's World War II Odyssey.* Annapolis, MD: Naval Institute Press, 1994.

Kido, Koichi. *The Diary of Marquis Kido, 1931–45: Selected Translations into English.* Frederick, MD: University Publications of America, 1984.

King, Ernest J., and Walter Muir Whitehill. *Fleet Admiral King: A Naval Record.* New York: W. W. Norton, 1952.

Kiyosawa, Kiyoshi. *A Diary of Darkness: The Wartime Diary of Kiyosawa Kiyoshi,* trans. Eugene Soviak and Kamiyama Tamie. Princeton: Princeton University Press, 1999.

Lawson, Robert. *U.S. Navy Dive and Torpedo Bombers of World War II.* St. Paul, MN: Zenith Press, 2001.

Layton, Edwin T., with Roger Pineau and John Costello. *"And I Was There": Pearl Harbor and Midway—Breaking the Secrets.* New York: William Morrow, 1985.

Leach, Douglas Edward. *Now Hear This: The Memoir of a Junior Naval Officer in the Great Pacific War.* Kent, OH: Kent State University Press, 1987.

Leahy, William D. *I Was There.* New York: Whittlesey, 1950.

Leckie, Robert. *Helmet for My Pillow.* New York: Bantam, 2010.

Lee, Clark. *They Call It the Pacific: An Eye-Witness Story of Our War Against Japan from Bataan to the Solomons.* New York: Viking Press, 1943.

Lee, Robert Edson. *To the War.* New York: Alfred A. Knopf, 1968.

Lindsay, Patrick. *The Coast Watchers: The Men Behind Enemy Lines Who Saved the Pacific.* North Sydney, NSW, Australia: William Heinemann, 2010.

Litoff, Judy Barrett, and David C. Smith, eds. *American Women in a World at War: Contemporary Accounts from World War II.* Wilmington, DE: Scholarly Resources, 1997.

———, eds. *Since You Went Away: World War II Letters from American Women on the Home Front.* New York: Oxford University Press, 1991.

Loewenheim, Francis L., Harold D. Langley, and Manfred Jonas, eds. *Roosevelt and Churchill: Their Secret Wartime Correspondence.* New York: Saturday Review Press / E. P. Dutton, 1975.

Lord, Walter. *Lonely Vigil: Coastwatchers of the Solomons.* New York: Viking Press, 1977.

Lotchin, Roger W. *The Bad City in the Good War: San Francisco, Los Angeles, Oakland and San Diego.* Bloomington: Indiana University Press, 2003.

Lucas, Jim Griffing. *Combat Correspondent.* New York: Reynal & Hitchcock, 1944.

Lundstrom, John B. *Black Shoe Carrier Admiral.* Annapolis, MD: Naval Institute Press, 2006.

———. *The First Team and the Guadalcanal Campaign: Naval Fighter Combat from August to November 1942.* Annapolis, MD: Naval Institute Press, 1994.

MacArthur, Douglas. *Reminiscences.* 1st ed. New York: McGraw-Hill, 1964.

Madsen, Daniel. *Resurrection: Salvaging the Battle Fleet at Pearl Harbor.* Annapolis, MD: Naval Institute Press, 2003.

Manchester, William Raymond. *American Caesar: Douglas MacArthur, 1880–1964.* Boston: Little, Brown, 1978.

———. *Goodbye, Darkness: A Memoir of the Pacific War.* Boston: Little, Brown, 1980.

Mason, Theodore C. *Battleship Sailor.* Annapolis, MD: Naval Institute Press, 1982.

———. *Rendezvous with Destiny: A Sailor's War.* Annapolis, MD: Naval Institute Press, 1997.

McIntire, Vice-Admiral Ross T. *White House Physician.* New York: G. P. Putnam's Sons, 1946.

Mears, Frederick. *Carrier Combat: A Young Pilot's Story of Action Aboard the Hornet in World War II.* New York: Ballantine Books, 1967.

Merillat, Herbert Christian Laing. *Guadalcanal Remembered.* New York: Dodd, Mead, 1982.

———. *The Island: A History of the First Marine Division on Guadalcanal.* Yardley, PA: Westholme, 2010.

Michener, James A. *Tales of the South Pacific.* Greenwich, CT: Fawcett, 1947.

Miller, Thomas Guy. *The Cactus Air Force.* 1st ed. New York: Harper & Row, 1969.

Morison, Samuel Eliot. *History of United States Naval Operations in World War II.* Boston: Little, Brown, 1947–1962.

    Vol. 5: *The Struggle for Guadalcanal: August 1942–February 1943.*

    Vol. 6: *Breaking the Bismarcks Barrier: July 22, 1942–May 1, 1944.*

    Vol. 7: *Aleutians, Gilberts, and Marshalls: June 1942–April 1944.*

    Vol. 8: *New Guinea and the Marianas: March 1944–August 1944.*

Morris, Ivan. *The Nobility of Failure: Tragic Heroes in the History of Japan.* Tokyo: Charles E. Tuttle, 1982.

Newcomb, Richard F. *The Battle of Savo Island.* New York: H. Holt, 2002.

Nitobe, Inazo. *Bushido: The Soul of Japan.* Tokyo: Charles E. Tuttle, 1969.

O'Kane, Richard H. *Clear the Bridge! The War Patrols of the U.S.S. Tang.* Chicago: Rand McNally, 1977.

———. *Wahoo: The Patrols of America's Most Famous World War II Submarine.* Novato, CA: Presidio Press, 1987.

Okumiya, Masatake, Jiro Horikoshi, and Martin Caidin. *Zero!* New York: E. P. Dutton, 1956.

Olson, Michael Keith. *Tales from a Tin Can: The USS Dale from Pearl Harbor to Tokyo Bay.* St. Paul, MN: Zenith Press, 2007.

Parshall, Jonathan, and Anthony P. Tully. *Shattered Sword: The Untold Story of the Battle of Midway.* Washington, DC: Potomac Books, 2005.

Peattie, Mark R. *Sunburst: The Rise of Japanese Naval Air Power: 1909–1941.* Annapolis, MD: Naval Institute Press, 2001.

Perry, Glen C. H. *"Dear Bart": Washington Views of World War II.* Westport, CT: Greenwood Press, 1982.

Perry, Mark. *The Most Dangerous Man in America: The Making of Douglas MacArthur.* New York: Basic Books, 2014.

Potter, E. B. *Bull Halsey.* Annapolis, MD: Naval Institute Press, 1985.

———. *Nimitz.* Annapolis, MD: Naval Institute Press, 1976.

Potter, E. B., and Chester W. Nimitz. *The Great Sea War: The Story of Naval Action in World War II.* Englewood Cliffs, NJ: Prentice-Hall, 1960.

Pyle, Ernie. *Last Chapter.* New York: H. Holt, 1946.

Radike, Floyd W. *Across the Dark Islands: The War in the Pacific.* New York: Presidio Press / Ballantine, 2003.

Raines, James Orvill. *Good Night Officially: The Pacific War Letters of a Destroyer Sailor: The Letters of Yeoman James Orvill Raines,* ed. William M. McBride. Boulder, CO: Westview, 1994.

Ralph, Barry. *They Passed This Way: The United States of America, the States of Australia, and World War II.* East Roseville, NSW, Australia: Kangaroo Press, 2000.

Raymer, Edward C. *Descent into Darkness: Pearl Harbor, 1941: A Navy Diver's Memoir.* Novato, CA: Presidio, 1996.

Reporting World War II. 2 vols. New York: Literary Classics of the United States, 1995.

Reynolds, Clark G. *On the Warpath in the Pacific: Admiral Jocko Clark and the Fast Carriers.* Annapolis, MD: Naval Institute Press, 2005.

Richardson, K. D., and Paul Stillwell. *Reflections of Pearl Harbor: An Oral History of December 7, 1941.* Westport, CT: Greenwood Press, 2005.

Rogal, William W. *Guadalcanal, Tarawa and Beyond: A Mud Marine's Memoir of the Pacific Island War.* Jefferson, NC: McFarland, 2010.

Rose, Lisle A. *The Ship That Held the Line: The USS Hornet and the First Year of the Pacific War.* Annapolis, MD: Naval Institute Press, 1995.

Rosenau, James N., ed. *The Roosevelt Treasury.* 1st ed. Garden City, NY: Doubleday, 1951.

Rosenman, Samuel Irving. *Working with Roosevelt.* New York: Harper, 1952.

Russell, Dale. *Hell Above, Deep Water Below.* Tillamook, OR: Bayocean Enterprises, 1995.

Russell, Ronald W. *No Right to Win: A Continuing Dialogue with Veterans of the Battle of Midway.* New York: iUniverse, 2006.

Sakai, Saburo, with Martin Caidin and Fred Saito. *Samurai.* New York: E. P. Dutton, 1956.

Schaller, Michael. *Douglas MacArthur: The Far Eastern General.* New York: Oxford University Press, 1989.

Sears, Stephen W., ed. *Eyewitness to World War II: The Best of American Heritage.* Boston: Houghton Mifflin, 1991.

Shenk, Robert, ed. *Authors at Sea: Modern American Writers Remember Their Naval Service.* Annapolis, MD: Naval Institute Press, 1997.

Sherman, Frederick C. *Combat Command: The American Aircraft Carriers in the Pacific War.* New York: E. P. Dutton, 1950.

Sherrod, Robert. *Tarawa: The Story of a Battle*. New York: Duell, Sloan & Pearce, 1944.

Sherwood, Robert E. *Roosevelt and Hopkins: An Intimate History*. New York: Harper & Brothers, 1948.

Shillony, Ben-Ami. *Politics and Culture in Wartime Japan*. Oxford: Clarendon Press, 1981.

Smith, Douglas V. *Carrier Battles: Command Decision in Harm's Way*. Annapolis, MD: Naval Institute Press, 2006.

Smith, Holland M., and Percy Finch. *Coral and Brass*. New York: Scribner, 1949.

Smith, Merriman. *Thank You, Mr. President: A White House Notebook*. New York: Harper & Brothers, 1946.

Smith, Rex Alan, and Gerald A. Meehl. *Pacific War Stories: In the Words of Those Who Survived*. New York: Abbeville Press, 2011.

Smith, S. E. *The Battle of Savo*. New York: Macfadden-Bartell, 1962.

Smyth, Robert T. *Sea Stories*. New York: iUniverse, 2004.

Solberg, Carl. *Decision and Dissent: With Halsey at Leyte Gulf*. Annapolis, MD: Naval Institute Press, 1995.

Sommers, Sam. *Combat Carriers, and My Brushes with History: World War II, 1939–1946*. Montgomery, AL: Black Belt, 1997.

Spector, Ronald H. *Eagle Against the Sun: The American War with Japan*. New York: Free Press, 1984.

Stafford, Edward Peary. *The Big E: The Story of the USS Enterprise*. New York: Random House, 1962.

Starr, Kevin. *Embattled Dreams: California in War and Peace, 1940–1950*. Oxford: Oxford University Press, 2002.

Sterling, Forest. *Wake of the Wahoo*. Riverside, CA: R. A. Cline, 1999.

Stevenson, Robert Louis, and Jenni Calder. *Island Landfalls: Reflections from the South Seas*. Edinburgh: Canongate, 1987.

Stillwell, Paul, ed. *Air Raid, Pearl Harbor! Recollections of a Day of Infamy*. Annapolis, MD: Naval Institute Press, 1981.

Stimson, Henry L., and McGeorge Bundy. *On Active Service in Peace and War*. New York: Harper & Brothers, 1947.

Stoler, Mark A. *Allies and Adversaries: The Joint Chiefs of Staff, the Grand Alliance, and U.S. Strategy in World War II*. Chapel Hill: University of North Carolina Press, 2000.

Tagaya, Osamu. *Imperial Japanese Naval Aviator 1937–45*. Oxford: Osprey, 2003.

Takeyama, Michio. *The Scars of War: Tokyo During World War II: The Writings of Takeyama Michio*, ed. Richard H. Minear. Lanham, MD: Rowman & Littlefield, 2007.

Taylor, Theodore. *The Magnificent Mitscher*. Annapolis, MD: Naval Institute Press, 1991.

Terasaki, Gwen. *Bridge to the Sun: A Memoir of Love and War*. Chapel Hill: University of North Carolina Press, 1957.

Tillman, Barrett. *Clash of the Carriers: The True Story of the Marianas Turkey Shoot of World War II*. New York: New American Library, 2005.

Toland, John. *The Rising Sun: The Decline and Fall of the Japanese Empire, 1936–1945*. New York: Random House, 1970.

Tolischus, Otto David. *Through Japanese Eyes*. New York: Reynal & Hitchcock, 1945.

Tregaskis, Richard. *Guadalcanal Diary*. New York: Random House, 1943.

Twining, Merrill B., and Neil G. Carey. *No Bended Knee: The Battle for Guadalcanal: The Memoir of Gen. Merrill B. Twining USMC (Ret.)*. Novato, CA: Presidio, 1996.

Ugaki, Matome. *Fading Victory: The Diary of Admiral Matome Ugaki, 1941–1945*, trans. Masataka Chihaya. Pittsburgh: University of Pittsburgh Press, 1991.

Vandegrift, A. A., and Robert B. Asprey. *Once a Marine: The Memoirs of General A. A. Vandegrift, United States Marine Corps*. 1st. ed. New York: W. W. Norton, 1964.

Victoria, Brian Daizen. *Zen at War*. New York: Weatherhill, 1997.

Weinberg, Gerhard L. *Visions of Victory: The Hopes of Eight World War II Leaders*. Cambridge: Cambridge University Press, 2005.

———. *A World at Arms: A Global History of World War II*. Cambridge: Cambridge University Press, 1994.

Werneth, Ron, ed. *Beyond Pearl Harbor: The Untold Stories of Japan's Naval Airmen*. Atglen, PA: Schiffer, 2008.

Westcott, Allan, ed. *Mahan on Naval Warfare: Selections from the Writings of Rear Admiral Alfred T. Mahan*. Mineola, NY: Dover, 1999.

White, William Lindsay. *They Were Expendable*. New York: Harcourt, Brace, 1942.

Wolfert, Ira. *Battle for the Solomons*. Boston: Houghton Mifflin, 1943.

Wooldridge, E. T., ed. *Carrier Warfare in the Pacific: An Oral History Collection*. Washington, DC: Smithsonian Institute Press, 1993.

Wukovits, John F. *One Square Mile of Hell: The Battle for Tarawa*. New York: NAL Caliber, 2006.

Yamashita, Samuel Hideo, ed. *Leaves from an Autumn of Emergencies: Selections from the Wartime Diaries of Ordinary Japanese*. Honolulu: University of Hawaii Press, 2005.

Yoshimura, Akira. *Battleship Musashi: The Making and Sinking of the World's Biggest Battleship*, trans. Vincent Murphy. New York: Kodansha International, 1999.

———. *Zero Fighter*. Westport, CT: Praeger, 1996.

Zich, Arthur, and the Editors of Time-Life Books. *The Rising Sun*. Alexandria, VA: Time-Life Books, 1977.

Articles

Arlen, Lorna. "The Year in Retrospect." *Paradise of the Pacific*, December 1944. (Reprinted in Dye, ed., *Hawaii Chronicles II*, p. 217.)

Baldwin, Hanson W. "Solomons Action Develops into Battle for South Pacific." *New York Times*, September 27, 1942.

———. "U.S. Hold in Solomons Bolstered; Damage to Japanese Fleet in Stewart

Islands Battle Strengthens Guadalcanal's 'Hell, Yes, We'll Stay' Stand." *New York Times*, November 3, 1942.

Beach, Edward L. "Culpable Negligence." *American Heritage*, December 1980. (Reprinted in Sears, ed., *Eyewitness to World War II*.)

"Bull's-Eye." *Time*, July 23, 1945.

Danton, Lt. J. Periam. "The Battle of the Philippine Sea." *Proceedings* (U.S. Naval Institute), Vol. 71, Part 2, September 1945.

Downes, Lawrence. "How a War Was Won and a City Vanished at Pearl Harbor." *New York Times*, December 7, 2006.

Clark, J. J. "The Marianas Turkey Shoot." *American Heritage*, October 1967. (Reprinted in Sears, ed., *Eyewitness to World War II*.)

Hammer, Captain Harry D. "Organized Confusion." *Proceedings* (U.S. Naval Institute), Vol. 73, Part 1, April 1947.

Hersey, John. "The Sinking of the Wasp." *Time*, November 2, 1942.

"Honolulu: Island Boomtown." *Paradise of the Pacific*, May 1944. (Reprinted in Dye, ed., *Hawaii Chronicles II*, pp. 186–89.)

"Interracial Marriage in Hawaii." *Paradise of the Pacific*, October 1944. (Reprinted in Dye, ed., *Hawaii Chronicles II*, p. 212.)

Kittredge, George William. "Savo Island: The Worst Defeat." *Naval History*, August 2002.

Kristof, Nicholas D. "Shoichi Yokoi, 82, Is Dead; Japan Soldier Hid 27 Years." *New York Times*, September 26, 1997.

Lake, M. "The Desire for a Yank: Sexual Relations Between Australian Women and American Servicemen During World War II." *Journal of the History of Sexuality*, Vol. 2, No. 4, 1992, p. 623.

Lamar, H. Arthur. "I Saw Stars." Fredericksburg, Texas: Admiral Nimitz Foundation, 1985.

Lippmann, Walter. "The Awkward Giant." *Washington Post*, August 25, 1942.

Lodge, J. Norman. "Halsey Predicts Victory This Year." Associated Press. (Reprinted in *New York Times*, January 3, 1943.)

"Mid-Pacific Stronghold." *New York Times*, December 27, 1943.

Ramage, James D. "Raid on Truk." Online at http://www.cv6.org/1944/truk/ (accessed October 4, 2014).

"Return Visit." *Time*, February 28, 1944.

"Sacrifice Will Win, Says Admiral King." *New York Times*, June 20, 1942.

Sherrod, Robert. "Marines' Show." *Time*, December 6, 1943.

" 'Shocking' Street Scenes at Night: Lord Mayor Disgusted." *Herald*, June 3, 1942.

Sullivan, Walter. "The Ship Ahead Just Disappeared." *New York Times Magazine*, May 7, 1995.

Trumbull, Robert. "All Out with Halsey!" *New York Times Magazine*, December 6, 1942.

———. "Big Bombers Won." *New York Times*, June 12, 1942.

————. "Repair: VI." December 19, 1942, 1. Unpublished dispatch (rejected by navy censor). Online at http://graphics8.nytimes.com/packages/pdf/opinion/20061207_pearl6.pdf (accessed April 4, 2013).

Vollinger, John. "The World War II Memoirs of John Vollinger." Online at http://www.janesoceania.com/ww2_johann_memoirs (September 12, 2012).

Wallin, Homer N. "Rejuvenation at Pearl Harbor." *Proceedings* (U.S. Naval Institute), Vol. 2, No. 526, December 1946.

"Washington in Wartime." *Life*, Vol. 14, No. 1, January 4, 1943.

Wilson, Cory. "War Workers as a Social Group." *Paradise of the Pacific*, August 1944. (Reprinted in Dye, ed., *Hawaii Chronicles II*, p. 201.)

Wilson, Willard. "Soldier and a Jukebox." *Paradise of the Pacific*, December 1944. (Reprinted in Dye, ed., *Hawaii Chronicles II*, p. 215.)

Zurlinden, Pete. "Prelude to Saipan, 15 June, 1944." *Proceedings* (U.S. Naval Institute), Vol. 73, Part 1, May 1947.

INDEX

Page numbers in *italics* refer to maps.